In his ambitious survey of the Indo-Aryan languages, Colin Masica has provided a fundamental introduction which will interest not only general and theoretical linguists but also students of one or more of these languages (Hindi, Urdu, Bengali, Punjabi, Gujarati, Marathi, Sinhalese, etc.) who want to acquaint themselves with the broader linguistic context. Generally synchronic in approach, concentrating on the phonology, morphology and syntax of the modern representatives of the group, the volume also covers their historical development, areal context, writing systems and aspects of sociolinguistics.

The survey is organized not on a language-by-language basis but by topic, so that salient theoretical issues may be discussed in a comparative context. At the same time a wealth of descriptive information is accessibly presented (all examples are in roman transcription), and the volume includes an inventory of languages and dialects, a detailed discussion of sub-classification schemes, and an extensive bibliography organized by language. This remarkable synthesis of research on Indo-Aryan will be an invaluable resource for all readers who have wished for a comprehensive handbook on this major language group.

Rauha
Mich. 7.95

THE INDO-ARYAN LANGUAGES

CAMBRIDGE LANGUAGE SURVEYS

This series offers general accounts of all the major language families of the world. Some volumes are organized on a purely genetic basis, others on a geographical basis, whichever yields the most convenient and intelligible grouping in each case. Sometimes, as with the Australian volume, the two in any case coincide.

Each volume compares and contrasts the typological features of the languages it deals with. It also treats the relevant genetic relationships, historical development, and sociolinguistic issues arising from their role and use in the world today. The intended readership is the student of linguistics or general linguist, but no special knowledge of the languages under consideration is assumed. Some volumes also have a wider appeal, like that on Australia, where the future of the languages and their speakers raises important social and political issues.

Already published:
The languages of Australia *R. M. W. Dixon*
The languages of the Soviet Union *Bernard Comrie*
The Mesoamerican Indian languages *Jorge A. Suárez*
The Papuan languages of New Guinea *William A. Foley*
Chinese *Jerry Norman*
Pidgin and creole languages, Volumes I and II *J. Holm*
The languages of Japan *M. Shibatani*
Celtic languages *D. MacAulay et al.*

Forthcoming titles include:
The languages of South-East Asia *J. A. Matisoff*
Austronesian languages *R. Blust*
Slavonic languages *R. Sussex*
Germanic languages *D. MacAulay et al.*
Romance languages *R. Posner*
The languages of Native North America *Marianne Mithun*

THE INDO-ARYAN LANGUAGES

COLIN P. MASICA

Department of South Asian Languages and Civilizations
University of Chicago

CAMBRIDGE
UNIVERSITY PRESS

Published by the Press Syndicate of the University of Cambridge
The Pitt Building, Trumpington Street, Cambridge CB2 1RP
40 West 20th Street, New York, NY 10011, USA
10 Stamford Road, Oakleigh, Melbourne 3166, Australia

First published 1991
First paperback edition 1993

Printed in Great Britain at the University Press, Cambridge

British Library cataloguing in publication data

Masica, Colin P.
The Indo-Aryan languages. – (Cambridge
language surveys).
1. Indic languages
I. Title
491′.1

Library of Congress cataloguing in publication data

Masica, Colin P., 1931–
The Indo-Aryan languages / Colin P. Masica.
p. cm. – (Cambridge languages surveys)
Bibliography
Includes index.
ISBN 0 521 23420 4 (hardback) 0 521 29944 6 (paperback)
1. Indo-Aryan languages. I. Title II. Series.
PK115.M37 1990
491′.1 – dc 19 88–37096 CIP

ISBN 0 521 23420 4 hardback
ISBN 0 521 29944 6 paperback

FP

CONTENTS

ILLUSTRATIONS

Maps

Figures

TABLES

PREFACE

The purpose of this book is to provide a general introduction to a fascinating field, both for those who are totally unacquainted with Indo-Aryan languages and for those who may have knowledge of one or more of them and want to acquaint themselves with the broader linguistic context. Since the focus is on that broader context, it has been decided to organize the presentation by topics, with respect to each of which the various Indo-Aryan languages are compared, rather than to give a series of thumbnail sketches of each language. Although with the aid of the index an overall basic description of each of the main languages (and a partial description of others) may be extracted from this, anyone whose sole interest is in a particular language would be better advised simply to read a good grammar of that language. (Here the linguistically subclassified Bibliography should be of help, as it will also with further reading.) It can be argued, however, that even such a person will find his understanding enhanced by a look at the language in question in a comparative context also.

Attempts to survey a field must still be selective, and even though an attempt has been made to cover the high points, much of interest (both with regard to topic and with regard to specific language-and-dialect data) has no doubt been omitted, whether by accident or by design. An attempt, perhaps inevitably not completely successful, has been made to keep the discussion simple and to avoid overly idiosyncratic terminology. The result is to do less than full justice to many technical issues. There is no space for that here. In general, priority has been given to simple presentation of facts rather than to the different theoretical analyses those facts may inspire (even though it can be argued that there is really no "theory-free" presentation of facts).

It should be added that this work involves essentially the collation and presentation of existing data, not original research. New data, however, keeps coming to light and new analyses keep appearing, even as this book goes to press. It is impossible for a work of this kind ever to be "complete" even in the sense of reflecting fully the state of knowledge at the time of its publication. The only solution is to adopt a cut-off point, with apologies for omissions (particularly from the Bibliography) tempered by pleasure in contemplating so much scholarly activity. (That is not to say that this book will not have other defects as well. I have often wondered why I should have written it: there are others more qualified. Perhaps I was the only one foolhardy enough to attempt it. I hope it will be useful nevertheless, and encourage interest and still more work in the Indo-Aryan field.)

ACKNOWLEDGEMENTS

First of all I would like to thank Cambridge University Press for its patience (this book was supposed to be written in two years and has taken something like seven), particularly Penny Carter for her unflagging encouragement. I owe much to W. S. Allen, who read the entire draft, and also to Peter Hook, who concentrated his attention on Chapters 1, 2, and 10, both of whom offered many helpful comments (failure always to heed which I alone am responsible for) and further encouragement (which often was needed). My thanks go also to Norman Zide, Clinton Seely, Edward Dimock, C. M. Naim, G. A. Zograph, Alice Davison, Eric Hamp, Douglas Varley, Elena Bashir, Charles Dent, David Magier, William Wallace, Howard Aronson, K. V. Subbarao, J. M. Lindholm, Paul Peranteau, Ranjit Chatterjee, David Gitomer, Vinay Dharwadker, William Alspaugh, Anvita Abbi, and Anuradha Saksena, for the contribution in one way or another (sometimes in the form of the gift or loan of valuable materials) of grist for my mill. Also to Rene Pomerleau, whose team kept my computer running, and who helped me set up the font of special characters needed for the draft, and to Alexis Papadopoulos, University of Chicago cartographer, who undertook the maps and several of the figures.

Finally, I am grateful to the National Science Foundation for a grant which among other things enabled me to take a year off from teaching (1985–6) to devote full time to this project.

NOTE ON TRANSCRIPTION

Of the several conventions in vogue for transcribing Indo-Aryan, the one adopted here is basically the "Standard Orientalist" transcription, as being most widespread and familiar (although by no means easiest for the typesetter). That is, so-called retroflex (or retracted) consonants are represented by letters with subscript dots (*ṭ*, *ḍ*, *ṇ*, *ṣ*), and etymologically long vowels by *ā*, *ī*, *ū*. ("Etymologically long" *ē*, *ō* are only consistently marked as such, however, in Sanskrit or where a contrast with equivalent short vowels exists in a language.) The Sanskrit "vocalic R" is represented as is traditional by *r̥*.

As in all commonly used transcriptions, *kh*, *gh*, *th*, *dh*, etc. represent *aspirated consonants* (as in "*bug-house*"), not fricatives. The symbol *c* represents a sound similar to English "ch" (see Chapter 5 for details), *ch* an aspirated version of the same, and *j* a sound similar to English "j" (not "y" as in IPA, which is represented by y).

Orientalist conventions are primarily a system of *transliteration* from the Indian scripts, based in turn upon Sanskrit. Where additional sounds are concerned, they have had to be augmented, either by simple extension of the conventions (*c̣*, *j̣*, *ẓ* for the retracted affricates and voiced sibilant found in some northwestern IA languages, *ṛ*, *ḷ* for retroflex flaps and laterals), or by use of phonetic symbols (*χ*, *γ*, *θ*, *ð*, *ɸ*, *ß* for velar, dental, and bilabial fricatives; *ŋ* for the velar nasal – even in Sanskrit; the palatal nasal, IPA [*ɲ*], is conventionally *ñ*]; *ʎ* for a voiceless lateral; *ɨ*, *ə* for high and mid unrounded central vowels; æ, ɒ, ɔ for lower front and lower back vowels; ɓ, ɗ, ʄ, ɠ for implosives). Palatalized consonants are indicated by ′, e.g., *t′*, *d′*, etc. Rounded front vowels are indicated by umlaut (*ö*). Prenasalized consonants are indicated by *n̆d*, *m̆b*. The affricates [ts, dz] are indicated inconsistently: as such (or as *ts*, *z*) in Chapters 5 and 10; as *ċ*, *j̇* (following Turner's conventions) in Chapter 6 (but never, as in Eastern European or Amerindian studies, as *c*, which always = č, i.e. [tɕ] [see above]).

Transliteration conventions have also been modified in the direction of greater phonetic transparency when the phonology has departed significantly from the "spelling" through merger, split, or phonetic change. Thus the symbol *a* generally indicates a short low central vowel, in some analyses indicated by *ə* (a symbol reserved here for a somewhat higher variety of central vowel, as found for example in Kashmiri). Where the equivalent vowel has become a backed and rounded vowel, however, as in Bengali, Assamese, and Oriya, it is represented by ɔ, ɒ or even *o* as appropriate. While the Sanskrit palatal and retroflex sibilants are represented conventionally by *ś*, *ṣ*, in languages with only one "hush" sibilant the symbol *ʃ* is used, regardless of the spelling.

A slight innovation, namely the use of the tilde to the right of a vowel, is employed for the indication of NIA nasalized vowels, e.g., *ā˜* (rather than *ā̃* or *āṁ*).

For further discussion, see Chapters 5 and 6.

1

Introduction

What claim do the Indo-Aryan languages have on our attention? Their foremost claim surely has to be the sheer numerical weight of the populations speaking them – possibly one-fifth of mankind. To the plea that these are largely accessible through English, it must be answered that no foreign language can afford full access to the hearts and minds of a people.

Many would say that English, which has been an intimate part of South Asian life for at least a century and a half (in some areas longer), helping to shape the minds of whole generations through schooling, and being shaped in its turn to express many features of South Asian life it was ill-suited to express initially, cannot justly be called a "foreign" language in the area. The whole question of the indigenization of English in South Asia is a fascinating study in itself.[1] Despite such adaptations, however, neither English nor Persian (which held sway in the subcontinent for a much longer period) can be as fully expressive of South Asian cultures as the languages which have been totally formed by those cultures. Both English and Persian have their primary base and formation elsewhere. In any case, knowers of English, however important in terms of absolute numbers and of international impact[2] and prestige constitute only a tiny minority (average 2.3 per cent[3]) of these populations.

It is perhaps to the deceptive convenience of English, however, that we owe the popular notion (more prevalent in America than in Britain) that the population of India, for instance, babbles chaotically in "hundreds of dialects," coupled with ignorance of the very existence of great languages (Bengali, Marathi, Hindi, and half a dozen others) of comparable age and demographic weight to the modern languages of Europe. Another factor in this ignorance is no doubt the degree of political unity the region has succeeded in retaining in the post-colonial period. It has not been Balkanized to any great extent, and most of these languages are accordingly subnational rather than the expressions of independent political entities. (Exceptions are Bengali in Bangladesh, Sinhalese in Sri Lanka – where it must contend with a substantial Tamil-speaking minority, and Nepali in Nepal –

where it is the official language and undoubted lingua franca but again not the mother tongue of all the population. Urdu is the sole official language of Pakistan but it is not the mother tongue of other than a small minority in that country, mostly migrants from North India concentrated in Karachi. It is, however, the preferred *literary* language of the numerically dominant Punjabi speakers.)

The speakers of these languages, in partnership with others brought into a common orbit via the unique cultural achievement that constitutes Sanskrit, have moreover been the creators of one of the great civilizations of the world, which merits the attention of all who would seek to follow and appreciate the human story. This Indic civilization once extended as far as Vietnam[4] and Indonesia, and contributed important components to the civilizations of China, Korea, and Japan as well, mainly through the vehicle of Buddhism.

The dazzling achievements of Sanskrit literature and thought, providing more than enough to digest as the West continues to make their acquaintance, together with the ignorance referred to above of the very existence of the modern languages, plus the availability of a small but meritorious literature from the area written originally in English (and a voluminous literature *about* the area in English) may account for the fact that the *literatures* of the modern Indo-Aryan languages remain practically unknown to the outside world. Yet many of them do possess flourishing modern literatures in most of the familiar genres, no doubt destined to expand further as literacy increases, as well as important pre-modern literatures in mediaeval and folk-genres meriting attention in their own right.

An aspect of Indo-Aryan that has, for some reason, excited more interest in continental Europe than in the English-speaking world is the fact that the speakers of these languages are our linguistic cousins, fellow members of the great Indo-European linguistic community. For British readers, a substitute has existed in the close historical ties between Britain and the former Indian empire, lately a subject of much renewed interest. (Of course the latter took in considerably more than Indo-Aryan, but Indo-Aryan lay at the heart of the matter, with three out of the four major centers of the empire, namely Calcutta, Delhi, and Bombay, in its territory.)

Apart from these general humanistic, practical, and sentimental concerns, there is a different set of reasons why Indo-Aryan merits attention. These have to do with the scientific study of language.

It is almost a commonplace that modern Western linguistic science took its birth from the discovery that the classical language of India, Sanskrit, is related to the classical and modern languages of Europe. This discovery is usually credited to Sir William Jones. Although Jones was actually neither the first to postulate a common origin for the Indo-European languages nor the first to add Sanskrit to their company (the former honor seems to go to the seventeenth-century Dutch scholar Marcus Zeurius Boxhorn, and the latter to the sixteenth-century English Jesuit Thomas Stevens),[5] it may be claimed that it was Jones's publication of his discoveries, which seem to have been largely independent, in the form of his presidential address to the Asiatic Society in 1786, that gave the impetus to Sanskrit studies in Europe, without which Indo-European philology would not have gotten very far.

Indo-European studies still form the backbone of historical linguistics, and the subsequent history of Indo-Aryan as a major branch of Indo-European, and one moreover whose development under the most diverse conditions can be followed almost continuously for 3,500 years, deserves a larger place in such studies than it is usually accorded. In the same address in which we find the much-quoted passage concerning the affinity of Sanskrit, Latin, and Greek, Jones made some remarks concerning modern Indo-Aryan, less often quoted, which may have a bearing on this situation:

> and this analogy might induce us to believe, that the pure Hindi, whether of *Tartarian* or *Chaldean* origin, was primeval in Upper *India*, into which the *Sanskrit* was introduced by conquerors from other kingdoms in some very remote age . . . (quoted by Grierson 1927, *LSI 1.1*:11)

In other words, he failed to perceive the relationship of Hindi to Sanskrit, and thought it was basically a pre-Sanskritic language of the "Tartarian" group, indigenous to India. It took a while to get matters straightened out: the first steps of correction overshot the mark, and took the Dravidian as well as the New Indo-Aryan languages to be descended from Sanskrit. All this may have contributed to the slowness with which the later development of Indo-Aryan found a place in Indo-European studies.

Materials for such studies are now relatively abundant, however (although there is naturally always more to be done), thanks to the labors of a remarkable company of scholars over the last hundred years, among which those of Sir George Grierson, especially the unparalleled achievement represented by the *Linguistic survey of India* (1903–27), and of Sir Ralph Turner, culminating in his *Comparative dictionary of the Indo-Aryan languages* (1966), deserve special mention as providing tools with which most other fields are not so conveniently blessed. A place of honor also goes to Suniti Kumar Chatterji (1890–1977), whose monumental *Origin and development of the Bengali language* (1926),[6] based on his 1921 University of London D.Litt. thesis, is basic reading for anyone interested in historical Indo-Aryan in general, and has served as a model for several similar studies.[7] Originally self-taught in European-style historical and comparative linguistics, Chatterji was enabled by a government of India scholarship to study in Europe under such masters as Meillet and Jules Bloch. In England, Grierson took a personal interest in his work.

This interest on the part of foreigners and foreign-trained native scholars joined itself to and was no doubt partly inspired by an indigenous tradition of grammar, phonetics, and lexicography of great sophistication and depth, unmatched in other parts of the world. The full implications of the rule-based Sanskrit grammar of Panini (fourth century BC) could not, perhaps, be properly appreciated in the West[8] until modern linguistic theory itself had evolved to such a stage, which was only recently, but in the field of phonetics the impact of Panini and of the ancient Indian phoneticians in general on Western linguistics was early (nineteenth century, another service of Jones) and profound (Allen 1953: 3–4). Somewhat later their influence may also be detected in American structuralist morphophonemics, e.g., in Bloomfield's description of Menomini (Allen 1962: 24). In India itself, the first real synthesis of the learning of the pandits and the scholarship of the West is represented by Sir R. G. Bhandarkar (1837–1925), the foremost Indian Sanskrit scholar of the nineteenth century, self-taught in the new philology. He seems not to have gone abroad until 1886, for the Vienna meeting of the International Congress of Orientalists, when he was a well-established scholar. As a measure of the influence of these two men, until recently at least Calcutta (Chatterji's seat) and Poona (Bhandarkar's seat) have remained the centers of historical research in Indo-Aryan.

Indo-Aryan presents special opportunities for the investigation of other linguistic problems also. One of these, which we may call areal or convergence studies, has to do with the phenomenon of linguistic change from a vantage point just opposite, as it were, to that of historical–comparative linguistics. That is, with focus on the results of the process rather than with antecedents, with external rather than internal motivation for change, and with spatial rather than (or in addition to) temporal relationships. As languages diverge from a common ancestor they may also – particularly where extensive migrations are involved – change in type, and come in some degree to conform typologically to new linguistic environments in which they find themselves.

Exactly how and why this happens is not fully understood (although reasonable hypotheses abound), but the history of Indo-Aryan offers ample scope for exploring the question. The fact that typological changes affecting New Indo-Aryan managed to disguise their Indo-European affinity for Jones is indicative of their suitability for this purpose. Moreover, not only is the history of Indo-Aryan itself relatively well documented, but the non-Aryan languages and stocks of the region are also fairly well documented and studied in comparison with such situations elsewhere. If it should be held that one important factor in the development taken by Indo-Aryan, or a particular branch of it, was the adoption of Aryan speech by non-Aryan speakers (Chatterji for one maintains that this was the case in East Bengal, Assam, Orissa, and South Bihar, among other places), this need not remain in the realm of pure speculation: the same thing can be observed going on today, e.g., in Halbi (the neo-Aryan speech of former Gond speakers in Bastar District in Madhya Pradesh) and in Nagamese (the Assamese-based pidgin of Nagaland in the extreme northeast, now creolizing), to name but two instances. The continuing spread of Nepali among Tibeto-Burman speakers both within Nepal and beyond it to the east is another case in point, complicated by the existence of a written standard.

The effects of super- as well as substrata on linguistic development can also be studied in Indo-Aryan in relation especially to Sanskrit, Persian, and English as prestige languages. To these should be added the influence of Modern Standard Hindi and Urdu on a number of languages and dialects, and indeed of standard literary languages on the spoken languages generally.

This brings us to the whole set of problems coming under the general heading of sociolinguistics. Here Indo-Aryan constitutes a vast laboratory almost without equal, albeit as yet little exploited. On the one hand, there is the complexly compartmentalized traditional caste society of India, socially segregated, occupationally specialized, hierarchically organized, yet interdependent. What effect does this have on language? For comparison, there are the other Indo-Aryan-speaking societies, minimally to maximally different: traditionalist but half-Tibetanoid Nepal, Muslim Pakistan and Bangladesh, Buddhist Sri Lanka, and speaking a language closely related to that of the latter, the Muslim Maldives. Within each of these, but especially in India, there is the contrast between rural and urban subcultures, the latter sometimes ancient, sometimes rapidly modernizing – and typically multilingual. There are striking differences in regional marriage patterns: for example, between the local exogamy of the North of India, bringing in women of different dialectal background, and the local endogamy of the South.[9]

Finally, there are the three quite distinct cases of Indo-Aryan languages taken completely outside the South Asian region: (1) the ancient migration of the Gypsies to the Near East and thence to Europe; (2) the largely nineteenth-century emigration of laborers and/or merchants to Fiji, Mauritius, East and South Africa, Guyana, Trinidad, and other spots in the Caribbean; (3) the mid-twentieth-century movement that has brought upwards of a million seekers of a better life to Britain (largely from the Punjab, in contrast to the nineteenth-century movement of laborers to the British colonies, mainly from eastern UP and Bihar). To these we should add the still more recent settlement of (until lately) mainly well-educated professionals from all areas in the United States and Canada. (A movement of Punjabi-speaking farmers at the beginning of this century to the west coast of North America, i.e. to British Columbia and California, is also worth noting. Another, very different case is represented by the Parya language of Soviet Tadzhikistan, whose existence also implies a migration, but the date of the latter is quite unknown.)

Modern facilities for travel and communication being what they are, the most recent migrations involving literate speakers are of sociolinguistic interest mainly from the standpoint of ordinary problems of language maintenance and adaptation to new expressive needs. The earlier transplantations of illiterate laborers, subsequently cut off from their roots, involve more specialized phenomena, including the evolution of new Indo-Aryan-based lingua francas to facilitate communication among people of different dialectal and language backgrounds. The arrival on the scene of zealous propagators of Modern Standard Hindi has further complicated the situation.[10] The case of the Gypsies, where a form of Indo-Aryan speech has been jealously guarded for centuries as a secret language of intra-group communication as well as a badge of identity in a semi-nomadic subculture, is unique.[11]

The multilingual nature of much of South Asian society presents special challenges to the sociolinguist. Participation of linguistically disparate regions in a common civilization, held together by such specific institutions as pilgrimages, as well as requirements of trade, led to the development of lingua francas, of which Hindustani is the most notable recent example. Sanskrit itself could be said to have played this role, as to a limited extent it still does among the traditionally educated elite. As a deliberately standardized and maintained yet flexible medium of elite communication Sanskrit is a fascinating product of the human spirit. In its heyday in the first millennium AD, it linked together – and synthesized elements from – an area much vaster than Indo-Aryan itself or even the subcontinent, and widely separated epochs of time. At the other end of the sociolinguistic spectrum, the expansionist character of Aryan society in a region full of other linguistic stocks has given rise to pidgins and creoles and mixed languages of every description.

As an effect both of superstrata and of a long literary tradition, some Indo-Aryan languages are characterized by a notable degree of *diglossia.* That is, the literary language is different from even the educated colloquial, not only in vocabulary but also in phonology and grammar. This has reached its extreme point in Sinhalese.[12] In some other languages (Bengali, Marathi), there has been a slowness on the part of well-established traditions to adjust to linguistic change, but such adjustments have eventually to some degree been made. The Sinhalese situation[13] is approached more closely in some of the non-Aryan languages of the region with long literary histories such as Tamil.

True diglossia, where the literary norm is nobody's spoken language, should be distinguished from the kind of bilingualism or bidialectalism where people are accustomed to use as their literary language a dialect or even a language which is not their own spoken language. This situation is naturally very common in Indo-Aryan South Asia where there are many more major dialects and spoken languages than there are literary languages, with each of the latter, even when it has its own corps of speakers, serving a number of the former.

This situation is hardly unique to South Asia, and the whole question of the formation of standard literary languages is one of general interest. Although it has been studied in other contexts, Indo-Aryan offers not only ample and diverse material for comparison but also processes amenable to concurrent observation. There is also the related question commonly referred to as language "modernization" – that is, "expansion to meet the needs of a developing society." What are these needs, and how are they being met in the meantime? Do some functions lend themselves to "language engineering" more than others? What options are in fact available? Although such questions may not be answered or even properly addressed here, they are sharply posed for further researchers by the sociolinguistic context of Indo-Aryan.

This book is an introduction only to Indo-Aryan, not to the other linguistic stocks in the South Asian region, which are mentioned only when they impinge directly on the development of Indo-Aryan. Moreover, our focus here will be on the modern languages, not on Sanskrit – again, except as necessary background for the former. For Sanskrit as such there are available several excellent books by competent authorities.[14]

2

The modern Indo-Aryan languages and dialects

Before proceeding further, it is appropriate that we identify more precisely the languages to be discussed. A brief survey of the modern Indo-Aryan domain in terms of contemporary political geography is therefore given here. Although this may not be necessary for all readers, it will no doubt be helpful to those less familiar with the area. It is followed by discussion of the problems of language vs. dialect in the Indo-Aryan context, of Hindi–Urdu, and of nomenclature, and supplemented by Map 1, as well as by a comprehensive alphabetical inventory of Indo-Aryan language and dialect names, living or dead, given in Appendix I. Because of the sheer number of names that will be met with in the literature (by those whose interest or work takes them beyond this book), the last is needed for reference purposes in any case: even the specialist is unlikely to be familiar with all of them.

2.1 **Indo-Aryan: a bird's-eye view**

The Indo-Aryan languages are a sub-branch of the Indo-European family, spoken today mainly in India, Pakistan, Bangladesh, Nepal, Sri Lanka, and the Maldive Islands by at least 640,000,000 persons (est. 1981). Although they are not the only languages spoken in any of these countries, their speakers in all cases constitute majorities. In the past, Indo-Aryan languages (distinguished here from the Nuristani languages [see Section 2.1.18]) extended also into eastern Afghanistan, where isolated remnants may still exist, and at a more remote epoch (the early centuries of the Christian era), also into Chinese Turkestan (Sinkiang).

The modern Indo-Aryan languages, properly and henceforth called NEW INDO-ARYAN (= "NIA", as against "MIA" for the preceding stage of MIDDLE INDO-ARYAN [see Chapter 3]), date from approximately AD 1000. The NIA languages are presently distributed as follows (for more details on each language see Appendix I):

2.1.1 A vast central portion of the subcontinent, consisting of the Indian states of Uttar Pradesh, Bihar, Madhya Pradesh, Rajasthan, Haryana, and Himachal Pradesh, plus the Union Territory of Delhi, is known as the "HINDI area", because the official and general written language, that is to say, that of administration, press, school instruction, and modern literature, is Hindi, sometimes called MODERN STANDARD HINDI, and the whole area is heir to the "Hindi literary tradition" – Hindi being used here in a different and wider sense, to refer to pre-modern literatures in **Braj** and **Awadhi**, and often to those in languages proper to Rajasthan and Bihar as well.

While Kellogg could in 1892 describe "**High Hindi**", as he called it, as "understood more or less through all the Hindi-speaking country, but in no place the language of the home," this is no longer accurate: Standard Hindi does have native speakers, especially in urban areas, and is fast encroaching on dialectal forms of speech, to the point where a student of the latter is now sometimes hard put to find "pure" informants.

From this the reader will not incorrectly draw the conclusion that there are other forms of speech "on the ground" in the Hindi area, particularly at the village level (but by no means excluding a good portion of the urban population), over which Standard Hindi is superimposed. These are the so-called **regional languages of the Hindi area**, sometimes less accurately called Hindi "**dialects**". Some of these are fairly closely related to Standard Hindi (and often, confusingly, also loosely called "**Hindi**" by their speakers); some are more distantly related to it. (The situation somewhat resembles that of an earlier historical period in the Italian-, Spanish-, or German-speaking areas of Europe, although the area and population involved in India is much greater, and the role of some of the regional languages or dialects is much larger in the pre-modern literary tradition. Another but looser analogy might be to China.)

The heartland of the Hindi area is the densely-populated Upper Ganges valley, corresponding to the state of Uttar Pradesh (which alone had 110,850,019 people in 1981), minus its hill areas, together with the Haryana region west of Delhi and adjoining areas of northern Madhya Pradesh and perhaps also northeastern Rajasthan. From west to east the regional languages here are: **Haryāṇvī** (formerly called **Bāngarū**) in most of Haryana State (formerly southeastern Punjab) and rural parts of the Delhi Territory; adjoining it in UP northeastward from Delhi up to the premontane Tarai and as far east as Rampur, and reaching across the Jamuna to include the northeastern portion of Haryana as far as Ambala, there is a form of Indo-Aryan speech with no settled name, despite its importance [see below]: Grierson called it **Vernacular Hindōstānī**; it has often been called **Khaṛī Bolī**; since the latter term is applied also to Colloquial Standard Hindi, Bahri

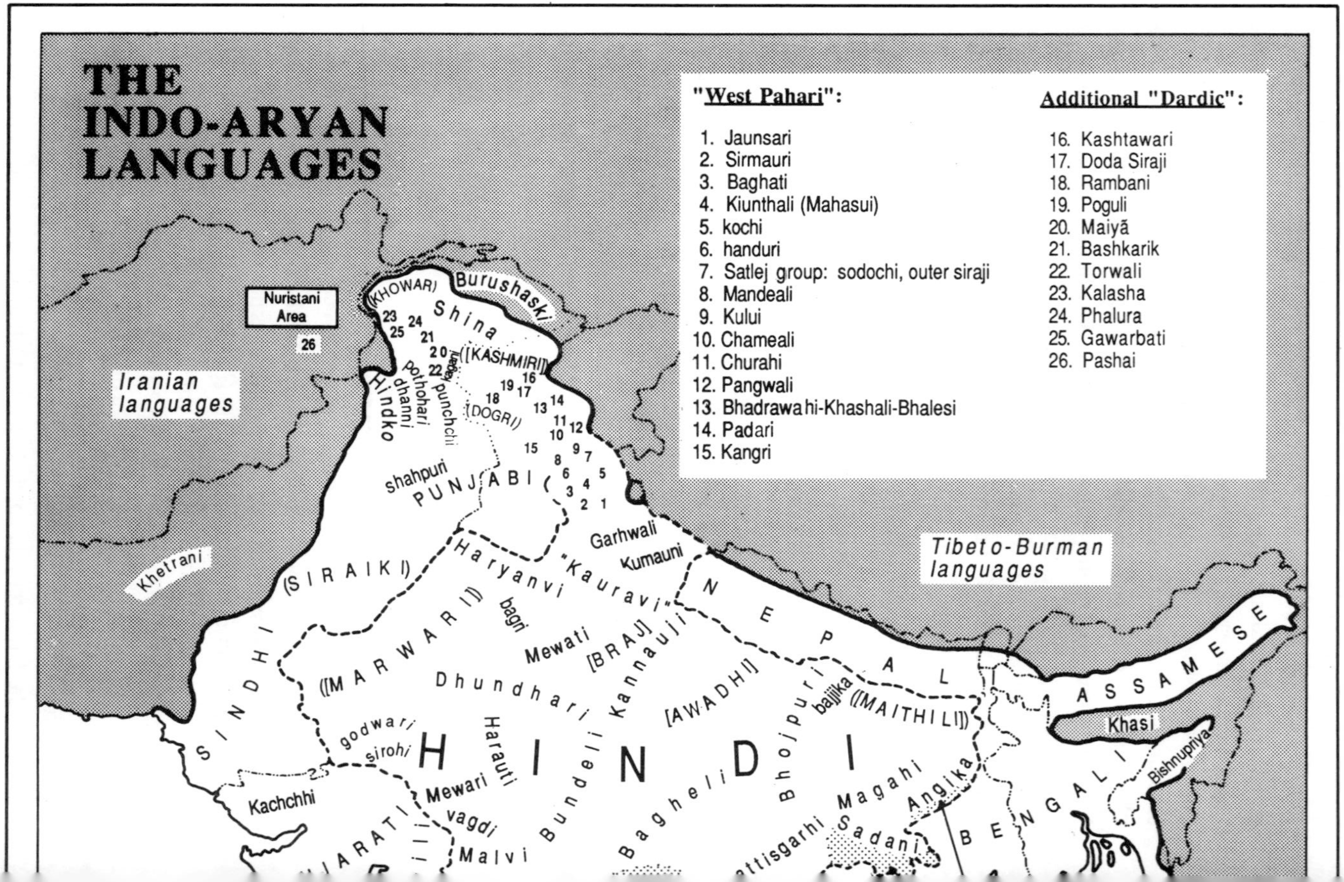
THE INDO-ARYAN LANGUAGES
"West Pahari":
1. Jaunsari
2. Sirmauri
3. Baghati
4. Kiunthali (Mahasui)
5. kochi
6. handuri
7. Satlej group: sodochi, outer siraji
8. Mandeali
9. Kului
10. Chameali
11. Churahi
12. Pangwali
13. Bhadrawahi-Khashali-Bhalesi
14. Padari
15. Kangri
Additional "Dardic":
16. Kashtawari
17. Doda Siraji
18. Rambani
19. Poguli
20. Maiyã
21. Bashkarik
22. Torwali
23. Kalasha
24. Phalura
25. Gawarbati
26. Pashai
Nuristani Area
26
Iranian languages
Tibeto-Burman languages
Khetrani
(KHOWAR)
Burushaski
Shina
([KASHMIRI])
Hindko
pothohari
dhanni
punchchi
(DOGRI)
shahpuri
PUNJABI
Garhwali
Kumauni
(SIRAIKI)
Haryanvi
"Kauravi"
NEPALI
ASSAMESE
Khasi
Bishnupriya
([MARWARI])
bagri
Mewati
[BRAJ]
Kannauji
[AWADHI]
Bhojpuri
bajjika
([MAITHILI])
Dhundhari
SINDHI
godwari
sirohi
HINDI
Harauti
Bundeli
Bagheli
Magahi
Angika
BENGALI
Kachchhi
Mewari
vagdi
Malvi
Sadani

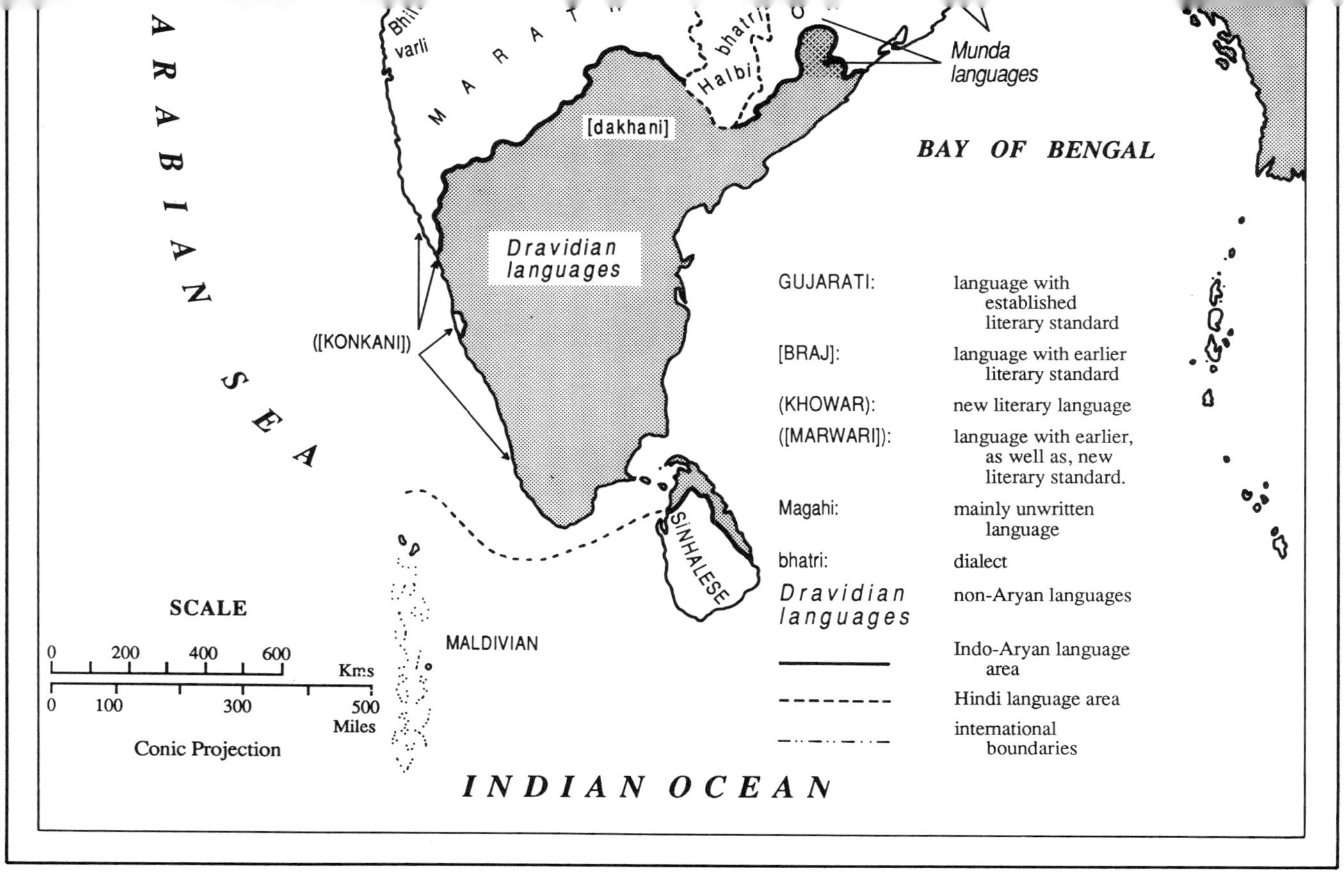

ARABIAN SEA
Bhil
varli
MARATH
bhatri
Halbi
Munda languages
[dakhani]
BAY OF BENGAL
Dravidian languages
([KONKANI])
SINHALESE
MALDIVIAN
INDIAN OCEAN
SCALE
0 200 400 600 Kms
0 100 300 500 Miles
Conic Projection
GUJARATI: language with established literary standard
[BRAJ]: language with earlier literary standard
(KHOWAR): new literary language
([MARWARI]): language with earlier, as well as, new literary standard.
Magahi: mainly unwritten language
bhatri: dialect
Dravidian languages: non-Aryan languages
Indo-Aryan language area
Hindi language area
international boundaries

Map 1 The Indo-Aryan languages

(1980) following Rahul Sankrityayan proposes to call it **Kauravī**, after the ancient land of the Kurus; southeast of Delhi, a broad area centering on Mathura but extending northeastward as far as Bareilly is the homeland of **Braj**; in a narrower band to the east, from Etawah and Kanpur up to Pilibhit is the closely allied **Kannaujī**; to the south of these in Madhya Pradesh from Gwalior as far as the tribal hinterlands of Chhindwara and Hoshangabad is **Bundēlī**, also similar to Braj; a more distinct language, **Awadhī**, prevails in east-central UP north and south of Lucknow; a variety of this known as **Baghelī** extends in Madhya Pradesh from Rewa to Jabalpur and Mandla; more isolated and therefore more strongly characterized is the **Chhattīsgaṛhī** further to the southeast on the borders of Orissa; eastern UP, including Varanasi (Benares), Azamgarh, and Gorakhpur, is occupied by various dialects of **Bhojpurī**, which extend into Bihar (Shahabad and Saran Districts, west of the rivers Son and Gandak respectively, and most of Champaran District).

Grierson classed "Vernacular Hindostani", Braj, Kannauji, and Bangaru (Haryanvi) together as "**Western Hindi**" and Awadhi, Baghelī, and Chhattisgarhi together as "**Eastern Hindī**", but put Bhojpuri into the more distantly related "**Bihārī**" group. The other principal "Bihari" languages/dialects are **Magahī**, spoken in central Bihar (south of the Ganga and east of the Son) and **Maithilī**, spoken north of the Ganga. The latter has a long literary tradition, the former none. Also in the "Bihari" group are **Sadānī** (or **Nagpuriā**) in South Bihar (Chota Nagpur) centering on Ranchi, **Angikā** in eastern Bihar (Monghyr, Bhagalpur, Santal Parganas, Purnea, according to Pandey 1979: Grierson, who calls it **Chhikāchhikī Bolī**, excludes Purnea), and **Bajjikā** in Muzaffarpur and part of Champaran Districts in northwest Bihar (S. Tivari 1964). Claims of independent status for the latter two, previously taken to be dialects of Maithili, are recent, as are their names, although the dialects themselves are ancient.

Leaving now the North Indian plain with its cultural extensions in the rougher country to its immediate south for Rajasthan, we find the main desert area west of the Aravalli range occupied by various forms of **Mārwāṛī**, among which the **Bāgṛī** of the Haryana border and the **Bhitrauti**, **Sirohī**, and **Godwārī** of the southern Aravalli foothills might be mentioned as distinctive. East of the Aravallis, **Mewāṛī** in the southeast has been classed as a dialect of Marwari but is also distinctive. (Southeastern Rajasthan south of Udaipur city, as well as the interior of the southern Aravalli range, are occupied by **Bhili** dialects which no one tries to affiliate to either Hindi or Rajasthani. The dialect of the former is known as **Vāgḍī**, or **Wāgḍī**.) Further northeast lies what Grierson called **Central Eastern Rājasthānī**, with two main representatives, **Ḍhuṇḍhāṛī** (or **Jaipurī**), centered on Jaipur, and **Hāṛautī**, centered on the Districts (former princely states) of Bundi and Kota. In the Alwar District of the extreme northeast, spilling over into the Gurgaon District of Haryana, is **Mewāṭī**. (In the area of Bharatpur, Dholpur, and Karauli just to the south, Braj extends into Rajasthan.) Outside of Rajasthan, the language of western Madhya Pradesh (Ujjain, Indore, Bhopal), **Mālvī**, is also classed with "Rajasthani". A far-southern dialect, **Nimāḍī**, isolated in the Satpura range between the Narbada and Tapti valleys in a tribal area, has developed special peculiarities.

The Himalayan areas of UP, except for the highest elevations, are occupied mainly by two languages (in various dialects), **Gaṛhwālī** and **Kumaunī**, grouped together by Grierson as "**Central Pahāṛī**" (Pahāṛī = "hill speech"). They are more closely allied to Rajasthani than to the Hindi of the plains. Further west in the mountains, in Himachal Pradesh and beginning already in the western part of Dehra Dun District in UP, lies the highly splintered group of Indo-Aryan dialects collectively known as "**Western Pahāṛī**". From southeast to northwest the main ones are **Jaunsārī** (in Dehra Dun), **Sirmaurī**, **Baghāṭī**, **Kiūṇṭhalī** (around Simla, now apparently known as **Mahāsuī**), **Haṇḍūrī**, **Kuḷuī**, **Maṇḍeāḷī**, **Chameali**, **Bharmaurī** (or **Gādī**), **Churāhī**, **Pangwāḷī**, and (continuing into Kashmir) **Bhadrawāhī**, **Bhalesī**, **Khashālī**, and **Pāḍrī**. These too bear some Rajasthani affinity, along with characteristic archaisms and innovations that are increasingly marked toward the northwest. Whether because of the complexity of the situation or because of greater linguistic differences, they are less commonly claimed as "dialects of Hindi" (e.g., neither by Kellogg 1938/1892 nor by H. Bahri 1980 – although Diack 1896 does indeed title his work *The Kulu dialect of Hindi*), even while Garhwali/Kumauni (and by Kellogg even Nepali) are so claimed. One reason may be the former closer affiliation of these areas politically with the Punjab. There have been reports of an attempt to concoct a "**Himāchalī**" language on the basis of these diverse dialects to serve, in the name of regional identity, as co-official language with Hindi, but it is too early to predict the outcome.

We may now leave the complexities of the "Hindi area" to survey, first the remainder of the contiguous Indo-Aryan territory by means of a rough *pradakṣiṇā* (clockwise circumambulation) of the Hindi area, then the non-contiguous languages.

2.1.2 East of "Central Pahari" along the Himalayas lies "Eastern Pahari", that is, **Nepālī**, an independent language by any standard *pace* Kellogg (who had very limited access to it), dominant not only in the kingdom of Nepal but recently also in Sikkim, the Darjeeling District of West Bengal, and parts of Bhutan.

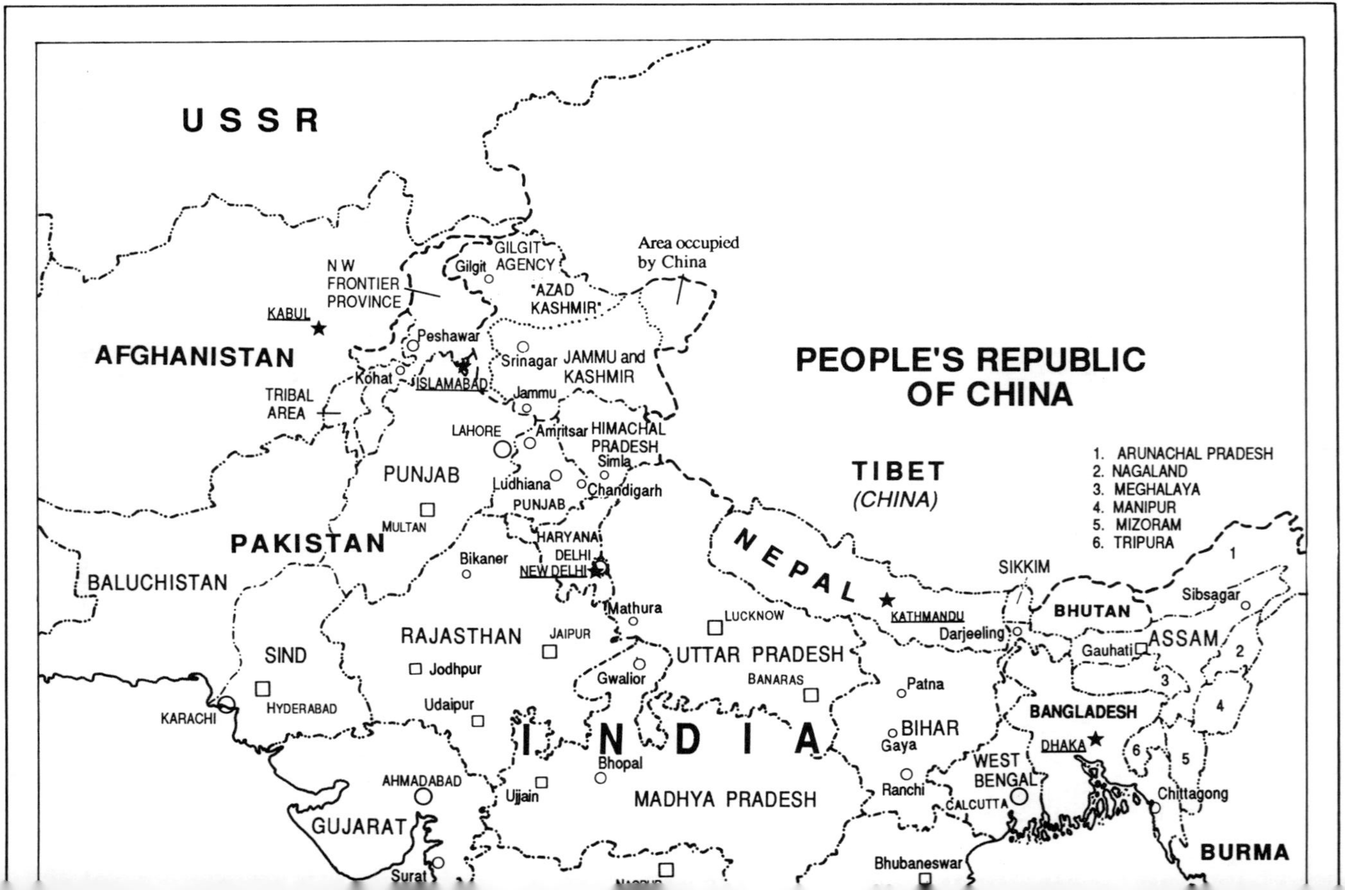

USSR
AFGHANISTAN
KABUL
N W FRONTIER PROVINCE
TRIBAL AREA
Peshawar
Kohat
ISLAMABAD
Gilgit
GILGIT AGENCY
'AZAD KASHMIR'
Area occupied by China
Srinagar
JAMMU and KASHMIR
Jammu
LAHORE
Amritsar
HIMACHAL PRADESH
Simla
Ludhiana
Chandigarh
PUNJAB
PUNJAB
MULTAN
PAKISTAN
BALUCHISTAN
HARYANA
DELHI
NEW DELHI
Bikaner
Mathura
SIND
HYDERABAD
KARACHI
RAJASTHAN
JAIPUR
Jodhpur
Udaipur
Gwalior
UTTAR PRADESH
LUCKNOW
BANARAS
I N D I A
Bhopal
Ujjain
MADHYA PRADESH
AHMADABAD
GUJARAT
Surat
PEOPLE'S REPUBLIC OF CHINA
TIBET (CHINA)
NEPAL
KATHMANDU
SIKKIM
Darjeeling
BHUTAN
Gauhati
ASSAM
Sibsagar
Patna
BIHAR
Gaya
Ranchi
WEST BENGAL
CALCUTTA
Bhubaneswar
BANGLADESH
DHAKA
Chittagong
BURMA
1
2
3
4
5
6
1. ARUNACHAL PRADESH
2. NAGALAND
3. MEGHALAYA
4. MANIPUR
5. MIZORAM
6. TRIPURA

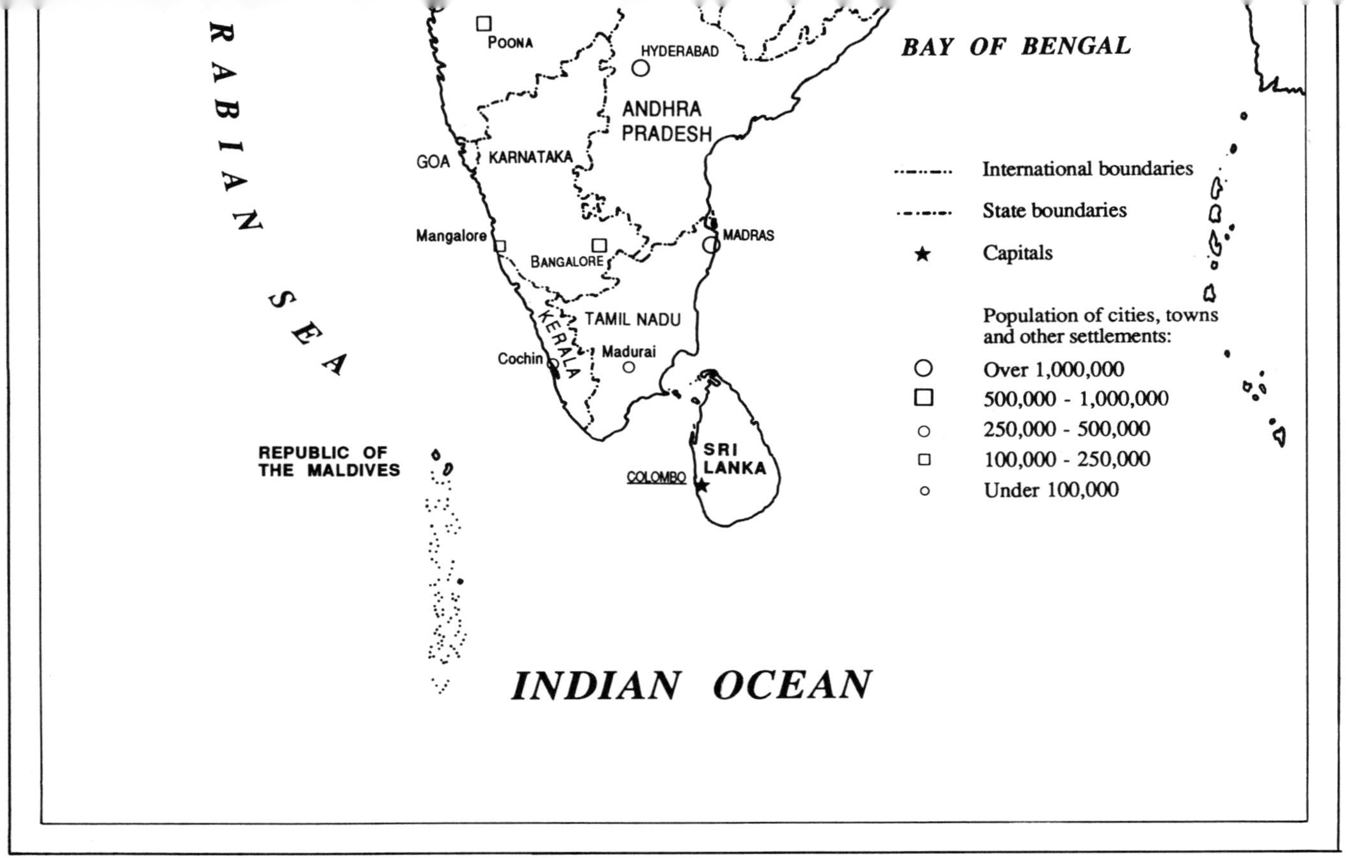
RABIAN SEA
BAY OF BENGAL
POONA
HYDERABAD
ANDHRA PRADESH
GOA
KARNATAKA
Mangalore
BANGALORE
MADRAS
TAMIL NADU
KERALA
Cochin
Madurai
REPUBLIC OF THE MALDIVES
SRI LANKA
COLOMBO
INDIAN OCEAN
International boundaries
State boundaries
Capitals
Population of cities, towns and other settlements:
Over 1,000,000
500,000 - 1,000,000
250,000 - 500,000
100,000 - 250,000
Under 100,000

Map 2 South Asia: Political boundaries

2.1.3 **Assamese** is the language of the Brahmaputra valley in far northeastern India. It was little known in most of the Tibeto-Burman and Khasi-speaking hill areas surrounding the valley, part of the old state of Assam but now largely separated politically as new states and territories. In one of them, however, Nagaland, a pidginized form of Assamese known as **Nagamese** is reported to have become a lingua franca.

2.1.4 Cut off from the Hindi area by the barrier of the Rajmahal hills, and from Assamese partly by the Khasi-Garo hills, both the homes of non-Indo-Aryan-speaking tribes, is the **Bengali** area, basically the great delta of the Ganges, now politically divided between the Indian state of West Bengal and the new country of Bangladesh. Bengali is also dominant in Tripura, an Indian territory to the east of Bangladesh, and Bengali speakers are numerous in Assam. The colloquial standard of Dhaka, the Bangladeshi capital, is different from that of Calcutta. The dialect of Chittagong, in southeast Bangladesh, is different enough to be considered a separate language.

2.1.5 Another Indo-Aryan language of the eastern frontier is **Bishnupriya Manipuri**, formerly spoken in Manipur (on the border with Burma), but driven from that area in the early nineteenth century and presently at home in the adjacent Cachar District of Assam, Tripura, and the Sylhet District of Bangladesh.

2.1.6 Southwest of Bengal, the delta of the Mahanadi is the center of the **Oṛiyā** language. Much of the state of Orissa is home to non-Aryan-speaking tribal peoples, a large bloc of which separate Oriya from Bengali. The interior Sambalpur lowland has a distinctive dialect. **Bhatrī** is an aberrant dialect of Oriya spoken by former Gond (Dravidian) tribesmen in the northeast of the former Bastar State, now a District of Madhya Pradesh.

2.1.7 Bhatri is transitional to the main Indo-Aryan language of Bastar (where Gondi dialects continue to be spoken), **Halbī**. The latter is in turn transitional to Marathi, of which it is sometimes considered an aberrant dialect.

2.1.8 **Marāṭhī** occupies the extensive rolling plateau of the northwestern Deccan from Nagpur to Nasik, Pune (Poona), and Kolhapur, as well as the lowland known as the Konkan below the raised rugged edge of the plateau (= Western Ghats) from north of Bombay (Thana District) to just north of Goa (Ratnagiri District). The dialects of the Konkan are distinct.

2.1.9 These are to be distinguished further from **Konkaṇī** proper, centered on Goa, but extending slightly to the north (Savantvadi) as well as to the south (coastal North Kanara District of Karnataka State), with an important outlier in South Kanara, centering on Mangalore, and another in Kerala, around Cochin. (For a documented discussion of the "Konkani–Marathi controversy", see Pereira 1971.)

2.1.10 Beginning already in the northern part of Thana District (north of Bombay) and stretching in an arc around the eastern and northeastern periphery of Gujarat is a zone of tribal peoples now speaking, whatever their original language(s), Indo-Aryan dialects mainly grouped together as "**Bhīlī**". As noted earlier, these extend into southern Rajasthan. Their closest affiliation is generally with Gujarati, but the southernmost, such as the **Vārlī** of Thana and the **Ḍangī** of the Dangs District (in southeast Gujarat), are closer to Marathi, and may be regarded as a bridge between the two major languages. (Except in the Nagpur area, the Marathi–Hindi boundary is by contrast a sharp one, marked also physically by the Satpura range, the home of non-Aryan, i.e. Munda-speaking, tribals.) East of Dangs are the Maharashtrian Districts of Dhulia and Jalgaon, formerly known as Khandesh, with a language, **Khāndeshī**, better known locally as **Ahirani**, which is transitional between Gujarati and Marathi.

2.1.11 To the north, **Gujarātī** is the language of greater Gujarat (including the Kathiawar peninsula) and also of an important component of the population of the city of Bombay. Beyond the Gulf of Kutch, however, the language, **Kachchhī**, is more closely related to Sindhi.

2.1.12 Across the Pakistan border, **Sindhī** is the language of the Lower Indus valley, below the narrowing of the valley above the Sukkur dam, and of the desert region to the east. It is more sharply bounded immediately to the west by the Kirthar range that marks the beginning of Baluchistan and Iranian speech. Karachi city, on the margins of the area in any case, is dominated by Urdu-speaking migrants from North India. The center of Standard Sindhi is the city of Hyderabad rather than Karachi.

2.1.13 The valley of the Indus and its tributaries in Pakistan north of Sind up to the Pir Panjal range on the frontier of Kashmir is occupied by a series of dialects known by various local names, and to outsiders first as "**Western Punjabi**". Noting that these – or some of these – had as much in common with Sindhi as with Punjabi, and differed strikingly from the latter in some features,

Grierson bestowed[1] the name "**Lahndā**" (from a Punjabi word for "western") on them collectively as a distinct "language". This has caught on only among linguists (who later began to prefer the feminine form **Lahndī**, matching the usual names of Indo-Aryan languages); it has no currency among the speakers themselves. It will accordingly be used here – for convenience, as there is no ready substitute – always in quotes.

Shackle, who has done more work in the area than any other recent linguist, has challenged (1979, 1980) the "Lahnda" construct even in terms of its convenience, as well as Grierson's subclassification of the dialects comprising it (which has long been found unsatisfactory), although without presuming to come up with a final scheme himself. The situation is complicated for indigenous scholarship by the rival claims of old (i.e. pan-Punjabi) and new language movements.

In any case, the area concerned is divided, physically and linguistically, into two unequal halves by the great escarpment of the Salt range above Mianwali and Sargodha, which bounds the western Punjab plain on the north. The linguistic self-consciousness of the southern (= Central Pakistan plains) dialects (**Riyāsatī–Bahāwalpurī**, **Mūltānī**, **Jhangī–Jaṭkī**, **Thaḷī**, etc.), centering on the ancient city of Multan and the former princely capital of Bahawalpur, has coalesced around the name **Sirāikī**,[2] a term unfortunately also applied to a variety of Sindhi (the name is from S. *siro* 'north, up-river'), doubly confusing because Siraiki is also spoken by many Siraiki settlers in Sind. Affiliated dialects are spoken also by segments of the population west of the Indus where the main language is Pashto. At the north end of the plains area, where linguistic and cultural distance from Multan is maximal, the dialect of Sargodha District, **Shahpuri**, which was taken by Grierson to be "standard Lahnda", is in fact transitional to Punjabi, if not indeed a dialect of that language (Shackle 1976: 8, 1979: 201). It has been suggested that the non-contiguous dialect **Khētrānī**, spoken by a tribe in northeasten Baluchistan, may be the remnant of a separate language, of "Dardic" affinity (see below).

In the broken hill country to the north of the Salt range are the more diverse dialects of "**Northern Lahndā**", Grierson's pioneering subclassification of which most experts agree is particularly unsatisfactory. The least problematic may be **Poṭhohārī** (*LSI* **Pōṭhwārī**), the dialect of Rawalpindi and Jhelum Districts (and thus of the southeastern hinterland of the new Pakistani capital of Islamabad).

To the west and north of this, that is primarily in Attock and Hazara Districts, and across the Indus in Kohat and Peshawar, both the dialectal and the terminological picture is much more confusing, with discontinuous dialects (due to migration and invasion), dialects with no settled name, and identical names applied to several different dialects. The worst of the latter is "Hindko", a term (basically meaning 'the language of the Indians' – as contrasted with Pathans) applied not only to several forms of "Northern Lahnda" but also to the Siraiki dialects of Dera Ghazi Khan and Mianwali Districts (also called **Ḍērāwāli** and **Thaḷī** respectively), and of Dera Ismail Khan (Northwestern Frontier Province). Shackle (1980), however, proposes to set up a group called **Hindko proper**, comprising four dialects of Attock District, corresponding more or less to three of its tehsils (**Awāṇkārī** to the southern Talagang tehsil, **Ghēbī** to the central Pindi Gheb tehsil, and **Chachhī** to the northern Attock tehsil, extending to the southernmost Haripur tehsil of neighboring Hazara) plus **Kohāṭī** of Kohat city beyond the Indus.

The "Hindko" of Peshawar city deserves separate classification according to Shackle, partly due to the influence of Punjabi via the Grand Trunk Road. Despite the fact that a majority of the inhabitants are Pashto-speaking, **Peshāwarī Hindko** has considerable prestige and has been cultivated for literature.

To the east of "Hindko proper" (and west of Pothohari), in western Jhelum District (Chakwal) the dialect is **Dhannī**; to the north of the latter (Fatehjang tehsil, Attock District), in the valley of the Sohan river, is the closely related **Sawain** or **Sohain**. From Abbottabad northward in Hazara District, east of the Upper Indus (in the Northwest Frontier Province), are the northernmost dialects of "Lahnda", also confusingly called "Hindko": Grierson distinguished **Hindkī of Hazara** (the main dialect); **Tināulī** in the southwest; **Ḍhūṇḍī-Kaiṛālī** in the east. Bailey 1915 described **Kāg̱ānī**, "spoken in the whole of the Kagan Valley" including Mansehra and Abbottabad, and "known as Hindko" – apparently the same as Grierson's "Hindki of Hazara". In the hills and mountains west and southwest of Kashmir (Pir Panjal) are **Chibhālī** and **Punchhī**. This northern area especially stands in need of more work, starting with an up-to-date survey.[3] Parts of Hazara are now Pashto-speaking.

2.1.14 This brings us to **Kāshmīrī** itself, essentially the language of the Vale of Kashmir, certainly not of the whole state of that name, the greater part of which (Ladakh, Baltistan) is Tibeto-Burman-speaking. Kashmiri influence, however, or the same tendencies that are shown by Kashmiri, are perceptible in bordering Indo-Aryan languages of both the "Lahnda" and "West Pahari" varieties. To the southeast on the Upper Chenab lies the smaller valley of Kishtwar, the language of which, **Kaṣhṭawāṛī**, has been called "the only true dialect" of Kashmiri. Beyond is the Bhadrawahi group of West Pahari mentioned earlier. Other dialects/languages of the Kashmir group lie between Kashmir and Jammu: **Pogulī**, **Ḍoḍā Sirājī**, and **Rāmbanī**.

2.1.15 The language of Jammu itself is **Ḍogrī**, once considered a "dialect" of Punjabi, now thought to be more closely related to West Pahari, and in any case now claiming independent language status. To the southeast in western Himachal Pradesh is the closely allied **Kāngrī**.

2.1.16 Finally we come to **Punjabi**, on the northwestern flank of the Hindi area, the language not only of Punjab State in India, but also of a major element in the population of Pakistan – some would say the "dominant" element, but this assessment is confused by continued use of the term "Punjabi" by some to cover both Punjabi and "Lahndi" speakers. Grierson fixed the boundary between "Lahnda" and Punjabi, admittedly poorly defined, at a line running north–south through Montgomery and Gujranwala Districts, west of Lahore, that is, well within Pakistan. (Following Shackle, we may call the Punjabi-speaking Lahore–Gujranwala–Sialkot area Central Punjab.)

Whatever validity Grierson's line may once have had has no doubt been disturbed by the great movements of population associated with Partition. However, H. Bahri seems to have been wrong in his prediction (1962: x) that Partition would have the eventual effect of shifting the uncertain boundary of "Lahndi" eastward to the new international frontier, presumably because Punjabi speakers in Pakistan would be cut off from influence from the main centers of the language in Eastern (Indian) Punjab. The reverse seems to have happened. Not only has Lahore proved to be a sufficiently strong center of Punjabi in its own right (see Shackle 1970), but the position of Punjabi in Pakistan in general has been strengthened by the large number of refugees from Eastern Punjab following Partition, as it had been earlier by the resettlements in the new Canal Colonies. These involved an influx of Punjabi speakers into the Siraiki-speaking area (to which the "Siraiki movement" is in part a reaction).

On the Indian side also, the situation is confused by the increasing identification of "Punjabi" with Sikhism, and the partly successful campaigns of the Arya Samaj to persuade Punjabi-speaking Hindus to return their mother tongue in the census as "Hindi". This is not to say that many Punjabi-speaking Hindus do not identify with the language also, but the number of speakers and their area of settlement is larger than official statistics indicate. Again, an up-to-date objective survey of the situation on both sides of the border is very desirable, but is unlikely for political reasons to be undertaken in the near future.

2.1.17 Although with Punjabi the circle is completed, there remain to be mentioned a number of Indo-Aryan languages northwest of "Lahndi" and Kashmiri, more or less contiguous with the main group (i.e. except where interrupted by recent intrusions of Pashto) but in important ways outside their "orbit", culturally and historically. These are generally grouped together as "**Dardic**". The most important is **Shina** (Ṣiṇā), spoken in several dialects in the basin of the Upper Indus (Chilas) and its tributaries (Kishenganga, Astor), beyond the mountains to the north of the Kashmir valley, from Gilgit to Palas in Indus Kohistan, that is to say, mainly in Pakistani territory. West of the Indus in Swat Kohistan are found **Bashkarīk** (= **Gāwrī**, in the Panjkora valley and at the headwaters of the Swat), **Maiyā̃** (on the right bank of the Indus, with a dialect **Kanyawālī** isolated in Shina territory in the Tangir valley to the northwest), and **Torwālī** (in the Upper Swat valley). Further west again, across another range of mountains, is the large Chitral valley, where the main language is **Khowār**. **Kalaṣha** survives in side valleys of southern Chitral. **Phalūṛa**, an archaic dialect of Shina, is or was spoken in some villages in southern Chitral. (Most of these, that is, excluding only Gilgit and Chilas, are presently in the northern reaches of the Northwest Frontier Province, Pakistan.) **Gawar-Bātī** is spoken on the Chitral–Afghan border, centering at Arnawai, where the Chitral and Bashgal rivers unite to form the Kunar. Other, already-fragile linguistic fragments, **Ningalāmī**, **Gṛangalī**, **Shumāshtī**, **Kaṭārqalā-Woṭapūrī**, **Sāvī**, **Tirāhī**, discovered by researchers in single villages in eastern Afghanistan, in some cases spoken by only a few families (or even a few old men), often a generation or more ago, may no longer exist, but are important for the linguistic history of the region. The encroaching language is everywhere Pashto. A larger collection of now mutually incomprehensible dialects, spoken further into Afghanistan in scattered valleys north of the Kabul river from the Kunar (Chigha Sarai) as far west as the Panjshir, centering in the region known as Laghman, constitutes what is left of the **Pashaī** language, apparently once much more widespread.

2.1.18 [In remote valleys higher up in the Afghan Hindu Kush are several additional languages, before the conversion of their speakers to Islam at the end of the nineteenth century collectively called "**Kāfirī**", a term now replaced by "**Nūristānī**", which were once grouped with "Dardic" on the basis of inadequate information. I follow more recent scholarly opinion (Morgenstierne 1961, 1973, Strand 1973, Fussman 1972, Buddruss 1977, Nelson 1986) in treating them as a group separate from Indo-Aryan, but it seems appropriate to mention them here. From east to west, they are: **Kati** (= **Bashgalī**) in the Upper Bashgal valley, with small enclaves in Pakistani Chitral, and the dialect **Kamvíri** lower on the Bashgal (Kamdesh); **Tregāmī** in three villages (as the name indicates) further to the southwest, between the Pech and the Kunar; **Waigalī** (= **Kalaṣha-alā**) in the Waigal valley (a northern tributary of the Pech); **Prasun** (= **Veron** = **Wasī-weri**) in six villages in the high valley of the Upper Pech; **Ashkun** between the Pech and the Alingar. In the drainage of upper tributaries (Kulum, Ramgel) of the Alingar and also of the Ktivi tributary of the Pech, Kati is again spoken, its continuity broken by Prasun. The whole Nuristan area was conquered by the Afghans only in 1896.]

2.1.19 The *non-contiguous* Indo-Aryan languages, that is, those based *outside* the contiguous Indo-Aryan area, may be listed as follows: **Sinhalese**, the principal language of Sri Lanka; **Maldivian** (= **Divēhī**), the related language of the republic of the Maldives (an archipelago in the Indian Ocean southwest of India); **Saurāshtrī**, the language of a community of silk-weavers centered at Madurai in the Tamil country; **Dakhinī**, a southern form of Urdu, insofar as it is centered at Hyderabad in the Telugu area; **Parya**, an Indo-Aryan language recently discovered in Soviet Central Asia (Tadzhikistan). Like the outlying dialects of **Konkaṇī** (and apparently also **Khetrānī** in Baluchistan) mentioned earlier, all of these are the result of pre-modern migrations of Indo-Aryan speakers – in the case of Sinhalese, as early as the fifth century BC. More recent migrations (i.e. both overseas and within India and Pakistan) have not yet resulted in distinct languages (and under modern conditions are not likely to), but unique *koines* have arisen in the course of the colonial experience in Trinidad and Fiji.

2.1.20 There remains a third category of Indo-Aryan languages to be noted, partly overlapping with the above (i.e. in some cases also non-contiguous) – those with *no specific territorial base*. The most important of these is **Urdū**, the language first of the Muslim population, mainly urban, of northern India; now the official language of Pakistan and a second language for all educated persons there; the southern form **Dakhinī**, mentioned above as having a base at Hyderabad, is also found spoken (along with Standard Urdu for formal purposes and by the more educated) by Muslims in cities and towns throughout the Deccan, and in Bombay.

Other such languages are **Gojri** (or **Gujuri**), spoken by semi-nomadic herdsmen found scattered at higher elevations in the hill areas mainly of Jammu–Kashmir (especially Punch District) and adjoining regions of Pakistan and on into Afghanistan; **Lamānī** (= **Banjārī** = **Lambādī**), spoken by another nomadic people (nowadays engaged mostly in construction) found primarily in Andhra Pradesh, Karnataka, and Maharashtra; both are of Rajasthani affinity. Finally there is **Romany**, the language of the Gypsies, not only non-contiguous but extra-Indian as well as non-territorial, although (as with the others) there are marked concentrations in certain areas, in this case in Eastern Europe (Yugoslavia, Eastern Slovakia).

2.2 "Language" vs. "dialect" in the Indo-Aryan context

We have managed to complete the brief survey above without really confronting a problem which nevertheless did unavoidably obtrude itself from time to time, namely the distinction between a *language* and a *dialect.* A few words may be said about it now.

The problem is that although the distinction is a common and indeed often a useful one, there is no generally accepted criterion for making it. Both terms are used, not only popularly but also by scholars, in several conflicting ways. There are two common senses in which the meaning of one term is linked with the other.

In Sense A, a *dialect* is a subvariety of a larger unit, which is typically a *language.* (It may in turn be subdivided into smaller units, or *subdialects.* These terms have equivalents in Indo-Aryan languages, e.g., H. *bhāṣā* 'language', *bolī* 'dialect', *upabolī* 'subdialect'.)

In Sense B, a *dialect* is unwritten, while a *language* possesses a **written "standard"** and a literature. (This distinction is then undermined by the usage *"the literary dialect"* in situations of diglossia, such as obtain in Sinhalese or Bengali. Inasmuch as this refers to a *subvariety* of a language, even if of a special kind, it may be said to hark back to Sense A.) To be sure, a (non-literary) dialect may also be written down (= transcribed) but this does not turn it automatically into a "language" in this sense: it should also have a (written) literature and a measure of official and cultural recognition, both elastic concepts. It is clear that the entailed status comes and goes, however, and therefore is primarily sociocultural rather than linguistic in nature. In contemporary India and Pakistan several erstwhile *dialects* (Dogri, Siraiki) are said to be "agitating for *language* status". Meanwhile, one-time literary *languages* such as Braj and Awadhi are said to have "reverted to *dialect* status" (Khubchandani 1983: 27, 168; his term is *vernacularization*).

Even on one side of the unclear boundary between *dialect* and *language* in Sense B, there are differences: one speaks of "developed" and "undeveloped" languages. Such differences are in part linguistic, invoving the development of certain specialized registers. While in principle not unquantifiable, such differences are more clinal than absolute. In modern Indo-Aryan every part of the cline is represented, depending on the length of time the *language* has been cultivated and under what circumstances. Thus Modern Standard Hindi, with its official status at two levels (provincial and national), has more developed registers than, say, Siraiki, until recently cultivated only for religious poetry, or Khowar, which has only recently been cultivated at all.

In view of the slipperiness of Sense B, it might appear that Sense A is the preferable one for the scientific study of language (using the latter word now in a third sense, Sense C). The terms of Sense A, however, are often taken (mainly in academic usage itself) to be purely relative, with different applications at different levels of abstraction: *x* is a dialect of language *L*, which is in turn a "dialect" of construct *G*, etc.; e.g., Sambalpuri is a dialect of Oriya, which is a "dialect" of Magadhan, which is a "dialect" of Indo-Aryan, which is a "dialect" of Indo-Iranian, which (like Germanic, Italic, etc.) is a "dialect" of Indo-European. Although it is the term *dialect* which suffers most, the higher constructs in each case might logically be called "languages", leaving us, it would appear, with no definable level of application for either term.

Even if it is granted that such usages are metaphorical extensions of terms normally and properly applied to a language and its subvarieties, there is unfortunately no universal criterion of linguistic distance for *languages* as against *dialects*, that is, of how different a speech-variety has to be from another to qualify as a separate *language*. Not that attempts to come up with such a measure have not been made. Nigam (1971: xxv–xxvi), for example, perhaps taking a cue from lexicostatistics, suggests that speech varieties sharing 81 per cent or more of **basic vocabulary** should be classed as *dialects*, less than 81 per cent as *languages*. H. Bahri (1980: 1–2), recognizing that "mutual intelligibility" is a relative rather than an absolute concept, suggests a more subtle breakdown: **mutual intelligibility** around 10 per cent = two languages historically related but geographically removed (Punjabi and Gujarati); up to 25 per cent = two languages in long cultural contact (English and French); 25–50 per cent = can be called "languages" or "dialects" (Rajasthani and Hindi); 50–75 per cent = two dialects (Braj Bhasha and Bundeli); around 90 per cent = subdialects (Sargujiya and Bilaspuri).[4]

No one has to my knowledge seriously attempted to apply either Nigam's or Bahri's criteria to problems of language and dialect identification in Indo-Aryan. Mutual intelligibility is an especially tricky concept to apply in a multilingual society such as that of South Asia, where familiarity (i.e. various degrees of "passive bilingualism") as well as purely linguistic distance must be reckoned with. Any attempt to apply it must reckon also with judgments like Morgenstierne's (1962: 21–4) that the Pashai dialects are "decidedly one language" despite their mutual *un*intelligibility, because they are "well-defined through phonetical, and especially through morphological and lexical peculiarities." (Speakers of the geographically fragmented Pashai dialects have few opportunities for contact and for thus acquiring that degree of passive bilingualism that is often a component even of inter*dialectal* mutual intelligibility.)

What happens in practice, of course, is that in parts of the world where a clean slate is not available for these exercises, rather than attempt them even linguists fall back for the most part on the conventional "languages" of Sense B, whatever their mutual linguistic distance, and whether mutually intelligible to a significant extent or not, for identifying the *dialect groupings* that are treated as languages in Sense A. In a continent like Europe, blessed with well-defined peninsulas and islands, and where the nation–state has become the norm, this becomes problematic linguistically only at a few points, such as the Dutch–German and Franco–Italian borders, where there is a true dialectal continuum. Elsewhere *language* in Sense A *and* Sense B correlates fairly well with geographical and political units.

South Asia, which bears many analogies to Europe, differs from it radically here: it is *shaped* differently. Lacking clearcut geographical units of the European type where dialectal variants can crystallize in semi-isolation, or longstanding political boundaries, the entire Indo-Aryan realm (except for Sinhalese) constitutes one enormous dialectal continuum, where continued contact inhibits such crystallization, and differentiated dialects continue to influence one another. The speech of each village differs slightly from the next, without loss of mutual intelligibility, all the way from Assam to Afghanistan. Cumulatively the differences are very great, but where do we draw the dialect, let alone the language, boundaries?

A careful dialect geography would no doubt show that the subdialectal continuum in fact does not present a uniform gradient, but is punctuated by both smaller (dialectal) and greater (language) bundlings of isoglosses. The *LSI* does not really constitute such a dialect geography, but it is a step in that direction. The region is not totally devoid of natural barriers – for the most part consisting of rough hill country.

Superimposed on this ground pattern are the literary languages of Sense B and their culturally-defined orbits. The relation of these to languages in Sense A is often problematic. Thus the Rajbangsi dialect of the Rangpur District (Bangladesh), and the adjacent Indian Districts of Jalpaiguri and Cooch Behar, has been classed with Bengali because its speakers identify with the Bengali culture and literary language, although it is linguistically closer to Assamese. So has the Chittagong dialect of southeastern Bangladesh, which differs from Standard Bengali more than Assamese itself does. There are limits to this, however: although Urdu is the preferred literary language of Kashmir and of Pakistani Punjab, no one would take Kashmiri or Punjabi to be dialects of Urdu (or of Hindi–Urdu).

As indicated in the preceding section, the real problem is with the vast "Hindi area", defined as the area within which Modern Standard Hindi is today the accepted written language. Are all forms of Indo-Aryan speech within it "dialects of Hindi"? Rejecting this as intuitively too much at variance with the proper scope of a *language* in Sense A (and not having to reckon with the subsequent further consolidation of the status of Hindi), Grierson proceeded to set up, as noted above in section 2.1.1, several artificial constructs at the level of "languages" in Sense A that he felt were needed to make linguistic sense of the situation: "Eastern Hindi", "Western Hindi", "Rajasthani", and "Bihari". (He also used the term "Pahari", but always with reference to a group; never, it seems, in the sense of "a" language.) The first two did not catch on at all; "Rajasthani" and "Bihari" did trickle down to some extent into popular usage – to the annoyance of Nigam who remarks regarding the census of 1961 that the terms should be discouraged: it "is not useful to have a blanket name," which only confuses the statistics. (The first is most often used, however, as a synonym for Modern Literary Marwari and the second for Magahi – usages which may owe nothing to Grierson.) The majority of "Bihari" and "Rajasthani" speakers still report their mother tongues under more specific and traditional names – Maithili, Bhojpuri, Marwari, Dhundhari, etc. – or simply as Hindi.

Another such Griersonian language construct was "Lahnda", discussed in section 2.1.13 above. Elsewhere, "normal" taxonomic problems exist, sometimes complicated by politics, on a scale appropriate to the subcontinent: is Konkani a separate language or a dialect of Marathi? Is Halbi a mixture of Oriya and Marathi, a dialect of Marathi, or a separate language? Is Khandeshi a dialect of Marathi or of Gujarati, or a separate language?

Often such problems correlate with transition areas. Even at the subdialectal level, Grierson tried to distinguish what he regarded as "mixed" and unstable forms of speech characteristic of such areas from "true dialects", presumably part of the underlying gradient. Certain cases might seem particularly to call for such a distinction, but dialect or language mixture has in fact been involved in the formation of most of the major NIA languages to some extent also. It is difficult to know where to draw the line. "Stability" is perhaps the key to the difference, but the sociolinguistic and historical variables involved in such stabilization need further study. Dialectal differentiation in an area geographically like that of Indo-Aryan cannot proceed in a "pure" form, i.e. without the peripheral dialects running up against neighboring languages, in any case, and mixed dialects in the zones of transition between major languages (and mixed subdialects in the zones between major dialects) are an inevitable result.

"Mixed" forms of speech involving *non-Aryan* languages or substrata are perhaps another matter, calling for special treatment as creoles. Such would include such "dialects" of Bengali as **Chākmā** (spoken in the Chittagong hills presumably by former Chin [Tibeto-Burman] speakers) and **Malpahāṛiā** (spoken in the Rajmahal hills by former Malto [Dravidian] speakers), as well as the aforementioned Halbi, whose speakers may or may not be former Gond [Dravidian] speakers (Trelang 1966: 359–60), and many others. The matter is complicated by the fact that, except for the first, these *also* typically involve transition zones between Indo-Aryan languages (Bengali/"Bihari" in the case of Malpaharia; Oriya/Marathi in the case of Halbi).

2.3 Hindi and Urdu

The ultimate anomaly in the what-is-a-language dilemma in Indo-Aryan is presented by the Hindi–Urdu situation. Counted as different *languages* in sociocultural Sense B (and officially), Urdu and Modern Standard Hindi are not even different dialects or subdialects in linguistic Sense A. They are different *literary styles* based on the *same* linguistically defined subdialect.

At the colloquial level, and in terms of grammar and core vocabulary, they are virtually identical; there are minor differences in usage and terminology[5] (and customary pronunciation of certain foreign sounds), but these do not necessarily obtrude to the point where anyone can immediately tell whether it is "Hindi" or "Urdu" that is being spoken. At formal and literary levels, however, vocabulary differences begin to loom much larger (Hindi drawing its higher lexicon from Sanskrit, Urdu from Arabic and Persian), to the point where the two styles/languages become mutually unintelligible. To the ordinary non-linguist who thinks, not unreasonably, that languages consist of words, their status as different *languages* is *then* commonsensically obvious, as it is from the fact that they are written in quite different scripts (Hindi in Devanagari and Urdu in a modified Perso-Arabic).

The latter is a factor of peculiar importance in *language-B* status in South Asia that has not yet been discussed: there is a widespread feeling that a self-respecting language should have a distinctive script (see Chapter 6). Some readers may be drawn to make a comparison with Serbo-Croatian (written in Roman and Cyrillic scripts), but the analogy is not quite apt: there are grammatical differences between these two – for example involving the use or non-use of an infinitive – which are not found in Hindi–Urdu, while on the other hand the lexical differences are not so massive and systematic. The Hindi–Urdu situation is apparently unique in the world.

What, then, is the subdialectal base of these two standard languages? Not surprisingly, it was that of the capital, Delhi, sometimes referred to as **Dehlavi**. It is often called **Khaṛī Bolī** (among various etymologies: < H–U. *khaṛā* 'standing', hence > 'stand[ard dialect]'). This would be appropriate, if this term were not also frequently applied to the country dialects north of Delhi, which present a number of phonological (*/ṇ, ḷ/*) and other features not found in the standard of the capital. (As noted in 2.1.1 above, Sankrityayan and Bahri therefore propose to call the former "Kauravi", reserving "Khari Boli" for the Delhi-based standard language, wherever it may be spoken.)

Like urban speech everywhere, and especially that of capitals, the language of Delhi was not based on one dialect in any case, but on a dialectal composite. Thus, along with "Kauravi", Hariyanvi, Punjabi, Rajasthani (Mewati), Braj and other influences have gone into the making of Khari Boli – the last especially during the century (1566–1658) when the imperial capital moved to Agra, in the heart of the Braj country. (Some scholars believe this dialectal fusion took place earlier in the Punjab, i.e. Lahore, which had been under Muslim rule for nearly two centuries, and was then brought to Delhi with the Muslim conquest in 1193, but the evidence for this is very thin from this remote and unsettled period. The proximity of the city to the Punjab is probably sufficient to explain the "Punjabi" elements in Khari Boli.)

This "standard" dialect was moreover not precisely equivalent to the speech of Delhi as such, but more specifically to that of certain *classes* and *neighborhoods* most closely associated with the Mughal court and its predecessors. Although reference to the latter fact is often made, based on statements in literary sources, what precisely this might mean in linguistic terms has not been spelled out. More importantly, a careful *linguistic* analysis of the aforementioned dialectal mixture has yet to be made.[6] Rai (1984), while fascinating, is deliberately "non-technical". He does make the observation, however, that at least at what he calls the Old Hindi stage (thirteenth–fourteenth centuries?) the contributing dialects

> were all in their initial, formative stage, when their identities were not sharply defined – and therefore mixing was easy . . . Any attempt to divide them or to contrapose them one to the other is likely to confuse the linguistic picture of the times altogether and get the researcher tied up in a whole lot of quite intractable problems.
>
> (p. 123)

Tiwari (1961) is more concerned with Hindi in relation to the general history of Indo-Aryan.

Once Khari Boli had taken on a stable shape in the capital, and had spread far and wide as a lingua franca, there were other influences, essentially superficial, on its *literary* development in later centers of literary activity such as Lucknow (Urdu) and Allahabad (Hindi). These too need to be investigated from a linguistic point of view. In summary, it could be said that although the *sociopolitical* history of Hindi and Urdu has been much studied and commented upon (see also Narula 1955, Brass 1974, Barannikov 1972, Chernyshev 1978), a proper *linguistic* history of them (as distinct from their MIA and OIA antecedents) still needs very much to be written.

Often enough even accounts of sociopolitical history are distorted by the attempts of partisans of one language/style or the other to establish its priority. In this they are aided by terminological confusion. Is Modern Standard Hindi really Urdu in Devanagari script relexified with Sanskrit *tatsamas* (see Chapter 4)? Or is Urdu really Hindi in Perso-Arabic script from which the *tatsamas* have been purged and replaced with Perso-Arabic terms? Both assertions will be found in the literature on the subject.

On the one hand, it is no doubt true that British administrators (and missionaries) played a role in promoting and even creating Modern Standard Hindi at the beginning of the nineteenth century by encouraging the development at Fort William College, in place of the old and limited Braj literary language, of a new prose standard in the Nagari script *"on the basis of Urdu"* – that is to say, on the basis of Khari Boli. This was in recognition of the fact that Urdu had conveniently spread as a lingua franca (as well as preferred language of the Muslim population) wherever in India Mughal influence had been felt,[7] as well as of the fact that the higher literary style of Urdu had evolved into something remote from Indian life, unintelligible to the masses, and that its script was not originally designed for an Indo-Aryan language, difficult to master, and not suitable for printing.

On the other hand, Urdu was not called *Urdu*[8] until around 1800.[9] In fact in earlier Urdu writing itself it was often called *Hindi*! But this is a term, as we have seen, of very different implications for different people. To the aforementioned Urdu writers, *Hindi* or *Hindavi* undoubtedly meant 'the language of India' – which for them happened to be Khari Boli, as contrasted with Persian, the language of the Muslim establishment. For protagonists of Modern Standard Hindi, however, the term includes all the earlier indigenous literary traditions of the present "Hindi area", predominantly in dialects (or languages) other than Khari Boli. Ordinary people in the area, particularly in Uttar Pradesh, also commonly call their non-Khari Boli spoken languages "Hindi". Since *Hindi* as a term is of Muslim (Persian) origin, derived from the river *Sindhu* 'Indus' (and meaning originally simply 'Indian'), it would be interesting to know just when and how they came to do this. In any case, if the linguistic history called for above is to be coherently written, it must have a clear focus – i.e. Khari Boli itself, with reference to the other languages of the "Hindi area" only insofar as they impinge on it.

Meanwhile, although for the British administration and many others the terms *Urdu* and *Hindustani* were essentially equivalent, *Urdu* in the eyes of some of its protagonists took on a special connotation of stylistic refinement and could not refer to "plain" Khari Boli/Colloquial Hindustani. (Rai [1984] refers to this development as "New Urdu".) Whether Urdu can maintain such a luxury in its new function as the national language of Pakistan remains to be seen, although proponents of this view are not wanting.

Many complex social and political forces, which we cannot go into here, have conspired to pull the two "styles" ever further apart. Their identity as separate languages may now be regarded as a cultural fact, however anomalous linguistically.

2.4 **Nomenclature**

Although European languages present a few instances of multiple or fluctuating names (e.g. *Ruthenian/Little Russian/Ukrainian*), these have now been largely sorted out. Linguistic nomenclature in the Indo-Aryan field, on the other hand, still constitutes a boulder-strewn path over which one must pick one's way carefully. Nomenclature complicates the Hindi–Urdu situation, as we have seen. (It is in fact even more complicated than just described: besides the once-ubiquitous *Hindustani* (now seldom used), the more specific *Dakani* or *Dakhini*, and the earlier *Hindui* and *Hindavi*, there was also *Rekhta* (< Pers. 'mixed' = 'the Hindustani or Urdu language' [Platts 1965 (1884)]), and its specialized feminine counterpart *Rekhti* '[imitated] women's speech'. "Hindi" in the broader sense, referring to all the speech varieties of the Hindi area, is of course equivalent to a plethora of more specific names.)

Elsewhere in Indo-Aryan, the name for a language or dialect one encounters may be its current official name (*Hariyanvi*), a popular name (*Laria* for Chhattisgarhi), its former name (*Bangaru* for Hariyanvi), a newly emerging name (*Siraiki*, *Angika*), a nickname bestowed by others (*Chhikacchiki Boli*, *Jangli*, *Hakki-pikki*), or a name with no popular currency bestowed by a researcher (*Lahnda*, *Central Eastern Rajasthani*). It may be the name, real or fancied, of a community, such as a caste, applied to the language it speaks: *Jatu* for Hariyanvi, *Jatki* for several subdialects of "Southern Lahnda", where Jats or Jatts are numerous; *Ahirani* (from the Ahirs, a caste of dairymen) for Khandeshi. Especially in the case of migrants long-established outside the territory of their mother tongue, there is a tendency to draw their identity from the fragment of their former society they can still see before them – a caste group, an occupation, or a remembered locality. Thus small groups of Marathi speakers outside Maharashta return their language under a number of strange names – *Bare*, *Burdi*, *Kamari*, *Koshti*, etc. Some Gujarati speakers in Mysore return their language as *Kshatriya*, while *Kshatri* is a name given to a form of Hindi spoken in Andhra Pradesh. *Khatri* is also an alternative name of Saurashtri, in Tamilnadu. (All three are from *ksatriya*, the warrior caste.)

Many languages/dialects have several names: thus *Hariyanvi/Bangaru/Jatu/Deswali*, and *Khandeshi/Ahirani/Dhed Gujari*. Political changes often have a surprisingly immediate effect on language names: with the dissolution of the old native state of Keonthal, near Simla, the major Pahari dialect name *Kiunthali* seems to have disappeared, and been replaced by the new coinage *Mahasui*, from the new District of Mahasu (in Himachal Pradesh).

More problematic for census takers is the situation where a single name is used for more than one language/dialect. There are at least four different sub-Himalayan dialects called *Siraji* (see entries in Appendix I). *Dangi* is a dialect of Braj in northeastern Rajasthan and a dialect of Khandeshi (or of Bhili) in south Gujarat. *Thali* is a dialect of Marwari in western Rajasthan, and a northwestern dialect of Siraiki in Pakistan. Significantly, these names are taken from common topographic features: *sirāj* 'mountainous country', lit. 'Shiva's kingdom' < *śiva-rājya*; *thal* 'desert' (also *thar*; cf. *Thareli*, a desert dialect of Sindhi); *ḍāng* 'heavily forested hill country'. *Pahari* (< *pahāṛ* 'mountain') is another such non-specific topographic term. One must be careful not to jump to conclusions, however. The name *Doabi*, for instance, refers not to the (Braj) dialect of the best known *doāb* ('interfluve') between the Ganges and Jumna in western UP, but to the (Punjabi) dialect of the Jalandhar *doāb*, between the Beas and the Sutlej.

The census often tells us something regarding the name speakers prefer for their language. For instance, they overwhelmingly prefer the old name *Dhundhari* to the more transparent *Jaipuri*, and *Marwari* to the more grandiloquent *Rajasthani*, although the latter has made considerable headway.

3

The historical context and development of Indo-Aryan

3.1 Genetic connections

The nearest relatives of Indo-Aryan are the **Iranian** languages immediately to the west. These include, besides **Persian** and related dialects in Iran: **Kurdish** and **Baluchi**; **Ossetic** in the Caucasus; **Gilaki**, **Mazanderani**, **Talishi**, and **Tati** along the southern and southwestern shores of the Caspian; **Pashto** and other languages in Afghanistan and adjoining areas of Pakistan (mainly the Northwest Frontier Province); and the Pamir group of archaic dialects (**Shugni**, **Sarikoli**, **Yazgulami**, **Wakhi**, **Ishkashmi**, **Munjani**, **Yidgha**) which extend into northeastern Afghanistan from Soviet Tajikistan (the main language of which, **Tajik**, is closely connected to Persian). Iranian languages once covered a much larger area, including most of Soviet Central Asia, large areas of southern Russia and the present-day Ukraine, and extending into Chinese Turkestan and even the Balkans. The area has contracted mainly as a result of the expansion of Turkic.

Older stages of Iranian are well documented in **Old Persian** (from the sixth century BC) and **Avestan**, Middle Persian (**Pahlavi**), **Parthian**, **Sogdian** (texts from both Soviet Central Asia and colonies in China), and **Khotanese** (Chinese Turkestan), and in more fragmentary form in other extinct dialects. Old Persian represents a Western Iranian dialect; Avestan, the language of the Zoroastrian scripture (the *Avesta*), called "Zend" by earlier writers, represents a Northeastern dialect. Until recently, the reforms of Zoroaster/Zarathushtra and the core of the *Avesta* were thought, on the basis of unreliable Sasanian traditions of the first millennium AD, to date from about 600 BC. A number of scholars now incline to a much earlier date, 1000 BC or before – even as early as 1700 BC (see Boyce 1979, Gnoli 1980). Among the arguments for an earlier date is the similarity of Avestan to Vedic Sanskrit (see below).

Together Indo-Aryan and Iranian constitute INDO-IRANIAN, a major branch of the Indo-European family. Within Indo-Iranian, Indo-Aryan is now clearly the weightier partner, both demographically and in terms of number of languages, despite the great territorial extension of Iranian. It also possesses records which are not only older in time but for the most part more archaic linguistically. (Even if the new arguments for an early date for portions of the original *Avesta* are accepted, the text as it now stands dates only from the Sasanian period [third to seventh centuries AD], and it appears to have been affected much more by the process of transmission before that date than was the text of, e.g., the *Rig Veda* during its transmission [the core of which in any case is probably older].)

From its earliest monuments Iranian is distinguished by a number of phonological innovations: (1) the loss of aspiration in voiced stops (∗*bh*, ∗*dh*, ∗*gh* > *b*, *d*, *g*); (2) the spirantization of voiceless stops in preconsonantal position (∗*p*, ∗*t*, ∗*k* + C > *f*, *θ*, *χ* + C); and, in most subgroups, (3) the opening of ∗*s* to *h* before non-occlusives. In a few respects, however, Iranian is more conservative than Indo-Aryan, e.g., in its retention of: (1) final consonant clusters (simplified in the oldest Indo-Aryan: $-C^1C^2\#$ > $-C^1\#$, Iranian *vāχʃ* > Skt *vāk*); (2) a diphthongal pronunciation of ∗*aι*, ∗*au* (> Indo-Aryan *ē*, *ō*: Iranian *haoma*, Skt *sōma*); voiced sibilants (lost in Indo-Aryan, in the case of ʒ turning a following *d* into the new sound *ḍ* in the process). In any case, Iranian is very important for comparisons that often throw light on Old Indo-Aryan morphology and semantics as well as phonology.

Within the wider confines of Indo-European, the closest affinities of Indo-Iranian in turn are with the so-called *Satəm*[1] languages on the one hand (Albanian, Armenian, Baltic, and Slavic), and with Greek on the other. With the *Satəm* languages in general Indo-Iranian shares two basic changes in the Late ∗IE consonant system: (1) loss of the labial element in the ∗*labiovelars* ($*k^w$, $*g^w$, $*g^wh$ > *k*, *g*, *gh*); (2) affrication ultimately leading in most cases to spirantization of the ∗*palatals*[2] (∗*kˆ*, ∗*gˆ*, ∗*gˆh* > ∗*ć*, *ǰ*, *ǰh*, thence > Skt *ś*, *j*, *h*; Iranian *s*, *z*; OPers. *θ*, *d*; Lith. *š*, *ž*; Slavic *s*, *z*).

With Slavic and partly with Baltic it also shares a peculiar rule (the "ruki" rule – or set of rules), affecting ∗*s* after ∗*r*, ∗*u*, ∗*k*, ∗*ι*. In these environments, *s* was retracted to *ṣ*, which remains in Sanskrit (and then developed to *ʃ* in Iranian and eventually to *χ* in Slavic). It also shares with Slavic a so-called Second Palatalization involving the new velar (originally labiovelar) series before front vowels (*k*, *g* > *č*, *ǰ* [the latter in Slavic then > *ž*]) – but this appears to have happened independently in the two branches.[3] Balto-Slavic and Indo-Iranian also have in common certain peculiarities of declension and conjugation and a number of special lexical items (e.g. words for 'holy', 'God', 'mountain', 'bright', 'dark', 'black', 'cold', 'to praise', 'fear', 'to be released', 'to call', 'to awaken').

With Greek,[4] Indo-Iranian shares another set of important common features of conjugation and declension, the most salient of which is the "augment" (prefixed *a-* in Skt, *e-* in Gk) as a sign of the past.[5] It also shares at least one phonological feature, the merger of *IE $\mathring{m}$,$\mathring{n}$ (syllabic nasals) with *a*: Skt *a̱-jñāta-*, Gk *a̱-gnōstos* vs. Eng. cog. *un-couth*.

3.2 **Migration hypotheses and associated problems**

Some of the special features shared with Greek seem to be common innovations rather than common preservations, presupposing a long period of close contact *after* the general Indo-European dispersal. This poses problems for the earlier location of the Indo-Iranian speakers and the route taken by them to India and Iran.

A prior location south of the Urals accords best with a proven exchange of vocabulary with Finno-Ugric (this language group may once have been located further to the south and east),[6] with the distribution of the prehistoric Andronovo culture (equated by some archaeologists with the Indo-Iranians), and perhaps also with the special relationship with Slavic. (Although the location of the Proto-Slavs even two thousand years later is not definitely known, it was certainly further to the west, probably in the Carpathian foothills and to the northeast of them. Their location at this early period is even more speculative. It is possible, however, that the Dnieper river served as a line of communication between Slavs and Indo-Iranians at this time just as it did much later between Slavs and Iranians [Scythians].)

This also accords with a migration route east of the Caspian, as does the existence of the group of languages now called **Nuristani** (section 2.1.18 above), thought to be an archaic offshoot of Proto-Indo-Iranian (see Chapter 8), in the Hindu Kush region of Afghanistan, and with archaeological evidence showing the displacement of the older culture in northern Iran around 3500–3000 BC (Gimbutas 1970).[7] It seems to be increasingly clear that the Indo-Iranians halted for a rather long period in northeastern Iran and Bactria before pushing on into either India or western Iran.

All this does not accord well with the Greek connection, however, insofar as the latter implies contact between Proto-Greeks and Proto-Indo-Iranians after they left the Indo-European staging area. The linguistic ancestors of the Greeks are assumed to have come from the north, via the Balkans. Estimates of the date of their arrival in Greece vary from 2500 BC to 1500 BC, with the weight of opinion inclining to *c.* 1900 BC (Wyatt 1970). In any case, they did not move eastward to colonize the coastlands of Asia Minor until the eighth century BC. Long before this, from the nineteenth century BC, the heartland of Asia Minor had been dominated by the Hittites, later joined by other groups of Indo-

European affinity, none of whom, except possibly the Phrygians, had any special relation to the Indo-Iranians. A temporary association of Proto-Greek and Proto-Indo-Iranian speakers (and Proto-Armenians) *prior* to their separate southward migrations (but after the departure of other Indo-European "dialect" groups, and a rupture of the Indo-Iranian connection with Balto-Slavic) is a possibility – indeed, it would seem, the only possibility, providing the datings can be harmonized.

Two bits of data that have long posed a problem are: (1) evidence of an Indo-Iranian ruling class (identified as such by their names and characteristic deities, known from cuneiform documents preserved mainly in Hittite archives) in the Mitanni kingdom, which flourished in northeastern Syria 1500–1300 BC; and (2) absence of any mention of Indo-Iranians in western Iran in Assyrian records prior to the tenth century BC. In other words, Indo-Iranians appear in northern Syria a full half millennium *before* their appearance in western Iran. How did they get there? If not from the east, certainly also not very plausibly from the west via Asia Minor (although this used to be suggested): this would have taken them through the Hittite domains from which we get most of the evidence for their presence in Mitanni; it is also at odds with indications of their presence at the same time or earlier in northeastern Iran and Bactria.

Burrow (1955) tried to solve the problem by bringing the Mitanni rulers-to-be straight over the Caucasus, in a movement separate from the main Indo-Iranian migration. This suggestion had the merit of placing them with the Hurrians, the rank-and-file of the Mitanni kingdom over whom they ruled (and whose language in the main they seem to have adopted, retaining only some proper names, names of deities, horsemanship and gambling terms): the Hurrians are thought to have come from the Caucasus.

To call these Mitanni kings "Indo-Iranians", however, is to beg an important question. There has been a controversy on this point among scholars since the discovery of the data in 1907. Some have held that these linguistic fragments are specifically *Indo-Aryan*. Others including Burrow (1955) held they represent undifferentiated *Indo-Iranian*, before the split between Iranian and Indo-Aryan.

The two views have implications for the history of the Indo-Iranian languages. An Indo-Aryan identification would demand an earlier dating of the Iranian/Indo-Aryan split; with it have also been associated speculations regarding the route taken by the Aryans to India (e.g., the Asia Minor route mentioned above), or, possibly a *back migration* of Aryans from India. (If the latter, the date of the Aryan settlement of India would have to be moved back far enough to allow not only for them to reach Syria by 1500 BC, but also for their language to have died out by then, leaving only the terminological residue noted above.) A Proto-Indo-

Iranian identification would allow a later date for the split, although it would not demand it, since the Mitanni fragments could represent a fossilized preservation of an earlier linguistic stage by a small group who left the main body before the split. There is no question of the Mitanni rulers representing the main body of Proto-Indo-Iranians, since their language was already dead.

By 1973 Burrow had accepted the cumulative arguments, best represented by Thieme (1960) and Mayrhofer (1966) (see also Mayrhofer 1973) that the Mitanni fragments are indeed Indo-Aryan (better called *Proto*-Indo-Aryan) and proceeded to reconstruct the scenario as follows to accord with the other evidence, including the new arguments for a much earlier date (1100 BC at the latest) for the reforms of Zoroaster:

1. The split between Indo-Aryan and Iranian-speakers occurred no later than 2000 BC, probably earlier.
2. The split was originally a north/south one, rather than east/west as might appear from the modern distribution of these languages.
3. The southern branch, the Proto-Indo-Aryans (the *Indo-* portion of the term being somewhat out of place, since they had not reached India yet), moved south, via Central Asia, first, occupying initially northeastern Iran, Afghanistan, and Bactria, but eventually moving also into northwestern Iran.
4. Such Proto-Indo-Aryan settlements in northwestern Iran, for which some circumstantial evidence exists (e.g., in hostile Zoroastrian references to *daeva*-worship in Mazanderan, and in a possible Indo-Aryan etymology for the name of Lake *Urmiya*), were a likely source for the antecedents of the Mitanni kings. Evidence for their language indicates a "Pre-Vedic" phase of Indo-Aryan.
5. Meanwhile, Proto-Indo-Aryans from Afghanistan and Bactria began moving (*c.* 1500 BC) into adjacent northwest India (now Pakistan), to which their center of gravity eventually shifted, and where the Vedic language and religion were further characterized.
6. A portion of the northern branch (= Proto-Iranians) then also moved south from Central Asia no later than the fourteenth century BC, into the areas in northeastern Iran and Bactria which had been left lightly occupied by the onward-moving Proto-Indo-Aryans; here Zoroaster was born and inaugurated his religious reforms. (Some of the Proto-Iranians – the Proto-Scythians – apparently remained in the steppe region, which they dominated in the first millennium BC.)
7. Fired by zeal for their new religion, the southern Iranians proceeded

to convert or extirpate remaining pockets (e.g., in northwestern Iran) of Proto-Indo-Aryans who adhered to the old Indo-Iranian religion, and eventually moved to occupy also southwestern Iran, where ultimately, in amalgamation with the high civilizations of the earlier inhabitants (Elamites and others), their great empire arose.

8. A few Proto-Indo-Aryan (according to Burrow) remnants found refuge in inaccessible valleys of the Hindu Kush and became the ancestors of the Nuristani ("Kafiri") tribes, isolated from the Vedic Aryans.
9. Despite identification of the Mitanni rulers as (Proto)-Indo-Aryans, there is thus no necessity and no basis for seeing in the Mitanni evidence any indication either of the route taken by the main Indo-Aryan group or of any back-migration of Indo-Aryans from the Punjab.

Burrow's hypothesis (*JRAS* 1973: 123–40) has been given in some detail because it seems best to satisfy the requirements of the varied kinds of evidence that must be taken into account: the archaeological evidence, the relationship between the Avestan and Vedic languages and religion, the distribution of Iranian peoples at a later period, the Assyrian and Hittite records, the existence of the Nuristani languages, and toponymic evidence.

The date most commonly accepted for the Aryan movement into India is 1500 BC – or broadly speaking, since it seems to have been a gradual, continuing movement, 1700–1200 BC. The only archaeological culture that so far might possibly be connected to the Aryans, the Painted Grey Ware culture of the Western Ganges valley, is dated (C – 14) to around the eleventh century BC (Thapar 1966: 30fn). This would represent a phase of settlement subsequent to the first phase centered on the Upper Indus and the valley of the Kabul river.

3.3 The traditional Indian view

It must be noted that all of this does not accord with Indian tradition, which retains no memory[8] of any migration from an earlier home outside India. (It does retain, in the *Ramayana* epic, a possible memory of Aryan penetration of the South of India, and also, in the story recorded in the *Satapatha Brahmana* of the stopping of the fire-god Agni at the river Gandak in Bihar, of their movement eastward down the Ganges valley.) This is not a matter for great surprise, as very few if any of the Indo-European peoples have any memory of their previous wanderings. What we know of any of these must be pieced together from stray observations of outside observers and inferred from philological evidence. Meanwhile, the traditions of each Indo-European people have become thoroughly intermingled with those of the previous occupants of their respective lands as they put down local roots and evolved newly composite cultures and identities.

Although spokesmen for the traditional Indian view continue to try to fight back with selective modern arguments, the philological evidence alone does not allow an Indian origin of the Aryans. In addition to the special relationship with Balto-Slavic and Finno-Ugric, neither of which is likely to have moved very far from its original location, there is the matter of the nature of the common vocabulary shared by Sanskrit with the rest of Indo-European, which points to a more northerly ultimate home.

Among many such examples, Friedrich (1970: 169) notes that the paucity of *IE tree words in Indic suggests "a movement into a radically different environment." The handful that were preserved ('birch', 'willow', possibly 'pine') are "northern" trees that have analogs somewhere in the Indian environment, if only in the Lower Himalayas and Hindu Kush. (The willow, of course, is also characteristic of the Bactrian intermediate home.) The Himalayan species of birch (*Betula utilis*, in English sometimes called the *Jacquemon tree*) is different from the European *Betula pendula*, but the *IE word (Skt *bhūrja* > H. *bhoj*, N. *bhuj*) seems to have been readily enough transferred to it. (The retention of this word in languages as far south as Marathi and Oriya, despite the fact that the genus *Betula* is not found outside the Himalayan zone, is probably due to the importance of *Betula utilis* in traditional Ayurvedic medicine.) Sanskrit also preserves an *IE word for 'snow' (*hima*), no doubt again with the aid of the Himalayan subenvironment (*himālaya* = 'abode of snow'), outside of which it is not part of the experience of Indo-Aryan-speaking peoples (apart from the Gypsies).

The names of things peculiar to India, on the other hand, are for the most part either borrowed or coined (rather than "primitive"), either of which may be taken as an indication that the thing in question is new to the speakers of a language. Typically Indian items for naming which Sanskrit resorted to *borrowing* include the banana (*kadalī* < prob. Austroas.); cotton (*karpāsa* < prob. Austroas.); pepper (*marica* < likely Austroas.); palm (*tāla* < Drav.); lotus (*kamala*, *kumuda*, *kuvalaya*, *nalina* < all prob. Drav., + *padma* < unknown, but not IE); sandalwood (*candana* < Drav.); banyan (*vaṭa* < prob. Drav. 'rope'); mongoose (*nakula* < prob. Austroas., showing typical prefix); lion (*siṁha* < unknown); peacock (*mayūra* < Drav. [see below, note 11]); and rice in various forms (*vrīhi*, *sāli*, *taṇḍula*, all < non-IE) – not to speak of other non-animal foodstuffs characteristic of the area.[9]

Sanskrit resorted to *description* when it came to: the mango (*āmra*) and tamarind (*āmlā*), both apparently < *amla* 'sour'; elephant (*hastin* = 'having a hand', apparently a calque on Drav.: cf. Tamil *kayam* 'elephant', *kay* 'hand'); buffalo (*mahiṣa* = 'the great one', possibly also a calque on Drav.); monkey (*vānara* = 'forest-er', cf. Malay *orang-utan* 'man of the forest'); cobra (*phaṇakara* = 'producing a hood'); python (*ajagara* = 'goat-swallower'); and possibly the tiger (*vyāghra* < √GHRA 'smell, sniff at something' > 'one who discerns by sniffing, the sniffer' – or a folk etymology along these lines of a Drav. loan-word, cf. Tamil *vēnkai*, Tel. *vēngi*); the list could be extended.[10]

None of this is in the least surprising – *unless* one is trying to establish that Indo-Aryan is indigenous to India. Dravidian, on the other hand, although some hold it also to be non-indigenous, apparently did possess "primitive" terms for a number of these and similar items. (A note of caution is necessary here, however. The native Dravidian vocabulary has not been reconstructed. Burrow and Emeneau's *Dravidian etymological dictionary* [1960] only assembles materials for it. Even the question of borrowing between Dravidian and Austroasiatic would take us too far afield, and it is possible that some of these items were borrowed from the language(s), now vanished, of some pre-Dravidian indigenous population of peninsular India.)

The Aryans of India have more excuse than most for their lapse of memory. Not only was their penetration of the subcontinent a gradual one, extending over many generations: it took place from an area immediately outside it, and not so different from the areas they first entered. They had moreover been settled in the former for a long period after leaving the ultimate Indo-European (or Indo-Iranian) staging area further to the north. Their immediate memory would have been of that more recent home, which moreover was not left entirely behind. It remained in a shadowy way in the Aryan orbit, seesawing between Indian and Iranian control until the spread of Islam and finally the rise of the European colonial empires in the nineteenth century which divided the world differently.

(Rather different scenarios for the Indo-European migrations have recently been proposed by Gamkrelidze and Ivanoff [1984], and as this book goes to press, by Renfrew [1988]. These proposals cannot be discussed here – critical reaction is still emerging. They do not (except in the case of one of Renfrew's alternative hypotheses) affect the basic point of the extra-Indian origin of the Aryans, and most of the preceding and following arguments still seem valid.)

3.4 The new linguistic environment

In any case, it is clear that the incoming Aryans did not find the subcontinent empty. Preceding them were peoples speaking languages of other linguistic stocks, some of which are still vigorously represented in the subcontinent today.

To what stock the language or languages of the highly advanced pre-Aryan

Indus valley ("Harappan") civilization, with its planned cities and as of this writing still undeciphered script, belonged is not clear. This civilization was centered in Sind and Gujarat, with extensions to the Punjab (including the major site of Harappa), northern Rajasthan, to northwestern UP, and even, as recent discoveries show, to a corner of Maharashtra. Sind and Gujarat seem to have been areas initially avoided by the Aryans, who may have kept closer to the cooler foothills in the first phases of their penetration, although violent confrontation with the Harappans in the Punjab is a possibility, particularly in the light of the vivid descriptions of attacks on fortified cities in the *Rig Veda*. The civilization seems to have continued peacefully in Gujarat until a comparatively late period, i.e. 800 BC (Fairservis 1975: 307), after which it dissolved into the subsequent culture, which makes that area one of prime importance in detecting any Harappan influence on Aryan language and culture.

A strong but as yet unproven contender for the language of the Harappans is the **Dravidian** stock, which we have already had occasion to mention. It is represented today by the great languages of culture of southern India (**Tamil**, **Telugu**, **Kannada**, and **Malayalam**), as well as by non-literary languages in east-central and northeastern India – and importantly for the Harappan argument, by a linguistic relic far to the northwest in Baluchistan, **Brahui**. This, along with the presence of Dravidian loanwords in Vedic (*khala* 'threshing floor', *mayūra* 'peacock',[11] etc.), as well as much more numerously in Classical Sanskrit, has been taken to indicate a former much wider distribution of Dravidian.

There have been other pre-Aryan archaeological cultures identified in India, evidently non-Harappan, about whose languages even less can be conjectured. These cultures include those of stockade-building cattle-breeders in Karnataka and of agricultural villagers in Maharashtra and southern Rajasthan.

A second major non-Aryan stock confronting the newcomers at some point, however, was the **Austroasiatic**, which, unlike Dravidian,[12] does have clear affinities outside the subcontinent, namely to the east, in the Indo-Chinese peninsula. It once prevailed there (prior to the Tai and Burmese invasions from the north), and there are located its major languages of culture (**Khmer** or Cambodian, **Mon**, and **Vietnamese**).

The Austroasiatic family is represented in India today by two branches. The **Muṇḍā** branch, formerly called **Kolarian**,[13] is presently concentrated in the forested hilly region in the northeast of peninsular India (in southern Bihar, Orissa, northeastern Andhra Pradesh, and border areas of West Bengal), with one outlying westerly representative (**Korku**) in the Mahadeo hills overlooking the Narbada valley, north of Maharashtra. Like Dravidian it must once have been more widespread. It is likely that a considerable portion of the peasantry in Bihar south of the Ganges, and in Orissa and parts of West Bengal (Chatterji 1926: 101, Mansinha 1962: 16) represents former Munda-speakers who have switched to Aryan (although Dravidian-speakers were and are also represented in these tracts). Grierson would go further. He saw a Munda substratum in North Bihar also, extending to Nepal and adjacent submontane tracts far to the west – largely on the basis of linguistic typology (*LSI 1.1*: 35, 132; *3.1*: 273). Munda is taken by some to be as plausible a candidate as Dravidian for the language of the pre-Aryan population of present-day Uttar Pradesh, but it must be noted that loanwords from Dravidian, which entered Sanskrit mainly at the time of the Aryan occupation of the Ganges plain (Burrow 1955: 386–7), are much more numerous than loanwords from Munda in Sanskrit. There is less reason still, in view of the eastward connections of the Munda stock, and lacking any positive evidence, to bring it further to the west as a candidate for the language of the Harappans.

The other branch of the Austroasiatic stock, **Mon-Khmer**, is now represented in India proper only by the **Khasi** language of the former hill region of Assam now constituting the new state of Meghalaya with its capital at Shillong. It seems always to have been fairly remote from the Aryan advance and not to have affected the results directly, except perhaps locally in the case of Assamese.[14] It may once have had a greater extension – but toward the east: it is closely related to the Palaung-Wa languages of parts of northern Burma and southern China, whose territory was constricted not by the spread of Indo-Aryan, but by the spread of Tibeto-Burman. There may be echoes of the matrilineal and quasi-matriarchal society of the Khasis in the Early New Indo-Aryan legends of the Land of Female Magicians, Kudali, supposedly lying somewhere in Assam.

Tibeto-Burman is the third major non-Aryan stock of which we must take note. Although it is represented by many languages, they are confined to the subcontinent's northern and eastern borderlands. It is apparently more recent in the latter area than Austroasiatic, whose continuity it interrupts. It too once occupied more extensive territories, including not only the entire Assam valley, which it still overlooks from the hills on all sides and from outposts within it, but according to Chatterji (1926: 79, 154) also East and North Bengal.

A fourth stock is represented by a single language, **Burushaski**, with no known affinities. It is spoken in two dialects by about 30,000 persons in Gilgit-Hunza in the extreme north of Pakistan, in the valleys of two upper tributaries of the Indus. Opinions differ regarding the former extent of this language, the speakers of which are among those select world mountaineers with fabulous longevities. Burrow (1954: 375) suggests it may always have been "an isolated unit in a remote mountain tract," although perhaps occupying a somewhat larger territory than at present. Grierson (1915, *LSI 8.1*: Introd. note), however, thought that it had occupied the "whole tract of country in which the Dardic languages are now spoken" – i.e. most of the Upper Indus system including Nuristan. A few Burushaski loanwords do occur in some of these languages: e.g., Shina *ʒākun* 'ass'; Shina of Dras *phu* 'fire'; Prasun *iul* 'belly'; and, curiously, the word for 'iron' (from Burush. *chomar*) in Kati, Waigali, Kalasha, Khowar, Gawarbati, Pashai, Gawri, Torwali, and Shina.

It should be noted that not only Dravidian and Munda, but also Tibeto-Burman and Burushaski have grammatical features that turn up in later Indo-Aryan. Prominent among the latter is the ergative construction (see Chapter 10).

(A fifth stock, the **Tai**, is also present today in the far northeast of India in the form of the **Khamti** language, but it is a latecomer to the area, much later than Indo-Aryan itself, and therefore was not part of the new linguistic environment in which Indo-Aryan found itself upon its arrival or during its subsequent spread.)

Hints of the existence of other stocks, since vanished, within the subcontinent come from the discovery of languages like **Nahali**, spoken by less than one thousand persons mainly in and around a single village in Nimar District, southwestern Madhya Pradesh (where a peculiar Indo-Aryan dialect is also spoken), the coreeee of which does not seem to be related to any of the stocks listed above, and from loanwords in Sanskrit and later Indo-Aryan that cannot be traced to any known indigenous non-Aryan or foreign source. Examples in Sanskrit are: *ikṣu* 'sugarcane'; *roṭikā* 'bread'; *śāli* 'rice'; *vrīhi* 'rice'; *kodrava* 'Paspalum millet'; *sūraṇa* 'a kind of yam'; *bhiṇḍā* 'okra'; *kusumbha* 'safflower'; *mendhikā* 'henna'; *khalla* 'leather'; *badara* 'jujube-plum'; *tinduka* 'round gourd-vegetable'; *siṁha* 'lion'; *padma* 'lotus'. In, e.g., Hindi, there are also: *bājrā* 'pearl millet'; *jwār* 'sorghum millet'; *cāval* 'rice'; *urad* 'black gram'; *supārī* 'betel-nut'; *rūī* 'cotton wool'; *hengā* 'harrow', etc. It should be noted that some of these items are culturally very important. (It is possible that some of these words, along with the products themselves, may be of African origin.) Many attributions to Dravidian or (especially) Austroasiatic in, e.g., Mayrhofer (1956–72), turn out to be mere guesses rather than etymologies.

Shifts in language have not been uncommon in South Asia, and in some cases seem to have occurred more than once, e.g., from Munda to Dravidian to Indo-Aryan, or from Mon-Khmer to Tibeto-Burman to Indo-Aryan. We see clearly only the most recent phases. Although hints of earlier phases are often still embedded in a language, inferences remain largely speculative. Grierson, for one, was not thereby deterred from some very elaborate speculation. For example, regarding **Pahari** languages, he concluded that they betray evidence of successive layers of Munda, Tibeto-Burman, **Khaśa** (originally Dardic, itself allegedly underlain by Burushaski), Gurjara (possibly of non-Aryan Central Asia origin), and Rajasthani elements (*LSI 1.1*: 179–81; *9.4*: 14–16) – in different proportions in different parts of the Pahari area, to which should be added latter-day influence from Punjabi in the west, Hindi in the center, and Maithili in the east.

Such was the new linguistic environment in which Indo-Aryan found itself, hardly a vacuum, already complicated by the presence and mutual encounters of preceding linguistic stocks. The picture would not be complete without noting that, whatever the occasion of their separation, the Iranian cousins of Indo-Aryan soon brought up the rear and came to adjoin it on the west, in places themselves spilling into the subcontinent proper. The precise sequence of these movements is not clear, but from the fact that Indo-Aryan now counts among its immediate neighbors, **Baluchi**, **Parachi**, and **Ormuri**, which are genetically *West* Iranian (related most closely to Kurdish), it seems that the present situation is not a simple continuation of the relationships that prevailed at the time of the first Aryan settlement.

The neighborhood is rounded out in northeastern Afghanistan by another set of cousins, the Nuristani languages already referred to, which according to modern opinion are either pre-Vedic Proto-Indo-Aryan (Burrow), or go back to the period of Indo-Iranian unity (possibly even earlier), and early lodged in the most inaccessible valleys of the Hindu Kush.[15] The knot of mountains at the northwest corner of the subcontinent is thus presently a refuge for an interesting array of linguistic relics: (1) the unclassifiable Burushaski; (2) the Nuristani languages; (3) the archaic East Iranian "Pamir" languages (beyond the Nuristani languages generally on the north side of the Hindu Kush); (4) the archaic Indo-Aryan "**Dardic**" languages (adjoining Nuristani on the south and east); (5) notably archaic dialects of Tibetan (**Balti**, **Ladakhi**) to the northeast of "Dardic"; and (6) the displaced West-Iranian Parachi and Ormuri. The intricate pattern of hidden valleys and mountain barriers in the Upper Indus system, and beyond the divide in the Upper Oxus (< Skt *akṣu*) system, seems to have provided ample opportunity to get lost for many small groups preferring such security to the greater pportunities and risks of life on the richer plains. The Pashto language has long been encroaching on many of these, however, and some of them are now reduced to dwindling islands in a sea of Pashto speech. A similar encroachment by Tajik is reported on the Soviet side.

3.5 Subsequent spread of Indo-Aryan in the subcontinent and beyond

Once inside the mountain barrier, Indo-Aryan quickly became the dominant factor in the subsequent linguistic history of the subcontinent, and influenced that of regions beyond it. The non-Aryan languages in the area that developed literatures did so (with the exception of the language of the Harappans – if indeed it had a literature and not just a system for recording commercial transactions) after the arrival of Indo-Aryan and under direct or indirect Aryan tutelage. This is true not only of the four Dravidian literary languages, but also of Tibetan, Burmese, Newari (in Nepal), Meithei (Manipur), and further east, of Mon, Cambodian, Cham (a language once prevalent in central-coastal Vietnam), Lao, Shan, Thai, and even faraway Javanese in Indonesia. It was, of course, no longer quite the same Indo-Aryan that had entered India, having absorbed meanwhile elements from the pre-Aryan stocks to the point where it could, in the form of Classical Sanskrit or Pali, indeed act as a unifying cultural force throughout this vast and diverse area.

Alongside the physical extension of the settlement of the Indo-Aryan speakers, there were thus two additional kinds of "Aryanization" that took place in the Indian realm. One involved the wholesale adoption of Aryan speech at all levels of society by an indigenous population. The other involved retention of non-Aryan speech in an Aryan garb and its cultivation under the tutelage of Sanskrit (or Pali). Although there was no Aryanization of the first type (involving migration of Aryan speakers) outside the subcontinent except initially in Sri Lanka, all three situations are to be found within it. The lines dividing them are not hard and fast ones, however. There were stages of transition between them, and coexistence of more than one type on the same territory (e.g., Nepali and Newari in Nepal). Moreover, former Aryan-speakers could and did get integrated into eventual "Aryanized non-Aryan" speech communities (particularly in South India).

Aryanization of the third type in some cases involved saturation of vocabularies with Indo-Aryan elements to such an extent that casual observers (such as early Europeans) and sometimes even native scholars could be misled as to the genetic affinities of such a language (e.g., Telugu) – particularly when Indo-Aryan itself had meanwhile also been transformed structurally by non-Aryan influences. Such an "Aryanized non-Aryan" language may actually have a higher proportion of Aryan vocabulary (presumably not, however, *basic* vocabulary – a relatively recent concept) than a genetically Aryan language which has subsequently come under heavy Perso-Arabic influence. Such languages are also in some sense in the Aryan orbit, and might be called the linguistic stepchildren of Indo-Aryan, in contrast with, as it were, its blood descendants. Only the latter are the subject of this book, but the others are part of the larger family picture.

Indo-Aryan settlement, with attendant Aryanization of the first type, apparently proceeded piecemeal via the northern Punjab first into and then down the Ganges valley. Bihar was Aryanized in some sense by the time of the Buddha (i.e. prior to the sixth century BC), although there seems to have been a relapse in Bihar south of the Ganges after the collapse of the great empires based in Magadha (Mauryas, Śungas, Guptas) – depopulation, infiltration of non-Aryan settlers probably of Munda affinity, and their slow re-Aryanization. Bengal was not Aryanized until the Gupta period (fourth century AD) or even later (Chatterji 1926: 76, 79). Orissa remained outside the Aryan pale, at least in the first sense, as late as the seventh century AD (Chatterji 1926: 78, based on remarks of the Chinese pilgrim Hsuan Tsang). In a sense the Aryanization of Orissa, Assam, and North Bengal is *still* under way, as is that of Nepal.

Some form of Indo-Aryan thrust southward – on the west side of the peninsula, not the east – is put by some authorities around the eighth century BC. One basis for this is the extension of the Northern Black Polished Ware, associated with the urbanizing period of the Aryanized culture of the Ganges valley, into the northwestern Deccan at about this time, when it replaced earlier microlithic and chalcolithic cultures (Thapar 1966: 25–6). The earlier Painted Grey Ware, mentioned above as possibly associated with the first wave of Aryan expansion into the Ganges valley, is not found in the Deccan.

Indo-Aryan speech established itself in Sri Lanka according to tradition in the fifth century BC, probably carried by settlers from the west coast (Gujarat), supplemented by later ones from somewhere in eastern India. From Sri Lanka it spread to the Maldives in the ninth or tenth centuries AD – unless we subscribe to the theory that these islands were settled at about the same time as Sri Lanka itself.

The vicissitudes of Indo-Aryan in the peninsula are complex. The Mauryan occupation of the south (third century BC) seems to have been without lasting linguistic effects. There are Asokan pillar edicts inscribed in Early Middle Indo-Aryan which are now deep in Dravidian-speaking territory. The so-called Andhra or Śatavahana empire (first century BC to second century AD), with its capital at Paithan in modern Maharashtra, is thought to have played a more significant role in the Aryanization of at least the northern half of the peninsula. It used a form of Middle Indo-Aryan as its administrative language. Yet it appears that subsequently an Aryanization of the third type, crystallizing around the Kannada and Telugu languages, arrested or delayed an Aryanization of the second type in the Deccan. Later dynasties ruling in what is now Maharashtra (Rashtrakutas, Yadavas) were Kannada-speaking and used Kannada in their inscriptions (along with Sanskrit) up to the eve of the Muslim conquest (fourteenth century). By that time they had begun to patronize Marathi also, and Marathi phrases or lines were beginning to appear in their inscriptions. The earliest of these is strangely from Sravana Belgola, now in the heart of the Kannada country.

Suddenly Marathi is everywhere. Where did it come from? It does not seem to be a simple scenario of Indo-Aryan pushing Dravidian southward, but rather of a longstanding bilingualism involving coexisting social groups, of which different ones had the upper hand at different times. During one phase of this process, apparently the upper hand went to the speakers of an "Aryanized non-Aryan" language (Kannada), while the Aryan speech itself, the ancestor of modern Marathi, meanwhile continued to make headway among the humbler strata of society.

The earlier Maharashtri Prakrit was cultivated under the Satavahanas, but it does not seem to have been the only language. There is some difference of opinion as to whether it is necessarily to be associated with Maharashtra. Sukumar Sen (1960: 20) writes, "There is no reason to assign Māhārāṣṭrī to a fixed dialect area." Most authorities seem to agree with Woolner, however, who holds (1975 [1928]: 5) that it is indeed "based on the old spoken language of the country of the Godavari, and contains many features that survive as peculiarities of modern Marathi." Similarly, Master (1964: 2): "There are already words in the *Sattasai* of Hala (*c.* AD 400–500) which are peculiar to Marathi." Bloch (1920: 32) speaks without hesitation of "la forme du moyen indien marathe". K. M. Munshi (1967: 21), however, citing various authorities, says that the ancestor of Marathi was further north in Asoka's day, was pushed south by the ancestor of Gujarati, and was not in any case the prevailing language of present-day Maharashtra, which until at least the ninth century was Kannada. This, he notes, explains the influence of both Maharashtri and Kannada *on Gujarati*. He reminds us that Gujarat itself (to say nothing of Maharashtra) is for some purposes, e.g., traditional classification of Brahmans into Pancha Gauda and Pancha Dravida orders, in the "Dravida" column.

The total picture may be quite complex: not all of the pieces are yet in place or well understood. (See Southworth 1971 for a speculative but enlightened reconstruction of some aspects of it utilizing the concepts of pidginization and creolization.) In some respects (i.e. morphologically) Marathi is paradoxically quite conservative. Another noteworthy feature is the presence of caste dialects: in this it somewhat resembles its Dravidian neighbors rather than its northern Aryan sisters.

Indo-Aryan languages have thus established themselves variously over Dravidian, Munda, Tibeto-Burman, and probably other substrata. (Peculiarities in Northwest Indo-Aryan – Sindhi, "Lahnda" – led Grierson [*LSI 8.2*: 1–7, 235] to postulate a "Dardic" substratum as well in that area. On the other hand, that was the area of the Harappan civilization, the discovery of which postdates Grierson's hypothesis, with its unknown language.) As noted above, that was not the only possible scenario: the earlier language could arm itself with Aryan weapons and survive as the ruling language.

There is a certain inexorability about the Indo-Aryan advance, however. The dynamics of the process can best be studied in Maharashtra, Orissa, Assam, and Nepal. In the latter, direct government intervention has been a factor: not only was Nepali officially promoted but the rival Newari language (cultivated under Sanskrit influence from the twelfth century) was banned during the Rana period (1846–1950). According to Grierson (*LSI 3.1*: 283) books in Limbu (another Tibeto-Burman language of eastern Nepal) were also forbidden and burnt when found.

3.6 **Foreign influences and contacts**

The subsequent external history of Indo-Aryan is not confined, however, to the gradual Aryanization (in all the above senses) of the subcontinent and its offshore islands. New elements continued to be added to the linguistic, cultural, and racial brew.

Most importantly, the Aryans could not close the northwestern gate behind them, and were followed in due course by a succession of further invaders from Central Asia and the Iranian plateau. Most of these were speakers of Indo-European or even more closely related Iranian languages and for the earlier period it is difficult to sort out their linguistic impact. In the pre-Muslim period it must have been in any case confined to the northwestern quadrant of the subcontinent, east as far as Mathura and south to Gujarat. First came the Achaemenid Persians (sixth century BC), then the Bactrian Greeks (second century BC), then the Śakas (first century BC), the Kushanas (first century AD), and finally the Hunas (fifth century AD), with possibly other peoples following in the wake of the last.

Among the latter are sometimes numbered the Gurjaras, who gave their name to Gujarat and to two districts in the Punjab (Gujrat, Gujranwala) and furnished an important early medieval North Indian imperial dynasty, the Gurjara-Pratihāras of Kannauj. Some have seen a Central Asian origin for the Gurjaras. S. K. Chatterji thought they might be "possibly Dardic." A key element in these speculations is the presence of the tribe or caste of herdsmen called Gujars. They are an important element in the population of Rajasthan and are also found in parts of western UP, Punjab, Himachal Pradesh, Kashmir, and beyond the Indus in Chitral (Pakistan) and on into northeastern Afghanistan. They are not found south of Gujarat. In the northwestern areas of their distribution, the Gujars have maintained their own language, as noted in the survey in Chapter 2 (section 1.20). The trail, in other words, seems to point northwestward. The only trouble is, Gujari is not a Central Asian language, or even a "Dardic" language: its closest relations are with Northeastern Rajasthani (Mewati). It is possible that they acquired this language after coming to India, subsequently migrating back in the direction from which they had come, but it is also possible that they are merely a group native to Rajasthan, some elements of which happened to come to power in the confused centuries after the Huna disruptions (and other elements of which later began to move northwestward). Their sudden historical prominence does not prove foreign origin: the appearance of the Marathas is equally mysterious. The ethnographic picture we have of India in earlier eras is very incomplete.

Of the early invaders, only the Hunas (= Huns), whose impact was mainly destructive, seem to have spoken a non-Indo-European language. The Śakas (= Scythians) spoke a language of Iranian stock. Concerning the Kushanas, who are of major cultural importance, there has been some confusion due to two senses of the word *Tocharian*. The Kushanas were descendants of a people known to the Chinese as *Yüeh-chi* and to classical and Arab writers as *Tocharians*, but their language was apparently a form of Scythian (Śaka) spoken in Chinese Turkestan. The mysterious Indo-European Centum language known as Tocharian was spoken by a neighboring people (hence the confusion) called by the Turks *Toghri*, who seem never to have left their oasis homes. (They called themselves *Arshi* [= Aryans?] and may be the people called *Wusun* by the Chinese.) Both usages are by now too well-established to hope to change them. There has been an attempt to clarify the confusion – by calling the Tocharian speakers *false* Tocharians and the Scythian-speaking Yüeh-chi (> Kushanas) *true* Tocharians – which would seem only to make things worse.

The later or Muslim phase of incursions from the northwest, beginning in the eleventh century (the Arab attempt at conquest in the eighth century was confined to Sind by a defense mounted by the above-mentioned Gurjaras), had a linguistic impact that was eventually felt in every corner of the subcontinent, although most deeply in the northwest. This was mainly through the agency of the Persian language, which became and remained the language of administration for nearly a millennium. The Turki (Eastern Turkic) speech of some of these invaders, however, which is known to have been retained domestically for several generations (e.g., by the Mughals), even though the court language was Persian, may also have had an impact greater than is generally conceded. Chatterji (1926: 21–3) writes (noting there are less than one hundred Turki loanwords in Hindi) that "it does not seem as if Turki exerted any influence on Indian languages."

However, he also notes (p. 214) that Persian was brought to India by Turks and in India betrays many indications of Turki usage. (See Masica 1981, and Chapter 10, for at least one area of *syntax* that may show Turki influence, albeit partly mediated and abetted by Persian.) The Muslims, significantly, were known as "Turks" in contemporary non-Muslim sources.

Meanwhile, the subcontinent had long been open to influences by sea as well. The Indus valley civilization was in touch with Mesopotamia by sea. On the evidence of the adoption of certain crop plants, there seems to have been contact between the west coast of India and northeastern Africa and/or South Arabia at an early date (prior to 1000 BC, when the aforementioned plants begin appearing in the Indian archaeological record). The borrowing may have extended to the names of these items in some instances. (One possibility is the word for 'lentil': H. *masūr*, Skt *masūra[-kā]*, *[-ikā]*, not satisfactorily explained, although Tamil *mutirai* 'pulse in general' is sometimes cited. The Amharic is *massar*.) There is also the matter of writing systems: the Ethiopic script operates on a principle similar to that of the Indic scripts (see Chapter 6).

Beginning in the first century AD, and continuing one way or another, with interruptions, until modern times (although the first phase ended in about the fifth century), there has been large-scale commercial contact between India and Southeast Asia. In addition to bringing Indian influence to these countries, there was a flow of new products and the names for them (e.g., cloves, Skt *lavaṅga* < Indonesian) back to India, which eventually became part of the common Indo-Aryan heritage.

Starting at the end of the fifteenth century, the sea brought influences from further afield – first the Portuguese, then the Dutch, English, Danes, and French. (There had been commercial contact between South India and Rome early in the Christian era, but this did not affect Indo-Aryan speaking areas, except possibly Sri Lanka.) Some of these were local or unimportant in their linguistic effects, but two, Portuguese and English, were more pervasive. Portuguese functioned for a long period as the lingua franca of trade between all Europeans and Indians; everyone coming out to India had to learn it, whether or not he learned anything else. Communities grew up which had a creolized Portuguese as their mother tongue. Some still exist in Sri Lanka and elsewhere. As is only to be expected, the impact of Portuguese is greater on the coastal languages (the reverse of that of Persian). This may be illustrated by the word for one ubiquitous New World import, the potato: Marathi, Gujarati *baṭāṭā*, Kannada *baṭāṭe*, but Hindi, Bengali *ālū*.

The impact of English may have been similarly coastal at first, but now it is everywhere: a typical urban conversation in any part of South Asia is sprinkled with English words. They may be avoided in serious writing, but such speech (and the more extreme form technically known as *code-switching*) is often caricatured in less-serious writing.

The impact of all of the maritime contacts – African, Southeast Asian, European, with the exception of English – has been exclusively lexical. The influences from the northwest, particularly that of Persian, have probably had grammatical (syntactic) consequences as well, at least in some languages, and especially in Hindi. It should be noted that the *lexical* impact of Persian has receded, however, from what was probably its high point in the eighteenth century, in most Indo-Aryan languages except Urdu, Sindhi, and "Lahnda". Many words current then did not take root (Chatterji 1926: 205). The impact of English has also been both lexical and syntactic, although the latter is difficult to disentangle from the larger question of the development of prose styles.

The catalogue of potential foreign influences would not be complete without mention of a third direction from which foreign incursions came, namely by land from the east. The Tai-speaking Ahoms, who already had a written language, conquered Assam in the thirteenth century and ruled for approximately six hundred years, until 1826. Whether because of their social habits or small numbers, their direct linguistic impact was minimal, confined to a handful of loanwords and place names, mostly of rivers in the immediate vicinity of Sibsagar (their capital), many of which do not survive today (Kakati 1962: 51). Indirectly Ahom did have an important impact on Assamese, however, by furnishing the model for the historical prose chronicle, the *buranji*, one of the glories of Assamese literature and unique in India. Not less importantly perhaps, the Ahoms also gave Assam and its language their name (*Ahom* and the modern Assamese *ɒχɒm* 'Assam' come from an attested earlier form *asam*, *acam*, probably from a Burmese corruption of the word *Shan/Shyām*, cf. "*Siam*": Kakati 1962: 1–4).

The Burmese incursions into Bengal and Assam in the eighteenth and early nineteenth centuries were too brief to have any direct linguistic effect. They did have an indirect effect, in that they led to British rule in Assam, and under it, the replacement of Assamese by Bengali in administration and education for the greater part of the nineteenth century, and thus a setback for Assamese.

3.7 The historical stages of Indo-Aryan

The long *internal* history of Indo-Aryan in India, spanning about 3,500 years, may be divided linguistically into three stages: Old, Middle, and New Indo-Aryan, conventionally (and henceforth in this book) abbreviated as OIA, MIA, and

NIA. These may be taken as corresponding roughly to the periods 1500 BC–600 BC, 600 BC–1000 AD and 1000 AD–present respectively.

These may be subdivided further into Early, Middle or 'Second', and Late, and attempts have been made (e.g., by Chatterji) to assign approximate dates to the latter also, but such attempts confront two additional problems: (1) a given linguistic stage was reached at different times in different areas – i.e. earlier in the east than in the west, which was more conservative; and (2) the literary languages on which our knowledge of the stages is based typically flourished (or at any rate are represented by surviving texts) at periods subsequent to those they represent linguistically, that is, when the vernacular had already evolved further. How much earlier the spoken language was current on which was based the literary dialect (represented by texts whose own date is often also uncertain) is under the circumstances a matter of guesswork.

Even if absolute dates are hard to come by, it can usually be said with a fair amount of certainty that a given literary dialect represents an "older" or a "younger" linguistic stage than another given literary dialect. A linguistic form *B* in such a sample usually has to be derived from a linguistic form *A* and not the other way around. On this basis, the older recorded forms of Indo-Aryan (several of which we have already had ample occasion to refer to) may be listed and classified as follows:

I.A. *Early OIA*

1. VEDIC: based apparently on a far-western dialect, perhaps influenced by Iranian; further substages may be distinguished, the language of Books II–VII of the *Rig Veda* being the most archaic, that of the *Brāhmaṇas* and *Sūtras* the least.

I.B. *Later OIA*

1. CLASSICAL SANSKRIT: based on a dialect of the midland (western Ganges valley, eastern Punjab, Haryana), although influenced by Vedic. Later literature was much influenced by MIA (with which it is contemporary), remaining OIA only in phonetics and morphology.

II.A *Early MIA*

1. AŚOKAN PRĀKRITS: various regional dialects of the third century BC (eastern, east-central, southwestern, northwestern), with the notable *exception* of the midland, recorded in the inscriptions of the Emperor Aśoka on rocks and pillars in various parts of the subcontinent.

2. PĀLI: language of the Hinayana Buddhist canon and other literature, apparently based on a midland dialect possibly influenced by the original eastern forms of the remembered Buddhist discourses, and subsequently by Sanskrit. Again, the language of the metrical portion of the canon proper, or *Gathas*, is more archaic than the language of the commentaries and other literature.
3. EARLY ARDHAMĀGADHI: language of the earliest Jain Sūtras. (Most Ardhamāgadhi represents a later MIA stage, however [see below].)

II.B. *MIA, Second Stage*

1. NIYA PRAKRIT: administrative language of an Indo-Aryan polity (i.e. besides the Scythian and Tocharian ones) in Chinese Turkestan, known from third century AD documents, "northwestern" in type but full of Iranian and other loanwords. Akin to this but somewhat earlier (first century) is what is sometimes called GANDHARI, the language of the Khotan manuscript of the *Dhammapada*.
2. ARDHAMĀGADHI: supposedly the ancient language of Kosala (= Oudh or modern eastern UP), known from the Jain canon (not finalized until the sixth century AD) and from early Buddhist dramas; of varying age.
3. LATER (= post-Asokan) INSCRIPTIONAL PRAKRIT: until replaced (fifth century) totally by Sanskrit in inscriptions.
4. MĀGADHI: language of Bihar, and presumably of the Mauryan Empire (fourth–second centuries BC); stylized subvarieties represented by the conventionalized speech of lower-class characters in the Sanskrit drama.
5. ŚAURASENĪ: the standard Prakrit of the drama; it represents the stage of midland speech succeeding Pali, *mutatis mutandis*; more conservative than Magadhi or Maharashtri; another variety was cultivated by Jains.
6. MAHARASHTRI (*māhārāṣṭrī*): a southwestern dialect, vehicle of lyric poetry (and in another variety, mixed with Ardhamāgadhi, of Jain literature); phonologically the most advanced of the Second Stage Prakrits.
7. SINHALA PRAKRIT: language of the Sinhalese inscriptions, from the first century BC.

(To these might be added BUDDHIST HYBRID SANSKRIT, a Middle

Indo-Aryan dialect in Sanskrit garb, vehicle of Mahayana Buddhist literature.)

II.C. *Late* (or *Third Stage*) *MIA*

1. APABHRAṀŚA: literary language (= WESTERN or ŚAURASENĪ APABHRAṀŚA) based on midland speech of a later stage than Sauraseni Prakrit; somewhat influenced by local usage when cultivated in other regions; the term is also used to indicate the Late MIA stage itself, transitional to NIA. Early NIA texts show admixture of Apabhramsa forms.
2. EḶU: "a sort of Sinhalese Apabhraṁśa" (Chatterji 1926: 15).

In several languages of the NIA stage there is also preserved enough older literature to warrant division into substages. As there are sometimes two, sometimes three of these, the terminology may become confusing. Thus what Kellogg (1875: 69) called "OLD" BAISWĀṚĪ – the language of Tulsidas's late-sixteenth-century *Rāmacaritamānasa* (also called "OLD" AWADHI, e.g., by Grierson 1904) – is equivalent to what is generally known as "MIDDLE" BENGALI, not to "OLD" BENGALI, which dates from the twelfth century. Further distinctions are sometimes usefully made: the language of the late fourteenth-century *Śrikṛṣṇakīrttana* (= "EARLY MIDDLE BENGALI") differs from that of sixteenth–eighteenth-century texts such as the *Caitanyacaritamṛta* (= "LATE MIDDLE BENGALI").

A modicum of order might be brought to this situation by postulating First, Second, and Third substages, analogous to those of MIA – with the understanding that a given substage may not be documented for a particular language (also the case, of course, in MIA). As in MIA, a given substage might be reached at different times in different parts of the Aryan area. The question at this point easily gets confused with that of *literary* stages. Thus the Third stage is connected with the development of modern prose styles under British influence, generally during the nineteenth century (in Bengali, Assamese, Oriya, Hindi, Gujarati, Marathi), but in some cases (Punjabi, Sindhi) not until the turn of the twentieth, and in others (Kashmiri) just now beginning. The Second stage is connected in a number of languages (Bengali, Assamese, Oriya, Marathi, Gujarati, Braj, Awadhi) with an efflorescence of Vaishnavite devotional poetry. Even if such stages are established on purely linguistic grounds, there is the matter of the cross-linguistic equivalence of the stages. Each NIA language has its separate history, and its linguistic stages may not be coordinate with those of another NIA language.

Finally it should be noted that Indo-Aryan historical linguistics is complicated, despite the documentation of various earlier stages, by the fact that the languages recorded at successive stages are often not in direct historical relationship with one another. This problem is not unique to Indo-Aryan, to be sure, but perhaps is present in a more acute form. Even when the *general* region of their provenance can be ascertained – and even this apparently simple matter is complicated by their use as literary languages far beyond those regions and by their acquiring in the process a certain composite quality – it was often a different dialect or dialectal mixture that formed the basis of the literary language at each stage. General comparisons can be made: e.g., Classical Sanskrit, Pali, Sauraseni Prakrit, Literary Apabhramsa, and various forms of Western Hindi (Khari Boli, Braj Bhasha) all do represent in a general way the language of the midland at various stages – but much qualification is necessary, especially with regard to Khari Boli.

Confusion of another sort, mainly at the popular and political levels but obtruding at the academic level as well, complicates the picture with regard to Hindi itself, as we have seen (Chapter 2, section 3). Academic as well as popular tradition includes under earlier Hindi the medieval literature in every language and dialect from western Rajasthan (*Ḍingaḷ*) to North Bihar (Maithili), but none of these stands in direct *linguistic* antecedence to Modern Standard Hindi. (The closest is perhaps the mixed dialect of the Nirguṇa poets sometimes called *sādhū bhāṣā* [see below] which at least incorporates some elements of Khari Boli.) Some of them even represent different branches of Indo-Aryan (see Chapter 8). The one language that is antecedent, namely Urdu, does not usually appear on the list, for reasons which have nothing to do with linguistics.

The most serious obstacle in the path of Indo-Aryan historical linguistics, however, is the paucity of data pertaining to the Late MIA and Early NIA periods, and the transition between them. For several major languages (Punjabi, Sindhi) there is no data at all from the Early NIA period; there is some literature in Old Bengali (the deliberately enigmatic *Caryā* songs), Old Marwari ("Old West Rajasthani"), Old Gujarati, Old Marathi (the monumental *Jñāneśvarī*, extant however in a late-sixteenth-century revision), Old Kashmiri (lyrics of the Saivite poetess Lalla), and more doubtfully, in Old Hindi (Nathpanthi tracts of very uncertain date, and two short fragments in the *Ādi Granth* of the Sikhs attributed to the Sufi saint Baba Farid, d. 1266 [Chatterji 1960: 199], along with some short pieces by Amir Khusrau, d. 1325); for Marathi, Oriya, and Sinhalese we are fortunate enough to have inscriptions in addition. Late MIA is mainly represented by a literary form of one language, that of the midland (Sauraseni Apabhramsa), which was employed for compositions from Bengal in the east to Punjab and Gujarat in the west (only sparingly in Maharashtra). Into its *local corruptions* one must try to read indications of the actual local language. These corruptions increase with time until in a few areas (North Bihar, eastern Rajasthan) a very mixed style of Apabhramsa and local Early NIA was in vogue. This was sometimes known as Avahaṭṭha in Bihar; in eastern Rajasthan it was semi-standardized as Pingaḷ. Even this kind of data is missing for many areas.

The MIA/NIA hiatus is crucial, for while there is uneven documentation for some phases of MIA also, the history of MIA is essentially one of the slow erosion of OIA forms. The NIA languages, on the other hand, emerge into the light of day with radically transformed systems. Many of the details of this process, certainly one of the aspects of the history of Indo-Aryan of greatest general interest for linguistics, seem unfortunately to be inaccessible.

3.8 Sociolinguistic aspects of the history of Indo-Aryan

With the exception of the Asokan inscriptions (which are not without their own problems) and a few others, the Niya Documents, and evidence (for MIA) in contemporary descriptive grammars we must rely for information regarding older stages of Indo-Aryan on compositions, most often in verse, in self-consciously literary languages. Their status as such affects the way the linguistic information they offer must be regarded, although it is of interest for its own sake. Many features of the formation and cultivation of Indo-Aryan literary languages have universal parallels; others seem peculiarly Indian, or at least to be present there in an especially exaggerated form.

Among the former is the fact that many literary languages, Indian and non-Indian, are a composite of several dialects rather than representing one dialect in a pure form. Among the latter is the persistent anachronism of the Indo-Aryan literary languages (certain modern NIA literary styles excepted), already alluded to above. Thus Classical Sanskrit, fixed by Panini's grammar in probably the fourth century BC on the basis of a class dialect (and preceding grammatical tradition) of probably the seventh century BC, had its greatest literary flowering in the first millennium AD and even later,[16] much of it therefore a full thousand years after the stage of the language it ostensibly represents (and well into the Second and even the Late MIA period).

The oldest Sanskrit inscription, that of Rudradāman, a Śaka king – a foreigner – in what is now Gujarat, dates only from AD 150. The habit of making inscriptions in Sanskrit thus gradually ousts that of making them in Prakrit and not the other way around. It is as if Latin had replaced (Old) French. (The replacement of Vulgar and medieval Latin by Classical Latin for some purposes at the time of the Renaissance may be a more apt analogy – except that the main body of "Classical" literature of Sanskrit *followed* this development rather than preceding it by more than a millennium as in the Latin case.) Almost rivalling Rudradāman's inscription in date is the great Sanskrit stele of Vo-canh (late second/early third century) in faraway Vietnam, which incidentally shows that Sanskrit had become the official language of the Indianized Indo-Chinese state of Fu-nan at about the same time that it was replacing Prakrit in that capacity in India itself. It was in fact native Aryan India, particularly the Aryan outpost in Maharashtra (later to become a bastion of Sanskrit), that held out against Sanskrit the longest (Warder 1972: 6). The cultivation of Sanskrit not only for literary and scholarly purposes but also for mundane communication has subsequently never stopped. All India Radio still maintains a news broadcast in Sanskrit.

Pali was developed in northern India before 200 BC, perhaps as early as the fifth century BC, but the bulk of its literature not only dates from a much later period (the first millennium AD, and in Southeast Asia from the second millennium), but was produced outside the subcontinent altogether, in Sri Lanka, after the eleventh century in Burma, and still later, also in Thailand.

The literary representative of the Late MIA stage, Apabhramsa, seems to go back – that is, there are several references to it even if no documents – to at least 600 AD, but its literature continues well into the NIA period: Vidyapati's compositions in Apabhramsa date from the fifteenth century.

Such removal in time and place of literary compositions from the points of origins of the languages employed in them inevitably introduces complications into their use as evidence for stages of linguistic development. Not only do contemporary forms creep in – often in phonological disguise (this is particularly true of vocabulary in Sanskrit) – but the supposedly artificially fixed languages do undergo some change in areas (such as syntax) not legislated upon in the prescriptive grammars. Sometimes these developments reflect authentic underlying historical trends in Indo-Aryan (e.g., the disuse of Sanskrit and Pali finite past tenses in favor of the participial construction with the subject in the instrumental), authenticated by the end produced in NIA; sometimes they are entirely artificial (e.g., the growth of noun compounding in later Sanskrit).

Anachronism is not the only source of artificiality in the data for the older stages of Indo-Aryan. The so-called Dramatic or Literary Prakrits (the main representatives of the Second MIA stage: Sauraseni, Magadhi, and Maharashtri) are highly stylized dialects prescribed for certain types of stage characters or literary genres, written according to formula. Although among themselves they represent somewhat different stages of linguistic evolution (as well as ostensibly different areas), not only were they in literary use together (often in the same composition), but also simultaneously with Sanskrit and partly Apabhramsa.

There has always been a tendency, and not only in India, to give a serious literary medium an enhanced air of respectability by approximating it to and buttressing it with forms taken from more prestigeful classical languages. An extreme example of this is the so-called Buddhist Hybrid Sanskrit, a MIA language so Sanskritized as to disguise its identity (affirmed by scholars only recently) and give the impression of merely ungrammatical Sanskrit.

The time-lag so characteristic of OIA and MIA literary languages is less pronounced in NIA literary languages, but it is nonetheless often present. In particular, literary Bengali, Sinhalese, Marathi, and Oriya (which, generally speaking, are the languages with the oldest continuing literary traditions) present a definitely archaic aspect when compared with modern spoken forms – in the first two cases to the point of diglossia. Literary Bengali or *ʃādhu bhāʃā* (not to be confused with the medieval Hindi *sādhū bhāṣā*) is based on the spoken language of the fourteenth and fifteenth centuries. This situation has been mitigated by the rise of a second Bengali literary norm (*colit bhāʃā*) based on the modern Calcutta Colloquial, somewhat analogously to Riksmaal/Bokmål and Landsmaal/Nynorsk in Norway. Its success no doubt owes something to the support of the great writer Tagore. In Marathi the situation has been mitigated by a recent spelling reform.

These situations are to be distinguished from those involving the use of another language entirely as a written language by a population: Urdu by speakers of Kashmiri, and of Punjabi and other languages in Pakistan; Modern Standard Hindi by speakers of Rajasthani, Bihari, Pahari, Punjabi, and also Munda languages in India; Nepali by speakers of diverse Tibeto-Burman languages in Nepal; also Bengali by speakers of Assamese for a period in the nineteenth century, and Marathi (and Dravidian Kannada) by some Konkani speakers. The Konkani situation is complicated by the failure of the seven modern Konkani dialects (several of which have been independently cultivated for literary purposes) to evolve a common standard, although some progress has recently been made (Pereira 1973).

One peculiarity of the traditional literary languages of the Hindi area is their specialization for different purposes. Braj was the appropriate vehicle for singing the praises of Krishna, whereas Rama was extolled in Awadhi. There was a logic to this based on traditional history: Krishna was associated with Mathura and Brindaban, the heart of the Braj area; Rama was king of Ayodhya, in the Awadhi area. Similarly, the popular epic the *Ālhākhaṇḍ* (a sort of Indian *Song of Roland*) is chanted in Bundeli, the dialect of the area where most of the action takes place and where the heroes are from. The Sant or Nirguṇa tradition of mystical poets, on the other hand, beginning with Kabir, has tended as noted above to prefer a fluid mixed dialect with a strong Khari Boli element favoring widest possible intelligibility. The implication, however, is that all four of these dialects were largely mutually intelligible, with a little repetitive hearing (which was not lacking), throughout northern India. (The same could not be said for the bardic literature in Ḍingaḷ, which was probably not much known outside of Rajasthan.)

A somewhat analogous case of dialectal specialization is found in the Bengali area, in the so-called Brajabuli literature of the Vaishnavas. The difference is that the latter is a completely artificial dialect, compounded of Maithili and Bengali, and associated with the Braj homeland of Krishna only by poetic convention.

Court patronage (including Muslim court patronage) was a factor in the emergence of some of the NIA literary languages, including Bengali, Braj, Nepali, Marathi, Assamese, Marwari, and Dakhini. Recently Khowar has been the beneficiary of such patronage. The fillip given to Modern Standard Hindi by the British administration at Fort William College might also be placed in this category. Where such patronage was lacking or directed elsewhere (e.g., toward Persian in Sind, Kashmir, Punjab, or toward Old Gujarati in Mewar in Rajasthan), the regional NIA literary language got off to a slower start.

Narula (1955) raises interesting questions regarding the formation of Indo-Aryan literary languages. For him, a modern standard language is the product of *regional integration* on a number of levels – economic and social primarily, permitting dialectal integration and the emergence of a clear *collective identity*. Anything else (e.g., Sanskrit) is a "*class jargon*". The conditions are close to being met in some of the outlying NIA linguistic regions – Bengal, Maharashtra, Gujarat – but according to him they are not met at all in the Hindi area, which is too large, unintegrated, and diverse. The various subregions of the area (e.g., eastern UP, western UP, Bihar, Rajasthan) themselves fall short of such integration, the attainment of which would be a normal and necessary stage before overall integration on such a grand scale can be contemplated. Such subregional integration, weak and slow in any case in comparison with Bengal, Gujarat, etc. (partly due to lack of clear geographical foci, partly to level of economic development) has now been thwarted by the imposition of Modern Standard Hindi, accordingly another "class jargon".

While it is on the whole still true that the body of Hindi speakers (and/or users) lacks a "collective identity" (there is not even any term for them) commensurate even with that conferred by the other linguistic foci in NIA, the clock cannot be turned back. Standard literary languages, once established, have their own effects both linguistic and sociological. They may even become normally spoken languages: this has happened in Germany and elsewhere under the influence of education. As it is, standard Hindi is demonstrably affecting the spoken dialects within its sphere in many ways – to the dismay of students of those speech-forms no doubt, but indicating that the process of integration is well under way. A lingering degree of integrational underdevelopment, however, is shown by responses, especially numerous in the Hindi area, to the language question in the census of India, giving a caste name, occupation, or village name as the respondent's "language".

Katre (1968: iii) voices concerns similar to Narula's about NIA in general:

> Our modern languages . . . as languages of culture, are at a distance from the common vernaculars of the people . . . they are still not national languages within their own sphere because of this linguistic distance between the majority of speakers and the minority of elites. It is essential that this distance be annihilated, through a widening process of education.

Part of the sociolinguistic gap Katre is referring to is due to the heavy overlay of learned borrowings from Sanskrit in most modern NIA standard languages (see Chapter 4). The pre-modern NIA literary languages show rather different sociolinguistic characteristics: the devotional and neo-epic literature was closer to the language of the people; in particular, the lexicon while not devoid of Sanskrit and Perso-Arabic loanwords was predominantly NIA, a far cry from the hybrid languages of today. The whole point of using the vernacular instead of Sanskrit or Persian was popular intelligibility. Similar needs, including religious proselytization, govern the emergence of European vernacular literatures, whose history parallels that of Indo-Aryan to a remarkable degree, given the differences between the two cultures.

Punjabi "identity" constitutes an interesting enigma from a sociolinguistic point of view. Psychoculturally it is a well-established identity, but sociolinguistically the situation is peculiar, due to a number of historical factors: the association of literary Punjabi with adherents of the Sikh religion, the successful attempts of the Arya Samaj to promote Modern Standard Hindi as a written language among Hindus in the Punjab, the use of Urdu as the official language in the Punjab by the British administration and in Pakistan. In some Punjabi families, each generation has a different primary written language. The second partition of the Punjab into the new states of Punjab and Haryana has not sorted out the problem, as recent events have shown. Whatever their (secondary?) identities, most Punjabis continue to speak Punjabi at home in any case.

A factor not yet discussed which erects further barriers between us and a true picture of Indo-Aryan linguistic history is that of *manuscript transmission*. The extant copies of older works are removed from the originals by many generations of recopying; the science of textual criticism and reconstruction is thus an essential adjunct to Indo-Aryan historical linguistics. As the senior Indian historical linguist S. M. Katre (1965: 16–18) points out, this factor can be exploited positively also: the very errors and emendations introduced by different generations into a transmitted text – even a Sanskrit text (particularly of the two great epics, the *Mahābhārata* and the *Rāmāyaṇa*) – may reflect the grammars of their own real spoken languages, and thus constitute another means, albeit a very indirect one, of gleaning some authentic information concerning the latter.

3.9 **Comparative reconstruction**

Another approach entirely to the history of Indo-Aryan is that afforded by the methods of comparative reconstruction. Abundant NIA descriptive material, relating to non-literary as well as literary languages, is available to work from. Earlier hypothetical stages arrived at by this method then need to be compared with the attested forms discussed above, which constitute authentic historical data, however problematic. Each type of data thus becomes a critique of the other: discrepancies help identify problems; agreements on the other hand yield strengthened guesses regarding the periods and regions affected by successive changes – always bearing in mind that developments in any spoken language are likely to antedate even their earliest written attestations, perhaps by centuries.[17]

Attempts that have been made to apply the comparative method to Indo-Aryan (Pattanayak 1966) underline the importance of the points chosen for departure. If these are unrepresentative the construct arrived at may be valid within the model but without actual historical validity. If they are insufficient in number the construct itself is questionable. As Katre has pointed out, there should be at least three independent witnesses. Unfortunately many forms are attested by less than that, and their ancestral form is accordingly problematic. A problem that particularly plagues NIA reconstruction is the flood of Sanskrit and Persian loanwords in the modern languages, in that they have often driven out many genuine NIA words, at least from urban standard speech. These must be sought, if they survive at all, in remote village dialects, or in medieval texts.

An additional problem is the prevalence of *Mischformen*, whose ancestry involves two or more competing words (Katre 1968: 34–8) – often due to interference from literary superstrata. A set of forms even more resistant to reconstruction are the *expressive* forms so characteristic of all Indic languages, Aryan and non-Aryan (see Chapter 4).

Even a balanced selection of subcontinental NIA languages when subjected to the method yields a set of reconstructed forms approximating *only to MIA*. To get beyond this it is necessary to add the archaic "Dardic" languages, Romany, and Sinhalese to the mix. These were beyond the pale of the evolving pan-Indic civilization and thus unaffected by MIA changes that spread to all contiguous languages participating in the latter.

4

The nature of the New Indo-Aryan lexicon

4.1 General considerations

Different languages by no means show equivalent lexical development. Different cultures have often quite different needs. A nomadic pastoral society will not need the same range of expressions as a traditional peasant society, for example, let alone an industrial society. Languages of hunting and gathering or of fishing groups have vocabularies that are highly developed in other ways. Supposedly all human beings have a core of common experience that is reflected in equivalent core vocabularies, but attempts to draw up such basic vocabulary lists still tend to betray hidden cultural biases, and even biases related to climate.

In this sense, most NIA languages are quite complex, in that the societies they serve are complex – highly differentiated occupationally and socially, urban as well as rural, and with elaborate ideological super- and substructures. Except perhaps for the kernel of the last, such was not always the case. The original Indo-Iranians (and Indo-Europeans) were a pastoral society, not exactly simple, but lacking any but the most rudimentary agriculture. This is clear from the fact that agricultural terms (that is, not referring to animal husbandry) are generally not primitive, but either borrowed from preceding peoples or independently coined – in every Indo-European group. In India they were taken from Dravidian, Austroasiatic, and stocks which can no longer be traced. (This fascinating subject will not be the focus of the discussion here. For further details see Masica 1981.) The same is true on the whole for the traditional industries (e.g., textiles) for which India is famous. This is related to the fact that Indo-European groups, including Indo-Aryans, apparently imposed themselves as a ruling class over various previously settled peasant societies, owing to their superior *military* technology. This in turn was largely related to their mastery of the horse.

Vocabularies of languages also differ in accordance with the different functional *registers* they have developed – also ultimately a matter of cultural need. In particular, the abstract vocabulary and other lexical apparatus (specialized conjunctions, sentence connectors, etc.) of *connected modern prose* are not things a spoken language is born with, so to speak, just as that function itself is in no way a "normal" (= universal or basic) function of language but rather a special superstructure. Such expressions have to be acquired or developed as a language comes of age as a modern literary medium and needs to develop such registers, something not every language is called upon to do. Indo-Aryan long ago adapted itself to the needs of the complex traditional society of India, but these new demands of the modern period were a challenge that began to confront NIA a little more than a century and a half ago.

The NIA languages were not completely devoid of any traditions of prose composition before the modern period. Examples of pre-modern prose include the *banis* or sayings of saints in Hindi and the hagiographical *vārtā* literature of the Vallabhite sect in Braj Bhasha,[1] the *janamsākhīs* or hagiographies of Guru Nanak in Old Punjabi, some of the Mahanubhava sectarian literature in Old Marathi, Jain didactic tales in Old Gujarati, and historical chronicles in Assamese, Sinhalese, and Rajasthani, along with a few commentaries and inscriptions. It would nevertheless be fair to say that pre-modern literary expression in NIA was mainly through poetry.

Moreover the existing meager prose was not modern prose. Briefly, the prose needs of a medieval society were different from those of a modern society and many of them were handled in any case by Persian and Sanskrit. In the words of S. K. Chatterji (1960: 108–9) pre-modern NIA prose was

> employed for simple narrative rather than for scientific or philosophical or reflective purposes . . . A simple style therefore sufficed, and prose, not having to grapple with complex situations in the thought world, could not draw out all the latent powers of the language . . . the vernaculars were not yet ready as finished instruments of expression, and this is . . . evidenced not only from the absence of good scientific and technical terms but also from the halting and not precise prose syntax of many NIA speeches.

A similar situation may of course be found in the early stages of English, Spanish, Russian, and other European literatures.

In the development of literary NIA we may usefully distinguish the following stages:

1. literary cultivation as such, albeit mainly for poetry, making demands necessarily already beyond those of an unwritten dialect; in

the case of most of the NIA literary languages this began in the pre-British period;

2. creation of a modern prose register, in most cases during the period of British rule; in some languages, however (e.g., Bengali and Urdu), it took place much earlier (i.e. at least a century) than in others (e.g., Sindhi and Punjabi);
3. confrontation with the full range of modern functions, e.g., terminological and administrative (which had previously been partly usurped by English) in the period since Independence – a period characterized by very rapid and uneven lexical expansion.

What was lacking lexically in NIA languages at any of these stages had to be supplied somehow – borrowed, created, or otherwise developed. There are several options available to a language in such a situation:

(a) The needed lexical apparatus can be borrowed outright (with appropriate phonetic modification) from a language that already has it;
(b) It can be developed from scratch (coined) out of the native resources of the language (the "Icelandic" or "Chinese" method);
(c) It can be "translated" – again, from a language that already has it – into more or less equivalent *morphemes* of the borrowing language (*calqued*): another, albeit hidden, form of borrowing;
(d) It can be *calqued*, but using morphemes not of the borrowing language itself but of a classical language (which can be [1] *cognate* or [2] *non-cognate*) from which the borrowing language is accustomed to draw vocabulary;
(e) It can be coined, but using the resources of a classical source language (again, [1] cognate or [2] non-cognate).

The term *cognate* needs some qualification. What is really meant is not merely "related", as Latin or Greek are ultimately to English, but "of the same subgroup", as Latin is to Romance languages, Classical Greek is to Modern Greek, or Church Slavonic is to Russian. Theoretically at least, material from such sources should lend itself more to a transparency of interpretation approaching that of "native" material, whereas material from a *non-cognate* source – which thus would include not only the Arabic element in Persian or the Chinese element in Japanese but also the Latin and Greek element in English – will be opaque in terms of its internal structure and learned as a unit. In practice the matter is not so clearcut: supposedly "cognate" material may well not be transparent without some education, whereas certain "foreign" formants may become so thoroughly familiar as to be for all practical purposes as transparent as native formants: e.g., *-able*, *-ize* in English.

Calquing may be complete or partial from a structural point of view, and according to some authorities it may be only "semantic". That is to say, when a word exists in another language of which the coiners of a new word are aware and the meaning of which they are trying to render, the resulting word may be viewed as a calque even though it does not show a morpheme-by-morpheme correspondence with the model. The very existence of a "model" makes the process a different one from true coinage-from-scratch. Such calques are more difficult to identify as calques than are formally equivalent calques, although the existence of a larger pattern of such borrowing may give a clue – as may evidence of the first appearance of the word in question in a context of translation.

The main options chosen by the modern NIA literary languages are (a), (d), and (e): having borrowed what they could from Sanskrit or, in the case especially of Urdu and Sindhi, from Persian and Perso-Arabic, often with modification of meaning, they then have proceeded to coin terms or create, for the most part on the basis of English (= Neo-Greco-Latin) models, calques using the same classical languages. To the extent they draw on Sanskrit, instead of wholesale borrowing directly from English (for example – although such borrowings do fill the urban colloquial as already noted), NIA languages could be said to be maintaining their Indo-Aryan character, but the above qualifications apply: the ideally cognate Sanskrit material (as well as the non-cognate Arabic material) is for the most part *not* transparent to the speaker of a NIA language without some education. Some common Persian loanwords, on the other hand (like common words of French origin in English, e.g., *pray*, *feast*), have become an indistinguishable part of everyday speech in many NIA languages as far as the average speaker is concerned.

4.2 The traditional analysis: *tadbhava* and *tatsama*

From a historical point of view, the word-store of almost any language includes items of two kinds: first, those inherited by direct transmission, generation to generation, from the original stock from which the language sprang, and second, those borrowed from other languages, living or dead, related or unrelated. NIA languages have borrowed from older IA literary languages (chiefly Sanskrit, and in the case of Sinhalese, also Pali), from non-Indo-European languages of the Indian subcontinent and environs, from "foreign" but neighboring languages such as Persian and Arabic (the former in some sense a cognate language), from

European colonial languages (chiefly Portuguese and English) and others, and last but not least, from each other.

The situation with respect to borrowed words is given a special twist in NIA, however, by: (1) the peculiar *cultural* relation of Sanskrit to most of the languages of the group, at least during part of their history, and (2) the consciousness of this relationship (which should not be confused with an understanding of it in terms of modern historical linguistics) on the part of the cultural elite. A traditional analysis of the IA vocabulary in terms of this relationship exists, the terminology of which has been adopted with various modifications by most foreign and modern South Asian scholars working in the field also. The resulting insights and confusions are something with which the would-be student of IA must learn to cope.

The key terms of the traditional analysis are three: *tatsama* (Ts.), *tadbhava* (Tbh.), and *deśya* (or *deśaja*, modern *deśī*). To these has been added a fourth, *videśī*. Basically, a *tatsama* ('the same as that', short for *saṃskr̥tatatsama* 'the same as Sanskrit') is a word that has the same form – or to put it more baldly, is *spelled* the same (pronunciation may vary) – as in Sanskrit, except for the absence of case terminations in nouns: e.g., *karma* 'deed, action'. A *tadbhava* ('originating from that', short for *saṃskr̥tatadbhava* 'originating from Sanskrit') is a word that has a different form, but which can be related to (that is, constructed out of) a Sanskrit prototype by means of definite phonological rules: e.g., Pali *kamma* (by assimilation of the *-rm-* cluster), Hindi *kām* 'work' (by simplification in turn of the MIA geminate with lengthening of the preceding vowel, plus weakening and loss of final vowel). A *deśaja* (lit. 'country-born', i.e. local) word cannot (or could not) be so related.

The terms were first applied to MIA, where, as Vertogradova (1978: 14) points out, they referred to all aspects of the structure, not just to the lexicon. They were later extended to NIA. There *tatsama* indeed has been made to refer to unmodified Sanskrit loanwords only, and *tadbhava* loosely to the inherited core stock of words. This is somewhat at variance with the traditional usage, which as we have seen envisaged a *comparison* but not a *history*. Moreover the comparison was of MIA with Sanskrit; equivalent phonological laws relating to NIA were not all worked out (indeed they are still being worked out); *tadbhava* in the meantime came to mean words inherited by NIA from MIA.

This was soon found to present problems from the point of view of historical linguistics. For one thing, the traditional *tadbhava* class included not only the original inherited word stock (provided it could be related to Sanskrit) but also Sanskrit *loanwords* from various periods *if* they had undergone any subsequent phonological modification – words like H. *bhagat* 'devotee; Vaishnava holy man'

<Skt *bhakta* 'devotee; shared' (from the root √BHAJ 'share; enjoy') also 'cooked' vs. H. *bhāt* 'boiled rice'. (The word *bhakta* itself also exists in H. as a Ts.) Both *bhagat* and *bhāt*, though obviously subject to different phonological processes, were indifferently Tbhs. according to the traditional analysis, since the only criterion was difference from Sanskrit.

Both Beames and Bhandarkar saw a need to distinguish between what they called "early/old" Tbhs. (words inherited "from the beginning", like *bhāt*, and "late/modern" Tbhs. (= "corrupted" Sanskrit borrowings) like *bhagat*. For the latter, Grierson later proposed the term *semi-tatsamas*, which acquired some currency. (Bhandarkar had clearly meant to indicate that his "modern *tadbhavas*" were once *tatsamas*.) It was even given an air of pseudo-antiquity by being Sanskritized into *arddhatatsama*.

Chatterji then emphasized the importance of recognizing the existence of *semi-tatsamas* in MIA also, from Pali onwards, on the ground that they exhibit phonological modifications different from those found in words inherited by MIA (e.g., insertion of a vowel rather than assimilation in the case of internal consonant clusters: Skt. *padma* 'lotus' > Pali *paduma*, later MIA *paüma*, rather than **pamma*[2]) as well as the necessity of distinguishing between *earlier* and *later* MIA *semi-tatsamas*, because of the survival of the effects of these in NIA. (For Beames, the "*late tadbhava*" category, in which he included words like NIA *rāt* 'night' < Skt *rātri*, could not have come "through Prakrit" since they exhibit consonants that were supposed to have been elided in the typical Prakrits according to the grammarians, e.g., Maharashtri *rāï*. The error here seems to lie in taking the literary Prakrits, and in particular the most "advanced" of them, Maharashtri, as representing a stage reached by MIA in general – or indeed as representing a natural language at all. A peculiar feature of them – and again, particularly of Maharashtri – is known to have been the generalization by rule of various phonological tendencies which in reality had not spread to all items potentially affected nor to all parts of the country. The word for 'night' and its cognates retain a */t/* in all NIA languages – including Romany – except Sinhalese and Maldivian.)

On the other hand, the traditional *tatsama* category also left something to be desired from the standpoint of scientific historical linguistics. It included words (such as *deva* 'god', *nāma* 'name', *ghāsa* 'grass', *bhara* 'load') which due to their already simple phonological structure were not subject to modification in Prakrit, but were nevertheless in all probability inherited, not reborrowed from Sanskrit. Moreover many words for which analogs could be found or could be created in Sanskrit were in fact *non-Aryan borrowings* at either the OIA or the MIA stage. That is to say, *tatsamas* included Dravidian and other loanwords established in

Sanskrit (e.g., *bala* 'strength', *piṇḍa* 'lump', probably *phala* 'fruit', *nīra* 'water') – many of which were also probably inherited in MIA, not borrowed from Sanskrit.

The term *tatsama* has also been used in a broader sense to refer to Pali borrowings in the context of Sinhalese, which at the same time has its full share of Sanskrit *tatsamas*. There has even been reference to Portuguese "*tatsamas*".

Finally, the *deśya* category was made up partly if not mostly of words that were not aboriginal at all but which happened to descend from OIA dialects other than the one on which Sanskrit was based – hence, part of the inherited native vocabulary. (To call them *tadbhavas*, however, would extend the meaning of that term in a way its originators had not intended.) Or, in some cases they turn out to indeed descend from (popular) Sanskrit itself, but through previously undiscovered phonological processes.

In light of all this it is not surprising that Turner threw up his hands at the entire *tatsama–tadbhava* terminology (Gune Lectures, 1960: 47–9) and suggested it be avoided at least in the context of historical linguistics, as more confusing than helpful. He pointed out yet another deficiency: the *tadbhava* category, even with the "semi-*tatsamas*" removed, did not distinguish between inherited words and words borrowed *from other NIA dialects* (usually Hindi). These also must be excluded from the lexical base on which the phonological laws of development of a given dialect are worked out.

Turner emphasized that the only distinction needed for diachronic descriptions is that between loanwords of all types on the one hand and inherited words on the other – primarily for the purpose of excluding the former from the calculations of the sound developments proper to each stage and variety of the language.

4.3 The Sanskrit element in NIA

An ever increasing influx of Sanskrit *tatsamas* is one of the most salient characteristics of NIA (at least, in those languages outside the dominantly Islamic culture sphere) and one which distinguishes it from MIA. Although borrowings from Sanskrit have taken place throughout the history of IA, in the MIA literary languages these were forced by convention to conform to the phonology of MIA, that is, to become *semi-tatsamas* (in the traditional terminology, "*tadbhavas*").

To use Bhandarkar's example, a word with consonant clusters like *prārthanā*, a common NIA (Hindi, Bengali, Gujarati, Marathi) Ts. meaning 'prayer; request', could not have existed in such a form in literary MIA: it had to become *patthanā* (Pali) or *patthaṇā* (Prakrit). While these could well have been inherited forms in MIA, the two Prakrit reflexes of Skt *praśna* 'question', namely *paṇha* and *pasiṇa*, may well represent inherited and borrowed forms respectively, since the latter is made to conform to MIA norms by a method (cf. *paduma* in section 4.2 above) different from the normal treatment of sibilant + nasal clusters, which is SN > NH (as exemplified by *paṇha*).

In NIA such rules were no longer applied, and we find not only in modern but in earlier NIA literature (e.g., Tulsidas, sixteenth century) words like *prārthit* 'requested' or *praśna* 'question', with no modifications.

The incidence of Tss. has varied among the NIA literary languages. A diagram in Beames (1871) arranging some of the major NIA languages on a basically west–east axis according to the increasing proportion of Tss. (from a minimum in Sindhi to a maximum in Bengali) may no longer be strictly accurate, due to the increased Sanskritization of Standard Hindi, and confrontation of NIA languages in general with modern register and terminological needs. Assamese (not included in Beames's scheme), which had been praised at the beginning of the century by Grierson for having resisted the kind of Sanskritization he found so pernicious in Bengali, has meanwhile succumbed. Even literary Sinhalese makes extensive use of Sanskrit. Meanwhile, the new colloquial-based *colit bhāṣ̃ā* standard has gained currency in Bengal.

It makes more sense to compare equivalent registers than to compare languages. It is no doubt still true in a general way to say that Marathi is more Sanskritized than Gujarati, and Hindi than Punjabi, and Sindhi the least. Part of the reason for this, however, is that Bengali, Marathi, and Hindi have been more utilized for "serious" purposes than some of the other languages mentioned, and have had accordingly to develop the requisite terminological resources.

The reason for Sanskritization that is usually advanced is the lexical poverty of NIA due to its previous non-use for "serious" purposes in favor of Sanskrit. Lexical poverty, that is, with regard to abstractions and other special requirements of high culture: in their own spheres, pertaining to everyday life, especially rural life, the NIA "vernaculars" were and are quite rich.

The objection that is usually advanced is that Sanskritization of certain literary languages has gone far beyond the meeting of such legitimate needs. It has involved the replacement of perfectly adequate existing NIA words by their Sanskrit (Ts.) counterparts, creating an exaggerated gulf between the colloquial and the literary language. To some extent the effects of this are not confined to the written languages; such replacements have spread to speech, first of the educated, and have even driven out the original words, threatening the language with impoverishment of another kind, the loss of what Beames and Grierson were fond of calling its stock of "honest" Tbhs.

This is particularly vexing to philologists, because only such words could be used as the basis of diachronic description: the Sanskrit loanwords are useless for this purpose. To be sure, inherited Tbhs. can still be turned up in remote village dialects, and in the older literature, but with a lot more trouble, at least in the former case. (The importance of relatively unSanskritized languages such as Sindhi, of intermittently cultivated languages such as Konkani and Rajasthani, and of relatively uncultivated languages such as the Central and West Pahari dialects or Bhojpuri for historical linguistics is greatly enhanced by their comparative richness in Tbhs.)

Chatterji's response to this (1960: 135) was to point out that a language does not exist "merely for the sake of its history." Sanskritization can be defended as binding NIA (and also the cultivated Dravidian languages, except for Tamil) together into a "cultural whole." As any foreign student of Indic languages knows, it is comparatively easy to go from one relexified literary language to another, once the Sanskritic key is mastered; village-level colloquials are quite another matter. The point is not lost on educated native speakers of NIA.

This procedure is not without its pitfalls, to be sure. Sanskrit loans do not always have the same meaning in every language, and there are "false friends" just as there are between cognate French and English words (*concurrence*, etc.) – perhaps fewer, since the *pandits* represent a force not to be reckoned with in Europe. To this writer's limited knowledge, there has been no thoroughgoing study of the subject.

There is also the matter of pronunciation. While Hindi and Marathi drop certain final short /*a*/'s, the assimilatory pronunciation of Bengali and of Assamese Tss. (let alone of Thai and other Southeast Asian borrowers – but that is beyond the scope of this book) sometimes makes a word difficult to recognize before one knows the "code": e.g.,

Ts. spelling	H. pron.	B. pron.	As. pron.
satya	[*sʌtya*]	[*ʃottɔ*]	[*χɒtyɒ*]
abhyāsa	[*ʌbhya:s*]	[*ɔbbhæʃ*]	[*ɒbhyaχ*]
ātmahatyā	[*a:tmʌhʌtya:*]	[*ãttohɔtta*]	[*atmɒhɒtya*]

(Note especially the last example above: Assamese shows fewer assimilations of Skt consonant clusters than Bengali – perhaps a testimonial to the more recent infusion of Tss. into Assamese.)

Sanskrit /*r̥*/ is generally pronounced [*ri*] in Hindi and Bengali and [*ru*] in Marathi, Sinhalese, and partly in Gujarati. The Skt cluster /*jñ*/ is variously rendered, but everywhere modified: Skt *jñāna-* 'knowledge' = H. [*gya:n*], B. [*gæ:n*], M. [*dnya:n*]. (The inherited Tbh. form of this word is by contrast represented by OG. *nāṇa*, and, with analogical replacement of /*n-*/ by /*j-*/ from related verbal forms, by H.-B. *jān*, M. *dzān*.)

As is usually the case with languages having such stratified vocabularies, traditional Tss. typically have a general, "higher", more abstract meaning, while corresponding Tbhs. have a "lower", more concrete or more specialized meaning. In the case of the Hindi pair *gyān/jān* (perhaps not the best example) the former has the meaning of 'knowledge, learning, understanding' in the general as well as in the Hindu religious sense, while the latter (not to be confused with *jān*-$_2$, a much more common Persian loanword meaning 'life, soul') is found only in set phrases and compounds such as *jān-pahcān* 'an acquaintance', *jānkārī* '(practical) knowledge, information, familiarity'. Marathi *dzān* means 'acknowledgement of favors and kindnesses' (Molesworth).

Hindi–Bengali *jān*-$_3$ 'a soothsayer, diviner' comes from Skt *jñani* 'knowing, wise'. There is also the Hindi–Bengali intimate imperative *jān!* 'know!' from the related verb (Skt 3sg. *jānāti*). The four *jān*'s – to which Bengali adds a fifth, the polite imperative of the verb 'go' – suggests a reason beyond lexical "poverty" why an infusion of Sanskrit into NIA became necessary: phonological erosion of the word resulted in numerous homonyms (even if they were not as pervasive as literary Maharashtri Prakrit would suggest).

Commonly it will be found that the Ts. has won the day, and the Tbh. is now archaic and/or dialectal. Hindi examples cited by Kellogg include the now standard Ts. *lābh* 'profit' and *krodh* 'anger' vs. Tbh. *lāh*, *lāhu*, *lāha* and *koh*, now practically confined to classical Hindi (and Marathi and Punjabi) poetry. (It is typical that the Tbh. stem is still current in Sindhi: *lāho*.)

Helping drive such words from modern speech and writing were not only Ts. like *lābh* and *krodh*, but also Persian loans like *fāydā* and *gussā*. This (and the ever-popular *jān* 'life' mentioned earlier) brings us to the second major source of supplementation of the NIA lexicon: Perso-Arabic.

Before proceeding, however, it should be noted that the Sanskrit element in NIA falls roughly into two categories: first are the words actually borrowed from Sanskrit – which existed in Sanskrit – to express perhaps "higher" but not alien concepts. Second are the words – generally complex words and belonging to a more recent stratum – which never existed as such in Sanskrit, but which have been coined from Sanskrit elements, often on foreign (English) models, in response to contemporary needs. This Neo-Sanskrit element will be discussed in a special section below.

Finally it should be noted that the Sanskrit element, whether traditional Tss. or Neo-Sanskrit, is not necessarily borrowed by each language directly. Much of it was borrowed by Hindi from Bengali, which had a head start in these matters, and by other languages subsequently from Hindi.

4.4 The "foreign" element in NIA: Perso-Arabic

As noted earlier, to the three MIA lexical categories traditional NIA philology added a fourth, *videśi*, that is to say, 'foreign' words. There had been extra-Indian borrowings even in Sanskrit (e.g., *kendra* 'center' from Greek) but these had not been distinguished as such. In the NIA period, however, this element came to loom too large to be ignored. The three principal sources of such vocabulary, Perso-Arabic, Portuguese, and English, made their appearance in roughly that order historically.

The PERSO-ARABIC element (or perhaps better simply the Persian element: Arabic generally was not drawn upon directly[3] at least not until recently, but came in through Persian in a Persian form) can be divided into three subcategories:

First, there are the loanwords, particularly those pertaining to administration and to the amenities of urban life, but by no means confined to those areas, found in most NIA languages, a legacy of the six centuries or more of Muslim rule in much of the subcontinent. (Chatterji points out that the former are particularly the legacy of Akbar's Hindu finance minister Todar Mal, who made Persian the language of the Mughal revenue administration in the later sixteenth century.) Naturally this legacy is strongest in the regions longest subject to Muslim rule, and weakest in the regions peripheral to it (Rajasthan, Nepal, Assam, and of course Sri Lanka). Although the administrative lexicon has begun to fade a little (in India, not in Pakistan), a significant portion of the vocabulary of everyday urban speech in some languages, above all in Hindi, remains Persian. Sanskrit Tss. are thus not the culprits in driving out inherited Tss. from these colloquials – they had already been driven out by Persian words.

Some of the Persian, as distinct from the Arabic, lexicon was no doubt aided in its assimilability by the fact that Persian is after all a close cousin of NIA. It may accordingly sometimes resemble native NIA vocabulary closely: e.g., Pers. *band* 'fastened' = NIA *bandh-*; Pers. *-stān* 'place' = NIA *sthān*; Pers. *jān* 'soul, life' = NIA *jan* 'living being'; Pers. *baccah* 'young one, child' = NIA *baccā*. Some words of ultimately Arabic origin are just as firmly embedded, however: *aurat* 'woman'; *lekin* 'but'; *bilkul* 'completely'. Affinity also aided in the assimilation of certain Persian suffixes, particularly the most common of them, the adjectival *-ī* (cf. Skt *-īya*: e.g., *hindustān-ī* 'Indian', *bhārat-īya* 'Indian'); the same cannot be said regarding Persian *prefixes* (*be-* 'devoid of (x)') similarly assimilated. The use of such formants is not confined to the Persian-derived lexicon: *jāpānī* 'Japanese'.

Second, in regions of dominantly Islamic culture (with the partial exception of

Bangladesh), Perso-Arabic elements have been the means used to provide the literary languages with the needed abstractions and apparatus of prose syntax, in the manner of Skt Tss. elsewhere. In the Hindi area, as we have seen, strong ties of cultural allegiance in both directions have produced the two modern literary languages, Urdu and Modern Standard Hindi, differentiated mainly at this level.[4] (Other differences, e.g., phonological, are mostly a by-product of this.)

The resulting difference is quite considerable. An inexact but convenient rough way to illustrate this in an identical context is provided by St Paul's list (Gal. 5: 19–22) of the "works of the flesh" followed by the "fruit of the Spirit" in their respective Hindi and Urdu translations:

English	Hindi	Urdu
fornication	*vyabhicār*	*harāmkārī*
impurity	*gande kām*	*nāpākī*
licentiousness	*lucpan*	*ʃahwat-parastī*
idolatry	*mūrtti-pūjā*	*but-parastī*
sorcery	*ṭonā*	*jādūgārī*
enmity	*bair*	*adāvate˜*
strife	*jhagṛā*	
jealousy	*īrṣyā*	*hasad*
anger	*krodh*	*ɣussā*
contentions	*virodh*	*tafrīqe*
dissension	*phūṭ*	*judāiyā˜*
heresies	*vidharm*	*bid'ate˜*
envy/spite	*ḍāh*	*buɣz*
drunkenness	*matvālpan*	*naχah-bāzī*
carousing	*līlā-krīṛā*	*nāc-rang*
love	*prem*	*muhabbat*
joy	*ānand*	*χuʃī*
peace	*mel*	*itmīnān*
patience	*dhīraj*	*tahammul*
kindness	*kṛpā*	*mehrbānī*
goodness	*bhalāī*	*nīkī*
faithfulness	*viśvās*	*īmāndārī*
gentleness	*namratā*	*hilm*
self-control	*sa˜yam*	*parhezgārī*

These terms do not represent a highly learned register (a number of Tbhs. are included), and were presumably chosen to be intelligible to a wide audience.

Nevertheless it is interesting that the translators ended up with only one term in common – appropriately enough *jhagṛā* 'quarrel, strife'.

Third, Perso-Arabic is the source which is mined (primarily by Urdu in its capacity as the official language of Pakistan, and by Sindhi) to create *neologisms* in response to burgeoning contemporary terminological needs, in the manner of Neo-Sanskrit.

4.5 The "foreign" element in NIA: Portuguese

PORTUGUESE was the first European language with which South Asia came in contact and it was accordingly the primary mediator of terms for the products, artifacts, and institutions of pre-industrial Europe (e.g., Western Christianity). Through Portuguese also came knowledge of the myriad products of the just-discovered tropical New World, which soon established themselves as an integral part of South Asian life in the course of what Crosby 1972 calls "the Columbian exchange". (Not all of these bear Portuguese or Portuguese-mediated Amerindian names in NIA; some have NIA descriptive names: e.g., H. *lāl mirc* lit. 'red pepper' = 'chillies'.)

Although Portuguese words are not as numerous as words of English or Perso-Arabic origin, they are often names of common objects ('key', 'window', 'towel'), and so well assimilated as not to be recognizably foreign. There are naturally more of them in the coastal languages, where there was direct contact with Portuguese, than in the interior languages, which they reached only by indirect means. They are most numerous in Konkani (a special case), then in Sinhalese (where the inventory differs somewhat from that on the subcontinent), after that in Marathi, Bengali, and Gujarati, then in Hindi–Urdu, and finally in other languages. They are found, however, even in Nepali (*cābī*, *bālṭī*, *mistrī*, etc.), where they penetrated presumably via Hindi. The forms of the words in the coastal languages tend also to be closer to the Portuguese original:

Portuguese + gloss	Sinhalese	Marathi	Hindi
chave 'key'		*cāvī*	*cābhī*
janela 'window'	*janēlaya*	[Beng. *jānālā*]	*janglā*
balde 'bucket'	*baldiya*	*bāldī*	*bālṭī*
camara 'room'	*kāmaraya*		*kamrā*
mestre 'artisan'		*mestrī*	*mistrī*
armario 'cabinet'	*almāriya*		*almārī*
couve 'cabbage'	*gōvā*	*kobī*	*gobhī*
batata 'potato'	*batala* *	*baṭāṭā*	

toalha 'towel'	*tuvaya*	*ṭuvāl* [Beng. *toale*]	*tauliyā*
camisa 'shirt'	*kamīse*	*khamīs*	*kamīz*
sabão 'soap'	*saban*	*sābaṇ*	*sābun***

Sinhalese *batala* refers to the *sweet potato*, the original (but generally confused) meaning of Amerindian *batata*. Sinhalese *artapal* 'white potato' is one of the few NIA loanwords from Dutch (<*aardappel*). There is some controversy regarding the last two items, since *sābun* and *qamīs* also exist in Arabic and Persian, which may have gotten them from Portuguese, or directly from Latin. The *-an*/*-aṇ* of the Sinhalese and Marathi words for 'soap' probably indicates Portuguese origin, however, as may the *-z* in the Hindi–Urdu word for 'shirt'.

An important role in the transmission of Portuguese lexical material to Indian languages was no doubt played by the Portuguese creoles once current in parts of coastal South Asia, including Bengal. Only self-contained lexical items were borrowed from Portuguese[5] (mainly nouns, in Konkani also a few verbs and other parts of speech), not morphemes or processes of word-formation – quite different from what obtained with Persian.

4.6 The "foreign" element in NIA: English

The role of Portuguese has since the nineteenth century been dwarfed by ENGLISH, now clearly the major foreign source of NIA lexical supplementation. Everyday English loanwords pertain especially to the institutions and artifacts of modern life: *ṭikaṭ*, *film*, *sinema*, *baink*, *hoṭal*, *sāikil*, *rel*, *āiskrīm*, *reḍio*, *bīyar*, *baiṭarī*, *kāfī*, *āfis*, *sṭeśan*, *bas*, *krikeṭ*, *cek*, *maniyārḍar*. Such words are known to all. A few are partially assimilated by way of folk etymology: *lālṭen* from Eng. *lantern*.

Casual educated urban speech goes far beyond this, however, and sprinkles its sentences liberally with English nouns, adjectives, and English-based verbs for most of which NIA equivalents exist. This is not a recent phenomenon. Grierson was already citing examples at the beginning of the century, e.g., from an attorney in court: *is position kā incontrovertible proof de saktā hū̃ aur merā opinion yah hai ki defence kā argument waterhold nahī̃ kar saktā hai* (*LSI 1.1*: 165 fn. 1). It is debatable whether the more extreme examples of this kind are to be called borrowing or codeswitching – although such linguistic behavior on the part of bilinguals is no doubt a source of loanwords in the "real" language. (Indeed Grierson gives his examples in the context of speculation regarding the origins of Urdu in quite similar circumstances, involving Persian–Hindi instead of English–Hindi bilingualism.)

Borrowing of English nouns and adjectives is easy enough, and the borrowing of verbs (sometimes incorrectly said to be non-existent, not only with regard to NIA languages but languages in general) is facilitated by a device for expanding the verbal repertoire common to most NIA languages and some others (notably Persian, also Japanese and Korean): a noun or adjective, usually abstract and typically borrowed, is combined with an "empty" verb (generally *do* for transitives and *become* for intransitives) which serves a verbalizing function similar to that of English *-ize* to produce a new abstract verb. English *verbs* are typically borrowed by incorporating them into the "nominal" slot of such complexes: e.g., H. *arenj karnā* 'to arrange', corresponding to *intizām karnā* and *prabandh karnā* with a Perso-Arabic noun and Skt Tss. respectively.

The question arises whether such "fillers" occupy the same rather fluid position in the lexicon in relation to a basically stable underlying NIA structure that involves one interchangeable element, i.e. occupied by Perso-Arabic, Sanskrit, or English material as circumstances dictate. This is not to suggest that there may not be different nuances of meaning or range of use among such triplets – or that there is always a triplet: a given English or Perso-Arabic or Sanskrit item in the N-slot may well convey something for which there is not even an approximate equivalent in the other sets. (Perso-Arabic material is moreover not used in all NIA languages to the extent it has been in the Hindi–Urdu area.) The point is that with the aid of a "floating layer" of borrowed material finer and finer distinctions can be made, and every need of a many-faceted culture met.

4.7 The "foreign" element in NIA: pronunciation

Foreign loanwords in NIA often reflect an earlier or dialectal pronunciation of the source languages, different from the standard pronunciation of those languages today. Thus the Persian element, even in Urdu (and Persian itself as it is read in the subcontinent) reflects a pronunciation of Persian current in the eastern part of the Persian domain (Central Asia, Afghanistan) perhaps five hundred years ago, not that of Iran today. This particularly affects the vowels. Thus [*ro:z*] not [*ru:z*] 'daily'; [*ʃe:r*] not [*ʃi:r*] 'lion'; and [*ʃahā:dat*] not [*ʃæhɔdǽt*] 'evidence'. The Arabic (and Turki) /*q*/ is kept distinct from /*γ*/: [*bá:qi*] not [*bɔγī*] 'remainder'.

Portuguese words reflect an earlier (and remaining northern dialectal) pronunciation of *ch-* as an affricate rather than modern standard [*ʃ*]. It is clear, however, that final *-o* and *-e* already had their high values [*u*, *ɪ*]. Thus *chave* > [*ca:vɪ*] or [*ca:bi*], never *[*ʃa:ve*]; *tabaco* > [*tamba:ku*].

The matter of English is more complex, because the question of spelling pronunciation as well as of Scottish and Welsh traders and teachers intrudes.

Words like H. *ṭamāṭar* 'tomato', however, suggest exposure to a so-called "*r*-less" dialect.

The extent to which foreign loanwords have retained sounds foreign to NIA (in the manner of French /ʒ/ in English) and affected the overall phonology of the latter is a matter for discussion in the next chapter.

4.8 NIA creativity: expressive forms

Borrowing does not exhaust the means by which the NIA lexicon has been enriched. NIA lexical creativity must also be considered. Attention is directed in this section to several highly productive types of *expressive* formation in NIA. On the basis of the standard languages, it might be thought that NIA is not particularly rich in *diminutive* and *augmentative* formations (compared with its Romance or Slavic cousins, for example). This may be an artifact of the literary language focus of many descriptions; in any case, there are some important exceptions to such a generalization.

First, there is the *multiple stem* phenomenon of the spoken dialects of the "Hindi area" (absent, except for a few fragments, from Standard Hindi and Urdu). In its classic form, the system is best developed in Eastern Hindi (Awadhi) and "Bihari", where a noun may have as many as four expressive stems: e.g., Magahi *ghōṛ/ghōṛā/ghoṛwā/ghoṛauwā*. (All mean 'horse', with various degrees of attitudinal coloration.) These are usually called the (1) *short weak*, (2) *short strong*, (3) *long*, and (4) *redundant* (or *longer*) forms respectively. In addition, there is a *reduced* stem, used in compounds, e.g., *ghuṛ-*. (For Maithili, where a *redundant* stem in *-abā* is common, Jha [1958: 275–6] has a slightly different classification.) Corresponding feminine or former feminine forms end in *-i/-ī/-iyā/-iyawā*.

In Western Hindi dialects, e.g., Bundeli (Jaiswal 1962: 61–2), one *redundant* formant (*-aiyā*) often does duty for both masculine and feminine. In both Eastern and Western Hindi, the stem vowel is usually reduced before the *long* and *redundant* stem-formants are added. This is not always the case in Braj (Kellogg 1938: 74), and it is not the case in Rajasthani (Bahl 1972: 39), where a *redundant* form seems to be absent, albeit with compensations (see below). (See also Chatterji 1926: 96, 658; Grierson 1903 [*LSI 5.21*: 26, 38, 50].)

Tiwari (1954a: 181) says there is no particular difference in meaning among these forms (in Bhojpuri), but according to B. Saksena (1971: 110) in Awadhi the *long* form (except in the eastern dialects, where it is the "general" form) "is used only familiarly and sometimes has a tinge of ... contempt." In Maithili also, according to Jha, "the long forms when used with reference to persons carry a sense of disrespect, while the redundant forms indicate that the speaker is not in a serious mood." With reference to inanimate objects no semantic difference is observed, but such usage is characteristic of "the speech of children and persons of the lower classes of society." Jaiswal makes similar comments regarding Bundeli, adding that the use of *long* and *redundant* forms, which is "rapidly declining in towns" (under the influence of Standard Hindi?) "may often suggest disgust, unconcern, or inferiority." Although the *redundant* forms seem generally to be regarded as vulgar, the *long* form may be used as a term of endearment, e.g., *biṭiyā* < *bēṭī* 'daughter'. It is called simply *diminutive* by Bahl. In any case, such forms have rarely been used in literature, except in dialogue portions of the recent genre of *ā̃calik* or "local color" novels.

In the eastern dialects of Awadhi (i.e. of Faizabad and Sultanpur), the *short* form is only used to denote a *class*. This is also the case in Rajasthani (Marwari), where according to Bahl forms like *khurpal/khurpalau* 'hoe' contrast as *generic/specific*.

In Awadhi *respectful long* as well as *longer* forms are also available: *ghoṛaū*, *ghoṛawaū*; *ghorīyaū*, *ghoṛiyawaū*. Saksena says these [augmentative?] forms are "sometimes found in tales and [are] particularly applied to powerful and big animals like lions and camels."

Affective *adjectival* stems also exist. They have been noted briefly by Tiwari for Bhojpuri and more extensively by Bahl for Rajasthani, who extends the analysis to participles as well. In both cases special affective suffixes seem to be involved, along with variations on the above system: in Awadhi *-k-*; in Rajasthani *-k-*, *-l-*, *-ṛ-*, often in combination: e.g., R. *moṭau* 'big' > *moṭorau/moṭaṛakau/moṭalau*; R. *likhiyau* 'written' (m.) > *likhiyoṛau/likhiyoṛkau/likhiyoṛlau* (Bahl 1972: 42).

Second, on a much wider basis in NIA it is found that the *common feminine or onetime feminine suffix -ī* (< OIA *-ikā*) when applied to nouns referring to inanimate objects denotes a *smaller* object than the corresponding word with *-ā/-au/-ō* (< OIA *-akaḥ*): H. *kaṭorā/kaṭorī* 'bowl/small bowl', *ṭokrā/ṭokrī* 'basket/small basket', *baṭṭā/baṭṭī* 'pestle/small pestle'.

Since the OIA suffix *-akaḥ* is said (Whitney 1950/1889: 467, Burrow 1955: 196) to have at least partially a *diminutive* force (retained in other IE languages), the use of this form of the m./f. contrast for the above purpose would appear to involve a (NIA?) reworking of this material. In any case, it is now quite productive and works both ways: H. *pothī/pothā* 'book/huge tome', *rassī/rassā* 'rope/thick rope' (< MIA *rassi* < OIA *raśmī*). In Bengali the suffix *-ā* (< OIA *-akaḥ*) may be augmentative in itself: *cā̃d/cā̃dā* 'moon/big round moon' (Chatterji 1926: 658–9). The *long* (and properly "*diminutive*") form of the f. suffix,

-iyā, is sometimes found instead of *-ī* in these contrasts: H. *ḍibbā* (*ḍabbā*)/*ḍibiyā* 'box/small box', *ciṛā*/*ciṛiyā* 'sparrow/any small bird'.

In NIA languages with three genders, e.g., Gujarati, the masculine may indicate an extra large object, while the neuter may have a pejorative connotation: *roṭlo*/*roṭlī*/*roṭlu˜* 'coarse bread or loaf/ thin round bread/ poor quality bread', *māṭlu˜*/*māṭlī*/*māṭlo* 'large pot/ small pot/ extra large pot' (Cardona 1965: 64).

Finding it difficult to draw a line between these and the preceding, Bahl treats them together, and maintains that the *main function* of the so-called gender affixes is not to denote sex, which is only incidental (the female of a species is usually smaller), but lies in this area. He draws attention to the fact that in Rajasthani at least the "gender" affixes are applied indifferently to both male and female *proper names* as part of the larger affective system, and proceeds to list fifty-three affective forms common to the male name Sohan and the female name Sohni (1972: 29–30).

4.9 NIA creativity: onomatopoeia and sound symbolism

Every language has its share of onomatopoetic formations, no doubt, but the whole South and Southeast Asian region is the focus of an unusually high degree of their development. It is characteristic of all the languages of the region: Dravidian, Munda, Mon-Khmer, and Indo-Aryan. In Indo-Aryan much of it goes back to MIA, but not, apparently, to OIA (Chatterji 1926: 371). Examples are indeed found in Epic and Classical Sanskrit literature, contemporary with living MIA, from which they are likely to have been borrowed. (For discussion, and a couple of isolated Vedic examples, see Hoffman 1952.) In any case, there is a pronounced increase with time, and no connection with *IE or even with Iranian.

It is an obvious *areal feature*, developed by Indo-Aryan in response to areal pressures. Emeneau, who treated the subject in an important article (1969, reprint 1980), concluded that meant diffusion from Dravidian (without prejudice to Austroasiatic, however, for which sufficient comparative data was unavailable). He came up with forty-six "areal etymologies", i.e. common to Indo-Aryan and Dravidian.

In addition to onomatopoeia of less structured types (sometimes difficult to identify as such in any language), what is characteristic, both of NIA and of the region, is onomatopoeia having the specific structure CVC-CVC, that is, with reduplicated stem. (In most of Dravidian, as well as in MIA and in certain NIA languages such as Oriya, the structure is CVCV-CVCV. The final vowel, usually *a* or *ɔ*, has been lost in most of NIA.) E.g., H.P.G.M.B. *khaṭkhaṭ* 'a knocking sound'; H.B. *jhanjhan*, M.G.P. *jhaṇjhaṇ* 'a jingling sound'; H. *balbal* 'a gurgling sound'.

Equally characteristic are the verb stem formations from these elements, either employing the denominative *ā*, *āu* (h. *khaṭkhaṭānā*, P. *khaṭkhaṭāuṇā* 'to knock or clatter' as in 'He knocked on the door' = H. *darvāze par khaṭkhaṭāyā*), or directly: M. *jhaṇjhaṇane˜*, G. *jhaṇjhaṇavu˜* 'to tinkle; to tingle'. Such stems with denominative *-āya* are already found in Classical Sanskrit. Characteristic NIA verbal nouns are then formed from these stems: H. *jhanjhanāhaṭ*, M.G. *jhaṇjhaṇāṭ* 'jingling'. Onomatopoetics may also be used in the preverbal slot of the NV-complex denominatives with *kar*: *jhanjhan karnā* 'to jingle'.

Onomatopoetic is a misnomer if it is taken to imply sound imitation only. These formations have a far wider reference, to sensations of many other kinds – visual and tactile: they include equivalents of Eng. *glitter*, *tingle*, *throb*, etc. Some interesting examples supplied by Chatterji include *bɔjbɔjā* 'sense of being moist and rotten', *pilpilā* 'sense of being overcrowded', *thikthikā* 'sense of teeming with maggots' (1926: 891). Hence the term *sound symbolism*, which unfortunately has been used (as has *phonaesthetics*) to refer to individual sounds or clusters (such as English *gl-*), a matter which no doubt also deserves closer examination in NIA. In the Austroasiatic field, G. Diffloth favors the term *expressives*, but that has already been employed above to denote diminutives and other affective/attitudinal formations.

The reduplication in these stems generally implies *iterativity* of the phenomenon in question. Variations on this theme include substitution of a different initial consonant, lengthening or nasalization of vowels, and addition of suffixes (usually *-ak*): *jhalmalānā* 'to be aglow with tremulous light'.

Nonreduplicated stems, typically with the suffix *-ak*, are available to express phenomena of a sudden, noniterative nature: *jhaṭak* 'jerk', *saṛāk* 'crack of a whip' (vs. *saṛāsar* 'repeated cracks of a whip'), *camak* 'flash, flare' (vs. *camcam* 'sparkle, glitter'). Such stems may be compatible with *grammatical* expression of iterativity or durativity, however: H. *dhaṛakā* 'it throbbed (once)'; *dhaṛak rahā thā* 'it was throbbing'. Cf. B. *dhɔṛkhɔṛ kɔrā* 'writhe, flutter', *dhūkdhūk kɔrā* 'palpitate', with reduplicated stems, vs. M. *dhaḍakne˜* 'bump into', with nonreduplicated *-ak* stem.

Most of these types are found in Dravidian as well (Emeneau 1980 [1969]: 261, 263). If they are borrowed, why are we discussing them under NIA creativity? It was basically the *pattern* that was borrowed, not the individual items. Even the few examples given above contain sounds – i.e. aspirates – not native to Dravidian. Although there are indeed a number of common etymologies, which may go back to the MIA period, they are dwarfed by the number of original formations peculiar to each language or confined to a few. Emeneau turned up forty-six possible "areal" (IA/Drav.) etymologies, but Chatterji counted over 125 such commonly used verb stems in Bengali, and mentions a list of 651 onomatopoetics given by Tagore. Bahl (1972) gives a chart of 277 "basic" (C-a-C) onomatopoetic "elements" used in Rajasthani. (Not every consonant can be used in combination with every other consonant: *kaṭ*, *kaṭh*, *kad* exist but not **kat*, *kath*, *kadh*.) These can then be varied as to vowel (*a*/*i*/*u*), suffix (*-ak*, *-āk*, *-ar*, *-al*, *-aṛ*), *gemination* of final consonant and reduplication vs. nonreduplication to produce already 277 × 90 = 24,930 "regular" possibilities, of which only 1,260 did not actually occur in his data. There were also a number of special types affecting only certain of these stem-classes. Chatterji also notes the extended possibilities in varying the internal vowel: *tɔktɔk* 'tick of a clock', *ṭikṭik* 'tick of a watch; mild nagging', *ṭukṭuk* 'gentle battering with a tiny hammer', *ṭæ̃kṭæ̃k* 'jangling; unpleasant remarks', *ṭukṭāk* 'gentle blows with alternation of sound', etc.

Etymologizing is further complicated by variability of consonants (especially initial consonants) in ways foreign to the regular sound laws of the language. Aspirate and nonaspirate, retroflex and nonretroflex, voiced and unvoiced consonants seem to interchange in semantically related sets of stems. A more appropriate undertaking would involve working out the semantics of the system of sound symbolism – a formidable task, partly because of the difficulty in defining the "referents" in a metalanguage (such as English) which is far less rich in such elements and was formed in a totally different cultural ambience. In using a NIA metalanguage it is difficult to avoid recourse to the terms themselves.

Unlike the *affective* forms discussed in the previous section, these so-called onomatopoetic formations are definitely part of the NIA literary languages. In *Materials for a medium-sized dictionary of Hindi verbs* (mimeographed, Chicago, n.d.), Bahl and his assistants culled 129 such verbs of the reduplicating type alone from a sample of contemporary Hindi literary and journalistic prose.

4.10 **NIA creativity: echo-formations**

The last category we propose to discuss here, *echo-formations*, is less overwhelming, but no less characteristic. What is involved is the following of a word, most often a noun, by a form which "echoes" it, replacing the initial consonant (sometimes also the following vowel) with a standard consonant (or CV sequence), which varies according to the language. The meaning is that of the basic noun "and things like that" almost but not quite equivalent to "*etc.*". According to Bahl (1972: 48) the meaning is "the speaker's manifest attitudinal lack of concern or care toward his collocutor or the thing referred to by him." The formation verges on the syntactic, since the members of the resulting "compound" can be interrupted by clitics (Cardona 1965: 166).

In Hindi the substitution involved is *v-* (> *u-* before back vowels): *pānī-vānī* 'water, etc.', *ghoṛā-uṛā* 'horses and the like'. In Bengali it is *ṭ-* (*ghoṛā-ṭorā*), in Maithili *t-* (*ghorā-torā*), in Gujarati and Sinhalese *b-* (*bhoḍo-boḍo, aśwayā-baśwaya*), in Marathi *bi-* (*ghoḍā-biḍā*), in Assamese *s-*, in Punjabi *b-*, in Dogri *m-*, in Rajasthani *ph-*, *v-*, *s-*, in Dakhani *gi-* (*khānā-ginā* 'food, etc.' also the general Dravidian formant).

There is again obvious evidence of an *areal trait*. The formation is not inherited from OIA and is well established in the other areal families. Within NIA, it seems to fall into two main dialectal types, an Eastern apical type, represented by Bengali, Maithili, and Assamese, and a Western labial type, in which Sinhalese is significantly included.

4.11 NIA creativity: modern neologisms

NIA lexical creativity includes the fashioning of new words to meet contemporary needs, whether out of Sanskrit, Perso-Arabic, NIA, or even English elements. Such words are generally complex: that is, they involve suffixes and prefixes (the latter otherwise alien to NIA structure, with minor exceptions); they are often compound as well, in which case they will be found largely to continue the types of compounding recognized in Sanskrit. (The Arabic elements drawn upon by Urdu, Sindhi, and other languages are an exception, since Arabic does not permit compounding. The coinages are instead *lexicalized phrases*, as in French.) Under this category of creativity should also be included words which did exist in the older languages but which have been invested with a new modern content, e.g., Skt *vijñāna* 'discrimination, discernment, worldly knowledge' > mod. NIA 'science; *-ology*'.

The preference of the standard languages for calques has already been referred to. It must not be imagined that the need for new words is confined to the translation of English terms, however. South Asian societies have their own situational needs calling for creation of new vocabulary. Some of the results are accordingly difficult to render into English, e.g., H. *chāyāvād*, the name of a Hindi literary movement of the 1920s and 1930s (< *chāyā* 'shadow' + *vād* 'talking' > 'exposition' > 'theory, doctrine' > mod. '*-ism*'.) An example based on NIA material is B. G. *gherāo/gherāv* 'the act, in a labor dispute, of surrounding management in their offices and not allowing them to leave until demands are met' (< *gher* 'to surround' + *-āo/āv*, NIA nominalizer).

In the area of modern technical terminology it appeared at one time self-evident that English (that is, the Greco-Latin based "international" terminology in its English form) would sweep the field, despite the ingenious but quixotic attempts of the indefatigable Dr. Raghu Vira and others to invent "Indian" (= Neo-Sanskrit) equivalents for such things as *benzylphenylacetate* (= *dhūpaladarśalaśaktīya*). For one thing, the South Asian scientific community had a vested interest in English as both its own natural medium of activity (partly a legacy, to be sure, of the fact that these subjects have until recently been taught and studied in the subcontinent above the school level almost exclusively through English[6]) and its channel of communication with the outside world. The latter in particular would seem to outweigh any advantage to be gained by transparency in a "native" terminology. The accelerating pace of scientific and technical advance moreover would make it more difficult today than ever before to *sustain* an independent terminology.

Nevertheless, more and more books are being published eschewing English terminology in favor of a national terminology, leaving the issue in some doubt (the issue here being, it must be emphasized, the matter of terminology *in NIA languages*, not the use of English as such). The question is as much one of cultural loyalty as of alleged easy comprehensibility. As Raghu Vira put it, there are three great classical sources in the world from which other languages build their higher vocabularies: Latin–Greek for Europe, Chinese for Eastern Asia, and Sanskrit for South and Southeast Asia (conspicuously omitting mention of a fourth, namely Arabic). Since the "word-building power of Sanskrit is at least equal to, if not superior to" these others, it would clearly be an act of cultural treason to import terms from another source – "opaque" terms at that. Moreover, such terminological development was actually mandated in the new constitution of independent India, as Vira read it.

Unfortunately the potential of Neo-Sanskrit for creating a unified pan-Indian terminology even at less ambitious levels has not been consistently realized. Urdu aside, languages preferring Neo-Sanskrit have often gone their own ways. E.g., 'international' is calqued in H. as *antarrāṣṭrīya* (< *antar* 'between' + *rāṣṭra* 'country' + *-īya* 'adjectival ending' cf. Russ. *mezhdunarodnyi* and Germ. *zwischenstaatlich*). Slightly different interpretations of the rules of Sanskrit morpheme combination give Marathi–Gujarati *āntarrāṣṭrīya*, with a long first vowel. The double *rr* in both cases is a violation of Sanskrit rules, however. A hypercorrect but little used Bengali formation tries to remedy this with a *visarga*. The usual Bengali rendering, however, is *āntɔrjātik* (from *jāti* 'tribe, genus' + a different adj. ending *-ik* (*a*)). Assamese has a different combination of these elements *ɒntɔrzātīyo*. Sinhalese has *jātyantara* as well as *antarjātika*, the former not a "full" calque. Such differences probably constitute no great barriers to mutual comprehension, in that an educated speaker is familiar with all the elements involved, however they may be put together. Trouble comes when such words end up with different meanings in different languages, e.g., *antarjātīya* in Sinhalese means, and not illogically, 'interracial'.

Typical of the current situation also is the presence in one and the same language of several competing neologisms for the same concept, especially in Hindi, where there is not one literary and publishing capital, but a number of widely dispersed centers. Barkhudarov (1963: 15960) illustrates the problem nicely by pointing to the existence of more than ten Hindi words (all Neo-Sanskrit) for 'linguist/philologist': *bhāṣāśāstrī*, *bhāṣāvaigyānik*, *bhāṣāvigyānī*, *bhāṣāvid*, *bhāṣātattvavid*, *bhāṣāśāstravid*, *bhāṣāvigyānvid*, *bhāṣāvigyānvettā*, *bhāṣāvidyāviśārad*, *bhāṣātattvaviśārad*, etc. Efforts by scholars to impose order on this creative exuberance have often resulted only in adding more words to the competition. (Much scholarly energy has also gone into concocting Neo-Sanskrit words designed to drive out established Perso-Arabic or English loanwords – with more success in the former than in the latter cases: e.g., *dvacakra*, lit. 'two-wheeler' for *sāikil*.)

It is true that from the standpoint of Sanskrit, some neologisms are less "correct" than others (although this is far from being the only reason for the proliferation of synonyms). Interestingly enough, it is often the "incorrect" forms (i.e. those that ignore certain rules of Sanskrit *sandhi*, like *antarrāṣṭrīya* above) that gain the greater currency – indicating (besides ignorance of Sanskrit) that perhaps for Neo-Sanskrit rules are operative that differ from those of Paninean Sanskrit.

Written prose does not form a single register. In the more formal registers of scholarly prose, NIA strives not only to be more correct but also purist, eschewing foreign loanwords. In the registers of popular journalism and the like, a more eclectic and spontaneous spirit prevails, and hybrid forms, combining Neo-Sanskrit, NIA, Perso-Arabic, and English formants, abound. Typical of many examples collected by Barkhudarov are *yuddha-parastī* (Skt–Pers.) 'militarism', *sarva-islām-vād* (Skt–Arabic–Skt) 'Pan-Islamism', *bijlī-karaṇ* (NIA–Skt) 'electrification', *ḍigrī-prāpt* (Eng.–Skt) 'possessing a higher degree', *upa-kameṭī* (Skt–Eng.) 'subcommittee', *harāmī-pan* (Pers.–NIA) 'baseness'.

Many neologisms are shortlived, coined for one occasion and not used again – or even stillborn, never making it off the lists of terminology-makers into actual usage. All of this adds further to the fluidity of these levels of the NIA lexicon. Yet, although the NIA lexicon may be fairly described, even more than is true for every language, as still in process, at the same time there is much that has been stabilized.

The whole subject is of obvious importance, both linguistically and socially, and deserves more attention – and careful monitoring – than it has received.

Outside of South Asia, so far it seems to have interested only Soviet scholars, whose works remain the best sources on the subject (Chelyshev 1958, Beskrovny 1960, Zograph 1960, Barkhudarov 1960, 1963, Barannikov 1962). Even then, attention has been focused mainly on Hindi and Urdu. A comparative study of actual usage in the context of NIA as a whole (which could profitably include the Sanskritized Dravidian literary languages) remains a desideratum.

4.12 **Common basic vocabulary**

If Tss. and Neo-Sanskrit provide a measure of lexical unity to the majority of NIA languages at one end of the scale, so also does basic Tbh. vocabulary at the other end. To end this chapter without stressing this also would be to neglect an important aspect of NIA lexicology and possibly to leave the reader with a distorted picture.

Table 4.1, consisting of some basic verbs (in the form of the stem, since infinitive or other endings would make the relationships less salient) and names of body parts in twelve of the main NIA languages, is accordingly provided as an indication of this level, from which readers may draw their own conclusions. It could of course be greatly expanded. From this much it should be clear, however, that there is a clear NIA lexical "identity" which is fairly easy to recognize, despite phonological developments in the individual languages and lexical replacements here and there. The aberrant status of Kashmiri and Sinhalese – at the same time occasionally preserving OIA features not preserved elsewhere – will be apparent (as will the close relationship of Romany).

Table 4.1 *Sample of common new NIA vocabulary*

	Sanskrit	Romany	Kashmiri	Sindhi†	Punjabi	Hindi	Nepali	Assamese	Bengali	Oriya	Gujarati	Marathi	Sinhalese
'ask'	PṚCCH-	phuč-	prutsh-, pritsh-	puch-	pucch-	puch-	puch-	pus-	puch-	puch-	pūch-	pus-	aha- (Mald. fuh-)
'come'	ĀṔ (AYA)-, ĀĪ-, ĀTY (ēti)	av-	yu-	ac-	āu-	ā-	āu-	āh-	ā-	ās-	āv-	yē-	ē-
'die'	MÁR- (Vedic), MRI (YÁ)-	mer-	mar-	mar-	mar-	mar-	mar-	mar-	mar-	mar-	mar-	mar-	mär-, mi-
'do'	KAR-	ker-	kar-	kar-	kar-	kar-	gar-	kɔr-	kɔr-	kɔr-	kar-	kar-	kara-
'drink'	PÍB-	pi-	co-	pi-	pī-	pī-	piu-	pi-	pi-	pi-	pī-	pi-	bo-, bī-
'eat'	KHĀ́D-	xa-	khyo-	khā-	khā-	khā-	khā-	khā-	khā-	khā-	khā-	khā-	ka-
'give'	DĀ-	de-	dyu-	ḍḍi-	de-	de-	di-	di-	dē-	dē-	āp-,de-	dē-	de-
'go'	YĀ́-	ǰa-	yu-, gatsh-	vañ-	jā-	jā	jā-	zā-	jā-	j-	jā-	dzā-	ya-
'hear'	ŚRU-(ŚṚN-)	sun-	buz-	suṇ-	suṇ-	sun-	sun-	xun-	ʃon-	suṇ-	sā̃bhaḷ-	aik-	āhe-
'see'	*DṚKṢ-, PAŚY-, VÍKṢ-	dikh-	vuch-, ḍes-	ḍḍis-	vēkh-	dēkh-	dēkh-	dēkh-	dækh-	dēkh-	jo-, dēkh-	pāh-, dēkh-	daki-
'sit'	ÚPAVIŚ-, VÁS-	bes-	bih-	veh-	baiṭh-	baiṭh-	bas-	bɔh-	bɔʃ-	bɔʃs-	bɛs-	bas-	iňda gan-
'speak'	*BOLL- (<√BRŪ?) VAD-		van-, bol-	cav-, bbol-	ākh-, bol-	bol-	bol-	bol-	bɔl-	bol-	bol-	bol-	kiya-
'take'-	LÁBH-, GṚHṆĀ́, NÁYA- ('lead')		ni-	ni-, vaṭh--	lai-	lē-	li-	ni-	nē-	nē-	lē-	ghē-	gan-
'ear'-	KÁRṆA-	kan	kan	kanu	kann	kan	kān	kān	kān	kānɔ	kān	kān	kaṇa
'eye'	ÁKṢI-, CÁKṢUS-	yakh	əchi	akh	akkh	akh	ā̃kho	sɔku	cokh	ākhi	ā̃kh	ḍoḷā	ähä
'foot'	PÁDA-, *PADARA-		khɔr	peru	pair	pair, pā ū	goṛo, pāu	pāo	pā	pā	pag	pāy	paya (Mald. fā)
'hand'	HÁSTA-	vast	athɨ	hathu	hatth	hāth	hāt	hāt	hāt	hātɔ	hāth	hāt	ata
'tongue'	JIHVĀ́	čhib, čib	zyav	jjibha	jibbh, jībh (H.)	jībh	jibro	zibhā	jib	jibh	jībh	jībh	diva
'tooth'	DÁNTA-	dand	dād	ḍḍandu	dand	dā̃t	dā̃t	dā̃t	dā̃t	dāntɔ	dā̃t	dāt	data

† A double initial letter is used to indicate the implosive initial consonants of Sindhi.

5

NIA descriptive phonology

5.1 Descriptive problems

Several types of problems complicate the description of NIA phonologies, and especially any attempt to give an overall account of them. These include: inadequacies in the data and in its analysis; alternative analyses of the same data; the status of borrowed elements; and problems posed by the existence and nature of NIA writing systems.

With regard to the first, in spite of the fact that a great deal of data has been collected on the languages and dialects of the subcontinent by dedicated scholars and other interested persons, both foreign and South Asian, much of this is inadequate from the phonological point of view. Lack of special training is particularly telling in the areas of phonology and phonetics. In some cases, however, it is a matter of the proper tools having not yet been invented. As Gumperz (1958) put it, many of the key studies (e.g., Grierson's work, including the *Linguistic Survey* itself; Bailey's work) were done "at a time when the phonemic principle was insufficiently understood." In other cases, it is not a question of the time, but of a particular writer not having grasped the difference between phonetics and phonology.

Many of the extant descriptions of NIA – and in the case of some languages and dialects the only ones available – are thus pre-phonemic or at any rate non-phonemic. In the presence of good phonetic data a certain amount of phonemic analysis is possible, but this is not the same as being able to elicit and compare minimal pairs, and the analysis is likely to be incomplete under such conditions. In some cases, however, the available data is not only non-phonemic but non-phonetic, that is, impressionistic and often spotty. The writer is usually familiar with the core Indo-Aryan system (see below) but may lack the means to accurately describe deviations from it, particularly unusual ones. He may be unduly influenced by the orthography if one exists. Finally, he may simply not be interested in giving a full account of the sounds of the language, since his focus is on another topic, or be able to under the circumstances (for example, a lucky but brief encounter with a speaker of a remote mountain dialect). Any information at all is worth something, and such accounts may still be capable of telling us something about phonology, but not very reliably and not everything we would like to know.

Even where there is an attempt to undertake a phonemic analysis, it may be that the analysis is lacking in rigor at certain points. A typical case is lack of attention to stressed vs. unstressed environments of vowels in setting up would-be contrasts. (This means that no true minimal pairs are cited, only purportedly similar environments, which in fact are not similar.) On the phonetic level also, the use of IPA symbols is no guarantee of the accuracy of the observations.

Even when applied rigorously, however (which may mean different things to different schools), phonemic analysis does not solve everything, and brings with it problems of its own. The reader may be familiar with the well-established case for the *non-uniqueness of phonemic solutions*. That is, many problems of phonemicization permit of alternative solutions, sometimes several. Each solution has its advantages and disadvantages, so that there is a trade-off among them. Opting for one solution rather than another always involves sacrificing some advantages for others on the basis of a value-judgment regarding their respective importance. In such a judgment, there is an element of arbitrariness, and often not a little linguistic fashion-of-the-moment. (This is assuming the judgment is made with full awareness of all the possibilities, which of course is often not the case. Some possibilities may be discovered by later reseachers on the language, or await new developments in linguistic theory before they suggest themselves.)

One of the simplest of such cases involves the selection of the distinctive criterion that distinguishes a phoneme or class of phonemes when phonetically there are several. In this process, certain phonetic facts about the language are arbitrarily subordinated and one might say suppressed. For example, certain vowels in NIA languages such as Hindi and Punjabi differ, according to some descriptions, in both duration and quality (variously called *close/open* or more recently *tense/lax* or *peripheral/centralized*). By making length the distinguishing factor, we obtain the vowels i/i:, a/a:, u/u:, and ignore the qualitative differences. By making quality the distinguishing factor, we obtain the vowels I/i, ə/a, U/u, and ignore the length differences.

For our purposes here, this poses a problem even greater than the suppression of certain phonetic facts in a given case. That is the *non-comparability* of different cases when different analytical options have been chosen. In the above cases, analyses of (for example) Hindi vowels according to length and of Punjabi vowels according to quality (assuming for the sake of argument that the underlying phonetic and distributional facts are indeed the same) cannot be simply juxtaposed. The apparent "difference" between the two languages this would show is an artifact of the analysis, and unreal.

Confining the discussion just to straightforward old-fashioned phonemics, other common examples of alternative analyses in descriptions of NIA involve analysis of: (1) aspirated consonants as clusters (of consonant + /h/) or as unit phonemes; (2) nasalized vowels as unit phonemes or as the corresponding oral vowels plus the suprasegmental phoneme */˜/ "nasalization"*; (3) long vowels as unit phonemes or as the corresponding short vowel plus the phoneme */:/ "length"*. (Whereas the previously cited rival analyses come up with the same "number of vowels," this option would reduce them by three. Still another proposed analysis should be mentioned: the long vowels as basic, plus a *"phoneme of shortness"*. Although this would also reduce the inventory by three, the basic inventory would be different.)

For one large group of analyses, done under the influence of a late phase of American structuralism, an implicit goal affecting the choice of analytical options was *minimalization of the number of "phonemes"*. Phonological theory at that point was groping toward the recognition of more basic functional units, culminating in distinctive feature theory and generative phonology. That recognition of deeper patterns need not necessarily affect the number of segmental units in this manner, however, is shown by the fact that Prague School phonology, where such concerns were early and paramount, was not averse to recognizing large numbers of segmental phonemes in a language, even while detecting deeper correlations among them. Such differences in approach, whatever their merits, obviously result in significantly different "phoneme counts." The latter are therefore significant only if there are theoretically equivalent analyses of all the languages being compared.

The non-occurrence of one or more members of an otherwise contrastive set of phones in a given position is again something which is handled differently in different descriptions (when it is noticed at all). That is, if, e.g., [*p*] and [*b*] generally contrast, but only [*p*] occurs in position X, it may be stated as: (1) an instance of */p/*, with a restriction on the occurrence of */b/*; (2) (less commonly, but occasionally there is a morphophonemic argument in its favor) an instance of */b/*, with a restriction on the occurrence of */p/*; (3) an instance of the "archiphoneme" */P/*, embodying the "neutralization" of the p/b contrast, but contrasting with t/d, k/g, etc. (There may be further subtleties: the actual phone that occurs in position X may be different from the dominant allophones of either */p/* or */b/*, and perhaps midway between them.)

The problem here again is to avoid solutions that either obscure significant cross-linguistic differences or create artificial ones. For instance, in a number of NIA languages, including Kashmiri, the *aspirate/nonaspirate* contrast is neutralized in final position. While in the other languages involved it is the aspiration that is dropped (as one might expect), in Kashmiri only the aspirates occur in final position – which may incidentally serve as a warning against overgeneralizations concerning "natural phonology". (A further problem is not to overcomplicate the morphology, and the "solution" most often chosen in practice is to interpret the given phone as */p/ or /b/* – or more relevantly for NIA, as *aspirate* or *nonaspirate* – according to its morphophonemic behavior.)

Another kind of distributional fact that does not show up in conventional "phonemic" analysis, except by way of supplementary statement (not always given), is one which affects more than one segment, however the latter is defined. That is, its domain is the syllable, or often the word, or sometimes even longer units. Typical examples in Indo-Aryan are (again) aspiration, nasalization, length, and vowel (and consonant) harmony. These will be discussed in their place; here it will suffice to note that the recognition of a *segment* embodying such a feature may not exhaust its phonological implications (positive or negative) elsewhere in the word: certain other sounds may be mandated (or excluded) accordingly.

The prosodic phonology developed by certain British linguists (following J. R. Firth) as a result of dissatisfaction with the neglect and even distortion of such facts in conventional phonemic analysis postulated two kinds or levels of basic units: *prosodic* (features having predictable relations extending beyond a single segment) and *phonematic* (segmental features having no such relations). (A word of caution is necessary here: the term *prosodic* is sometimes also loosely used – in what must be called *non*prosodic descriptions – not in the above sense but as a synonym of *suprasegmental* – referring to stress, intonation, and juncture, or even to features abstracted from individual segments without syntagmatic implications.) The *phonematic units* thus also present, like the *phonemes* of the structuralists referred to earlier, a minimalized inventory, but for a different reason: the systematic allocation of some phonological features to a different type of unit. It would no doubt be revealing if NIA phonology could be presented in prosodic terms, but that will not be possible here. Although perhaps more Indo-Aryan languages have been analyzed in these terms than other languages, still most of them have not been, and as Allen (1954) points out, there is no way an existing *phonemic* description can be "translated" into a *prosodic* description: "the selection and allotment of criteria [from the primary phonic data] are governed by different theories in the two cases." The most that can be done is to try to indicate in what follows some of the salient syntagmatic phonological relations that could benefit from such analysis. (For examples of application of prosodic theory to Indo-Aryan materials, see Allen 1951, 1953, 1954.)

Phonological *symbols* themselves may be a source of confusion. One of the problems with phonemic transcriptions is that there is always a tendency to read common IPA values into the symbols, although they were not chosen for this purpose. (There is an even greater danger of this with a prosodic transcription.) In any case, different descriptions may use different symbols for the same sounds, or the same symbols for different sounds, without implying any analytical disagreement.

The main task facing the compiler of a book such as this, then, is to attempt to "translate" arbitrarily differing analyses into common terms to facilitate comparison and generalization – terms that will bring out genuine phonological – and important phonetic – differences as well as similarities. Regarding the symbol problem, the proper path for this kind of handbook would seem to lie in trying to represent phonological units, not in the fashion appropriate for the transcription of a single language (i.e. with the simplest symbols consistent with maintaining its system of contrasts), but by cross-linguistically transparent symbols reflecting the phonetic qualities of dominant allophones. For example, Bengali–Oriya–Assamese */a/* will be transcribed */ā/*, which is its phonetic as well as historical equivalent in the other NIA languages, even though in the Eastern group the *length* mark (¯) is redundant, lest it be confused with the centralized short vowel [ə] of those languages (and Sanskrit), conventionally transcribed */a/*. The Bengali equivalent of the latter will be transcribed */ɔ/* rather than */a/* (except where it has merged with */o/*), to bring out its phonetic character.

5.2 **Secondary subsystems**

In addition to the foregoing problems which linguists create in part for themselves (and each other), there are problems which arise from the special historical and sociolinguistic circumstances of NIA. As noted in Chapter 4, almost all languages have loanwords. Not all languages have loanwords constituting the basis of a prominent and unassimilated phonological subsystem not shared by all speakers, however, as do a number of NIA languages.

The question of *tadbhavas* vs. *tatsamas* and other borrowings has been discussed in the preceding chapter. From the standpoint of *historical* phonology, attention has to be focused on the *tadbhava* or inherited element in a language. Borrowings, particularly intact borowings (*tatsamas*), from Sanskrit and foreign languages have no place in it. From the standpoint of *descriptive* phonology the problem is quite different. A Persian or English or even a Sanskrit loanword – let alone a loanword from another NIA language such as Hindi – may be the only word for a thing, known to all or most speakers, and hence synchronically "part of the language." Its pronunciation, however, may vary (in the degree to which its alien phonology is altered or retained) with parameters of social class, education, urban–rural residence, even religion and occupation. The question becomes then partly one of norms: *whose* phonology are we describing?

In a part of the world where social differentiation is strongly developed and in fact greatly elaborated, and where moreover certain classes are characterized by bi- or multilingualism, such questions assume a greater than usual importance. Someone versed in Sanskrit, English, or Persian, especially by virtue of family or caste tradition, is more likely to try to maintain elements of the phonology of such a language, and use more vocabulary borrowed from it, than a speaker ignorant of these languages. It would be misleading to accept such a mixed idiolectal or acrolectal phonology as the norm of a language without further qualification.

Even when – as is often the case – the so-called standard or literary standard language has a large Sanskritic or Persian lexical component, the careful pronunciation of the Sanskrit or Persian scholar will differ from the natural pronunciation of the merely educated or literate. There is often a continuum, in conjunction with the above-mentioned extra-linguistic as well as personal factors, from the consistent maintenance of borrowed distinctions to their complete assimilation, with a wide zone in the middle where they freely vary or vary with situation. In such circumstances, it is advisable to set up a *coexistent phonological subsystem* to take proper account of the special status of such sounds.

Not all borrowed distinctions are of an elitist type. As noted above, a loanword may be the only designation for a common object. Such a loanword *may* retain elements of its alien phonology among a wide enough range of speakers to be said to constitute a stable element in the general linguistic system, and to the point of affecting the whole. (A literary loanword may also, it is true, be the only designation for a given concept or object, but it may not be a *common* concept or object, hence not part of the linguistic competence of many speakers. Often enough also in NIA languages, a literary loanword is an *alternative* designation of a common concept or object, which already has a colloquial name.)

One example will have to suffice at this point. In Hindi (and a number of other NIA languages), there are two phones, a voiced retroflex stop [*ḍ*] and a retroflex flap [*ṛ*], generally in complementary distribution. The former occurs initially, after its homorganic nasal [*ṇ*], and geminated. The latter occurs intervocalically, finally after vowels, and preconsonantally. The common English loanwords *radio* and *road*, however, generally pronounced [*re:ḍiyo:*] and [*ro:ḍ*], introduce the phone [*ḍ*] contrastively (albeit not producing minimal pairs) into the intervocalic and final postvocalic environments previously occupied exclusively by [ṛ], thus rendering the earlier allophonic distinction "phonemic", according to one criterion for deciding such matters. (Some investigators, e.g., Misra 1967, maintain that the phonemic split was accomplished long before this through the agency of forms such as */niḍar/* 'fearless', used by Tulsidas as early as the sixteenth century. One problem with this, apart from the definition of *Hindi* – Tulsidas wrote in Awadhi, occasionaly in Braj, although the word is also found in Modern Standard Hindi – is that it involves a morpheme boundary: *ni-* 'negative prefix' + *ḍar* 'fear'; the [ḍ] is thus, if not word-initial, at least morpheme-initial.) Here again the resolution is not absolute: some rural speakers may indeed, as is sometimes reported, say [*re:ṛiyo:*] and [*ro:ṛ*]. The question then becomes: can they be said to be speaking "Standard Hindi"? How do we define the latter for phonological purposes? (One common-sense approach is that represented by Ohala [1983]: Standard Hindi is "the dialect spoken by educated urban speakers in casual conversation.")

Such speakers would not only maintain the contrastive distribution of the phones [ḍ] and [ṛ] in words like */roḍ/* and */reḍiyo/* (which, as is often the case with foreign influence on phonology, involves not the borrowing of new sounds, but the *redistribution of previously existing* sounds taken to be equivalent to the foreign sounds: the English source words themselves, of course, contained no retroflexes). They would also maintain the distinctiveness of the borrowed segments */f, z, ʃ/*. They would not, however, maintain the purely Sanskrit segments */ṇ/* and */ṣ/* (confined to Formal Literary Hindi, and normally assimilated to */n/* and */s/*), or the purely Perso-Arabic segments */q, χ, γ/* (confined to Urdu speakers, and normally assimilated by Hindi speakers to */k, kh, g/*).

Admittedly such parameters, while representing a real and growing sociolinguistic reality, are at the same time both arbitrary and somewhat vague. Speakers who fail to consistently maintain */f, z, ʃ/* (confusing them with */ph, j, s/*) are by this definition substandard, although these are "foreign" sounds; a few of the same speakers (non-urban with a Sanskritic education) may overshoot the mark in the direction of superformality by maintaining */ṇ, ṣ/*. The mention of Urdu is a reminder of the *urban* component of this definition, of the former position of Urdu in the towns of North India, and of the curious fact that for native speakers of Urdu (who are mostly Muslims – as distinct from speakers of Urdu as a second language, who could be anybody) the maintenance of */f, z, ʃ/* is *not* correlated with level of education or sophistication, but is characteristic of all social levels.

Another approach is represented by Misra (1967) who prefers to speak of *overall pattern* in Modern Standard Hindi (in which he apparently means to include Urdu as well as Formal Sanskritized Literary Hindi, with all the attendant phonological distinctions, real or theoretical, of both, along with certain local features and English loanwords) vs. *common core* (excluding all such borrowed distinctions on the ground that they are not maintained with equal consistency by all speakers). Ohala also hedges by proposing to mark all morphemes as +/− *native*, on the ground that even Standard speakers whose speech maintains /*f*, *z*, *ʃ*/ are aware that "many non-standard Hindi speakers" do not have these segments, which lie therefore outside the *common core* (a term she also employs).

It is a concept we shall have to make at least implicit use of here also. In an overall description of NIA phonology, we are in any case interested not just in Standard Hindi and its definitional problems, but in the characteristics of the *vernacular base* – "common core" if you will – onto which these additions have been grafted. Although the Hindi (–Urdu) problem may be especially complex in its many sociolinguistic and regional variations, similar problems confront the description of every NIA language and dialect to some degree, and particularly the description of every language with a literary standard, which almost always entails a large borrowed lexical and therefore phonological element.

Not unconnected with the problems involving the status of borrowed elements are some of the problems posed by the existence of writing systems. An established orthography has many advantages, no doubt, but it is often an additional source of problems for the linguist. One of these is spelling pronunciations. Where a writing convention preserves the original spelling of loanwords, there is often a tendency to see in the spelling a norm of correctness, especially if the orthography is otherwise more or less phonemic, and to attempt to produce, or to feign to hear, distinctions which do not really exist in the language. This is especially the case with Sanskrit loanwords, not only because of the enormous prestige of Sanskrit, but because of its thoroughgoing codification and its perceivable organic and orthographic relations to New Indo-Aryan. The special pharyngeal and dental letters[1] in Arabic loanwords on the other hand, while preserved in spelling in those languages using the Perso-Arabic script, were already shorn of their phonetic significance in Persian before reaching Indo-Aryan. (The use of [*f*, *z*, *ʃ*, *χ*, *γ*, *q*] by Urdu speakers and certain others in the northwest of the subcontinent cannot be ascribed to spelling, since these sounds seem really to have been borrowed at the colloquial level, i.e. they are used by illiterates.)

5.3 The NIA consonants

Despite the fact that there are more of them, it will be easier to discuss the NIA consonants first, since the vowels and allied phenomena present problems better understood in the light of the consonants (although to a smaller extent the reverse is also true).

5.3.1 *Stop positions*

The *basic Indo-Aryan system* of stops (which is also that of Sanskrit) theoretically involves five distinctive tongue positions: labial, dental, "retroflex", palatal, and velar: */p, t, ṭ, c, k/*. The "retroflex" position */ṭ/ may* involve retroflexion, or curling back of the tongue to make the contact with the underside of the tip, or merely retraction; the point of contact may be alveolar or postalveolar (i.e. in any case non-dental). According to Allen (personal communication) the distinctive quality arises "more from the shaping than from the position of the tongue."

The affricated stop */c/* is traditionally included as involving a distinct tongue position (blade in contact with hard palate) in addition to its (almost unavoidable) affricated release. It is not quite the same sound as English "ch" (=[*t*+*ʃ*]), despite the fact that some descriptions represent it as [*č*] or even as [*tš*] or [*tʃ*] (a more accurate *phonetic* representation would be [*cʃ*]), or defy the tradition by setting up a separate subsystem of affricates.

There is a tendency in some languages and dialects to pronounce the */c/* as an alveolar (or "dental") affricate [*ts*],[2] e.g., in Nepali, Eastern and Northern dialects of Bengali (Dacca, Maimansing, Rajshahi), the Lamani and Northwestern Marwari dialects of Rajasthani, the Kagani dialect of "Northern Lahnda", Kumauni, and many West Pahari dialects (not, however, the Chamba dialects, Mandeali, Jaunsari, or Sirmauri). This does not affect the basic number of articulations, which remains five in these languages as well as in all Hindi dialects, Punjabi, Dogri, Sindhi, Gujarati, other Rajasthani dialects (except Southern Mewari), Oriya, Standard Bengali, the Bihari languages, and even in Sinhalese.

In some languages with the [*ts*] tendency, a [*č*] phone is retained in certain positions: before front vowels (especially */i/*), before */y/*, or when geminated. In Marathi and Konkani this complementation is upset by dialect mixture and other factors which reintroduce a [*č*] into environments occupied by the erstwhile [*ts*] allophone, thus producing a *č/ts* contrast in those environments: M. */cār/* 'four', */tsārā/* 'fodder'. Internal developments in some West Pahari languages (∗*tr*, *t* > *č*) have reintroduced a [*č*] and produced a *č/ts* contrast there also. There is thus a system with six distinctive stop/affricated stop articulations instead of five in Marathi, Konkani, certain West Pahari dialects (Bhadrawahi, Bhalesi, Padari; the Simla group; the Satlej group; possibly also the Kulu group), and also in Kashmiri.

The addition to this repertoire of a retroflex (or retracted) affricate */c̣/* (=[*ṭṣ*]) brings the number of distinctive articulations to a maximum of seven (excluding the borrowed postvelar /*q*/) in a number of NIA languages of the Dardic group: Shina, Bashkarik, Gawarbati, Phalura, Kalasha, Khowar, Shumashti, Kanyawali, and Pashai.

The [*ts*] pronunciation of /*c*/ in some NIA dialects has progressed to [*s*], in which case we can no longer speak of a stop articulation and, barring other developments, the inventory is *reduced* by one. This has taken place in the Southern Mewari dialect of Rajasthani, in the Chittagong dialect of Bengali (as described by Uchida), and in Assamese. (It has happened in Sinhalese as well, but there have been other sources of a secondary /*c*/.)

Assamese, alone among NIA languages except for Romany, has also lost the characteristic IA *dental/retroflex* contrast (although it is retained in spelling), reducing the number of articulations, with the loss also of /*c*/, to three. (Romany retains the palatal /*č*/ and thus a four-way system of inherited distinctions. Some Romany dialects have augmented this with a borrowed /*ts*/.)

The Chittagong dialect is in danger of losing /*p*, *k*/ through spirantization in many positions (> [*f*, *χ*]). Thus only /*t*, *ṭ*/ are fully stable in this dialect.

5.3.2 *Nasals*

The ancient Indian phoneticians accurately observed that there were five nasal stop articulations [*m*, *n*, *ɳ*, *ɲ*, *ŋ*] corresponding to the five oral stops of Sanskrit. Although five alphabetic symbols were duly provided (in Orientalist practice generally transliterated *m*, *n*, *ṇ*, *ñ*, *ṅ*), these were not all equally functional. They were often dispensed with in predictable environments through use of *anusvāra*. Excluding secondary subsystems (e.g., the alleged presence of /*ṇ*/ in *tatsamas* and semi-*tatsamas* in acrolectal Maithili), among modern languages and dialects Dogri, Kacchi, Kalasha, Rudhari, Shina, Saurashtri, and Sindhi have been analyzed as having a full complement of five *phonemic* nasals (/*m*, *n*, *ṇ*, *ñ*, *ŋ*/) – in the case of the last two nasals generally as the result of the loss of the stop from a homorganic nasal + stop cluster (*ñj* > *ñ*, *ŋg* > *ŋ*), although there are other sources as well.

A phonemic retroflex /*ṇ*/, phonetically often a nasalized flap [*ṛ̃*], is found throughout the western half of NIA from Konkani north to West Pahari inclusive (i.e. also in Marathi, Gujarati, Rajasthani, Punjabi, "Lahnda", Sindhi, Dogri, and Haryanvi). Except for Oriya, it is absent from the northeast (Bengali, Assamese, Nepali), from Sinhalese, and from the Hindi area east of Haryana (although according to Gumperz's field observations it is found in the northwest of the Vernacular Hindustani ["Kauravi"] area, around Saharanpur). It is found in Kumauni but only subphonemically in the more Hindi-influenced Garhwali. It is not found in Kashmiri, but is present in most of the other "Dardic" languages (Shina, Khowar, Kalasha, Bashkarik, etc.).

Complementing this predominantly western distribution of */ṇ/* is a northeastern focus of occurrence of a phonemic velar nasal */ŋ/*, which characterizes Bengali, Assamese, Nepali, Maithili, and Bhojpuri. There seems to be no disagreement over its phonemicity in these languages or in Sinhalese, Kacchi, Sindhi, or Dogri.

It has also been listed, however in some descriptions of Marathi and its dialects, of Kumauni, Khowar, Kalasha, Shina, and Rudhari, and – with some hesitation – of Punjabi, Siraiki, Oriya, and Lamani, as well as of Modern Standard Hindi (MSH). Disagreement regarding its status in these languages (and in Sanskrit and Romany) seems to hinge on whether it contrasts in its very restricted distribution (vs. its much wider distribution in the groups mentioned earlier) with a cluster [*ŋg*], and if not whether to treat it phonemically as such a cluster (although phonetically the stop is missing): cf. Emeneau (1946) vs. Misra (1967). The cluster argument is reinforced by the presence of other homorganic nasal + stop clusters in similar environments, and by free as well as morphophonemically conditioned variation of [*ŋ*] and [*ŋg*]. Misra offers the MSH contrast */maŋnа/* 'ask', */manna/* 'accept', while conceding the possibility of an alternative analysis */mangna/*[3] for the first item. Mehrotra (1964), however, offers */pəŋkhi/* 'small fan' (also 'bird') vs. */kənkhi/* 'squint'. Here */pəngkhi/* for the first is harder to justify.

Phonemic or not, [*ŋ*] is a common and characteristic sound in NIA languages, although more common in some languages than in others. In Nepali and Assamese (and probably other languages of the northern and eastern frontiers) the occurrences and environments of the sound are swelled by loanwords from Tibeto-Burman.

Somewhat similar arguments are made regarding the status of */ñ/* vs. clusters */ny/* and */nj/*, the latter being one of its sources as noted above. It is a less common sound, but evidently present in Maithili, Bhojpuri (noted by Tiwari [1960] although not by Shukla [1981]), Sinhalese, Kacchi, Sindhi, Siraiki, Dogri, Kashmiri, Shina, Kalasha, and the Rudhari dialect of West Pahari (bordering the Kashmir group). In Punjabi (and to some extent also in Siraiki) it is still in stylistic or dialectal variation with [*ñj*]. Misra (1967) includes */ñ/* in his "overall pattern" for MSH (not in the *common core*) on the ground that it can be said to contrast with a cluster */-ny-/* for the "rather small number" of Hindi speakers who have it (perhaps MSH–Bhojpuri or MSH–Maithili bilinguals?) through the agency of Sanskrit *tatsamas* containing the latter. Chaudhuri (1940–44) found that the North Bengali Rajshahi dialect contained an */ñ/* phoneme (and not the usual Bengali */ŋ/*).

5.3.3 *Laterals and flaps*

Although OIA was allegedly once divided into three dialects, a Northwestern dialect with only /r/ (exemplified by Early Vedic), an Eastern dialect with only /l/ (exemplified by Magadhi Prakrit), and a Central dialect with both /r/ and /l/ (exemplified by Classical Sanskrit), such a situation did not continue typologically, and all NIA dialects have both sounds. Some have expanded inventories in this area. Leaving aside aspirates (see 5.3.7 below), these include /ḷ/, /ṛ/, and /λ/.

A retroflex flapped lateral /ḷ/, contrasting with ordinary /l/, is a prominent feature of Oriya, Marathi–Konkani, Gujarati, most varieties of Rajasthani and Bhili, Punjabi, some dialects of "Lahnda" (Bahri 1963: 135–6, 143–5), most dialects of West Pahari, and Kumauni (not in the Southeastern dialect described by Apte and Pattanayak), as well as Hariyanvi and the Saharanpur subdialect of Northwestern Kauravi ("Vernacular Hindustani") investigated by Gumperz. It is absent from most other NIA languages, including most Hindi dialects, Nepali, Garhwali, Bengali, Assamese, Kashmiri and other Dardic languages (except for the Dras dialect of Shina and possibly Khowar), the westernmost West Pahari dialects bordering Dardic (Bhalesi, Khashali, Rudhari, Padari) as well as the easternmost (Jaunsari, Sirmauri), and from Sindhi, Kacchi, and Siraiki. It was once present in Sinhalese, but in the modern language has merged with /l/.

The retroflex flap [ṛ] is often taken as an allophone of /ḍ/, with which it often stands in complementary distribution: initial, geminate, and postnasal for [ḍ]; intervocalic, final, and before or after other consonants for [ṛ]. It has, however, come to contrast with [ḍ] in at least some environments in Punjabi (*sāṛī/sāḍī* 'burnt'/'our,fsg.'), "Lahnda" (*naṛī/vaḍī* 'reed'/'big,f.'), Sindhi (*jhāṛū/pāḍū* 'tree'/ 'ruin'), in Modern Standard Hindi (as noted earlier) (*nīṛaj/niḍar* 'bird'/'fearless', *toṛ/roḍ* 'break!'/'road' < Eng.), and in Bengali (primarily through English loans, cf. Ferguson and Chowdhury 1960). It may be or is reported as phonemic also in Shina and some other Dardic languages, Dogri, Rajasthani (except Southern Mewari, Lamani, and Gujuri), various Western Hindi dialects (Haryanvi, Braj, Bundeli), and in several West Pahari dialects, notably the westernmost. It remains subphonemic in Marathi, Gujarati, Eastern Hindi, Bhojpuri, Maithili, Kumauni, Kashmiri (where it is found mainly in rural speech), and probably also Nepali. (This is on the basis of its lack of contrast with [ḍ]. Some analyses focus instead on its contrast with [r]: see below.)

The sound is absent altogether from Assamese, East and North Bengali dialects, and Bishnupriya – in all of which it has merged with /r/ – and from Sinhalese and Romany. It has also merged with /r/ in the Hindu subdialect of Multani Siraiki, and is on the verge of merging with /r/ in Maithili. On the other hand [ṛ] varies with [ḷ] in Wotapuri, and **/ḷ/ becomes* [ṛ] in Dogri, and merges with

/*r*/ in Southern Mewari. All five sounds [*ḍ*, *ṛ*, *ḷ*, *r*, *l*] are closely related descriptively and also historically (see Chapter 7), and should be studied together. As important as the contrast of [*ṛ*] with [*ḍ*] is its contrast with [*r*], strongly maintained in some languages, lost in others as we have just seen. It should also be noted that /*ṛ*/ is present phonemically in some languages (Western Hindi, Sindhi, Bengali, the Khashali–Bhalesi–Rudhari group of West Pahari) that lack /*ḷ*/ and absent from some (Oriya, Marathi, Gujarati) that possess /*ḷ*/. In such languages there is more latitude in the phonetic realization particularly of the former: the so-called /*ṛ*/ of some Hindi and Urdu speakers has in fact a strong lateral coloring. On the other hand, Punjabi, "Lahnda" dialects, Rajasthani, Haryanvi, and possibly certain West Pahari dialects (e.g., Kochi) maintain a contrast between /*ṛ*/ and /*ḷ*/ and between these and /*ḍ*, *r*, *l*/.

That leaves the voiceless lateral /*λ*/. This is not a characteristic NIA sound and is confined to the far northwest. There, however, it has been independently noted by investigators of Bashkarik, Gawarbati, Katarqalai, Shumashti, Torwali, and Glangali.

5.3.4 *Fricatives*

Indo-Aryan languages are notoriously poor in native fricatives. In NIA the most widespread pattern consists of one voiceless sibilant, generally [*s*], plus /*h*/. In Standard Bengali, the dominant sibilant allophone is [*ʃ*] (becoming [*s*] before dental consonants). Although this is a Magadhan inheritance, it is not maintained in other modern Magadhan (Eastern NIA) languages (e.g., not in Assamese, Oriya,[4] or "Bihari") although there is perhaps a trace of it in the free variation of [*ʃ*] and [*s*] in modern Maithili.[5] (Pandit 1954: 44 reports a single sibilant phoneme that is phonetically [*ʃ*] also in the Northern Saurashtra dialects of Gujarati. This is an unrelated development.)

Certain NIA languages, however, maintain a two-way distinction *s*/*ʃ* in inherited words. In one type, best represented by Marathi, a near-allophonic distribution of [*s*] before back vowels and (secondary) [*ʃ*] before front vowels is disturbed by contrasts (often of uncertain origin, but strengthened by Sanskrit, Persian, and Hindi loanwords) before the central vowels: *sāḷu*/*ʃāḷu* 'hedgehog'/'a variety of grain sorghum'. In another type, the development of a secondary *s* from **ch* has also introduced a contrast in the East Bengali dialects of Dacca and Chittagong, which originally had [*ʃ*] in all prevocalic environments. (In some East and North Bengali dialects, this [*ʃ*] has become [*h*].) In Dogri, **ch* has developed to [*ʃ*], again introducing a contrast with common NIA *s*.

In a third type, however, which includes Kashmiri, most West Pahari dialects (except the Punjabi-influenced Mandeali and Chameali), Kumauni, and

Romany, the *s/ʃ* distinction is for the most part not secondary but inherited from OIA. In Gujarati also, the *s/ʃ* distinction once thought (Turner 1921, Chatterji 1926) to be allophonic in origin (like Marathi) has been shown by Pandit (1954) to involve a preservation of OIA */ś/* in certain environments (before front vowels and */y/*) – */*s/* having for the most part, unlike Marathi, remained [*s*] in those environments. (There have been a few redistributions and analogical extensions, which is also true of the Himalayan cases.)

A *s/ʃ* distinction is now well-established in the *overall systems* of Standard Hindi–Urdu, Punjabi, and Sindhi, but the */ʃ/* is found exclusively in loanwords from Sanskrit, English, and above all, Persian. No distinction is made in ordinary speech between Sanskrit */ś/* and */ṣ/* in *tatsamas*, both merging with the Persian */ʃ/*, although there is naturally a retroflex allophone before retroflex consonants: [*ṣṭ*].

A three-way distinction */s, ś, ṣ/* is maintained by a number of Dardic NIA languages beyond Kashmiri: Shina, Bashkarik, Torwali, Phalura, Kanyawali, Gawarbati, Khowar, Kalasha, and Pashai. The systems are made up in part of preservations of OIA distinctions, and in part of secondary developments from clusters.

It remains to discuss */h/*. It occurs in almost all NIA languages (one exception being the Chittagong dialect of Bengali) but is much more frequent in some (certain Rajasthani dialects) than in others (Punjabi), due to historical developments. The question of a voicing opposition in the *h* category will be taken up below. The complex relation of Indo-Aryan *h* to features such as tone, murmur, and glottalization is properly a matter for historical phonology, but see also 5.4.5 below.

Other fricative sounds do occur in NIA languages, either as secondary allophones in a few languages or in loanwords in some languages. (See 5.3.7, and 5.3.9 below.) Voiced fricatives will be dealt with in section 5.3.6 below. The */w/* phoneme, often transcribed as V, has an allophone in some languages that could be described as labiodental fricative. It will be dealt with in the next section, under semivowels. An interdental fricative */θ/* is very untypical of IA, but is reported from Pashai dialects.

5.3.5 *Semivowels*

The semivowels */y/* and */w/* are a somewhat shaky part of the NIA inventory. In a number of languages their occurrence is practically restricted to semi-predictable intervocalic glides. Their position is weakest in the east (where in Bengali the two are confused in writing), strongest in the west. There is a phonetic as well as a historical difference between the Eastern glides, late in origin and sometimes optional, and Western preservations of original OIA semivowels. The Western

/w/ in particular has a distinctive [*v*]-like allophone (although the contact is typically a loose one, between the upper teeth and the *inside* of the lower lip) before front vowels: the Eastern glide does not occur in such environments. There are often several possible phonemic interpretations of the glides: (1) */y, w/* as above; (2) automatic and hence not to be noted at all; (3) "non-syllabic" */i, u/* or even */e, o/* and thus an element in rising or falling diphthongs. For example, *eya*, *ea* or *ei̯a*; *ay* or *ai̯*.

For orthography, the choice is often a matter of convention rather than dictated by the phonology. Thus in Marathi, according to Bloch (1920), **y* "has no existence . . . outside of *tatsamas*" and is only an orthographic device for *i, e* in a falling diphthong. Hindi in modern Nagari also prefers to *write* Y, W, while the Gurmukhi orthography of Punjabi prefers sequences of vowel symbols: H. SWAMI vs. P. SOAMI. However, both */y/* and */w/* do exist in Hindi *outside* of diphthongs (i.e. initially), albeit only in deictics (again, leaving aside loans). In Marathi (except in the word *yeṇe* 'come') and Gujarati only */w/* so occurs, but it is more widespread. In Bengali neither occurs.

A nasalized [*w̃*] occurs in the Harauti dialect of Rajasthani (Allen 1957a), Bengali (Ferguson and Chowdhury 1960), Marathi, Hindi, and probably other languages. It is usually (perhaps not in Hindi) best treated as an allophone of */m/*.

5.3.6 *Voicing*

A voicing opposition in the basic stop series, */b, d, ḍ, j, g/* vs. */p, t, ṭ, c, k/*, is found among all NIA languages without exception (in contrast with, for example, Tamil). However, it does not always cover all the *additional affricate* articulations noted in section 5.3.1. For example, Khowar and Gawarbati have no **j* to match their */ç/*. Bashkarik and Kanyawali have voiceless */ts, c, ç/* but only */j/*, no **dz* or **j̣*. Shina has */j̣/* as well as */j/* but no **dz* to match its */ts/*. On the other hand, Kalasha and Phalura do have the full complement of */dz, j, j̣/* to go with */ts, c, ç/*, and most six-position languages have */dz, j/*.

A [*dz*] very easily passes over to a [*z*], however. That seems to be what has happened in the Shina case. In a number of other languages, including Kashmiri and Marathi, a positional (intervocalic) or free variation of [*z*] with [*dz*] is recorded. Descriptions differ as to which is taken as basic. This poses a problem for the phonemicizer: is a voiced sibilant phoneme to be posited, or, bearing pattern congruence in mind, an affricated stop with – perhaps most of the time – a sibilant allophone? In Assamese, at least, the situation is clear: the affricates, both voiced and voiceless, have passed over completely to fricative status, and the system has been restructured into one with *s/z* instead of **c/j*. Other cases present more of a problem because only the voiced member is affected (**dz* > [*z*] but *ts* remains) and the overall system is one of contrast in stops, whatever the particular phonetic realities.

Nasals, flaps, laterals, and semivowels all occur only in voiced versions, except for the voiceless lateral /λ/ of the far northwest mentioned earlier. Fricatives, i.e. sibilants, are another matter, however. Although exclusively voiceless sibilants are the Indo-Aryan norm, a voicing opposition in the sibilants does now exist in Assamese, as a result of the transformation of the affricates noted above, and is well-established in a number of languages of the northwest: Shina, Pashai, Kanyawali, Khowar, and Kalasha have *s/z*, *ʃ/ʒ*, *ṣ/ẓ*; Gawarbati, Bashkarik, Mayan, and Phalura (and Romany) have *s/z*, *ʃ/ʒ*; Torwali has *ʃ/ʒ*; *ṣ/ẓ*; Kashmiri and Tirahi have *s/z*. Here again, as with the affricates, there are occasionally gaps in the system: Kashmiri, for instance, has no **ʒ* to match its /*ʃ*/; Gawarbati has no **ẓ* to match its /*ṣ*/; more strangely, Torwali has no **z* to match its /*s*/. An *s/z* opposition has also developed in Chittagong Bengali.

The IA /*h*/ is traditionally considered a voiced ([*ɦ*]). An opposition of voiced/voiceless *ɦ/h̥* has developed in certain Rajasthani (Southern Mewari and North-western Marwari) and non-standard Gujarati dialects, however, where **s* has developed into a voiceless [*h̥*].[6] Since this has happened elsewhere in NIA, it is possible that such an opposition exists or has existed (it is perhaps inherently not very stable) in other NIA dialects also.

Several languages, among them Standard Hindi and Urdu, acquire a secondary voicing opposition in fricatives through Persian loanwords, most commonly *s/z*. In Khowar, however, even the *χ/γ* is of native origin, and is only augmented by loans.

5.3.7 *Aspiration*

An aspirated series of both voiceless and voiced stops, producing a four-way contrast /*p*, *ph*, *b*, *bh*/ at all five basic points of articulation, is the normal (and distinctive) NIA as well as Sanskrit pattern.

As noted earlier, a number of modern analyses prefer to treat the aspirates as clusters, generally to minimize the total number of phonemes. At the same time it is admitted (e.g., Gumperz 1958, Ferguson and Choudhury 1960, Hai 1958) that – in many of the languages at least – they pattern in most respects *like* single consonants (e.g., in their combinatorial and other occurrence propensities and in their effects on vowels [see below]). If taken as clusters, in some languages they would be the only *initial* clusters. (Distributional considerations may occasionally weigh in favor of the opposite conclusion, e.g., in Lamani, where aspirates occur only initially.) Finally, there is the testimony of the Pan-Indian writing system itself (see Chapter 6), which in all its varieties has implicitly recognized the unitary status of these segments by providing them with unitary symbols. The borrowed Perso-Arabic script in its Urdu version represents them as consonant + *h* (of a special type), but in its Sindhi version special unitary symbols (with dots) have been invented.

As with voicing, the extension of this pattern to the expanded articulation series is incomplete in some cases. For example, of the languages with seven articulations, Kanyawali lacks aspirate equivalents of /*c*, *ç*, *j*/, Shumashti of /*ts*, *c*/, and Kalasha and Phalura of /*dz*, *j*/. (Gawarbati, Kalasha, Phalura, and Shina have a full complement of seven *voiceless* aspirates, however: /*ph*, *th*, *ṭh*, *tsh*, *ch*, *çh*, *kh*/.) Of the languages with six articulations, the Himalayan group (including Kashmiri) generally has a full complement of voiceless aspirates, but the voiced aspirate series, in those dialects that have it, often seems to be missing a member, **jh* or **dzh*, or in the case of Torwali, **jh*. In the southern group, Marathi and Konkani have a complete voiced series, but are missing a **tsh*.

Some of these apparent gaps among the aspirate affricates seem to be due not to such a phone not having evolved but to its having evolved further into a fricative, losing its stop element. Thus the erstwhile Marathi–Konkani **tsh* has become a pure [*s*] and (losing also its aspiration) has merged with the original /*s*/ phoneme. Marathi /*dzh*/ is frequently heard as [*zh*] (aspirated [*z*]), but since there is no aspiration opposition among sibilants, it remains distinct, systemically part of the stop oppositions.

A more significant variation is the absence of the *voiced* aspirate series in some languages, reducing the system to a three-way contrast /*p*, *ph*, *b*/. This is the pattern in Punjabi, some "Northern Lahnda" dialects (e.g., Kagani, "Hindko" of Hazara), Kashmiri and most other Dardic languages (Shina, Bashkarik, Gawarbati, Khowar, Katarkalai, Shumashti, Tirahi), a few West Pahari dialects ("the Simla dialects as a whole," according to Bailey), and Romany. It is also reported from the East Bengali of Dacca (Pal 1966a) and the dialect of Chittagong (Učida 1970). Except for the latter, it is a phenomenon of the northwest. (Voiced aspirates are retained, however, in most West Pahari dialects, most "Lahnda" dialects, in Dogri, and in the Kashtawari and Rambani dialects of the Kashmiri group, and in the Dardic Maiyã and Kalasha.) Voiced aspirates are absent from *non-initial positions* in several varieties of Rajasthani (Allen: personal communication).

Absence (in the sense of elimination) of the voiced aspirates is often correlated with the presence of TONE (e.g., both in Punjabi and in the Bengali dialects mentioned above). This is not always the case, however (e.g., in Kashmiri or Romany), nor is the converse true: the presence of tone does not always mean the absence of the voiced aspirates (e.g., in Dogri, various "Lahnda" dialects).

Phonemic aspiration has been entirely lost in Sinhalese and Maldivian, and in the Kasargod dialect of Marathi, spoken in the north of Kerala (Ghatage 1970). (It has not been lost, however, in the Saurashtra language domiciled in the heart of the Tamil country. Cf. Dave 1976.)

There is a natural tendency (cf. Greek, Iranian) for aspirates to evolve into fricatives, especially voiceless aspirates ([*ph* > *f*, *th* > *θ*, *kh* > *χ*]). On the whole this tendency has been *resisted* in NIA, and the aspirates are firmly in place as such. Bengali and its dialects constitute an exception. Even in Standard Bengali there is a tendency to pronounce /*ph*/ as a bilabial fricative [*ɸ*], and also /*bh*/ as its voiced equivalent [*β*]. In the East Bengali dialects and especially in the dialect of Chittagong that is carried much further, to the velar stops and to both aspirated and unaspirated stops (**kh, k* > *[χ]*, **ph, p* > *[ɸ]*, **g* > *[γ]*). The tendency occasionally crops up elsewhere: Gujarati /*ph*/ varies with [*f*], and medial /*bh, dh, gh*/ have variants [*β, ð, γ*]; in Garhwali initial /*ph-*]/ and final /*-p*/ tend to become [*ɸ*] (Chandrasekhar 1970); the contact of /*ph, bh*/ is described as "weak" also in Nepali (Korol'ev 1965). In what Shackle calls substandard Siraiki /*kh, g*/ tend to become [*χ, γ*]. In Marathi also, there is a tendency to weaken or spirantize *postvocalic* /*bh, dh*/ and *intervocalic* /*jh*/ (> [ʒ]) (Lambert 1943).

On the other hand, contrastive aspiration has *extended* its domain to *nasals*, *laterals*, *flaps*, and even *semivowels* in a number of NIA languages. Here again analytical opinions differ (unit vs. cluster), but initial /*mh-, nh-*/ occur in Marathi, Konkani, most dialects of Rajasthani, Kumauni, Braj, and the Saurashtra language, and the sounds are found non-initially also in Gujarati, Sindhi, other Hindi dialects, the Bihari languages, Kalasha, and most West Pahari dialects. A /*ṇh*/ occurs in Gujarati and some West Pahari dialects, and a /*ŋh*/ occurs in Maithili, Bhojpuri, and Chhattisgarhi. In contrast to all these languages, where aspirated nasals are very much part of colloquial speech, in Bengali they belong to an artificial *acrolectal* pronunciation and are ordinarily converted into plain *geminated* nasals (**brɔmhɔ* = [*brɔmmho*] > /*brɔmmo*/).

An aspirated /*lh*/ is found in Maithili, Bhojpuri, Chhattisgarhi, Braj, Standard Hindi, Nepali, Kumauni, Gujarati, various Bhili and Rajasthani dialects, Konkani, certain Marathi dialects (Warli, Kudali), Sindhi, Siraiki, and Kalasha. It seems to be absent from Oriya, Assamese, Punjabi, Dogri, Kashmiri, and most other Dardic languages (except Kalasha). It does not turn up in the available West Pahari material. (Its absence in some though not all of these languages, along with the absence of aspirated nasals, is in line with the *absence of voiced aspirates generally*, e.g., in Kashmiri and Shina.) Although it occurred in Vedic, [*ḷh*] is apparently a rare sound in NIA. It is reported only for Gujuri and the rural dialect of Northwestern Hindi studied by Gumperz (1955a).

An aspirated /*rh*/ occurs in Maithili, Bhojpuri, Braj, Bundeli, Chhattisgarhi, Gujarati, Bhili, Hindi, Kumauni, Nepali, Marathi, and Siraiki. An aspirated retroflex flap *ṛh* occurs as a phoneme or as an allophone generally in the same languages that have its unaspirated counterpart as a phoneme or allophone. Kumauni and several varieties of Rajasthani (Marwari, Mewari, Harauti) are exceptions: they have *ṛ* but no **ṛh* (Allen: personal communication). These sounds (*lh*, *rh*, *ṛh*) occur in Bengali under the same restricted circumstances as described earlier for *mh*, *nh*, *ŋh*.

Finally /*wh*/ (or [*vh*]) is a characteristic sound of Marathi and its dialects. It is also reported by Shackle (1976) for Siraiki, by Trail (1970) for Lamani, by Allen for Mewari, and unavoidably in various accounts of Marwari (Marw. *vheṇo* 'to be'). A word *whittar*, *whītar* 'inside' (cf. H. *bhītar*) turns up in *LSI* and other accounts of some West Pahari dialects (Mandeali, Inner Siraji), but possibly the transcription *wh-* is meant to indicate a /*bh*/ with weakened occlusion, as in Bengali.

Ghatage (1965) records a /*yh*/ in the Kudali dialect of Marathi.

5.3.8 *Other correlations, and special sounds*

Perhaps the most famous set of additional consonants are the *implosive* voiced stops of Sindhi: /ɓ, ᶑ, ʄ, ɠ/. Such an opposition is not quite confined to Sindhi, but is found only in NIA dialects immediately adjacent to it. In Kacchi and Siraiki ("Southern Lahnda"), there is the same set as in Sindhi; in dialects of Marwari a slightly different one: /ɓ, ɗ, ᶑ, ɠ/ (Allen 1957b). According to Bahl (1972) (and Magier 1983) the Marwari sounds in question are "*glottalized*", not implosive, consonants, and Bahl counts only /*b*ˀ, *d*ˀ, *ḍ*ˀ/. One never knows, in regard to Rajasthani, whether the writers are referring to the same subdialects and therefore to the same phenomenon. It may be relevant that the Thareli dialect of Sindhi, adjacent to Rajasthani, is sometimes said to lack the Sindhi implosives. On the other hand, the latter are sometimes referred to, e.g., by Turner (1924), as "*preceded* by glottal closure." According to Allen (personal communication): "Much depends on the definition of 'glottalisation'. Implosives also are glottalised in that they are 'glottalic suction stops' as opposed to 'glottalic pressure stops' ('ejectives') e.g. in the definitions of Pike, Catford."

The Sindhi implosives (glottalized suction stops [see above]) have been but should not be confused with a set of *glottalized pressure* stops (ejectives) found in some East Bengali dialects (and Bishnupriya) *in place of the voiced aspirate series*: /*b*ˀ, *d*ˀ, *g*ˀ/ in the Maimansingh dialect, /*b*ˀ, *d*ˀ, *ḍ*ˀ, *dz*ˀ, *g*ˀ/ in the Chittagong dialect (according to Goswami 1940–4). In both dialects, **h* itself has become a glottal stop /ʔ/. (The Sindhi sounds have nothing to do historically with the aspirates.) Glottalization is often connected with TONE and in the East Bengali cases seems to be related to the evolution of tone from the voiced aspirates. Indeed, Uchida's analysis perceives tone rather than glottalized consonants in the Chittagong dialect. (Chatterji claimed that the Dacca dialect also had glottalized voiced stops, a point which is disputed by Pal [1966a].)

Another famous set of exotic sounds are the *prenasalized stops* of Sinhalese, usually transcribed as /*m̆b*, *n̆d*, *n̆ḍ*, *n̆g*/. They are apparently confined to that language in NIA (although I should add that I have been unable to find any good account of Maldivian phonology). Some analyses (e.g., Fairbanks, Gair, and De Silva 1968, Geiger 1938) prefer to split the nasal element from the stop and speak of distinctive *half-nasals*. In the Sinhalese writing system, there is a unitary symbol for /*m̆b*/ but /*n̆d*, *n̆ḍ*, *n̆g*/ are written with symbols analyzable into nasal + stop components.

Kashmiri is unique in subcontinental NIA in possessing an almost complete set of *palatalized* consonants (C/C′), including stops, nasals, flaps, laterals, and sibilants. Missing from the correlation are only the palatal consonants themselves (/*c*, *ch*, *j*, *ʃ*/). Not surprisingly, North Russian Romany also possesses a set of palatalized consonants (Ventzel 1983). According to one analysis (Zakhar'in 1974), Kashmiri also possesses an opposition of *labialization* (C/C°), affecting consonants other than voiceless stops.

Finally, there is a peculiar set of *laterally-released* apical stops in the northwest West Pahari dialects Bhadrawahi and Bhalesi: /*ṭλ*, *ṭhλ*, *ḍλ*, *ḍhλ*/.

5.3.9 *Secondary consonants*

Borrowed consonants fall chiefly into three subsets, partially overlapping:

1. those from Persian (in its Central Asian pronunciation): *f*, *v*, *ʃ*, *z*, *χ*, *γ*, *q*, fairly well established in the languages of predominantly Muslim populations (though not equally in all) and in the case of *f*, *v*, *ʃ*, *z*, of some others as well, preeminently common Hindi; all seven of the sounds mentioned are characteristic of Urdu, but *∗q* and *∗γ* are lacking or not well established in Sindhi, "Lahnda", and Kashmiri, and *∗q* is lacking in Dakhani Urdu;

2. those from Sanskrit, confined by contrast to careful and somewhat artificial pronunciations of rather restricted educated circles of mainly Hindi and Marathi (not Bengali) speakers: *ṇ* in some languages which do not normally have it (such as Hindi and Maithili), and *ṣ*, when there is an attempt to differentiate it from *ś* in *tatsamas* (rather than pronounce it vulgarly as *kh*, or assimilate both to *ʃ*); to these should perhaps be added the nasalized *w̃* used in the traditional rendering of *anusvāra* in *tatsamas* before voiced consonants and *s*, *ʃ*, *r*, *v*, *h* in Marathi: e.g., *saṁrakṣaṇ* 'protection' > [*səw̃r əkṣəṇ*];

(Romany) (palatalized:)

p	t	(ts)	c	k	p′	t′	k′
b	d	(dz)	j	g	b′	d′	g′
ph	th		ch	kh			
m	n					n′	
(f)	s		(ʃ)	(χ)	(f′)	s′	
v	(z)		(ʒ)	h	v′	z′	
	r	l				l′	
			y				

Shina

p	t	ṭ	ts	c	ç	k
b	d	ḍ		j	j̧	g
ph	th	ṭh	tsh	ch	çh	kh
m	n	ṇ		ñ		ŋ
(f)	s	ṣ		ś		
	z	ẓ		ź		h
	r	l ṛ				
w				y		

Kashmiri (palatalized:)

p	t	ṭ	ts	c	k	p′	t′	ṭ′	ts′	k′
b	d	ḍ		j	g	b′	d′	ḍ′		g′
ph	th	ṭh	tsh	ch	kh	ph′	th′	ṭh′	tsh′	kh′
m	n			ñ		m′	n′			
	s			ʃ			s′			
	z					h	z′			h′
	r	l					r′ l′			
w				y		w′				

Siraiki

p	t	ṭ	c	k
b	d	ḍ	j	g
ph	th	ṭh	ch	kh
bh	dh	ḍh	jh	gh
ɓ	ɗ		ʄ	ɠ
m	n	ṇ	ñ	ŋ
mh	nh	ṇh		
(f)	s		(ʃ)	(χ)
	(z)			(γ) h
	r l	ṛ		
	rh lh	ṛh		
w			y	
wh				

Punjabi

p	t	ṭ	c	k
b	d	ḍ	j	g
ph	th	ṭh	ch	kh
m	n	ṇ	[ñ	ŋ]
(f)	s		(ʃ)	
	(z)			h
	r l	ṛ ḷ		
w			y	

Nepali

p	t	ṭ	c*	k
b	d	ḍ	j*	g
ph	th	ṭh	ch*	kh
bh	dh	ḍh	jh*	gh
m	n			ŋ
mh	nh			
	s			h
	r	l		
	rh	lh		
[w]			(y)	

Assamese

p	t	k
b	d	g
ph	th	kh
bh	dh	gh
m	n	ŋ
	s	χ
	z	h
	r	l
[w]		

Figure 5.1 Representative NIA consonant systems

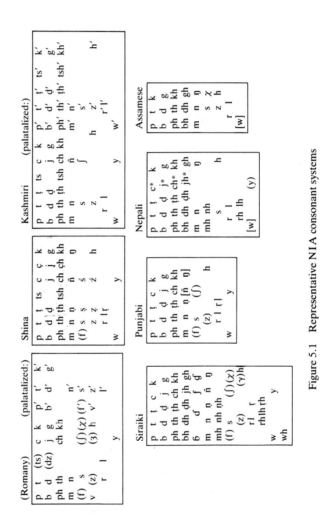

Sindhi

p t ṭ c k
b d ḍ j k
ph th ṭh ch kh
bh dh ḍh jh gh
ɓ ɗ ʄ ɠ
m n ṇ ñ ŋ
mh nh ṇh
(f) s (ʃ) (χ)
(z) (γ)h
r l ṛ
rh lh ṛh
w y
wh

Marwari

p t ṭ c k
b d ḍ j g
ph th ṭh ch kh
bh dh ḍh jh gh
ɓ ɗ ɗ̣ ɠ
m n ṇ
mh nh
s h
r l ṛ ḷ
w y
wh

Hindi

p t ṭ c k
b d ḍ j g
ph th ṭh ch kh
bh dh ḍh jh gh
m n
(f) s (ʃ)
(z) h
r l ṛ
ṛh
([w]) ([y])

Bengali

p t ṭ c k
b d ḍ j g
ph th ṭh ch kh
bh dh ḍh jh gh
m n
ʃ h
r l ṛ
[w] [y]

Gujarati

p t ṭ c k
b d ḍ j g
ph th ṭh ch kh
bh dh ḍh jh gh
m n ṇ
mh nh ṇh
s ʃ h
r l ḷ
rhlh
w y

Marathi

p t ṭ |ts |c k
b d ḍ dz j g
ph th ṭh ch kh
bh dh|ḍh dzh|jh gh
m n ṇ
mh nh
s ʃ h
r l ḷ
rhlh
w y
wh

Oriya

p t ṭ c k
b d ḍ j g
ph th ṭh ch kh
bh dh ḍh jh gh
m n ṇ
s h
r l [ṛ]ḷ
[ṛh]
[w] [y]

Sinhalese

p t ṭ c k
b d ḍ j g
m̆b n̆d n̆ḍ n̆g
m n ñ ŋ
s h
r l
w y

Figure 5.1 (*cont.*)

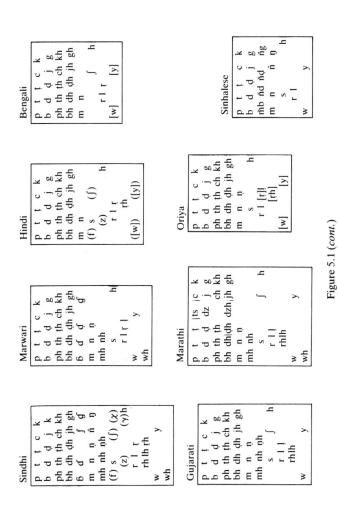

3. those from English, fairly widespread in educated urban speech, especially in the north and west, where English and Persian influences reinforce each other: *f*, *v*, *ʃ*, *z*; it should be noted that not all the exotic consonants in originally English loanwords are incorporated into NIA speech: *θ, ð, ʒ are almost always replaced by NIA /*th*, *d*, *j*/ or *jh*; the last happens to have in Marathi an intervocalic allophone approximating the English sound.

One characteristic of the secondary phonemes is that they do not enter into the correlations of aspiration, palatalization, or even voicing discussed earlier, unless they accidentally encounter a preexisting partner, or bring one with them. For example, an aspirated **qh* is a perfectly possible phoneme, one existing in various Caucasian and Amerindian languages, but it is not found in NIA.

Another characteristic of the secondary phonemes is that, except in Urdu, where they are as it were part of the very definition of the language, they are to varying degrees always liable to be replaced by a native NIA sound by at least some speakers: *f* by /*ph*/, *v* (where this sound is foreign) by /*b*/ or even /*bh*/, *z* by /*j*/, *χ* by /*kh*/, *q* by /*k*/, *γ* by /*g*/, *ṣ* by /*s*/, /*ʃ*/ or *kh*, *ʃ* by /*s*/, *ṇ* by /*n*/.

5.3.10 *Overview of NIA consonant "systems"*

Although the reader can piece together the complete consonant systems of various NIA languages from the foregoing discussions, those of the major languages and a few others are spelled out in Figure 5.1 for quick reference and comparison. Parentheses indicate consonants found only in loanwords; square brackets indicate those with "very low functional load." The arrangement is roughly geographical.

5.4 **NIA vowels and associated features**

Vowel descriptions often disagree more than consonant descriptions, and the number of distinctive segments ascribed to a particular language in various accounts may vary alarmingly, even with respect to plain oral vowels and leaving aside such features as nasalization, register, and tone. (For simplicity's sake, the latter will be dealt with separately here and not included in the basic vowel inventories.) For one thing, vowels are describable along what is essentially a continuum, and merge into one another in a way consonants do not. It is an area where special training or the lack of it can make a big difference in the number and identification of discriminated sounds. More disturbingly, there is evidence (Fox 1978) of individual differences in vowel perception irrespective of training or background. Finally, vowel phones in some languages do vary considerably in relation to neighboring consonants, position in the word, and stress, as well as nasalization and tone. Identifying the contrastive parameters of the vowels themselves thus puts the phonemic principle to the sorest test.

It should also be noted that NIA orthographies sometimes diverge considerably from the phonologies in this area, and it is sometimes difficult for the educated investigator to disengage his or her perceptions from the written norms. On occasion the divergence is so great as to be plain to all, but other cases may leave room for doubt. Many of the best and most detailed accounts are written by educated native speakers "using myself as informant." While we must be grateful for these, a great desideratum is for more accounts based on wide and objective surveys, especially of the unsuspecting. While one problem with some accounts is lack of true minimal pairs or even minimal environments for the contrasts claimed, a problem with some others is the citation of minimal pairs that may contrast only in spelling, or perhaps in what may be called a reading pronunciation, misidentified as "speech".

5.4.1 *NIA oral vowel systems*

It will be convenient first to present a typology of NIA vowel systems in the conventional manner as whole systems of contrasts. Except for the five-vowel system /*i*, *e*, *a*, *o*, *u*/ found only outside the subcontinent in European Romany, the minimal NIA vowel system is a *six-vowel system*. (Ventzel [1983] posits a six-vowel system for North Russian Romany also, but the sixth vowel, a high unrounded central /*ɨ*/, behaves suspiciously like a variant of /*i*/ after nonpalatalized consonants.)

The subcontinental six-vowel system has two subtypes: one is the *Oriya type*, with parallel front and back vowels /*i*, *e*, *a*; *u*, *o*, *ɔ*/; it is also found in Bishnupriya. The other is the *Nepali/Marathi type*, with a height contrast in the central vowels: /*i*, *e*; *a*, *ə*; *o*, *u*/. It is also found in Lamani and Sadani. Both Nepali and Marathi have been analyzed differently (e.g., Clark identifies two additional lower-mid front vowels /*ɛ*, *æ*/ in Nepali – which would make a remarkably asymmetrical system) but these are the most common views of those languages. The Marathi higher central vowel is considerably higher than the Nepali one, particularly in its lengthened final-position allophone. (Some would consider the latter a phoneme, bringing the Marathi total to seven. The question hinges mainly on whether to consider the vocalic release after final consonant clusters a vowel, and thus an allophone of /*ə*/ contrasting with final [*əː*], or automatic.)

Otherwise the quintessential *seven-vowel system* is that of Bengali, with differentiation of lower-mid vowels both front and back: /*i*, *e*, *æ*; *a*; *ɔ*, *o*, *u*/. Some dialects (Rajshahi, Maimansing, perhaps Chittagong, but not Dacca) appear to have reduced systems. (Učida finds additional long vowels */a:, ɔ:, o:/* in the Chittagong dialect.)

There are several types of *eight-vowel systems*, chief among which are the Gujarati (*/i, e, ε; a, ə; ɔ, o, u/*) and, with four parallel front and back vowels, the Assamese (*/i, e, ε, a;* ɒ, *ɔ, o, u/*). Halbi and Bhatri seem to exemplify a third type with contrasts in the high vowels instead of in the lower-mid vowels: */i:, i, e:; a:, a; o:, u, u:/* (Telang 1966). The same subtype is reported for Garhwali by Chandrasekhar (1970), and seems to characterize the Chameali and Gadi (Bharmauri) dialects of West Pahari. Kalasha may also have an eight-vowel system, although the phonetic vs. phonological character of Morgenstierne's account is not clear. Although Warli is of the Gujarati type, the Bhili of Dangs (Kulkarni 1976) has a system with three front and three central vowels of different heights but only two back vowels: */i, e, ε; ɨ, ə, a; o, u/*. It is impossible to tell from the available materials (overdifferentiated?) what the vocalic phonology of other Bhili dialects might be. It may well be the same as Gujarati (i.e. there seems to be something analogous to the Gujarati contrast in the lower-mid vowels, but Jain [1971] posits several other vowels as well).

A *nine-vowel system* in NIA generally involves contrasts also in the high vowels (i/I, u/U, or i:/i, u:/u, or i:/I, u:/U – three ways of describing the same thing), although the Harauti dialect of Rajasthani has it only in the back set (Allen 1957b). There is usually asymmetry in the lower-mid vowels in the nine-vowel systems: either the back contrast is lacking or the front. Dogri (Shankar 1931) has /i:, I, e, æ; ə, a:; o, U, u:/, i.e. no *ɔ to match its /æ/. Rudhari (Varma 1936) has a similar system: /i, I, e, ε; ə, a; o, U, u/, as do apparently several other West Pahari dialects (Mandeali, Pangwali, Khashali, Churahi) as well as Siraiki (Shackle 1976). The Shodochi and Surkhuli dialects of West Pahari on the other hand have *o:/ɔ* but not **e:/ε*. Finally there are *symmetrical* systems in some West Pahari dialects (Jaunsari, Shoracholi, Kului) which have both the front and the back mid-vowel contrasts but lack **ə*. Although nine-vowel systems thus seem to be characteristic of West Pahari, the reader is cautioned that the materials on which these conclusions are reached are not very satisfactory. In particular it is not clear from them what the phonetic value of the segments represented as *ai*, *au* is in these dialects. If monophthongal as in most of northwest India, we may be dealing with eleven-vowel systems here – assuming the "short" and "long" *e*'s and *o*'s of the accounts are indeed contrastive and not determined.

The symmetrical *ten-vowel system* of Hindi and Punjabi (/i, I, e, æ; a, ə; u, U, o, ɔ/ – often represented as */ī, i, e, ai; ā, a; ū, u, o, au/*) is considered the *normative* NIA system, in that it is "closest" to Sanskrit – that is, has the same number of distinctions, except for the loss of the vowels **/r̥, r̥̄, l̥/*. The diphthongs *ai*, *au*, conventionally counted as part of the Sanskrit inventory of "vowels" (though not of NIA inventories, being properly relegated to the category of diphthongs), are monophthongized to æ, ɔ in these languages, although in eastern (i.e. Bihari) pronunciations of common Hindi (and in some acrolectal pronunciations of *tatsamas*) a diphthongal element is retained (Harris 1966).

It is also generally agreed that the *quantitative* distinctions of Sanskrit (i:/i, u:/u, etc.) have been replaced, or are at least accompanied, by *qualitative* distinctions (not only in these systems but in some of the "reduced" systems already discussed). Even for Sanskrit, Panini had noted that the contrast conventionalized as *a/a:* was in reality already a qualitative distinction, [*ə*, *a:*]. It is possible, however, that a qualitative difference accompanied all the length distinctions from the beginning, or at least had intruded by the time of contacts with the Greeks. (Cf. Bloch 1965: 35.) Because it is the traditional basis of the system, one still occasionally finds the NIA vowels also stated in terms of quantitative contrasts (see above). (Ohala [1983] says she is forced to do so because of the constraints of generative phonology. We shall in fact do the same in the remaining sections of this book for reasons of typographical convenience and clarity as well as etymological comparability.)

This system is shared also by Sindhi and (Northern) "Lahnda" (according to some analyses – according to others Sindhi lacks /ɔ/), Kacchi, and most varieties of Rajasthani, including Gujuri (although Magier [1983] reports the collapse of the higher and lower mid-vowels, both back and front, in many varieties of Marwari, also noted by Grierson in *LSI 9.2* as a "general Rajasthani tendency," observable even in Malvi).

Certain West Pahari dialects (Sirmauri, the Rampuri and Rohru subdialects of Kochi, Baghati, Bishshau, Inner Siraji), and some Dardic dialects (Phalura, Maiya, Gawarbati) seem to have a ten-vowel system in which the distinctions are filled out not by monophthongized **ai*, *au* (if these are also present, they would produce a twelve-vowel system) but by "*short/long*" (and at the same time qualitatively *lower/higher*) *e/e:*, *o/o:* = [*ɛ/e:*, *ɔ/o:*] contrasts. (In the language of the plains, monophthongized **ai*, *au*, as well as undifferentiated mid-vowels, are all supposed to be long vowels, [*æ:*, *ɔ:*, *e:*, *o:*].) According to Buddruss (1960), the ten-vowel system of the Dardic language-fragment Wotapuri is still mainly quantitative; quality distinctions do not always accompany the length differences, except in the case of *a:/a* (as in Sanskrit) and apparently also *e:/e*, *o:/o* (unknown to Sanskrit). A similar system is noted by both Pandit (1972) and Učida (1979) for the Saurashtri of South India.

Systems with eleven vowels generally involve adding something to the "Himalayan" system with the length-differentiated mid-vowels. In Padari, Bhadrawahi, and Kiunthali it is a long rounded front vowel */ü:/*. In Northeastern Pashai dialects there seems to be a contrast in height between short central vowels *a/ə*. There is a similar contrast in Kumauni (where according to Apte and Pattanayak [1967] it is the lower mid-vowel that is long and the higher that is short, *ɛ:/e*). In Bhojpuri according to Shukla (1981) there is an /æ/ in addition to /*ɛ, e:*/ – and to the diphthong */ai/*. According to Katre (1966), Konkani has an /*ɔ*/ contrasting with /*o, o:*/ as well as with */au/*.

According to Varma (1935) and Jaiswal (1962), Braj and Bundeli have a *twelve-vowel system* in which both of the above additions are made – in this case, however, representing monophthongizations of **ai, au* > [æ, ɔ]. Varma (1948) describes what is apparently a twelve- (or possibly a thirteen-) vowel system of a rather different sort in the Bhalesi dialect of West Pahari: /i:, I, (e), *ɛ*, *æ:*, a:; ɔ, *(ɔ:)*, o, U, u:, *ü*, *ö*. (The vowels in parentheses may not be phonemic.) Varma (1938) noted a similar system (with two front-rounded vowels) in neighboring Bhadrawahi. Bashkarik (Kohistani Dardic) seems to have a twelve-vowel system with three height and/or length distinctions in the front-mid vowels (*e:/ɛ/æ:*) – possibly also in the back (*o:/o/ɔ:*, which would = thirteen) plus the front-rounded vowel */ö:/*. Accounts of Khowar listing three central and three back-mid (*ɔ, o, o:*) vowels, but not front-mid, may be subphonemic.

An *authentic thirteen-vowel system* is found in Sinhalese, however. It is based mainly on quantity: */i:, i, e:, e, æ, æ:, a:, a, ə, o:, o, u:, u/*. The exception is the *ə/a* distinction, based on height, which is not distinguished in writing, and therefore not included in Geiger's account. (Some writers, e.g., Fairbanks, Gair, and De Silva [1968], posit a long as well as a short *ə:/ə*, but the long variety occurs only in English loanwords, e.g., *ʃə:t* 'shirt'.)

NIA languages with a larger number of vowel phonemes may also exist. It is a question primarily of Kashmiri and Shina, regarding both of which there are widely differing accounts. Grierson thought he heard front-rounded vowels [*ü, ü:, ö*]. Most modern analyses, however (e.g., Bailey 1937, Handoo 1973, and Kachru 1973), hold these to be *un*-rounded *central* vowels, [*ɨ, ɨ:, ə, ə:*]. Kashmiri thus has (at least) three contrasts in height in the central vowels (including the low-central vowels *a/a:*). There are at least three contrasts also in the back vowels (*/u:, u; o:, o; ə/*), but possibly only two (*/i:, i; e:, e/*) in the front vowels. Kachru and Handoo but not Bailey or Grierson distinguish *ɔ/ɔ:*; this would bring the phonemic total to sixteen. The phonetic descriptions make clear, and Zakhar'in (1974) has established experimentally, that the vowels distinguished by length in the above account also differ in quality (height).

According to Zakhar'in, however, the number of actual phonemes is much fewer (around ten): [*i, i:, e, e:*] are allophones of the central vowel *phonemes /ɨ, ɨ:, ə, ə:/* in the vicinity of palatal consonants. (This would posit a very odd vowel system, with only central and back vowel phonemes.) The problem, or rather the challenge, of Kashmiri (to which we shall have to return) is that the relationship of sounds is such that the regularities of the phonology can only be stated in a way that obscures the phonetics of the language, while the regularities of the grammar can only be stated in a way that departs from phonology in the conventional sense in the direction of morphophonemics.

With regard to Shina, Bailey reduced the twenty vowels he distinguished in his 1924 account to fourteen upon further analysis in 1925: /i, I, e, ɛ, æ; u, U, o, *(ɔ)*, ɒ; ə, ʌ, ɤ, a/. (The sound (ɔ) belongs mainly to loanwords. The /U/ phoneme has a front-rounded allophone [*ü*]; /i, I/ have retracted allophones [ɨ, ɪ̈] in the vicinity of the *retroflex* affricates and sibilants (*ç, j̣, ṣ, ẓ*). Schmidt and Zarin (1981), analyzing the Palas dialect, come up with twelve vowels, none of which is back-unrounded, high-central, or front-rounded (although wide variation in vowel *allophones* is noted): /i:, I, e:, ɛ, æ:, æ, a:, ʌ, o:, ɔ, u:, U/. (They actually posit six vowels, /*i, e, æ, a, o, u*/, + /:/, occurring with all vowels, which are described as having the other phonetic shapes above when *not* so cooccurring.)

Ghatage describes both the Kasargod dialect of Marathi (1970) and the Konkani of the Chitrapur Saraswats of South Kanara as having a large number of vowels, eighteen and fourteen respectively, albeit with suspicious positional restrictions, especially in the first case.

5.4.2 *Further remarks on vowels*

The above presentation of NIA vowel systems has been in a simple order of increasing complexity. From the standpoint of an historical typology, they may be subcategorized rather differently: those that have preserved what might be called the basic system (Standard Hindi and Punjabi); those that have *reduced* that system (the Eastern group, Marathi, and Gujarati), mainly by collapsing the distinctions in the high front and back vowels; and those that have *expanded* that system in various ways (e.g., Sinhalese, Kashmiri, many Pahari dialects, and non-standard Western Hindi dialects themselves according to some accounts).

The presence of "geminated vowels" (*ii, ee, oo, uu*, etc.) allegedly belonging to only one syllable (cf. Goswami 1966: 97) in such languages as Assamese and Bengali is a reminder that a degree of conventionality governs even these analyses. Such vowels are not usually (an exception is Učida's analysis of the Chittagong dialect) counted as "long" vowels perhaps because they are fairly recent evolutes, and are often still *spelled* as two vowels separated by an (unpronounced) glide. If new long vowels are to arise in these languages, they would no doubt do so in precisely this manner, as they have already many times in NIA (see

Chapter 7). In Oriya according to Pattanayak and Das (1972) such geminates are "pronounced as two syllables." The line between the two perceptions is perhaps very fine, and the question in general deserves a careful phonetic investigation.

Purely systemic comparisons can be misleading, Hindi, Bengali, and Gujarati /ɔ/, for example, are different phonetically, historically, and in their written representation. The first is a long vowel, the result of monophthongization of the diphthong **au*, which remains its written symbol. (In Bengali this has evolved instead into the diphthong /*ou*/.) The second is a phonetic development of the vowel **a* (> [ɔ], therefore etymologically equivalent to Hindi and Gujarati /ə/, and as the "inherent vowel" represented by zero graphemically. The origin and status of Gujarati /ɔ/ is more complicated (see Pandit 1955–6a, Cardona 1965): while partly a development (not uniform) of *early* NIA **au*, it also goes back to MIA **u*, *o* in closed syllables, to combinations with **h* (**aho*, *ahu*, *uha*, *oha*) and to other sources. Its employment varies dialectally and stylistically. It is generally not differentiated from /*o*/ in spelling; AU is unavailable to represent it, as there is a more recent /*əu*/ diphthong in the language (in Tss.). This last, however, is also beginning to be pronounced [ɔ], perhaps under Hindi influence. The contrast *ɔ*/*o* obtains only in initial or monosyllables. Gujarati /ɔ/ is less open than the Hindi or Bengali sound.

Analogous remarks apply to the lower-mid front vowels in these languages. Again the symbol *ε*, used in some descriptions for the Hindi sound instead of *æ*, in that case denotes a more open sound than the same symbol in descriptions of Gujarati (E is also used for the latter). Neither the Bengali nor the Gujarati sounds have the slight diphthongization sometimes heard in the Hindi sound. Although the sources of Bengali /*æ*/ are partly similar to those of Gujarati /*ε*/ (whereas **ai*, the source of Hindi *æ*, has developed in Bengali into /*oi*/), it has become a more open sound, and by virtue of a number of additional sources, e.g., sequences of **ya*, *yă*, vowel harmony, etc., it is more firmly established in the language.

Expansion of the system has been by way of elaboration of distinctions in the mid-vowels and in the central vowels, and by adding such refinements as front-rounded vowels. The last are very rare in NIA, turning up only in a few West Pahari and Dardic dialects, where they are also marginal. (Jordan-Horstmann [1969] detects an [*ü*] in the Sadani language of South Bihar, but she phonemicizes it as a cluster /*ui*/.) Higher central unrounded vowels are somewhat more common, and characteristic of Marathi and Kashmiri.

Commonest of all, however, and also most problematic, are further distinctions, or alleged distinctions, in the mid-vowels, often posited as *e*/*e:* and *o*/*o:*, albeit with qualitative differences attached. On the one hand. there is often a suspicious restriction of occurrence of the "short" vowel to certain environments (e.g., closed syllables, unstressed syllables) plus certain form classes (e.g., pronouns). The former goes back to MIA, where the phonemic status of the short mid-vowels is therefore also problematic. On the other hand, since the Northern scripts have no way of clearly representing such vowels, should they develop, *orthographic hesitation* between e/i and o/u is often an indication of their presence, at least phonetically. One of the great desiderata in IA linguistics is a thoroughgoing overall clarification of the phonological status of the "short" mid-vowels in those NIA languages where they have been noted (Pahari dialects, Dardic languages, several Hindi dialects, Bhojpuri, Konkani – in Sinhalese there appears to be no problem, although it might be worth including for the sake of comparison), and in MIA.

Secondary subsystems involving borrowed sounds (as distinct from sporadic individual code-mixing) play a much more minor role among NIA vowels than among consonants. The main case worth noting is Marathi, where the vowels */ɔ/* and */æ/* (in English loanwords) and */ɨ/* (in Sanskrit *tatsamas* with an original *ṛ) may be said to constitute a secondary subsystem – noted, moreover, by special written symbols. (To these might be added the long */əː/* in Sinhalese mentioned earlier – if one vowel can constitute a subsystem.) Marathi has no native [ɔ] or [æ] phones, as the diphthongs */ai, au/* remain phonetically diphthongs. In Hindi, Bengali, and other languages which do have these sounds, the vowels in English loanwords are simply assimilated to them. (In Hindi, the short [ɛ] in English words merges with */æ/*.)

It is possible to speak of another kind of secondary subsystem, however, consisting not of borrowed sounds but rather of native sounds of marginal status. In Bengali, for example, there are rare but undeniable contrasts between, e.g., *E/e* in [*chEle*] 'boy' and [*chele*] 'if (it) covers', and between *I/i* in [*kIntu*] 'but' and [*kintum*] 'I used to bring/would have brought' (Clinton Seely: personal communication). In Nepali there are the additional vowels (*/ɛ, æ/*) noted by Clark (1977), which are in fact colloquial pronunciations of the sequences */Cya, Cyā/* respectively. Cases like the former can sometimes be taken care of by positing junctures: */kin–tum/* vs. */kintu/*, while those like the latter can be "interpreted" as a sequence (historically underlying or otherwise), as Jordan-Horstmann does with Sadani [*ü*] = */ui/*, although this is not always the most satisfactory solution.

5.4.3 *Diphthongs*

Diphthongs, defined as combinations of vowel sounds within one syllable, should be distinguished from sequences of vowels constituting more than one syllable (see section 5.5.2 below), although accounts of NIA phonologies do not always do so. To do so most rigorously perhaps would require showing contrasts between diphthongs and corresponding vowel sequences, e.g., *ai̯/aï*, but although this can be and in fact has been done with regard to some NIA languages, it is not always possible, or necessary to establish the reality of the diphthong (any more than it is necessary to show contrasts with sequences of C + /*h*/ to establish the reality of aspirated consonants). To add to the confusion, vowel sequences often *evolve into* diphthongs – in NIA (as contrasted with, for example, English or Spanish) they are in fact the main historical source of the latter – and in such circumstances there are naturally very many borderline cases.

Another question involves so-called rising diphthongs ([*u̯a*, *i̯a*, *i̯e*], etc.) vs. sequences of the "semiconsonants" /*y*, *w*/ + vowel. As this is partly a matter of particular phonological doctrine (and the rigor of its application) rather than of any phonetic differences, both interpretations are found in accounts of some NIA languages. In other cases, there is more justification for the diphthongal interpretation, namely when the glides occur *only postconsonantally* in such combinations (e.g., C + *u̯a*, *i̯a*, etc.) and never initially. Such is the case in Bengali, for example, where moreover the glides are often treated as "non-syllabic" *e̯*, *o̯*, rather than **i̯*, *u*. In languages where the semivowels pattern more like consonants – e.g., occur initially and in the case of *w* have consonant-like allophones (as noted earlier the phoneme is often representable as /*v*/) – it seems more appropriate to treat such sequences as simple vowels preceded by consonant clusters of the type C*w*-, C*y*-.

Sanskrit had only the two diphthongs /*ai*/ and /*au*/, for which special symbols were eventually provided in later Brahmi. While inheriting this writing convention for what now may be pronounced as diphthongs (in the Eastern languages as phonetically *different* diphthongs, [*oi*, *ou*]) or as a simple vowel (usually [*æ*, *ɔ*]) the NIA languages generally have an *expanded inventory of falling diphthongs* (except for Sinhalese, which has no diphthongs, and Kashmiri, which along with some West Pahari dialects has only /*ai*, *au*/). These naturally have to be represented in other ways, either as sequences of vowels (which may also represent disyllabic sequences) or of vowel + the semivowels /*-y*/ and /*-w*/. As there is a reluctance in some descriptions to recognize any diphthongs other than the traditional two (and therefore to go into the question at all), it is difficult to be exhaustive in comparisons, but it is clear enough that the Eastern languages have the greatest number of true diphthongs (*as well as* disyllabic vowel sequences): in Bengali, for instance, Ferguson and Chowdhury (1960) recognize /*āi̯*, *āe̯*, *āo̯*, *ei̯*, *oi̯*, *ui̯*, *āu̯*, *eu̯*, *ou̯*, *iu̯*, *ɔe̯*, *æe̯*, *ɔo̯*/ (also /*ii̯*, *oo̯*/), contrasting most of them with identical disyllabic sequences. Marathi, on the other hand, seems to have only a few diphthongs, but they include contrasts such as *əw*/*āw*, *əy*/*āy* which are unknown to, for example, Hindi. In Gujarati, Cardona (1965) notes several diphthongs (phonemicized as V + *y*, *w*, e.g., *āy*, *āw*, *ew*) along with diphthongal allegro pronunciations of forms with lento disyllabic variants (*āy* = *ā-i*, *āw* = *ā-u*, *ew* = *e-u*) – a situation typical also of Hindi, Punjabi, Marathi, and other languages (which present such forms as *gāy* ‘cow’/*gā-ī* = *gāy* ‘sang’).

5.4.4 *Nasalization*

Nasalized vowels are a very prominent characteristic of most NIA languages. There are two kinds of vowel nasalization in NIA, namely the predictable (in the neighborhood of nasal consonants, nonfunctional but often noted in Indian descriptions in keeping with traditional attention to syntagmatic phonetic detail) and the unpredictable or contrastive. The latter tends to be phonetically stronger. While phonetically conditioned nasalization is prosodic or suprasegmental by definition, contrastive nasalization is by no means so.

A purely segmental phonology would of course recognize the inherently nasalized vowels as additional vowels, as in French, but no doubt in the name of phoneme economy most modern accounts of NIA seem to prefer to posit instead one “phoneme of nasalization” to be combined with the basic vowels. The disadvantage of this is that there must be an accompanying statement telling *which* of the basic vowels (and diphthongs) may take this feature, an exercise which is sometimes neglected in favor of a blanket statement to the effect that “all vowels may be nasalized.” This may on occasion be true; often it deserves closer scrutiny, and sometimes involves confusion of the two kinds of nasalization noted above. There may also be disagreement as to what form such a statement should take, and as Ohala (1983) points out, even over the phonetic facts involved. For some examples of such disagreement regarding Hindi, see Dixit (1963), according to which there is no nasalized **e˜* or **o˜* – a statement no doubt related to the effect of nasalization on vowel quality; Misra (1967) and Kelkar (1968), according to which there is phonemic nasalization of *all* vowels; Narang and Becker (1971), according to which *all* vowel nasalization is *predictable*; and Ohala (1983), according to which there is phonemic nasalization of the “long” vowels – *i:˜*, *e:˜*, *æ:˜*, *a:˜*, *ɔ:˜*, *o:˜*, *u:˜* – finally and before voiceless stops only, but predictable nasalization of long vowels before voiced stops – because of the presence of an unrecognized homorganic nasal consonant, and of short vowels – I˜, *ə˜*, U˜ – generally. That is, according to Ohala short nasalized vowels are (with certain exceptions, as always) predictable either phonetically – there is an unrecognized homorganic nasal consonant following – or morphologically (or both). What is involved in the latter is a morphophonemically reduced form of a basic form having a *long* nasalized vowel, e.g., */sı˜cnā/* ‘to be irrigated’, derived intransitive of */sī˜cnā/* ‘to irrigate’. In the opinion of this writer, Ohala’s analysis, complex though it is, is the best. It also makes good use of laboratory phonetics. She notes that the unnaturalness of the short nasalized vowels is confirmed even for the handful of unpredictable cases by the tendency among the less educated either to denasalize them, */ha˜snā/* 'laugh' > */hasnā/* or to insert a homorganic nasal consonant. See also Shackle (1976: 17) on Siraiki and Gill and Gleason (1969: 23) on Punjabi.

In any case, there are real, not theoretical, differences in the domain of vowel nasalization among different NIA languages. In general nasalization is stronger, phonetically and systemically, in the west (where it tends to play not only a lexical but also a morphological role, e.g., in Hindi, Punjabi, Gujarati, Rajasthani, Sindhi, "Lahnda" and Siraiki, Nepali, and Konkani) than in the east. In Bengali, where it has only a lexical role, it is absent altogether from some East Bengali dialects (Dacca, Maimensing), and in the Calcutta Standard affects only six of the seven vowels (not */ɔ/* – or only rarely) and (marginally) only one of the many diphthongs (*ɔe˜* or *oi˜*). In Oriya there are no such restrictions.

Nasalization is absent from Sinhalese and from most Marathi dialects (although present in Konkani, and retained until recently in Marathi spelling). It is also absent from Romany. Nasalization is not reported from most dialects of Pashai (Morgenstierne 1973b) or from Tirahi, but seems to be present in most other Dardic and Pahari languages, including Kashmiri (Kachru [1973] gives many minimal pairs). In Gujarati, there is only one nasalized mid-vowel, front and back, corresponding to the two oral mid-vowels. It is generally taken to be closer to the lower variety, thus */ɛ˜, ɔ˜/*. There is a similar tendency in Rajasthani, without, however, destroying the contrast in every case (Magier 1983; see also Allen 1957b). Allen (personal communication) notes that the phonetic effects of nasalization on vowel quality vary with different forms of Rajasthani: Marwari */o + ˜=ɔ˜/*, but Harauti */o + ˜=u˜/*.

5.4.5 *Tone and murmur*

Contrastive tone is reported from several NIA languages and dialects, among them Chittagong and Dacca Bengali, Shina, Khowar, Gawarbati, Bashkarik, "Lahnda", Rajasthani, Dogri, several West Pahari dialects (Kochi, Shodochi, Bishshau, Rudhari, Khashali), and possibly Wotapuri, but undoubtedly the classic case of tone in NIA is Punjabi. There are two distinctive tones in Punjabi contrasting with the neutral tone: the High (or High-Falling) /ˋ/ and the Low (or Low-Rising) /ˊ/. (Some would say there are three tones, including the neutral or "Mid" tone as one of them.) Favorite examples of the contrasts are */koˊ ṛā/* 'leper', */koˋ ṛā/* 'horse', and ("Mid" or unmarked tone) */koṛā/* 'whip'.

Punjabi tone is definitely prosodic (and thus resembles – in terms of its acoustic impression as well as structurally – Scandinavian rather than Chinese or – even less – African or Mesoamerican tone) in that its domain (described by Gill and Gleason in terms of an "onset" and a "tail") normally *extends over two syllables* – although a monosyllable may also have tone. As Shackle (1972) points out, words without one of the distinctive tones (or, in other terms, with the neutral "tone") are far more common than words with them. To anticipate the discussion in Chapter 7 for the sake of greater clarity here, this is because Punjabi tone has clearly evolved from certain kinds of aspiration, and is therefore found *only* in words whose equivalents in other NIA languages have voiced aspirates, aspirate nasals or liquids, or */h/* itself. (For example, the Hindi equivalents of the words above are */koṛhī/* – with a different suffix, */ghoṛā/*, and */koṛā/*.) Bahl (1969) observes further that tone (that is, tone *onset*) is found only on stem vowels and those of certain (stem-forming) derivational suffixes, never on inflectional endings.

According to Bahl, Punjabi tone was first noticed by Bailey in 1913, and not fully described until B. D. Jain's 1934 accounts, which were restated by Bahl in phonemic terms in 1957. The late recognition of Punjabi tone by scholars is undoubtedly related to the way it is represented in writing (see Chapter 6). Regarding some of the other languages mentioned, analyses are (with the exception of "Lahnda", thanks to the work of Bahri on the Awankari dialect, and again of Bahl) less complete; sometimes all we have is someone's observation that tone seems to be distinctive in a language.

Such statements call for caution. As Pike points out in his classic treatise on the subject (1948: 46), "the student is certain to hear pitch phenomena in any language which he studies, since all languages have their words spoken on some pitch, whether or not these pitches are organized into a tonal system." Nevertheless, there is good reason to suspect the development of tone in those NIA dialects which have, like Punjabi, lost or modified the system of voiced aspirates. This is not the whole story, however. Leaving aside exceptional cases like Sinhalese and Romany, where other factors are clearly responsible, the two phenomena (loss of the voiced aspirates and tone) overlap considerably, but do not coincide. Even in the immediate neighborhood, Kashmiri lacks both the voiced aspirates and "tonemes", while in certain "Lahnda" dialects (Awankari) and in the Haryanvi form of Western Hindi both occur. In the case of several Dardic language-fragments on the verge of extinction (Shumashti, Wotapuri, Tirahi, Pashai), or even of West Pahari dialects now much influenced by Standard Hindi, it may be impossible ever to clarify the situation.

In Rajasthani, both the High-Falling tone noted for Marwari – where it plays an important *morphological* role – by Magier (and several predecessors, going back to Asopa in 1896, who used for it the Vedic term *udātta*), and the Rising tone noted by Allen for South Mewari do seem to go back to an **h*, whether original or itself derived from an earlier **s*. Both also entail a phonetic lengthening of a "short" vowel without losing its qualitative opposition to the corresponding "long" vowel. (In Awankari "Lahnda", according to Bahri 1963, tone-bearing vowels are *shortened*.)

Obviously allied to the phenomenon of tone in NIA is that of *murmur*, both typologically, in that this type of voice quality contrast (nowadays generally called a *register* contrast, a use of this term differing from Pike's) typically goes with tonal systems (areally and systemically), and historically, in that it too is related to historical voiced aspirates and **h*. Sometimes it is called *breathy voice*; it should be distinguished from *whisper*, which is voiceless. It has been described mainly for Gujarati (Pandit 1955–6b), where Dave (1967) notes not only eight murmured vowel segments contrasting with eight clear vowel segments, but also six further *murmured nasalized* segments contrasting with the six unmurmured nasalized vowels – making twenty-eight contrastive vowel segments in all. Pandit, followed by Cardona (1965), prefers to regard it as an allophone of /*h*/ – originally postvocalic but now "simultaneous with the vowel" and accompanied by a lowering of pitch.

Historically it is clearly related to postvocalic **h*. A favorite contrastive set (with the first example showing *murmur*) is /*bā̱r*/ 'outside' vs. /*bār*/ 'twelve' and /*bhār*/ 'burden', corresponding with Hindi /*bāhar*, *bārā*, *bhār*/. It has spread to other environments, however. Pandit notes final voiced aspirates alternate with murmured preceding vowel + plain voiced stop: /*vāgh*/ 'tiger' = /*vāhg*/ (= [*vā̱g*]). In a number of cases there is no H in the spelling, e.g., /*mā̱ro*/ 'my', written simply MARO. This recalls the closely related Rajasthani (Marwari) form /*mhāro*/, and Grierson's observations (*LSI*) that in some West Pahari dialects the aspiration of initial aspirates, or some of them, is *transferred to the right of the following vowel*: C*h*V > CV*h*. Further investigation of these dialects for possible murmur phenomena is in order. (In Gujarati itself, it should be noted, initial aspirated non-nasal stops are never followed by, and presumably never produce, murmured vowels. Aspirated nasals thus constitute a different category in this respect.)

Murmured vowels have also been noted in Marathi (Kelkar 1958, Lambert 1943). Marathi also has murmured/breathy *diphthongs*: /*pā̱y̱je* = *pāyhje*/ 'wants, needs'. In both Gujarati and Marathi, the murmured segments are in free variation with unmurmured vowels (or in some cases with vowel + postvocalic /*h*/), especially among educated speakers.

Whispered vowels, alluded to above, have been noted in NIA only in the Western dialects of Awadhi (Saksena 1971: 74–7); although some descriptions of the Kashmiri so-called *mātra* vowels may appear to indicate something similar ("inaudible", etc.), these are better described as lost entirely, but leaving effects on preceding consonants and vowels – e.g., palatalization, umlaut – that may make it analytically convenient still to posit them as occurring. Saksena notes that the whispered vowels of Awadhi "do not make a syllable". The same is noted (Peter Hook, personal communication) with regard to the ultrashort final vowels of Shina.

5.4.6 *Stress*

NIA languages are syllable or *mora*-timed rather than stress-timed, and although stress patterns differ from language to language, stress is generally predictable, if not always simply so. Assamese, for which Goswami (1966) demonstrates the existence of a phonemically contrastive stress (*bān'dhɒ* 'you fasten' vs. *'bāndhɒ* 'friend'; *'pise* 'he is drinking' vs. *pi'se* 'then'), seems to be an exception to this. Shackle (1976) also notes a few cases of lexically contrastive stress in Siraiki (*'itlā* 'so much' vs. *it'lā* 'informing', although stress is generally predictable). (Some, e.g. Gumperz [1958], would insist on its phonemicity, albeit limited, in Standard Hindi also, citing such pairs as *'patā/ba'tā* 'information/tell!'. It could be argued, however, that the position of stress in the second item is *morphologically* predictable, in that the stem-forming {*-ā*} of causative and denominative verbs is always stressed.)

To say stress is predictable does not mean it always falls on a particular syllable, as in Polish or Finnish. Chatterji (1926) does describe such a stress pattern (initial syllable of the phrase or breath group) for Standard Bengali, but emphasizes that this generalization does not seem to apply even to other Bengali dialects, let alone a sister language such as Oriya. Regarding the latter, Pattanayak says it is evenly stressed, a characterization sometimes also applied to Marathi (Lambert 1943); stress in these languages is in any case weak. A weak initial stress is also the dominant tendency in Sinhalese and Nepali.

For the remaining languages (Hindi, Gujarati, Punjabi, etc.), rather complicated sets of rules are necessary, involving the number of syllables, whether they are open or closed, and the nature of their vowels. A number of different formulations have been made. Those by foreigners sometimes confuse the prominence of long vowels with stress. Despite attempts (e.g., by Grierson) to formulate one overall set of rules, sometimes said to be roughly "those of Classical Latin",[7] it is clear that each language has its own peculiarities: Hindi *ga'rīb*; *nuk'sān* 'poor'; 'loss' vs. Gujarati *'garib*, *'nuksān*. Those modern analyses that do not recognize traditional vowel quantity are forced to state their stress rules in a form quite different from those that do (cf. Cardona 1965 vs. Master 1925 for

Gujarati, and various analyses of Hindi). In general, Hindi and Punjabi permit more final stresses than other NIA languages.

Regarding the alleged survival of Vedic stress position in Marathi (Turner 1916), see Chapter 7.

An interesting form of *emphatic* "stress" occurs in Bengali, Marathi, and perhaps other languages (although it is not characteristic of Hindi). It involves *geminating a medial consonant*, e.g., Marathi *ātā* 'now' > *āttā* 'now!' (Kavadi and Southworth 1965: 20). Sometimes this effects a quasi-phonological change: Bengali *bɔṛo* 'large' > *bɔḍḍo* 'enormous' (Clinton Seely, personal communication).

5.5 **Distributions**

If we compare the phonemic inventories of Sanskrit with, say, Modern Standard Hindi, we notice a few minor differences – loss of the syllabic liquids (*r̥*, *r̥̄*, *l̥*), reduction of the sibilant system from three to two (if we include borrowed items), monophthongization (incomplete in some subdialects, and, one could say, a subphonemic matter in any case) of the diphthongs /*ai*/ and /*au*/, quasiphonemic emergence of the allophones [*ṛ*] and [*ṛh*]. The differences may be greater or fewer if we compare various other NIA languages. The overall impression, however, might be one of relatively great stability, especially for the Midland group. If we look at the privileges of occurrence of the OIA and NIA sounds, however, a quite different picture emerges, which will form the subject matter of this section.

5.5.1 *General positional privileges*

Sanskrit words (or rather, words in isolation, i.e. utterances) could end in any vowel, short or long, but only in very few consonants (*p*, *t*, *ṭ*, *k*, *ḥ*, *m*, *n*, *ṁ*, rarely *l*, *ṅ*, *ṇ*). No aspirates, voiced stops, semivowels, sibilants, palatals, or -*r*, and almost no final clusters[8] were permitted. When such sounds (and clusters) occurred etymologically, they were assimilated or reduced to the sounds just listed when in final position.

NIA languages generally show no such pattern. Although a few languages (mainly Oriya and, with certain qualifications, Sindhi) permit only vowels finally (continuing and extending a pattern that became dominant in the MIA period), the majority permit a much wider range of final consonants than OIA did. Hindi for example allows all the sound types forbidden in Sanskrit: aspirates (*sāth* 'with'), voiced stops (*sab* 'all'), semivowels (*gāy* 'cow'), sibilants (*ras* 'juice'), palatals (*kuch* 'some', *lāj* 'bashfulness'), and /-*r*/ (*kar* 'do!'), as well as certain clusters (*khaṇḍ* 'piece') – the number of which is vastly increased if we consider, as we must, the borrowed Persian and Sanskrit[9] vocabulary which is the lifeblood of Modern Standard Hindi (e.g., *band* 'closed' < Pers., *kaṣṭ* 'trouble' < Skt).

An exception is Sinhalese, which, although it has in other respects departed very much from the OIA pattern, has ended up with a restricted set of permitted finals oddly similar to those of Sanskrit: vowels, the voiceless stops (minus the palatal) /*p*, *t*, *ṭ*, *k*/ (*pot* 'book'), nasals (*dæŋ* 'now'), /*l*/ (*pol* 'coconut'), along with /*s*/ (*kes* 'hair') and /*y*/ (*lamay* 'children').

Certain NIA languages besides Sindhi and Oriya have retained final vowels lost elsewhere: Kashmiri, Awadhi, Maithili, the southern dialects of Konkani, Sinhalese. This is a historical statement, and does not imply that all words in those languages end in vowels. Although it is no doubt a fact that, partly indeed because of these preservations, vowel endings are much more common than in, for example, Hindi or Punjabi, it is easy enough to find words ending in consonants in these languages (cf. the Sinhalese examples above).

In Oriya, on the other hand, in addition to the retained historical vowels, the vowel /*-ɔ*/ has been *added* to words ending in a consonant to produce the vowel-final pattern referred to – a situation reminiscent of the neighboring Dravidian Telugu (where the "euphonic" vowel is *-u*). Sindhi is somewhat problematic, because not all investigators hear the final vowels similarly added to, for example, all Perso-Arabic loanwords in that language according to Grierson (i.e. is it *āvāz* 'noise', *sarkār* 'government', or *āvāzŭ*, *sarkārŭ*?) – who remarks that they are "hardly audible" (*LSI 8.1*: 22). Suggestions that the final short vowels in Southern Konkani are later accretions, again influenced by Dravidian word phonology, are rejected by Katre (1966) on the ground that all Konkani dialects had them in the sixteenth century. The form of loans like *moṭərə* 'car' (Ghatage 1963), however, suggests such a process is somehow operative in any case. The addition of an utterance-final vowel is noticeable in some varieties of rustic speech even in the Hindi (especially Braj) area, far from any immediate Dravidian influence.

Words can *begin* with either a consonant or any vowel in both Sanskrit and NIA (in contrast with the common Dravidian pattern where vowels other than *a*-, *ā*- are preceded by consonantal glides – although this pattern occasionally shows itself in some dialectal forms of NIA). Sanskrit, however, despite its interdict on final clusters permits quite a number of *initial clusters*, even some with three consonants (*str*-, *sty*-). Many of these of course find their way into NIA in *tatsama* vocabulary, but in most NIA languages in non-borrowed vocabulary initial clusters are severely restricted. In many of them indeed the question of whether they exist at all is bound up with the treatment of semivowels and diphthongs, since what is involved is exclusively C*y*V- (or C*i*V-) and C*w*V- (or C*u*V-) sequences (as in Hindi *pyālā* [*piālā*] 'cup', *gwālā* [*goālā*] 'milkman'). A wider range of initial clusters is found in Northwestern NIA (Dardic and West Pahari dialects) and to a lesser extent also in "Lahnda", Punjabi, Sindhi, and Gujarati.

Arguments over the phonemic status of a number of individual sounds and classes of sounds hinge on their positional freedom of occurrence. Thus the aspirated nasals *mh*, *nh*, *ṇh*, *ŋh* have a stronger claim to such status in languages where they occur initially (Marathi, Konkani, Rajasthani, Braj, Kumauni, Jaunsari, Kiunthali, Mandeali, Chameali, Kalasha – along with dialectal Hindustani or "Kauravi"), than in languages where they occur only medially and/or finally (Standard Hindi, Awadhi, Bhojpuri, Chhattisgarhi, Maithili, Bundeli, Sindhi, "Lahnda"), and these in turn more than in languages where they are also rare (Nepali, Gujarati) or unstable (Bengali, Oriya). Analogous remarks apply to the aspirated liquids (*lh*, *rh*). The fact that closely related dialects (e.g., of rural and standard "Hindustani" [see Bahri 1980 and Gumperz 1955a, 1958]) differ with regard to apparent positional constraints suggests caution in drawing large conclusions from such differences – or perhaps suggests the importance of giving due attention to sociolinguistic and particularly to rural/urban dimensions in these matters.

Where alternative analysis as a cluster is not an option, restriction to non-initial positions is of course no bar to phonemic status, e.g., generally for */ṇ, ḷ, ṛ, ñ, ŋ/* in languages where they are otherwise contrastive. In certain West Pahari dialects (Kiunthali), */ṛ/* does occur initially (as it does in Pashto); in others (Kochi), */ṇ/* occurs initially. Initial */ñ-/* (alternatively analyzable as */ny-/*) is not uncommon in Kumauni. Initial *ḷ-* is found in the Sinhalese spellings of about seventy-five words, but does not represent in the modern language a sound different from */l/*.

The palatal consonants are subject to severe positional restrictions in a few languages. In Sinhalese *-cc-*, *-jj-*, *-ññ-* and in Dacca Bengali *-cc-*, *-cch-*, *-jj-*, occur mainly only medially and geminated. On the other hand the retroflex stops occur in all positions including initial position.

More diagnostic are the positional restrictions affecting the semivowels *y* and *w*. In the eastern languages, as we have seen, they are restricted to intervocalic, postconsonantal, and postvocalic positions, where they are interpretable as satellite vowels, so that their existence as phonemes is questionable. In a Central group including Hindi, Kumauni, Nepali, and Eastern Rajasthani (also Malvi), they occur initially, but only in *deictic* forms (such as demonstrative pronouns, words for 'here', 'there', etc.). Then there is a long Western belt, stretching from Sinhalese through Konkani, Marathi, Gujarati, at least some varieties of Marwari,[10] Sindhi, Punjabi, and "Lahnda" to West Pahari and Kashmiri, where */w-/* ("*v-*") occurs initially also in non-deictic words, as a full-fledged consonant. Occurrences of */y-/* are very limited except in Sinhalese and Kashmiri (and Shina, Phalura, Bashkarik, Maiyan, Torwali, etc.). In the other languages mentioned (including West Pahari and even certain Dardic languages such as Khowar,

Kalasha, and Gawarbati) such *$*y$-'s are mostly represented by /*j*-/, as in the rest of NIA. The ever-present tendency for [w-, v-] to become [b-] subtracts a number of Dardic and West Pahari dialects (Khowar, Shina, Bashkarik, Bhadrawahi, Bhalesi, Pangwali, Churahi, etc.) from the wider /*w*-/ distribution. Some Romany dialects show /*b*-/, others *v*-/.

In some accounts of certain NIA languages (including Hindi) reference is made to the non-occurrence of the aspirates in final position, or to deaspiration or weakening of the aspirates in that position. This is often a phonetic rather than a phonological statement, or if one prefers, a morphophonemic statement, in that aspiration reappears when a vowel ending is added; it is thus similar to final devoicing in, for example, German. It should be distinguished from the canonical restriction of aspirates to certain positions in the word, or of the number of aspirates permitted in a word, which is often a prosodic matter (see section 5.5.2) and characteristic only of certain languages.

The short vowels, that is /*i*, *u*, *a*/ (also analyzed as /I, U, ə/), in languages where they contrast with /*i*:, *u*:, *a*:/, do not occur finally *except* in Sindhi, Konkani, Maithili, Awadhi, and Sinhalese. (Short /-*e*, -*o*/ apparently occur finally in unstressed particles in West Pahari dialects.) *Only* the short vowels, however, occur before *geminated* consonants in Punjabi and Standard Hindi (as in the literary Prakrits). No such restriction applies in northwestern dialectical Hindi ("Kauravi", Haryanvi – again see Gumperz 1958), where any vowel may occur before geminates. According to Turner this is also true of "Lahnda", but examples are few: most words conform to the restriction. There are exceptions even in Punjabi: *gāṭṭā* 'neck, throat', alongside the regularized *gāṭā*; *gāḍḍī* 'cart', alongside the regularized *gəḍḍī* (H. *gāṛī*). Alleged exceptions involving /*ē*, *ō*/, however, (H. *ekkā* 'one-horse cart') raise the question of whether these traditionally "long" vowels are not actually short in this position. (See Turner 1967 and Učida 1977.)

5.5.2 *Cooccurrence possibilities and constraints*

As already noted, in many NIA languages *initial clusters* are restricted in *tadbhava* words to sequences of C + semivowel (Cy-, Cw-): Hindi, Nepali, Kumauni, Bhojpuri, Maithili, Rajasthani, Bengali, Assamese, Oriya. (In the last three the semivowels are customarily interpreted as vowels, sometimes even as syllabic vowels.) In some languages (Sinhalese, Maldivian, Konkani) even these sequences do not exist. Another group of languages tolerates also sequences of C + *r*-: i.e. *tr*- (Marathi, Punjabi; even Bengali, Assamese, and Oriya have *tr*- in the word for 'thirty' = B. *triʃ*); *tr*-, *dr*- (Gujarati) or *tr*-, *dr*- (Sindhi); also other C*r*- ("Lahnda", Kashmiri, Dogri, some West Pahari dialects, Shina, Phalura, and, much more plentifully, Khowar, Kalasha – and Romany). Finally, Kalasha and

Khowar have a few instances of *s* + C-, even of *s* + CC-; more than a few, if a prothetic vowel is ignored, e.g., *istri:ʒa* 'woman', *ispra:p* 'sleep, dream', *istonim* 'groan' (Morgenstierne 1973a).

Sanskrit and English loanwords add to this list of initial cluster *types* (as distinct from *examples*) only moderately (Perso-Arabic loanwords not at all): C*r*- clusters in languages that do not already have them; C*l*- clusters; *kṣ*- (often assimilated to *ch*-); but, most notably, clusters involving the sibilants as first member, i.e. *s*C-, *ś*C-, and *s*CC-. While these are *spelled* STH-, SN-, SPH-, etc. they are often, when the second member is a stop, pronounced with a prothetic vowel, e.g., /*strī*/ 'woman' = [istrī], /*sṭeʃan*/ 'station' = [*isṭeʃan*]. (The Punjabi tendency is to break up the cluster with an epenthetic vowel = [*saṭeʃan*].)

Final clusters, native or borrowed, are not allowed in some NIA languages, including Bengali, Sinhalese, Nepali, and Braj. In Gujarati and probably most varieties of Rajasthani only borrowed final clusters are found. Other languages (Hindi, Marathi, Punjabi, Kashmiri, West Pahari dialects, "Lahnda", Assamese) generally permit at least native clusters of homorganic nasal + consonant (*-nd*, *-ṇḍ*, *-ṇṭh*, *-mp*, *-ŋg*, etc.). Such clusters exist in the languages previously mentioned also (except in Gujarati, where the nasal consonant has become a nasalized vowel), but they are not final, being followed, as in the vowel-ending languages (Oriya, Sindhi), by a vowel. (In Sinhalese even these are confined to borrowed items.)

Punjabi, "Lahnda", and certain West Pahari dialects ostensibly permit final *geminates*: P. *jhakk* 'duststorm', *ṭhiṭṭh* 'bad', *rukkh* 'tree'. If these are indeed long (rather than "tense") consonants, they would seem impossible to pronounce without some kind of vocalic release, however slight, but such release can no doubt be considered nonsyllabic and the double consonants therefore still "final".

Some languages of the Dardic group (Kalasha, Khowar, Gawarbati, Phalura, Pashai, Shumashti, rarely also Shina – but not Kashmiri) permit final clusters of sibilant + stop, generally *-st* and *-ṣṭ*: Kal., Gaw. *hast*, Kho. *host*, Pash. dial. *hāst*/*hōst* 'hand' (= H. *hāth*, < Skt *hasta*); Kal., Phal., Shina dial. *aṣṭ*, Kho. *oṣṭ*, Gaw. *ōṣṭ* 'eight' (= H. *āṭh*, < Skt *aṣṭa*).

Such *-SC#* clusters are, however, amply supplied to the other languages (at least to those which permit final *-NC#*) through both Persian (*dost* 'friend') and Sanskrit (*kaṣṭ* 'trouble') loans. Unlike the situation obtaining with initial clusters, both Perso-Arabic and Sanskrit (as well as English) loans considerably augment the overall NIA inventories of final clusters, adding not only such types as *-r*C#, *-l*C#, and *-pt#*, and types involving the borrowed phones *f*, *χ*, and *z* (*-ft#*, *-χt#*, *-fs#*, *-bz#*, etc.), but more unlikely types, such as *-nm#*, -C*r#*, -C*y#*, *-gn#*,

-bd#, *-Cw#*, and even involving -CCC# and -CCCC# (*-str#*, *-ntr#*, *-gdhy#*, *-rtsy#*, etc.). Like the geminates noted earlier, many of these are impossible to pronounce without a vocalic release (or epenthetic vowel). Their status as final clusters depends on the phonological status given to that vowel, i.e. an allophone of some vowel (generally */-a/*, that is, *-ə*), or "automatic" (= no status). As such a decision is somewhat arbitrary, various descriptive accounts will be found to differ in their treatments. For languages like Bengali and Oriya, the vowel in question is fully recognized, if only because the neutral vowel has evolved phonetically to [ɔ] or even [*o*], which may be harder to ignore.

NIA languages typically have large inventories of *medial* clusters, including not only the above types but many others unknown to OIA. (There are some exceptions, e.g., Sinhalese. It should be noted also that *written tatsama* clusters are greatly simplified in Bengali *pronunciation*, according to assimilatory rules recapitulating those of Prakrit.) In some languages, e.g., Hindi, Marathi, Nepali, there seem to be almost no constraints on medial sequences of two consonants. Many of these are sequences of a special type, however: i.e. they cross morpheme boundaries. An epenthetic vowel may intervene under certain circumstances, and is counted as a syllable in traditional meters. The question therefore arises as to whether these are "true clusters" – although many modern descriptions reckon them so. (Indication of the epenthetic vowel in transliteration, however, as has been done with the name of the Janata, or "People's", Party in India = *jan-tā* – perhaps to avoid identification with the Anglicized version of the word *junta*? – results in mispronunciation by the uninitiated: i.e. most English-speaking newscasters (outside India) have pronounced the party name as [**jə'nātə*] rather than [*'jənəta*].)

There remain in any case many medial clusters that do not involve such considerations. Prominent among them are geminates, "long" consonantal segments which some descriptions (Ohala 1983) indeed opt to classify as "phonemes" in their own right. Although historical simplification of such double consonants (which were a hallmark of MIA) affected most of NIA east and south of Delhi, many NIA languages still have at least a few of them for various reasons. Sindhi is an exception, as is Garhwali (Chandrasekhar 1970). They are marginal and "conspicuously highflown" in Oriya according to Pattanayak and Das (1972). They appear to be absent from Kashmiri. Their number and frequency vary greatly in the remaining languages. In Gujarati and Marathi they are uncommon, except, for morphological reasons (also involving a morpheme boundary), *-vv-* in the former. They are most numerous in Punjabi, "Lahnda", West Pahari (where the historical change mentioned above did not operate) – and Bengali, because of *tatsama* clusters simplified in this manner. They are also frequent in Sinhalese. Standard Hindi, having undergone much influence from neighboring Punjabi and Bangaru (Haryanvi), occupies an intermediate position between these languages and Braj, where the historical simplification has largely triumphed.

NIA languages differ considerably in the *sequences of vowels* they permit, although all seem to permit them. Because of lack of any uniform criteria in the descriptive literature for distinguishing vowel sequences from diphthongs, and for dealing with semivowels, it is difficult to make detailed generalizations. It will be roughly accurate to say, however, that permitted vowel sequences increase from southwest to northeast in NIA, reaching a maximum in Assamese, where as many as five vowels (constituting three syllables) may follow one another in succession: *χuāiei* 'just having caused somebody to sleep' (Goswami 1966: 106). Elsewhere, there has been a tendency to oppose the vowel hiatus widely tolerated in Late MIA, either by merging the vowels or inserting one of the glides (*y*, *w*) between them. This process has been unable, however, to keep up with loss of medial consonants and genesis (through this and other means) of new vowel sequences.

Cooccurrence constraints may also affect segments not immediately adjacent to one another. There are notable instances of this in NIA affecting both vowels and consonants.

In the first case, one possibility is *vowel harmony*. NIA furnishes at least two clear-cut examples of this phenomenon, both involving not the adaptation of the vowel of a suffix to the vowel of the stem, as in Turkish, but the adaptation of the vowel of the stem to the vowel of a suffix, and consequent morphophonemic variants of stems. The simpler case involves Standard Bengali, in which many stems show a higher or lower alternate vowel *i*/*e*, *e*/*ā*, *o*/*ɔ*, *u*/*o*, depending upon whether a suffix with a high vowel (*i*, *u*) follows or otherwise: *kena* 'to buy'/*kini* 'I buy'; *nɔṭ* 'actor'/*noṭi* 'actress' (Dimock 1957). (In the Standard Colloquial, the conditioning vowel has dropped out of certain verbal endings, producing what now must be regarded as a partly morphologically conditioned alternation. See Chapter 9.)

The other principal case is Kashmiri. This is much more complicated, not only because the phonology in terms of which it must be stated is itself much more complex (and as noted earlier, the formulations of Grierson, Bailey, Kachru, and Zakhar'in, to name a few, also *differ* drastically), but also because the *effects* are more complicated: stems show *more than two* allomorphs in many cases, and consonantal as well as vowel changes: e.g., 'fat' = msg.nom. *v'oth*, fsg.nom. *v'əth*, mpl.nom. *veth'*, fpl.nom. *vechi* (B. Kachru 1973). Declensional differences further complicate the analysis: Kashmiri does not have an agglutinative morphology like that of Bengali. This is not the place to attempt a solution of the interrelated phonological, morphological, and morphophonemic riddles of Kashmiri, but as an example of the problem, let us take the adjective 'big'. Grierson (1911, repr. 1973) gives the following forms:

	SG		PL	
	M	F	M	F
Nom.	*boḍ*^{u}	*büḍ*^{ü}	*baḍ*^{i}	*bajĕ*
Dat.	*baḍis*	*bajĕ*	*baḍĕn*	*bajĕn*
Ag.	*baḍ*^{i}	*baji*	*baḍyau*	*bajyau*
Abl.	*baḍi*	*baji*	*baḍyau*	*bajyau*

According to his analysis the changes in the stem vowel in the masc. and fem.sg.nom. (*a* > *o*, *a* > *u*) are triggered by the final *mātra*-vowels –^{u}) and –^{ü}) respectively. Grierson admits that these vowels are "often quite inaudible . . . yet there are few words in Kashmiri the sound of which is not affected by them," and goes on to compare them with the silent final -E of English, e.g., *mat*, *mate*. Since they do not actually exist as *segments*, they are dispensed with in the transcriptions of Bailey and others. Bailey (1937) gives the following version of the same paradigm:

	SG		PL	
	M	F	M	F
Nom.	*boḍ*	*bɜḍ*	*bɜḍ*^{i}	*baji*
Dat.	*bɜḍis*	*baji*	*bɜḍen*	*bajen*
Ag.	*bɜḍi*	*baji*	*baḍyau*	*bajyau*
Abl.	*baḍi*	*baji*	*baḍyau*	*bajyau*

Without the fictional *mātra*-vowels (except for the ^{i}-matra, which is transcribed as palatalization of the preceding consonant, /'/), the stem-vowel alternations *baḍ/boḍ/bɜḍ* are inexplicable phonologically, and are reduced to morphologically or even lexically conditioned variants. (There are certain other differences in the transcriptions as well: Bailey hears a different stem-vowel in the Dative and Agentive Masculine Singular and in the Masculine Dative Plural, which might be difficult to explain in terms of vowel harmony in any case, and does not hear the difference between the Feminine Dative Singular + Nominative Plural on the one hand and Feminine Agentive + Ablative Singular on the other which is transcribed by Grierson.)

Further cases of stem-vowel change of this sort are noted by Grierson (*LSI 9.4*) for Kumauni and West Pahari dialects, increasing in number toward the west as one approaches Kashmiri. He calls it, confusingly, "*epenthesis*", but it is clear from his account that he does not mean this in the currently accepted sense of "insertion of an etymologically unjustified vowel or semivowel to ease a difficult transition." The vowel is changed, not inserted, and it is not etymologically unjustified insofar as it is conditioned by a historically present succeeding vowel. When the conditioning vowel is still present, e.g., in Churahi *khāṇā* 'to eat' > fem. *khaiṇī*, or Kumauni *mero* 'my' > pl. *myara*, it may be proper to speak of vowel harmony, but it is difficult to do so when the conditioning vowel is no longer present, e.g., in Kiunthali *bauhṇē* 'sister' (ag.sg.) > nom.sg. *bü̃hṇ* (from **būhṇī* < **baihṇī*).

Vowel harmony in any case does not exhaust the kinds of vowel conditioning in NIA. For example, in Hindi (and some other languages), a suffix with a "long" (= "peripheral") vowel added to a stem (nominal or verbal) results in the shortening (= "centralization") of the stem vowel if it is long ("peripheral"): *pīnā* 'to drink' *pilānā* 'cause to drink', *cūhā* 'rat' > *cuhiyā* 'small or female rat; mouse'. (Such considerations testify to the convenience of the traditional *long/short* analysis for certain purposes.) An apparent exception such as *gherāv* 'lock-in' (a technique employed by workers against management in a labor dispute) is a loanword from Marathi, where such a rule does not apply. Hindi purists would accordingly prefer *ghirāv*.

The rules of diphthongization (*vṛddhi*) that affect *tatsama* stems in most NIA languages when a *tatsama* suffix is added (*itihās* 'history' > *aitihāsik* 'historical', *bhugol* 'geography' > *bhaugolik* 'geographical') must be ascribed to morphological rather than phonological conditioning, applicable moreover only within the *tatsama* subsystem.

There remains to be noted the fact of prosodically conditioned distribution of *consonantal* features. This in particular affects the distribution of aspirates in some languages, most notably certain forms of Rajasthani. As described by Allen (1957b), the constraints include: (1) only one aspirate per word in Harauti, South Mewari, and some forms of Marwari; (2) voiced aspirates and /*h-*/ initial only in Harauti and Mewari of Udaipur; (3) all aspirates initial only in South Mewari. Trail (1970) notes aspirates as initial only also in Lamani. No such restrictions obtain in most of the rest of NIA (East Bengali dialects are an exception), where aspiration must therefore be reckoned as a non-prosodic feature: cf. forms like H. *chāch* 'buttermilk', *ṭheṭh* 'pure', *ḍhū̃ḍh* 'search' (which would be prohibited also in Sanskrit). Such forms are found also in at least written Marwari and Jaipuri ("Central Eastern Rajasthani") – cf. the popular name of the latter dialect, *ḍhū̃ḍhāṛī*. The situation suggests that additional careful phonetic observations, focusing on aspirates, are needed in various parts of the Rajasthani area (and perhaps the Gujarati, Bhili, and Pahari areas as well).

5.6 Areal and typological comparisons

Typologically, NIA languages can be said to be characterized by the non-universal phonological features of distinctive *retroflexion*, *aspiration*, and *nasalized vowels*, despite the fact that a few NIA languages are lacking (generally because of loss) one or more of these. (Assamese and Romany lack retroflexion, Sinhalese lacks aspiration, and Standard Marathi and Sinhalese lack nasalized vowels.)

Retroflex consonants are clearly a pan-South Asian areal feature which NIA shares with Dravidian, Munda, and also certain nearby Tibeto-Burman and Eastern Iranian languages (and Burushaski). Just as clear is the concentration of this feature (in terms of both systemic development and lexical and textual frequency) in the west and south of the subcontinent (that is, in Western and Northwestern NIA – and adjacent Eastern Iranian languages such as Pashto – and in Dravidian) and its fadeout toward the northeast. The latter makes it difficult to connect the sporadic manifestation of the feature in Southeast Asia (Vietnamese) and Indonesia (Javanese), as well as its strong development in Australian languages, with the Indian phenomenon.

It has been customary to treat the voiced and voiceless aspirate stop series as part of the same basic aspirate/nonaspirate correlation, and there are some good reasons for doing so, one being that the historical development of Indo-Aryan itself has as it were conspired to construct parallel sets. At the same time, it is clear that the voiced aspirates (and their further correlates, the aspirated nasals and liquids) are phonetically quite different (in fact at variance with some common definitions of aspiration), and this difference is responsible for the connection of the voiced and not the voiceless series (and of /*h*/ which in IA goes with the former and not the latter) with tonal and register phenomena. (In spite of these differences, the voiceless series has been capable of transmutation into the voiced series at certain points – i.e. early MIA – in the history of IA, and the two participate equally in *Grassman's Law* mandating deaspiration – in Sanskrit – when two aspirates succeed each other in a word.)

A *voiceless* aspirate/nonaspirate correlation is not uncommon among world languages, and in the NIA case is part of a larger areal configuration, involving this time not the Indian subcontinent (Dravidian lacks it), but areas (mainly Sino-Tibetan) to the north and east of it. *Voiced* aspirate stops are extremely rare, however, and Indo-Aryan is their main area of current manifestation, although they have been reconstructed for proto-languages (including Indo-European) once encompassing other areas.

Nasalized vowels are again not uncommon among world languages, but they are not characteristic of Central or Northern Eurasia, of Southwest Asia, or Southeast Asia, or indeed of Dravidian (except as a recent and restricted subphonological development in some languages, mainly Tamil and Telugu). Indeed among the neighbors of NIA they are found only in certain Tibeto-Burman and Munda languages, and Baluchi.

It remains to take note of particular phones. The retroflex affricates and sibilants found in certain NIA dialects of the extreme northwest are found also (some or all of them) in neighboring Burushaski, Nuristani languages (Kati, Waigali, Ashkun, Prasun) and Eastern Iranian languages (Pashto, Wakhi, Ishkashmi), and, further afield, in Chinese. The *ts/č* opposition characteristic of a wider group in the northwest (including Kashmiri and many West Paḥari dialects) is shared for the most part with the same languages. The same, partly allophonic, opposition in Marathi and Southern Oriya is shared with neighboring Telugu and northern Kannada dialects.

Although development of tonal and register distinctions may be concentrated in those parts of the area generally closer to non-Indo-Aryan languages having these features, it cannot be said that the development follows any adjacency principle: those NIA languages where tone developments are strongest (e.g., Punjabi) are not in immediate contact with tone languages, while those that are (e.g., Assamese, Nepali, Kashmiri) have not developed such features at all. The nearest focus of *register* distinctions lies in Southeast Asia, far from Gujarati.

Finally, the *prenasalized stops* of Sinhalese are foreign to South Asia, finding their nearest parallels in East Africa and Indonesia. The lack of aspiration and of nasalized vowels in Sinhalese, however, and the developed opposition of length in all the vowels, reflect the situation in South Dravidian.

6

Writing systems

The would-be student of Indo-Aryan is confronted by perhaps three dozen scripts that are or have been in use in the Indian area, either for Indo-Aryan languages themselves or for other languages of the area (Dravidian, Tibeto-Burman, Austroasiatic) with which he might want to examine lexical and typological relationships. It is true that, except for Perso-Arabic (used with various modifications by Urdu, Sindhi, and occasionally Punjabi, and newly by Khowar, Siraiki, and sometimes other languages), Roman (used to write Konkani since the sixteenth century, and to write a number of non-Aryan tribal languages since the nineteenth), and the peculiar script used by Maldivian (constructed out of Arabic numbers and other elements), all these scripts have a common root in the Brahmi script of the third century BC Asokan inscriptions.

6.1 **Origins of Brahmi**

The origin of the Brahmi script itself is still a matter of controversy, which can be touched upon only briefly here. Most Western scholars have assumed it to be derived from a Semitic prototype, usually North Semitic, although a few have favored South Semitic, or an unknown progenitor of them both. Precise and incontrovertible connections have not been demonstrated. It would be conceded in any case that the script had undergone considerable refinement and improvement in India, apparently at the hands of persons well-versed in phonetics. These included the systematic provision of symbols for sounds peculiar to Indian languages, the elimination of any phonetically redundant symbols (in contradistinction to what happened with the more recent adoption of the Arabic script by Urdu), and especially the provision of symbols for vowels, lacking in the early Semitic scripts.

With few exceptions, Indian scholars have held to theories of the indigenous origin of Brahmi, and generally of its high antiquity as well. In the absence of any concrete, that is, archaeological, evidence (a few alleged pre-Asokan finds that would bring it back even to the fifth century BC have been shown to be either wrongly dated or highly questionable) the latter assumption rests entirely on literary references and logical deductions. That is, it is held (by some Western as well as by most Indian scholars) that the "perfection" of the script implies a long evolution; that the subtleties of Paninean and other grammatical and phonetic analyses imply writing as a tool; that the compilation and editing of Vedic and other texts do likewise; that references – in comparatively late works, some of them foreign – to the god Brahma as the inventor of the Brahmi script imply a sacral character, and association with the ancient Vedic religion, its texts and its Brahmanical priesthood. (For a comprehensive overview see Nowotny 1967.)

The discovery in the 1920s of the Indus valley or Harappan civilization of *c*. 2500–1800 BC with its still-undeciphered script added new fuel to these speculations, and sparked a series of enthusiastic attempts to derive the Brahmi script from the Harappan. None of these has found general acceptance. For one thing, they imply decipherment of the Harappan script itself and identification of its language as a preliminary. Success in these endeavors has not been conceded either. (One of the most recent and ambitious attempts is that of Rao [1982], who claims the language is Aryan, rather than Dravidian as a number of other would-be decipherers have assumed.)

Another serious obstacle to any attempt to link the Brahmi script with the Harappan is the time-gap between the two, which may amount to 1,500 years. Although recent discoveries in Gujarat and elsewhere extending the time-span of the Harappan civilization after the destruction or decline of the Indus valley cities may narrow the gap somewhat, it still remains formidable. Despite these difficulties, it may be said that derivation of Brahmi from the Harappan script – somehow – remains the most popular view in India. It was held even by the late S. K. Chatterji. The more zealous would go further and turn the tables on all theories of foreign origin, deriving not only the Kharoṣṭhī script – a rival script current in northwest India and Central Asia from the time of Asoka until about the fourth century AD, generally conceded to be derived from Aramaic – but all West Asian and therefore all alphabetic scripts from "Proto-Brahmi" and Harappan. For a more balanced view of the whole problem, see Goyal 1979.

The contention that no archaeological evidence of writing has been found for the period between the Harappans and the Asokan edicts because writing was done only on perishable materials is of course inherently impossible to refute. It is not very tenable, however. As S.P. Gupta (1979: xxi) points out, "archeology all over the world has proved that once a script is born it can never confine itself to one medium." It is unheard of that any people having a script never use it on hard materials.

The alleged literary evidence generally involves either mistaken inferences (references to "texts", meter, phonetics, or even numbers do not necessarily imply a script) or ascription of unacceptably early dates to sources of probable post-Asokan date. As Goyal points out, it often also involves selective suppression of much clearer indications of the *non*-existence of writing in some of the very same sources – Greek writers and the Buddhist Vinaya literature, for example. (E.g., Megasthenes, the Greek ambassador to the Maurya court a quarter century before Asoka, states categorically that the Indians "have no knowledge of written letters.")

Inference of the existence of writing from the feats of textual preservation and analysis accomplished by the ancient Aryans does an injustice to the remarkable mnemonic powers developed by them. While it is true that these do not preclude the existence of writing, they render it less necessary. Particularly in the area of religious texts, both the Brahmanical and the early Buddhist traditions concur in according primal sacrality to the orally-transmitted text, not the written text. The notion of a sacred *written* text is very late in India – the seventeenth-century *Guru Granth Sahib* of the Sikhs – and appears to reflect foreign, that is, Islamic, influence. (For a different view see Bronkhorst 1982.)

Regarding the alleged necessity of writing for the grammatical and phonetic analyses of Panini and his predecessors, the opposite argument can be made, as Goyal again points out: the scientific organization of the Brahmi script implies an existing *prior* analysis, which could then be given systematic written form – possibly by a single individual or small group assigned the task. Examples are not wanting elsewhere: the Cyrillic, Armenian, Georgian, Tibetan, and Korean scripts were all consciously devised (although not necessarily, except perhaps the last, on the basis of such a thoroughgoing phonological analysis). Panini, as an inhabitant of the far northwest, knew of the existence of books and of the Greek and possibly other scripts (which incidentally would seem to exclude a date for him earlier than the fourth century B C) but not the Brahmi script, nor apparently did he make use of any script himself.

Brahmi was originally used for writing Prakrit, not Sanskrit. It was only applied to Sanskrit some four centuries later, so far as is known, and then at first only for "secular" – administrative, literary, and scientific – purposes. The sacred texts so long preserved in oral memory were, it seems, finally set down in writing – reluctantly – only at a comparatively late date. While the tradition of Panini and of the ancient phoneticians did no doubt influence the formation and refinement of the script, all this is a far cry from the notion of a sacred script devised by the Brahmanical priesthood to preserve its sacred texts.

At the Asokan stage, the Brahmi script was not completely perfected or settled. (Notions of its perfection seem to involve a projection back onto Brahmi of features belonging to later scripts.) Certain symbols, namely the long vowels Ī, Ū, AI, AU along with R̥, R̥̄, L̥ – more necessary for Sanskrit than for Prakrit – seem to be missing. Symbols are given different shapes and different orientations, even in the same inscription. Geminated consonants – a prominent feature of Prakrit – are not indicated. The great innovation of the Brahmi script, its indication of vowels other than A ([ə]) by modifications added to basic consonant symbols, is as yet far from clear or consistent. This suggests, not a long prior evolution, but a script still in the experimental stage. The absence of significant regional variation in Asokan and even later Brahmi also suggests its relative newness.

While the independent invention of writing in ancient China, Egypt, Mesopotamia, and Central America – to which should be added the Indus valley – shows that such invention is certainly possible, the Brahmi script is in a different category. Those scripts bear no resemblance to one another, but the resemblance of a number of Brahmi symbols to symbols in Western Asian scripts, particularly the North Semitic, is too close to be entirely fortuitous. (Some even resemble Roman letters, although the values are different: e.g., "E" is /*j*/, "D" is /*dh*/, "I" is /*ṇ*/, upsidedown "T" and "V" are /*n*/ and /*g*/. In spite of the fact that it would seem there are only a limited number of basic shapes to draw from, such coincidences do not embrace Chinese ideographs or Mayan hieroglyphs.) It is also noteworthy that the resemblance is there at the beginning, and becomes less and less as Brahmi evolves into the Gupta, Kutila, Nagari and other later scripts.

The crux of the matter is what is meant by "invention." Totally new, with no antecedents? Or a creative use of pre-existing elements? One of the objections to the North Semitic origin theory has been that similar symbols do not correspond phonetically. It may be pointed out that this is also true of certain symbols among the daughter scripts of Brahmi, known to be related. For example, a Gurmukhi S (ਸ) is like a Nagari M (म), a Gurmukhi DH (ਧ) is like a Nagari P (प), and a Gurmukhi M (ਮ) is like a Nagari BH (भ). A possibility that does not seem to have been considered seriously enough, however, is the use, once the decision to construct a writing system had been made (probably inspired by awareness of the existence of other such systems), of ready-made symbols that might have come within the purview of the "inventor(s)" – North Semitic, South Semitic or whatever – as graphic building blocks, as it were, without regard to the phonetic value they may have had in other languages. (Sequoia, for example, made such use of Roman letters in constructing the Cherokee syllabary.) Further symbols could be constructed as needed by analogy with these – and this seems to have been done when it came to representation of the distinctive retroflexes and aspirates of Indo-Aryan, as a comparison particularly of the former with their dental counterparts will suggest. This is indeed invention, particularly when proceeding according to a prior phonological blueprint, but it is not invention "from scratch": it draws on existing materials. It is also quite different from "adopting" a foreign script.

As a final footnote to the question of foreign connections, it should be noted that, whereas the South Semitic or Himyaritic script seems to have but a very weak claim to any influence on Brahmi, the reverse is not true. The case is persuasive that one of the genuinely original innovations of the Brahmi script, namely the indication of vowels through modifying signs attached to the consonants, was taken to South Arabia and Axum by Indian traders. Vowel symbols do not appear in the Axumite inscriptions before the third century AD, and when they do, they are similar in principle (as the vowel signs of the Ethiopic script still are) to those first worked out in Brahmi 600 years earlier. It is the signs themselves, and the principle behind them (replacing a vowel /*a*/ taken to be otherwise inherent in the unadorned consonant), that are similar. The phonetic *values* given to each sign often differ. Double consonants are not indicated in the Ethiopic script to this day, just as they were not indicated in Brahmi. (See Chatterji 1968.)

6.2 **Evolution and diversification of Brahmi**

In any case, the Brahmi script did exist, and is – if not as old as some would wish – of quite respectable antiquity. What is remarkable is that the Brahmi script has changed so much, evolving into such a multitude of mutually unintelligible forms. The differences are not superficial (like those between "Gothic" and ordinary Roman), but at least comparable to those among Roman, Greek, Cyrillic, and even Armenian. The graphemic inventories of those alphabets differ, however: in the Indian scripts they are, with minor exceptions, *theoretically the same*. Both the degree of formal difference and the underlying common principle may be seen in Tables 6.1 and 6.2.

Although such evolution may be perfectly natural, it should be noted that the Roman and Greek scripts did not undergo comparable changes over the same time-span. It must be recalled also that not only the Brahmi script but even the later Gupta script had become totally illegible to contemporary Indian scholars by the nineteenth century, and required international collaborative efforts at decipherment over several decades before success was finally attained in the 1830s.

The reasons for the difference are not hard to find. The political unity India attained under the Mauryas was not approached again until the end of the seventeenth century under Aurangzeb, some nineteen hundred years later. There was no centralized Universal Church to maintain the unity of the written word in the meantime, as there was in the West, nor one sacred written text, as in the Islamic world. The Brahmans – themselves regionally divided – maintained the

Table 6.1 *The Indian* varṇamālā *("garland of letters") in Brahmi and daughter NIA scripts*

	Brahmi	*Gurmukhi (= Punjabi)*	*Takri (Chameali)*	*Gujarati*	*Devanagari*	*Bengali (+ Assamese)*	*Oriya*	*Sinhalese*
A	𑀅	ਅ	𑚀	અ	अ अ	অ	ଅ	අ
Ā	𑀆	ਆ	𑚁	આ	आ आ	আ	ଆ	ආ
I	𑀇	ਇ	𑚂	ઇ	इ	ই	ଇ	ඉ
Ī		ਈ	𑚃	ઈ	ई	ঈ	ଈ	ඊ
U	𑀉	ਉ	𑚄	ઉ	उ	উ	ଉ	උ
Ū		ਊ	𑚅	ઊ	ऊ	ঊ	ଊ	ඌ
Ṛ				ઋ	ऋ ऋ	ঋ	ଋ	ඍ
E	𑀏	ਏ	𑚆	એ	ए	এ	ଏ	එ
AI		ਐ	𑚇	ઐ	ऐ	ঐ	ଐ	ඓ
O	𑀑	ਓ	𑚈	ઓ	ओ ओ	ও	ଓ	ඔ
AU		ਔ	𑚉	ઔ	औ औ	ঔ	ଔ	ඖ
*								
KA	𑀓	ਕ	𑚊	ક	क	ক	କ	ක

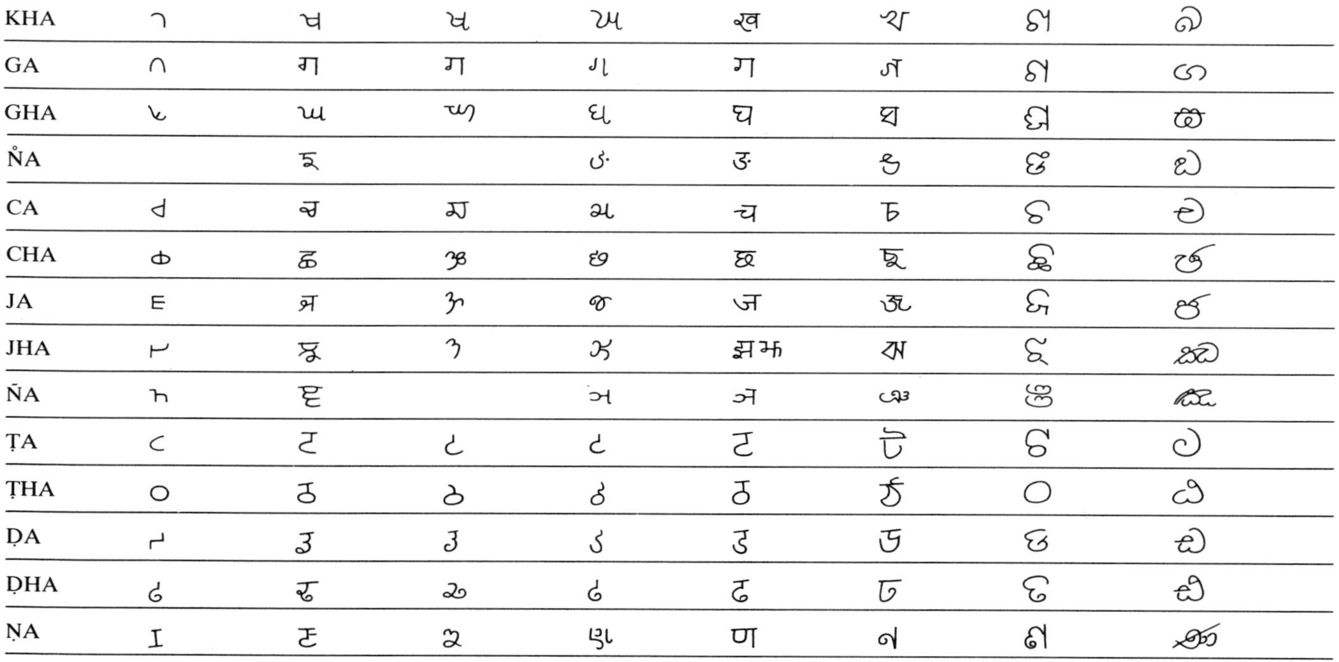
KHA
GA
GHA
ṄA
CA
CHA
JA
JHA
ÑA
ṬA
ṬHA
ḌA
ḌHA
ṆA

Table 6.1 *The Indian* varṇamālā *("garland of letters") in Brahmi and daughter NIA scripts* (continued)

	Brahmi	*Gurmukhi (= Punjabi)*	*Takri (Chameali)*	*Gujarati*	*Devanagari*	*Bengali (+ Assamese)*	*Oriya*	*Sinhalese*
TA	𑀢	ਤ	𑚙	ત	त	ত	ତ	ත
THA	𑀣	ਥ	𑚚	થ	थ	থ	ଥ	ථ
DA	𑀤	ਦ	𑚛	દ	द	দ	ଦ	ද
DHA	𑀥	ਧ	𑚜	ધ	ध	ধ	ଧ	ධ
NA	𑀦	ਨ	𑚝	ન	न	ন	ନ	න
PA	𑀧	ਪ	𑚞	પ	प	প	ପ	ප
PHA	𑀨	ਫ	𑚟	ફ	फ	ফ	ଫ	ඵ
BA	𑀩	ਬ	𑚠	બ	ब	ব	ବ	බ
BHA	𑀪	ਭ	𑚡	ભ	भ	ভ	ଭ	භ
MA	𑀫	ਮ	𑚢	મ	म	ম	ମ	ම
YA	𑀬	ਯ	𑚣	ય	य	য়	ଯ ୟ	ය
RA	𑀭	ਰ	𑚤	ર	र	র ৰ	ର	ර
LA	𑀮	ਲ	𑚥	લ	ल	ল	ଲ	ල

VA	𑀯	𐨬	𑀯	व	व	ব ৱ	ཝ	ව
ŚA	𑀰	𐨭	𑀰	श	श	শ	ཤ	ශ
ṢA	𑀱		𑀱	ष	ष	ষ	ཥ	ෂ
SA	𑀲	𐨯	𑀲	स	स	স	ས	ස
HA	𑀳	𐨱	𑀳	ह	ह	হ	ཧ	හ

* Sinhalese has additional vowel letters, representing Æ, Ǣ, E, O (vs Ē, Ō).

Table 6.2 *The modifying vowel signs* (mātrās), *exemplified with "KA"*

	Brahmi	Ethiopic*	Gurmukhi	Takri	Gujarati	Devanagari	Bengali	Oriya	Sinhalese
KĀ	𑀓𑀸	ቃ	ਕਾ	𑚊𑚭	કા	का	কা	କା	කා
KI	𑀓𑀺	ቅ kĕ	ਕਿ	𑚊𑚮	કિ	कि	কি	କି	කි
KĪ	𑀓𑀻	ቂ	ਕੀ	𑚊𑚯	કી	की	কী	କୀ	කී
KU	𑀓𑀼		ਕੁ	𑚊𑚰	કુ	कु	কু	କୁ	කු
KŪ	𑀓𑀽	ቁ	ਕੂ	𑚊𑚱	કૂ	कू	কূ	କୂ	කූ
KṚ					કૃ	कृ	কৃ	କୃ	කෘ
KĒ	𑀓𑁂	ቄ	ਕੇ	𑚊𑚲	કે	के	কে	କେ	කේ
KAI			ਕੈ	𑚊𑚳	કૈ	कै	কৈ	କୈ	කෛ
KŌ	𑀓𑁄	ቆ	ਕੋ	𑚊𑚴	કો	को	কো	କୋ	කෝ
KAU			ਕੌ	𑚊𑚵	કૌ	कौ	কৌ	କୌ	කෞ

* Ethiopic ḲA is given for comparison. (Sinhalese has additional vowel *mātrās*.)

Sanskrit language, it is true, but they wrote it, when they did so, in the various regional scripts, the triumph of Nagari in this area being quite recent. Writing was not a religious monopoly in India, nor, as has already been noted, was it regarded as particularly sacrosanct by the religious establishment, or by the population at large. It has been associated rather with commercial record-keeping. Many have been the manuscripts lost through use as kindling by villagers indifferent to the value of the written word.

Briefly and with some oversimplification, the evolution of Brahmi proceeded as follows: during the six centuries following Asoka, the script, while still essentially "Brahmi", developed subtypes conventionally called "Northern" and "Southern". The "Northern" type led to the Gupta script of the fourth and fifth centuries AD, which in turn developed in the northwest into the Sharda (*śāradā*) script, in the center into the Kuṭila ("bent") script of the sixth to tenth centuries (also called *siddhamātr̥ka*, "provided with complete vowel signs"), out of which developed at various points the Early Nāgarī and Proto-Bengali scripts. (The Tibetan script was deliberately developed from a Gupta prototype in the seventh century.) A popular variant of Sharda (which became and remained until recently the script of Kashmiri Brahmans) was the Laṇḍā script of the Hindu mercantile and clerical communities of Punjab and Sind, out of which Angad, the second Sikh Guru, is said to have fashioned the Gurmukhī script in the sixteenth century, making various improvements. Another set of variants of the Sharda type, widely used until recently in small states of the western Himalayas (now Himachal Pradesh and Jammu), goes by the general name of Ṭākrī. It too was the basis of improved scripts, such as Ḍogrī and Camĕāḷī. (Other subvarieties, documented by the *LSI*, include the Jaunsārī, Sirmaurī, Kōcī, Kuḷuī, and Maṇḍeāḷī scripts.) Early Nagari was the basis of Modern Nāgarī, the Kaithī script (from Kayath < Kayastha, the name of a caste of writers and clerks) current until recently in Bihar and eastern UP, the related Gujarātī script (adopted in Gujarat only in the nineteenth century), and the Modi script invented for Marathi by a minister of Shivaji in the seventeenth century. Proto-Bengali gave birth to the Maithili, Modern Bengali (settled in the seventeenth century: Assamese is a nineteenth-century variant), and Oriya scripts, as well as the Manipuri and Newari scripts for two Tibeto-Burman languages.

The "Southern" current of development led to the closely related Kannada and Telugu scripts on the one hand and through the Pallava script to the Grantha, Malayalam, and Tamil scripts on the other. (The first was used for writing Sanskrit in the Tamil country.) A third line of development led to the Sinhalese script. There were also several developmental dead ends, known only from inscriptions and other documents. The Pallava script was also the ultimate source of various Southeast Asian scripts: Mon-Burmese, Cambodian (Khmer), Thai, Lao, Javanese, Balinese, and scripts used in Celebes and Sumatra. They do not concern us here, except that a script of Khmer type is or was used to write the Chakma "dialect" of Bengali, spoken in the hills back of Chittagong.

All the scripts in the "Southern" group are characterized by rounded letters in contrast with the more angular shapes of the "Northern" group. It is said this evolved from the use of palm leaves as writing materials with a metal stylus, which would tear the leaves unless it avoided lines parallel to their veins. This is also true of the Oriya script, which therefore bears a superficial resemblance to a "Southern" script and looks very different from the Bengali. A close examination of the forms of the letters, along with the principles of *conjunct* formation (see below) will reveal its true affinities, however. The Nagari-derived Modi script is also of cursive type, possibly for the same reason.

The terms "Northern" and "Southern" are somewhat misleading. The "Northern" Nagari script makes its debut not in the north, but in Maharashtra under the Rashtrakutas in the eighth century. The early post-Asokan scripts from the area of Gujarat, on the other hand, are of "Southern" type.

What may have been the high water mark of script differentiation unfortunately coincided with the introduction of printing, which had a tendency to accentuate and freeze many minor differences, for example between the Telugu and Kannada scripts. There seems to have even been a scramble for distinctive type faces, springing from a widespread feeling in the region that "language"-status (in sociolinguistic Sense B [see Chapter 2]) demands a distinctive script.

By mid-twentieth century, however, the tide seemed to have turned, economic rationalism and still newer technologies partly outweighing budding chauvinisms at least in this sphere. Carried to one form of logical conclusion, this would dictate the use of the Nagari script (or Perso-Arabic in Pakistan). Nagari (literally the "city" or "metropolitan" script < *nagar* 'city', also called Devanagari) is the official script of Hindi, Marathi, and Nepali, and of the new (or revived) literatures in Rajasthani, Dogri, Maithili (and other Bihari dialects), and Pahari dialects (e.g., Kumauni) when written. The Maithili, Kaithi, Landa, Newari, Modi, Dogri, Chameali (and other Takri-type) scripts have all largely given way to it.

Manipuri has adopted the Bengali script, however, and Kashmiri the Perso-Arabic, while emigrant Sindhis in India after considering the Nagari have recently opted to retain the Perso-Arabic in order to maintain the unity of the language. Nagari shows no sign of displacing the native scripts of Bengali, Assamese, Oriya, Gujarati, Punjabi (Gurmukhi), Sinhalese, or Maldivian. It is even less likely to displace the scripts of non-Indo-Aryan languages in the area (with the exception of the recent-vintage Roman orthographies of certain tribal languages).

The continued vitality of the old prejudice is shown by the attempt of S. V. Raykar in 1965 to buttress the claim to full *language* status for Konkani through the invention of a distinctive script,[1] which has so far not found acceptance. (Meanwhile the language is written in the Roman, Nagari, Kannada and Malayalam scripts.) Other major languages employing the Nagari script, such as Marathi and Nepali, manage through writing conventions to look as different as possible from Hindi: e.g., postpositions are written attached to the preceding noun in the former languages, generally as separate words in Hindi;[2] consonant clusters of a certain type are treated differently in Hindi and Nepali (see below). The Tamil and Telugu scripts have been pressed into service for the Indo-Aryan Saurashtra language centered at Madurai (which also has or had its own script, said to be of the Modi type). Should the need arise to look at the past, which for the philologist can hardly be avoided, materials in the Kaithi, Sharda, Takri, Old Nagari, Maithili, Modi, and other scripts may be confronted. (It may be noted in passing, and should be apparent from the samples in Table 6.1, that the Nagari script is one that has gone furthest from Brahmi, at least among the "Northern" scripts. The other scripts, particularly Gurmukhi, often retain letters more similar to those of Brahmi.)

6.3 **Legacy of Brahmi**

All of this variation presents – to the investigator – difficulties of merely a mechanical sort, a burden on the visual memory. Brahmi had certain peculiar characteristics, however, bequeathed to its successors in India and elsewhere, which sometimes present other difficulties. These included the inherent vowel, the attached sign for other vowels, and the compound ligature – the so-called *conjunct* character – for consonant clusters (necessitated by the inherent vowel assumption). We shall consider problems connected with these in a moment.

A further problematic legacy of Brahmi is the close connection it soon developed with the phonology (and phonetics) of Sanskrit as worked out by the phoneticians of ancient India (even though, as noted earlier, Brahmi was probably originally employed for writing Prakrit). The sophistication of their analysis, and the resulting precision of the alphabet as adapted for Sanskrit, coupled with the prestige of Sanskrit itself, imparted to the system a special rigidity. It was a question of the *system* and its underlying categories, not of the form of letters as such.

The very order of the alphabet, as learnt and recited by every schoolchild, is systematic and logical, unlike the arbitrary order of European and Semitic alphabets. First come the vowels: the basic vowels, long and short, A, Ā, I, Ī, U, Ū, followed by the syllabic liquids and (according to traditional analysis) diphthongs R̥, R̥̄, L̥, Ē, AI, Ō, AU, and finally the vowel-like nasal Ṁ and whisper Ḥ. (Excessive symmetrizing zeal sometimes adds a long L̥̄, which never occurs in any real word, to match the rare L̥.) Then come the series of stop consonants with their manner modifications (aspirate, voiced, nasal) in an order following that of the passage of the breath out of the body, i.e. starting with the back of the mouth and of the tongue, ending with the lips: K, KH, G, GH, Ṅ; C, CH, J, JH, Ñ; Ṭ, ṬH, Ḍ, ḌH, Ṇ; T, TH, D, DH, N; P, PH, B, BH, M. Then the semivowels and liquids (which behave similarly for certain purposes in Sanskrit) in the same order: Y, R, L, W ("V"); finally, the sibilants Ś, Ṣ, S (again theoretically back to front: dorsopalatal, retracted-apical, dental apical) and the isolated voiced H.[3]

There was a bit of phonetic overkill in the system: the sound represented by Ḥ (in Nagari, :) could be taken as an allophone of S, for example, and the palatal and velar nasals Ñ, Ṅ were largely predictable. Concerning Ṁ (also transliterated Ṃ), there is some controversy as to whether it represents a homorganic nasal consonant (therefore an alternative way of writing the specific nasal consonants as the first element in clusters), a nasalized vowel, a nasalized semivowel, or all of these according to context; there are actually two terms involved, *anusvāra* and *anunāṣika*, and, eventually, two symbols as well (in Nagari, a dot over a vowel, and the same with a half-moon under it: ं , ँ) but their usage and mutual delimitation is not consistent in different ancient authorities and seems also to have changed with time (for a more detailed discussion, see Allen 1953: 39–46). An intervocalic lateral flap allophone [Ḷ] of Ḍ is described for some Vedic texts and represented by a special symbol (Nagari ळ).

In any case, according to some, all possible sounds had already been described and provided for in this system, as Sanskrit was the original and perfect language. Hence it was difficult to provide for or even to conceive of *other* sounds, unknown to the phoneticians of Sanskrit. (It should be noted that the phoneticians did describe certain other sounds *qua* sounds – bilabial fricatives, for instance – which, being either sporadic or completely predictable, never were represented in the writing system.)

Inevitably, sounds alien to Sanskrit do exist in the NIA and other languages using Brahmi-derived scripts. Sometimes they have been ignored in writing; sometimes they have been provided for in a way typical of many scripts (e.g., Roman, Arabic), that is, via *diacritics* or *ligatures* (and ignored in the recitation of the alphabet); rarely have new symbols been invented. The favorite diacritic in the "Northern" scripts is the *subscript dot* (̣), e.g., Hindi ज = /J/, ज़ = /Z/. It is used for the near-allophonic intervocalic flaps [ṛ, ṛh] corresponding to /ḍ, ḍh/ in Hindi, Bengali, and Oriya[4] (Ḍ = ड, ড, ଡ; Ṛ = ड़, ড়, ଡ଼); in the Gurmukhi script used for Punjabi it has a special symbol (ੜ); in Marathi and Gujarati it is ignored; in Nagari as used for Rajasthani (Marwari) ड represents Ṛ, while a special symbol ॾ is used for Ḍ (= [ɖ]). The widespread NIA /ḷ/ is represented by local versions of the Vedic ळ in Marathi, Gujarati (ળ), Sinhalese (ළ), and Oriya (ଳ); by a subscript dot (under Nagari L) in Rajasthani; and commonly ignored in Punjabi (Gurmukhi). In some Rajasthani and Braj manuscripts a dot distinguishes /V/ (व़) from /B/ (व).

Additional vowels are less easily accommodated in this fashion, because vowels have to be written in *mātrā*-form (already a kind of diacritic) to begin with when not syllable-initial. Subscript dots are preempted by the consonants to which the vowel-*mātrās* are attached, and superscript dots by nasalization. The *mātrās* can of course be modified in other ways, or additional ones invented; it is partly a question of how strong the need is. Long vs. short Ē/E and Ō/O are distinguished only in the "southern" scripts, i.e. in NIA only in the Sinhalese: the long vowels are represented by the addition of diacritics (a "flag") to the symbols for the short vowels (Si. එ/ඒ; ඔ/ඕ). (The Dravidian scripts follow a similar strategy.) The new Sinhalese vowels *æ*, *ǣ* are also represented by "flags" added to A: අ, ඇ, ඈ = a/æ/ǣ, but the Bengali /æ/ is either written YĀ or not differentiated from E. In Marathi, the vowels /æ, ɔ/, found only in English loanwords, are indicated by the diacritic ˇ over Nagari A, Ā: अ‍ॅ, ऑ. Gujarati *e*/*ɛ* and *o*/*ɔ* are not distinguished in writing.

Where there is no new contrast, and a graphemic segment merely reflects a changed phonetic value, generally no change is made. Thus the symbol originally representing the Sanskrit diphthong /*ai*/ represents /*æ*/ in Hindi, /*oi*/ in Bengali.

An extreme example of this or perhaps better an example of a radical revalorization is the indication of *tones* in Punjabi by the graphemes that originally stood for voiced aspirate stops, aspirate nasals and liquids (all lacking in the modern language), and /*h*/: briefly (omitting certain qualifications), the High Tone is indicated by a following aspirate letter or letter-combination of these categories and the Low Tone by a preceding one. It accordingly took scholars some time to clarify what was actually going on, phonologically and phonetically, since *as written*, Punjabi looks much like any other NIA language.

As noted earlier (Chapter 5), the Gujarati murmured vowels are partly represented by the postvocalic H to which they are most simply related historically (*ba̤r* written BĀHAR), but unrepresented when their origin is more complicated (*ma̤ro*[5] written MĀRO not *MĀHRO). Not all exotic sounds have had to be represented in the Brahmi-type scripts, either because they occur in unwritten dialects or because the languages in question use non-Brahmi scripts.[6] An exception are the implosives, found in Rajasthani as well as Sindhi. In the former they are usually represented in Nagari by the signs for the ordinary unaspirate voiced stops (B/ ब, D/ ड़, etc.; the ordinary voiced stops themselves are uncommon and are represented in other ways (dotted letters, etc.). The peculiar Sinhalese prenasalized stops are basically written as ligatures (see below) – too complex to reproduce here, as are the aspirated nasals and liquids of Marathi and other languages.

In all of the above an essentially etymological principle prevails: the new sound is represented by the sign of its historical antecedent. This causes no problems once the phonetic key is held – unless phonological splits, mergers, or reassignments are also involved. Thus the grapheme *A/অ (as the "inherent vowel" often not written at all [see below]) may represent, in Bengali, not only its phonetic evolute [ɔ], but also /o/ with which it has merged in some positions, or zero, and to the non-native speaker it is not always clear which.

The writing systems have also had difficulty in recognizing the *loss* of distinctions that were part of the system, except perhaps as a mispronunciation. Thus only the Gurmukhi script recognizes Indo-Aryan phonological history (see Chapter 7) by reducing the sibilant symbols to a single S – although this necessitates the use of a dotted symbol for Persian and English loanwords with /ʃ/ in Modern Punjabi. Other scripts continue to use three sibilant symbols (at least in *tatsama* words) even though they may pronounce all of them the same (e.g., as [ʃ] in Bengali, [s] in Oriya, or [χ] in Assamese).

Nor has the inventory of vowel symbols been reduced in languages (Bengali, Gujarati, Marathi, etc.) where distinctions such as *i/ī* and *u/ū* have been lost. Preservation of such distinctions in writing forces even native speakers to resort to dictionaries for correct spellings.

Sanskrit was not the only indigenous phonology to cast its shadow over subsequent orthographies. According to Pandit (1954), the spelling of Old Gujarati was influenced by that of literary Apabhramsa, which was based on the Midland variety of that late stage of MIA – a variety with only one sibilant, /s/. Since Old Gujarati like Modern Gujarati presumably had two, /s, ʃ/, the old spelling failed to represent all its phonemes.

The assumption by the Brahmi script of an inherent vowel /a/ in each consonant required a method for eliminating it when two or more consonants formed a cluster (or when an utterance ended in even one consonant) – situations untypical of Prakrit, for which the script was first used, but common enough in Sanskrit. (In Prakrit all words ended in a vowel, and clusters were mainly geminates, which were not represented in early Brahmi, and homorganic nasal + consonant, which could be represented by *anusvāra*.) Although a vowelless consonant could be represented by using the sign known as *virāma*, this was used mainly for final consonants, and the main device used to adapt the script to write Sanskrit clusters was the conjunct character. This typically (in the more common case of clusters of only two consonants) consisted of half of one character (either the first in the case of horizontal conjuncts or the second in the case of vertical conjuncts) attached to a narrowed version of the whole of another character, e.g., in Nagari S (स्) + T(a) (त) = ST(a) (स्त); K (क) + L(a) (ल) = KL(a) (क्ल). There were also, however, a number of special conjuncts, resembling neither of their ostensible component letters (e.g., KṢ, JÑ), or not simply derivable from them, and special forms of letters (notably R, Ś) used only in conjuncts. This cumbersome system (but less cumbersome for handwriting than for printing) has been inherited by all daughter scripts except the Tamil, where the *virāma* principle has prevailed. It is very much attenuated in the Gurmukhi script, where there remain only special signs for aspirates (not pronounced as such in Punjabi [see above]), R, and two equivalents of *anusvāra* (called *tippi* and *bindi*) for homorganic nasal consonants – plus a special sign (*addak* = ˇ) analogous to the Arabic *shaddah* (ّ) for geminates.

The inherent A is not pronounced under two different sets of circumstances in NIA. In the first it was absent originally: in *tatsama* vocabulary with clusters in Sanskrit (H. *vyakti* 'person', *strī* 'woman'), in borrowed vocabulary (Perso-Arabic and English) with clusters in the original languages (H. < Pers. *dost* 'friend', H. < Eng. *sṭeʃan* 'railroad station'), and in a few *tadbhava* words with preserved clusters (H. *pyār* 'love'). In the second, it has been lost in the later NIA period, e.g., finally in languages like Hindi and Punjabi (H. *ghās~~a~~* 'grass'), between morphemes in many instances (H. *kar~~a~~-nā* 'to do'), and even in *tatsama compounds* (H. < Skt *sah~~a~~-yog* 'cooperation').

Orthographic conventions differ with regard to these cases. Except for Gurmukhi and its relatives, the various Neo-Brahmi scripts used in NIA represent *tatsama* clusters (however they may be *pronounced*, e.g., in Bengali), inherited *tadbhava* clusters, and morpheme-*final* Perso-Arabic clusters through conjuncts. (Increasingly in print, especially journalistic print, perhaps basically because of the limitations of typewriters, horizontal conjuncts are replacing vertical ones, e.g., Nagari KLa is क्ल rather than क्ल, and the *virāma* device – called *halant* in Hindi – is used where this is not feasible, e.g. TTa is ट्ट rather than ट्ट.)

On the other hand, consonant combinations, particularly across morpheme boundaries, resulting from loss of **a* – or other short vowel – in NIA are generally not written with conjuncts in most NIA languages. (They are so written in Nepali, however: H. *kar-nā* करना 'to do', B. *kor-bo* করব 'I shall do', but N. *gar-nu*

गर्नु 'to do'.) Some view these new combinations as pseudo-clusters. At any rate they are clusters of a different class; the recently lost vowel is for some purposes psychologically still present: it is counted as a syllable in traditional meters, and even (lightly) pronounced in many styles of singing. (See Ohala 1983: 138–9 for further qualifications.)

This is also true of a lost *final* vowel: the *virāma* device is generally not used (and reserved for hypercorrect representation of *tatsama* with original consonant endings, e.g., H. < Skt *vidyut* 'lightning, electricity' = विद्युत्, but commonly simply विद्युत). Another type of cluster not represented as such (i.e. where neither a conjunct nor *virāma* is used) is found in Arabic loans (through Persian) of the type *matlab* 'meaning', *maʃhūr* 'famous', particularly numerous in colloquial Hindi; here the vowel was not lost in NIA, but already deleted according to the rules of Arabic morphology.

Ohala (1983: 117–54) has shown that it is not necessary, at least for Hindi, to indicate the deletion of $*a$ in such cases. It is *automatic* according to general *phonological rules* (which moreover are continuing to evolve), internalized by the native speaker, making a simpler basic orthography possible. Whether such rules can be worked out for other NIA languages (e.g., whether the Nepali orthography is required by Nepali phonology, or needlessly complex) remains to be seen. It may well be that the possibility of such rules makes the Neo-Brahmi scripts better suited to most NIA languages than to Sanskrit, and it is mainly the layer of Sanskrit loanwords that makes the complex system of conjuncts necessary.

Assumption of an inherent vowel together with the *mātrā* system of vowel signs (which essentially substitute other vowels for the inherent vowel) has another consequence, deriving from the fact that these presuppose consonants. When a word (or a syllable) *begins with a vowel* the latter has to be written some other way. This is normally through use of a complete set of "full" vowel characters (although long/short pairs are obviously related, the former generally being an elaboration of the latter). A more economical solution would be to use a neutral vowel "carrier", in the manner of Arabic *alif*, with the modifying vowel-*mātrās* in usual fashion. The logical choice for such a carrier would be the character used for the inherent vowel (normally short A) when initial, i.e. A, Ā, I, Ī, U, Ū, E would be अ, आ, अि, अी, अु, अू, अे (in Nagari) instead of अ, आ, इ, ई, उ, ऊ, ए. So far this solution has been tried primarily in Marathi, in the so-called Savarkar script, and has not prevailed even there, although "increasingly used in magazines and text books" (Berntsen and Nimbkar 1975b: 13). The Gurmukhi script shows a similar tendency, however, in that it employs what are essentially *three* vowel carriers (perhaps not coincidentally corresponding to the three long vowel signs of the Arabic script, although used differently), with the regular *mātrā* signs (and certain other economizing conventions) rather than a set of syllable-initial vowel signs, i.e. A, Ā, I, Ī, E, U, Ū, O = ਅ, ਆ, ਇ, ਈ, ਏ, ਉ, ਊ, ਓ.

6.4 Perso-Arabic script for NIA languages

Unlike Brahmi, the Perso-Arabic script was not designed for IA languages and requires some modification to fit them. Due to the fact that diacritics (dots, etc.) are already an integral part of the script, representation of additional sounds is fairly easily accomplished, however, at least as far as consonants are concerned, through the use of additional or different diacritics – perhaps more easily than with Brahmi. Since the script is neutral with regard to the presence or absence of a short vowel, rather than implying it as with Brahmi, the way is open for the use of simple letter combinations as well (e.g., cons. + H for aspirates in Urdu). Different languages do not use the same devices, however. Although the standardized Kashmiri orthography follows the conventions of Urdu where possible (wisely, since Urdu is the main written language in Kashmir) – as does that of Punjabi when written in Perso-Arabic, the differences between Urdu and Sindhi are significant. (See especially the retroflexes, aspirates, and K in Table 6.3 below.)

As noted earlier (Chapter 5, note 1), redundant Arabic graphemes (with no attempt at distinctive articulation) are preserved in the spelling of Arabic loanwords in most languages using the Perso-Arabic script, just as redundant Neo-Brahmi letters are preserved in the spelling of Sanskrit loanwords in most languages using Neo-Brahmi scripts – although there are more such letters in Perso-Arabic. Attempts to simplify the orthographies by spelling words as they sound (i.e. using a single T, S, and Z for all *t*'s, *s*'s, and *z*'s) have occasionally been made, but have not met with general acceptance, since the Arabic language is as sacrosanct for Muslims as Sanskrit is for Hindus.

Vowels are always a problem for languages other than Arabic using the Arabic script, particularly when a language has many vowels. Short vowels are usually not represented at all. There is ambiguity in representation of long vowels also, since the few available symbols are made to do multiple duty. Although (in Urdu) final /*ē*, *ai*/ have been distinguished from final /*ī*/ (ی) by a special device (ے), they are not distinguished from each other, nor are any of the three distinguished word-internally. One symbol also represents *ū*, *ō*, *au*. These can be disambiguated through the use of diacritics, but normally these are not used. In the official (post-1950) Kashmiri version of Perso-Arabic (cf. Handoo 1973), representation has somehow been found (mainly via an elaborate system of diacritics) for all of the many vowels of that language. (According to Peter Hook's

Table 6.3 *NIA Consonants in Perso-Arabic script: Urdu vs. Sindhi*

	Urdu	*Sindhi*		*Urdu*	*Sindhi*
p	پ	پ	*ǰh*	جھ	جه
t	ت	ت	*gh*	گھ	گه
ṭ	ٹ	ٽ			
č	چ	چ	*ɓ*		ٻ
k	ک	ڪ	*ɗ*		ڏ
			ʄ		ڄ
b	ب	ب	*ɠ*		ڳ
d	د	د	*m*	م	م
ḍ	ڈ	ڊ	*n*	ن	ن
ǰ	ج	ج	*ṇ*		ڻ
g	گ	گ	*ñ*		ڃ
			ŋ		ڱ
ph	پھ	ڦ			
th	تھ	ٿ	*y*	ی	ي
ṭh	ٹھ	ٺ	*r*	ر	ر
čh	چھ	ڇ	*ṛ*	ڑ	ڙ
kh	کھ	ک	*l*	ل	ل
			v	و	و
bh	بھ	ڀ			
dh	دھ	ڌ	*s*	س	س
ḍh	ڈھ	ڍ	*h*	ہ	ھ

Note: This does not include all of the letters of the Perso-Arabic alphabet as used in Urdu and Sindhi, or in the proper order. Other letters are found only in Perso-Arabic loanwords. The vowel signs are also omitted.

impressions, and from what I can discern from neo-Kashmiri materials in the University of Chicago Library, these do seem to be commonly used when the language is written today.)

The Maldivian script, called Tana or Thaana, although written from right to left and employing certain Arabic diacritics and numerals as the basis of some of its signs, is a completely original invention (inventor unknown) rather than in any sense a modification of the Arabic script. According to De Silva (1969), Tana is phonologically quite efficient, "perhaps the most scientific alphabet in South Asia."

6.5 **The Roman script for NIA languages**

Although the Roman script has long been the basis of more or less standard systems of *transliteration* of Indian languages, and has been advocated for general use on various grounds by the late J. R. Firth and S. K. Chatterji (1960: 304–15), it has been seriously employed only for one language, Konkani. (It might be noted in passing, however, that several anthologies of Kashmiri poetry have been published using the Roman script.) In contrast with the transliteration systems of the Orientalists and also with Portuguese, its immediate model (but like the systems devised by Firth and Chatterji), the Roman orthography devised for Konkani in the sixteenth century eschews diacritical marks. Retroflexes are indicated by doubling the consonant (*/māḷo/* 'floor' = mallo), final nasal vowels by V + m (as partly in Portuguese): */pitā̃/* 'I drink' = pitam. This necessitates the use of a hyphen to indicate geminates (*/māllo/* 'beaten' = mal-lo, */kāḷḷo/* 'took' = kal-llo, and of a double -mm to indicate final */-m/*. (Examples are from Pereira 1973.) As can be seen from the above examples, there is no indication of vowel quantity. A characteristic mark of Roman Konkani is the use of the letter x to indicate a hush sibilant */ʃ/*, as in Portuguese: Barhdexi, Saxtti = */barhdeʃi, saʃṭi/* (names of Goan Konkani dialects). Aspirates are written as C + h.

7

Historical phonology

7.1 **Introduction**

The philological importance of Indo-Aryan has already been alluded to at the beginning of this book: the long recorded history and extensive differentiation of the group offer historical linguists a unique opportunity to practice their craft. Although there is still much to be done, they have taken advantage of that opportunity; as a result, a good deal is known about both the historical phonology and the historical morphology of Indo-Aryan. The former is essential for understanding the latter, and ultimately the great typological changes undergone by Indo-Aryan. Its generally accepted fundamentals accordingly need to be included in a handbook of this type, even though many details that a book devoted exclusively to the subject would need to cover have to be glossed over.

The materials that make this knowledge possible are not ideal. They are incompletely representative in regional terms (a complaint conceivable only in the presence of so many records), unreliable (as semi-artificial literary languages) as direct testimonials to contemporary speech, and basic phonological correspondences are overlaid by waves of mutual borrowing, particularly from and into prestige languages, both spoken and written, and above all from (and into) Sanskrit.

The extensive augmentation of the lexicon with Sanskrit at all subsequent stages of Indo-Aryan (but particularly in New Indo-Aryan) has not, however, managed to obscure the essentials of the phonological evolution of the inherited element. Unlike the mutual borrowings among the regional languages, which require a bit more effort, the Sanskrit element is generally readily identifiable. Its main effect is to make it more difficult, by driving out many inherited words (particularly from the standard languages), to provide illustrative lists of phonologically equivalent words in the various languages.

(The other main source of lexical suppletion in New Indo-Aryan, namely Persian, has a similar effect for some languages, as already noted in Chapter 4.

The Persian element – and of course particularly the Perso-*Arabic* element – is also generally readily identifiable, although the close kinship of Iranian and Indo-Aryan occasionally provides some superficially similar results: e.g., in Hindi, Pers. lw. *band* 'closed', native Indo-Aryan *bandh-* 'tie(d)'; Pers. lw. *bacca* 'child', native Indo-Aryan *bāchā* 'calf'. Borrowing from Iranian becomes a delicate matter primarily on the northwest frontier of Aryandom, where geographical contiguity as well as linguistic relationship is a factor.)

Indo-Aryan historical phonology can be presented most conveniently by dealing first with what might be called its main or "focal" line of development. This is usually divided into a Middle Indo-Aryan phase (with several subphases) and a Common New Indo-Aryan phase. Then we shall go backward and look, first at languages that do not share some of the Common New Indo-Aryan developments, then at languages that do not share some of the Middle Indo-Aryan developments. We may then proceed to look at (mainly later) developments peculiar to specific languages or language groups.

It again must be stressed that this history is that of the inherited element, not of the borrowed element, albeit Indo-Aryan, insofar as the two can be separated. In the case of the *tatsama* or borrowed Sanskrit element it generally though not always can be, but separation of *later Indo-Aryan* borrowings from the strictly inherited element is one of the delectabilia of Indo-Aryan philology. Borrowed elements also have a history, unless they are very recent – even borrowed Sanskrit elements. Hence the category of *semi-tatsamas*. That history can be revealing, confirming as it often does certain general tendencies operative throughout Indo-Aryan development. Nevertheless it is imperative that it be carefully distinguished from that of the inherited element, except where particular strands of the two histories have merged: that is, where material is borrowed early enough to undergo the same later developments as inherited material. This, of course, is one of the principal methods of determining the date of such borrowings.

A couple of examples may make such abstractions clearer. Marathi words containing *ch* (such as *chāp* 'stamp', *chātī* 'chest', *chabilā/chabēlā* 'pretty') must be loanwords from a Midland language (i.e. Hindi) during the later NIA period, since all earlier *ch*'s became *s* (or *ś*) in Marathi. In Sinhalese, both MIA *c* and MIA *ch* regularly become *s*, but there are a number of words in which an intervocalic original *c* behaves like *j*; that is, it shows up as *d* rather than *s*: Skt *prācina* 'eastern' = Si. *pädum* (vs. Skt *marica* 'pepper' > Si. *miris*). Geiger (1938: 50–2) concludes that this is due to the migration into Ceylon of a group of speakers whose MIA dialect had voiced all single intervocalic voiceless stops (VÇV > VÇV) – a widespread MIA development (see below). For them *-c-* had become *-j-*, and this habit of theirs came to infect many (in fact, most) intervocalic *c*'s – prior, however, to the development that changed all *j*'s, whether original or < **c*, to *d*. As a third example, we may take the Greek loanword "drachma", which shows up in Sanskrit (via a conservative Northwestern Prakrit dialect preserving initial clusters with *r*) as *dramma-*. It was early enough to participate in subsequent changes (see below), simplifying the initial cluster (> ordinary Prakrit *damma*), then reducing the medial geminate with lengthening of the preceding vowel, and thus giving Hindi *dām* ('a small coin'; > 'price'), exactly like a native word such as *drākṣā-* 'grape' > *dakkhā* > *dākh*. This contrasts with a "semi-*tatsama*" such as *bharam* 'illusion' (<Skt *bhrama-*), where the C*r*- cluster is treated quite differently.

"Focal" may not be the best term, but it is difficult to come up with a better one: "mainstream", perhaps? "Central" will not do, as this term has a more specific reference in Indo-Aryan linguistics (usually to the language of the *midland*, i.e. to that chiefly represented by present-day Hindi and its dialects, sometimes with the addition of Gujarati). Although that group is involved, so is the Eastern group (Bengali–Assamese–Oriya), and in many respects also the Southern group (Marathi–Konkani); in short, everything except the Northwestern group and Sinhalese, and even these are affected by some of the developments. In that many of the phenomena in question show increasing intensity and earlier development down the Ganges valley, "Gangetic" would be a tempting term, were it not for the fact that many of the developments are equally characteristic of Marathi. It might simply be said that the developments in question represent the "typical" pattern of Indo-Aryan phonological evolution – an elastic concept. Deviations from it are "peripheral", generally both in a geographical and in a historical sense.

No attempt will be made here to deal systematically with the relation of Old Indo-Aryan to Indo-Iranian or Indo-European phonology. Interested readers might begin with Burrow 1955 and Bloch 1965.

At the risk of some repetition of material already alluded to in Chapters 5 and 6, it will, however, be necessary to take a closer look at the phonology of Old Indo-Aryan itself, since that will be the effective starting point for our comparisons. For practical purposes, that means OIA as represented by Sanskrit and especially by Vedic Sanskrit, although it should be kept in mind that there must have been spoken dialects of OIA other than those represented by these literary languages, and some features of later Indo-Aryan undoubtedly go back to them.[1] Such dialectal differences may have been slight, but occasionally significant for later developments. It must also be remembered that later Sanskrit is host to numerous contemporary Prakritic and non-Indo-Aryan loanwords, which cannot be taken as indicative of original OIA phonology.

7.2 Review of OIA phonology

Old Indo-Aryan had the following *consonant* system:

1. *Five stop articulations*, voiceless and voiced: *p/b*, *t/d*, *ṭ/ḍ*, *c/j*, *k/g*. Of these, the retroflex *ṭ*, *ḍ* are uncommon in early Sanskrit and occur mostly under special conditions, namely:

a. after the retroflex sibilant *ṣ* (*aṣṭā* 'eight') or its lost voiced counterpart **ẓ* (*nīḍa-* 'nest' < **nīẓḍa*, cf. Polish *gniazdo*);

b. as a morphophonemic substitute for root-final *ch*, *ṣ*, *ś*, *j*, *h* finally, in compounds, and before certain inflections beginning with consonants:

√PRACH 'ask'	>	*aprāṭ* (3sg. aorist, Vedic)
ṣaṣ- 'six'	>	*ṣaṭ* (nom.)
		ṣaḍbhis (instr.)
√DVIṢ 'hate'	>	*advēṭ* (3sg. imperfect)
viś- 'habitation'	>	*viṭ* (nom. sg.)
samraj- 'emperor'	>	*samrāṭ* (nom. sg.)

c. possibly after a lost (on Indo-European evidence) **r̥* (*kaṭu-* 'bitter, sharp-tasting' ~ Lith. *kartús* (supposedly ~ √KR̥T 'cut', MIA and later forms of which show no retroflex; Dravidian lw. according to Burrow), *gaṇḍa-* 'goiter' < *gr̥nda-* according to Morgenstierne); after an existing *r̥*, it should be noted, Sanskrit *t remains t*: *kr̥tá* 'done';

d. (rarely) *before* a lost *r*: the only sure case, and that by contamination, seems to be the post-Vedic (but Paninean) root √ḌI (>*ḍayatē*, Vedic √DI > *diyati*) and its derivatives (*uḍḍayana-*'flying up') – supposedly by contamination with √DRU 'to run'; other examples, e.g., *āṇḍa-* 'egg' (~OSlav. *jeⁿdro*), *daṇḍa* 'stick' (~Gk. *dendron*), *caṇḍa-* 'fierce' (~Vedic *candra* 'bright'), *paṭṭa-* 'slab, tablet' (~Vedic *pattra-* 'wing/feather' > 'leaf') are disputed or speculative: the first seems more likely because of conservative NIA forms like Kalasha *ōṇḍrak* and "Lahnda" *āṇḍṛā*; there is no such support for *daṇḍa-* according to Turner; *khēṭa-* 'village' (Mahabharata), if indeed from *kṣētra-* 'field', would be a MIA form;

e. practically never initially in the older language.

Alternatively, *ṭ/ḍ* are found in loanwords, or at any rate newer words of uncertain origin, both of which become increasingly numerous in the post-Vedic literature from the epics (*Mahābhārata–Rāmāyaṇa*[2]) onward, in environments other than those above, including initially: *tāḍa-* 'blow' (*Atharva Veda*), *kuṭumba-* 'household' (*Chāndogya Upaniṣad*, seventh century BC), *kaṭāha-* 'saucepan with handles, wok' (*Mahābhārata*), *aṭavī-* 'forest' (*Rāmāyaṇa*), *ṭanka-* 'spade, hoe, chisel' (*Rāmāyaṇa*), *jaḍa-* 'stupid; cold' (*Manu*, second century), *biḍāla-* 'cat' (*Manu*), *aṭṭa-* 'tower' (Kālidāsa, fifth century), *ḍimbha-* 'newborn child' (Kālidāsa), *ḍambara-* 'sonority' (*Harṣacarita*, seventh century), *ḍōmba-* 'man of low caste living by singing and music' (*Kathāsaritsāgara*, eleventh century), *capēṭā-* 'slap' (*Kathāsaritsāgara*), *ṭakkarā-* 'blow on the head' (*Rājataranginī*, twelfth century). It should be noted, however, that the majority of pan-Indo-Aryan etyma involving initial *ṭ-*, *ḍ-* go back to forms not found in Sanskrit literature of any period, or frequently even in Prakrit, possibly because of their popular or technical character.

Although less restricted, the segments *c*, *j* are unlike the other stops in several respects: unlike the others (even *ṭ*, *ḍ*) they do not replace each other as voiceless and voiced equivalents in euphonic combination with following voiceless and voiced segments, and they cannot occur finally. They revert instead to *-k*, *-g*, their (pre-Aryan) etymological sources, and participate in these relations in that guise. A few instances of *-j*, however, become instead *-ṭ/-ḍ* as noted above. Chatterji (1926) as well as Allen (1953) interpret the statements of the ancient phoneticians to mean that these segments were at the beginning pure palatal stops (i.e. something between [k^y, g^y] and [t^y, d^y]), acquiring their later affricated pronunciation first in the east, according to Chatterji.

The segment *b* is infrequent in Old Indo-Aryan (although not as rare as in Indo-European), many of its occurrences being secondary (due to Grassmann's law of dissimilation of aspirates: √BHI 'fear' > 3sg. pres. *bibhēti*, √BHR̥ 'carry' > 3sg. pres. *bibharti*, and prior to OIA itself, √BANDH < *BHANDH 'bind', √BUDH < *BHAUDH 'wake', etc.) or in loanwords (*bila* 'hole', *bilva* 'wood-apple'). The etymology (and Indo-European vs. borrowed character) of many common words with *b* is disputed: *bala-* 'strength', *bāla-* 'young', *bindu-* 'drop', *bija-* 'seed'.

2. *Two aspirate series* (voiced and voiceless) corresponding to these: *ph/bh*, *th/dh*, *ṭh/ḍh*, *ch/jh*, *kh/gh*. Interestingly enough, it is the typologically marked *voiced* series that is by far the more common (except for *jh*, and also *gh*, since it has often evolved into *h*). The most frequent aspirate overall is *bh*; the least frequent initially is *th*, for which there are few if any good cases, but the sound is well-established in medial position because of its use in verbal inflection (*-tha* is the 2nd person sg. Perfect Active ending as well as the 2nd person pl. Present Active ending, and *-th-* also appears in most 2nd person dual endings, both Active and Middle) as well as in certain ordinals (*caturtha* 'fourth') and in some common adverbs (*atha* 'then', *kathaṁ* 'how, why', *tathā* 'in that way') and nouns (*gāthā* 'song', *pr̥thivī* 'earth', *śapatha-* 'curse').

The honor of the rarest aspirate overall goes easily to *jh*, represented by only one word in the *Rig Veda* and, to quote Whitney (1950 [1889]: 16), occurring "hardly half-a-dozen times in the whole older language [and] where found, it is either onomatopoetic or of anomalous or non-Indo-European origin." According to Whitney again (who made a count), *ph* and *ḍh* are tied for second place.

Although *ch* is more frequent, both *ch* and *jh* at this stage have the character of barely established units pulled in, as it were, to complete the symmetry of the system, *ch* as a development of the sequence **sk^*, and *jh* mainly through onomatopoeia. Both have the peculiarity of occurring medially only in geminated form, *-cch-*, *-jjh-*.

The retroflex aspirates *ṭh*, *ḍh* share the restricted character of their unaspirated counterparts. The former exists almost exclusively in the cluster *-ṣṭh-* in the older language (including the superlative ending *-iṣṭha*, which gives it a relative textual if not lexical frequency); the words *kaṇṭha-* 'throat' (*Śatapatha-Brāhmaṇa*), *pīṭha-* 'stool' (*Gṛhya-Sūtra*), *kaṭhina-* (Suśruta) 'hard, stiff', *maṭha-* 'ascetic's hut' (*Mahābhārata*) are thought or known to be of non-Aryan origin, while the roots √PAṬH 'read' and √LUṬH 'roll' and their derivatives are considered Prakritisms. The voiced *ḍh* is produced by the combination of suffixes with initial dentals (e.g., the personal endings *-ti*, *-te*, *-thas*, *-thās*, *-tha*, *-ta*, *-tam*, *-tu*, *-tām*, *-dhi*, *-dhve-*, *-dhvam*, passive participle *-tá*, infinitive *-tum*, etc.) with the final *-h* of a certain class of roots:

√	+*-tum* (Inf.)	+*-ta* (Ppl.)
RUH 'rise'	*roḍhum*	*rūḍha-*
SAH 'prevail'	*sōḍhum*	*sāḍha-*
VAH 'carry'	*voḍhum*	*ūḍha-*

There are no initial occurrences of *ṭh-* or of *ḍh-* until a late period.

3. *Five nasals* corresponding to the five stop positions are described by the traditional grammarians, namely *m*, *n*, *ṇ*, *ñ*, *ŋ* (the last usually transcribed *ṅ*, by Whitney *ṅ*). Only three of these (*m*, *n*, *ṇ*) really contrast functionally (*kāma* 'love', *kanā* 'girl', *kāṇa* 'one-eyed'), and only two (*m* and *n*) can occur initially. The units *ñ* and *ŋ*, the palatal and velar nasals, are essentially to be found only preceding stops of the same classes (*ñc*, *ñch*, *ñj*, *ñjh*, *ŋk*, *ŋkh*, *ŋg*, *ŋgh*), or in the case of *ñ*, also *following* such stops (*jñ*, *cñ*) in a few words.

Since the sequence *-jm-* also occurs, albeit rarely (Vedic *ōjman-* 'vigor'), a marginal case could be made for the phonematicity of *ñ* on that basis. A marginal case could also be made for *ŋ* on the basis of the fact that it can stand alone (or geminated) finally (and thus contrast with *m*, *n*), as an obligatory abbreviation of the cluster *ŋk*, mainly in nom. sg. masc. forms of adjectival derivatives of the root √ANC: *pratyañc* 'opposite', nom. sg. *pratyaŋ* (before a following vowel *pratyaŋŋ*). It can also stand alone as a combinatorial substitute for *k* (often itself a substitute for *c*) before *m*, *n*: *vāŋmaya* 'consisting of speech' (*vāc*), 'rhetorical'; *r̥ŋmaya* 'consisting of verses of praise' (*r̥c*).

The OIA retroflex *ṇ* is considerably more frequent than its non-nasal stop counterparts. Most often it results from the operation of a rule changing *n* to *ṇ*, with certain qualifications (a vowel, nasal, or semivowel must immediately follow, and a dental, retroflex, or palatal must not intervene) after a preceding *r*, *r̥* or *ṣ* anywhere in the word: voc. sg. *brahman* (no vowel follows, although *r* does precede at some distance), but instr. *brahmaṇā*. This leaves *ṇ* in contrast with *n* "segmentally" as it were, although perhaps not "prosodically". Other *ṇ*'s, however, came into the language through loanwords, particularly in the sequence *ṇḍ* (*tuṇḍa-* 'beak', *kaṇḍu-* 'the itch').

Attempts to relate some intervocalic *ṇ*'s to "swallowed" *r̥* or *r* are disputed as was the case with *ṭ*, *ḍ* above: e.g., *guṇa-* 'thread' from **gr̥-ṇa* '*twisted, intertwined'; *koṇa-* 'corner' from **kaurna-* ~ ?Gk. *kyrtos* 'curved, bent' (Burrow and others claim a Dravidian origin). More promising[3] are cases involving a swallowed IE **l*: *kāṇa-* 'one-eyed' from **qol-nos* ~ Old Irish *coll*; *kuṇi-* 'having a withered arm' ~ Gk *kyllos* 'crippled'; *pāṇi-* '(palm of) hand' from **pālni-* ~ Lat. *palma* (forms with *r* do occur in Nuristani and in Kalasha). There are rival Dravidian etymologies for the first two cases but Mayrhofer finds them unconvincing.

4. There was *another nasal*, not part of the five-fold scheme, the so-called *anusvāra* (lit. "after-sound"), here represented by *ṁ*. Its exact nature is in dispute: a nasalization of the vowel, a nasalized semivowel following the vowel? Whatever it was, it was not a stop, yet it counted as a consonant in determining the weight of a syllable metrically.

5. OIA as represented by Sanskrit had a typologically unusual (and some would say, unstable) set of *three sibilants*, plain, palatal, and retroflex: *s*, *ś*, *ṣ*.

6. There were *no voiced fricatives* except possibly *v*, which is traditionally classed as a semivowel – and with very good reason, as its interaction morphophonemically with *u* is basic to the system. There was, however, a voiced *h*, described by some as a "glottal buzz" and put in a class by itself. Its closest relation in the

system is to *gh*, from which it partly developed. (Its other principal source at this period was Indo-Iranian **ʒ'h* [or **z'h*] < *IE *ǵh*, the aspirated voiced palatal.)

There was also a *voiceless* "h", called *visarga* ("emission") and traditionally represented by *ḥ*. It was not an independent phoneme but an allophone of *s* finally – and, inconveniently, also of *r*.

7. There were traditionally *four semivowels*, with which were classed, for morphophonemic reasons, the liquids: *y*, *r*, *l*, *v*. That is, as *y* and *v* were the non-syllabics corresponding to *i*, *u*, so were *r*, *l* in relation to *r̥*, *l̥* (see below).

There is a good deal of confusion between *r* and *l* in Sanskrit, resulting in doublets sometimes differentiated semantically, sometimes not. This is because Classical Sanskrit, itself based mainly on a Central dialect that preserved a distinction between *r* and *l*, was influenced by the prestige of Vedic, based on a Northwestern dialect that had only *r*, and, to a much lesser extent, also by an Eastern dialect that presumably had only *l*.

Vedic also had the retroflex laterals *-ḷ-*, *-ḷh-*. They were not part of the semivowel system but rather intervocalic allophones of *ḍ*, *ḍh*, although represented in some manuscripts by special symbols.

8. The above consonants could be combined in the following *initial clusters*: *ps-, py-, pr-, pl-, br-, tm-, ts-, ty-, tr-, try-, tv-, dy-, dr-, dv-, dvy-, cy-, jñ-, jy-, jv-, kṣ-, kr-, kl-, kv-, gr-, gl-, bhr-, dhy-, dhr-, dhv-, ghr-, mr-, ml-, sk-, skh-, st-, sty-, str-, sth-, sn-, sp-, sph-, sm-, sy-, sr-, sv-, śc-, śm-, śy-, śr-, śv-, hr-, hv-, vy-, vr-.*

9. *Medially*, almost all the above groups could occur, and in addition *-pt-, -ptr-, -pn-, -pp-, -pph-, -psy-, -bj-, -bd-, -bdh-, -bb-, -tk-, -tkr-, -tkv-, -tkṣ-, -tkh-, -tt-, -ttn-, -ttr-, -ttv-, -tth-, -tn-, -tp, -tpr-, -tpl-, -tph-, -tsn-, -tsy-, -tsv-, -dg-, -dgr-, -dgh-, -dd-, -ddy-, -ddr-, -ddh-, -ddhm-, -ddhv-, -dn-, -db-, -dbr-, -dbh-, -dm-, -ṭṭ-, -ṭṭh-, -ḍḍ-, -ḍḍh-, -ḍy-, -ḍr-, -ḍv-, -cc-, -cch-, -cchy-, -cchr-, -cñ-, -jj-, -jjy-, -jjv-, -jjh-, -jm-, -jr-, -kk-, -kṇ-, -kt-, -ktr-, -ktv-, -kth-, -kn-, -km-, -ky-, -kṣṇ-, -kṣṇy-, -kṣm-, -kṣy-, -gg-, -gj-, -gdh-, -gdhr-, -gn-, -gny-, -gm-, -gry-, -thn-, -thy-, -dhn-, -dhm-, -khy-, -ghn-, -ghm-, -mn-, -mp-, -mpr-, -mph-, -mb-, -mbh-, -mm-, -my-, -nt-, -nty-, -ntr-, -nth-, -nd-, -nddh-, -ndr-, -ndh-, -ndhy-, -ndhr-, -nn-, -nm-, -ny-, -nv-, -ṇṭ-, -ṇṭh-, -ṇḍ-, -ṇḍy-, -ṇḍr-, -ṇḍv-, -ṇḍh-, -ṇṇ-, -ṇm-, -ṇy-, -ṇv-, -ŋk-, -ŋkt-, ŋkr-, -ŋkṣ-, -ŋkṣy-, -ŋkh-, -ŋg-, -ŋgh-, -yy-, -rk-, -rkh-, -rg-, -rgy-, -rgr-, -rgh-, -rghy-, -rŋg-, -rc-, -rch-, -rj-, -rjy-, -rjh-, -rḍhy-, -rṇ-, -rṇy-, -rt-, -rtt-, -rttr-, -rtm-, -rty-, -rtr-, -rts-, -rth-, -rd-, -rddh-, -rdr-, -rdv-, -rdh-, -rdhm-, -rdhr-, -rdhv-, -rn-, -rp-, -rp-, -rb-, -rbh-, -rm-, -rmy-, -ry-, -ry-, -rl-, -rv-, -rs-, -rsv-, -rṣ-, -rṣṭy-, -rṣṭr-, -rṣṇ-, -rṣm-, -rṣy-, -rh-, -lk-, -lg-, -ld-, -lp-, -lph-, -lb-, -lm-, -ly-, -ll-, -lv-, -lh-, -vv-, -ṣk-,*

-ṣkr-, *-ṣkv-*, *-ṣṭ-*, *-ṣṭy-*, *-ṣṭr-*, *-ṣṭv-*, *-ṣṭh-*, *-ṣṭhy-*, *-ṣṇ-*, *-ṣp-*, *-ṣpy-*, *-ṣph-*, *-ṣm-*, *-ṣmy-*, *-ṣy-*, *-ṣv-*, *-hṇ-*, *-hn-*, *-hm-*, *-hy-*, *-hi-*. (In addition, *anusvāra* [*ṁ*] and *visarga* [*ḥ*] could occur followed by various consonants in compounds.)

The majority of these involve morpheme boundaries "-" (as do also many medial instances of those in the previous group), which are as a rule very clear in Sanskrit. (The main exceptions are *r* + C: *mārga-* 'road', *varṣa-* 'rain', *tarku-* 'spindle', *dīrgha-* 'long', etc., and combinations of homorganic nasal + stop, NC: *danta-* 'tooth', *candra* 'moon', *ambara* 'circumference', *aṅga* 'limb', etc.) Of these in turn a good many are due to two common affixes: the past passive participle suffix *-ta*/*-na* (√LIP 'smear' > *lip-ta*, √MUC 'release' > *muk-ta*, √LABH 'obtain' > *lab-dha*, √BHUJ 'bend' > *bhug-na*) and the verbal prefix *ud-* 'up' (*ud-bhavati* 'comes up', *ud-ghāṭayati* 'opens up', *ut-kūrdati* 'jumps up', *ut-khanati* 'digs up', *ut-kvathati* 'boils up', *ut-patati* 'flies up', etc.).

Although the second list contains some geminates, geminates are not very typical of OIA. The rules of euphonic combination (*sandhi*) do produce a number of geminates across morpheme boundaries – again, most often involving the same two affixes mentioned above (√MAD + *-ta* = *mat-ta*, √BUDH + *-ta* = *bud-dha*; √BHID + *-na* = *bhin-na-*, *-ud-* + √DYUT = *ud-dyōta-*, *ud-* + √CAR = *uc-carati*). Gemination also appears to have an emphatic function (still noticeable in India) in a few adverbs: *ittham* 'thus!'. The optional gemination of any consonant after *r* (*karta*/*kartta*) may perhaps belong here, in the sense of deliberately "distinct" speech. Gemination appears in onomatopoeia: √HIKK 'hiccup'. Aside from these, however, and a few referring to body parts likely to be subject, according to Turner, to irregularities due to taboo (*vṛkka* 'kidneys', *majjan* 'marrow') – and, of course, *-cch-*, *-jjh-* which occur no other way – for the most part there are no stems involving internal geminates in Sanskrit except for plant, animal, and tribal names of obscure or definitely non-Aryan origin, mainly showing up in the later literature and especially in the medieval lexicons, medical treatises, etc. Such forms as *kukkura* 'dog' (in the fifth-century drama *Mṛcchakaṭikā*) following earlier *kurkura* (*Atharva-Veda*) must be regarded as Prakritisms. Judging by the *CDIAL*, the vast majority of common IA etyma involving geminate stems do not occur in Sanskrit literature at all. (That is to say, neither the geminate itself, as reconstructable from NIA and/or citable from Prakrit, occurs in Sanskrit nor any stem containing a dissimilar cluster that might be anterior to it.)

10. *Finally*, Sanskrit permitted no clusters (except in a handful of root-forms, mainly confined to the *Veda*, involving *r* + C: aorists *vark* and *avart*, imperfect *amārṭ*, nom. sgs. *ūrk*, *suhārt*), and only a limited number of single consonants: *p*,

t, *ṭ*, *k*, *m*, (*ṁ*), *n*, (*ṇ*, *ŋ*, *l*,) *ḥ*. Clusters that would occur were reduced to the first member, which in turn was assimilated to these.

The *vowel* system of Old Indo-Aryan was fairly simple on the surface, but there were hidden complexities underlying it:

1. There were three short vowels *a*, *i*, *u*, three long vowels corresponding to them *ā*, *ī*, *ū*, and seven additional vocalic segments *ē*, *ō*, *āi*, *āu*, *r̥*, *r̥̄*, *l̥*.

a. *i*, *u*, *r̥*, *l̥* were the syllabic equivalents of the semivowels *y*, *v*, *r*, *l* respectively; *a* was in another category, purely vowel (in a sense the only one) without such equivalence; it corresponded, however, to Late Indo-European (i.e. Greek) **e*, **o* as well as **a*.

b. *ē* and *ō*, although phonetically purely monophthongal, were considered diphthongs along with *āi*, *āu*, and with some reason: before other vowels they resolved, under the rules of euphonic combination (via their ancestral forms **ai* and **au*, differing from *āi*, *āu* in the length of the first element) into *ay*, *av*; (*āi*, *āu* similarly became *āy*, *āv*); by the same rules *ē*, *ō* were *produced* by juxtaposition of independent *-a* + *i-* or *-a* + *u-*. (Most post-Whitney Sanskritists write *ai*, *au* for *āi*, *āu*, since the two do not contrast as such in the language; Whitney himself, but not Turner, writes *e*, *o* for *ē*, *ō*, since there are no contrasting short vowels of this caliber in Sanskrit; while the convenience of these practices is understandable, they make some of the euphonic rules less transparent.)

2. Basically OIA (or at any rate, Sanskrit as codified by Panini) did not tolerate hiatus between vowels, with only a handful of exceptions. Otherwise, wherever a situation arose where vowels would succeed each other, hiatus was avoided by: (a) converting any element capable of it (i.e. including components of diphthongs or etymological diphthongs [see above]) into its corresponding semivowel; (b) merging the two vowels into one; or (c) dropping one of them. (Vedic rules are slightly different.)

3. OIA also had an accentual system, allegedly based on musical pitch. The main or "raised" (*udātta*) tone of a word could fall on any syllable. Its placement was not predictable phonologically, although it often was morphologically. It was indeed often a part particularly of the derivational morphology, distinguishing otherwise homophonous forms by its placement (e.g., agent nouns, masculine and accented on the suffix, from neuter nouns denoting an object or action, accented on the root: *brahmán-* 'one who prays', *bráhman-* 'prayer'; or cf. *priyé* 'dear' mas. loc. sg. vs. *príye* fem. voc. sg.).

All authorities, on the basis of the descriptions of the ancient Indian phoneticians, insist on the "pitch" rather than "stress" character of the accent. It is noted that it had no effect on meter or on syllable reduction. That is, neither was an unaccented syllable necessarily reduced (see below) nor did the presence of the accent save a syllable from being swallowed in external sandhi: *ná* 'not' + *tú* 'but' + *ēvám* 'thus' = *ná tvēvám* 'but not thus'; *rā́jā* 'king' + *ā́sīt* 'was' = *rā́jā"sīt* '(the) king was'. (However, a stress accent, which often typically also involves a change in pitch, need not entail reduction of unstressed syllables as in English or Russian. A stress *accent* should be distinguished from stress *timing*.)

Some authorities hold that the so-called musical phase, in which unaccented syllables were not in danger of reduction, was preceded by a stress phase in which that did happen (Burrow 1955), and also succeeded, at least in some areas, by a stress phase (Pischel 1981 [1900], Turner 1975 [1916]). In any case, Vedic Sanskrit does not seem to have been *tonal* in the sense that Chinese or even Modern Punjabi are tonal; that is to say, it did not use *contrasting* tones (since there was really only one tone[4]) to distinguish lexically between roots.

The important point for our purposes here is that the Vedic accent was frequently on a different syllable than in the Latin-like system, based on quantity, that later took over, and it played a role in the grammar. Authorities differ as to how long the old pitch accent maintained itself (i.e. even in the speech of the educated). Did it entirely disappear after Panini, fourth century BC (Bloch)? Or did it survive him by a few centuries (Coulson)? Was it dead by the time of Patanjali (second century BC), or was it certainly alive in his time (Burrow)?

Although attention to the Vedic accent is vital from the standpoint of comparative Indo-European linguistics, its importance for Sanskrit itself may be judged by the fact that many modern grammars of the Classical language, where for many forms it is unknown in any case, find it possible to ignore it entirely. It is marked only in Vedic texts, and the data is reduced further by the fact that verbs in main clauses were not accented. One might legitimately extrapolate to analogous forms, but most Sanskritists scrupulously avoid doing this, marking the accent only when the actual word is so attested in a Vedic text.

4. Closely related to the accentual system, however, and overlapping the semi-vowel-vowel equivalence system (*saṁprasāraṇa*) alluded to above,[5] there was another set of morphophonemic relations among the vowels themselves, built upon the old Indo-European system of three quantitative grades of the basic vowel (**e* = OIA *a*): *normal*, *reduced*, and *strengthened*. In Sanskrit in combination with the system of semi-vowels and "diphthongs" it resulted in the set of relations known as *guṇa* and *vr̥ddhi* shown in Table 7.1.

Table 7.1 *Vowel grades in OIA*

Reduced ("zero")	*Normal* (*guṇa*)	*Strengthened* (*vr̥ddhi*)
-,*a*, *ā*	*a*, *ā*	*ā*
i, *ī*	*ē* (**ai*)	*āi*
u, *ū*	*ō* (**au*)	*āu*
r̥	*ar*	*ār*
l̥	*al*	(*āl*)

A sample of the effects of this system on OIA morphology is illustrated in Table 7.2.

The traditional Indian system, still widely used, takes the reduced rather than the normal (*guṇa*) grade as basic, and derives the others through two successive processes of strengthening. Modern comparative linguists would start with the *guṇa* grade for several reasons, by no means all of them comparative. First of all, the reduced and *vr̥ddhi* grades are derivable most simply by dropping the key vowel *a* (either as such or as a component of the "diphthongs" *ē*/**ai*, *ō*/**au*) from the *guṇa* forms in the first case and lengthening it in the second. (Where the result of dropping the *a* would be unpronounceable, as in **bhktá*, it is kept.) Second, the same process produces, in combination with *saṁprasāraṇa* and regular consonantal alternations, such forms as *uktá*, ppl. of √VAC 'speak' and *iṣṭá*, ppl of √YAJ 'sacrifice' (*vac* – *a* = *vc* = *uc* > *uk*/*Ç*). These are not normally considered part of the *guṇa* system because it cannot predict *va*, *ya*, *ra* (vs. *ō*/*av*, *ē*/*ay*, *ar*) starting from *i*, *u*, *r̥*. In reverse, both are handled equally well.

The system would be tighter still if it could be said that the *guṇa*-grade root bears the accent, but this is by no means always the case; many factors have disturbed such a simple relationship, even in verbal conjugation, where its remnants are most apparent. See Table 7.2 below. It may at least be said, however, that reduced-grade roots are *un*accented (even if all unaccented roots are not reduced), which is helpful in explaining forms such as those in the first column of Table 7.2, especially past participles.

The *vr̥ddhi* grade was at first less regular in its application, but it is this grade which is greatly elaborated in its use in later Sanskrit, being applied regularly to the first syllable of words in connection with the use of certain very productive secondary suffixes, an application which is very much alive in the *tatsama* portion of the vocabulary of all NIA languages today: *itihāsa* 'history' + *-ika* = *aitihāsika* 'historical', *bhūmi* 'earth, ground' + *-a*, *-ya* = *bhauma*, *bhaumya* 'terrestrial'.

There is much more to be said concerning the OIA phonological system,

Table 7.2 *Effects of vowel grade system on OIA morphology*

Reduced	*Guṇa*	*Vr̥ddhi*
ápaptat 'fell' (Aor.)	*pátati* 'falls'	*papā́ta* 'fell'
jagmé 'went' (Mid. Pt.)	*gamíṣyati* 'will go'	*jagā́ma* 'went'
bhaktá 'shared'	*bhájate* 'shares'	*babhā́ja* 'shared'
kr̥tá 'done'	*karṓti* 'does'	*cakā́ra* 'did'
jitá 'conquered'	*jētum* 'to conquer' (*jáyate* 'conquers')	*ájāiṣīt* 'conquered' (Aor.)
rugṇá 'broken'	*rokṣyati* 'will break'	*árāukṣīt* 'broke' (")
śrutá 'heard' (ppl)	*śrotum* 'to hear'	*áśrāuṣīt* 'heard' (")
	śravya 'hearable'	*suśrāva* 'heard'

particularly with regard to its rules of euphonic combination and other morphophonemic alternations, but it is hoped that the above account will be enough to enable the non-specialist reader to follow the ensuing developments with better understanding. (For further details, consult the standard grammars and the vast specialized literature on the subject.) For our purposes here, its salient features may be summarized as follows:

1. OIA had numerous initial and medial clusters of unlike consonants, but very few consonants that could occur finally.
2. Its inventory of sounds was very similar to that of some of the NIA languages, but some of them were much more restricted in occurrence, in terms both of position and frequency.
3. It had a very complicated system of morphophonemics, involving historically conditioned alternations, vowel grades, and shifting accentuation, all interacting with phonologically conditioned alternations; the single morpheme *vac* 'speak', which is not untypical, had for example the following allomorphs as a result of these: *vac*, *vak*, *vāc*, *vāk*, *vāg*, *vāŋ*, *voc*, *vag*, *uc*, *ūc*, *uk*.
4. Despite the action of some of these forces across morpheme boundaries, the latter remained relatively transparent.

7.3 MIA or "Prakritic" developments[6]

The following is not meant to substitute for a full account of Middle Indo-Aryan phonology, which is a field in itself. The interested reader is referred to authorities such as Pischel, Geiger, Bloch, Woolner, Sen, Chatterji, Tagare, Katre, Burrow, and Turner, along with more recent work such as that of Elizarenkova and Junghare. Since a basic understanding of the MIA developments is essential for understanding the evolution of New Indo-Aryan, however, a brief outline of them must be given here.

Greater dialectal differentiation had taken place in MIA than in OIA, and much of this is represented in the MIA records. There are naturally still important gaps, to say nothing of distortions, in those records, inscriptional as well as literary. In the earliest, namely the Asokan inscriptions of the third century BC, the all-important Central dialect group is not represented: those in its area are of Eastern dialect type. The Central group at the Early substage is probably more or less represented by Pali, however, and at a slightly later point (first century AD) by one of the dialects ("Old Sauraseni") in Asvaghoṣa's Buddhist drama. At the Second substage, the stylization and artificiality of the Literary Prakrits has already been noted, and we still miss a Northwestern representative in this set, possibly by accidental non-survival of its records. Even there, we do have at the beginning Kushana and other inscriptions, the Kharoshthi Dhammapada, and the Niya administrative documents. At the Late or Apabhramsa substage it is the Central group that is represented at the expense of the others, except in Sri Lanka. All in all, combined with fragments of descriptions of still other dialects by medieval grammarians, it is a remarkable record, even if incomplete.

The mainstream (Central–Eastern + Southern) developments of the Middle Indian stage, although they generally involved nothing unexpected, greatly transformed the phonological heritage of OIA. The changes typically involved the *distributions* of sounds rather than the *inventory* of sounds, but the latter was also affected.

(In what follows, for convenience of reference only and with no pretension of scientifically ordered rigor, the MIA phonological developments will be assigned a "reference number", **#MIA-n**. The common developments characteristic of NIA will likewise be labeled **#NIA-n** – both with the understanding that such developments may have occurred earlier in some IA dialects, later in others, but that **#NIA-n** developments follow and presuppose **#MIA-n** developments. Other cataloguing labels will also be used; they will be defined in the proper place. NB All bold-faced paragraph numberings are part of the subcataloguing system. E.g., **#MIA-8** below refers to reduction and assimilation of medial clusters; [#MIA-8b](**3**) refers to a particular assimilation.)

First of all, there were phonemic *losses*:

#MIA-1. The vocalic liquids *r̥* and *l̥* were lost, replaced by *a*, *i*, *u*.

Sanskrit	*Pali*
r̥ṣi 'inspired singer'	*isi*
r̥ṇa 'debt'	*iṇa*

gr̥ha 'house'	*gaha*
kr̥mi 'worm'	*kimi*
mr̥ga 'animal; deer'	*maga*; *miga*
bhr̥jjati 'fries, parches'	*bhajjati*
pr̥cchati 'asks'	*pucchati*

In a few cases, the loss of *r̥* seems to have caused retroflexion of a following dental (*nr̥tate* 'dances' > *naṭate*) but in most it did not (cf. *ghr̥ta* 'ghee' > *ghata*; *tr̥tiya* 'third' > *tatiya*; *mr̥ta* 'dead' > *mata*; *mr̥du* 'soft' > *mudu*; *pr̥thula* 'broad' > *puthula*; *kr̥ttikā* 'the Pleiades' > *kattika*). The usual substitution, as will be seen, was *a*; *u* appears mainly when there is a preceding labial, but not regularly. In Prakrit as distinct from Pali, initial *r̥-* sometimes became *ri-*: *r̥kṣa* 'bear' > *accha*, *riccha*; *r̥ṣabha* 'bull' > *usabha*, *risabha*; *r̥ṣi* > *isi*, *risi*.

#MIA-2. The three sibilants *s*, *ś*, *ṣ* were reduced to one, generally *s* (but *ʃ* in the east):

Sanskrit	*Pali*
śiṣya 'pupil'	*sissa*
sasya 'grain'	*sassa*
śaśa 'hare'	*sasa*
kēśa 'hair'	*kēsa*
dēśa 'country'	*dēsa*
dōṣa 'fault'	*dōsa*
dāsa 'slave'	*dāsa*

#MIA-3. The diphthongs *āi*, *āu* were lost, becoming *ē*, *ō* as **ai*, **au* had done before them (by first becoming [*ai*, *au*]):

Sanskrit	*Pali*
āuṣadha 'herbs'	*ōsadha*
gāura 'white, light yellow'	*gōra*
kāuśika 'owl'	*kōsika*
tāila 'oil'	*tēla*
vāira 'enmity'	*vēra*
śāila 'rocky'	*sēla*

[MIA-3]**a**. Although technically not involving the loss of a phoneme, the change (with a few lexical exceptions [see below]) of the sequences *aya* and *ava* to *ē* and *ō* respectively is related to the above and may be noted here. Since the former is among other things the OIA causative morpheme and the latter a common prefix ('down, off') these changes have a wide effect:

Sanskrit	*Pali*
māpayati 'measures, builds'	*māpēti*
rōpayati 'plants'	*rōpēti*
bhājayati 'distributes'	*bhājēti*
avakāśa 'opportunity'	*ōkāsa*
avatāra 'descent'	*ōtāra*
avakirati 'pours out'	*ōkirati*

#MIA-4. These changes took effect in the Early MIA stage, here represented by Pali. A further loss, of the semivowel *y* (partly involving its merger with *j* initially and in most clusters), was completed in the Second MIA stage, but there is evidence (Chatterji 1926: 249–50) that it had already acquired at least a fricative pronunciation [ʒ] in the Early MIA period.

Sanskrit	*Prakrit*
yama 'god of death'	*jama*
yava 'barley'	*java*
yuddha 'battle'	*juddha*
yaḥ 'which' (rel. pn.)	*jo*

Medially it was usually simply dropped: *niyama* 'rule' > *ṇiama*; *sarayu* 'n. of river' > *saraū*; *payōdhara* 'woman's breast' > *paōhara*; *prayōga* 'use' > *paōa*; *prayukta* 'used' > *paütta*; *chāyā* 'shade' > *chāā*. The appearance of a prothetic *y* (*ēva* 'indeed' > *yēva*), and of a *-y-* as a transition between vowels in place of a lost consonant (including **y* itself) in some phases of Prakrit (*āhlāda* 'joy' > *alhāya*) and the replaceability of both this and etymological *y* by *v* in some situations (*jiyā* 'bowstring' > *jīā*, *jīvā*, even in Pali: *āyudha* 'weapon' > *āvudha* [Geiger 1916: 60, with further examples; see also Allen 1962: 61, 71]), together with the practice of writing Y for J in some dialects (e.g., Magadhi, as still in Modern Bengali), make the interpretation of recorded *-y-*'s (e.g., *māyā* 'illusion', *dayā* 'compassion', *kiyā* 'action' < OIA *kriyā* – all possibly Sanskritisms) problematic.

Sometimes, however, medial *-y-* became *-jj-* (via **-yy-*), particularly in the case of the passive morpheme *-ya-*: *dūyatē* 'is tormented' > *dujjaï*; *pīyatē* 'is drunk' > *pijjaï*; cf. *pēya* 'rice gruel' > *pēa*/*pejjā*. The sequences *-yy-* and *-ry-* became *-jj-* in any case: *śayyā* 'bed' > **śēyyā* > *sejjā*; *kārya* 'duty' > *kajja*.

#MIA-5. The case for *new* phonemes is marginal, at least in "focal" MIA – although there seem to be some new *phones*:

(MIA-5]**a**. The best case might be for *ñ* (if this was not accorded phonemic status earlier because of the marginal *jñ/jm* contrast in Sanskrit), since initial *jñ-* (as well as *ny-*) became *ñ-* and medial *-jñ-* (and *-ny-*) became *-ññ-*, giving it greater freedom of occurrence. This happened, however, only in Pali (and less regularly, in the Northwest Prakrit, outside the "focal" area): *jñāna* 'knowledge' > Pali *ñāna*; *nyāya* 'method' > *ñāya*; *ājñā* > *aññā* 'recognition', *anya* 'other' > *añña*.

[MIA-5]**b**. A case might also be made for recognizing the new aspirated nasals *mh*, *nh/ṇh* as unit phonemes (rather than clusters), since they occur initially (at least in several forms of Prakrit, barely in Pali) where otherwise only single consonants are permitted [see below]. The bulk of the evidence is on the other side of the argument, however, as will shortly be seen. The case for *lh*, *vh*, *yh*, *ñh* is yet more doubtful, either because their distribution is more restricted or because they vary with unaspirated forms. In any case "YH" probably = [*jh*].

[MIA-5]**c**. The reappearance of *ḷ*, *ḷh* as (written) intervocalic allophones of *ḍ*, *ḍh* in Pali (cf. Vedic) does not yet qualify them as phonemes. At least the first of these substitutions also obtained in Prakrit (Pischel 1981: 199) but was represented in writing simply by L, or by vacillation between L and Ḍ: e.g., Skt *pīḍā* 'pain' > Pa. *pīḷā*, Pkt *pīḍā/pīlā*; Skt *tāḍa* 'blow; latch, bolt' > Pa. *tāḷa*, Pkt *tāla*; Skt *uḍu* 'star' > Pa. *uḷu* 'lunar mansion', Pkt *uḍu*; Skt *garuḍa* 'n. of mythical bird' > Pa. *garuḷa*, Pkt *garuḍa/garula*; Skt *ṣōḍaśa* 'sixteen' > Pa. *sōḷasa*, Pkt *sōlaha*. Chatterji suggests that the Greek transcriptions of MIA *-ḍ-*, *-ḍh-* as R early in the Christian era show that the general present-day flapped pronunciation ([*ṛ*, *ṛh*]) of those segments in intervocalic position had already evolved, however they were written.

[MIA-5]**d**. Another new feature of interest, albeit also still allophonic, is the development of short *e*, *o* vowels before double consonants. While no new symbols were devised for these sounds in the Northern scripts, vacillation in writing between E and I and between O and U is testimony to their existence, along with inference from the new overall sound-pattern of the language [see below].

The remaining MIA developments, which perhaps play the greater role in reshaping the appearance of the MIA word, have to do with the *redistribution of existing* sounds:

#MIA-6. OIA *final consonants* were dropped; *-m*, *-n*, however, were usually but not always preserved as *anusvāra* (*ṁ*); *-aḥ* became *-ō* or *-a*, but *-ē* in the east (*dēvaḥ*, *saḥ* nom. sgs. of 'god', 'he' > Magadhi *dēvē*, *ʃē*, otherwise *dēvō*, *sō*). It sometimes appears that *anusvāra* takes the place of lost final consonants other than *m*, *n*, but it is also added sporadically to original final vowels. Cf. Skt *samyak* 'together, properly' > Pali *sammā*, Pkt *sammaṁ*; Skt *yāvat* 'until' > Pa. *yāva(ṁ)*; Skt *paścāt* 'behind' > Pa., Pkt *pacchā*; Skt *kartum* 'to do' > Pa. *kattuṁ*; Skt *idānīm* 'now' > Pa. *(i)dāni*, Pkt *(i)dāṇi(ṁ)*; Skt *kim* 'what?' > Pkt *ki(ṁ)*. All MIA words thus *end in vowels* or *anusvāra*.

#MIA-7. MIA words as a rule *began* only with a vowel or a single consonant. A few clusters (mainly C + *l*, also sometimes C + *r*, *y*, *v*, *m*, *n*) were broken up (and thus had their constituents preserved) by the insertion of a so-called *svarabhakti* vowel (*klēśa* 'distress' > *kilēsa*: according to Sen (1960) this is *semi-tatsama* rather than normal MIA treatment, but with *Cl-* it is the only treatment). *Most OIA initial clusters*, however, were *reduced* to one consonant – either (a) to one of the component consonants or (b) to a different consonant.

[MIA-7]**a**. The first case included the C*r*- clusters and most C*v*- clusters, as well as some C*y*- clusters, all of which were reduced to the preceding C-element:

Sanskrit	*Pali*
prabhu 'lord'	*pabhu*
trasati 'trembles'	*tasati*
drava 'running'	*dava*
krandana 'lamenting'	*kandana*
grāma 'village'	*gāma*
bhramara 'bumblebee'	*bhamara*
dhruva 'fixed'	*dhuva*
ghrāṇa 'smelling'	*ghāṇa*
mrīyate 'dies'	*mīyati*
vrīhi 'rice'	*vīhi*
śruta 'heard'	*suta*
sravati 'flows'	*savati*
tvac 'skin'	*tacō*
dvīpa 'island'	*dīpa*
jvara 'fever'	*jara*
kvaṭhati 'boils'	*kaṭhati*
dhvani 'sound'	*dhani*
śvaśura 'father-in-law'	*sasura*
svajana 'kinsman'	*sajana*
cyavate 'perishes'	*cavati*

jyōtiṣa 'astrology'	*jōtisā*
vyaya 'expense'	*vaya*
śyāma 'dark'	*sāma*
syālaka 'wife's brother'	*sālaka*

[MIA-7]**b**. The second case includes a few exceptions to the above: e.g., *dv-* and *dvy-* sometimes > *b-* (particularly in combinations of the number 'two': *dvādaśa* 'twelve' > *bārasa*, and more often in Prakrit than in Pali). More important are two other developments.

[MIA-7b](**1**) In the first, the combination of dental + *y* yields *new palatals* (*ty-* > *c-*, *dy-* > *j-*, *dhy-* > *jh-*):

Sanskrit	*Pali*
tyāga 'abandonment'	*cāga*
dyūta 'gambling'	*jūta*
dhyāna 'meditation'	*jhāna*

[MIA-7b](**2**) In the second development, *new instances of initial voiceless aspirates* arose from OIA *s* + C- (*s* + C- > C*h*-):

Sanskrit	*Pali*
spṛśati 'touches'	*phusati*
stana 'udder'	*thana*
skandha 'shoulder'	*khandha*

As may be seen from the last example, the old late-*IE rule ("Grassmann's Law") prohibiting more than one aspirate in a stem was abrogated in the process.

[MIA-7b](**3**) Additional instances of initial voiceless aspirates were produced by dropping the *s* in initial *s*C*h*- clusters:

Sanskrit	*Pali*
sphōṭa 'boil, pimple'	*phōṭa*
sthala 'dry land'	*thala*
skhalati 'stumbles'	*khalati*

The sequence *str-* also gave *th-* (or *itth-*): *strī* 'woman' > *thī*, *itthī*.

[MIA-7b](**4**) New instances of initial aspirates were not confined to *ph*, *th*, *kh*. The sequence *sth-* often gave *ṭh-* rather than *th-* (*sthāna* 'place' > *ṭhāna*, *sthāpayati* 'establishes' > *ṭhāpēti*).

[MIA-7b](**5**) New instances of *ch-* also arose through related developments involving OIA sequences of C + sibilant (vs. sibilant + C). The rare *ts-*, *ps-* became *ch-*, while further *ch-*'s came from what appears to be MIA dialectal treatment of the important group *kṣ-*. The "normal" treatment of this cluster in the center and east is *kh-*, but according to Bloch (1920: 112) there is no MIA or NIA dialect in which there is not some representation of both treatments, "often in the same words."

[MIA-7b](**6**) In a few cases, due apparently to differential OIA dialectal preservation of one of the antecedents of *kṣ-* (Indo-Iranian **yz'h-*) surfacing in the records at this time, Sanskrit *kṣ-* corresponds also to MIA *jh-*.

Sanskrit	*Pali*	*Prakrits*
tsaru 'sword handle'	–	*charu*
psāta 'hungry'	*chāta*	*chāya*
kṣurati 'cuts, scrapes'	*khurati*	*churaï*
kṣubdha 'shaken'	*chuddha*	*khuddha/chuddha*
kṣētra 'field'	*khetta*	*chetta/khetta*
kṣata 'wounded'	*khata*	*khaya/chaya*
kṣīna 'worn away'	*khīṇa*	*khīṇa/chīṇa/jhīṇa*
kṣarati 'trickles'	*kharati*	*kharai/jharaï*

[MIA-7b](**7**) Finally, the sequence sibilant + nasal (SN) could be said to yield a new class of aspirated nasals (N*h*). It is less securely established in initial than in medial position: initial *sm-* more often gives *sum-*, *sam-* or simply *s-*; *sn-* gives *siṇ-*, *saṇ-*, *nah-* as well as *ṇh-*, *ṇ-*:

Sanskrit	*Pali*	*Prakrit*
snāna 'bathing'	*(sināna/nahāna)*	*(saṇāna)/ṇhāṇa*
snāru 'sinew'	*n(a)hāru*	*ṇhāru*
snūṣā 'son's wife'	*(suṇisā)*	*ṇhusā*
snēha 'affection'	*(sinēha)*	*(saṇēha)/ṇēha*
smaraṇa 'remembrance'	*saraṇa*	*s(um)araṇa*
smita 'smile'	*mihita/sita*	–
śmaśāna 'cremation place'	*susāna*	*masāṇa/susāṇa*

If the examples with inserted vowels are taken (with Sen 1960: 36–8, 42) to represent *semi-tatsama* treatment, they may be disregarded. Prakrit *mhi* 'I am' and *mho/mha* 'we are' (from *(a)smi*, *smaḥ*) are enclitic forms, not truly initial.

#MIA-8. *Medial clusters* are treated slightly differently. They are generally not (at the MIA stage) reduced to a single consonant, but to *two-consonant sequences* (if consisting of three or more consonants) of *sharply limited types*: geminates, stop + corresponding aspirate, nasal + homorganic consonant, and nasal +

aspirate. (The prevailing two-consonant pattern is an argument for treating the last as a sequence of two consonants rather than as a unit phoneme, which is of course the opposite conclusion from that to which pattern congruence argument based on initials would lead [see above]. In other words, such evidence is conflicting: if treated as a cluster, N*h* would be the *only* MIA initial cluster type, but if treated as a unit phoneme, N*h* would be the *only* case where OIA medial clusters do not end up as a two-consonant sequence in MIA.)

Reduction to the above types involved, besides reduction of -CCC- and -CCCC- to -CC-, extensive and drastic assimilations of OIA heterogeneous clusters, including those across morpheme boundaries.

[MIA-8]**a**. Sequences of *two unlike* stops or nasals (-C^1C^2-) were reduced to *geminates of the second* stop or nasal (-C^2C^2-):

Sanskrit	*Pali (Pkt)*
bhakta 'meal, food'	*bhatta*
siktha 'beeswax'	*sittha*
dugdha 'milk'	*duddha*
ṣaṭka 'set of six'	*chakka*
ṣaṭpada '*having six feet'	*chappada* 'bee'
ṣaḍguṇa 'sixfold'	*chagguṇa*
utkara 'rubbish'	*ukkara*
utkhāta 'dug up'	*ukkhāya* (Pkt)
utpāta 'sudden portent'	*uppāta*
utphālayati 'opens wide'	*upphālēti*
mudga 'mung bean'	*mugga*
udghāṭayati 'opens'	*ugghāṭēti*
udbhāsayati 'illuminates'	*ubbhāsēi* (Pkt)
sapta 'seven'	*satta*
śabda 'sound'	*sadda*
labdha 'taken'	*laddha*
ṣaṇmāsika 'half-yearly'	*chammāsiya* (Pkt)
unmīlayati 'opens eyes'	*ummīlēti*
nimna 'low'	*ninna*

[MIA-8]**b**. Sequences of stop (P), nasal (N), or sibilant (S) + *y*, *r*, *l*, *v* generally gave *geminates of the first* element (-P, N, S + *y*, *r*, *l*, *v*- > -PP, NN, SS-):

Sanskrit	*Pali (Pkt)*
aśakya 'impossible'	*asakka*
yōgyā 'exercise'	*joggā* (Pkt)

rucyatē 'is pleasant'	*ruccati*
ājya 'clarified butter'	*ajja*
truṭyati 'is broken'	*tuṭṭaï/ṭuṭṭaï* (Pkt)
supyatē 'sleeps'	*suppati*
ramya 'enjoyable'	*ramma*
dṛśya 'visible'	*dassa*
manuṣya 'human being'	*manussa*
rahasya 'secret'	*rahassa*
cakra 'wheel'	*cakka*
anugraha 'favor, grace'	*anuggaha*
vajra 'thunderbolt'	*vajja* (Pkt)
ōḍra 'n. of people'	*oḍḍa* (Pkt)
rātrī 'night'	*ratti*
nidrā 'sleep'	*niddā*
vipra 'Brahmin'	*vippa*
sahasra 'thousand'	*sahassa*
aśru 'tear'	*assu*
viklava 'alarmed'	*vikkava* (Pkt)
pakva 'cooked; ripe'	*pakka*
prajvalati 'ignites'	*pajjalati*
priyatva 'being dear'	*piyatta*
īśvara 'lord'	*issara*
sarasvati 'n. of goddess'	*sarassaī* (Pkt)

There are some special assimilations to be noted in this group:

[MIA-8b](**1**) If the stop is aspirated, the resulting geminate is also aspirated: *vyāghra* 'tiger' > *vaggha* (Pkt), *abhra* 'cloud' > *abbha*, *labhyatē* 'is taken' > *labbhati*;

[MIA-8b](**2**) As with initial clusters, the sequence dental + *y* yields palatals – except that in this case they are geminates: *satya* 'truth' > *sacca*, *kathyatē* 'is spoken' > *kacchati*, *adya* 'today' > *ajja*, *madhya* 'middle' > *majjha*.

[MIA-8b](**3**) the sequences *-dv*, *ḍv-* (but not *-tv*, *dhv-*) often give *-b(b)* in Pali, *-vv-* in Prakrit: *udvahati* 'lifts' > *ubbahati/uvvahaī*, *udvartatē* 'swells' > *ubbattati/uvvattaī*, *ṣaḍviṁśati* 'twenty-six' > *chabīsati/chavvīsaṁ* (but *śādvala* 'grassy' > *saddala*, and *adhvan* 'road' > *addha-*); the labial element also assimilates the nasal articulation in e.g., *dhanvan* 'bow' > *dhamma* (Pkt);

[MIA-8b](**4**) the sequences *-ṇy-*, *-ny-* gave *-ññ-* in Pali, *-ṇṇ-* in Prakrit: *araṇya* 'forest' > *araññalaraṇṇa*, *śūnya* 'empty' > *suññalsuṇṇa*;

[MIA-8b](**5**) the sequences *-mr-*, *-ml-* often gave *-mb-* rather than *-mm-*: *tāmra* 'copper' > *tamba*, *amla* 'sour' > *amba*, *amra* 'mango' > *amba* (but *dhūmra* 'smoke-colored' > *dhumma*).

[MIA-8]**c**. Stops, nasals, or sibilants *preceded* by *r*, *l* also generally *assimilate those elements* and result in geminates:

Sanskrit	*Pali (Pkt)*
karkaśa 'rough, hard'	*kakkasa*
mārga 'road'	*magga*
argha 'price'	*aggha*
carcarī 'kind of song'	*caccari* (Pkt)
mūrchā 'fainting'	*mucchā*
kharjūrī 'date-palm'	*khajjūrī*
arpita 'entrusted'	*appita*
durbala 'weak'	*dubbala*
garbha 'womb'	*gabbha*
karṇa 'ear'	*kaṇṇa*
dharma 'right'	*dhamma*
darśayati 'shows'	*dassēti*
varṣa 'rain'	*vassa*
ulkā 'meteor'	*ukkā* (Pkt)
phalgu 'spring season'	*phaggu*
alpa 'small'	*appa*
gulpha 'ankle'	*goppha[ka]*
balbaja 'a coarse grass'	*babbaja*
gulma 'thicket'	*gumma* (Pkt; Pali *gumba*)

(MIA-8c](**1**) The most important special assimilation in this group involves the sequence *r* + dental, which sometimes yields a retroflex, sometimes a dental geminate, rather unpredictably – except that the retroflex does not result when the prefix *nir-* ('un-') is involved: *varti* 'wick' > *vaṭṭi/vatti* (Pkt), *ardha* 'half' > *aḍḍha/addha*, *vartatē* 'moves, exists' > *vattati/vaṭṭati*, *vardhatē* 'increases' > *vaḍḍhati*, but *nirdōṣa* 'faultless' > *niddōsa*, *nirdhana* 'poor, unwealthy' > *nidd-hana*, and *kartavya* 'duty' > *kattabba*, *alagarda* 'water-snake' > *alagadda*.

[MIA-8]**d**. Of semivowel-liquid combinations, *l* assimilates *y*, *r*, *v*; *v* assimilates (with development to *-bb-* in Pali) *y* and *r* (preceding or following); and *y* assimilates *r* (with development to *-jj-* in Prakrit):

Sanskrit	*Pali/(Pkt)*
kalya 'liquor'	*(kallā)*
durlabha 'rare'	*dullabha*

bilva 'wood-apple'	*billa*
sarva 'all'	*sabba/(savva)*
tīvra 'sharp'	*tibba/(tivva)*
dravya 'property'	*dabba/(davva)*
kārya 'action'	*kayya/(kajja)*

[MIA-8]**e**. Combinations of sibilant (S) + stop (P) and stop + sibilant normally yield aspirated stops, as with initial clusters, except that they are geminated (SP, PS > PP*h*). In some cases the expected aspiration is missing, however. (These include but are not limited to situations involving the same prefix *nir-*, here in its allomorph *niṣ-*, that failed to produce retroflexion in section #MIA-8c(1) above.) The combination of sibilant (S) + aspirated stop (P*h*) gives a geminated aspirate (SP*h* > PP*h*) in all cases.

Sanskrit	*Pali/(Pkt)*
puṣkara 'blue lotus'	*pukkhara* (Pkt)
puṣkala 'abundant'	*pukkala* (Pkt)
turuṣka 'olibanum'	*turukkha (Pkt turukka)*
apaskara 'faeces'	*avakkāra* (Pkt *avakkhara*)
niṣkarman 'inactive'	*nikkamma*
niṣkālayati 'drives out'	*ṇikkālēi* (Pkt)
paścima 'western'	*pacchima*
aṣṭā 'eight'	*aṭṭha*
kuṣṭha 'leprosy'	*kuṭṭha*
vastu 'thing'	*vatthu*
puṣpa 'flower'	*puppha*
niṣpīḍayati 'squeezes'	*nippīḷēti*
niṣphala 'fruitless'	*nipphala*
bṛhaspati 'Jupiter'	*bihapp(h)aï*
aspṛṣṭa 'untouched'	*appuṭṭha* (Pkt)
āsphālayati 'strikes'	*apphālēi* (Pkt)

[MIA-8e](**1**) As is the case initially, the combination *-sth-* often yields a retroflex rather than a dental aspirate: *āsthā* 'condition' > *atthā/aṭṭhā* (Pkt), *upasthāka* 'attendant' > *upaṭṭhāka*, *avasthāna* 'position' > *avaṭṭhāna* (Pkt also *avatthāṇa*).

[MIA-8e](**2**) Again analogously to the initial cases, clusters of stop + sibilant (*kṣ*, *ts*, *ps*), which are somewhat more common medially, typically give *-cch-* (*vṛkṣa* 'tree' > *vaccha*, *vatsa* 'calf' > *vaccha*, *apsaras* 'nymph' > *accharā*), with the first more often giving *-kkh-* (*bhikṣu* 'mendicant' > *bhikkhu*).

[MIA-8e](**3**) Where a morpheme boundary is involved, however, the combination *-ts-* usually gives *-ss-* in Pali and in some forms of Prakrit (*utsarati* 'escapes' > *ussarati*, Pkt *ussaraï*, *utsāha* 'energy' > *ussāha*, Pkt *ucchāha*). The combination **t-ś*, already *-cch-* in Sanskrit according to sandhi, is treated differently in MIA: *ucchrayati* 'raises' (<**ut-srayati*) > *ussēti*, *ucchīrṣaka* 'pillow' (<**ut-śīrṣaka*) > *ussīsaska*, Pkt *ussīsa*. The combination *-ḥś-*, which occurs at the junction of compounds, also gives *-ss-* (*niḥśēṣa* 'complete' > *nissēsa*). (For further details on the fate of *visarga* in compounds, see Pischel 1981: section 329.)

[MIA-8]**f**. As noted at the beginning of this section, the combination sibilant + nasal (SN) normally results in aspirated nasals (N*h*) – but ungeminated, constituting already in themselves as it were the required two consonants (N + *h*):

Sanskrit	*Pali/(Pkt)*
grīṣma 'summer heat'	*gimha*
kr̥ṣṇa 'dark blue'	*kaṇha*
aśman 'stone'	*amha*
vismaya 'wonder'	*vimhaya*
praśna 'question'	*paṇha* (Pkt; Pali *pañha*)
prasnava 'flow'	*paṇhava* (Pkt)

[MIA-8f](**1**) There are some exceptions, particularly at the Pali stage: OIA *vismarati* 'forgets' > Pali *vissarati*, Pkt *vimharaī/vissaraī* > cf. Mod. Gujarati *visarvũ*, Marathi *visarnẽ*; *raśmi* 'rope' > Pali *rasmi/raṁsi*, Pkt *rassi* > cf. Mod. Hindi *rassī*.

[MIA-8]**g**. Further cases of -N*h*- are produced by metathesis of the sequences *-hn-*, *-hṇ-*, *-hm-*: *cihna* 'sign' > *cinha*, *udgr̥hṇāti* 'takes up' > *uggaṇhāti*, *brahman* 'priest' > *bamha* (also *baṁbha*). The same metathesis of the sequences *-hl-*, *-hv-*, *-hy-* produces *-lh-* (*āhlāda* 'joy' > *alhāya*), Pali *-vh-*/Pkt *-bbh-* (*jihvā* 'tongue' > *jivhā*, *jibbhā*), and Pali *-yh-* (= [ʒ*h*]?)/Pkt *-jjh-* (*guhya* 'secret' > *guyha*, *gujjha*).

[MIA-8)**h**. Homorganic nasal + stop combinations are generally preserved (in Prakrit with *anusvāra*), while nasals *following* stops are usually assimilated into geminated stops, in both cases with the regular vowel-shortening:

Sanskrit	*Pali/(Pkt)*
aŋkuśa 'elephant-hook''	*aŋkusa*
jaŋghā 'shank'	*jaŋghā*
khaṇḍa 'broken'	*khaṇḍa*
kaṇṭha 'throat'	*kaṇṭha*
antara 'interior'	*antara*

andha 'blind'	*andha*
lamba 'pendent'	*lamba*
aṣṭāŋga 'having eight parts'	*aṭṭhaŋga*
śānti 'peace'	*santi*
śaknōti 'is able'	*sakkōti*
agni 'fire'	*aggi*
abhimathnāti 'whirls'	*abhimatthati*
āpnōti 'reaches'	*appōti*
vanāgni 'forest-fire'	*vaṇaggi* (Pkt)
ātman 'self'	*attā*/*appā* (Pkt)

[MIA-8h](**1**) Sometimes it is the nasal (particularly *m*) that assimilates the stop, however: *tigma* 'pungent' > *tigga*/*timma*, *padma* 'lotus' > Pkt *pomma*, *yugma* 'pair' > Pkt *jugga*/*jumma*; as noted earlier, OIA *jñ* > Pali *ñ-*, *-ññ-*, Pkt *ṇ-*, *-ṇṇ-*. In the instance of *ātman* 'self' > Pkt *appā* (and a few similar cases), the *m* affects the place of articulation of the stop (as did *v* in the cases of *dv* > *b*/*bb*).

[MIA-8]**i**. Clusters of *three or more* consonants may be divided into those ending in *-v* or beginning or ending in *r* (-CC*v*-, -*r*CC-, -CC*r*-), in which *r* and *v* are usually lost with no effect on the remaining assimilations (although *r* + dental occasionally produces retroflexion), and a residue ending in *-y* (which may effect palatalization) or nasals (which are sometimes retained):

Sanskrit	*Pali*/*(Pkt)*
utkvathita 'boiled out'	*ukkaṭṭhita*
tattva 'reality'	*tatta*
uddhvaṁsatē 'is diseased'	*uddhaṁsati*
ujjvalati 'blazes up'	*ujjalati*
dr̥ṣṭvā 'having seen'	*diṭṭhā*
lōptra 'loot'	*lotta*/*lutta* (Pkt)
utkramati 'ascends'	*ukkamati*
udgrahaṇa 'taking out'	*uggahaṇa*
ardra 'wet'	*adda*
vardhra 'thong'	*vaddha*
mantra 'spell'	*manta*
candra 'moon'	*canda*
puṇḍra 'var. of sugarcane'	*puṁḍa* (Pkt)
caŋkramaṇa 'walkabout'	*caŋkamaṇa*

niṣkramati 'goes out'	*nikkamati*
rāṣṭra 'country'	*raṭṭha*
vastra 'clothes'	*vattha*
pārśva 'side'	*passa*
tīkṣṇa 'sharp'	*tiṇha/tikkha* [w. sem. dif.]
lakṣmī 'good fortune'	*lakkhī*, Pkt *lacchī*
alakṣya 'invisible'	*alakkha*
jyōtsnā 'moonlight'	*juṇhā/joṇha* (Pkt)
pārṣṇi 'heel'	*paṇhi*
matsya 'fish'	*maccha*
vartman 'wheel track'	*vaṭṭa* (Pkt; Pali *vaṭuma*)
kartya 'to be cut off'	*kacca* (Pkt)

#MIA-9. The reductions and assimilations of consonant clusters discussed above, which eventually prevailed throughout the focal area, were early enough so that most examples could be taken from Pali. The remaining important MIA phonological development affecting consonants belongs to the Second or "Middle Prakrit" period (or at any rate, is mainly recorded then) and does not characterize Pali. It concerns the treatment of *single intervocalic stops*. These are progressively weakened until in the stage represented by Maharashtri with the exception of the retroflex series (*ṭ*, *ṭh*, *ḍ*, *ḍh*) they for the most part either disappear altogether (unaspirated stops) or do so leaving behind a residual *-h-* (aspirated stops).

The process of weakening was presumably more or less as follows: first, voicing of voiceless stops (*k*, *kh*, *c*, *ṭ*, *ṭh*, *t*, *th*, *p*, *ph* > *g*, *gh*, *j*, *ḍ*, *ḍh*, *d*, *dh*, *b*, *bh*: *śōka* 'sorrow' > *sōga*, *kapha* 'phlegm' > *kabha*); second, spirantization of voiced stops, derived or original (>*γ*, *γh*, *ʒ*, *ð*, *ðh*, *β*, *βh*: *sōga* > *sōγa*, *kabha* > *kaβha*, *mṛdu* 'soft' > *miðu*); third, reduction of these to a weakly articulated *ẏ* (*"ya-śruti"*) or *v̇* (*soẏa*, *kav̇ha*, *miẏu*); finally, disappearance of even that residue of the stop element (*sōa*, *kaha*, *miu*).

Evidence for each of these stages may be found in the MIA records, though of course not necessarily for every word. The voicing stage lingered longer in the areas (the east and midland) represented by Magadhi and Sauraseni, and *-d-*, *-dh-* were in fact standardized for the latter, but eventually these areas too caught up with the progressive southwest. For the retroflexes, the process stopped there, and they were preserved as stops, or at any rate as flaps (*karpaṭa* 'rag' > *kappaḍa*, *pāṭha* 'reading' > *pāḍha*). (Original *-ḍ-*, as will be recalled, had become phonetically [*ḷ*]; original *-ḍh-* was preserved.) The spirantization stage is represented, according to Chatterji, by vacillation in writing a voiced stop, semivowel, or nothing (*bhāga* 'portion' > *bhāga/bhāa*, *ābhira* 'n. of a herding people' > *ābhīra/ āhīra*). (It is also represented explicitly, outside the focal area, in the Niya documents written in Kharoshthi script. See Burrow 1937, Sen 1960, Katre 1965.) The *-ẏ/v̇-* stage is represented in Jain manuscripts, in prescriptions of medieval grammarians such as Hemacandra (who held that *-ẏ-* was proper between *a* and *ā*), and perhaps in the frequent preservation of *-p-*, *-b-* as *-v-*, even in Maharashtri. (It may not be strictly correct, however, to equate these *v*'s with the *v̇*-glide that may stand for other consonants, or with the *ẏa-śruti*.) For further examples (mainly from *CDIAL*) see below:

Sanskrit	*Prakrit*
nakula 'mongoose'	*naula*
trilōka 'the three worlds'	*tilōa*
tyāga 'abandonment'	*cāya*
nagara 'town'	*nayara*
vacana 'speaking'	*vayaṇa*
śauca 'cleanness'	*sōa*
vraja 'cattleshed'	*vaya*
bhōjana 'food'	*bhōaṇa*
markaṭa 'monkey'	*makkaḍa*
mr̥ta 'dead'	*maya/mua*
avalōkita 'looked at'	*ōlōia*
kadala 'banana'	*kayala*
dvīpa 'island'	*dīva*
apāra 'boundless'	*avāra*
alābu 'bottle-gourd'	*alā(v)u*
śabara 'tribe in Deccan'	*savara*
nakha 'nail'	*ṇaha*
mēgha 'cloud'	*mēha*
kaṭhina 'hard'	*kaḍhiṇa*
kathayati 'says'	*kahēi*
pr̥thula 'broad'	*pihula*
krōdha 'anger'	*kōha*
viphalati 'splits open'	*vihalai*
śubha 'auspicious'	*subha/suha*

A vulnerable consonant could escape these fates through gemination: *saphala* 'fruitful' > *sahala/sapphala*. The vulnerability of intervocalic consonants varied along a cline, with the stops (and among the stops, the velars) at the weak end and, surprisingly, *r* and *h* at the resistant end. Between these extremes, *-s-*, *-l-*, *-m-*, *-n-*, *-ṇ-*, and the retroflex stops, were rarely lost entirely, but they were subject to phonetic weakening and modification.

#MIA-10. A conspicuous feature of Prakrit is the apparent *merger of all nasals* except *m* (and those preceding stops, homorganic or other, represented by *anusvāra*) with *ṇ*. While some (e.g., Bloch) hold that this was partly artificial, that graphic initial Ṇ- represented a dental [*n*], Chatterji suggests that initial *ṇ*- was redentalized in the Apabhramsa or Third MIA period. Tagare (1948: 74–5) calls our attention to the fact that "eminent text-critics like Pischel, Vaidya, Jain, and Upadhye have set an editorial tradition of levelling all *n* to *ṇ*" in their editions of Apabhramsa manuscripts, in which the actual state of affairs is very different, with much vacillation between the two. In any case, NIA has initial *n*-, not *ṇ*-, but the merger of medial *-n-* with *-ṇ-* seems real enough on the basis of NIA evidence (i.e. western NIA languages preserve *-ṇ-*).

[MIA-10]**a**. There is also the matter of the geminated nasals. In the standard (= non-Jain) Prakrits, the *-nn-*, *-ṇṇ-*, *-ññ-* of Pali were all merged graphically as *-ṇṇ-*. In the Jain languages (Ardhamagadhi, Jaina Maharashtri, Jaina Sauraseni), which also write initial *n*-, they are generally represented by *-nn-* (Pischel 1981: sec. 224, 225). From the NIA evidence, this seems closer to the phonological truth: *n* and *ṇ* were indeed merged in Middle Prakrit, but with complementary allophones [*ṇ*] intervocalically and [*n*] initially and geminated. (Cf. also the development of *-l-*, *l-*, *-ll-*, discussed in section 7.4.)

#MIA-11. It remains to discuss the vowels. The assimilation of the OIA diphthongs and certain other sequences has already been mentioned. Otherwise they were fairly stable, *except for one major rule*, already in place in Pali, *that sweepingly affected the quantity of long vowels*. The new rule (Geiger called it the "Two-Mora Rule") was that only short vowels could occur before two consonants; a long vowel could be followed by only one consonant. This resulted, as the attentive reader will already have noticed in many of the preceding examples, usually in the *shortening of OIA long vowels before clusters* (*vīdhra* 'clear sky' > *viddha*, *kārya* 'action' > *kajja*). In the rather infrequent alternative treatment, *the long vowel could be preserved at the expense of the consonant cluster* (*dīrgha* 'long' > *dīgha*).

It was this rule, which applied to all vowels including the erstwhile diphthongs, that produced the new, albeit positionally restricted short *e*, *o* of MIA: *nētra* 'eye' > *netta*, *yōgyā* 'exercise' > *yoggā*/*joggā*. Although we can represent such vowels easily enough in Roman transcription, this was not possible in the northern Indian scripts; MIA writers' discomfort with this situation is often indicated by their using sometimes E, sometimes I, and sometimes O, sometimes U: *lōptra* 'loot' > *lOtta*/*lUtta*, *śrēṣṭhin* 'distinguished man' > *sEṭṭhi*/*sIṭṭhi*.

Finally it is this rule which constitutes the best argument against recognizing MIA *-mh-*, *-ṇh-*, etc. as unit phonemes: OIA long vowels are shortened before them as before any *cluster* (*grīṣma* 'summer heat' > *gimha*, *ślēṣman* 'mucus, phlegm' > Pkt *silemha*/*silimha*).

The third MIA or Apabhramsa stage saw two further general phonological developments:

#MIA-12. Intervocalic *-m-* was weakened to a nasalized *-w̃-* (although Tagare 1948 disputes the generality and distinctiveness of this change): OIA *grāma* 'village' > Pali/Pkt *gāma* > Ap. *gāw̃a*.

#MIA-13. Final long vowels were shortened:[7] *sandhyā* 'twilight' > Pkt *saṁjhā* > Ap. *saṁjha*. The latter involved some not unnatural shifts in quality in this weak position: *-ē* > *-i*, *-ō* > *-u*, *-aṁ* > *-u*. These show up primarily in inflected forms: Skt *putraḥ* 'son' (nom. sg.) > Pali/Pkt *puttō* > Ap. *puttu* (*putta*); *putrē* (loc. sg.) Pali/Pkt > *puttē* > Ap. *putti*; *putrēna* (instr. sg.) > Pali *puttēna* > Pkt *puttēṇa(ṁ)* > Ap. *puttẽ*/*puttiṁ*; *asmad-* 'us' (obl. case base) > Pali/Pkt *amhē* 'we/us' (nom./acc.) > Ap. *amhi*; but note also *adya* 'today' > Pali/Pkt *ajja* > Ap. *ajju*, *vinā* 'without' > Pkt *viṇā* > Ap. *viṇu*.

#MIA-14. There were other, more sporadic developments in the phonological history of MIA that are more difficult to deal with briefly, although they too had their cumulative effect on the later languages. These included spontaneous *nasalization*, spontaneous *retroflexion*, spontaneous *aspiration*, and spontaneous *gemination* – "spontaneous" in the sense of not clearly motivated by the preexisting sequence of sounds.[8]

#MIA-15. Among the other factors that need to be considered is the new Latin-like stress system referred to earlier. Although it came to characterize Classical Sanskrit, it may be considered a MIA development.[9] Briefly, the new stress fell on the first long syllable, up to the fourth from the end, starting with and going backwards from the penult. In other words, it never fell on the final syllable, whereas the Vedic accent frequently did so. Already in Pali, this resulted in a weakening and confusion of the vowel in the post-accentual syllable (Vedic *candramā́ḥ* 'moon' > Cl. Skt *cā́ndramāḥ* > Pali *candimā*).

7.4 **Summary of the effects of the MIA changes**

As a result of the MIA developments, Indo-Aryan was transformed from the very Indo-European-looking language of the OIA stage into something that at one point looked, especially with regard to its syllabic structure of (C)V(:)/(C)VCC, its restricted cluster-types (geminates and homorganic nasal + stop), its obligatory final vowels, its lax intervocalic consonants, and its final nasals turned into nasalized vowels, rather like Dravidian, even like Tamil. This analogy must not be pushed too far, however. For one thing, aspiration, which is foreign to Dravidian, remains a prominent characteristic, surviving as we ha seen the disappearance of the stop-element itself in intervocalic aspirated stops. In Second Stage MIA and beyond, successions of vowels with unremedied hiatus become a prominent characteristic. This is as intolerable in Dravidian as it had been in Sanskrit. The dominant new penultimate stress-pattern of MIA is also not that of Dravidian, which generally has initial stress.

The following additional general effects of the MIA changes on the OIA phonological system should also be noted:

1. The position of the voiceless aspirates in the system is greatly strengthened, especially in initial position where they had been weak, as a result of the *s* + C > *Ch* rule.
2. The position of the palatals, aspirated and unaspirated, is strengthened by the assimilations involving dentals + *y* as well as by the merger of *y* with *j*, and the particularly shaky position of OIA *ch* and *jh* is strengthened in addition by the assimilations of *kṣ*, *ts*, *ps*, *śc*, *hy* and the development of *ṣ*- as *ch*- in forms connected with 'six'. The greatest proliferation of new *jh*'s, however, is in the scores of words, many of them onomatopoetic or "expressive", that appear without known antecedents for the first time in MIA. These include such NIA lexical staples as Pkt *jhuṭṭa* 'false', *jhullaï* 'swings', *jhuṁpaḍa* 'hut', *jhōliā*/*jholliā* 'bag'.
3. Apart from the great increase in retroflex *ṇ*'s brought about by the merger of medial -*n*- with -*ṇ*-, the incidence of retroflex *stops* is also augmented by assimilations, even if not universal, involving *rt*, *r̥t*, *st*, *rth*, *sth*, *rd*, *rdh*, *dr*, *tr*, and also C*rat(h)* (*prathama* 'first' > Pali *paṭhama*, *grathna* 'bunch' > Pkt *gaṭṭhiyā*), as well as by "spontaneous" retroflexion. One result is the secure establishment of these segments in *initial* position, from which they had been excluded in older Sanskrit (and also in Proto-Dravidian).
4. As compared with that of OIA, the MIA vowel system (*i*/*ī*, [*e*/*ē*], *a*/*ā*,

[*o*/*ō*], *u*/*ū*) is more symmetrical (although [*e*/*ē*] and [*o*/*ō*] are only positional allophones), and begins to approximate the Dravidian system.

5. The reduction of sibilants from three (which were distributionally skewed in any case: cf. Allen 1978: 92–4) to one achieves greater stability, and again approaches Dravidian (in the sense that these languages generally do not have *more* than one sibilant, although some of them have "less" than one, i.e. where [*s*] is an allophone of /*c*/).
6. The clear sense of morpheme boundaries which had obtained in Sanskrit in spite of sandhi is effectively lost as a consequence of the sweeping assimilations and losses involving medial consonants and consonant groups in MIA.
7. These assimilations also resulted in numerous homonyms, not only in the extreme case of Maharashtri (in which, e.g., *maa* = *mata* 'thought', *mada* 'intoxication', *maya* 'made of', *mr̥ga* 'deer', *mr̥ta* 'dead'), but already in Pali, where *passa* = 'one who sees' (<*paśya*) + 'side' (<*pārśva*), *ummagga* = 'emergence of the desire for knowledge' (<**unmagna*) + 'wrong way' (<*unmārga*), and derivational niceties were effaced in *agga* = 'top' (*agra*) + 'topmost, best' (<*agrya*). This led among other things to supplementation with pleonastic suffixes such as *-ka*, *-ika*, *-ia*, *-la*, *-lla*, *-illa*, *-ulla*, *-āia*, *-āna*, the use of which increased with time.
8. The redistribution of long and short vowels according to the "Two-Mora Rule", along with the loss of *r̥*, played havoc with the *guṇa-vr̥ddhi* system and thus with another part of the morphology. (See Turner 1975 [1923] for further discussion.)
9. Although MIA languages still had some sandhi rules, mainly between members of compounds, the absence of final consonants and of obligatory sentence sandhi meant that the system was vastly simpler than that of Sanskrit. Pali still has some traces of sentence sandhi, always facultative, and only between closely related sentence elements: verb and object, adjective and noun, adverb and verb. The short allomorphs (*'va*, *'pi*, *'ti*) of certain enclitics (*iva*, *api*, *iti*) as well as those with prothetic *y-*, *v-* represent "frozen" sandhi forms (Geiger 1916: 72). One interesting feature of Pali sandhi is the occasional reappearance of "lost" final consonants. Geiger gives *ētad-avōca* 'this one said' (vs. normal *ētaṁ*) among other examples (1916: 76).

7.5 MIA local and other qualifications

Even within the focal zone, the MIA developments described did not prevail everywhere or at the same time. Many of these local and temporary (and perhaps also scribal) differences are of no consequence for the later languages, and so are ignored here. For example, *kṣ* becomes *śk* in standard Magadhi, but this does not matter, as the *kh* treatment eventually prevailed in the Eastern group. Some local features did hold their own, however:

#MIA-LQ-1. The Eastern (Magadhi) substitution of *ʃ* instead of *s* for *ś*, *ṣ*, *s*, and of *ē* instead of *ō* for *-aḥ* have already been mentioned, and continue to affect the descendants of Magadhi, although modified by further language-particular developments.

#MIA-LQ-2. Another Magadhi feature, the universal substitution of *l* for *r*, has left only a few traces (in terms of forms with *l* in place of Sanskrit *r*) in the daughter languages, a few more in Assamese than in Bengali (As. *lāi*, Beng. Or. *rāi* 'black mustard-seed' < *rājikā*). The Magadhan forms with *l* (which are well-attested in inscriptions as well as in the stylized language of the drama and in the descriptions and prescriptions of the grammarians throughout the MIA period) were apparently overwhelmed later on by Midland and Sanskrit influences. Since the essential thing was the *loss* of the *r/l distinction*, not the [l] quality itself, another remnant of Magadhan "l" (according to Chatterji) may be "Bihari", especially Bhojpuri, forms with *r* instead of *l*: *phar* 'fruit' (<*phala*), *har* 'plow' (<*hala*), although these languages too have both /r/ and /l/ today. (Such *r*-forms, however, reach Eastern Hindi and even Braj.) (For the vexed question of *ḷ* vs *l* vs *ḍ* vs *ṛ* vs *r*, which is not a specifically Magadhan problem, see section 7.8.)

#MIA-LQ-3. The new predictable ("long-penultimate") accent apparently did not apply to Maharashtri, nor therefore to modern Marathi in terms of its phonological effects. Instead, something like the Vedic accent continued to prevail, transformed into stress. First put forward by Pischel in his monumental grammar of the Prakrits (1981: sec. 46, sec. 79–82 – where it is also claimed for Ardhamagadhi and the other Jaina languages, and for "poetical Apabhramsa"), this theory has been disputed from various standpoints[10] by Bloch, Jacobi, and Grierson, but supported, with modifications, in an important article by Turner (1975 [1916; also 1923]), and more recently by Southworth. The modifications mainly concern the accentuation of verbs (on the first syllable, vs. no accentuation in main clauses in Vedic) and a shift of accentuation from the final to the initial syllable at some point. The resulting pre-Marathi system with many initial stresses (which should be labeled "Vedic-derived" rather than "Vedic") differs from the later Sanskrit and derived systems most tangibly by not automatically accenting a long penult, and from neighboring Dravidian systems of initial stress (which it approaches) by *sometimes* accenting the penult (where Vedic had it). The main result seems to be the shortening of penultimate (and other) long vowels that were not accented in Vedic:

Sanskrit	*Maharashtri*	*Other Pkt*
útkhāta 'dug up'	*ukkha(y)a*	*ukkhāya*
prásida 'quiet'	*pasia*	*pasīda*
kumārá 'boy'	*kumara*	*kumāra*
sthāpáyati 'establishes'	*ṭhavēi*	*ṭhāvēi*

This shortening related to the position of the Vedic accent, apparent but not always attested in MIA texts, seems to account for a series of regular differences between Marathi and other NIA languages: M. *kũvar* vs. H. *kũwār*; M. *mhasan* 'cremation ground' vs. H. *masān* (<*śmaṣāná*); M. *āphaḷṇē* 'to throw down violently' vs. Guj. *aphāḷvũ*, N. *āphālnu*, As. *āphāliba* (<*ā́sphālayati*).

#MIA-LQ-4. There were other developments, not treated above, which, although not lacking their own regularities, were restricted morphologically rather than regionally. One that should be mentioned is the Late MIA opening of *s* to *h* primarily (although not exclusively) in certain *inflections*: OIA *-asya* gen. sg. masc. > Pkt *-assa* > Ap. *aha*/*-ahu*; OIA *-sya-*/*-iṣya-* fut. > Pali/Pkt *-ssa-*/*-issa-* > Ap. *-ha-*/*-iha-*. (See Turner 1975 [1927].)

7.6 The Common NIA developments

The reader who is acquainted with a NIA language, especially Hindi, will have already begun to recognize many forms in the products of the MIA changes. To produce all of the modern forms, however, another set of developments was required. The characteristic NIA developments were as follows:

#NIA-1. The MIA geminates (-CC-) were reduced to single consonants with compensatory lengthening of the preceding vowel:

MIA	*Hindi*	*Bengali*	*Marathi*
satta 'seven'	*sāt*	*ʃāt*	*sāt*
bhatta 'cooked rice'	*bhāt*	*bhāt*	*bhāt*
duddha 'milk'	*dūdh*	*dūd(h)*	*dūdh*
aṭṭha 'eight'	*āṭh*	*āṭ*	*āṭh*

tikkha 'sharp'	*tīkh(ā)*	*tīkha* (MB.)	*tīkh*
j(h)uṭṭha 'false; lie'	*jhūṭh*	*jhūṭ*	*jhūṭ*

#NIA-2. This was sometimes accompanied by spontaneous (and regionally random) nasalization of the vowel. (In some cases this goes back to Prakrit):

MIA	*Hindi*	*Bengali**	*Gujarati*
mugga 'mung bean'	*mū̃g*	*muŋ/mug*	*(mag)*
assu(āsu, aṁsuya) 'tear'	*ā̃sū*	–	*ā̃su*
akkhi 'eye'	*ā̃kh*	*ā̃kh(i)*	*ā̃kh*
uṭṭa 'camel'	*ū̃ṭ*	*(uṭ)*	*ū̃ṭ*
sappa 'snake'	*sā̃p*	*(sāp)*	*(sāp)*

(* Bengali having lost the distinction between *ī/i* and *ū/u*, its spelling of these vowels is often arbitrary.)

#NIA-3. Final vowels were generally lost, as may be seen from the above examples. Even long final vowels were lost (having been first shortened in the Apabhramsa stage – #MIA-13):

MIA	*Hindi*	*Bengali*	*Marathi*
jibbhā 'tongue'	*jībh*	*jib*	*jībh*
ṇiddā 'sleep'	*nī̃d*	*nīd*	*nīd*
rattī 'night'	*rāt*	*rāt*	*rāt*
lajjā 'shame'	*lāj*	*lāj*	*lāj*

#NIA-4. In the case of the MIA -VNC- sequences, the vowel was lengthened and nasalized and the nasal was dropped:

MIA	*Hindi*	*Bengali*	*Gujarati*
kampa- 'tremble'	*kā̃p-*	*kā̃p-*	*kā̃p-*
ganṭhi 'knot'	*gā̃ṭh*	*gā̃ṭh*	*gā̃ṭh*
bandha 'bond; dam'	*bā̃dh*	*bā̃dh*	*bā̃dh*
sañjhā 'twilight'	*sā̃jh*	*sā̃jh*	*sā̃j*

#NIA-5. Loss of unaccented vowels (in terms of the new long-penultimate stress system as well as earlier in Maharashtri and Ardhamagadhi in terms of the alleged Vedic-derived system) *in other positions also* is now common (more so in some languages than others). E.g., initial vowels in words of three or more syllables: *apāra* 'the near bank' > Pkt *avāra* > H. *vār*; *araṇya* 'wilderness' > Pkt *araṇṇa* > Guj. *rān* (> the "Rann of Cutch"); *abhiṣēka* 'anointing of a king' > (Pkt *abhisēa*)

> Si. *bisev*; also medial vowels: *susthira* 'very firm' > Pkt *sutthira* > H. *suthrā*; Pkt *uttāvala* 'impetuous' > G. *utāvḷū*; *utkuṭaka* 'sitting on the hams' > Pkt *ukkuḍuya* > M. *ukḍā*; sometimes even accented ones: *kṣurapra* 'scraper' > Pkt *khurappa* > P.H.B. *khurpā* (but Or. *khurapā*).

[NIA-5]**a**. This may produce new aspirates: *gardabha* 'ass' > Pkt *gaddaha* > B. *gādhā*; *vigraha** 'a division of land' > Pkt *viggabha* > H. *bīghā*; Pkt *kaḍāha* (**kaḍāhī*) 'cauldron' > M. *kaḍhāī*.

[NIA-5]**b**. It also may produce new internal clusters: *argala* 'door bolt' > Pkt *aggala* > N. *āglo*; **lappasīka* 'a sweetmeat' > Pkt *lappasiyā* > P.H. *lāpsi*, G.M. *lāpśī*. (See Chatterji 1926: 330–4.) The majority of such new NIA clusters, however, are at morpheme boundaries, particularly between verbal stems and affixes that, with loss of unaccented "thematic" vowels (often accompanied by other vocalic extensions), come to begin with consonants (H. *kar-nā* 'to do' < OH. *karana*, H. *kar-tā* 'doing' < OH. *karata*, H. *kar-vā-* 'cause to be done', OH. *karavā-*; Coll. B. *kor-bo* 'I shall do' < Sadhu Bhasa *koribo*; Coll. B. *kor-lām* 'I did' < Sadhu Bhasa *korilām*). Or, they involve the pleonastic (or sometimes diminutive) extensions *-l-*, *-n-*, *-r-*, *-ḍ-* (*khasa* 'scab' > H.P. *khasrā*; *pakṣa* 'wing' > Pkt *pakkha* > H. *pākhṛā*; *dīpa* 'lamp' > Pkt *dīva* > H. *dīvlā* 'small lamp'). At least the former are regarded as pseudo-clusters by some, not only because of the script (they are not written with conjunct letters, except in Nepali), and because the lost vowel "counts" in certain types of meter and is pronounced in certain types of singing (like mute "e" in French), but on the more cogent ground that the most basic *assimilations* (voicing, articulatory position, transfer of aspiration) *do not take place* within them: cf. H. *lagtā*, *paṛtā*, *dekhtā*. Otherwise, most of them do pass phonetic muster as bona fide clusters in most contexts.

In a still more arguable set of cases, a stem vowel itself (in polysyllabic stems involving short vowels, especially *a*) comes and goes, depending on the suffixation: H. *samajhnā* 'to understand' > *samjhā* 'understood'. This too produces clusters, albeit unstable ones. As noted in Chapter 6, the most recent treatment (synchronic) of this "schwa-deletion" phenomenon in Hindi is in Ohala 1983. I am unaware of any attempt to deal with it (and medial vowel loss in general) in systematic fashion either descriptively or historically across all NIA languages.

#NIA-6. *Successions of vowels* (known technically in the literature as *udvṛtta* = "opened" vowels) left in hiatus by the loss of intervocalic single consonants in the Second MIA stage *coalesced into new long vowels and diphthongs* – a process already under way[11] in the Later MIA (Apabhramsa) stage, but now more general. Alternatively, the separate vowels could be preserved by the use of *śruti*-glides (*ẏ*, *v̇* = [*w*], and in some languages, particularly Sinhalese, also *h*). There is great inconsistency across and even within languages in the way these are (or are not) represented in writing. Punjabi (in Gurmukhi script) writes vowels in hiatus. Marathi tended to prefer *v* where other languages had *y*. Certain languages (Assamese, Oriya, Maithili, Awadhi, to some extent Bengali) tolerated successive vowels better than others, and experienced less reduction. The details thus varied from language to language. (For Assamese, see Kakati 1962: 117–40; for Awadhi, Saksena 1971 [1937]: 61–84; for Bengali, Chatterji 1926: 338–56; for Bhojpuri, Tiwari 1960: 30–3; for Gujarati, Turner 1975 [1921]: 109–114; for Hindi, Misra 1967 and – very exhaustively – Učida 1977; for Marathi, Bloch 1920: 71–81; for Sinhalese, Geiger 1938: 15–18.) Nevertheless, certain general observations may be made:

[NIA-6]**a**. *Vowels of like quality* coalesced: MIA *cittaāra* 'painter' (<OIA *citrakāra*) > G. *citārɔ*; MIA *duuṇa* 'double' (<OIA **duguṇa*) > H. *dūnā*. Sometimes this was in spite of *śruti*-glides: MIA *ayaṇa* 'eating' (<OIA *adana*) > Or. *āṇa* 'dough; broth'; MIA *kaṁṭaya* 'thorn' (<OIA *kaṇṭaka*) > H., B. *kāṭā*; Si. *ahasa* 'sky' > Si. *āsa* 'sky'.

[NIA-6a](**1**) At times the glides in *aya*, *ava* seemed to possess more reality, either contracting to new diphthongs *ai*, *au* (thence to monophthongs *ɛ*, *ɔ* in some languages), or developing like their OIA predecessors as far as *ē*, *ō*: MIA *mayaṇa* 'mynah bird' (<OIA *madana*) > H. *mainā* > *menā*; MIA *avara* 'other' (<OIA *apara*) > H. *aur* > *ɔr*; but MIA *kayala* 'banana' (<OIA *kadala*) > H. *kēlā*; MIA *ṇayara* 'city' (<OIA *nagara*) > Raj. *-ṇēr* (as in Bika*ṇēr*); MIA **khava-* 'lose' (<OIA *kṣapa-*) > P.H.G. *khō-*. Turner (1921, 1975, [1925b]) explains the difference between *e/ɛ* and *o/ɔ* – at least for Gujarati – in terms of inherited words vs. later loanwords: in the former the process has had time to go further.

[NIA-6a](**2**) Glides after *ā* sometimes remained to give rise to diphthongs of a new type [*āi*, *āu*], often written *āy*, *āv* since the scripts have no way of distinguishing diphthongs other than [*ai*, *au*] from disyllabic sequences of vowels (for which in transcription we have the option of the dieresis, *oi* vs. *oï*): OIA *rājā* > MIA *rāā*, *rāya* > NIA *rā*, *rāy*, *rāv* > *rāo*.

[NIA-6]**b**. In the case of *unlike* vowels in succession (in hiatus or with *śruti*-glides) the first was generally dominant, at least to the extent that something of it remained in a subsequent rising or falling diphthong, whereas the second was sometimes lost altogether. Treatment was often dependent on position in the word, and on morphological status.

[NIA-6b](**1**) Thus *ia*, *iya*, *iā* often gave *ī* at the end of a word (*ghia* 'ghee' > H.B.M. *ghī* (vs. Or. *ghiɔ*); *jhōliā* 'bag' > H. *jhōlī*; *amiya* 'nectar' > G. *amī*), but internally the *a* or *ā* element remained (*pivāsā* 'thirst' > Ap. *piāsa* > H.G.M.

pyās; Or. *piāsɔ*, N. *piyās*) – that is, when it was accented. As Turner (1921) points out, *unaccented a* may also be lost: *ṇíama* 'rule' > G. *nīm* (B. *neo*, H. *nēm*); *sīala* 'cold' > H. *sīl(ā)*, G. *śīḷā*.

[NIA-6b](**2**) When the first vowel is *ē* or *ō*, it may oust the other vowel or itself become a semivowel *y* or *w* in the same accentual circumstances as above: *thōa* 'a little' (+ *-ḍ-*) > H. *thō(ṛā)*, but *gōvāla*/*gōália* > H. *gwāl*.

[NIA-6b](**3**) OIA sequences of *aCi* and *aCu* > MIA *aï*, *aü* (which were very frequent, especially the first) became the main sources of new NIA diphthongs *ai*, *au*, later monophthongized to *ɛ*, *ɔ* in some languages (see Turner 1975 [1925b]) (spelled with E, O in Gujarati and with AI, AU in Hindi): *pratijñā* 'promise' > OH. *paija*, M. *paij* 'wager'; *catuṣka* 'square' > H. *cauk*, G. *cɔk*.

[NIA-6b](**4**) In final position, especially in desinences (most importantly in the 3d sg. pres. of verbs: Skt *-ayi*, Pkt *-aï*), *-ai*, *-au* become *-ē*, *-ō*.

[NIA-6b](**5**) Otherwise, in Marathi *ai*, *au* are either retained as diphthongs or in some cases are reduced to *ā*, and in Bengali and other Eastern languages they develop phonetically into *oi*, *ou*.

7.7 Effects of the Common NIA changes

As a result of the general NIA developments, typical NIA languages look superficially a bit more like Sanskrit again, or perhaps one should say Indo-European, and less like Dravidian, to the extent that, in contradistinction to MIA, they have:

1. many words ending in consonants (more in fact than Sanskrit);
2. a number of words with stress on the final syllable, primarily in such words (as a result of the loss of final syllables in penultimately stressed words)[12] – unless a newer (tertiary) stress system has intervened;[13]
3. restored, albeit in different contexts, the Sanskritic diphthongs *ai*, *au*, although in some NIA languages these have been subsequently again monophthongized or otherwise phonetically altered;
4. clusters of unlike consonants, at least medially (initial and final clusters in Sanskrit and Perso-Arabic loanwords do not concern us here).

At the same time, as a result of the same changes, NIA has a number of *new* characteristics:

1. final consonants normally occur only after long vowels;

2. there are, besides *ai*, *au*, several new diphthongs, unknown to Sanskrit;
3. the inventory of new medial clusters (or pseudo-clusters) only partly overlaps with that of Sanskrit, including many new types and lacking some of the old ones;
4. NIA has a much more extensive and centrally established (non-marginal) system of nasal vowels.

The NIA developments did not all take place at the same time. The geminate-reduction and vowel-lengthening seems to have been first, followed by coalescence of vowels in hiatus (in at least some of its phases), and last of all by loss of final vowels, which is not yet complete in some languages (see below, 7.9.1), and of certain unaccented medial vowels, the phonological status of which is sometimes still disputed.

7.8 Special developments

#SD-1. The reduction of geminates and lengthening of vowels applied to *-nn-*, *-mm-*, *-ll-*, *-ss-* as well as stops. These geminates yielded ordinary single consonants in NIA in the usual fashion (Pkt *kaṇṇa* = probably [*kanna*] 'ear' > B.H.G.M. *kān*, Pkt *kamma* 'work' > B.H.G.M. *kām*, Pkt *galla* 'cheek' > B.H.G.M. *gāl*, Pkt *passa* 'side' > H. *pās*). The *single intervocalic* instances of these consonants, however, were not lost like their stop counterparts but underwent special phonetic developments which moreover have left different results in different NIA languages. Behind all of them, no doubt, lies the same articulatory "*weakening*" (Bloch 1965: 80, 82) which affected the single intervocalic stops. These, it may be recalled, "weakened" through stages of voicing, fricativization, and semivowel glide to final disappearance (#MIA-9). In the cases now under consideration, however, this "weakening" took other forms, due to the phonetic nature of these segments.

[SD-1]**a**. The passage of *-n-* to *-ṇ-* in Middle Prakrit, while graphic Ṇ- and -ṆṆ- apparently represented [n, nn], has already been noted (#MIA-10). Alternatively, -ṆṆ- may indeed have represented [ṇṇ], or both [ṇṇ] (at least in the case of antecedent *-rṇ-*) and [nn], and become dentalized (or merged with the dental version) in *Late* MIA (Bloch 1920: 138; Turner 1975 [1924]: 220), just before its reduction in NIA. In any case, it uniformly[14] results in *-n-*, *-n#* in NIA. Retroflex *-ṇ-* (<OIA *-n-*, *-ṇ-*) has remained [ṇ], and a separate phoneme, in NIA languages west of Hindi (except Kashmiri) and even in Kumauni, Hariyanvi, and north-western Kauravi ("Vernacular Hindustani") dialects. It has merged with dental *-n-* in Eastern and Western Hindi (except for the above-mentioned dialects), the

Bihari languages, Bengali, and Assamese, but is preserved in Oriya. (Thus: Sindhi–Punjabi–Rajasthani–Gujarati–Marathi–Oriya *pāṇī* 'water' – a favorite example with speakers of these languages – vs. Hindi–Nepali–Bengali–Assamese *pānī/pāni*.) This, along with its probable presence in Old and Early Middle Bengali (Chatterji 1926: 523–7), would seem to confirm the generality of the change of *-n-* to *-ṇ-* in continental MIA despite the absence of the latter sound from the modern Gangetic languages.[15]

[SD-1a](**1**) The story in Sri Lanka is a different one: although *n* and *ṇ* have merged in modern Sinhalese, there was apparently no such merger in Sinhalese Prakrit or early Sinhalese, original *n* being retained as such (Geiger 1938: 62–5).

[SD-1]**b**. As noted earlier (#MIA-12), *-m-* became a nasalized bilabial semivowel [*w̃*] in the Late MIA period (with certain exceptions to be noted later); in NIA the nasality moved to the preceding vowel, leaving -Ṽ*v*-; with the loss of the nasality in modern Marathi (clearer after the recent orthographic reform), and sporadically elsewhere, often only *v* is left: Pkt *ṇāma* 'name' > M. *nāv*. Or the *v* may be dropped, leaving only the nasalization: P. *nā̃*. Or ultimately both may go, as in Awankari *nā*.

[SD-1]**c**. MIA *-l-*, *-ll-* present more problems. In NIA, the first gives *ḷ* and the second gives *l* in much the same range of languages as *ṇ* and *n* from Prakrit *-ṇ-*, *-ṇṇ-* (except that the retroflex *ḷ* is absent from not only Kashmiri but from most other Dardic dialects as well, and from Sindhi): Punjabi-Rajasthani-Gujarati–Marathi *phaḷ*, Oriya *phɔḷɔ* 'fruit' = Hindi–Nepali *phal*, Bengali–Assamese *phɔl*. That seems simple enough. However, in the absence of graphic indication of *ḷ* in Middle Prakrit, there seems to be some question regarding the date and generality of the shift *-l-* > *-ḷ-*. Did it characterize all of Middle Indian, or was it only a regional (and late) development? The Prakrit grammarians (mainly Hemachandra) describe it only for the allegedly Northwestern Paiśācī, but as noted above the modern Dardic languages do not exhibit it (although most *West Pahari* dialects do). Chatterji's view is that the *-l-* > *-ḷ-* shift was indeed characteristic of "most" MIA (including Magadhi, which applied it also to secondary *-l-*'s derived from OIA *-r-*), and that subcontinental NIA languages which fail to show it have *redentalized* the *-ḷ-*, exactly as they did the *-ṇ-*. Alternatively, some of them have developed it further to *-r-*: these include primarily Sindhi on the one hand (Pkt *thala* 'dry ground' > S. *thar*ᵘ 'the Thar or Indian Desert' vs. G. *thaḷ*; S. *phar*ᵘ 'fruit' vs. G. *phaḷ*) and Eastern Hindi–Bihari on the other (Mth. Mag. Bhoj. *phar*, OAw. *phara* 'fruit'). This is taken to be further evidence of the generality of an *-ḷ-* stage. Although there are a number of *l* > *r* shifts in the history of Indo-Aryan without benefit of *ḷ*, these are sporadic, whereas this is systematic and general in the dialects concerned.

[SD-1c](**1**) Sinhalese again stands apart, in that its former *ḷ*, now merged with *l*, came from MIA *-ḍ-* (<OIA *-ṭ-*, *-ḍ-*) not from *-l-*, which was preserved.

[SD-1]**d**. All of this is further complicated by the fact that intervocalic -**ḍ-* (not -**ṭ-*, unless subject to early voicing) became *-ḷ-* much earlier in an Aryan dialect represented by Vedic, and most NIA languages inherit some words (not always the same ones) with *-ḷ-* (or with *-l-* in languages which lack *ḷ*) from such a source: OIA *pīḍayati* 'presses' (perf. *pipīḷē*) > MIA *pīḍai/pīlaī* > OG. *pīḍaī* (G. *pīṛvũ*), M. *piḷṇē*, Kho. *peḷik*; OIA *taḍāga* 'pond' > Pkt *taḍā(g)a/talāya/talāva* > G.M. *taḷāv*, H.N.B. *talāu*.

[SD-1]**e**. In much of NIA, MIA *-ḍ-* (<OIA *-ṭ-*, *-ḍ-*) became, at least allophonically, [*-ṛ-*], which is what represents the non-*ḷ* variant in most languages today: OIA *gaḍa* 'ditch, hole' > B. *gɔṛ*, O. *gɔṛɔ* vs. M. *gaḷ*, Kho. *gōḷ*. (Often both variants are represented in a language, with or without semantic differentiation: OIA *naḍa/naḷa/nala* 'reed' > L. *naṛ*, *naḷā*, P. *naṛā* 'cane', *nal* 'bamboo tube', B.H. *naṛ*, *nal* 'reed', etc.)

[SD-1]**f**. In the Bihari and Eastern (and even some Western) Hindi dialects, Nepali, Assamese, and East Bengali dialects (and partly in Kashmiri also), this [*ṛ*] has merged, no longer allophonically, with */r/* – and thus, in the first two, also with -**ḷ-* (>*-r-* according to #SD-1c above)!

[SD-1]**g**. MIA *-ḍḍ-* has also, and contrary to the general rule, become *-ṛ-* (thus merging with *-ḍ-* in Standard Hindi, Bengali, Gujarati, Marathi, Central Pahari, eastern West Pahari and Rajasthani dialects, and Oriya – and with *-r-* in Assamese and Romany). MIA *-ḍḍ-* is differentiated as *-ḍ-*, however (in accordance with the rule), in the *"r"*-languages (Nepali, Eastern Hindi, Bihari), and in the *"l"*-language, Sinhalese. (See especially Turner 1975 [1926a].)

In short, although many NIA words with *-l-*, *-r-* seem paragons of stability, coming down practically unaltered from OIA times (e.g., H. *gal* 'throat', Si. *kara* 'hand'), others have more complicated histories, even apart from the sporadic confusion of these two sounds directly with each other from early times. It might be helpful to tabulate some of these correspondences (see Table 7.3 below).

[SD-1]**h**. *-s-* need not detain us long. It weakens to *-h-* regularly only in Sindhi, "Lahnda", and partly in Punjabi: MIA *āsā* 'wish' > S. *āha* (H. *ās*); MIA *purisa/purusa* 'man' > S. *purihu* (H. *purus*); MIA *sāsa* 'breath' (OIA *śvāsa*) > S. *sāhu*, L.P. *sāh* (H. *sās/sā̃s*). This specifically intervocalic weakening should not be confused with the more general weakening of *s* in all positions (including initial and geminated) found in some other NIA languages (Sinhalese, Kashmiri); in those under discussion here, initial *s-* and geminate *-ss-* are resistant according to the general rule for consonants: MIA *sassū* 'mother-in-law' > S. *sasu*, L. *sass* (vs. K. *haʃ*, Si. *suhul*).

Table 7.3 *MIA and NIA intervocalic* nasals and liquids: "normal" correspondences*

MIA:	*-ṇ-*	*-ṇṇ-*	*-m-* *-w-*	*-mm-*	*-l-*	*-ll-*	*-ḍ-*	*-ḍḍ-*	*-r-*
NIA:									
Sindhi	*-ṇ-*	*-n-*	*-̃w-*	*-m-*	*-r-*	*-l-*	*-ṛ/(l)-*	*-ɗ-*	*-r-*
Gujarati	*-ṇ-*	*-n-*	*-m-*	*-m-*	*-ḷ-*	*-l-*	*-ṛ/(l)-*	*-ṛ-*	*-r-*
Marathi	*-ṇ-*	*-n-*	*-w-*	*-m-*	*-ḷ-*	*-l-*	*-ḍ/(ḷ)-*	*-ḍ-*	*-r-*
Oriya	*-ṇ-*	*-n-*	*-̃w-*	*-m-*	*-ḷ-*	*-l-*	*-ṛ/(ḷ)-*	*-ṛ-*	*-r-*
Hindi	*-n-*	*-n-*	*-̃w-*	*-m-*	*-l-*	*-l-*	*-ṛ/(l)-*	*-ṛ-*	*-r-*
Bengali	*-n-*	*-n-*	*-̃w-*	*-m-*	*-l-*	*-l-*	*-ṛ/(l)-*	*-ṛ-*	*-r-*
Assamese	*-n-*	*-n-*	*-̃w-*	*-m-*	*-l-*	*-l-*	*-r/(l)-*	*-r-*	*-r-*
Maithili	*-n-*	*-n-*	*-̃w-*	*-m-*	*-r-*	*-l-*	*-r/(l)-*	*-ḍ-*	*-r-*
Nepali	*-n-*	*-n-*	*-̃w-*	*-m-*	*-l-*	*-l-*	*-r/(l)-*	*-ḍ-*	*-r-*
Sinhalese	*-n-*	*-n-*	*-m-*	*-m-*	*-l-*	*-l-*	*-*ḷ > l-*	*-ḍ-*	*-r-*

* "Intervocalic" in Early NIA > often final in later NIA, due to loss of final vowels. (The *-w-* is variously written: -V, -U, -O.)

#SD-2. It is sometimes claimed that there were certain definable circumstances under which the vowel-lengthening rule did not apply (at least in the central group), even though following geminates were reduced, namely, when the geminate was followed by a long vowel, e.g., MIA *kappūra* (<OIA *karpūra*) 'camphor', MIA *ucchāha* (<OIA *utsāha*) 'energy'; MIA *kappāsa* (<OIA *karpāsa*) 'cotton' > H.G. *kapūr*, *uchāh*, *kapās* – vs. M. *kāpūr*, *kāpūs*, B. *kāpās*. A similar stricture would apply to the nasal + stop environment: MIA *mandāra* 'coral-tree'; MIA *tambūla/tambōla* 'betel-leaf' > H. *ma(n)dār*, *tambol*, G. *tāboḷ*, vs. M. *mā(̃)dār*, B. *mādār*, M. *tābūḷ*, B. *tābū(l)*. The further qualification is needed that the word must be originally of *more than two* syllables, because, as we have seen, MIA *jibbhā*, *jaŋghā* > H. *jībh*, *jāgh*. Although the end product does represent a common difference between NIA languages of the Central group (i.e. Hindi, and less consistently Gujarati) and some of the others, it is more likely the result of a process akin to the later Hindi rule which shortens all stem vowels before suffixes containing long vowels (in turn related to larger factors of word rhythm – cf. Bloch 1965: 46–7), then of failure of the Early NIA rule to apply. Cf. Old G. *ūchāh* > Mod. G. *uchāh*, and see Turner 1975 (1921): 106 (sec. 23.3). On the other side of the argument is the fact of preservation of the nasal consonant (vs. its reconstitution?) in H. words like *sindūr* 'vermilion', *hiṇḍōl* 'swing', *tambōl*.

7.9 Exceptions to the mainstream developments

Some IA languages and dialects did not participate in all of the innovations described in the preceding two sections, thus preserving older forms and distinctions. Although it is generally the northwest that is most conservative, the pattern of each conservation is different, and needs to be looked at separately. They will be taken up in the reverse order to which the innovations were presented, i.e. starting with the most recent.

7.9.1 The first conservation to be considered, that of final vowels, is an exception to the generalization about the northwest, no doubt because the innovation concerned is so recent. As we have seen, original long vowels were shortened in Late MIA and lost (along with original short vowels) in NIA. Except for certain pronominal, numerical, and other special forms, all final vowels in inherited words in the focal NIA languages are derived from coalescence of Late MIA sequences of vowels. The loss of original final vowels was a very recent development, however – known to be after the sixteenth or even the seventeenth century in certain of the languages concerned. Therefore it is not surprising to find that the process is incomplete in various ways in widely scattered NIA languages, implying no special connection among them: Konkani (southern dialects only), Sindhi, Oriya, Maithili, Awadhi, rustic dialects even of Western Hindi (Braj, Kanauji). Different vowels are preserved in different languages, in different functions, and to different degrees.

Thus Maithili has ultrashort $^{-a,-i,-u}$, of which the last two are often inaudible and confused with $^{-a}$ (Jha 1958: 88–90); Awadhi (Western dialects only) has rather *-i̥*, *-u̥*, *-e̥*, described by Saksena (1937) as "whispered", yet becoming ordinary short vowels under certain circumstances. Something similar affects Braj *-i*, *-u* in some dialects (Dh. Varma 1935: 50). A "half-pronounced" final *-i* is reported also from the Ballia dialect of Bhojpuri (lost in the Banaras dialect) by Tiwari (1960). (The short *-i*/*-i̥* which is the marker of the absolutive participle in these dialects comes from a sequence of vowels, MIA *-ia*. Similarly the 2sg. imperative in *-u* comes from the sequence *-ahu*.) Again in the Bihar group, it appears that the newly emergent Angika language (Grierson's Chikachiki Boli) also preserves original final vowels, sometimes even strengthening (lengthening) them. Final vowels are lost in the remaining Bihari speeches, Magahi and Sadani (Nagpuria) except that final *-i* is "preserved" in the latter by being in effect transposed to the preceding syllable: *āig* 'fire' (<**āgʹ* < MIA *aggi*), *dāil* 'split pulse' (<MIA *dāli*), *rāit* 'night' (<MIA *rattī*). This occurs occasionally elsewhere in NIA (most frequently in Assamese) but appears to be regular in Sadani.

In Sindhi, ultrashort $^{-u,-a,-i}$[16] distinguish masculine nominative, oblique, and locative respectively (or in the last two cases, also feminines). The Kacchi dialect has lost the final vowels. In Southern Konkani, where such vowels have been attributed (wrongly, see Katre 1966: 9–13) to Dravidian influence, *-u* and *-a* distinguish old masculines (*hātu* 'hand' < *hattō* < *hastaḥ*) and neuters (*phaḷa* 'fruit' < *phalam*). A better candidate for Dravidian influence might be the -ɔ that is added to all Oriya words not ending in another vowel, like the *-u* of neighboring Telugu. In many cases this -ɔ (which is not pronounced in the Sambalpuriya or Western Oriya dialect, according to Tripathi 1956–7:77) corresponds to an etymological *-a*, in others it does not. (Similarly, the addition of *-u* to words of Perso-Arabic origin in both Braj and Sindhi – *jwābu*, *naukaru* – cannot be described as the retention of an etymologically justified vowel: something else, indeed resembling Dravidian, is also going on.) Oriya does, however, preserve other vowels: *rāti* 'night' (<MIA *rattī* < OIA *rātrī*), *sāsu* 'mother-in-law' (<MIA *sassū* < OIA *śvaśrū*). It may be taken therefore to preserve Late MIA -**a* (>[-ɔ]) as well, though extending it analogically to other forms.

Kashmiri is often added to the list of final vowel preservers. Insofar as this is based on a misinterpretation of Grierson's so-called *mātrā* vowels, it is not correct. The latter do not constitute syllables in the modern language (Bailey 1937: 6), although they may have done so at the time of composition (late eighteenth century) of the Kashmiri *Ramayana* (Morgenstierne 1973 [1941]: 286); they are detectable only from their effects on "preceding" consonants and vowels and are thus one of several possible devices for representing (in this case, historically and indirectly) features of the latter. There are some real vowel retentions in present-day Kashmiri also: *gara* 'house' (spelled *garə* by Bailey and *gari-* by Kachru), *atha* 'hand' (= *athə* < OIA *hasta*), *dāñě* 'paddy' (spelled *daani* by Bailey and *da:ni* by Kachru) < OIA *dhānya*; more widely, the many "Ablatives" in *-i* (*gari* 'at home'), which contrast with $^{-i}$*-mātrā*: *guri* 'from the horse' ≠ *gur*^{i} (= [gur']) 'horses'. These are a long way from constituting a general retention of old final vowels, however: cf. Oriya *muḷɔ* 'root', Sindhi *mūr*^{u} (= 'capital'), K. *mūl*; Oriya *āṭhɔ* 'eight', Sindhi *aṭh*^{a}, K. *öṭh* (= @ Bailey ззṭ*h*). This is generally the case in Dardic, although there may be retentions in conservative dialects like Phalura (*çhītru* 'field' < *kṣētra*; cf. Shina *çeç*, Kalasha *çhetr*; H.B.P. *khēt*).

7.9.2 The earliest[17] and most characteristic NIA development, namely the shortening of MIA geminates with compensatory lengthening of the preceding short vowel (#NIA-1), did not obtain (usually – there are always exceptions) in areas of the northwest centering on Punjabi and "Lahnda"; thus, MIA *aggi* 'fire', *satta* 'seven' > H.B.G.M. *āg*, *sāt*, but P.L. (and W. Pahari) *agg*, *satt*. (A final geminate is usually pronounced with a very short [-ə] release.) Many such forms are to be found in Standard Hindi itself, which is thus revealed to be less purely a language of the Central group than dialects such as Braj: MSH.

makkhan, Braj *mākhan* 'butter'; MSH. *pakkā*, Braj *pākā* 'ripe'. Such forms have commonly been attributed to borrowing from Punjabi, but as Učida (1971) has shown, their origin is more likely in the Hariyanvi and "Kauravi" dialects of Western Hindi immediately west and northwest of Delhi, prominent in the dialect mixture that went into Standard Hindi (although themselves describable as transitional to Punjabi). Precisely which Dardic and West Pahari dialects preserve the geminates (e.g., Kashmiri does not, but the Rambani, Poguli, Kashtawari, and Doda Siraji dialects of the Kashmir group apparently do; Gilgiti Shina does not, but Guresi Shina does) and in which words, is too complex a matter to be gone into here, but it may be noted that the Gojri language, of Rajasthani affinity, is among the preservers, in contrast to the dialects of Rajasthan proper.

It is convenient for mainstream NIA to speak of the shortening of geminates and the lengthening of the preceding vowel as two aspects of a single process, but Sindhi, which has the former without the latter (Oriya *ākhi* 'eye', H.G. *hāth* 'hand' = S. *akhi*, *hathu* < MIA *akkhi*, *hattha*), shows that the two are not necessarily linked. Similarly, although the evolution of VNC into V:˜C looks like a related process in mainstream NIA (and in Punjabi, where neither process takes place), again Sindhi separates it: MIA *danta* 'tooth' > H.B.G. *dā̃t*, P. *dand*, S. *ɗ̣andu*. (For S. *ɗ̣* and S.P. *-nd* see next section; the retention of the short vowel and nasal consonant are the points under discussion here.)

7.9.3 In this connection, it will be justifiable to break a strict reverse-chronological order to note that Sindhi, some "Lahnda" and Punjabi dialects, and some Dardic and West Pahari dialects also show evidence of a much earlier retention, that of long vowels before double consonants (shortened in conjunction with the simplification of clusters in Pali and mainstream Prakrit), whether the latter were subsequently reduced or not: OIA *pārśva* 'side' > MIA *passa*, but S. *pās*^{u}, L.P. *pāssā*; OIA *mārga* 'road' > MIA *magga*, Pothwari L. *magg*, but S. *māḍu*; OIA **ārta* 'flour' > H. *āṭā* but P. *āṭṭā*; OIA *āṇḍa* 'egg' > MIA *aṇḍa*, but P. *āṇḍā*. (See Turner 1967.) Thus in Sindhi both long and short vowels occur before double consonants that have been shortened, but the former always (except in borrowed Midland forms!) represent original long vowels, in contrast with mainstream NIA where they may represent OIA short vowels that have been lengthened (or long vowels that were shortened and then re-lengthened). In literary Punjabi, which like literary Hindi represents a dialectal mixture, both types are found: *āṭṭā*, *āṇḍā*, *gājjar* alongside *allā* (<OIA *ārdra*), *magg*. Forms such as *gāḍḍī* 'cart' are also found in some Hindi ("Kauravi") dialects northwest of Delhi (see Učida 1971 and Gumperz 1958) and in some West Pahari and Dardic dialects, as are also, in the latter, forms of the Sindhi type.

7.9.4 Turning now to Late MIA innovations, intervocalic *-m-* is preserved in Sinhalese, most Dardic languages including Kashmiri and Shina, and, in certain positions (i.e. except in the preaccentual syllable and in inflectional suffixes: see Turner 1975 [1921]: 131) in Gujarati (also certain adjacent dialects of Rajasthani, such as Mewari): thus OIA *grāma* 'village' > Si. *gama*, K. *gām*, Kal. *grom*, Kho. *gram*, Savi *grām*, Bshk. *lām*, G. *gām* (vs. H.S. *gāu*, M. *gāv*). (See Table 7.3.)

7.9.5 Moving back to Second Stage MIA innovations: initial *y-* is retained, again by Sinhalese, Kashmiri, and certain other Dardic languages: OIA *yantra* 'device, contrivance' > Si. *yat* 'mill', Phal. *yāndr*, Sh. *yo̱r*; K. *yend*[a]*r* 'spinning-wheel'; OIA *yava* 'barley' > Si. *yava*, Sh. Bshk. *yō*. (Some Dardic dialects, including Kalasha and Khowar, have the transitional sound ʒ here instead.)

7.9.6 Intervocalic *-t-*, *-d-*, lost in the Literary Prakrits except for Sauraseni, lasted longer in the northwest; *-t-* and possibly also *-d-* are represented by *l* or *r* in modern Romany dialects (see Turner 1926b), and *-t-* only, by *r* in Khowar and *l* (sometimes evolving further into *u*) in Kalasha: OIA *bhrātr̥* 'brother' > Eur. Rom. *phral*, As. Rom. *bar*, Kho. *brār*; OIA *śata* 'hundred' > Eur. Rom. *ʃel*, Kho. *ʃor*, Kal. *ʃau* (<**ʃal*, found as a loanword in Shina); OIA *hr̥daya* 'heart' > Eur. Rom. *yilo* (<**hidaa*), but Kho. *hardi*, Kal. *hīṙa* (affected by *r̥t* > *ṛt*). OIA 3sg. *-ti* > Kho. *-r-*: *baṣir* 'it rains' < *varṣati* (with change of conjugation: Morgenstierne 1947: 20, Grierson 1906: 18).

7.9.7 Reduction of the three OIA sibilants to one did not take place in the northwest. All three are retained as such (with some redistribution in occurrence) in Shina, Phalura, Khowar, Kalasha, Bashkarik, Gawarbati, and some Pashai dialects (Morgenstierne 1973b: 34), as well as in the Shahbazgarhi inscription of Asoka and in the Kharosthi documents. Other Dardic dialects, European and Syrian Romany, and most West Pahari dialects (as far east as Jaunsari, but apparently excluding such dialects as Mandeali and Kochi) have retained two (as *ʃ*, *s*). At least in Kashmiri, this does not necessarily entail a complete merger of two of the original three sibilants, however: partly *ś* (but also intervocalic *-ṣ-*) has become *h*. (Nor does this entail a merger with **h*, which in some positions is dropped. The complicated historical phonology of Kashmiri stands in great need of a full working out. Meanwhile the following may be suggestive:)

OIA *s* = K. *s*:	OIA *ś* = K. *h*:
sapta 'seven' > *sath*	*śata* 'hundred' > *hath*
ghāsa 'grass' > *gāsa*	*daśa*' 'ten' > *dɜh*
dāsa 'slave' > *dās*	*keśa* 'hair' > *kīh*
	śuŋga n. of plant > *honga*
OIA *s* = K. *h*:	OIA *ś* = K. *ʃ*:
divasa 'day' > *doh*	*dēśa* 'country' > *dīʃ*
OIA *-rṣ-* > K. *ʃ*:	OIA *-ṣ-* = K. *h*:
varṣa 'rain' > *woʃ*	*viṣa* 'poison' > *vih*
	vēṣa 'dress' > *vīh*
OIA *-ṣC-*, *-śr-* = K. *ʃ*:	OIA *h* = K. Ø:
puṣya 'n. of plant' > *pōʃ*	*hasta* 'hand' > *atha*
śvaśru 'mother-in-law' > *haʃ*	*hala* 'plow' > *ala*
aśru 'tear' > *oʃ*	*hara* 'necklace' > *ara*

Elsewhere in NIA the presence of more than one sibilant in native vocabulary is a secondary development after reduction to one: either originally allophonic and rendered marginally contrastive through borrowings (e.g., in Marathi), or the result of the evolution of other sounds, mainly **c*, *ch*, into sibilants (in East Bengali dialects) – although Pandit has argued that some instances of *ʃ* in Gujarati are historical (<OIA **ś*).

7.9.8 Sibilants are retained in clusters in some far Northwestern languages (not including Kashmiri or most Shina dialects), and in Romany. Mainly it is a question of *-st-*, *-ṣṭ-* in medial position: OIA *aṣṭā* 'eight' > Kal. *aṣṭ*, Kho. *oṣṭ*, Phal. *áṣṭ*, Gaw. *ōṣṭ* (but K. ɜɜṭh); *hasta* 'hand' > Kal. *hast*, Kho. *host*, Gaw. *hast*, Rom. (E.) *vast* (but K. *atha*, Sh. *hat(h)*). In Kalasha and Khowar, initial *st*, *sth*, *sn* and even *sk* partly survive also (with aid of a prothetic vowel), and *śv* by transformation into *iśp-*, *isp-*: OIA *stamba* 'bunch' > Kal. *istam*; OIA *sthōra* 'pack-horse' > Kho. *istōr*; OIA *snāta* 'bathed' > Kho. *isnár*; OIA **skabha* 'peg' > Kal. Kho. *iskow*; OIA *śvēta* 'white' > Kho. *iśper*; *śvaśru* 'mother-in-law' > Kho. *iśpreṣi*, Kal. *isprɛs*. Medially also cf. OIA *pr̥ṣṭha* 'back' > Kal. *piṣṭ*; OIA *aśru* 'tear' > Kho. *aśrū*.

7.9.9 The survival of stop + *r* clusters, while also centered in the northwest, is more widespread, extending in the case of dental + *r* to "Lahnda" and Sindhi (which turns them into *ṭr*, *ḍr*) and in the case of a few items with *tr* also to Gujarati and even to Bengali and the Eastern group (*triṁśat* 'thirty' > K. *trah*, S. *ṭrīh̃*, L. *trīh*, G. *trīʃ/tīʃ*, B. *triʃ*, A. *triχ*). Survival of *kr*, *gr*, *ghr*, *pr*, *br*, *bhr* is more restricted, but still fairly widespread in the Dardic group, and sporadic in adjacent West Pahari dialects, Romany, "Lahnda", and Punjabi.

> OIA *kr*: *krīṇ-* 'buy' > Kho. *kren-*, Phal. *krin-*, Sh. *krin-*; *krūra* 'cruel' > K. *krūr*, Khaś. *krūrā* (L. *kurāṛā*); *krōśa* 'shout' > K. *kruh*, Bhal. *kro*
>
> OIA *gr*: *grāma* 'village' > Kho. *gram*, Kal. *grom*, Phal. *grām*, Sh. *girōm*, Cameali (WP) *grā̃*, Khaś. *grā̃o*; *grīva* 'neck' > Kal. *gŕä*, Sh. *grī*; *grīṣma* 'summer' > Kho. *griṣp*
>
> OIA *ghr*: *ghrāṇa* 'smelling' > Kal. *grũ*, Phal. *grhōṇ*; **ghraṇiṣya* 'sun's heat' > Kho. *graniś*
>
> OIA *pr*: *pratōlī* 'gate, main street' > WPah. *prauḷ*, *proḷ*; **prabhāla* > Kal. *pralik*, Phal. *prāl*, Gaw. *plāl*
>
> OIA *br*: *brākati* 'bleat' > Kho. *braγ*, Sh. *brã*
>
> OIA *bhr*: *bhrātṛ* 'brother' > Kho. *brar*, Tir. *brā*, Phal. *brho*, Gaw. *blāya*, Khas., L.P. *bhrā*, Rom. (E.) *phral (phal)*; *bhrū* 'eye-brow' > Kho. *bru*; **bhrāśa* 'flame' > K. *brāh*

7.9.10 One of the oldest IA assimilations, that of the peculiar cluster *kṣ*, is sometimes loosely stated to be to "*(c)ch* in the northwest and southwest and to *(k)kh* elsewhere", albeit with much mutual borrowing. While *kṣ* may indeed have merged with OIA *ch* (and undergone further evolution with the latter) in Marathi and Sinhalese and areas of West Pahari, this merger does not appear to have taken place further to the northwest. There in many languages it appears as *ç(h)*, and contrasts with **ch* (which often has developed to *ċ(h)* [ts(h)]. This may fairly be called a retention, since *kṣ/ṭṣ/ç(h)* are almost the same thing:

> OIA *kṣ* = *ç(h)*: *kṣīra* milk > Kho. Kal. Gaw. *çhir*, Phal., Bshk. *çhīr*; *akṣi* 'eye' > Phal. *açhi*, Sh. *açhī*, Maiya *āçhī*; *kṣētra* 'land' > Kho. *çhetur*, Kal. *çhetr*, Phal. *çhītru*
>
> OIA *ch* = *ch*: *chāyā(°akā)* 'shade' > Sh. *chas*, *chāi*, Kal. *chak*, Kho. *chaγ*, Phal. *chɛi*; *chidyatē* 'is cut' > Sh. *chijoiki*; *pṛcchati* 'asks' > Kal. *phuc-* (with shifted aspiration)

In Kashmiri and possibly some other nearby dialects, OIA *kṣ* > *ch*, but OIA *ch* > *ċh* [*t*sh]: *akṣi* > K. *achi*, *mōkṣita* 'set free' > K. *mucha*; but **chāyikā* 'shade' > K. *ċāy*, **chāpa* 'young of animal' > K. *ċav*, *pratyaya* 'belief' > K. *poċ*.

In a fashion similar to **kṣ*, the cluster *ts* has been "reinterpreted as a phoneme" *č* in some northwestern languages such as Kalasha and Phalura (in which **ch* generally > *ch*, not **čh*, giving three articulations).

7.10 Regional and language-specific innovations

The remaining phonological features of NIA involve innovations with more restricted distributions than those defining the Indo-Aryan mainstream. These are mostly of fairly recent (i.e. NIA) origin, although a few, particularly some of those pertaining to Sinhalese, go back to an earlier period. They fall into two types: a) innovations shared by several contiguous languages (constituting a group smaller than or other than the mainstream group); b) innovations that are language-specific, although they may turn up independently in more than one language. This section can only survey the more important cases of the latter. The two types overlap: a given innovation may both have spread regionally and occur independently elsewhere.

#RI-1. That is certainly true of the first such innovation to be noted, the passage of OIA *v-* to *b-*. This is characteristic of such a large group of mainstream languages (including Hindi,[18] Eastern Rajasthani, Kumauni, Nepali, the Bihari group, Bengali, Oriya, Assamese) that it may seem arbitrary not to include it among the defining features of the latter. This has not been done because it is not shared by Marathi or Gujarati, which do share the more fundamental mainstream feature of VCC > V:C.

Skt	*H.*	*B.*	*G.*	*M.*	*P.*
varṇa 'color'	*bān*		*vān*	*vān*	*vann(agi)*
vaṭa 'banyan'	*baṛ*	*baṛ*	*vaṛ*	*vaḍ*	*vaṛ*
vartayati 'twist'	*bāṭ-*	*bāṭ-*	*vāṭ-*	*vāṭ-*	*vaṭṭ-*
vivāha 'marriage'	*byāh*	*biyā*	*vivāh*	*vivāh*	*viāh*

A band of languages retaining original *v-* runs from Sinhalese up the west coast of India through Sindhi, "Lahnda", and Kashmiri (=[*w-*]), and separates the mainly central–eastern group of *b-* languages, which extends as far as West Pahari and Dogri, from a second locus of *v-* > *b-* innovation in further Dardic (including the in many respects highly conservative languages Kalasha, Khowar, and Shina). Beyond these again, *v-* is retained by Pashai dialects, Asian Romany, and Gawarbati–Shumashti (although lost altogether before *-i-* in the latter two: OIA *varṣa* 'rain' > Gaw. Shum. *wāṣ*, but OIA *viṣa* 'poison' > Gaw. *iṣ*). European dialects of Romany independently develop *v-* > *b-*. Back on the other side of the line, Punjabi, basically a *v-* language, shows mixed forms due to Central influence, while some dialects of Western Rajasthani (Marwari) maintain the *v-*/*b-* contrast by changing the latter to implosive ɓ-, even while changing the former to (normal) *b-*. (Some other Marwari dialects, including Mewari, maintain *v-*: see Allen 1957b, Magier 1983.)

#**RI-2**. The second localized innovation to be noted, the voicing of voiceless stops after nasals, is definitely centered outside the mainstream area, in the northwest (Punjabi, Sindhi, Kashmiri, further Dardic, West Pahari, with Gojri and Romany) although it does also affect both Central Pahari and Nepali (in those cases where Hindi forms have not subsequently ousted forms native to the language). It is one of the most characteristic differences between Hindi and Punjabi:

Skt	*H.*	*P.*	*S.*
aŋka 'mark'	*ā̃k*	*aŋg*	*aŋgu*
pañca 'five'	*pā̃c*	*pañj*	*pañja*
kaṇṭā 'thorn'	*kā̃ṭā*	*kaṇḍā*	*kaṇḍo*
danta 'tooth'	*dā̃t*	*dand*	*ɗ̣andu*
campa 'n. of tree'	*cā̃p*	*cambā*	*cambo*

Although the development is quite old (found in the Karoshthi documents) isolated enclaves in the region have resisted it, among them Gawarbati and the Bhadrawahi–Khashali complex in northwest West Pahari. Some Dardic languages (Khowar, Shina, Bashkarik), however, have carried the process a step further and dropped the stop, or dropped it in some forms (e.g., the Kashmiri present participle in *-n* < *∗-nd* < *-nt*).

#**RI-3**. Again in the northwest and adjacent areas, the characteristic Indo-Aryan feature of aspiration has undergone various special developments:

[RI-3]**a**. In most Dardic, including Kashmiri, the voiced aspirates have lost their aspiration. That this is a recent development is shown by the retention of voiced aspirates in Kalasha, Phalura, and some dialects of the Kohistani group (Maiyã, Kanyawali, Torwali), and by older informants or in earlier accounts of Tirahi, Gawarbati, and Bashkarik.

[RI-3]**b**. In Kalasha and Phalura there are some historically unmotivated[19] voiced aspirates: OIA *jānāti* 'knows' > Kal. *jhon-*, Phal. *jhan-*. These should be distinguished from cases in the same languages where aspiration, voiced or otherwise, occurring later in the word has been *transferred* to the initial consonant: OIA *bandhati* 'binds' > Kal. *bhon-* (cf. also Eur. Romany *phand-*), OIA *pṛcchati* 'asks' > Kal. *phuc-* (cf. Eur. Romany *phuc-*, Arm. Romany *puch-*). It is not clear whether this in turn is related to the phenomena noted by Allen (1957b) for certain Rajasthani dialects, particularly Harauti, where, in a revival and modification of Grassman's Law permitting only one aspirate per stem (if indeed it ever was suspended in this area as it was in Early Central MIA) voiced aspirates occur only initially, and non-initial aspiration is often transferred to initial unaspirated voiceless stops: *kathā* 'story' (Tss.) > *khatā*. (There is also some unmotivated aspiration of initials: > *phāṇī* 'water'.) Non-initial voiceless aspirates do occur, albeit infrequently, in both Kalasha and Phalura: Kal. Phal. *muṭh* 'bullock with stunted horns' (<OIA **muṭṭha*), Kal. *maçhērik*, Phal. *māçhurī* 'bee' (<OIA **mākṣikakara*), and aspiration is transferred to voiced as well as voiceless initials (cf. *bhon-* above). The precise conditions remain to be stated. Similar phenomena obtain also far to the south, in Konkani: only initial aspirates are tolerated, non-initial aspiration is shifted to the initial consonant (Ko. *dhai* 'curds' (<OIA *dadhi*, vs. H. *dahī*), Ko. *phāttōru* 'stone' (< OIA *prastara*, vs. H. *patthar*), and there are instances of unmotivated initial aspiration (Ko. *dhūra* 'far' < OIA *dūra*).

[RI-3]**c**. Metathesis of aspiration in the opposite direction, transferring the aspiration of an initial stop to the next postvocalic position, was reported for some West Pahari dialects by Grierson as noted previously (Chapter 5). This may be related to tonal phenomena (see below).

[RI-3]**d**. Final aspiration and pre-consonantal aspiration (-C*h*C-), along with medial *h-*, tends to be lost in a number of NIA languages, including Bengali (Chatterji 1926: 441), Nepali (Turner 1975 [1921]: 119), Gujarati, and Marathi, whether or not this is reflected in spelling. It is best preserved in Hindi:[20]

Pkt	*H.*	*B.*	*N.*	*G.*	*M.*
hattha 'hand'	*hāth*	*hāt*	*hāt*	*a̤th**	*hāt*
saṁbujjhai 'understands'	*samajh-*	*ʃɔmɔj(h)-*		*samaj-*	*samaj-*
vahū 'son's wife'	*bahu*	*bou* (cf. Ku. *bau*)		*va̤u**	*vahū*
bāhira 'outside'	*bāhar*	*bāire*	*bāira*	*bā̤r**	*bāher*

*(see below)

[RI-3]**e**. In Kashmiri, on the other hand, there are secondary (voiceless) aspirates in *final* position: OIA **varta* 'round stone' > K. *waṭh* (Sh. *băṭ*, L.P. *vaṭṭā*). Since all unaspirated voiceless stops are replaced by aspirates in this position[21] the matter is regarded as phonetic rather than phonological by some students of Kashmiri.

[RI-3]**f**. Immediately south of Dardic, the voiced aspirates (and non-initial *h*) also are lost in Punjabi, leaving in their wake the prominent tone phenomena of that language. Where a voiced aspirate preceded a stem vowel there is the modern "low tone" (`); where it followed, there is the "high tone" (´). (In disyllabic stems, a former intervocalic aspirate usually affects the following vowel.[22]) This is most easily illustrated by comparison with Hindi, which retains the aspirates concerned:

	H.	*P.*
'horse'	*ghōṛā*	*kō`ṛā*
'brother'	*bhāī*	*pā`ī*
'sunshine'	*dhūp*	*tu`pp*
'washerman'	*dhōbī*	*tō`bī*
'no'	*nahī*	*náī*
'milk'	*dūdh*	*dúdd*
'study'	*paṛhnā*	*páṛnā*
'tongue'	*jībh*	*jī́b*
'taught'	*paṛhāyā*	*paṛā`yā*
'story'	*kahānī*	*kā`ṇī*

While loss of aspiration in the Dardic group results in *unaspirated voiced* stops, it will be noted that in Punjabi the transformation of aspiration into tone *devoices* as well as deaspirates preceding (but not following) stops. What the historical relationship of aspiration is to alleged tone in "Lahnda" and West Pahari dialects, where voiced aspirates are preserved, or in Dardic dialects, where they are deaspirated, are questions needing further research. Needless to say, the tones of Punjabi, which seem to be a recent development, bear no relation to the old Vedic tonal accents.

[RI-3]**g**. The *murmured vowels of Gujarati (and Marathi), described in Chapter 5, are another development of (postvocalic) voiced aspirates and *-h-*, possibly in the direction of tone, still in process as it were. It therefore merits careful monitoring.

#RI-4. Completely unrelated to the above phenomena is the total loss of consonantal aspiration (not, at the beginning, of *h*) in Sinhalese, which goes back to the Sinhalese Prakrit period (*c.* 200 BC–400 AD) and doubtless reflects the areal model of neighboring Dravidian Tamil which lacks aspirates. The early date of this loss meant that the intervocalic aspirated stops of OIA did not leave a residual *-h-* upon their disappearance as in the rest of Indo-Aryan (since they were no longer aspirates at that point), but only a hiatus. Where contraction did not result, the latter was filled, rather more frequently than elsewhere (or at any rate with more lasting results), by euphonic *-y-*, *-v-*, or *-h-* – the last between identical vowels, just as in the case of non-aspirates (Geiger 1938: 46):

OIA	*Pkt*	*Si*
likhati 'writes'	*lihaï*	*liyanu*
sukha 'welfare'	*suha*	*suva*
śākhā 'branch'	*sāhā*	*sā*
mukuṭa, *makuṭa* 'diadem'	*maüḍa*	*muhuḷa*
kadala 'banana'	*kayala*	*kehel*

Modern Sinhalese *h* thus does not necessarily represent OIA **h* (which tends to be lost in initial position, a very rare development elsewhere: OIA *hanati* 'strikes' > Si. *annavā*, OIA *hasta* 'hand' > Si. *ata*, OIA *hr̥daya* 'heart' > Si. *laya*) and never represents, in the strict sense of the word, an OIA aspirate. Other sources of Sinhalese *h* are OIA **s* and **c*, **ch*, in that order chronologically, with those of more recent origin less likely to be dropped, and often forming doublets with *s* (Geiger 1938: 82–93): OIA *chandra* 'moon' > Si. *sam̆da*, *ham̆da*.

#**RI-5**. This brings us to consider two sets of developments which are prominent on the peripheries of Indo-Aryan. On the northeast, the common MIA sibilant opens universally to *χ* initially and to *h* non-initially[23] in Assamese (OIA *śaśaka* 'hare' > A. *χɒhā*), and to *h* generally in North Bengali and initially in East Bengali (Chatterji 1926: 143–4) and partly in Bishnupriya Manipuri (K. P. Sinha 1981). In compensation as it were, MIA *ch*, *cch* (in Assamese also *c*, *cc*) becomes *s* in largely the same languages and dialects, and *jh*, *jjh* (in Assamese also *j*, *jj*) become *z*: MIA *chā(y)ā* 'shade' > A. *sā*, MIA *vaccha* 'calf' > A. *bāsā*, MIA *jāla* 'flame' > A. *zāl*. (In East and North Bengali, *c*, *j* remain in an intermediate stage as [*ts*, *dz*].)

In the south, as already noted above, MIA *s* (OIA *ś*, *ṣ*, *s*) frequently (but never finally) becomes *h* in Sinhalese (and still more often in Maldivian): 'hare' = Si. *sā(vā)/hā(vā)*, MIA *vāsai* 'rains' > Si. *vasinavā/vahinavā*, Md. *veheni*, MIA *satta* 'seven' > Si. *hata/(sata)*, Md. *hat* (vs. Si. pl. *gas* 'trees', *des* 'countries'). The palatal stops *ch*, *c* (previously reduced to *c*) become universally *s*: MIA *chā(y)ā* > Si. *seya*, MIA *vaccha* > Si. *vas(s)ā*. (New palatals arise from combinations such as *-tiy-*; voiced *j* is treated differently: see below.)

In Marathi and Konkani MIA *s* remains, later splitting allophonically to [*ʃ*, *s*], but *ch* also became *s* (with the same allophones) while *c*, *j*, *jh* progressed (before non-front vowels) only as far as [*ts*, *dz*, *dzh*] (conventionally represented as *ċ*, *j̇*, *j̇h*). Later borrowings with [*c*, *j*, *jh*] before non-front vowels have rendered these allophones phonemic, as they have arguably those of *s*: MIA *chā(y)ā* > M. *sāuḷī*, MIA *chura* 'razor' > M. *surā*, MIA *calaï* 'goes away' > M. *ċaḷ-*, MIA *jāla* > M. *j̇āḷ*, MIA **jhaggaḍa* 'quarrel' > M. *j̇hagḍā*.

Further to the north, in North Gujarati, Western Rajasthani (S. Mewari, NW Marwari, see Allen 1957b), and Bhili dialects (those of the Rajasthan–Gujarat–Madhya Pradesh border areas, not those of Dangs on the south) MIA *s* again goes to *h* and *c*, *ch* both to *s* (in NW Marwari only to [ts, tsh]). As noted earlier, in Sindhi, "Lahnda", and sometimes in Punjabi, *intervocalic -s-* goes to *-h-*, but *c*, *ch* remain.

Finally, in the northwest proper, in much of Dardic, West Pahari, and even in Nepali there has been a general phonetic shift of *c*, *ch* as far as [ts, tsh], and *j*, *jh* to [dz, (dzh)] (or even to *z*), in some of the former rendered contrastive by borrowing, the emergence of new *c*, *ch*, *j* (or ʒ), or by some other mechanism (the details remain to be worked out): OIA *candra* 'moon', *chāyā* 'shade', *jān-* 'know' > K. *ċandar*, *ċhāy*, *zān-*, but OIA *caṇa* 'chickpea', *kṣap-* 'be ruined', *vīkṣ-* 'see', **yōṭa* 'pair' > K. *cana* (lw.), *chap-*, *wuch-*, *jūr*. (A regular source for *ch* in Kashmiri is OIA *kṣ*: see 7.8.10 above. Another regular source, not only for *ch* but for *c*, *j* as well, is *ṭ*, *ṭh*, *ḍ* before front vowels in inflection, and *k*, *kh*, *g*, and even *l*, in similar environments: msg. *boḍ* 'big', *vɔzul* 'red' > fpl. *baji*, *vɔzaji* – vs. OIA *ḍimba* 'body' > K. *ḍemb*, *ḍimbur*.) In Kashmiri only, however, have partly OIA *ś* and *-ṣ-* gone to *h*: OIA *śāka* 'potherb', *śvaśru* 'mother-in-law', *śiras* 'head', *māṣa* 'bean' > K. *hākh*, *haʃ*, *hīr*, *māh* (vs. e.g., Sh. *śā*, *śắṣ*).

#RI-6. The vowel *a* has developed a rounded and backed pronunciation ([ə > ɒ > ɔ]) in three quite separate areas: the east (centering on Bengali), the northwest, and Konkani. At the approaches to the foci of this phenomenon, for example in Bihari and West Pahari, it might be described as merely phonetic, but when it reaches the point where in some environments merger with /o/ takes place, as is the case in Bengali when [i, u] follow or followed in the next syllable, or in some cases finally, phonology is affected as well. Even without this, the phonological system of the Eastern group has been affected, if not by the above phonetic change alone, then by it in combination with the loss of the length distinction between the high vowels *ī*, *i* and *ū*, *u*. Together they resulted in a total restructuring of the Eastern vowel systems, making it no longer tenable to consider /ɔ/ the "short equivalent" of old /ā/:

OIA	*Bengali*	*Oriya*	*Assamese*
ī ū	*i u*	*i u*	*i u*
i u			
ē ō	*e o*	*e o*	*e o*
a			
(āi) (āu)	æ ɔ		ɛ ɔ
ā		*a* ɔ	
	a		*a* ɒ
(r̥, l̥)			

Although where /*a*/ remained [ə] the restructuring has been less radical, the distinction in the high vowels has been lost elsewhere as well, e.g., in Marathi, Gujarati, and probably Nepali. It is in fact maintained (qualitatively rather than quantitatively, most observers contend) only in Hindi, Punjabi, Sindhi, and other languages of the northwest. (In Sinhalese length distinctions are entirely secondary and do not represent a preservation.)

The low front and back vowels of NIA languages that have them do not, of course, represent OIA *āi*, *āu*, which merged with *ē*, *ō* early in the MIA period. In Hindi, Punjabi, and Gujarati they arise from monophthongization of similar but much later sequences of vowels produced by the Late MIA loss of intervocalic consonants. In the Eastern languages, on the other hand, where such sequences became *oi*, *ou* (also *ā*, *ō*, etc.), the sources of the open vowels are rather, for Bengali /æ/, mainly MIA *e*, *ē* lowered due to vowel harmony and related causes, and for Bengali–Assamese–Oriya /ɔ, ɒ, ɔ/, mainly MIA *a* as noted above. In Assamese, it appears (synchronic schematization aside) that /ɛ, ɒ/ represent "normal" *ē*, *a* and /e, ɔ/ are products of raising due to vowel harmony or umlaut. Such factors are also clearly operative in Kashmiri, Bashkarik, and other Dardic languages.

#RI-7. It would be useful to distinguish historic *umlaut*, defined as a change in vowel quality in the basic form of a word due to the influence of following vowels that may no longer exist, from *vowel harmony*, defined as synchronic variability of a stem vowel in the course of inflection, hence part of morphophonemics (and of the subject matter of the next chapter) – although the latter also has a history. In Bengali and even more in Kashmiri *both are significantly present*. For Bengali, Chatterji (1926) pinpoints epenthesis (or anticipation of a following vowel) as an important stage in the evolution of historic umlaut, still current in East Bengali, (and, as noted earlier, in Sadani): B. *rākhiyā* > *rāikhyā* > *rekhe* 'having kept'.

Grierson notes that the same phenomenon gradually increases in the West Pahari approaches to Kashmiri.

It is however at the third periphery of the Indo-Aryan world, in Sinhalese, where historic umlaut (together with other vowel mutations) has gone the furthest, often leaving the Sinhalese word with a complement of vowels very different from its NIA sisters. The vowels *a*, *o*, *u* in originally heavy syllables (Geiger 1938: 18) when followed historically by *i* (or by *y*), have been fronted (again through a presumed epenthetic stage) to *ä*, *e*, *i*: OIA *pāniya* 'water', *kōkilā* 'cuckoo', *bhūmi* 'earth' > Si. *pän*, *kevilī*, *bim*. In originally light syllables, there has been *assimilation* to the vowel of the following syllable: OIA *purāṇa* 'old', *kapi* 'monkey', *karuṇā* 'mercy' > Si. *paraṇa*, *kivi*, *kuluṇu*. There has also been what Geiger calls *vowel-levelling* – assimilation of two unlike vowels to an intermediate third vowel: OIA *vihāra* 'monastery' > Si. *vehera*. Finally, there has been replacement of vowels in weak, unaccented syllables with other vowels.

#RI-8. Throughout the northwest, beginning with Sindhi and including "Lahnda", Dardic, Romany and West Pahari, there has been a tendency to transfer of *r* from medial clusters to a position after the initial consonant: OIA *karma* 'work' > Kal. *krum*, Sh. *krom*, Phal. *krām*; OIA *dīrgha* > S. *ḍrigho*, L. *drigghā*, Phal. *drigo*.

#RI-9. In Sindhi, MIA *g*-, *-gg-*, *j*-, *-jj-*, *ḍ*-, *-ḍḍ-*, *d*-, *-dd-*, *b*-, *-bb-* became the implosives (*ɠ*, *ʄ*, *ᶑ*, *ɓ*) peculiar to that language (and neighboring Siraiki), while new normal stops arose from other sources (including loanwords, OIA *y*-, *-vy-*, clusters with nasals and *r*, original *d*- [see below], and deaspiration of initial aspirated voiced stops according to Grassman's Law: see Turner 1924a). Similar developments affected Marwari (Allen 1957b).

The above may be considered the most important *recurrent* peripheral phenomena in Indo-Aryan historical phonology. What remains is essentially language-specific. The following are among the more striking and important:

#RI-10. In Sinhalese, all original long vowels were shortened. (New long vowels have been formed by contraction of vowel sequences.)

#RI-11. Again in Sinhalese, MIA *j*, *jh* (including a layer of former *c*'s which had somewhere undergone voicing) went to *d*: OIA *jān-* 'know', *pūjā* 'worship', *ācārya* 'teacher' > Si. *dannu*, *puda*, *aduru*.

#RI-12. In Maldivian, *p* has become *f*: OIA *pāniya* > Md. *fen*.

#RI-13. In Sindhi, dentals in clusters preceding *r* (original or resulting from metathesis, see section 7.9.9 above) became retroflexes: OIA *traya-* 'three', *drākṣā* 'grape' > S. *ṭrē*, *ḍrākha*. (See Turner 1924b.) In addition, all other surviving *d*'s became retroflex (implosive) *ɗ̣*'s, except when preceded by *n*: OIA *danta* 'tooth' > S. *ɗ̣andu* (Bloch 1965: 61).

#RI-14. In a number of Northwestern languages, C + *r* clusters were neither retained as such nor simplified, but coalesced into new consonant types. In Shina, *dr*, *bhr*, *vr* yielded *ẓ* (or *j̣*), while *tr*, *pr*, *str* gave *ç*. In Gawarbati, some Pashai dialects, and partly Bashkarik the voiceless clusters *tr*, *kr* and (except in Bashkarik, which here follows Shina: Morgenstierne 1940: 216) also *pr* give the voiceless lateral *λ* (OIA *putra* 'son' > Bshk., Savi *puλ*, Gaw. *pūλ*) while their voiced counterparts give ordinary *l* (*drākṣā* 'grape', *grāma* 'village' > Bshk. *laçh*, Bshk. Gaw. *lām*). In the Bhadrawahi–Bhalesi cluster of West Pahari dialects, the products are peculiar laterally-released apical consonants *ṭλ*, *ḍλ*, *ḍhλ* (three sets because voiced aspirates are preserved and clusters involving them seem to be treated differently): OIA *traya* 'three', *haridra* 'turmeric', *bhrū* 'eyebrow' > Bhal. *ṭλā*, *haiḍλ*, *ḍhλu*. They have other antecedents also: OIA *plīhā* 'spleen', *guṇa* 'thread' > Bhal. *ṭλɛi*, *ḍλuṇo* (Varma 1948: 15–17).

#RI-15. In European and Armenian Romany, voiced aspirates became unvoiced aspirates: OIA *dhūma* 'smoke', *ghr̥ta* 'ghee', *bhrātr̥* > Rom. *thuv*, *khil*, *phral*.

#RI-16. Kashmiri has developed a complete set of *palatalized* consonants (in addition to new palatal consonants), mainly from postconsonantal MIA *-i* and *-e*.

7.11 Conclusions

Demarcations in time and space are not only a practical but a theoretical necessity in historical linguistics, but there is an element of arbitrariness, or at any rate of generalization, in such demarcations. In the Indo-Aryan field we are dealing to a large degree with long-term general tendencies that have been operative over much or even all of its history. While it is appropriate to fix as the period of a certain sound change the one when its effects seem to have been most general, in almost every case, its beginnings can be discerned in a few forms much earlier, and then be seen to have gradually gathered momentum. In space also, changes not yet characteristic of an area (particularly if they are "mainstream" changes) will be found to affect some words in it: e.g., VCC > V:C in Punjabi. Turner has called attention to this phenomenon in two important articles, *Anticipation of normal sound-changes in Indo-Aryan* (1975 [1937]) and *Early shortening of geminates with compensatory lengthening in Indo-Aryan* (1975 [1970]).

Although Indo-Aryan has its special peculiarities (such as the tendency to retroflexion, and the tenaciousness of aspiration), and it is these which have perhaps attracted most attention, many of its historical tendencies have been, if not universal, at least common in Indo-European, and students of Romance, Germanic, or Slavic will each find much that is very familiar.

Reconstruction, or even simple etymologizing, still presents many challenging problems, due to borrowing from related and unrelated languages, *Mischformen* and vague but persistent areal influences. Attention is called in this regard to two works of S. M. Katre, *Some problems of historical linguistics in Indo-Aryan* (1965) and *Problems of reconstruction in Indo-Aryan* (1968).

8

Nominal forms and categories

8.1 Introduction: "forms and categories" vs. "morphology"[1]

At this point in a traditional grammar we would turn to what is commonly called "morphology", a description of the inflections and derivational affixes that affect the forms of words. For the NIA languages, whose paradigms achieve their contrasts through various combinations of *inherited synthetic* elements, *new agglutinative* elements, and *analytical* elements, an account confined to the first of these, or even to the first and the second, would be fragmentary, and not give much of an idea of how these languages actually work. For that, the whole system of contrasting forms at the subphrasal level must be examined, heterogeneous though they may be, along with the grammatical categories they imply.

To be sure, we can still call this subject "morphology", if we adopt, e.g., Zograph's suggested (1976) more flexible definition of the latter (or more precisely of *inflection*, taken to be the central concern of "morphology"), that is, as including certain analytical elements (e.g., case particles, auxiliary verbs) entering into *paradigmatic contrasts*. There are compelling reasons to do so. For one thing, the line between such analytic elements and agglutinative affixes is uncertain, particularly since the former are generally ancestral to the latter, through gradual phonetic reduction and adhesion to the stem. (The exceptions are a few affixes borrowed from non-Aryan sources in such languages as Assamese, and affixes of synthetic origin to be discussed below.) A good example is the Bengali genitive suffix *-er*, from the earlier particle *kēra*, found as such in Apabhramsa, Awadhi, Maithili, Khashali, Romany, etc., and thought to come in turn from OIA *kārya* via MIA epenthetic form **kāira*. (See Chatterji 1926: 753.)

It becomes a question, therefore, of stages in a common historical process, wherein it is difficult to determine the precise point of transition from independent particle to suffix. Complicating the problem is the tendency, as older erstwhile analytic elements assume a suffixal value, to spawn a further, outer layer of secondary analytic elements.

Too much importance should not be given to mere conventions of writing in this connection. As noted in Chapter 6 (note 2), the Marathi practice is to write many secondary as well as primary postpositions as suffixal to the noun they govern, while the prevailing Hindi practice (in the case of nouns) is to write certainly the former, and also the latter, as separate words: M. *mulāsāṭhī*, H. *baccē kē liyē* 'for the child'; M. *mulālā*, H. *baccē kō* 'to the child'. In Bengali, where the erstwhile primary postpositions are generally admitted to have graduated to affixal status, secondary postpositions are written as separate words: B. *cheleke* 'to the child', *cheler jɔnne* 'for the child'.

Leaving aside for a moment the question of their demarcation vis-à-vis analytic elements, agglutinative elements themselves clearly must be included in even a conservative treatment of NIA morphology. There is accordingly often talk of a "new morphology" and an "old morphology". However, the line between these two is also blurred. This is because some inherited morphological elements have come to be wrenched free of their original environments and applied agglutinatively to all members of a class, sometimes in new functions. A common example is the Gujarati plural suffix *-o* (of unclear but certainly morphological rather than lexical origin[2]), now added to all nouns capable of pluralization, in most cases replacing the inherited declensional plural but in one subclass of nouns added redundantly to it, thus making an etymologically double plural: *ghar/gharo* 'house/houses', *chokrī*[3]/*chokrīo* 'girl/girls', but *chokro* 'boy', old pl. *chokrā*, new pl. *chokrāo*. In the same language, the inherited instrumental suffix *-e*[4] comes to be added agglutinatively *after* the new agglutinative plural just mentioned: *chokrāoe* 'by the boys'.

The three kinds of elements have also amalgamated in various ways to give new forms, as in the Bengali locative suffix *-te*, derived from the older locative postposition *-ta* (cognate with M. *-ā(˜)t* < OIA *antar* 'the inside') + the locative suffix *-e* (or **-ahi*), thus a double locative. Such pleonastic, or "strengthened", elements are common in NIA, and already in Late MIA.

In view of the fact that a good many of the units in these systems have either disputed or uninvestigated etymologies, a purely historical approach to the subject becomes problematic. Due to extensive and repeated analogical restructuring, reborrowing, and cross-linguistic influences accompanying the phonetic decay of old inflections, the course of development from OIA to NIA is anything but a straight line. It is difficult not only to separate the old morphology from the new, as noted above, but even to identify them. Their identification indeed often depends on the view taken in the etymological disputes just mentioned. The Marathi Restricted Dative in *-s*, for example, is according to the traditional view (Beames, followed by Grierson and others) derived from the OIA genitive *-sya*, hence a survival of the old morphology. Bloch (1920: 198–9) rejects this derivation on both semantic and formal grounds: for him the form (of unclear origin) is a "postposition". As Turner (1975 [1927, 1937], 1960) was at pains to point out, the uncertainties are compounded by abnormalities in the phonetic development of frequently used forms, and especially of terminations.

Under such conditions the history of NIA morphology is thus necessarily not only fragmentary and uncertain, but also very complex. Among other things, evidence in the form of literary remains from all stages and subvarieties of Indo-Aryan has to be weighed. Since the primary purpose of this book is to give the reader an overview of Indo-Aryan languages as functioning systems, a basically structural approach will therefore be adopted instead. Historical information will be relegated to subordinate commentary. The reader with a special interest in Indo-Aryan historical morphology is directed to the now classical writers on the subject: Hoernle, Beames, Bhandarkar, Grierson, Tessitori, Geiger, Bloch, Chatterji, Tiwari, Saxena, Jha, Turner, Katre, Kakati, Pandit – with a warning that he will not find an explanation for everything, and that some of the pioneering derivations in earlier works have been rejected by later writers.

The decision to include analytic elements in the "morphological" description, however, does raise the question of the boundary with syntax, or to put it another way, the question of the scope of the so-called paradigms. A degree of arbitrariness will be found in most descriptions. Zograph (1976) notes that from four to sixteen or more "forms" have been attributed to the same noun in different accounts of the same language.

Phonological criteria might be invoked to establish the boundary: the particles and auxiliaries in question are typically unstressed, that is, they are subordinated to the stress of the word to which they are attached. Elements that fail to meet this criterion (i.e. by having an independent stress) could be excluded from the paradigm accordingly. I know of no attempt to apply such a measure across the board in Indo-Aryan. In the absence of one anything said remains impressionistic and speculative, but it is likely that this criterion too would fail us, by including material we might wish to exclude, and perhaps also by excluding some material we might on other grounds wish to include, and worst of all by varying with the stress pattern of each particular language.

Alternatively, since a "word"-like unit might seem to be what is in order we could employ the criterion of *adhesion* which has been invoked in that context,[5] that is, the non-insertability of other elements between the ones in question. The "adhesion" criterion would need certain qualifications if applied to Indo-Aryan, where for example *emphatic particles* will be found to be insertable in positions where nothing else can be. However, in the matter of setting up Indo-Aryan paradigms (particularly verbal paradigms) – as with those of English – we may have to admit that we are indeed dealing with more than one "word" in any case. Perhaps "word" is not the issue, but a certain level of "*forms*" rather, intermediate between *word* and *phrase*, for which an appropriate term is wanting.

Syntax itself can help us at least to focus the problem. As Zograph notes, it is essentially a question of the rightward boundary of the erstwhile inflectional form, not of the leftward boundary. NIA languages are in the main syntactically left-branching languages, certainly so at the clause and phrase levels. That is, modifier normally precedes modified.

Recent linguistic theory would have us take the rightmost grammatical element (e.g., tense auxiliary, case particle) as the proper head of the constructions under discussion here (i.e. *hai* in H. *khātā hai* 'he eats', *liyē* – or perhaps just *-ē* – in *baccē kē liyē* 'for the child'), with the lexical element subordinate to and dependent upon it. This appears to have the merit of maintaining a consistency in left-branching in the NIA system, and identifying the head with the element which establishes the syntactic function of the construction. (The actual rightmost *surface* element in NIA verbal constructions is generally an agreement morpheme, however. To really maintain the aforesaid consistency it may have to be dealt with differently.)

If we adopt instead the view that for some purposes at least the "head" of these constructions is the lexical base (the term *lexical head* indeed seems to be finding acceptance lately) something interesting emerges. Material to the left of the head so conceived (e.g., the noun, adjective, or lexical verb) is generally attributive and subordinate, i.e. related to it purely syntactically: H. *baccā/choṭā baccā* 'child/small child', *acchā/bahut acchā* 'good/very good', *ānā/jaldī ānā* 'come/come early'. Material to the *right* of the lexical base modifies its general meaning in a quite different way, limiting and contextualizing it: H. *ā-* 'come', *ānā* fut. imper. + verbal noun, *ātā hai* 'he comes', *ā rahī hai* 'she is coming'. It thus has *potential* claim on "inflectional" status, in Zograph's sense. Or we may simply say that this provides a way to initially differentiate syntax from material more conveniently treated paradigmatically in Indo-Aryan. The three kinds of elements found in this potential "inflectional" material to the right of the base, the inherited synthetic, new agglutinative, and analytical, are moreover basically found in that order, although as noted above, an element originating in one category may develop as a member of another.

The above right-of-head criterion does not set apart morphology as such in the traditional sense. The latter generally includes derivation, and there are, along with numerous suffixes, a few derivational *prefixes* in Indo-Aryan (most of them borrowed from either Sanskrit or Persian, but sometimes detached from these lexical strata, particularly in the latter case, and used productively) – i.e. left-of-head elements. Derivation in general will receive cursory treatment here as compared with traditional grammars, except for certain borderline cases (derivational according to some analyses, paradigmatic according to others). For exhaustive lists of "formative affixes" (and information on their histories), with which traditional treatments of morphology usually begin, the reader is again directed to the classic historical grammars of various NIA languages.

The syntactic demarcation of potential "inflection" elected above comes at a price if followed consistently, which is always the best policy. The expression of such matters as definiteness and negation becomes (potentially) paradigmatic/ "inflectional" in some NIA languages (Bengali) and syntactic in others (Hindi). This may, however, involve a difference worth noting in any case.

The above approach does not solve the problem, as will be apparent below: it merely narrows it. Perhaps some will be quick to point out that the adoption of a generative approach would avoid much of the difficulty, i.e. beginning with syntax and not worrying at all about any syntax/morphology distinction. That option has not been chosen for several reasons: (1) it would overburden the text, already loaded with more data than there is room for, with much redundant apparatus; (2) it would (or should) require a much tighter degree of control of all the languages involved – an impossible task; (3) it would render the data less accessible, which would defeat our purposes here. For this handbook, it will be better to try to maintain a division between morphology and syntax, albeit with modifications.

A slight departure will be made from tradition, however, in the manner of presentation of the data. Rather than in conventional tables, it will be presented here by means of the special standardized chart (Figure 8.1), in which the position of each language corresponds roughly to its geographical position. (The reader is referred to the basic map of the Indo-Aryan languages, Map 1.) This will facilitate areal comparisons and discussion of the mutual influences so important in Indo-Aryan. An actual map would be not only more cumbersome and inflexible, but also misleading, in implying a uniformity or even a degree of knowledge not justified given the diversity of dialects on the ground.

In Figure 8.1, languages named represent only their standard dialects when such may be said to exist, or unless otherwise specified. Any further dialectal qualifications will be made in the "Comments" following each chart. The *language names* following their conventional abbreviations in the basic chart below will be replaced in the actual figures by the data under consideration. Although the "boxes" representing the various languages will have to be expanded or contracted to accommodate the data, their spatial relationships will remain approximately the same. It is hoped that the reader will quickly get accustomed to them, and in the process unconsciously assimilate the geographical relationships within Indo-Aryan, if they are not already familiar.

The items in square brackets, [D] and [WPah], referring to the Dardic and West Pahari groups of dialects respectively, are for orientation purposes only. Inclusion of data from these highly splintered groups in the main chart would overcomplicate the latter. Reference will be made to them (and, where necessary, to other dialects and languages not on the chart, including Romany) separately, when they are of special interest. The above scheme, while not complete, does include all the principal NIA languages plus representative regional languages of the Hindi area, necessary to a balanced picture. The "Lahnda" dialects are represented by the southern form Siraiki, mainly because of the latter's incipient status as a literary language and the availability of Shackle's comprehensive sketch, but still symbolized by "L." rather than "S." or "Si." to avoid confusion with Sindhi and Sinhalese. Despite its importance and official status, Urdu is not included because: (1) it lacks a clearly defined territorial base, and (2) for our purposes here it would for the most part simply replicate Hindi.

In certain cases, for example when the data is very complex, it may be possible to represent only the main literary and official languages (excepting Urdu), as in Figure 8.2.

This account of NIA morphology will not depart from tradition in another respect, however, and that is in the presentation of nominal morphology first. It will be found that all accounts of NIA, traditional or modern, philological or structuralist, follow this order, and for a very good reason. The verb may be the heart of the NIA sentence, but in many (not all) of the NIA languages it partakes of certain nominal inflections, and its description is simplified if these are understood first.

In NIA, nominal inflections are those which characterize primarily nouns, pronouns, adjectives, and in some languages, also certain numerals and adverbs. As just noted, some of them may also occur secondarily with certain verbal forms. Beyond this fact, the latter are best treated with verbs. The nominal inflectional categories are *gender*, *number*, *case*, and *definiteness*. While *case* is found in all NIA languages (by the definition of inflection here adopted), *gender* is not universal, *definiteness* characterizes only certain languages, and there is reason to question the universality of the category of *number*. *Gender* and *number*, as well as *case*, but not *definiteness*, characterized both OIA and MIA.

8.2 Gender

The first NIA nominal category that needs to be looked at is gender, despite the fact that it does not characterize all NIA languages. Grammatical gender in NIA

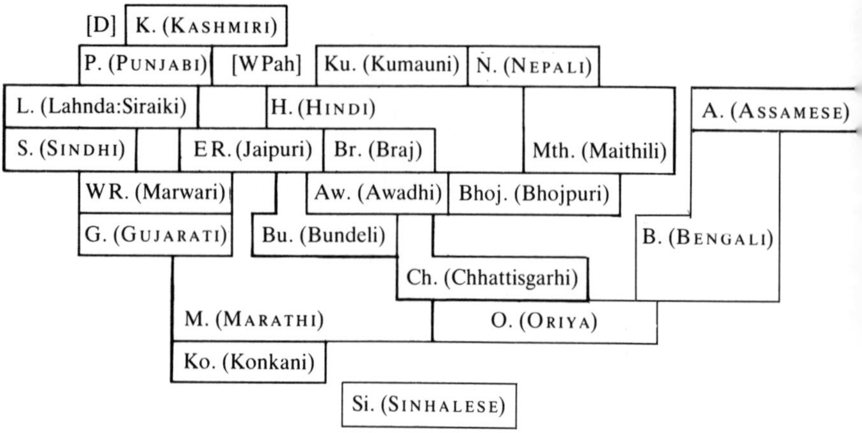

Figure 8.1 Basic template of NIA languages in spatial relationships

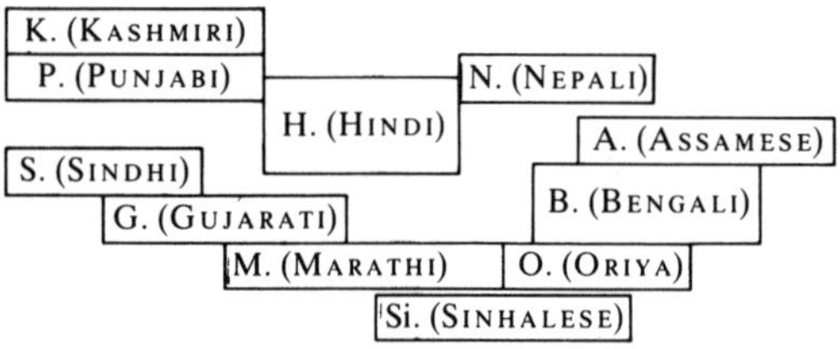

Figure 8.2 Reduced template of NIA languages in spatial relationships

is both a syntactic and a morphological category, in that its existence is essentially established through the *agreement* of forms in different words, binding them together syntactically.

Mere formal differentiation for sex – or other semantic purposes (see Chapter 4) – without such agreement, as in B. *dhopā/dhopānī* 'washerman/washerman's wife', *bāgh/bāghinī* 'tiger/tigress', is something else entirely, akin to Eng. *prince/princess*, *manager/manageress*, a part of *derivation*, no matter how productive. Such "feminine affixes", particularly those derived from OIA *-inī*, *-ānī*, are indeed very common in all NIA languages, due to a social need to distinguish the female members of various occupational groups as well as female kin, but – perhaps to belabor the point – despite occasional confusion on this subject in popular NIA language manuals (and even in a few more serious works), their presence does not in itself mean that a given language "has gender".

Gender in NIA often entails declensional differences. It is sometimes also reflected in obligatory pronoun choices – although pronominal differentiation for gender (e.g., *he/she/it*) is not as common in NIA as in European languages. This chapter will focus on the morphological aspects of gender; its syntactic ones – precisely what agrees with what in the context of a sentence – will be addressed in Chapter 10.

In the NIA languages that have it, gender is an inherent and classificatory property of one class of words (nouns) and a variable or inflectional property of others (adjectives, certain verbal forms, sometimes pronouns and adverbs, and one extremely important postposition). NIA languages also differ as to which of the latter are capable of gender agreement, and whether it is required or optional, and resulting differences in the *domain* of the category are also important.

Quite analogously to the Romance languages, the subclasses of nouns pertaining to each gender may or may not have overt markers of that status. Their identification depends in any case on the contrasts in the variable words qualifying them. The latter do have such markers – usually but not necessarily a suffix. (With one marginal exception, in Sinhalese, there are no gender-marking *articles* in NIA.) When nouns do have overt markers, they are generally the same as those of the variable words. Such nouns are often called *marked* nouns. (Other terms that will be encountered are *thematic*, *strong thematic*, *extended*, *augmented*, and *enlarged*. The first is very common but particularly confusing since in the broader context of Indo-Aryan it also refers to Sanskrit nouns with the suffix *-a-*, the descendants of which are precisely *un*-marked nouns in most NIA languages.) Unmarked nouns probably outnumber marked nouns, although the latter include many words of high frequency.

It is most convenient to present the gender contrasts that exist in each language by means of the markers that represent them (on variable words – the most reliable source – and on marked nouns) in the Direct Case ("Nominative") singular, as in Figure 8.3.

M = Masculine N = Neuter F = Feminine ANIM = Animate INAN = Inanimate

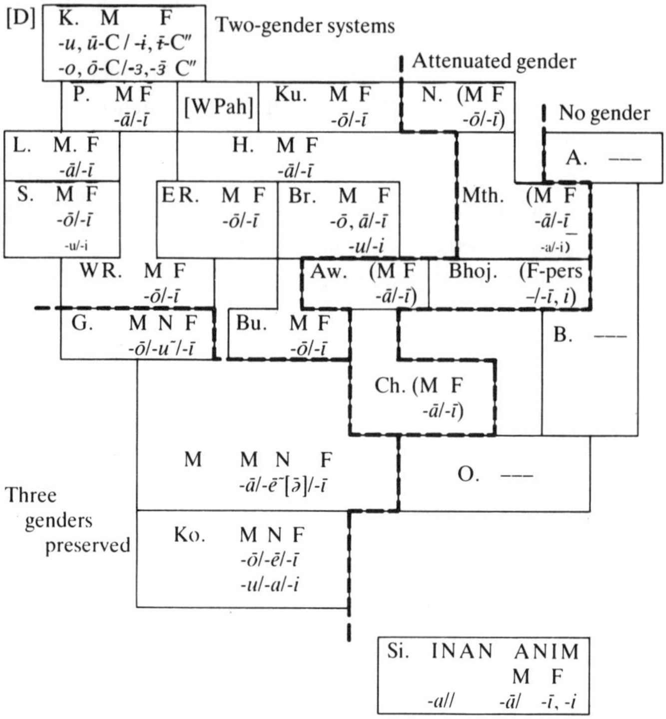

Figure 8.3 NIA gender markers: Direct Case singular

Comments on Figure 8.3

1. There is an obvious general decline in the strength of gender from west to east in NIA. Sanskrit had three genders, preserved in Pali and Prakrit, albeit with the beginnings of confusion of the Masculine and Neuter (always close in any case), particularly in Eastern Prakrit (Magadhi, Ardhamagadhi; see Pischel 1981: sec. 356–8; also Geiger 1916: 78), and quite advanced in Apabhramsa (Tagare 1948: 105–6; Pischel 1981: sec. 359). In NIA, three genders are preserved only in parts of the west: on the chart, in Gujarati, Marathi, and Konkani; also in dialects in their vicinity not on the chart (Bhili, Khandeshi – not, however, in Halbi); finally, in the Bhadarwahi–Bhalesi–Khashali group of extreme northwestern West Pahari, a discovery made by Siddheshwar Varma in 1928.
2. It is sometimes held that Sinhalese also preserves the three genders of OIA, but this is misleading. The system has been completely restructured into one based on "natural" gender (as in neighboring Dravidian), with the basic division between *inanimates* on the one hand (the so-called Neuter, whose membership therefore includes the inanimate Masculines and Feminines of OIA as well as most Neuters of OIA) and *animates* on the other, secondarily divided into Masculine and Feminine. (There is a hint of a tendency for such a restructuring in popular Sanskrit itself as used in South India, judging from numerous loanwords in Dravidian languages with the Neuter ending *-am*, *-amu* refer-

ring to inanimates, which are not Neuter in proper Sanskrit: e.g., Telugu *ankamu* 'number', *tapamu* 'heat, hot season', *deśamu* 'country' = Skt *ankaḥ*, *tapaḥ*, *dēśaḥ*.) Moreover, gender is primarily a declensional phenomenon in Sinhalese; syntactic agreement is very marginal, and confined to the literary language. Adjectives are invariant, even in Literary Sinhala. Declensional differences (between animates and inanimates) are preserved, however, even in the Colloquial. Animates and inanimates also select different existential verbs (*innavā* and *tiyenavā* respectively) and numerals.

3. The most widespread NIA system is a two-gender system, in which the old Masculine and Neuter have merged. (That is not to say that there have not been some reassignments of OIA gender, even in languages preserving three genders, usually because of phonetic or semantic analogy. E.g., the NIA descendants of OIA *agni-* 'fire', which is Masculine, are mostly Feminine, no doubt because of the *-i*.) This new Masculine/Feminine system dominates the Central and Northwestern heartland of Indo-Aryan, including the West Pahari dialects other than those mentioned above, and extends to Romany and most of Dardic (and even beyond, to the Nuristani languages).
4. To the east, it begins to attenuate, already in the band of languages represented on the chart (with parentheses) by Awadhi (the least attenuated), Nepali, Maithili, Bhojpuri, and Chhattisgarhi, to which may be added Bagheli, Magahi, and Angika. There gender accord typically is restricted to female animates (so that the system is essentially restructured as *zero/+Fem*), optional or loose even then (e.g., in Chhattisgarhi), and greatly reduced in syntactic scope. Many adjectives as well as verbal participles which have the extension in *-ā/ō* further west here end in consonants: H. *chōṭā*, *hamārā*, *dekhtā* ('little, our/my, seeing') = *choṭ*, *hamār*, *dekhat*. To some of these, particularly the verbal forms, may be added in Bhojpuri and Magahi the Feminine suffix *-ī*, *i* (and in Maithili the ultrashort and prone to disappear $^{-i}$), but we cannot speak about Masculine agreement in such cases. In Nepali, the ending is a neutral *-o*, changeable to *-ī* with Personal Feminines in more formal style (Matthews 1984).
5. In Maithili, however, there is also agreement of extended adjectives with extended nouns in the case of ordinary/diminutive as well as animate pairs with *-ā/-ī*: *karikkā ḍālā*, *ghoṛā* / *karikkī ḍālī*, *ghoṛī* 'black basket, horse/black small-basket, mare'. In Angika, there seems to be a contrast *-ɔ/-ī* (P. Pandey 1979: 23).
6. The genitive postposition, however, an unfailing indicator of the gender system further west, is typically invariant in these languages (Bhoj. Ch,*-kē* , Bagh.*-kar*, Mag. Mth.*-k* vs. H.*-kā/-kē/-kī*). Angika, however, shows a regular contrast for animates: *-rɔ/-rī*, *-kɔ/kī*, *-kerɔ/-kerī*.
7. Although Awadhi (and Western Bhojpuri, e.g., of Banaras) often show gender agreement similar to that of (Western) Hindi, in the southern extensions of Eastern Hindi, namely Bagheli and Chhattisgarhi, this is greatly attenuated, in the latter almost to the point of disappearance – completely so from the verb. The influence of Standard Hindi as the official language of this region is now a factor confusing the situation, and it may often be a question of the revival or even of the introduction of gender agreement rather than of its preservation.
9. Finally, gender has disappeared altogether in Bengali, Assamese, and Oriya, to which may be added Bishnupriya, and apparently also Sadani (Nagpuria) from the Bihari group. (Sanskritisms such as *sundarī nārī* 'beautiful lady' stand outside the real grammatical systems of these or any NIA languages.) Far from being aberrant, this Eastern loss of gender can be seen as the most natural outcome of the phonological erosion of OIA terminations in the absence of compensatory developments, and in particular in the absence of strengthening of the sense of gender from the side of the verb, when the participial element in the new verbal system did not develop with gender-sustaining extensions. It is significant that gender is *also lost at the other extremity of Indo-Aryan*, in the in many respects very archaic Khowar and Kalasha languages.
10. In the languages which have retained the Neuter, a nasal element connected with the *-am* of the Neuter Sg.Nom.–Acc. of Sanskrit is often still apparent: Gujarati–Bhili[6]*-ũ*, Bhadarwahi *-õ*, Formal Marathi + Konkani *-ẽ* (Informal Marathi = [-ə̃], a sound significantly still *spelled* with *anusvāra* in the Reformed Spelling). The *-u* of Bhalesi and

Khashali (like that of Gujarati) reflects the labializing influence of OIA *-m*. (The Masculine marker is *-o* or *-a* in these dialects.) In some unwritten dialects like Khandeshi, the nasal has finally disappeared but the short vowel of the Sanskrit Neuter (*-a-*) has been kept, evidently protected by the nasal (and possibly also by a final accent in one type of Middle Indian) for a sufficiently long period. In this way, even the Sinhalese Inanimate retains an organic link with the Sanskrit Neuter (Geiger 1938: 104).

11. The common M/F endings *-ā*, *-ō*/*-ī*, on the other hand, do not represent OIA endings as such, but are *rebuilt* forms. That is, although the dominant later Sanskrit thematic stems with Masc. Sg. Nom. in *-as* did have a common external sandhi form in *-ō* (before voiced consonants including nasals, semivowels, and *h*, and before following *a-*), which gave rise to the general Pali and Prakrit (Sauraseni–Maharashtri) ending *-ō*, as we have seen in Chapter 7, this *-ō* weakened to *-u* in Late MIA (Apabhramsa), and finally disappeared in most of NIA. (In Eastern MIA, that is, Magadhi and Ardhamagadhi, *-as* became *-ē* rather than *-ō*, and this *-ē* may be partly responsible for certain case-like phenomena in Assamese and dialectal Bengali, of which more presently.)
12. The modern Masculine *-ā*, *-ō* marker develops rather from the common Sanskrit suffix *-akas* (originally a diminutive, later a meaningless "extension") similarly weakened via > *-akō* > *-agō* > *-ahu*, *-aō* to *-au* (the last still current in older and dialectal forms of Western Hindi), and thence, according to the usual account, in different languages variously to *-ō* or to *-ā*. A certain degree of areal patterning will be apparent in this differentiation, which may not be without some historical significance. The *-ō* development links the Central Pahari area and Nepal with Rajasthan and Gujarat, and the latter also to the Braj–Bundelkhand area on the one hand and Cutch and Sind on the other, all except the last areas of medieval Rajput dominance. The *-ā* development connects Standard Hindi more closely with Punjabi and dialects to the west (including most West Pahari dialects, spoken after all in an area once known as the Punjab Hill States) as far as the Pashai of Afghanistan rather than with its immediate Western Hindi group neighbors Braj and Kannauji (which have both *-ō* and *-ā* in nouns, *-ō*, *-au* in adjectives). However, *-ā* rather than *-ō* is the normal development of the suffix further down the Ganges valley, from eastern UP to Bengal, although it is less frequent and not necessarily an agreement marker. The Marathi and Sinhalese developments may be coincidental.
13. The ubiquitous modern Feminine marker *-ī* largely comes in a similar way from the Sanskrit Feminine extension in *-ikā* (in this case possibly retaining more of its diminutive sense) rather than directly from OIA Feminines in *-ī*, which was likewise subject to weakening. Its evolution was no doubt influenced, however, by the existence of a Feminine in *-ī*, at times restrengthened, in all periods of the language. Tss. in *-ī* join the modern descendants of *-ikā* declensionally, whereas Tss. in *-ā* do not join those of *-akas* because they are for the most part Feminines. (Masculine Tss. in *-ā*, such as *rājā* 'king', *pitā* 'father', based on Nominatives of stems in *-an* and *-r̥* likewise do not join Tbhs. in *ā* declensionally, but go rather with the "Unmarked" Masculines.) There are no Tss. in *-ō*.
14. Those NIA languages which have not lost their original final vowels, namely Sindhi, Konkani, Maithili, and to some extent Braj, have a second set of gender markers, generally *-u*/*-i* (ultrashort$^{-i,\ -u}$ in Sindhi and Maithili), which do hark back to OIA thematic Nominatives in *as* > *-ō* and Feminines in *-is*, *-ī*. In languages where these vowels have been lost, we have "unmarked" nouns ending in consonants whose gender assignment is generally dependent on the lost vowels: H. *dās* (m.), *rāt* (f.); S. *dās*^{u}, *rāt*^{i}. (Additional unmarked subclasses involve nouns, both Tss. and Tbh., ending for various reasons in long vowels that in NIA terms do not match their inherited gender assignment, such as the Tss. Feminines in *-ā* referred to above, or words like *hāthī* 'elephant', m., from an OIA stem in *-in*.)
15. In Kashmiri, it is a matter of final vowels (whether original or from extensions is not always clear) having epenthetically influenced the internal vowels of a word (sometimes only in the last syllable, sometimes in all – usually not more than two – syllables) as well as the preceding consonant (and sometimes earlier consonants in a type of domino-

effect, all of which is represented by C > C'' on the chart) before disappearing. A residual *-u* caused rounding of historical *-a-*, *-ā-* to *-o-*, *-ō-*; a residual *-i* caused centralization of (*-a-*, *-ā-*) to *-ɜ-*, *-ɜ̄-* and of *-u-*, *-ū-* to *-ɨ-*, *-ɨ̄-*, along with concomitant consonant alterations inadequately describable as affricatization (*t* > *ts*, *d* > *z*, *l* > *j*, *n*> *ñ*). At least the vowel changes are a classic case of umlaut and could be so represented (as it indeed was by Grierson), were it not for the fact that the symbols *ü* and *ö* have for most people a phonetic value ("front rounded") which is far from that of the Kashmiri sounds.

16. Similar umlaut phenomena in the gender system are found in some Dardic neighbors of Kashmiri, mainly dialects of the Kohistani group (Bashkarik, Torwali). In this case the contrast is back/front rather than back/central: Bshk. *gōr/gēr* 'horse/mare', *ucuṭ/iciṭ* 'small (m/f)'. Elsewhere in Dardic, however, the system is either a conventional *-ā/-ī* (Southern Pashai), *-o/-ī* (Shina, Phalura, Gawarbati, Shumashti, Northeastern Pashai),[7] or grammatical gender has been lost altogether (Khowar, Kalasha, Maiyan).

As noted earlier, gender may be represented not only by agreement phenomena but also by pronoun substitutes, particularly 3rd-person pronouns, whatever their nature (in IA they tend to be demonstratives or correlatives rather than true personal pronouns). In Sanskrit, the three genders are clearly reflected both in the 3rd person singular (Nominative) forms *sas/tat/sā* (m/n/f) and in the plural forms (*tē/tāni/tās*). In cases other than the Nominative (and the Accusative Plural), the Masculine and Neuter merge. This system is preserved in Pali and Prakrit as (sg.) *sō/taṁ/sā*, (pl.) *tē/tāni/tā(yō)* (Pali), *tē/tāiṁ/tā(ō)* (Pkt). Magadhi, however, has *śē* (and Ardhamagadhi *sē*) rather than *sō*, swallowing the Neuter, and with the same form also in the plural. Analogical (to nouns) Feminine forms in *tī-* make their appearance particularly in Maharashtri. The NIA contrasts are illustrated in Figure 8.4 below.

8.3 Number

Number may seem like a straightforward category, but there are a few complications. First, it may or may not have a syntactic (agreement) dimension: in Bengali, Assamese, and Sinhalese it does not. If present, the agreement may be of two kinds: a) agreement (of adjectives, participles, etc.) involving nominal markers of the type discussed in the previous section; b) agreement involving personal verbal endings that distinguish number but are distinct from the nominal markers. Languages may show number agreement of both kinds (as in Hindi and Marathi) or of only the second kind (as in Oriya). We are concerned only with markers of the first kind in this chapter.

Second, it may have a declensional dimension, that is, show different forms with different historical subclasses of nouns. Conversely, it may take the form of an agglutinative affix, attached without distinction to all nouns, or perhaps several

M = Masculine N = Neuter F = Feminine IN = Inanimate
AN = Animate (or vs. Human, Animal) HUM = Human
< > = common (no differentiation) + = Correlative only

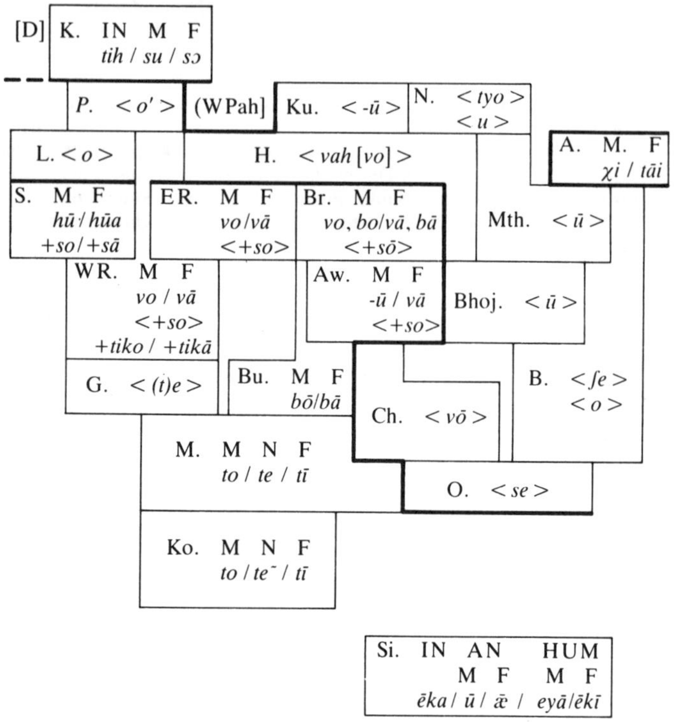

Figure 8.4 Gender in pronouns: third singular (= remote demonstrative/correlative) forms

Comments on Figure 8.4

1. This picture differs from that in Figure 8.3 in several respects. Not all the languages that show gender agreement of adjectives and participles have gender-differentiated pronouns: notably Hindi, Punjabi, "Lahnda", and Gujarati do not. On the other hand, some languages without gender agreement do have such pronouns, notably Assamese. (The reference there is to natural gender, both human and animal: it could hardly be otherwise.) Although such differentiation is absent in other Magadhan languages, and in Nepali–Kumauni and Chhattisgarhi–Bagheli, it is present in a broad band west of these, in Awadhi, Braj–Bundeli, all Rajasthani dialects (and Garhwali), and Sindhi. In all except the last these seem to be analogically constructed rather than preserved forms, and in the case of the Western and Eastern Hindi dialects mentioned, quite recent, i.e. they do not occur in the older literature (which shows only the undifferentiated *vaha*, *sō*, *su*).
2. After the apparently recent defection of Gujarati (Old Gujarati preserved at least a Neuter in *ta˜*), the threefold distinction of Sanskrit is preserved only – and then only with

considerable remodelling – by Marathi and Konkani (and by certain Bhili and Khandeshi dialects adjoining Marathi: not, however, by Vagdi or other more northerly Bhili dialects). There are threefold systems also in Kashmiri and Sinhalese (in the latter, actually a fivefold system), but these appear to be partly innovations (Neuter = Inanimate) rather than merely preservations of the old system.

3. The other locus of preservation of the OIA Neuter in the Bhadarwah subgroup shows a twofold contrast MF/N in the nominative singulars of pronouns (Bhalesi *o/un*, *tɛ/ten*), but a different contrast MN/F in the oblique cases (Bhalesi agentive *'ɔ˙ni/ɔ˙si*, *'teni/'tesi*). Several other West Pahari dialects, which do not otherwise distinguish a Neuter, do so in a three-way contrast in the oblique cases of pronouns (relative and interrogative as well as proximate and far demonstrative): Kiunthali *tĕs/tĕssau/tĕtthī*, Shodochi *tĕs*, *tĕs/tĕtth/taiā*, Mandeali *tĕs/tiddhī/tĕssā* (*LSI 9.4*: 566, 655, 723). The (undifferentiated) nominative is *sē* (Kiunthali and Mandeali) or *sau* (Shodochi). Some other West Pahari dialects (Churahi, Kului, Baghati) distinguish two genders (M and F) in the oblique cases but not in the nominative. All of this reverses the usual NIA pattern of differentiation in the nominative, merger in oblique cases. (Still other West Pahari dialects follow Punjabi and Hindi in showing no gender at all in the pronoun: Sirmauri, Chameali, Pangwali, Padri.)
4. There is nothing special about Dardic beyond Kashmiri: only Shina (*oh/eh*) and its offshoot Phalura (*hɛso/hɛse*) show gender in the pronouns. The others have versions of undifferentiated *so* or *o*. Romany, however, has (M/F) *yov/yoi* (demons. *odova/odȯya*).
5. The other point to be noted about these pronouns is that alongside the survival of forms connected with OIA *sa-* and its oblique stem *ta-* (in Bengali–Assamese–Oriya, Marathi–Gujarati, most of West Pahari and Dardic, and in the capacity of correlative [see Chapter 10] in Sindhi, Rajasthani, and various dialects of the Hindi area), we have the appearance and increasing dominance of a form *o*, *ū*, *vo* in the northern plains band of languages from Bengal to Afghanistan, differentiated for gender only in Rajasthani and recently in some Hindi dialects (and in a different way in some West Pahari dialects [see above]). Turner (*CDIAL*), following uncertain indications in Pischel (1981: sec. 432), derives it from OIA *asāu* 'that' (oblique stem *amu-*) > Pkt *aho*, but the MIA textual frequency of this is much too low to account for the sudden and widespread appearance of the above-mentioned forms in NIA after the twelfth century. Chatterji (1926) favors an Indo-Iranian form **ava-* represented by a solitary form in Vedic (and not in Sanskrit or MIA), on the assumption – which is rather extreme – that it was current in spoken dialects but unrecorded throughout the preceding two millennia. Another possibility, favored by history (diffusion clearly after the Muslim conquest of the north) and geography, and given equal probability by Bloch, is simply the convenient Persian *ō* (modern *ū*) 'he, she, it' (from the same **ava-*), perhaps reinforced by Turkic *o*. (Prothetic [v-, w-] before [o] is a common tendency in some NIA as well as in Dravidian languages.) The only thing against it is the dogma that such basic forms are not readily borrowed. There is every indication that they can be, or at least can influence the course of indigenous evolution. Possibly this "foreign" element (after all, Persian and NIA are closely related, which may facilitate such borrowing) coalesced with and gave new life to surviving fragments of *asāu*.

affixes, correlated with subclasses established on a semantic rather than a historical basis. Hindi and Marathi, and partly also Sinhalese, are examples of the first type, Bengali and Oriya of the second, while Gujarati is moving from the first to the second.

Third, it may be obligatory or optional. The new agglutinative affixes, especially in the Eastern languages, tend to be optional. In those Eastern languages, such as Bengali, with optional suffixes and no agreement, it is open to question whether number exists as an inflectional category, as distinct from a notion capable of facultative expression. Originally plural verbal forms in Bengali as well as in Maithili and Assamese now have a different function – that of *honorificity* (Chatterji 1926: 936, Jha 1958: 473, Kakati 1962: 349–51). Number is an obligatory category in *pronouns* in these languages, however.

One feature may be quickly disposed of. There are only two numbers, singular and plural, in NIA at best. OIA had three, but the old dual quietly disappeared at the beginning of MIA as a result of various phonological changes, in particular

< > = no declensional differences M1, F1 = marked subclasses
M2, 3, F2, 3, 4, etc. = unmarked subclasses
Ø = zero marker (direct plural same as singular)
+ = marker *added* to sg. (with morphophonemic adjustments)
− = marker *replaces* ending of sg.

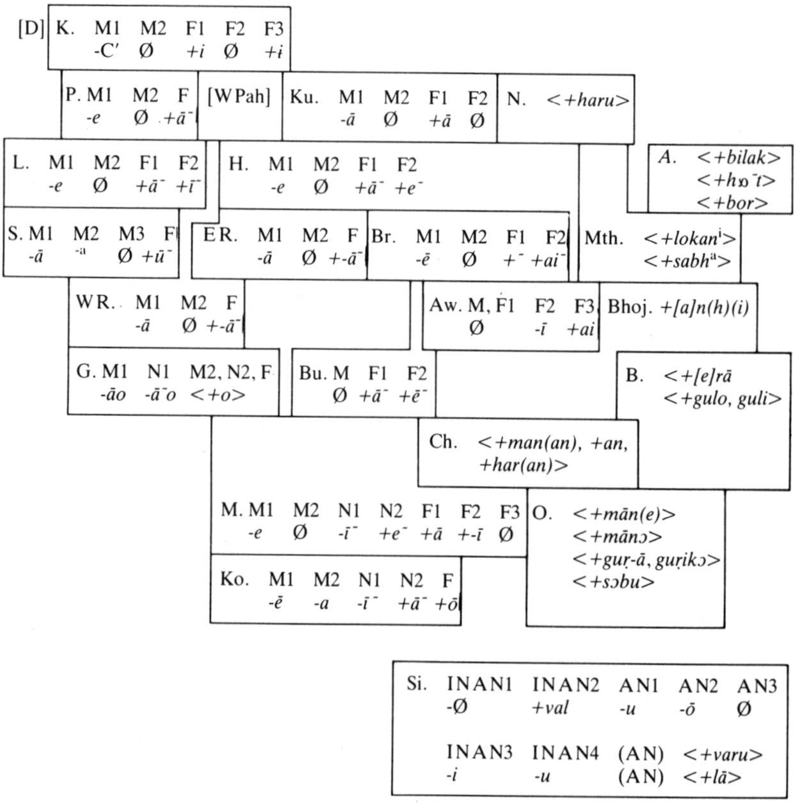

Figure 8.5 Direct case plural markers: NIA declensional types

Comments on Figure 8.5

1. In order to bring out cross-linguistic parallels more clearly, morphophonemic rules belonging to each language have been assumed in the above presentation. Traditional paradigms sometimes ignore them (and differ accordingly from the above), but they rightly need to be abstracted and placed in their own section of a description. Since they are proper to each language (although some general tendencies are also discernible), an exhaustive account of them cannot be given here. They might be divided for our purposes into those involving: a) the manner of joining the suffix to the stem, that is, treatment of stem-finals, and b) pre-final modifications of the stem itself.
2. The first is often essentially a matter of spelling, although there are small phonetic adjustments involved also. The most typical example involves the addition of the plural allomorph *-ā˜* (Marathi *-ā*) to marked feminines in *-ī*. Depending on the conventions of the language, the result may be *-īā˜* (Punjabi), *-iyā˜* (Hindi), *-yā˜* (Rajasthani), *-yā* (Marathi), e.g., the favorite example, 'mares': sg. *ko`ṛī*, *ghoṛī* or *ghoḍī* > pl. *ko`ṛīā˜*, *ghoṛiyā˜*, *ghoṛyā˜*, *ghoḍyā*. In all the above languages except Hindi this is really the same ending as is used with unmarked feminines (in Marathi, with one subclass of unmarked feminines): R. *bāt/bātā˜*, P. *gall/gallā˜* 'thing/things', M. *veḷ/veḷā* 'time/times'. Finals in *-u*, *ū* undergo analogous modifications: M. *sāsū/sāsvā* 'mother-in-law/mothers-in-law'.
3. Final consonants may also be affected, however. In Marathi, /*-ċ*, *-j̇*, *-j̇h*, *-ṡ*/ become /*c*, *j*, *jh*, *s*/ before the plural suffix *-ī*, *-ī˜*: *las/laʃī* 'vaccine/vaccines', *mhais/mhaʃī* 'buffalo/buffaloes', *māj̇hā/mājhī˜* 'my' (msg/npl).
4. Examples of the second type include the vowel-shortening in stem syllables before long-vowel suffixes which is found with variations in a number of N I A languages. In Hindi it applies only to derivational, not to inflectional suffixes (although the *dropping* of the vowel /*a*/ in words of the form CV*Ca*C before such inflections, as in *saṛak/saṛkē˜* 'street/streets' might be considered a related rhythmic phenomenon). In Marathi, however, it does apply to *ī*, *ū* before inflections (even in foreign words), at least in monosyllabic stems, along with some disyllabic ones, although the orthographic change is at present only subphonemic since the long and short high vowels do not really contrast in that language: *phīt/phit+ī* 'ribbon/ribbons', *mūl/mul+ē˜* 'child/children', *bahīṇ/bahiṇ+ī* 'sister/sisters'. A greater number of disyllabic stems *drop ī* or *ū* in the second syllable, as well as *a* as in Hindi: *kulūp/kulp+ī˜* 'lock/locks', *reʃīm/reʃm+ī* 'silk/silks'. Bhojpuri is another language where morphophonemic stem-vowel shortening is prominent: *ghōṛā/ghoṛani* 'horse/horses' (*LSI*), *rāti/ratiē* 'night/nights' (Shukla 1981).
5. A peculiarity of Kumauni is the diphthongization of the stem vowels /*e*, *o*/, rather in the manner of Spanish (*ie*, *ue* < *e*, *o*): *celo/cyàlà* (represented by Apte and Pattanayak as *cɛla*) 'son/sons', *ghoṛo/ghwàṛà* 'horse/horses'. Along with the change of /*u*, *o*/ to /*a*/ in the second syllable of disyllabic stems (*jiboḍo/jibaḍa* 'tongue/tongues') this is ascribed by Apte and Pattanayak to the operation of vowel harmony, a factor which grows increasingly prominent through West Pahari and culminates in Kashmiri.
6. Changes of both stem vowel and final consonant in Kashmiri may here be treated as morphophonemically conditioned, since in contrast with the Masculine/Feminine alternations, there is in the plural inflection a real suffix (or in the case of M1 nouns, where the mark of the plural is palatalization of the final consonant [represented by C´ in Figure 8.5], at least a tangibly final feature) to do the conditioning. The "suffix" (C) ´ may be said to trigger the same centralization of stem-vowels (*o* > *ɜ*, less consistently *u* > *i̵*) as in the gender distinctions (*brōr/brɜ̄r´* 'cat/cats'), while the F1 suffix *-i* entails a change – less easily explained – of f.sg. *-ɜ*, *ɜ̄-* to *-a*, *ā-* along with alterations of final consonants (*l* > *j*, *d* > *z*, *ṭ* > *c*, etc.): *pɜṭ/paci* 'board/boards', *lɜr/lari* 'house/houses'.
7. Figure 8.5 attempts to show the major and regular patterns. There are a number of special cases, exceptions, or minor classes which are not represented, especially in Marathi, Konkani, and Kashmiri. In combination with irregularities in other aspects of inflection (the classes in Figure 8.5 represent only *plural types*) these could bring the number of declensional classes in Marathi to close to two dozen. The contrast with the

Eastern languages, which have *no* declensions as such (and no morphophonemic nominal stem-alternates), or even with Hindi, which has four (or perhaps five, counting diminutives like *ciṛiyā/ciṛiyā˜* as a special type) but admits no irregularities, is striking. (Marathi plural inflections are given in their Formal Written forms, for purposes of historical comparison [see below]. Colloquially, *-ē˜*=[ə] and *-ī˜*=[*i*].)

8. Sinhalese, however, presents an exceedingly complex picture, combining features of both the Western synthetic and eastern agglutinative systems. The symbol -ø in Figure 8.5 represents the *subtraction* of the Nominative singular ending to form the plural: *potā/pot* '(the) book/books'. The AN1 suffix *-u* when substituted for the singular entails gemination and other morphophonemic changes in the preceding (stem-final) consonant: *putā/puttu* 'the son/sons', *minihā/minissu* 'the man/men'. The INAN3 suffixes *-u/-i* have precisely the opposite effect, i.e. reduction of geminates: *vatta/vatu* 'plantation/plantations', *pætta/pæti* 'side/sides', *væssa/væhi* 'rain/rains'. The <+*lā*> suffix is added to kinship terms, <+*varu*> has an honorific connotation.
9. Eastern dialects of Awadhi have generalized the ending +*ai* for all nouns, according to Saksena (1971: 115). Northern Bhojpuri (Gorakhpur) as described by Shukla (1981) has a different system from the one given in Figure 8.5: +*[a]wē*, *ē*, *iē* – possibly all predictable variants of a single ending +*ē* (cf. E. Awadhi +*ai*).
10. The most common West Pahari system has *-ē* for M1 nouns, no plural marker for M2 and F1 nouns, and +*ī* or +*ī˜* for F2 nouns. Bhadarwahi and Jaunpuri have +*ā˜* for F1 nouns; Baghati has +*ā* for all Feminines. For both marked and unmarked Neuters Bhadarwahi has +*ā˜*, like dialectal Gujarati: *ghar/ghar+ā˜* 'house/houses'. (Standard Gujarati has *ā˜* for marked Neuters in *-u˜* only: *chokru˜/chokrā˜(o)* 'child/children' but *ghar/ghar+o*.)
11. Except for Shina, which has a system based on *-ē* (M1), +*i* (M2) and +*ĕ* (M3 and F), with many irregularities, morphophonemic modifications of stem, and minor classes (Bailey 1924), the other principal Dardic languages show an unsettled mixture of zero-marking of the direct case plural, borrowed Persian inflections (+ *ān*), suppletive plurals, and collective suffixes analogous to those of the Eastern languages – in other words little in the way of inherited, even if remodeled, synthetic material.
12. Romany, however, shows a more conventional NIA system: *-e* (M1), + *a* (M2, F1, F2), *-i* (F3 – apparently made up of non-Indian loanwords, e.g., *felda/feldi* 'field/fields').
13. The history of the synthetic forms shows considerable remodeling and transfer of forms from one class to another. Largely because of the different historical evolutes of the extended nominals (in M. *-akas*, N. *-akam*, F. *-ikā*), resulting as noted earlier in the NIA marked classes, the NIA direct plural inflections are often more complicated than those of Sanskrit. The Sanskrit system can be reduced essentially to the two endings MF +*as* and N + (V:*n*)*i*, with a few morphophonemic rules for their combination with the stem (e.g., *-a* + *-as* = *-ās*, *-ā* + *-as* = *-ās*, *-ī* + *-as* = *-yas*, *-i* + *-as* = *-ayas*, *-u* + *-as* = *-avas*, *-a* + -[V:*n*]*i* = *-āni*, *-u* + -[V:*n*]*i* = *-ūni*, etc.). In Prakrit this had already resulted in *-ā* from *-ās* vs. *-ō* from *-as*, and the analogical extension of the *-ō* to thematic Feminines (*mālā/mālā* > *mālāō* 'garland/garlands'). The Neuter had undergone an epenthetical shift of the *-i* to produce *-āiṁ*, *-ūiṁ*, *-īiṁ*.
14. A notable NIA development was the transfer of this ending, in languages which did not preserve the Neuter, to the Feminine, to give e.g., Braj +*ai˜* (*bāt/bātai˜*), Hindi +*e˜* (*bāt/bāte˜*), ultimately applied also to Ts., Perso-Arabic, and English loanwords: H. *bhāṣāe˜* 'languages', *kitābe˜* 'books', *moṭare˜* 'cars'. Thence by analogy it may have nasalized the extended Feminine ending in +*ā* > +*ā˜* as well. Or possibly the *extended Neuter* ending ∗*-akāni* > ∗*-aāiṁ* itself in some form was also transferred.[8] Another explanation for Feminine plural *-ā˜* is transfer from the Oblique (but why Feminines?). See, however, Bloch 1965: 175 (influences of both forms may be responsible). Analogical levelling has in any case taken place in languages like Punjabi, Sindhi, and Rajasthani, reducing the Feminine plural endings to one. In languages which have retained the Neuter, the nasal component of the plural is confined to the latter (subsequently denasalized in Marathi) and the Feminine remains uncontaminated by it: H. *ghoṛiyā˜*, M. *ghoḍyā* 'mares'.

15. Meanwhile, the extended Masculine in **-akās* resulted in *-e* (Hindi, Punjabi, "Lahnda", Marathi, Konkani, Shina, most West Pahari) or *-ā* (Gujarati, Rajasthani, Sindhi, Central Pahari, vestigially in Nepali), depending on whether the MIA reductions proceeded through **-aya* or **-aa*.[9] The *un*extended original thematic ending *-ās*, Prakrit *-ā*, in Late MIA shortened to *-a*, survives in Sindhi and in Konkani (S. *hath*^{u}/ *hath*^{a} 'hand/hands'). Elsewhere such nouns now have zero-ending (H. *hāth/hāth*). The *-ō* endings characteristic of Feminines and non-thematic Masculines in Prakrit have similarly been reduced to *-u* and then lost: as noted above, new systems of Feminine plural suffixes have been constructed from Neuter and extended stem elements.
16. In contrast with the synthetic endings discussed above, the new agglutinative plural suffixes in Eastern and Northwestern NIA (and optionally also Gujarati *+o*: Cardona 1965: 66–8) are not employed when the idea of plurality is *already conveyed* by a numeral or other quantity expression ('many', etc.; in Gujarati also by an inflected adjective). They imply no case (the synthetic endings are Direct Case): the various case endings, including the so-called Nominative of Assamese and dialectal Bengali, are attached to them (see section 8.4). They may be attached only to the last of a series (under circumstances not fully explored).
17. These "plural-formative words" (as Jha calls them) are often common to a wide area. Oriya *mān(e)* is echoed by Chhattisgarhi, Halbi, and Sadani *man*. Bengali *gulo/guli* (the latter is an affective/diminutive) may be related not only to Western Assamese (Kamrupi) *gila*, but possibly also to Gawarbati *gila*, Khowar *gini*, etc. in the far northwest. One of the most common such formatives derives from OIA *sarva* 'all': this lies behind not only the characteristic Bihari *sabh* (used in Magahi and Bhojpuri as well as Maithili), but also Nepali *haru*, Malvi (SE Rajasthani) *hōr (ō)*, and Chhattisgarhi *har*. The word *lōg* 'people' is also in wide use for clarifying the plural of persons, not only in Bihari and Awadhi, but in colloquial Hindi itself. It barely makes sense to speak of suffixation here; facultative compounding with words expressive of quantity is a more accurate description, originally perhaps of all these formatives. (Bengali *-[e]rā*, according to Chatterji, comes from a strengthened Genitive originally preceding a now lost noun of multitude such as *sab*.) Commonly different formatives were favored (or experimented with) at different periods of a language. (For a more radical view of these formatives and the category in question, see Dasgupta 1985.)
18. Finally, it must be pointed out that in languages other than those of the Eastern type just discussed, Plurality is quite generally marked in the Oblique case (see section 8.4) even when it goes unmarked, in certain subclasses, in the Direct case. Even in the Direct case, it is often marked in the larger context of the Noun Phrase (i.e. on the adjective) when it is not marked on the noun itself: H. *baṛā makān/baṛe makān* 'large house/large houses'.

the change of /*āu*/, its most characteristic ending, to /*ō*/, making it homonymous with the singular nominatives of the common class of *-a* stems.

The semantic subclasses involved in agglutinative plural marker selection are most typically persons vs. non-persons, but there is often an honorific sense also and the "classes" (and in some cases the markers themselves) are not rigidly fixed. Insofar as these senses are clear they are indicated by vertical positioning (personal, honorific above vs. inanimate, contemptuous above) in Figure 8.5.

The declensional differences involved in gender classes, referred to at the beginning of the preceding section, may now be seen emerging in the direct case (= "nominative") plural markers. As may be seen, not only do different genders entail different markers, but marked and unmarked subclasses within each gender, and sometimes further subtypes of unmarked nouns, do so as well. There have, however, been some consolidations and simplifications, to different degrees in different languages.

8.4 Case

In NIA as in any language, case is vitally a syntactic as well as a morphological category. Its markers establish the function of the NP in the sentence (or partly in the case of the Genitive, within another NP). These *functions* will be dealt with in Chapter 10; our concern here is with the casal *forms*, insofar as they can be abstracted from the functions which help define them. Even as a form-category, however, case is easily the most problematic nominal category in NIA, whether for cross-linguistic, historical, or single-language descriptive analysis.

In OIA case was also a complex matter, mainly for two reasons. First, oblique case inflections varied with declensional type as well as gender and number. The result was a blurred collection of endings rather than a system made up of clearly-marked distinctions. The main ones of Classical Sanskrit, themselves much simplified from the Vedic language, are given below (as resultant forms, i.e. not subjected to analysis, since these were the basis of further developments).

Second, even if there were some distinctive endings amid the many overlapping

Table 8.1 *Sanskrit declension (= final stem vowels plus case markers)*

	singular	dual	plural
Nominative	*-Ø, ā, ī, as, us, is, ūs, i, u, am*	*-au, ī, ū, ē, inī, unī*	*-ās, ayas, avas, yas, vas, āṁsī, āni, īṇi, ūni*
Accusative	*-am, im, um, ūm, i, u, ām, -Ø*	*-au, ī, ū, ē, inī, unī*	*-ān, īn, ūn, ṝn, īs, ūs, as, ās, āṁsi, āni, īṇi, ūni*
Instrumental	*-ā, ēna, inā, unā, yā, vā, ayā*	*-bhyām, ābhyām, abhyām, ibhyām, ubhyām, ōbhyām, ībhyam, ūbhyam*	*-bhis, ibhis, ubhis, ībhis, ūbhis, ābhis, ais*
Dative	*-ē, āya, ayē, āyai, yai, inē, unē, avē, vai*	[same as Inst.]	*-bhyas, ēbhyas, ābhyas, ōbhyas, ṝbhyas*
Ablative	*-āt, as, ās, inas, unas, yās, vās, āyās, ēs, ōs*	[same as Inst.]	[same as Dative]
Genitive	*-asya, as, ās, inas, unas, yās, vās, āyās, ēs, ōs*	*-ōs, ayōs, yōs, vōs, inōs, unōs, ayōs*	*-ānām, ām, īnām, ūnām, ṝnām*
Locative	*-i, ē, au, ini, uni, yām, vām, āyām*	[same as Gen.]	*-ṣu, su, ēṣu, iṣu*
Vocative	*-Ø, a, ē, ō, i, u*	*-āu*	*-as, i, ūni, īni, avas, ayas, yas, vas, ās*

ones, the functions of the formal cases themselves also overlapped to a disturbing degree. As Bloch notes (1965: 155–6):

> Thus the person to whom something is given can be expressed by the genitive, dative, or locative; the person spoken to, by the accusative, dative, locative, or genitive; the place, by the instrumental or the locative, and similarly circumstance and time, by the same cases and also by the accusative. The instrumental and the ablative express at once cause, separation, and comparison and the genitive and instrumental are equivalent to one another when used with gerundives, words expressing resemblance, verbs meaning 'to fill', etc. These confusions . . . are both the indication and the cause of the disorganisation of the system.

The system indeed began to break down in MIA, as a result both of internal pressures and of phonological erosion, until there was so little left that it could barely fulfill the functions that a case system has to fulfill. One form of Late MIA (Apabhramsa) presented something like the picture presented in table 8.2.

These late MIA forms should be viewed recalling that one of the phonological developments characterizing NIA (Chapter 7) was the loss of final short vowels.

The system which arose in NIA to meet the resulting need presents difficulties of quite another sort. There are at least three *layers* of forms with case-like functions (here I, II, III) in most NIA languages, typically made up of inherited synthetic, new agglutinative, and quasi-analytic elements. Depending both on the language and on scholarly predilections, descriptions have recognized either two layers of affixes and one of postpositions, or one layer of affixes and two layers of postpositions. A second layer of affixes (= secondary affixes) can be equated in a general way cross-linguistically with a first layer of postpositions, but not in its particulars. That is, one of the problems confronting comparison is that a function managed in a given layer in one language is managed in a different layer in

Table 8.2 *Case endings in Late MIA (excluding "obvious Prakritisms")*

	singular	plural
Nominative	*-u, a, aṁ*	*-a, ai˜*
Accusative	[same as Nominative]	
Instrumental	*-eṁ, iṁ, he, hi*	*-(e)hi˜, ehi, ahi˜*
Ablative	*-hu, ahu, aho*	*-hu˜, ahu˜*
Genitive/Dative	*-ho, aho, ha, su, ssu*	*-na, ha˜*
Locative	*-i, hi, hiṁ*	*-hi˜*

another language. For example, the Agentive function, taken care of by the Layer II postposition *-ne* in Hindi, is indicated by Layer I affixes in Sindhi (the General Oblique) and Kashmiri (an organic Agentive/Instrumental).

Here it becomes necessary to make a number of delicate distinctions. Although there is considerable overlap at certain points, the problem of the layers should be separated from questions both of general typology ("synthetic"/ "agglutinative"/ "analytic") and of etymology (i.e. the question of the etymology of Marathi *-s*, discussed in section 8.1 above, has nothing to do with the fact that it now clearly functions on Layer II), and the latter from each other. An attempt at some definitions – or at least at some characterizations – of the layers is in order.

Layer I mainly consists of bits of inflectional material inherited from MIA/ OIA, although not without some shift of function (e.g., the Kashmiri *-as* inflection, said to go back to the OIA Genitive in *-asya*, is now clearly a Dative[10]) and rearrangement of forms. It is not always clear what particular inherited inflections Layer I elements represent: with the very great phonological reduction and analogical consolidation of the old declensional system over the MIA period their etymologies are often in dispute.

However, such "primary" affixes (certainly the most salient of them, the General Oblique) are often characterized, despite all the levelling, by declensional differences and by singular/plural differences (e.g., the same Kashmiri Dative is *-is* for another subclass of masculine nouns in the singular, *-i* for feminine nouns in the singular, and *-en* or *-[a]n* in the plural; the Punjabi Locative is *-e* in the singular, *-ī˜* in the plural).

They may be found only in one number, or only with one declensional subclass: e.g., the Punjabi Ablative in *o˜* (*kheto˜* 'from the field') occurs only in the singular; the Sindhi Locative in $^{-i}$ (*ɗ̣ēh*^{i} 'in the country') occurs only with "unmarked" masculines in $^{-u}$ and feminines in $^{-a}$; the Sinhalese Genitive in *-ehi* > *-ē* occurs only with singulars of the inanimate class. (In the remaining noun classes in these languages the function in question is expressed by Layer II elements.)

Layer I elements attach directly to the base, with morphophonemic adjustments which are occasionally complex.

Finally, *adjectives*, where they are declined, take only Layer I case affixes. (Therefore, any case affix occurring with an adjective may be considered a Layer I affix, although not all Layer I affixes may so occur, and this is no help in languages that do not decline adjectives.)

Layer II may be defined as (a) attached to the base indirectly, through the mediation of a Layer I element; and/or (b) invariant for all nouns and the same for both numbers. Here the complementarity of the conditions needs to be invoked for cases like the Marathi Dative and Instrumental suffixes *lā/nā* and *nē˜/nī˜*, which do vary for number (the latter no longer in speech) but are attached via a Layer I element (the Oblique):

vimān 'plane' (N2)
Obl. sg. *vimān-ā*, Obl. pl. *vimān-yā* ˜
Dat. sg. *vimānā-lā*/ Dat. pl. *vimānyān-nā* 'to the plane/planes'
Inst. sg. *vimānā-ne*˜/ Inst. pl. *vimānyān-nī*˜ 'by plane/planes'

Conversely, Assamese cases like the Dative (*-[ɒ]k*) and Locative (*-[ɒ]t*), are not added via any Layer I element, but they do not vary with number. The Hindi "primary postpositions", such as *se* (Instrumental–Ablative), *ko* (Dative), and *me*˜ (Locative), satisfy both conditions: they are added to the General Oblique (which has a zero-allomorph with several subclasses of nouns in the singular) and are the same in both numbers: *vimān* [Ø] *se*/*vimān-o*˜ *se* 'by plane/planes'.

Layer I is in fact as good as missing in Assamese (a handful of vestigial Locatives occur,[11] but play no role in declension) as in a number of other Eastern languages, but it is desirable for reasons of functional parallelism in a cross-linguistic study as well as for internal typological reasons to still treat the basic Assamese (and similar) case-markers as belonging to Layer II. In generally the same Eastern languages, these affixes can be separated from the base by definiteness markers (8.5) as well as by the new plural formants (8.4): Assamese *mānuh-ɒk*/*manuh-bilāk-+ɒk* 'to (a) man/to men'.

It must be stressed that the absence of elements *functioning* at Layer I does not necessarily mean the absence of *etymologically* primary affixes. There is such an affix in Assamese, the Agentive (sometimes called "Nominative") *-e*/*-ī*, which apparently represents a fusion of the old Instrumental *-ēna* with the old Magadhi Nominative in *-ē*. It now functions as an agglutinative suffix on Layer II, however (*mānuh-e*/*mānuh-bilāk-e* 'the man/men [Ag.]').

Morphophonemic variation, while not entirely absent at Layer II, tends to be of a simpler order than in Layer I, most often involving a support vowel used with consonant stems and dropped with vowel stems, or vice-versa, so that some affixes have the shape [V]C(V . .), some [C]V(C . .): Bengali Genitive *-[e]r* (*guru-r* 'teacher's', *bāgh-er* 'tiger's'), Locative *-[t]e* (*bāṛi-te* 'at home', *ghɔ-e* 'in the house').[12]

Typologically, a Layer II element may be either an agglutinative suffix or an analytic particle. As noted earlier, the line between the two is not clear and at least in part conventional. Etymologically, it is usually a much reduced (typically to one syllable or less) and unrecognizable form of a once independent word, but it may also be, as already noted, a primary inflection which has been dislodged from Layer I and come to function on Layer II (that is, unrestrictedly, and separated from the base by a Layer I element if available or by a plural formant). The Gujarati as well as the Assamese Agentive (both in *-e*) have such an origin.

Under certain conditions, which need more investigation,[13] Layer II elements function as true clitics, that is, as suffixes to a phrase rather than a word as such. For example, they often occur only with the last of a series: H. *rām, śyām, aur mohan ko* 'to Ram, Shyam, and Mohan'. This is never true of Layer I elements.

Layer III in turn would be definable as mediated by a Layer II element, most often a Genitive (in some language also a Dative, Ablative, or even an Agentive or Locative). However, since in a number of NIA languages such an element is *optional* (particularly when it is a Genitive: H. *laṛke ke sāth* 'with the boy', B. *chele-r ʃɔnge*, but G. *chokrā nī sāthe/chokrā sāthe*, P. *muṇḍe de nāl/muṇḍe nāl*), to be usable such a criterion would have to be reformulated to read "*potentially* mediated". In a number of languages the mediating Genitive is obligatory with pronouns (where the possessive adjective is equivalent to the Genitive) even when not with nouns: H. *me-re sāth*, B. *āmā-r ʃɔnge* 'with me', but also G. *mā-rī sāthe*, P. *me-re nāl*.

Even such a modified criterion is not universally applicable, however: in Marathi, the Genitive tends to be omitted with pronouns not referring to persons (*mā-jhyā-barobar* 'with me'/*tyā[ċ] barobar* 'at the same time ("together with that")', *tyā-ċā sāṭhī* 'for him'/*tyāsāṭhī* or *tyā-ċā sāṭhī* 'for/on account of that'[14]). Moreover, in Marathi the pronominal criterion is a double-edged sword. Under certain conditions, elements which belong in Layer II may also be mediated by a Genitive: Abl. *mā-jhyā-hūn* 'from me', Instr. *mā-jhyā-ne˜* 'by me', even Gen. itself *mā-jhyā-cyā-ne˜* (Katenina 1963: 129–31). Sometimes the use or non-use of the Genitive connector involves slight differences of meaning or emphasis: *gharā bāher/gharā-ċā bāher* 'out of the house/outside of the house' (Kavadi and Southworth 1965), or merely rhythmic considerations (in some languages, but by no means in all, there is said to be a tendency to use the Genitive with longer postpositions).

Fortunately there are some additional criteria characterizing a Layer III element, especially vis-à-vis a Layer II element:

(a) It lacks morphophonemic variants, may be longer than one syllable, and usually retains a fairly transparent connection with an independent word (most often a noun, sometimes an adjective or participle), of which it is generally a (sometimes obsolescent) primary (Layer I) case form. It often entails a variable Genitive (see below) connector in such a case form as well: H. °*ke pīche* 'behind' < Oblique form of *(°kā) pīchā* '(its) rear', G. *(° nī) puṭhe* 'behind' < Locative form of *puṭh* 'back', M. *(-cyā) māge (˜)* < Instrumental form of *māg* 'track' (< OIA *mārga* 'road'); cf. *māgīl* 'previous, hinder'. In cases where, e.g., the Oblique has a zero-allomorph, there is nothing distinctive about the postposition itself, but the connecting Genitive, if present, is in the Oblique (contrastive in Hindi only if the underlying noun is masculine): H. *°ke andar* 'inside of' < *°kā andar*.

(b) It is semantically more specific. E.g., as compared with a more diffuse Locative on Layer II or perhaps Layer I, Layer III typically mediates such concepts as 'on top of', 'under', 'behind', 'inside of', 'near', etc.: in Hindi -*°ke ūpar*, -*° ke nīce*, -*°ke pīche*, -*°ke andar*, -*°ke pās*, where °, representing General Oblique, is Layer I, the Genitive postposition *ke* is Layer II, and *ūpar* etc. are the Layer III elements. Compare the more general H. Layer II particles *mẽ* 'in' and *par* 'on, at', and the even more general Bengali Locative suffix -*[t]e* 'at, in, on, (from, by, etc.)'. (The Bengali Locative, or more properly Instrumental-Locative, also functions as an Instrumental with Inanimates, and is really the product of fusion of two cases, both originally primary, *plus* a Locative postposition.)

There are, however, some borderline cases, typically involving elements which do *not* bear any resemblance to a functioning lexical item, e.g., the Punjabi instrumental-sociative postposition *°nāl*, the Marathi sociative °-*ʃī* and allative °-*kaḍe*, the Assamese allative -*[ɒ]lɔi* – and elements such as Marathi °-*sāṭhī* meaning 'for', have a substantially grammatical function, yet may in some cases take an optional Genitive linkage, and in relation to another postposition (clearly belonging to Layer II) are more specific. On the other side of the problem are postpositions like Hindi *mẽ* ('in'), *par* ('on'), and *tak* ('up to'), which fulfill all the formal requirements of Layer II elements in terms of lexical opacity and non-Genitive linkage, but are too many (as well as a bit too specific) for a basic case function like Locative (as compared, again, with Bengali -*te* or Marathi -*t*).

It is not surprising that the boundary between Layers II and III is somewhat fuzzy when it is considered that Layer III is the recruiting ground for Layer II. It is to be expected that at any given time there will be some elements in a state of transition.

Certain complex formations raise the question of a *Layer IV*. One involves phrases of the type (cited by Zograph 1976) H.–U. *°kī χidmat/sevā mẽ* 'for, to' (lit. 'in service of'), M. °-*cyā yogā-nẽ* 'in connection with', which have Layer II case markers (instead of Layer I case markers) following lexical nouns (*χidmat* 'service', *yog* 'connection'). The question is, especially where the noun has primarily a relational rather than a concrete signification, are these a further type of postposition (or subtype perhaps, on the "active periphery" of Layer III), or are they simply oblique case nouns, albeit abstract ones, preceded by Genitive modifiers X-*kī*, X-*cyā*, as in *rām ke ghar mẽ/rāmācyā gharāt* 'in Ram's house'? The issue is complicated by items like H. X° *ke bāre mẽ*, 'about, concerning', where the Persian loanword *bārā*, *bārah* 'time, turn' (normally *bār*) is not common outside of this context in the extended meaning 'subject' (unlike *viṣay* in the partial literary equivalent X° *ke viṣay me˜*). In short, another indeterminate boundary arises because of the occurrence of some items mainly in the context of such phrases.

Although postpositions of the type of H. ^{ke}*liye* 'for' are commonly called *compound postpositions* (in contrast to those like *par* 'on' which are called *simple*), another question arises regarding postpositions that are truly "compound", i.e. made up of two significant parts: sequences like H. °*me˜ se*, G. °*mā˜thī* 'from in, from among' on the one hand, and P. *vicc-o˜* 'from inside', *kol-o˜* 'from near', S. *m-ā˜* (= *mē˜+-ā˜*) 'out of', *vaṭ-ā˜* 'from (a person)', M. *khāl-ūn* 'from under', *var-ūn* 'from on' on the other. Those of the first type, with a final Layer II element, are perhaps best treated not as units but as a special instance of the clitic function of the second element, here as suffixed to a postpositional phrase (G. *ghar-mā˜* 'in the house' + *thī* 'from' = *gharmā˜thī*), but in the case of those of the second type, which have a final Layer I element, there are difficulties in the way of such a treatment in that Layer I elements by definition cannot act as clitics. Are such sequences then to be ascribed, by virtue of their semantic complexity, to a Layer IV or to a special sublayer of Layer III, or, in cases where both elements belong to Layer II, even to a special sublayer of Layer II? Undue multiplication of distinctions on Layer II is to be avoided, since, as will be noted, this is the primary locus of basic case markers.

Perhaps it simply needs to be recognized that the way to preservation for a Layer I element lies in cliticization, and attachment to a postposition may be seen as a first step in such a process, which need not entail forfeiture of Layer I status (although suffixation to a postpositional phrase represents a significant expansion of function). Sindhi is particularly problematic in this regard, in that the Layer I element in question, *ā˜* ("Ablative"), while imparting semantic complexity to some postpositions, is simply the necessary adverbializing formant in other cases (^{je}*aggīā˜* 'in front of', ^{je}*hēṭhā˜* 'under'). And what of °*khā˜* 'from, than', more common in Ablative–Sociative function than *-ā˜*, but related formally to °*khē* 'to' in the same way that *mā˜* and *tā˜* ('out of', 'from on, away from') are related to *mē˜* 'in' and *tē* 'on'? And what then of °*khā˜-pō*^{i} 'after', °*khā˜aḏ̄ē* 'before'?

Finally, there are cases like B. *pɔrjɔnto* 'up to', *ɔnujāī* 'according to', *dhore* 'during' (for others see Seely 1985, Page 1934), generally recognized as postpositions, but which attach to the noun directly, without benefit of linking elements (even optionally) from either Layer I or Layer II. Should phrases with these be treated in some other way, perhaps as adverbial compounds? Such elements, which are "true" Layer III postpositions (i.e. preceded by linkage elements) in some other N I A languages, shade in turn into such elements as M. *-artha* 'for', in *udāharaṇārtha* 'for example'.[15]

There is a question on Layer I of the status in the system of vestigial old case forms other than the General Oblique when, as is often the case, they are found only with a limited set of words and are replaceable with Layer II forms except in certain fixed phrases. They can be viewed as having assumed the aspect of lexicalized adverbs. (The most widespread cross-linguistically are Locatives, followed by Instrumentals and Ablatives: M. *ghar-i*, WRaj. Aw. Mth. *ghar-e*, P. *kàr-e*, Or. *ghɔr-e*, etc. 'at/to home'; M. *gharūn*, P. *kàro*˜ 'from home/the house'.) The question is, how limited is too limited? All but the historically preoccupied may be content to accept a single item, such as *ghare*, as synchronically a lexical adverb, but what about primary Locatives said to be "restricted" to words referring to places and times? What if such expressions are functionally very basic and frequent? What if such endings are applied also to borrowed words (cf. Sindhi *ʃahar*^{i} 'in the city', *vaqat*^{i} 'at the time')?

At this end of the case spectrum also there would thus seem to be an indeterminate continuum, this time between lexicalization and productivity. In the representations of case that follow, such primary case remnants will accordingly not be excluded, but will be placed in parentheses if truly restricted to a "small" lexical set, a somewhat arbitrary judgement.

Zograph remarks that all the aforementioned levels cannot represent *case*, at least not in the same sense. Investigators' judgements have varied. Some with strong historical predilections have recognized *case* only in the inflectional fragments on Layer I, however restricted lexically or functionally. This is hardly a tenable position for NIA. Most would agree with Zograph that the locus of NIA case-marking lies with the agglutinative suffixes and particles of Layer II. Nevertheless it is undeniable that, in some languages at least, Layer I retains some case-marking capacities, and that, in almost all the languages, certain case-marking functions extend also to Layer III: not only is there what might be called the finer locative tuning of the particular local "cases", but there are also "extended" datives (benefactives?), ablatives, and instrumentals marking either basic general syntactic functions themselves (as alternatives to Layer II markers), or some special aspect of them. Not all Layer III postpositions lend themselves immediately to such interpretations, to be sure, but even the most recalcitrant can generally be seen as some extension of (usually) an instrumental or locative function.

Except for the fact that in NIA the elements involved occur in successive layers to the right of the base, this whole problem of case-marking and adpositions, including the matter of indeterminate boundaries of the system and of its component subsystems, is not unlike that found in familiar European languages. It is more precisely paralleled, however, by the situation in neighboring Dravidian.[16] There also are to be found a Layer I (an Oblique form, e.g., Telugu *illu*/*iṇṭ*-, Tamil *vīṭu/vīṭṭ-* 'house' – not found with all nouns, or, if preferred, with a zero-allomorph, just as in NIA), a Layer II (the basic case affixes, attached to the Oblique form if it exists: *iṇṭi-ki*, *vīṭṭu-kku* 'to the house'), and a Layer III (more specific "postpositions", added to various Layer II affixes – which may be optional: *vīṭṭu-kku mēlē* 'above the house'). See Arden 1937: 74–7; 1942: 125–7.

By way of anticipation, a further parallel lies within NIA itself. The layered build-up of basic case markers and specialized postpositional extensions, with its indeterminate boundaries, is strikingly similar to the relation between markers of aspect and *Aktionsart* in the verbal system.

It is axiomatic that a language should be described in terms of its own system of contrasts, not in terms of some external framework (even that of the Sanskrit grammarians). When comparing a number of languages, however, it is necessary to compromise this principle to the extent of providing a framework large enough to accommodate the contrasts of all the languages being compared, and therefore larger than required by some of them individually. (In addition, in describing NIA case systems, the matter of the layers often results in contrasts absent in one layer showing up in another.) This larger framework within which the contrasts of individual languages may be displayed to advantage, will be drawn in what follows from the *collective maximum* of NIA formal case contrasts on the *Layer II* level. This will generally accommodate Layer I contrasts also, with certain exceptions which will be given special treatment. It might be possible to work out a cross-linguistic system of Layer III contrasts as well. That will not be attempted here but only suggested, by giving certain Layer III markers as extensions of Layer II categories.

The oblique cases with distinct Layer II markers in one NIA language or another are Dative (or Dative–Accusative), Agentive (or Ergative), Instrumental, Sociative (or Comitative), Ablative, Locative, Genitive, and Vocative. Maximal differentiation (seven of the eight) appears to be in Marathi (°*-lā/nā*, °*-ne/nī*, °*-ʃī*, °*-hūn*, °*-t*, °*-ċā**, °*-no*) and Nepali (°*-lāī*, °*-le*, °*-sita/sa˜ga*, °*-bāṭa*, °*-mā–*, °*-ko**, *-ho*), in both of which the Agentive and Instrumental are combined. (Asterisks indicate "declinable" markers, variable for gender, number, and sometimes case itself.) It is generally in the *Ag/Instr/Soc/Abl* area that categories may be variously collapsed: e.g., Hindi combines Instrumental, Sociative, and Ablative (°*se*) while differentiating Agentive (°*ne*).

The Nominative (or Direct – as contrasted with Oblique [see below]) would accordingly be the unmarked case – except for the fact that in some forms of NIA it too is marked (with an *-e*: in East Bengali dialects a legacy of Magadhi *-ake* < OIA *-akas*; in Oriya animate plurals ultimately from the Vedic Instrumental plural in *-ēbhis*, according to Chatterji 1926).

Since at this point we are interested in case forms, not case relations, labels are drawn from traditional morphology rather than case theory. In general (that is, with some overlap) distinct forms do imply potentially distinct functions (on Layer II, less clearly on Layer III). Nepali, with an overabundance of what seem to be Layer II elements, is problematic here: in the Ablative area there are *-dekhi* and *-bhandā* as well as *-bāṭa* (see above), with partially different functions, while Sociative *-sita* and *-sa˜ga* are apparently completely synonymous.

It should be noted that (in contrast with Sanskrit, and also with Dravidian) there *is no Accusative case* in NIA (except possibly in some forms of colloquial Sinhalese, where Gair detected what may be an Accusative).

The status of the Genitive as a true case form (as against an "adjectival form of a noun") has been challenged. It was not recognized as a *kāraka* (which, however, has to do with case *relations*) by the Sanskrit grammarians. It lacks obvious differentiated equivalents in Layer III. However, it does act in several NIA languages as a suffix to a phrase, not just to a noun: M. *āplyā-jyavaḷ-cī* (*vastre*) '(the clothes) which [he had] with him', G. *tɛm-nā-mā˜-nā* (*ek*) '(one) among them' (Lambert 1971: 246), H. *mez par kī kitābe˜* 'the books on the table' (Subbarao 1984: 189). It also marks grammatical relations on the clause level as well as on the phrase level in Bengali at least. It is attached via an Oblique (see below) where this exists, like other Layer II case markers. All things considered, it is convenient to treat it as a formal case even while recognizing its special characteristics. Chief among them is its capacity to inflect like an adjective (in languages where adjectives inflect), in agreement with the noun which the Genitive phrase modifies, and the existence of special equivalent forms (possessive adjectives) in the pronominal paradigm.

The Vocative is essentially a Layer I phenomenon, except for plural forms in Marathi (*mulg-yān-no* 'Boys!'), Nepali (*chorā-harū ho*), and Sinhalese (*minisu-n-i* 'People!'), where it shows typical Layer II mediated attachment. Elsewhere it often coincides with the Nominative or with the Oblique, but it has distinct forms in Punjabi and Sindhi (and in the Hindi plural *-o* as contrasted with Oblique plural *-o˜*: *bhāiy-o aur bahan-o* 'Brothers and sisters!' – a common speech-opening formula). Since the Vocative plays no role in syntax, and is thus marginal to the case system as such, it will not be dealt with further here.

Before proceeding with a more detailed examination of the remainder of the NIA case spectrum in the above framework, it is necessary to deal with a peculiar Layer I element that does not fit in it, namely the General Oblique, already unavoidably referred to. In many NIA languages the General Oblique occurs *only* before Layer II elements (except in a few fossilized expressions, such as H. *bhūkho˜ marā* '[I'm] dead of hunger' – if indeed this oft-cited example is not a fragment of some other primary case: cf. the P. Ablative in *-o˜*). In a synchronic description of such languages (as of Dravidian languages) it is thus sometimes treated as an "Oblique Base" rather than as a "case" at all, since it really has no casal function.[17] In a few (principally Northwestern) NIA languages, however, it does have independent syntactic functions, chiefly agentive. As an important building-block of NIA case systems, it must be reckoned with in any case. Its forms are shown in Figure 8.6.

— = no contrast with Nominative
{ } = no contrast, but Nominative historically < Oblique
: = vowel-lengthening ˜ = *anusyāra*
an., AN = animate INAN = inanimate

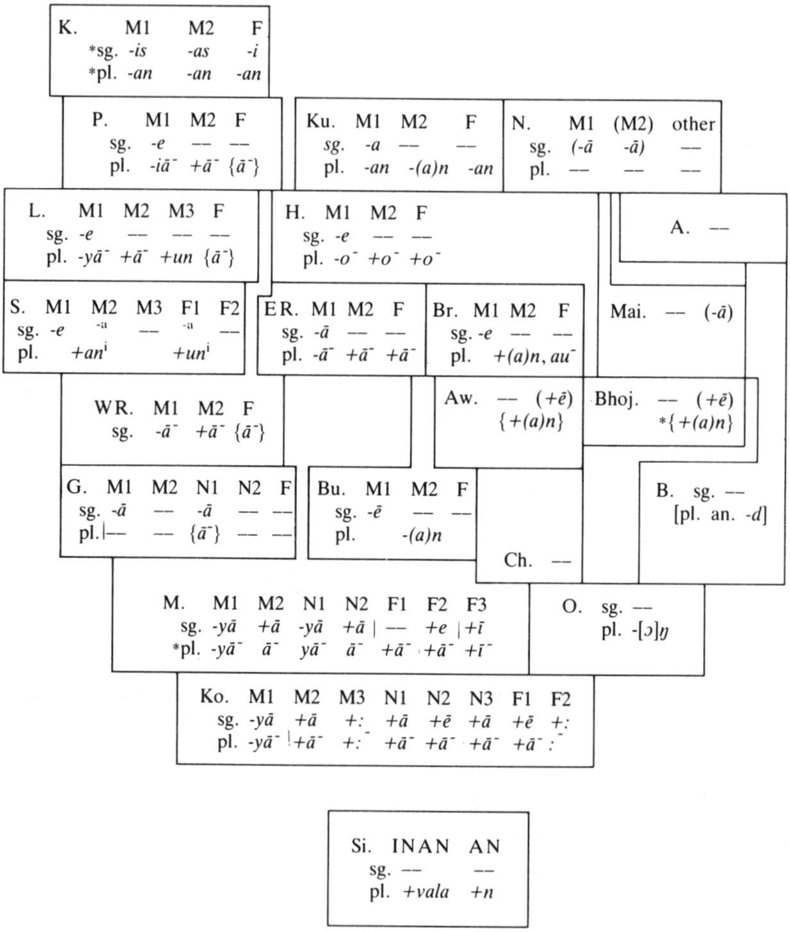

Figure 8.6 NIA case markers, Layer I: the General Oblique

Comments on Figure 8.6

1. The ubiquitousness of the nasal element (in the form of -˜ or -*n*, and generally as -*ā*˜ or -*an*) as the distinctive marker of the Oblique plural throughout NIA, even in distant Sinhalese, will be apparent. Outside the chart it is represented also in Romany (-*en*),

Kalasha (*-en*, *-an*), Khowar (*-an*, *-ān*), and more sporadically elsewhere in Dardic. (It is apparently missing in Shina and in a number of West Pahari dialects, although present in Mandeali and Bhadarwahi.) Most authorities trace this nasal element back to the OIA Genitive plural in *-ānām*. Regarding the nasal element in Marathi, see below (4).

2. In some dialects transitional to the Eastern group, this *-an* (or *-an(h) i*) has spread to the Direct plural, erasing the distinction: dialects of Awadhi, Bhojpuri, Magahi (Aryani 1965: 16), and in earlier forms of Maithili, now lost according to Jha (but cf. the modern plural formant *lokan*[i]). In Bhojpuri (starred), *-(a)n* has replaced the Direct plural in the "standard" dialect described by the *LSI*, but not in the Northern (Gorakhpuri) dialect described by Shukla 1981.
3. In Sinhalese, the Nominative sg. in *-ā* (Figure 8.3) is also an old Oblique (<MIA Genitive in *-āha*: Geiger 1938: 95–6).
4. The declensional scheme for Marathi could be elaborated further (cf. Konkani) by including, under each of the gender classes, further subclasses (mainly consisting of Tss. and other loanwords) ending in vowels, with no Direct/Oblique contrast in the singular. The Oblique used to be formed by lengthening the vowel, if short: *pati/patī* 'husband', *vastu/vastū-* 'thing' (but *rājā* 'king', *ċākū* 'knife', no change). With the loss of length contrast in the high vowels, this was purely graphic, and has been done away with in the new spelling (*patī*, *vastū*). The plural Oblique, formed by adding *anusvāra* to the vowel (*patī˜*, *vastū˜*, *rājā˜*) is – like the rest of the Marathi plural Oblique – partly but not purely graphic, in that the *anusvāra* (˜), which is otherwise silent, does come alive (in the form of a homorganic nasal) before common suffix-postpositions beginning with certain consonants: *paṭīn+na* 'to the husbands'.
5. The starred Kashmiri forms given are Datives rather than General Obliques, but they are the closest thing to the latter in the language, both in function (as the most common although not the only base for postpositions) and, as will be apparent from the plural at least, in form (for the good reason that they probably also go back to the OIA Genitives in *-asya* and *-ānām*).
6. It would be tempting to treat the Bengali animate plural forms with *-d-*, *-di-*, (= *-dig-* in older *sādhu bhāṣā*) as Obliques, since they form a base for all the oblique cases in the plural: *mee/mee-ra* 'girl/girls' (Nom.), *mee-ke/mee-d-er-(ke)* (Dat.), *mee-r dārā/mee-d-er dārā* (Inst.), etc. They would be unique (together with Sinhalese inanimate *-vala*) in that *-d-* is a secondary rather than a primary form. They are unique in any case (and recent), but the analysis is also messy. Although the *-er* element would seem to be the same as the Genitive suffix (see Figure 8.7), *-der* works as a unit in clitic function: *cor-ḍākāt o dūṣṭo lok<u>der</u> (nirmūl korlen)* '(He extirpated) thieves, dacoits, and wicked people' (Bender and Riccardi 1978: 69). The optionality of the Dative *-ke* with these plural forms, with the result that the Genitive normally does duty for the Dative (–Accusative) as in the above example, need not detain us, since it accords with the tendency to substitute the Genitive for the Dative that comes to the fore again and again in Indo-Aryan – in Sanskrit, in sister NIA dialects (Kashmiri, and everywhere in the plural), and elsewhere in the syntax of Bengali itself (see Chapter 10).
7. Particularly in the plural where they are most widespread and uniform, the Oblique endings are not extra morphological baggage devoid of function. Their function is apparently to mark plurality itself, in a context where it may be particularly important to do so. In the Nominative, verbal agreement may serve to indicate plurality (in many of the languages at least) even where plural marking is spotty. Significantly, those languages which lack regular Oblique plurals (Gujarati, Assamese, Nepali) have case-independent agglutinative plural marking instead.
8. Attention is called to the peculiar Oblique singular suffixes of Awadhi, Bhojpuri, and Maithili (also to be found in Magahi and Angika). According to Shukla 1981 and from what can be gleaned from the *LSI*, they are phonologically conditioned so that they often occur with nouns which do not have overt Oblique-marking in other NIA languages: H. *khet ko*/ Bhoj. *khẽt-e ke* 'field' (Dat.), H. *ghar ko*/ Aw. *ghar-ai*, *ghar-e ka*, Mag. *ghar-e ke* 'house' (Dat.). These are optional except with certain verbal nouns (where in Maithili–Magahi the suffix is *-ā*: Mth. *dēkhab* 'to see, seeing' > *dēkhab-ā sau˜* 'from seeing').

I = Layer I II = Layer II

( ) = occasional inflections
° = (preceding) Oblique linkage

inflected forms displayed as follows:

SG: MDir, (NDir), FDir / MObl, (NObl), FObl / additional case forms
PL: MDir, (NDir), FDir / MObl, (NObl), FObl / additional case forms

" = form identical with form directly above
+ = form identical with Direct Case equivalent for gender
(or, in Kashmiri, with preceding oblique case)

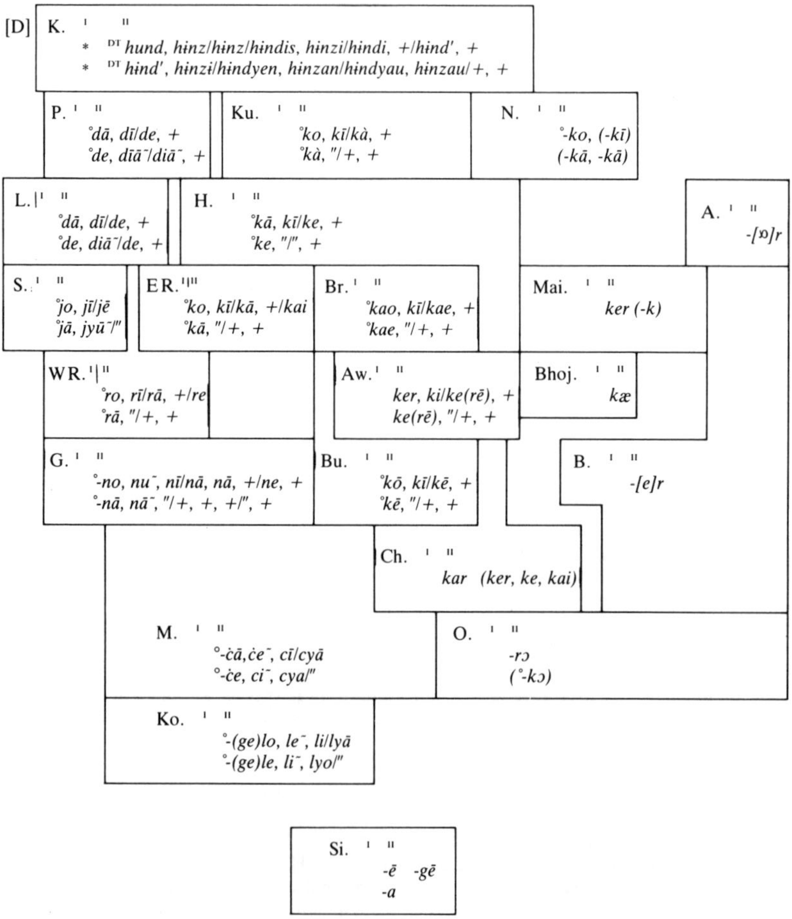

Figure 8.7 Genitive case markers in NIA

Comments on Figure 8.7

1. Two layers are basically sufficient to display N I A Genitive marking, although it could be argued that certain other declinable (= adjective-forming) postpositions (often with such meanings as "like", e.g., G. $^{(na)}$*jevu*˜, Siraiki $^{(de)}$*savā*˜, H. *jaisā*, but sometimes with local and other meanings) constitute Layer III equivalents of Genitives. (The K. declinable postposition *kyut* 'for' goes formally with this group but semantically with the Dative.)
2. In Rajasthani and Gujarati, the additional case is Agentive–Locative. In Kashmiri, the oblique categories are Dative, Ablative, and Agentive, in that order.
3. The Kashmiri Genitive is even more complicated than indicated above. There are two other markers besides the one given, *-uk** and *-un**, both fully declined. The first goes with masculine *inanimates (kary-uk sɔn* 'bracelet's gold', *gāma-ci barādrī manz* 'in the village's brotherhood'), the second with masculine *proper names* (*rām-un gur* 'Ram's horse'). These restrictions, together with the complex morphophonemics of their addition (allegedly to the Ablative, but with peculiar truncations), make them close to being Layer I markers. The "general" Genitive, used with plurals, feminines, and animate masculines (i.e. not with inanimate masculines), is not without such features also, however. It is added to a modified form of the Dative, from which its allomorph *sund* acquires (see Figures 8.6, 8.8 and Grierson 1973: 34) an *s*- after masculine singulars: *guri hund zyon* 'mare's birth', but *mǝ̄likɨ-sɨnzɨ kathɨ* 'owner's words' (Bailey 1937: 26, 28). (In the presentation of the paradigm of *hund* above, I follow Bailey with slight symbol modifications. Grierson has *hond/handis/handⁱ*, etc.)
4. Elsewhere on Figure 8.7 the Genitive is purely a Layer II marker, except in Sinhalese, where the Layer I markers *-ē*, *-a* go with Inanimates while the Layer II marker *-gē* goes with Animates (plus Tss. Inanimates). The Layer II markers in *k*- and *-r*, *r*- (the latter including most West Pahari dialects, besides Rajasthani), along with Sindhi *jo* and Marathi *-ċā* (also found as an alternative form in Konkani: *-ċo*) may all go back to various nominal forms of OIA √KR̥: *kārya*, *kr̥ta*, **kr̥tya* (contamination of *kr̥tvā*), via *kēra*, *kāra*, *kajja*, etc., although Chatterji favors the adjectival suffix *-kka* as the source of, or at least an influence on, the *k*- forms, since a single *k* in medial position (medial once it became a suffix) would normally have been lost (as in Bengali *-er* from *kera*). In the West Pahari dialect Shodochi, both the *-r*- and the *k*- have been lost, giving *-au**, *-ō** (declinable: vs. Dardic [see below]). Romany still shows *kero* (or *kiro*); note also Maithili, Awadhi, Chhattisgarhi, Bhadarwahi.
5. In the "Dardic" languages beyond Kashmiri, however (not shown), we have what certainly seems to be Layer I marking of the Genitive, preserving primary inflections: Shina *-ăi* (sg.), *-o* (pl.); Khowar *-o* (sg.), *-an*, *-ān* (pl.); Kalasha *-as* (sg.), *-an* (pl.), SW Pashai *-as* (sg.+pl.), Bashkarik *-an* (pl.+sg.), Gawarbati *-ana* (pl.+sg.). Some of these forms also double as General Obliques (cf. probable origin of N I A Oblique) or Datives (cf. Kashmiri).
6. In Oriya *-kɔ* is found with personal nouns only (following plural-Oblique *-ɔŋ*-) and has an honorific connotation: *bhɔgɔbānɔŋkɔ*. The Bhojpuri form is from Shukla 1981.

N I A languages differ as to whether they treat (on Layers I and II) agentive, instrumental, sociative, and ablative functions as one case or several. E.g., in Hindi, °*ne* marks the active agent, while °*se* marks the passive and causative agent + instrumental, ablative, and some sociative functions, but in Marathi °*-ne/nī* marks *both* active agent and instrument, while ablative and sociative have separate markers °*-hun* and °*-ʃī* respectively, and the passive agent takes a Layer III marker °*-kaḍūn*. Hence it will be convenient to treat these cases together in Figure 8.9. In a number of languages the Locative also overlaps these areas in form, but because of its different syntactic role and Layer III extensions it is best treated separately (Figure 8.10).

I = Layer I II = Layer II III = Layer III

° = (preceding) Oblique linkage
DT = (preceding) Dative linkage
de, ke, (etc.) = (preceding) Genitive linkage
PN = pronouns only
* = inflected form

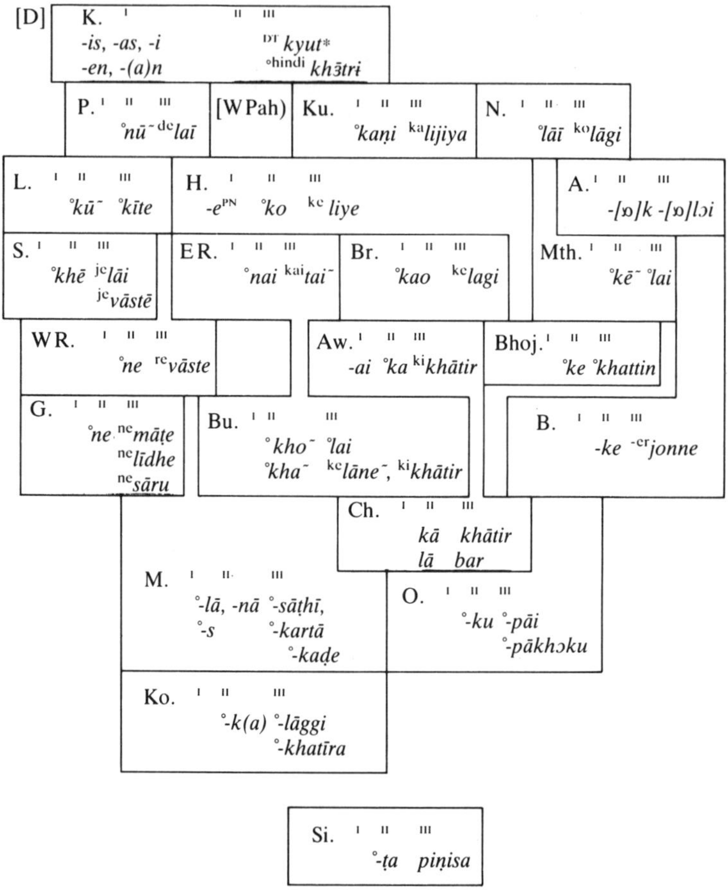

Figure 8.8 Dative case markers in NIA

Comments on Figure 8.8

1. West Pahari Layer II Dative markers include *-kh* (Jaunsari), *khē* (Sirmauri, Baghati, Kiunthali), *be* (Kului, Inner Siraji), *bo* (Bharmauri), *lai* (Shodochi), *jō* (Mandeali, Chameali, Bharmauri, Bhadarwahi-Bhalesi), *jē* (Pangwali), and *nī* (Churahi, Khashali).
2. Dardic Layer II Dative markers include *ka/ke/ki* (Shina), *ka* (Bashkarik), *ke* (Torwali, Gawarbati), *kai* (Kalasha), *te* (Khowar). Romany has *ke/ge*.
3. The Layer III markers shown generally mean 'for' and 'in order to'. In some cases (Nepali, Shodochi, Marathi) a form of the marker most often in question (*lā*, *lai*, *lɔi*, *lāi*, *lagi*, *lāgi*, *lāggi* – all derived, according to Bloch, from the MIA past participle of the root

√LAG 'be in contact with, adhere, stick') has been promoted to the status of the general Layer II marker. The sense of the forms with *khātir* is closer to 'for the sake of'. The *khātir* and *vāste* forms (both of Arabic origin) are found in Hindi and Urdu and other languages besides those indicated, but occupy a less central position.

4. In most NIA languages there are no primary (Layer I) Datives, but such forms are prominent in Kashmiri and Gawarbati (*-an*, *-ā*). They are also to be found in Pashai dialects (*-ai*), in Khowar (*-a*), and even in some Awadhi dialects, in Khowar mainly and in Awadhi exclusively in the sense of an *allative* ("motion to"), although Awadhi *-ai* had wider dative functions in the old literary language. (Pashai *-äi* seems to have been agglutinized, i.e. it is added also after plural formants: *ādam-an-ai* 'to the men'). Even in Hindi–Urdu, there is the *-e*, *-e˜* of the alternate Pronominal Datives (*mujh-ko/mujhe*, *us-ko/use*, *ham-ko/hame˜*, *tum-ko/tumhe˜*, *un-ko/unhe˜*, etc.) Although these forms mostly go back to inflectional material that is not specifically Dative (e.g., the Hindi forms to the Old Hindi Oblique in *-hi* from a MIA Locative in *-ahi*) it is likely, according to Morgenstierne, that in Khowar *-a* there is a preservation of the OIA Dative *-āya* itself, elsewhere long since lost.
5. Functionally, the inflected Kashmiri postposition *kyut* 'for' (connected with OIA *kr̥ta*) is parallel to the other Layer III Datives shown. There are therefore no Layer II Datives in Kashmiri.
6. It will be apparent that the most widespread Layer II marker is *ko*, *khē*, *ke*, *kai*, *ka*, *ku*, *-kh*, *-ɒk*. It has allomorphic variants in some languages. Among those not shown are Konkani *kā* (with pronouns), Awadhi *kā* (phonologically conditioned: see Saksena 1971: 215), Oriya *ki* (after bases ending in *-i*). The origin of these forms has been the subject of much controversy. It is not even clear whether they are to be ascribed a common origin. Related or not, a pattern of convergence toward this set of forms may be noted, which extends even to Dravidian, most strikingly in the case of Oriya *-ku/-ki* and the *-ku/-ki* of neighboring Telugu. Etymological theories, which overlap with those concerned with the Genitive markers, target OIA *kr̥ta*, *kārya*, *kakṣa* and the pleonastic/adjectival extension *-ka*, *-kka*. Chatterji and Grierson agree in seeing in many such Datives (also G. *-ne* vs. *--no*$_*$) a Genitive form inflected for the Locative. Such use of a Genitive as a Dative would repeat on Layer II what had happened earlier with the OIA/MIA inflections, and on Layer I in the northwest.
7. Markers with *-n* seem to be confined to an area from Gujarat to slightly beyond Punjab. The marker *te* (Khowar) is also found in Kumauni (*tɛ˜*, *thɛ˜*), in Old Marathi (*teṃ*, *theṃ*, and as a Layer III form (^{ri}*taī˜*, ^{re}*tēī˜* 'for') in West Pahari dialects (Kului, Churahi, Shodochi) and also in Hindi ^{ke}*tai˜*, *tāī* (with the meaning 'up to', more commonly *tak*). Bloch (1920: 200–1) connects the obsolete Marathi forms with among other things Gujarati, Punjabi, and Oriya Ablatives, possibly derived ("malgré la déviation du sens" in the latter cases) from OIA *artha* 'purpose'. Kumauni *kaṇī* is found also (*kani*) in the Khashali dialects of West Pahari (S. Varma 1938: 29).

Primary *Locatives* survive in many NIA languages, either as vestigial fragments or as forms usable with a fair number of words. The usual form is *-e* (Punjabi plural, Marathi *-ī˜*, Assamese allomorph *-i*, *-y*), which does not represent the Sanskrit Locative *-e* but must come from MIA forms such as *-ahi*, *-ahiṁ*. Locatives in *-ai* survive in Rajasthani and in *-hi* in Maithili. The original OIA Locative in *-ē*, *-i* may survive in the palatalized consonant of such vestigial Kashmiri forms as *nɜl´* 'on the neck' – from Nom. *nāl*. As mentioned above, the primary Locative has for phonological reasons merged with the Instrumental in a number of languages, either as a Layer I or a Layer II form.

NIA languages have in most cases nevertheless found it necessary to develop more distinctive Layer II Locative markers as well as more specific markers on Layer III. Many of the latter will be found to be nouns in the (primary) Locative case. A few languages distinguish motion vs. rest: Assamese, by appending *-ɒlɔi*

I = Layer I II = Layer II III = Layer III
AG: = Aagentive IN: = Instrumental SO: = Sociative AB: = Ablative
° General Oblique (as linker or as case marker)
KE, DE, CYĀ, ER, etc. = Layer II linker
(implying preceding Oblique where found)
AB, DT = Layer I (Ablative, Dative) linkers (in Kashmiri)

K. I II III
AG: -C', -n; -au IN: ^{AB}*kin'*
AB: -i, -ɨ; "
" SO: ^{AB}*sɨit'* AB: ^{DT}*path(ɨ)*

P. I II III
AG: °*ne* IN/SO: ^{de}*nāl* IN: ^{de}*rahī˜*
AB: *o˜* AB: °*to˜* AB: ^{de}*nālo˜* AB: ^{de}*kāraṇ*

N. I II III
AG/IN: *-le*
AB: *bāṭa, dekhi*
-bhandā
SO: *-sita (sa˜ga)*

H. I II III
AG: °*ne* AG/IN: ^{ke}*dvārā*
IN/AB/SO: °*se* SO: ^{ke}*sāth*
AB: ^{ke}*kāran*
^{ki}*taraf se*

A. I II III
AG: *-e* IN: ^{ɒr}*dārā,*
IN: *-ere* ^{ɒr}*hɔtuwāɪ*
SO: ^{ɒr}*χɔite*
AB: ^{ɒr}*pɒrā*
^{ɒr}*kɔɪ*

S. I II III
AG: ° AG/AB: °*vaṭā˜*
IN: *-e˜* SO/IN: °*sā˜* IN: ^{je}*zarīē, vasilē(sā˜)*
AB: *-ā˜* AB: °*khā˜* AB: ^{je}*sababā˜*
°*tā˜*, °*mā˜* AB: $^{\text{khā˜}}$ *vaṭhī˜*

Mth. I II III
IN: *-e, e˜* IN/AB: *sa˜* IN: ^{k}*dvārā*
(-hɪ) IN: *bute* *deā*
SO: *lāgal* SO: ^{k}*saŋge*
jɔ̄re ^{k}*ṭhā˜*
AB: ^{k}*kārane*

G. I II III
AG/IN: *-e,* °*ē*
IN/AB: °*thī* IN: ^{ni}*vaḍe, vati*
SO: ^{ni}*sāthe, joḍe*
AB: ^{na}*kartā˜*
^{ne}*kāraṇe*

B. I II III
IN: *te* AG/IN: ^{ke}*die*
^{er}*dāṛā*
IN: ^{te}*kore*
AB: *theke*
SO: ^{er}*ʃoŋge*

M. I II III
AG/IN: °*-ne˜, nī˜*
IN: *-e˜, -ī˜*
AB: *-ūn* AB: °*-hūn* AB: °*-ātūn*
SO: °*ʃī˜* SO: ^{cyā}*barobar*
AB: °*-mūle˜*
AB: °*-pekṣā*

O. I II III
IN: *-e* IN: *-re* IN: *dārā, dei*
IN: ^{re}*kɔri*
AB: *-u* AB: *-ru* AB: *ṭhāru, ṭhiru*
SO: ^{re}*sāŋge,*
^{re}*sāŋgɔre*

Si. I II III
AG: ^{ta}*kiəla*
AB/IN: *eŋ, -iŋ* IN: °*-gen* IN: *lavā,* °*visin*
SO: ^{t}*ekka*/°*ha* SO: $^{\text{(hā)}}$*samaga*
AB: °*keren* AB: ^{ē}*iṅdəla*/^{ē}*siṭa*

Figure 8.9 Agentive/Instrumental/Sociative/Ablative in the main NIA

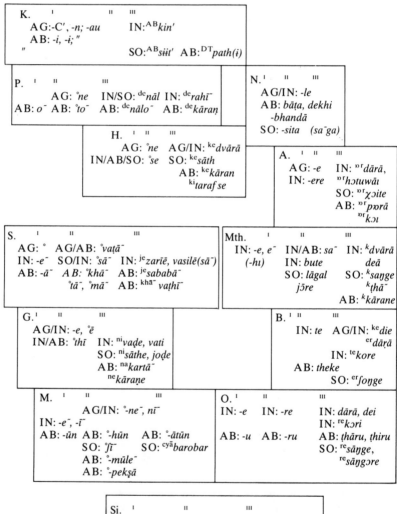

Comments on Figure 8.9

1. The complexity of the data on Figure 8.9 makes it possible to display only the "main" NIA languages (plus Maithili) in the space available. It is hoped that from these the reader may nevertheless get an idea of how this group of functions is differentiated or combined, and distributed over the three Layers, in various languages. (Only Nepali, among those shown, does not make much use of the Layer option here (all markers are Layer II), although it does so elsewhere, in the Dative area for example: see Figure 8.8.)
2. Primary (Layer I) Instrumental affixes, derived from OIA *-(ak)ēna*, are found (sometimes retaining a nasal element) in Kashmiri, Sindhi, Marathi, Sinhalese, Oriya, and Maithili as shown, and also in Magahi and Bhojpuri, Konkani, Bhili dialects, Rajasthani (*-ai*), Garhwali (*-n*), Dogri (*-ə˜*, *-i˜*), almost all West Pahari dialects (generally *-ē*, although Jaunsari has *-ē˜* and Bhadarwahi *-ɛi˜*), and in the Dardic group in Gawarbati (*-e*, *-i*), Khowar (*-en*), and Kalasha (*-an*). (They are apparently absent from Pashai and Shina, and from Romany.) In many cases they double as an Agentive: not, however, in Marathi (which employs a Layer II suffix in this function, the Layer I suffix being primarily adverb-forming) or in Sindhi (which uses the General Oblique). "Lahnda" (Siraiki), which lacks a Layer I Instrumental, also uses its General Oblique as an Agentive, as do some forms of Rajasthani in the plural. In the Kului, Mandeali, and Chameali dialects of West Pahari, the Agentive (or Agentive–Locative) coincides with the Obliques of M1 nouns (*ghōṛē*) and in all plurals but not in singular M2 (*ghar-ē*, *hāthī-ē*) and feminine (*bēṭī-ē*) nouns, where an extension in the direction of agglutination may be seen to have taken place.
3. Full agglutination of the suffix, and concomitant transfer to Layer II, can be seen in Assamese and Gujarati – incomplete in the latter in that it can still be used both ways, that is, either added directly to the stem or to an Oblique: *ghoḍo* > *ghoḍe*, *ghoḍāe*.
4. It has in many cases merged with a primary Locative after loss of its distinctive nasal element (e.g., in Rajasthani, West Pahari, and Oriya), or even retaining that element (Dogri). As noted earlier, in Bengali it has also merged with a *secondary* Locative. In Gujarati, however, there remains a shadow of a distinction between the two in that the homonymous Locative *-e* does not behave like a Layer II suffix, that is, it is only added directly to its noun.
5. A distinct Layer I Ablative survives (in the singular only) in Oriya (*-u*) and in the west: Marathi (*-ūn*), Sindhi (*-ā˜* – in the plural this is used agglutinatively), Siraiki (*-ū˜*, *-yū˜*), Punjabi (*-o˜*), Dogri (*-ā˜*, *-ā*), Gojri (*-ū˜*), Kashmiri (*-i*, *ɨ* – distinctive for masculine nouns only), Kalasha (*-ou*, *-ani*), and Khowar (*-ār*). In Sinhalese it is the same as the Instrumental (*-eŋ*, *-iŋ* – used only with Inanimates, although in both numbers).
6. The most widespread Layer II marker in these functional areas is that represented by H. *se*, found in various forms (*sa*, *sa˜*, *sau*, *sō*, *sō˜*, *sū˜*) throughout the Hindi area from Bihar to Rajasthan and beyond, in Sindhi (*-sā˜*), Marathi (*-ʃī˜*), even in Sinhalese (*-hā*, Literary) and Khowar (*sum*). In Pahari it seems to be found only in the far western Bhalesi dialect (*sɛi˜*); possibly Kumauni *hɛi*, *hai* also belongs here. Turner is uncertain whether to derive some of these from OIA *sama* 'equal' or *sa-hita* 'accompanying', but traces only Sinhalese *-hā* and Bashkarik *-sah* to OIA *saha* 'together with'. Functionally this element tends to combine instrumental, sociative, and ablative; in Marathi it is only a Sociative; in Shina, a suffix *-se*, possibly of different origin, is only Agentive. (Hindi-area *se*, etc. is an agentive marker also, in passive, causative, and potential constructions.)
7. Where this element is absent or much restricted (Marathi, to some extent Sindhi), these functions are divided among several postpositions, e.g., P. *to˜*, *nāl*, B. *-te*, *theke*, N. *-le*, *-bāṭa*, *-dekhi*, *-bhanda*, *-sita*, *-sa˜ga*, M. *-ne˜/nī˜*, *hūn*, *-ʃī˜*. The Marathi postposition *-ne˜/nī˜* combines Agentive and Instrumental (like Gujarati *-e*, Nepali–Kumauni *-le*); Hindi–Punjabi *ne* is only Agentive.
8. Outside the context of certain predicates of "interaction", Sociative is marked mostly on Layer III, with secondary postpositions which Turner traces back either to *sārtha* 'caravan' (H. ^{ke}*sāth*, *G.* ^{ni}*sāthe*, K. ^{AB}*sɨɨt*, also Torwali, Shina, W. Pahari, etc.) or *saṅga* 'contact' (B. $^{-er}$*ʃɔṇge*, O. $^{-re}$*sānge*, etc. Marathi $^{-cya}$*barobar*, from Persian *barābar* ('breast to breast'), is peculiar to that language.

9. Instead of simple 'from' several Western NIA languages (plus Oriya and Sinhalese) seem to favor what might be called Delocal Ablatives of the type 'from in', 'from on', 'from under', 'from near', etc.: M. *-ātūn*, *-varūn*, *-khālūn*, *-pāsūn* (and many others); S. *mā̃/manjhā̃*, *tā̃*, *hēṭhā̃*, *vaṭā̃*; P. *(vi)ccõ*, *utõ*, *khalliõ*, *kolõ*, even G. *mā̃-thī*, *par-thī* (more frequent than equivalent Hindi expressions). The primary Ablative suffixes, especially the sharply restricted M. *-ūn*, have as their main function the formation of such complex postpositions. Only a few of these are represented on Figure 8.9.
10. An interesting mirror-image of these cases, namely "directive-datives" ('towards-in', 'towards-on', 'towards-behind', 'towards-near') was discovered by Siddheshwar Varma (1938) in the remote Khashali dialect subgroup of West Pahari (°*-mā̃nī*, *-tirīnī*, *-pāī-īṇī*, *-kānī* – cf. Kumauni).
11. It has been noted by Morgenstierne for Khowar, and applies equally to a number of other languages, that in the area of these as well as other case functions the prevalent pattern is the use of Layer I markers with *inanimates* and of Layer II markers with *animates*.

and *-ɒt* or *-e* respectively; Oriya, by appending *-ku* and *-re*; and Sinhalese, by appending *-ṭa* and (less consistently) *-ē*; as noted above, Oriya and Sinhalese add 'motion *from*' to this system. (See also reference to Khashali above.)

At least the Layer II forms generally have some quasi-grammatical as well as "local" functions.

In Figure 8.10 below which illustrates the essence of this marking system, space considerations again make it possible to include only the principal NIA languages.

8.5 **Definiteness**

The fourth category that enters into NIA inflection, Definiteness, is one that is unknown to Sanskrit and MIA, and affects only a minority of the NIA languages. In these, however, it is an important and inescapable feature. The remaining NIA languages are by no means without definiteness marking, but it is marked syntactically, not morphologically. (For Hindi *ko* in this syntactic function, see Chapter 10.)

There are two types of NIA morphological definiteness marking, the Eastern (Bengali–Assamese–Oriya) type and the Sinhalese type. Both affect only *singular* nouns, along with numerals and some pronouns. Terminology can be confusing in this area (see Masica 1986), but in both cases also, it is a matter of *specifying*, through suffixes, the status of a noun in discourse as *identified* (previously mentioned or known = "definite") or as *unidentified* (new = "indefinite").

The Sinhalese type involves the suffixed "Indefinite Articles" *-ek* (Animate) and *-ak* (Inanimate, sometimes also Feminine), derived from the numeral 'one' (OIA *ēka*), but not identical with it, since *eka* 'one' occurs as a numeral *before* the noun (with or without the suffix). Nouns without them are deemed to be Definite (Identified): *lamayā/lamayek* 'the boy/a boy'; *pota/potak* 'the book/a book'. They impart the same sense of Specified–Indefinite (Unidentified) to numerals: *lamay*

° = preceding Layer I linker (General Oblique or other)
°° = preceding Layer II linker (Genitive or other)

sample of typical local cases displayed thus:

'inside/outside'
'on, above/under, below'
'in front of/behind'
'near'

K. I II III
°°manz/nebar
°°pyaṭh/tal
°°brō̃ṭh/pɨt' (pat)
°°niʃ

P. I II III
(-e) [sg] *°-cc* *°°andar, vicc/bāhar*
-ī̃ [pl] *°-te* *°°uppar, utte/khalle, heṭh*
°°sa'mṇe, agge/picche
°°kol

N. I II III
°-mā *°-bhitra/bahira*
°-māthi/muni
°-aghāḍi/pachāḍi
°-nira

H. I II III
°me˜ *°°andar, bhītar/bāhar*
°par *°°ūpar-nīce*
°°sāmne, āge/pīche
°°pās

A. I II III
(-e) *-ɒt* *°°bhītɒr/bāhire*
°°opɒrɒt/
°°āgɒte/pisɒt
°°osɒrɒt

S. I II III
-i *°mē˜* *°°andar/ɓāhirā˜*
°tē *°°mathā˜/heṭhā*
°°sāmhū˜, aɗīā˜/puṭhīā˜
°°vējhō, bharsā˜

Mth. I II III
-e *me* *°°andara/bāhara*
-hi *°°upara-nīcā˜*
°°āgū/pāchū
°°kāta

G. I II III
-e *°mā˜* *°°andar/bāhar*
°par *°°upar/nīce, heṭhe*
°°sāme, āgaḷ/puṭhe, pāchaḷ
°°pāse, kane

B. I II III
-[t]e *°°bhītɔre/bāire*
°°opor(e)/nīce
°°ʃāmne/pechone
°°kache

M. I II III
-ī *°-t* *°°-āt, madhe/bāher*
°°-var/khālī
°°-samor, puḍhe/māge
°°-pāʃī(˜), javaḷ

O. I II III
-e *-re* *mɔddhɔre/*
upɔre/
āgɔru/
pakhɔre

Si. I II III
-ē *°kerehi* *°°ætule/*
(kerē) *°°uḍa/yaṭa*
°°issara/passe
°°laṅga

Figure 8.10 Locative and local case markers in the main NIA languages

dennā/lamay dennek 'the two boys/two boys'. Certain usages with a suffixed *-ek* in Assamese, Oriya, and other languages (O. *mās-ek* 'a month or so') may indicate the origins of such a system.

The Eastern type uses specifier suffixes (sometimes called "articles" – Kakati calls them *enclitic definitives* or *numeratives*) derived from a numeral-classifier system (B. *-ṭā*, *-ṭi*, *-khāṇā*, *-khāni*; O. *-ṭa*, *-ṭi*; A. *-to*, *-zɒn*, *-khɒn*, *-khɒni*, *-gɒs*, *-dāl*, etc.) which itself is most elaborate and intact in Assamese, and clearly of non-Aryan origin. (It is a prominent feature of mainland Southeast Asian languages.) Added to nouns these suffixes specify Identified status (B. *cheleṭi* 'the child'); added to numerals preceding nouns they specify Unidentified status (B. *ekṭi chele* 'a child'). The distinctions among the suffixes involve not gender, which is absent in these languages (although animacy is relevant), but size, shape, affect, etc. Use of an element with numerals does not imply its use as a suffixed specifier to nouns: B. *ægjon bhɔdrolok* 'a gentleman', but not **bhɔdrologjon* 'the gentleman'.

In both types, case suffixes follow these elements in declension: B. *cheleṭike*, *cheleṭir* 'to the child, the child's'; Si. *kaḍē-ṭa* 'to the shop'/*kaḍē-ka-ṭa* 'to a shop'.

8.6 **Adjectives**

Even where adjective inflection is the rule, only one class of adjectives ("variable") is inflected; the rest are invariable. The variable class is nevertheless important, not only because of frequency but because its inflections are shared by the ubiquitous Genitive postposition (Figure 8.7) and in part by participles which play a vital role in the verbal system (see Chapter 9). They also play a role in marking plural or oblique status in situations where this is not marked on the noun itself (e.g., especially nouns of the M2 class such as *dukāndār* 'shopkeeper', *hāthī* 'elephant').

Adjectives are inflected for gender, number, and case, i.e. not for definiteness. (Maithili "definite adjectives" referred to by Jha 1958 seem to be merely variable adjectives [pp. 284–5], and/or adjectives used as nouns [p. 360].) Adjectival case inflection is confined to Layer I cases. Typically this means an opposition only of Direct/General Oblique (H. *choṭā ghar/choṭe ghar se* 'small house/from the small house'), but in languages with additional Layer I cases adjectives may reflect these too: G. *nānuˇ ghar/nānā̜ ghar-thī/nāne ghare* 'small house/from the small house/in the small house'. In Kashmiri this means inflection for Dative, Ablative, and Agentive, masculine and feminine, singular and plural – sixteen combinations in all (e.g., *ɜmis bɜḍis hihis ʃāhzādas* 'to this big-like prince', Bailey 1937: 37).

There are, however, various neutralizations in the adjectival declension. In many languages, number is neutralized in the masculine oblique (H. *choṭe ghar meˇ/choṭe gharoˇmeˇ* 'in the small house/houses'). In Marathi, both number and gender are neutralized in the Oblique: all adjectives are made to end in *-yā*. Number (as well as case) is neutralized in the feminine in Hindi and Gujarati (H. *baṛī kitāb/baṛī kitābeˇ* 'big book/books') but not in Punjabi, Sindhi, or Marathi (P. *vaḍḍī kitāb/vaḍḍīāˇ kitābāˇ*). In Nepali, gender (when observed at all) is generally neutralized in the plural: *rāmro choro/rāmrī chorī/rāmrā choraharu, choriharu* 'good son/good daughter/good sons, daughters'. (Generally the adjectival inflections are the same as those shown for the Genitive marker in Figure 8.7. Greater elaboration is sometimes found in Sindhi for the Oblique; in Figure 8.7 only the simplified uniform obliques are given.)

Some NIA languages do not inflect adjectives at all: Bengali, Assamese, Oriya, and Sinhalese do not. In languages of the transitional belt (Nepali, the Bihari group, the Eastern Hindi group) inflection is truncated and often optional, and in any event only for gender and/or number, not for case.

OIA (= *IE) comparative and superlative inflections of adjectives do not survive in NIA (except as isolated lexicalized forms). Comparison is expressed through a syntactic construction.

8.7 **Pronouns**

In most but not all NIA languages personal as well as some other (relative, interrogative, indefinite) pronouns show distinct Oblique vs. Direct bases, and in the 1st and 2nd persons special adjectival forms in lieu of Genitives. A few languages have special forms for the 1st and 2nd person Agentives (in Gujarati arguably for the 3rd person, interrogatives, and relative as well). In other languages (Hindi, Punjabi) these Agentives have ousted old Nominatives. As mentioned earlier, Hindi has special forms for the Dative.

A number of NIA languages lack 3rd person personal pronouns, using deictics (demonstratives) instead. These are differentiated for a minimum of two categories (distant/proximate) and in some languages for as many as four: e.g., Sinhalese *mēka/ōka/araka/ēka* 'this one, that one (by you), that one (yonder), that one (not in sight, only spoken about)'. They may be differentiated for gender as well (see Figure 8.4). The Bhadarwahi–Khashali dialect group is unique in distinguishing gender in 1st and 2nd person plural pronouns: Bhad. *ʌs/ʌsāˇ* 'we (m.)/we (f.)' (S. Varma 1938: 8).

Marathi, Gujarati, and some forms of Rajasthani (Marwari, Harauti) conform to a Dravidian pattern in distinguishing 1st person *exclusive* vs. *inclusive* pronouns: M. *āmhī/āpaṇ*, G. *ame/āpaṇ*, Marw. *mheˇ/āpāˇ*.

An *honorific* system of varying elaborateness is superimposed on the pronoun system: use of plural for singular, use of special forms of nominal origin. The basic pronominal declension may be illustrated as in Table 8.3.

Table 8.3 *1st person pronouns*

	SG 'I/me/my'					PL 'we/us/our'				
	Dir.	Ag.	Obl.	Dat.	Gen.	Dir.	Ag.	Obl.	Dat.	Gen.
Sanskrit	*aham*	**mayā*	**mām*	*mahyam*	*mama*	*vayam*	**asmābhiḥ*	**asmān*	*asmabhyam*	*asmākam*
Kalasha	*ā*	–	*mai*		*mai*	*abi*	–	*homa*		*homa*
Shina	*ma*	*mas*	*ma*	*maṭ*	*mai˜*	*be*	*bes*	*aso*	*asoṭ*	*asei*
Kashmiri	*bɨ*	*me*	*me*	*me*	*myōn**	*as*	*asi*	*asi*	*asi*	*sōn**
Romany	*me*	–	*man*		*miro**	*ame*	–	*amen*		*amaro**
Punjabi	*mai˜*	*mai˜*	*mai˜*		*merā**	*asī˜*	*asi˜*	*asā˜*	*(sānū˜)*	*sāḍā**
Siraiki	*mæ˜*	*mæ˜*	*mæ˜*	*(mækū˜)*	*mædā**	*asā˜*	*asā˜*	*asā˜*	*(sākū˜)*	*sādā**
Sindhi	*mā˜, āū˜*	*mū˜*	*mū˜*		*mu˜hinjō**	*asī˜*	*asā˜*	*asā˜*		*(asā˜jo*)*
Gujarati	*hu˜*	*me˜*	*mārā*	*(mane)*	*māro**	*ame*	*ame˜*	*amārā*	*(amne)*	*amāro**
W. Raj.	*[mhū˜]*	*mhai˜*	*mha*		*mhāro**	*mhe*	*mhe*	*mhā˜*		*mhā˜ro**
E. Raj.	*mai˜*	*mai˜*	*mū˜, ma*		*mhāro**	*mhe*	*mhe*	*mhā˜*		*(mhā˜ko*)*
Braj	*hau˜*	*(mainai˜)*	*mo*	*moy*	*merau**	*ham*	*(hamnai)*	*ham*	*hamai˜*	*hamārau*
Kumauni	*mai˜*	*(mai˜le)*	*mai˜*		*mero**	*ham*	*(hamale)*	*haman*		*hamaro**
Nepali	*ma*	*(maile)*	*ma*		*mero*	*hāmī*		*hāmī*		*hāmro**
St. Hindi	*mai˜*	*(mai˜ne)*	*mujh*	*mujhe*	*merā**	*ham*		*ham*	*hame˜*	*hamārā**
Awadhi	*mai*	–	*ma(h)i*		*mor**	*ham*	–	*ham*	*hamai*	*hamār**
Bhojpuri	*ham*	–	*hamrā*	*hamrā*	*hamār*	*hamran*	–	*hamran*		*(ham-rankæ)*
	ham	–	*ham*	*hamme˜*	*hamār*	*hamman*	–	*hamman*		*(ham-mankæ)*
Maithili	*ham*	–	*hamrā*	*hamrā*	*hamar*	*ham-sabh*	–	*ham-sabh*		*hamsabhak*
Assamese	*mɔi*	*mɔi*	*mo*	*(mok)*	*(mor)*	*āmi*	*āmi*	*āmā*	*(āmāk)*	*(āmār)*
Bengali	*āmi*	–	*āmā*	*(āmāke)*	*(āmār)*	*āmrā*	–		*āmāder*	*āmāder*
Oriya	*mu˜*	–	*mo*	*mote*	*mo*	*āme*	–	*āmɔ*	*(āmɔku)*	*āmɔ*
Marathi	*mī*	*mī*	*mājhyā*	*malā*	*mājhā**	*āmhī*	*āmhī*	*āmcyā*	*āmhālā*	*āmċā**
Konkani	*hā˜v*	*hā˜ve*	*maj-*	*mākā*	*magelo**	*āmi*	*āmi*	*āmc-*	*āmkā+*	*āmgelo**
Sinhalese	*mama*	–	*mā*	*maṭa*	*magē*	*api*	–	*apa*	*(apaṭa)*	*apē*

Comments on Table 8.3

1. The symbol – means that the case in question (generally the Agentive) does not exist as such in the language; a blank space means the case is formed by simply adding the regular case particle used with nouns to the Oblique stem as given; parentheses ( ) indicate certain idiosyncrasies within this principle (e.g., addition of the regular case particle to something other than the normal Oblique); * indicates a form inflectable for gender and number.
2. In the line of Sanskrit given for comparison, the Instrumental is given in the Agentive column and the Accusative in the Oblique column.
3. The forms of the 1st person pronouns may be taken as representative of those of the 2nd person pronouns also, where questions of honorificity (e.g., H. *tū/tum/āp*) complicate the picture with regard to number (the old plural being used as a singular in many cases) with a confusing lack of sociolinguistic equivalence of forms cross-linguistically (e.g., H. *tum* is familiar, M. *tumhī* is respectful; among old singulars M. *tū*, P. *tū˜* are less rude than H. *tū*). Old plurals *may* have plural reference or may require supplementation with an agglutinated indicator of plurality (*-log*, *-sabh*).
4. This problem is not entirely avoided even in the pronouns of the 1st person, where old plurals have come to be used as singulars in many languages, especially in the east. The old singulars are now archaic or dialectal in Bengali (*mui*), Maithili (Obl. *mohi*), Bhojpuri (*me˜/mo-*), etc. As noted earlier, another common displacement has been that of the Nominative by the Agentive (< Instrumental), in Hindi, Punjabi, and also in Braj (*mai˜* for *hau˜*), W. Rajasthani (Marwari: *mhai˜* for *mhū˜*), and elsewhere. Indeed the present Direct forms in Assamese and Bengali (Kakati 1962: 312–13), and probably of Marathi (cf. Bhadarwahi Dir. *au˜*, Ag.-Obl. *mī˜*), also hark back to Instrumentals.
5. The history of pronouns is also characterized by irregularities of phonetic development (Turner 1960, Katre 1965, 1966). OIA *aham* is most clearly reflected in Konkani *hā˜v* (also *āu˜*, in Mangalore Konkani), G. *hu˜*, Braj *hau˜*, Old Bengali *hāu˜*, Bhadarwahi *au˜*, and Kalasha *ā*. OIA *vayam* is reflected in Shina *be* and in K. *bi-* (singular). Note the apparent preservation of the *s* of the OIA oblique cases in the plural forms of Punjabi, Siraiki, and Sindhi. The *ham* forms are not from *aham* but from the oblique base *asm-* (or Vedic *asmē*) > **amh-* (cf. Marathi, Rajasthani) > **hamm-* (Tiwari 1961: 450).

Interrogative pronouns, like interrogative words in general, generally begin with K- in NIA. (Exceptions are the words for 'what' in Sinhalese, Gujarati, Sindhi, Romany, and Shina: *mokakda*, *ʃu˜*, *chā*, *so*, and *jēk* respectively; the first merely involves a prefix.) Most NIA languages (unlike Sanskrit, except as implied by the Neuter) distinguish between animate and inanimate (or personal and impersonal) interrogatives ('who/what') in the Direct but not always in the Oblique cases.

Indefinite pronouns also begin with K- (being derived from OIA interrogatives) and make a person/thing distinction ('someone/something').

Alone among IE languages, NIA has preserved (except in Sinhalese, Romany, and the Dardic group beyond Kashmiri) distinct *relative pronouns* (Bloch 1965: 197), rather than using forms derived from interrogatives. The distinction extends to subordinating conjunctions (*when*, *where*, etc.), with complete sets beginning (most generally) with J- paralleling the interrogatives with K-.

This discussion would not be complete without reference to the *pronominal suffixes* (or enclitic pronouns) found in certain languages mainly on the western periphery of NIA, e.g., in S., L., and most elaborately in K. (Hook and Koul 1984b: 123–35): *-s, -kh, -n, -vɨ, -kh* indicating subjects of intransitives and patients of transitives; *-m, -th, -n, -vɨ, -kh* indicating agents of transitives in non-ergative tenses and patients of transitives in ergative tenses; *-m, -y, -s, -vɨ, -kh* indicating experiencers or recipients (see Chapter 10), often in combination. Thus *tse on-u-th-as bɨ yōr* 'you brought me here' vs. *tsi- ch-u-s-ath bɨ yōr anān* 'I am bringing you here' (ibid. 127-8). Cf. S. *āndomā̃se* 'I brought him', *likhiāī̃va* 'written by him for you' (Egorova 1966: 51). Although this phenomenon owes much to the influence of neighboring Iranian, it must not be forgotten that OIA itself had a set of enclitic pronouns. For a full discussion see Emeneau 1980 (1965): 136–57.

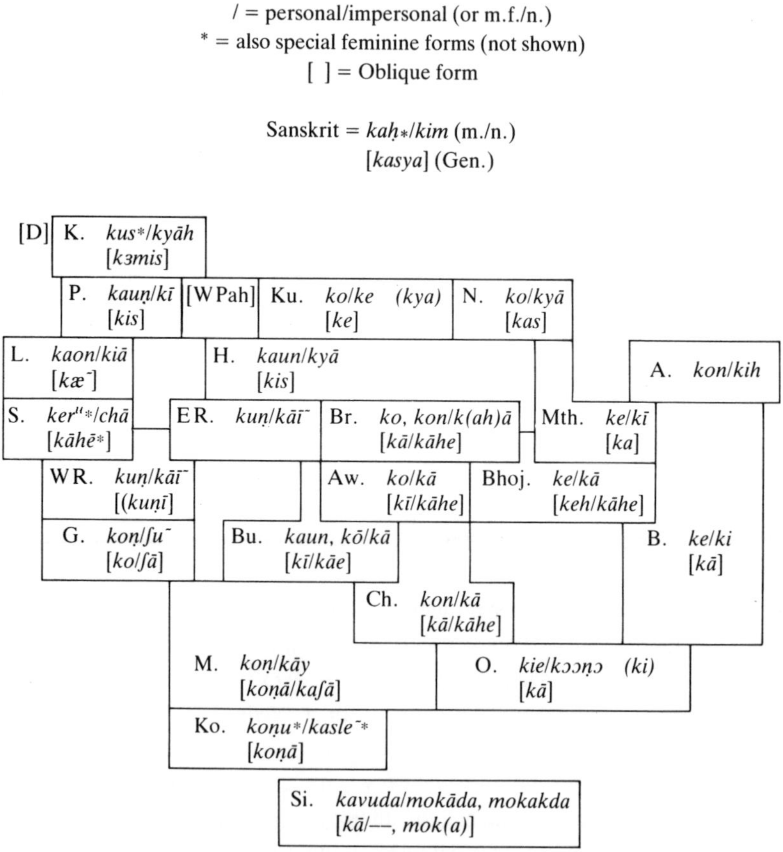

Figure 8.11 NIA interrogative pronouns: *who, what?*

Comments on Figure 8.11

1. In addition to feminine forms ($_*$ – primarily where short final vowels have been preserved, in K., mainly as "shadows" with effects), a number of languages, mainly in the center and west, also have special *Oblique plural* forms for the personal interrogative, e.g., K. (*kaman*, Dat.), P.H.Br.Aw. *kin*, S. *kane*, *kine*, Siraiki L. *kinhã̄*, Bhoj. *kinhan(ī)*.
2. Forms analogous to S. *ker*$^{u}_{*}$ are found also in P. (*ke´ ṛā*$_*$), Multani (*kerhā*$_*$), and some West Pahari dialects (Mandeali *kēhṛā*$_*$), but mean 'which' [adj.] (in the latter case, 'like what'). On the other hand, the *kaun*, *kon* "animate/personal" forms generally also can mean 'which' when used adjectivally (sometimes with an extension, as in H. *kaun sā*$_*$). Some languages have *kon* forms (meaning 'who, which') in addition to those given above (e.g., N. *kun*). In Oriya, the other hand, *kɔɔṇɔ* refers to *in*animates ('what?').
3. Sinhalese distinguishes between persons (*kavu-*), animals (*mokā-*) and inanimate objects (*mokak*). The *-da* is the general interrogative particle.
4. Note that pronominal forms typically preserve Layer I *case* marking even in languages (e.g., in the east) where this has otherwise been lost.

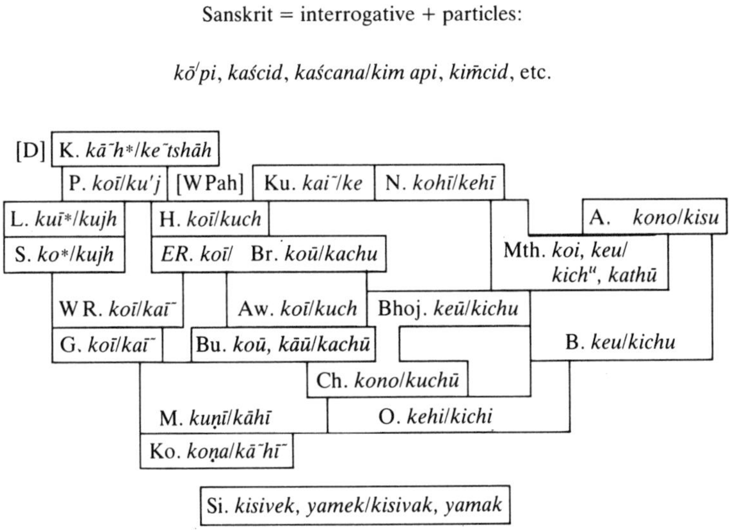

Figure 8.12 NIA indefinite pronouns: *someone*, *something*

Comments on Figure 8.12

1. Forms of the inanimate indefinite *kachu*, *kichu* (<OIA *kiṁcid*) are found as alternate or archaic forms in languages other than those shown (e.g., Awadhi).
2. Gender differentiation ($_*$) is present in the personal indefinites in Sindhi and "Lahnda" (feminine = S. *kā*, L. *kaī*).
3. Direct/Oblique case differentiation is also present in some languages for the personal indefinite, e.g., H. *koī* [*kisī*], B. *keu* [*kāu*], S. *ko* [*kāhē*].

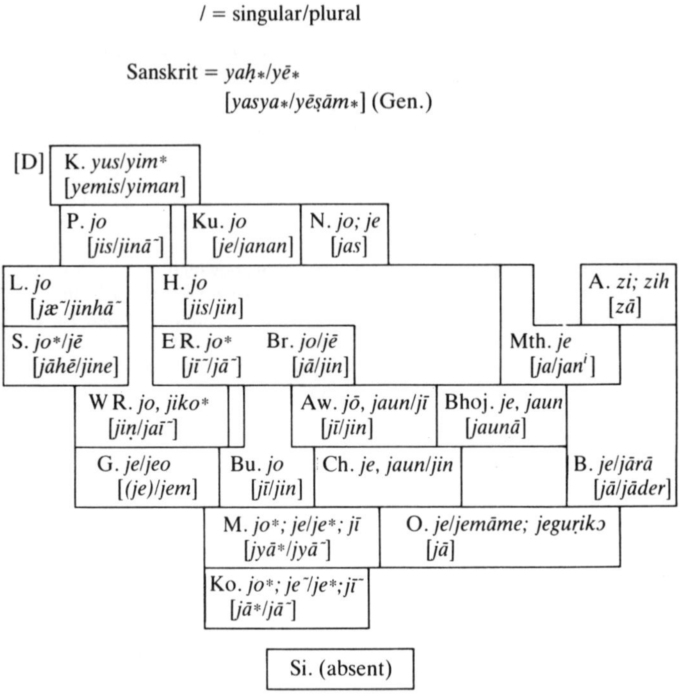

Figure 8.13 NIA relative pronouns: direct and [oblique)

Comments on Figure 8.13

1. The asterisk again indicates there are additional *feminine* forms (not shown), e.g., in S. and WR. *jā*, in M. and Ko. *jī*. A semicolon (;) separates masculine from *neuter* (or personal from *impersonal*) forms, e.g., in N. and A.
2. The declension of relative pronouns, like that of interrogatives, closely parallels that of demonstrative or "third person" pronouns, which are given only in their Direct Case singular forms in Figure 8.4 ("Gender in pronouns"). E.g., H. *jo* [*jis/jin*], *kaun* [*kis/kin*], *vah (vo)* [us/un] 'that/those', *yah* [*is/in*] 'this/these'.

9

Verbal forms and categories

9.1 **Introduction: the basic NIA system**

The development of the NIA verbal system has been in many ways similar to that of the nominal system – although the verbal system is a much more complex thing. In both cases, an OIA system with functionally unclear categories and an often meaningless profusion of forms, further eroded (both phonetically and otherwise) in the MIA period, has in NIA not only been "repaired" but "rationalized": formal distinctions have been sorted out and more sparingly employed to signal, on the whole, real functional distinctions. From a typological and historical point of view these new systematized paradigms are made up of various combinations of inherited-synthetic, neo-synthetic/agglutinative, and so-called analytic (discrete) elements.

The NIA verbal paradigm, like the nominal, normatively involves successive layers of "inflectional" elements to the right of the lexical base (H. *[maĩ] jā rahā thā*, B. *[āmi] jāchilām* '[I] was going') although in some Northwestern languages certain analytic elements may be transposed to the left of it[1] under special conditions (negation or with certain question words):

P. *mai jāndā sā̃* 'I used to go'
mai na` ĩ sā̃ jāndā 'I didn't used to go'

S. *hū kam karē thō* 'he is working'
hū kam na thō karē 'he is not working'
hū chā thō karē 'what is he doing?'

In one language, Kashmiri, one set of such elements is normally[2] found to the left of the base but under special conditions to the right of it): *(bɨ) chus/ōsus gaċhān* 'I am/was going' (also = 'I go/used to go').

With these minor qualifications, the basic plan of the NIA finite verb may, with a little squeezing (i.e. positing zero markers) be expressed by the following formula (*c* standing for an element of CONCORD):

V + Asp + *(c)* + T/M + *(c)*

That is,

VERB STEM + Aspect Marker + (CONCORD) + Tense/Mood Marker + (CONCORD)

The two concord markers are bracketed because one or the other may be absent in one paradigmatic form or another in one NIA language or other. Not, however, both, except in one major language, Colloquial Sinhalese. On the other hand, both are present in many paradigmatic forms in a number of languages. Although positing a "zero marker" here would not be as well-motivated as may arguably be the case with the other categories, it will better maintain the parallelism of the paradigms and therefore the clarity of the presentation if we put an "X" in the positions indicated when concord is altogether absent.

The above formulation of the NIA system, although it may have certain universal resonances (e.g., with respect to the typical status of tense indicators vs. aspect indicators in terms of distance from and/or independence of the verbal base in most languages), is not based on any such considerations, but is derived strictly from an extrapolative comparison of the NIA languages themselves, keeping in mind both forms and functions. It remains a norm, to which there are exceptions in NIA itself (typically in peripheral languages), but central enough so that these may be usefully treated as deviations. It is important in any case for the purposes of this book that an attempt be made to cut through the jungle of conflicting terminologies in extant descriptions of individual NIA languages and identify the common features sometimes hidden by them. Those features only emerge when, with due apologies to local traditions and to the preferences of individual authors (which may be well-founded), the conflicting terminologies are replaced by a uniform terminology and viewpoint. In settling on that terminology, however, the most prevalent traditions in Indo-Aryan linguistics have been taken into account. Radical innovation at the expense of ready intelligibility would serve no useful purpose: the goal is merely greater consistency. As a further concession to intelligibility, attention will be called to well-established language-particular nomenclature that differs from the one used here.

Like the nominal system, the verbal system is a dynamic one, but the cutting edge of its refinement is not the furthermost rightward boundary (as might appear with the nominal system, where it is primarily the rightmost category of Case that is expandable[3]), but rather the potential for further differentiation within each constituent category (including CONCORD and the VERB STEM itself). The expansion of each category may indeed be partly achieved through "rightward" increments within it, but it may also be through "vertical" substitution of elements. With each category having its independent potential, there is thus no general rightward progression from general to specific, as might appear to be the case with the nominal system, nor is there a general rightward progression from inherited synthetic through agglutinative to analytic elements, any of which may be found utilized at various points (i.e. within each constituent category) in the final string.

The above formula does not cover *non-finite* forms. They play an unusually important role in NIA syntax (which strains toward, although it does not quite attain, the Dravidian ideal of one finite verb per complex sentence). It is often customary to deal with them first in NIA descriptions, not so much for this reason perhaps as because of the role they play as formal components of finite verbal expressions themselves. Doing this exhaustively, however, entails dealing with subordinate and derived expressions prior to dealing with the basic or main clause expressions which are in a sense their source. In departing from that tradition to give precedence to the latter, we still have to deal with those forms that enter into finite expressions as forms. A full inventory of non-finite forms as such, however, will be deferred until a later part of this chapter, and the main discussion of their syntactic role until Chapter 10.

Before discussing language-specific paradigms, a bit more needs to be said about each of the basic "inflectional" categories, that is, CONCORD, Aspect, and Tense/Mood.

9.2 Concord

While by no means a definitional prerequisite, concord (or "agreement"), often rather complex, is characteristic of most NIA finite verbal expressions. Some of these complexities are syntactic – the question of which sentence element or elements the verb agrees with: as far as possible, discussion of these will be deferred till Chapter 10. Other complexities, however, are indeed morphological, and sufficient to occupy our attention in this section.

The essence of these is that in most NIA languages there are several sets of concord suffixes, used with different tenses or other components, a situation not unfamiliar from the Romance languages (Spanish *habl-o* 'I speak', *habl-é* 'I spoke', *habl-e* '[that] I speak', *est-oy hablando* 'I am speaking', etc.) – except that in NIA for the most part it is possible to separate the concord suffixes from the markers of the tenses themselves (Bengali *bol-ch-i* 'I am speaking', *bol-l-um* 'I spoke', *bol-b-o* 'I shall speak'). It is in fact possible to the point where in those cases where it cannot be done it is worth positing zero markers (B. *bol-ø-i* 'I speak') to maintain the parallelism. That is not to say there are not cases where use of suffixes from one set rather than another *in conjunction with* other markers does not differentiate certain forms: M. *jā-t-o* 'he goes', *jā-t-ā* 'if he had gone'. But the concord marker itself does not inherently connote any tense, mood, or aspect; those in question are found in other combinations also (M. 3s. *jā-o* 'may he/she go', *j-āyċ-ā* 'he used to go'). Certain *imperative* endings do stand as exceptions to this, marking in effect person and "mood" simultaneously: B. 3c. *jā-k* 'may he/she go'; M. 1s/pl. *jāū* '[let] me/us go'. (The personal ending *-ū[˜]*, though common in other NIA languages such as Hindi, is not found otherwise in Marathi.)

NIA concord-sets may be personal or (except in the Eastern group) "nominal" – that is, adjectival (showing gender and number in the manner of variable adjectives in the language), or a combination of these (e.g., showing adjectival concord in certain persons, usually the 3rd, or showing gender differences in a manner different from adjectives).

Personal endings (henceforth PC) are traditionally further distinguished as *primary* and *secondary*. "Primary" endings (PC-I) are those which are attached directly to the stem, and descend at least in part (that is, not without some analogical restructurings, compensatory innovations, and other vicissitudes) from the thematic endings of the Sanskrit Present Active (*-āmi*, *-asi*, *-ati*; *-āmas*, *-atha*, *-anti*). The imperative endings (PC-i) are also attached directly to the stem, but except in the case of the 2s., which is *-ø* everywhere but in Sindhi as a result of the reduction of an earlier *-a*, these are generally "secondary", that is, late, formations.

The "secondary" endings (PC-II, in some languages several sets = PC-IIa, PC-IIb, etc.) are those which have been attached to various aspect and tense formants as part of a process of resynthesization. They generally have a more checkered (and disputed) history, often including influence or admixture of adjectival endings, which is not part of the history of PC-I. (They have nothing to do with the secondary endings of Sanskrit, which have left no trace, except possibly in Khowar and Kalasha: see Morgenstierne 1947: 22–3.) In some cases a relationship to enclitic pronouns seems apparent, particularly when languages in which such pronouns are a living reality (Kashmiri, Sindhi) are considered (see Figure 9.1 below).

The adjectival endings (henceforth AC) are only to be expected in systems which are built heavily on participles. (They are absent from the eastern group only because, or to the extent that, adjectives in general have lost the capacity for agreement there.) These endings too are "secondary" in the sense that they generally are not part of the basic forms (which also occur without them) and represent added elements. Nevertheless it is useful to distinguish them from the personal endings.

Sometimes a *"tertiary"* personal element is added to otherwise purely adjectival endings: 2sg./2pl. *-s/-t* in Marathi *kelā-s/kelī-s/kele-s*; *kelā-t/kelī-t/kele-t*[4] 'you (sg./pl.) did X' (M/F/N – according to gender of [the patient] X); or the nasal increment ˜ in Hindi 1, 3 Fpl. *gaī˜* 'we/they (F) went' (singular *gaī*, vs. adjectival feminine, where sg. = pl.: *acch-ī* 'good'). When such sets are adjectival except for this limited personal increment, we may label the concord AC+. When such increments are added to an adjectival subset (marked in Figure 9.1 with { }) of a mixed set, we will mark it { }+. When such elements are found elsewhere, whether by direct inheritance or by analogical extension, they will not be marked, since further unravelling of the processes by which PC-II sets were (or are being) formed is a more delicate matter.

The details are properly a matter for syntax, but it may be noted here that whether through such tertiary elements, the capacities of the two basic CONCORD slots themselves, or the use of multiple enclitic pronouns, it is possible in some NIA languages for a verbal expression to "agree with" (or refer to) more than one sentence element at once (as in the Marathi case above). In a Kashmiri example from Hook and Koul 1984b: *ch-us-an-av chaliināvān* (*-us* = 1sg.M., *-an* = 3sg., *-av* = 2pl.) 'I am having him wash (clothes) for you'.

There is for the most part only one "conjugation" in NIA. Exceptions are Sinhalese, where thematic vowels (*-a*, *-i*, *-e*) and past participle formation but not personal endings are affected (see Geiger 1938: 138–43, Hendriksen 1949), and Marathi and Sindhi where intransitive and transitive verbs (roughly speaking – there is also some apportionment on phonological grounds) take different PC-I endings derived from the Prakrit reflexes of Sanskrit ordinary thematic vs. causative stems: 3sg. *-ati* vs. *-ayati* > Pkt *-aï* vs. *-ēï* (it will be recalled that OIA *-aya-* becomes MIA *-ē-*) > M. *ċāl-e* 'he, she, it used to go' vs. *kar-ī* 'he, she, it used to do'. (In Sindhi the 3sg. has been regularized, but other persons of transitives shown an *-i-*: *ḍor-ā˜* 'I may run', *mār-iā˜* 'I may beat'.) This affects only that part of the total conjugation in these languages which either retains PC-I endings (i.e. only the Old Past Habitual and Future in Marathi, and the Subjunctive, Conditional, General Present, and Imperative in Sindhi) or is formed with the aid of the Imperfective participle, the suffix for which is also affected: M. *ċāl-at*, *kar-īt*, S. *hal-ando*, *kar-īndo* 'going, doing'. (The modern apportionment of verbs hardly implies, of course, that all transitive verbs in Marathi and Sindhi come from OIA causatives. They merely provided, it would appear, a semantic and formal nucleus around which the verbs of these languages were sorted into two classes.[5])

Grierson posits three "conjugations" for Kashmiri, but these appear to have a syntactic rather than a morphological basis: the endings, when they are present, are the same.[6] Bailey (1924), however, recognizes two conjugations for Shina that do involve some minor phonetic differences in inflection which may be related to the Sindhi–Marathi phenomena. There is some indication of inherited conjugational differences also in Gawarbati (Morgenstierne 1950), Kalasha (Morgenstierne 1965), and Khowar (Morgenstierne 1947: 19–21). The last case (Kho. *mār-īm* 'I kill' – cf. M., old spelling, *mār-ī˜* – vs. *bri-um* 'I die') is clearly related to the question of causative/noncausative OIA stems.

In Figure 9.1 below, the symbols 1 2 3 4 5 6 will be used to indicate 1sg. 2sg. 3sg. 1pl. 2pl. 3pl. *or their equivalent slots* respectively, to avoid confusion while maintaining historical parallelism in a situation where the old plural has taken on an honorific (singular) function, exclusively in some languages (Bengali), particularly in others.

9.3 **Aspect**

The category of Aspect is at the heart of the NIA verbal system, morphologically (it is the "innermost" inflectional element, not counting secondary stem increments, which in any case are arguably "derivational": see section 9.6 below) and historically. Approaching the subject from the basic standpoint of "tenses", as is still often done after European models (with discussions of "Imperfect", "Preterite", or of different types of "Present"), as if Tense and Aspect could not be separated, or as if the former were the axis of the system, clearly misses a major structural feature.

Lienhard (1961: 27) observes that the rebuilding of NIA verbal systems, after the almost complete destruction of the old system of tenses in the course of the MIA period, proceeded first (that is, in the Early NIA period) by establishing aspectual distinctions, to which the refinements of tense (and mood) were only later added. This accords with what is known of such processes in the context of pidgins and creoles (Bickerton 1981), child language (Ferreiro 1971), and early Indo-European itself (Kuryłowicz 1964).[7]

In view of the importance which the Indo-Aryan developments would seem to hold, both in their cross-linguistic extensiveness and in their documentable history, for the universal study of aspect, it is surprising that they have not attracted more attention. For one thing, the subject of aspect itself is in its infancy, and as Hook (1978a) notes, "shows little of the cutting, moving and insertion that lends itself so well to transformational analysis," the dominant theory and method in linguistics in recent decades. For another, the basic Indo-Aryan aspect–tense combinations for the most part lent themselves with relative ease to translation into, for example, English, and thus seemed to offer no particular challenge – unlike aspect in Slavic languages.

That is not to say that nothing at all has been done. Major exceptions of monograph length (not necessarily devoted exclusively to the subject, or to Indo-

I = primary personal concord II (a, b) = secondary personal concord
AC = adjectival concord AC+ = adjectival concord + pers. increment
{ } = partial adjectival concord / = gender contrast (M/F/N)

K.	I	IIa	IIb	AC
1	-ɨ	-s	-m	-u/ɨ
2	-akh	-kh	-th	-u/ɨ
3	-i	-Ø	-n	-u/ɨ
4	-av	{-C′/i}	-Ø	-i/e
5	-iv	-vɨ	-vɨ	-i/e
6	-an	{-C′/i}	-kh	-i/e

P.	I	AC
1	-ā˜	-ā/ī
2	-e˜	-ā/ī
3	-e	-ā/ī
4	-īe	-e/īā˜
5	-o	-e/īā˜
6	an	-e/īā˜

Ku. I	II	AC
-ū˜	-yū˜	-o/i
-ai	-ai/ī	-o/i
-Ø	{-o/i}	-o/i
[=1]	-ā˜	-ā/i
-au	-ā	-ā/i
-an, au	-à/in	-ā/i

N. I	IIa	IIb	AC
-ū˜	-u	-e˜	-o/ī
-es	-as/es	-is	-o/ī
-os	-a/e	{-o/ī}	-o/ī
-au˜	-au˜	-au˜	-ā
-e	-au/yau	-au	-ā
-ūn	-an/in	-e/in	-ā

L.	I	AC
1	-ā˜	-ā/ī
2	-e˜	-ā/ī
3	-e	-ā/ī
4	-ū˜	-e/iā˜
5	-o	-e/iā˜
6	-in	-e/iā˜

H. I	AC
-ū˜	-ā/ī
-e	-ā/ī
-e	-ā/ī
-e˜	-e/ī˜
-o	-e/ī˜
-e˜	-e/ī˜

A. I	IIa	IIb
-o˜	-o˜	-(i)m
-ɒ	-i	-i
-e, y	-Ø/-e	-ɒ
[= 1]		
-ā	-ā	-ā
[= 3]		

S.	Ia	b	II
1	-ā˜	-yā˜	-usi/asi
2	-ī˜	-ē˜	-ē/ia˜
3		-ē	{-ō/ī}
4	-ū˜	-iū˜	-āsī˜/iūsī˜
5	-ō	-yō	-au/iū˜
6	-an	-in	{-ā/iū˜}

Br. I	AC
-ao˜	-ō/ī
-ae	-ō/ī
-ae	-ō/ī
-ae˜	-ē/ī˜
-ao	-ē/ī˜
-ae˜	-ē/ī˜

Mth. I	IIa	IIb
-ī	-hu˜	-i
-ae˜	-ae˜	-ae˜
-ae	-aka	-aka
	-Ø/-i	
[=1]	[=1]	[=1]
-aha	-aha	-aha
[=3]	{-anhi / -āha-īha}	-tha/thi

WR.	I	II	AC
1	-ū˜	-ū˜	-o/ī
2	-e	-ī	-o/ī
3	-e	-ī	-o/ī
4	-ā˜	-ā˜	-ā/ī
5	-o	-o	-ā/ī
6	[=3]	[=3]	-ā/ī

Aw. I	II	AC+
-au˜	-eu˜/iu	-ā/ī
-ai	-isi̥	-ā/ī
-ai	isi̥	-ā/ī
-ī	-en	-ē/ī
-au	-eu/iu	-ē/ī
-ai˜	-ini̥	-ē/ī˜

Bhoj. I	IIa	IIb	IIc
-ī˜	-ī˜	-ī˜	-ī˜
-u	-e	-e	-e
-o	-e	-asi	Ø/i
[=1]	-ī˜jā˜		-ī˜jā
-a	-a/-ū		-a/-ū
-asa	-ansa˜/isa˜		-esa˜/isa˜

Figure 9.1 Concord suffixes used with NIA verbal forms

G.	I.	AC
1	-u˜	-o/ī/u˜
2	-e, y	-o/ī/u˜
3	-e, y	-o/ī/-u˜
4	-īe	-ā/ī/ā˜
5	-o	-ā/ī/ā˜
6	[=3]	-ā/ī/-ā˜

Bu.	I	II	AC+
	-au˜	-au˜	-ō/ī
	-ē	-at, ai	-ō/ī
	-ē	-ai	-ō/ī
	-ē˜	-an, ai˜	-ē/ī˜
	-ō	-au	-ē/ī
	-ē˜	-ai˜	-ē/ī˜

B.	I	IIa	IIb
	-i	-ām	-o
	-(i)ʃ	-iʃ	-i
	-e	-o	-e
	[= 1]		
	-o	-e	-e
	-(e)n	-en	-en [=H2, 3]

Ch.	I	IIa	IIb
1	-au˜	-eu˜	-au˜
2	-as	-es, ē	-ē
3	-ai	-is	-ai, ī
4	-an	-en	-an
5	-an	-eu	-au
6	-ai˜	-in	-ai˜

M.	Ia	b	IIa	IIb	AC+
1	-e˜	-ī˜	-o˜/-e˜	-o˜/e˜	-ā/ī/e˜
2	-as	-īs	-os/es	{-ās/īs/e˜s} +	
3	-e	-ī	-o/e/e˜	{-ā/ī/e˜}	-ā/ī/e˜
4	-ū˜		-ō˜	-ō˜	-e/yā/ī˜
5	-ā˜		-ā˜	-ā˜	-e/yā/ī˜
6	-at	-īt	-āt	{-e/yā/ī˜}	-e/yā/ī˜

O.	I	IIa	IIb	IIc
	-e	-i	-i	-i
	-u	-u	-u	-u
	-e	-ā	-ɔ	-i
	-u˜, e	-u, e	-u˜, ā	-u˜
	-ɔ	-ɔ	-ɔ	-ɔ
	-ɔnti	-e	-e	-ɔnti

Ko.	I	II
1	-ā˜	-ō˜/ī/-e˜
2	-āsi	-osi/ī/-e˜(i)
3	-ā	{-o/ī˜/e˜}
4	-āu˜	-eu˜
5	-āt(h)	-yāth
6	-āt	{-e/yo/ī(˜)}

Si.	I	IIa	IIb
1	-mi	-emi	-emi
2	-hi	-ehi	-ehi
3	-yi	-eya/ī	-ēya/āya
4	-mu	-emu	-emu
5	-hu	-āhu	-āhu
6	-ti	-ōya	-ōya

Figure 9.1 (*cont.*).

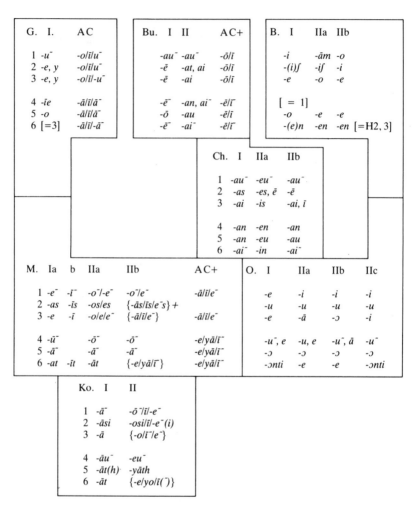

Comments on Figure 9.1

1. To recapitulate, (PC) I or *primary* personal endings are added directly to the verb stem to form "tenses", varying from language to language, which are thus derived from the old Sanskrit Present Indicative. (The stem is sometimes referred to as the "root" and the corresponding tenses accordingly as "radical" tenses, but this is something of a misnomer, since by no means all NIA stems are roots, as we shall see; on the other hand it is important to make a distinction between these "bare" stems and so-called participial stems.) (PC) II or *secondary* personal endings are added not to the stem but to an intermediate, usually participial, suffix. Some languages have several sets (IIa, b, c), going with different suffix types; others (including Hindi, Punjabi, "Lahnda", Braj, and Gujarati) have no secondary personal endings. In these languages person is marked in the verb *only in the primary-derived* forms, and by the auxiliary when it involves such a form. AC are the adjectival endings, pure or with marginal increments, shown by some verbal forms. Ia b refers to different conjugations reflected in the system of primary endings. The bracketed 3p forms under Mth. are transitive and intransitive respectively, but this is not sufficient to posit separate "conjugations", especially since the forms in question are secondary (IIa).
2. Inspection will show there are various neutralizations among these forms in person, in gender, and in number. Only neutralizations of the category of number are specifically noted, by such symbols as [= 1], [= 3], signifying "equivalent to 1", "equivalent to 3". Particularly in the Eastern group, 1, 3 and 5 can be either singular or plural; 6 (the original 3rd plural) is often purely honorific (although in Oriya it can also denote *animate* plurals); a missing 4 (original 1st plural) has often contributed to the form of 1.
3. Nepali has an additional set (IIc) of secondary endings, those of the Presumptive Future, for which there was no room on the chart: *-ā/ī*, *-ās/is*, *-ā/ī*; *-āu˜*, *āu/iu*, *ān/in*.
4. The complexities of Bhojpuri are of a different sort. While in most NIA languages originally plural endings (5 and 6) double as plurals and honorific singulars (or often in the case of 5, as "ordinary" against "familiar/disrespectful" which = 2), or assume wholly the honorific function, in Bhojpuri not only are there *three* degrees of honorificity in the third as well as the second person, but plurality and honorificity are kept distinct to some extent. The distinctly plural endings also have longer and shorter variants: e.g., in IIa-6, *-ansanhi*, *ansan*, *ansa˜*, *ansa/isanhi*, *isani*, *isa˜*, *isa* (cf. Mth. IIa-6). Leaving out the latter complication, the full range of PC-I endings is as follows: Second Familiar *-u* (sg.), *-asa˜* (pl.); Second Ordinary *-a* (sg., pl.); Second Honorific *-ī˜* (sg., pl.); Third Familiar *-o* (sg.), *-asa˜* (pl.); Third Ordinary *-asu* (sg.), *-o* (pl.); Third Honorific *-ī˜* (sg., pl.). In the secondary endings these distinctions are further complicated by gender, e.g., II-b, Third Ordinary *-ani*, *ē/ī* (sg.), *-ø* (pl.). Bhojpuri exhibits great dialectal diversity. The above account is based on Tiwari 1954a.
5. The Marathi endings of the old written standard have been given, as these better facilitate comparison. The new written standard, reflecting in part the long-prevailing pronunciation of the *Desh* (Deccan Plateau), though not always that of Coastal Maharashtra, does away with all markers of nasalization in these endings, which effaces the distinction between (PC-I and IIa) 1 and 3, as well as between Neuter Singular and Masculine Plural among the AC+ and IIb endings. The colloquial standard (which may also be written) preserves the latter distinction as *ə/e*. The colloquial standard also optionally adds a *-t* increment to AC-6 and to IIb-5.
6. There may well be further sets of Konkani secondary endings, but I forbear to give any because my sources represent different dialects. Those given (based mainly on Katre 1966) represent Goa Christian Konkani, a conservative type.
7. The Sinhalese endings (also suffixed to nouns: Geiger 1938: 143) are Literary Sinhala. Colloquial Sinhalese has no verbal concord.
8. In Sindhi and Maithili the final short vowels are of the "ultrashort" variety, $^{\text{-i, -a, -u}}$˜, i.e. Mth. IIb-6 = *-th*^{a}/*th*^{i}. In some accounts of Sindhi $^{\text{-i}}$ is omitted, i.e. the II-1 endings are taken to be *-us/as*.
9. A full history of even the PC-I endings would be too complex to attempt to lay out here.

Sanskrit *-āmi*, *-asi*, *-ati*, *-āmaḥ*, *-atha*, *-anti* developed through Pkt *-āmi*, *-asi*, *-ai*, *-amo*, *-aha*, *-anti* to Apabhramsa *-au˜(-āmi)*, *-asi(-ahi)*, *-ai*, *-ahu˜*, *-aha(-ahu)*, *-anti(ahī)*. The develoment of Assamese–Marathi 1sg. *-o˜*, Punjabi–Sindhi 1sg. *-ā˜* and of Hindi–Punjabi–Gujarati–Bengali–etc. 3sg. *-e* from the latter through simple monophthongization, and of Nepali 1pl. (4) *-au˜*, Konkani *-āu˜* through loss of /*-h-*/, is clear enough, as is the potential for confusion between 1 and 4 (1st sg./pl.). A number of other developments, e.g. 2pl. (5) *-o* from Ap. *-ahu*, are merely combinations or variants of these. The retention of 3pl. (6) *-anti* in Oriya and of its /*-n-*/ element in several other languages (Punjabi, "Lahnda", Sindhi, Kumauni, Nepali, Bengali, Kashmiri) is worth noting; in Marathi–Konkani–Sinhalese it was the *-t-* element that was retained. Not all NIA languages represent a stage subsequent to Apabhramsa or even Prakrit. The apparent retention of OIA 2pl. (5) *-atha* in older Konkani (Katre 1966: 146) is a case in point. Hook 1987c reports a similar form (*-ath*) in Poguli; there may be other north-western retentions.

10. The retention of several endings in their non-monophthongized (i.e. Apabhramsa) form is a striking characteristic of dialects of part of the "Hindi area": Braj, Awadhi, Maithili, Magahi, Chhattisgarhi, secondary endings in Bundeli. (The spellings "ae", "ao" used by S. Varma 1935 and Jha 1958 may represent attempts to avoid confusion with "ai", "au", often used to represent monophthongized [ɛ, ɔ] in Khari Boli, Punjabi, etc., and thus to emphasize the diphthongal pronunciation.)
11. Note also the characteristic Eastern Hindi (Aw., Bagh., Ch.) II-3 in *-is(i̯)*: *kahis*/*cale-gaïs* 'he said/went away'.
12. Space did not permit the inclusion on the chart of Eastern Rajasthani forms. In Dhundhari (Jaipuri) they are essentially the same as in Western Rajasthani, except that *-ai* (cf. Braj) is preferred to WR. *-e*. In Harauti and Malvi, however, there is no secondary conjugation (there being no *-s-* or *-h-* Future), and *-e* is preferred to *-ai*.

Aryan) are Lienhard 1961 as mentioned above, Pořízka 1967–69, Hook 1974, and R. Chatterjee 1980. Articles and reviews by A. K. Pal (1966b, 1970), Svetovidova (1968), Chatterjee (1975, 1979), Hook (1978a, b), and Pořízka (1982) also deal with it. All of the foregoing are concerned only with Hindi or Bengali. Recent descriptions of a few other languages (Trail 1970 on Lamani, Magier 1983 on Marwari, S. Verma 1985 on Magahi) have given more explicit attention to aspect than had heretofore been the case. To my knowledge there is as yet no study of the subject, typological or historical, that concerns itself with Indo-Aryan as a whole.

The main thrust of the contributions cited first above (Lienhard excepted) has been to uncover a new locus of quasi-aspectual functions in the so-called "compound verb" (see section 9.8 below), unfortunately at the expense of neglect or even denial of aspectual functions in the basic morphology. The urge to relate Indo-Aryan phenomena to those of Slavic (and to attempts to interpret the latter in Western languages) has been confusing. Possibly the analogy of Slavic verbal prefixes to Indo-Aryan *vector verbs* (second members of compound stems) has led to the identification of an important dimension of the function of the latter (although there is by no means universal agreement as to the precise function of the former). The complexities and subtleties of (North) Slavic and particularly Russian "aspect", however, are partly due to lack of a tense-auxiliary (see next section), which Indo-Aryan has. A Slavic model for Indo-Aryan is therefore misleading and unnecessary, however important it may be to consider under general aspectology.

A second thrust of much recent work is devoted to the identification of privative (+/−) oppositions. If a particular form, for example the compound verb, is determined to be "marked" for a category such as Aspect, its opposite, in this case, the simple verb, has to be "unmarked". There are other ("equipollent") kinds of opposition, of course, but these seem to be found less interesting. There is also the matter of the correct identification (and definition) of the category involved. Is it really Aspect? The only kind of Aspect? In any case, attempts to locate aspectual function in the Indo-Aryan vector verb have led to corollary assertions that non-compound Indo-Aryan verbs are "unmarked" *and therefore aspectually neutral.*

What then are we to make of the regular *morphological* oppositions found in simple (non-compound) verbs in NIA – by most accounts "aspectual" in a more conventional sense? Examples cited to buttress the notion of their aspectual "neutrality" are (1) marginal (90 per cent of the time, a particular aspectual value is clear enough), and (2) subject to alternative interpretations. E.g., two favorites with Pořízka (taken from the Hindi writers Nagarjun and V. Prabhakar respectively): *lalcanmā jab tak jiyā, jī jān se merī sevā us ne kī* 'Lalchanma took care of me with all his soul as long as he lived', and *patnī ne kaī bār kahā, par vah ṭāl gaye* 'His wife told him about it several times, but he put off doing anything', may seem incompatible with *perfectivity* if the latter is defined as the "completion of a particular act", but they are not so if we adopt a more comprehensive definition of perfectivity (cf. Comrie 1976: 16–24) as "viewing" an action "as a whole", from "outside" it. The fact of its duration or even its repetition is immaterial if that is not the focus of our attention. It is not the nature of the action but the perspective from which we view it that lies at the heart of aspectual distinctions. (In the first sentence above, for example, the contrasting Imperfective form *sevā kartā thā* 'used to take care of' cannot for such reasons be substituted,[8] despite its apparent semantic plausibility.) Care must be taken here not only not to be hamstrung by imperfect definitions with their subjective cross-linguistic pitfalls, but also to avoid confusion with features, such as punctuality, that belong rather to the *lexical* properties of *individual verbs* – even though such lexical features clearly interact with grammatical categories such as Aspect.

Another bit of evidence sometimes cited in favor of the localization of aspectuality in the compound verb is the fact that certain Hindi–Russian dictionaries often render Hindi compound verbs by Russian perfectives and simple verbs by imperfectives (the "unmarked" member of the Russian opposition, according to one widely-received interpretation). Hook (1978a) has caught one anomaly here, however: while Russian perfectives are textually more frequent than imperfectives, Hindi compound verbs are less frequent than simple verbs. Moreover, if Russian insight into these matters is to be given special weight, it should also be noted that in the grammatical sketches often appended to Indic–Russian dictionaries (and elsewhere), Russian specialists usually interpret the basic NIA *morphological* oppositions in aspectual terms, as I intend to do here. (See also Zograph 1976.)

In view of the controversial nature of this area (although it may not be a controversy all are aware of) and the fact that much more work needs to be done, both historically and cross-linguistically, what follows should hardly be taken as the final word on the subject. The positions taken here are in part constrained by the need to try to present a coherent general account of NIA verbal morphology, the subject of this chapter.

Therefore, I relegate (with Lienhard and partly with R. Chatterjee, if I understand them correctly) the compound verbs to the domain of *Aktionsart*, and consider it useful to try to maintain a distinction between the latter and Aspect. The border between the two is sometimes fuzzy, not least because *Aktionsart* forms are often a source from which the Aspect category replenishes and expands itself (as in the movement of the V + *rahā* forms from the category of *Aktionsarten* to that of Continuous Aspect markers in Hindi and several other NIA languages). Until such a revalorization (and generalization) takes place, however, they belong more to the domain of derivation, that is, to lexicon, than to grammar: (1) however ubiquitous and productive, they are not predictably the same for all verbs; (2) they do modify the meaning of the verb itself, however subtly and in many cases untranslatably, which purely grammatical elements should not do. In this they are indeed like the Slavic prefixes, which according to the usual analyses happen to be closely bound up at the same time with the matter of grammatical Aspect, and like the German prefixes, which are not.

There is, however, an alternative view of Aspect in Slavic itself (see Aronson 1985 with further references) that may be more to the point: it would establish the primary locus of Aspect in Slavic in the *suffixes* rather than in the prefixes. Adopting this viewpoint we might concede that whatever abstract grammatical value *is* imparted by the Slavic prefixes *collectively* (as against their individual values as *Aktionsart* formants) may indeed be analogous to the one imparted by the Indic verbal vectors collectively. A further analogy is provided by the set of so-called resultative verbs (*-lái*, *-chyù*, *-dàu*, etc.) in Chinese (Mandarin) alongside the Perfective suffix *-le*. It seems that we need a *name*, other than "aspect" (however readily the latter comes to mind), for the distinctive collective function fulfilled by all these elements. (For further discussion see section 9.8.)

We turn, then, to Aspect as embedded in the suffixal morphology. NIA languages make use of two participles of OIA origin, the so-called Past Passive Participle in *-ta*, *-na*, *-ita* and Present Active Participle in *-ant-*, *-at-*, along with the plain stem of the verb, to develop their basic Aspect systems. Already built in, as it were, to the respective semantics of these components were the basic distinctions Perfective/Imperfective/Unspecified, or *completed* (more precisely "viewed" as "complete"), *not-completed* (or "viewed" as "in process"), and, logically, *not-yet-begun.*

A number of languages add further refinements, the most common being a splitting of Imperfective into *Iterative* and *Durative.* Since these terms are not always used with the same meaning, we shall use here the common and unambiguous terms *Habitual* and *Continuous. "Progressive"* is often used for the latter (and is to be preferred according to Comrie), but in the context of NIA that term is better reserved for a type of secondary formation, common to almost all the NIA languages, meaning to "go on doing" something, against some kind of resistance, e.g., "He went on talking, despite the interruptions." (It is formed, much as in English, by use of the verb *go* with the Present Participle.) Another set of terms, found in descriptions based on "tense", is (Present) *"Indefinite"* (= Habitual-General) vs. *"Definite"* (= Continuous). They are used by some authors, however, in precisely the reverse senses.

The Habitual/Continuous distinction, which appears to be spreading, is found in Hindi, Nepali, Bhojpuri, Magahi, Bengali, Oriya, Marathi, Eastern Rajasthani, Lamani, Gojri, Braj (optional), Bundeli, Punjabi, a few West Pahari dialects (Kului, Mandeali), Sindhi, and, with some qualification, in Assamese. It seems to be absent (on the paradigmatic level: the distinction can if necessary of course be made, as in French *être en train de*) in Kashmiri, most West Pahari dialects, Garhwali, Kumauni, Marwari, Gujarati, Sinhalese, and Awadhi.

The basic participial Aspect markers noted above evolved historically as follows. Except for special forms coming down from clusters formed with *-ta*, *-na* (G. *dīṭhu˜*, L. *ḍiṭṭhā* 'seen' < OIA *dr̥ṣṭa*; S. *ḍino*, OH. *dīnhā* 'given' < OIA **dinna*) which are retained in some NIA languages, mostly Northwestern, and especially in Sindhi (another center of retention is Sinhalese), the {*Perfective*} marker developed from the productive form of the suffix in later Sanskrit, *-ita.* By the regular processes of phonological attrition in MIA and NIA this became *-ia* and thence *-i* or *-y-*, the form found in most Central and Northwestern languages today (see Figure 9.3). The Sinhalese *-u* from an earlier *-*ī* (as shown by umlaut-effects: *tava-/tævu* 'heat/heated') as well as some of the *-i* participial suffixes – others are *svarabhakti* vowels according to Geiger – have the same origin. The extreme weakness of this element made it prone to disappear entirely, as possibly in Awadhi (where, however, it may lurk in some of the PC-II endings: 1sg. Unspecified Perfective *dēkhẹu˜* 'I saw' vs. 1sg. Contingent Future *dēkhau˜* '[if] I see').[9] In Standard Hindi (and in Jaunsari, Sirmauri, Kiunthali, etc.) it is retained only with vowel stems: *khā-y-ā* 'eaten', *ga-y-ā* 'gone' (cf. Aw. *gawā*) but *likh-ā* 'written'.

(This has led to some formulations in which the mark of Perfectivity is said to lie in the CONCORD suffixes themselves, and the residual *-y-* is treated as an automatic intervocalic glide. The *-w-* in Awadhi *gawā* is indeed such a glide. From a cross-dialectal as well as a historical perspective, it is better that we accord *-y-*, *-i-* its proper status. Moreover, Perfectivity cannot reside in the CONCORD suffixes as such, which occur in other, non-Perfective contexts. Because of the presence of a fair number of inherited participles in some languages as noted above, the Perfective marker is best represented by a morphophonemic symbol {-Y-}, which is to be understood as standing both for "regular" forms developing from *-ita* – directly or analogically – and for so-called "irregular" forms stemming from *-ta*, *-na*. Loss of *-y-*, *-i-* from all but a few contexts in languages such as Standard Hindi may be indicated by using the symbol {*-(y)-*}.)

Even in languages where the *-y-* is fully alive after consonant stems (which include "Vernacular Hindustani" or "Kauravi" as well as Hariyanvi and Punjabi) it merges with Feminine and other CONCORD suffixes beginning with front vowels: P. *likh-i-ā* 'written' (Msg.), but *likh-ī/likh-e/likh-īā˜* (Fsg./Mpl./Fpl.); N. *gar-y-o/ gar-y-au˜* 'he did/we–you did', but *gar-e˜* 'I did', *gar-ī* 'she did', etc.

All these threats to the integrity of the morpheme apparently led in the east and south (Bhojpuri, Maithili, Assamese, Bengali, Oriya; Marathi, Konkani) to its being shored up by the extension *-illa*, *-alla*, resulting in a modern {*-il*, *-l*} or {*-al*} Perfective marker in those languages. In the Bihari group (Bhojpuri, Maithili, Magahi, also Sadani) and in Marathi–Konkani these forms (like their {-Y-} counterparts to the west and north) are with certain qualifications employed in Tense-specified (so-called "Perfect") as well as Tense-unspecified (so-called "Simple Past" or "Preterite") contexts (see section 9.4 below). (The qualifications are that in Maithili *transitive* "Perfects" use the form *-ane* instead of *ala*, and in Bhojpuri – as reported by Tiwari 1960 – there is an alternative "Simple Past" form in *-u-* alongside the one in *-al-*: *dekh-u-ī˜* or *dekh-al-ī˜* 'I saw': possibly a simple phonetic development.[10]) In Bengali–Assamese–Oriya, however, the "Perfect" tenses utilize the Conjunctive Participle instead (A., O. {*-i*}, B. (Sadhu Bhasa) {*-iyā*}, (Colit Bhasa{*-e*}), which also implies prior completion: B. *dekh-l-um* 'I saw', but *dekh-e-chi*, *dekh-e-chilum* 'I have seen/had seen'.

The development of the *-ant*, *-at* suffix as an {*Imperfective*} (or Habitual, or Continuous) marker has been a simpler affair, at least as far as form is concerned.

Its most common reflex is {*-t-*}, with {*-atị*} in Awadhi, {*-it*} or {*-ait*} in the Bihari group, and {*-ite*} in Sadhu Bhasa Bengali: H. *dekh-t-ā*, Aw. *dekhatị*, Bhoj. *dekh-it*, Mag. *dekh-ait*, B. (Sadhu) *dekh-ite* 'seeing'. In the group of Northwestern languages where /t/ is voiced after /n/, the reflex is {*-(n)d-*}, with loss of /n/ after consonant stems: P. *jā-nd-ā* 'going', *vekh-d-ā* 'seeing'. In Sindhi we have the fuller form {*-and-*, *-īnd-*}: *pas-and-o* 'seeing', *mār-īnd-o* 'striking'. In Kashmiri ({*-ān*}), Kumauni ({*-an-o*}, reduced form {*-a˜*}), and Sinhalese ({*-n-*}), it is the /n/-element which has been preserved.

In Assamese and in Middle and dialectal Bengali, the form is {*-i*}, obviously in danger of confusion with the Conjunctive Participle in {*-i*}, used to form the Tense-specified Perfectives (see above). According to Chatterji (1926), this Imperfective {*-i-*} is not to be traced to {*-ite*}, but perhaps to a Locative of a verbal noun, exemplified also in Mth. {*-ai*} (otherwise interpreted as an optional reduction of the form in {*-ait*}). In Standard Colloquial (Calcutta) Bengali, the two basic Aspects are re-separated: Perfective-marking (Conjunctive Participial) {*-i*} becomes {*-e*}, while Imperfective {*-i*} is dropped (leaving behind, however, a *higher-vowel variant* of the preceding stem as a token of its former presence): *dekh-e-che* 'he/she has seen', *dekh-che* (Sadhu *dekh-ite-che*) 'he/she is seeing, looking', vs. *dækh-(ø)-e* 'he/she sees'. (In the Past Habitual, a {*-t-*} is retained: *dekh-t-um* 'I used to see' vs. Pf. *dekh-l-um* 'I saw'.)

In Assamese, the potential for confusion remains: *dekh-i-so˜* can mean either 'I am seeing' (B. *dekhchi*) or 'I have seen' (B. *dekhechi*). In practice, the difficulty seems to be resolved by (1) using the form with the Present auxiliary (1sg. *-so˜*) in an Imperfective (Continuous) sense and the form with the Past auxiliary (1sg. *-silo˜*) in a Perfective (Pluperfect) sense, while using the Unspecified Perfective in *-il*, *-ile* in contexts where other NIA languages would use a Present Perfective; and (2) using the full rather than the contracted form of the auxiliary to disambiguate Imperfective meaning, especially in the Past: *dekhi asilo˜* 'I was seeing' (vs. *dekhisilo˜* 'I had seen/saw'). The Assamese aspectual system needs closer study, ideally in an areal context.

The Oriya Imperfective marker is {*-u-*}: *jā-u-c(h)i* 'I am going', *jā-u-thili* 'I was going' (vs. Pf. {*-i-*}: *jā-i-c(h)i/jā-i-thili* 'I have/had gone'). Regarding its origin, Tripathi (1962: 179) says that "scholars are doubtful," but notes that "identical forms are used in Asokan inscriptions at Girnar" (on the opposite side of India). Oriya also possesses an *adjectival* Present Participle in {*-ɔntā*} (among Tripathi's examples: *jiɔntā māchɔ* 'the living fish'), remarkably close to its Skt prototype, but this is used only as a Conditional in the verbal paradigm itself.

The final short vowels of the ancestral OIA forms having been lost, the participial forms dealt with above are commonly extended with AC suffixes (when they are not graced with PC-II suffixes). However, they do occur without them, the Imperfective in {*-t*} in Marathi, Gujarati (Conditional sense), Bhojpuri, Magahi, and Sadani (in Maithili the final short vowel is not lost); in {*-ān*} in Kashmiri; and the Perfective in {*-il*} in the 3sg. of intransitive verbs in Assamese (*uthil* 'he/she arose').

As will already be obvious from the above discussion, the available aspectual *markers* must not be confused with the aspectual distinctions themselves. The latter are sometimes marked in different ways in conjunction with different tenses. The notion of Markedness (to be distinguished from the use of *markers* as such, although the two are naturally interrelated) can be very helpful in understanding how the pattern of marking (confusing terms, but they seem unavoidable) has developed in each language. However, it must be understood in a dynamic fashion, as a process of successive differentiations interacting with situational probabilities and linguistic needs, with the principle of economy tempered by the drive toward symmetry and regularity. These several components have been active to varying degrees in different NIA languages, with slightly different results accordingly, although the broad lines of development are similar.

That is, the first aspectual feature to be marked, theoretically and also historically in IA, is Perfectivity (by the descendants [see above] of the *-(i)ta* participle, already widely substituted for the finite verb in what could be described as this function in Classical Sanskrit), opposed initially merely to (unmarked) Non-Perfectivity, represented by the plain stem (found in the so-called Old Present as well as in the Imperative), which could be used not only for "non-completed" (imperfective) action but (with or without further Tense-indication) for action not yet begun (future or hypothetical). Even without Tense-specification, Perfective and Non-Perfective are naturally linked to past and non-past time implication respectively.

The first point at which further elaboration was called for in this rudimentary inherited system is therefore likely to have been the indication of Non-Perfective in the past, a "marked" function at this level (since the natural and most frequent, hence "unmarked", association of past action is with completion). Here the Present Participle in *-anta*, heretofore a non-finite form, furnished a ready-made marker with appropriate semantic content. This stage, with {-Y-} marking Perfective, {*-t-*} marking Non-Perfective in the past, and {ZERO} for Non-Perfective in the present, contingent, and (with Tense-marking) "definite" future, is still found in Marwari (see Magier 1983) and, with some qualifications (see below), in Gujarati.

An apparent anomaly which is only apparent is the use of this Non-Perfective marker {*-t*} to indicate also the so-called Past Conditional or Contrafactive

(Magier's more apt term) in all NIA languages except Kashmiri, Sindhi, Assamese, and Oriya (in which last it is a "Present" Conditional (Tripathi 1962: 190–3). At first glance, this might seem to belong to the category of "mood" rather than "aspect" and to demand separation from such a thing as Past Imperfective on semantic grounds. That would be to impose our external preconceptions on the situation, however. As far as NIA is concerned, the two have always been linked. (Languages now lacking this form of Contrafactive, which goes back at least to MIA (cf. Chatterji 1926: 959, Prakash 1975: 286, Tripathi 1962: 193), have in most cases had it in the past, and replaced it with various circumlocutions.) In some modern languages, such as Hindi, Marwari, Punjabi, and Bengali, the Contrafactive and what has typically (though not in Marwari) become a Past Habitual are identical in form. (It may or may not be relevant that both can be conveniently rendered by English *would* + *V*. Magier 1983: 165 calls attention also to the use of the French Imperfect as a contrafactive.) In other languages (where a more general Past Imperfective meaning is typically retained) they are minimally differentiated, e.g., by use or non-use of a Tense-auxiliary, and/or of different sets of concord suffixes (in Gujarati, Bhojpuri, Awadhi, most of West Pahari): G. *āvto (hato)* 'used to come, was coming'/*āvat* 'would (have) come; (if) X had come'.

Another option for indicating Non-Perfective in the past, employed by some varieties of West Pahari (Jaunsari, Kiunthali, Sirmauri, Baghati) and also of adjacent "Kauravi" and Hariyanvi, was to extend use of the unmarked Old Present to the past, while adding an explicit marker of Past Tense. Something similar may have characterized the oldest stratum of the Marathi system, where the Old Present (although without any special marking of Tense) now has almost exclusively a Past Habitual function (except residually in proverbs and idioms), having meanwhile been crowded out of its original function by newer participial forms (cf. Bloch 1920: 235–7).

At the next stage, perhaps, the forces of analogical levelling came into play, extending the {*-t-*} marker to the present. In some languages (Nepali, Bengali [Sadhu], Mandeali, Kului, also the equivalent {*-u*} marker in Oriya) it came to indicate (with the aid of a Present Tense-marking auxiliary, the system of which was by then developing [see section 9.4]) Continuous Aspect – quite in keeping with its function as a non-finite form. It stood in contrast with the unspecified Old Present, to which was thus left indication of the Habitual–General (in the present) and Contingent Future. (Indication of the Continuous in the past was then typically achieved through symmetrical use of a Past Tense-marking auxiliary, contrasting with the Tense-*unspecified* {*-t-*} forms that still stood for [past] Habitual/Contrafactive.)

In other languages (Awadhi, Bhojpuri, Maithili, earlier stages of Hindi and

Punjabi, Garhwali, Kashmiri), it took over the Habitual function in the present also, leaving to the markerless Old Present the indication of potential (= future) action only. Gujarati has also moved in this direction, with the {*-t-*} forms taking over not only in all T/M combinations except the Present: *āve che*, but *āvto hato*, *āvto hɔy*, *āvto haʃe*, *āvto hot* (see section 8.5), but also in the Present Negative (*āvto nathī* 'doesn't come/isn't coming'). Full regularization (*āvto che* instead of *āve che*) is already found in dialects.

This development, however, left the Habitual/Continuous distinction unspecified, the need for which has been supplied to varying degrees in some of the languages concerned by use of the Perfective of the verb *remain* (in most languages, {*rah-*}) in construction with the Conjunctive Participle (short form, if there is one – in Hindi and Punjabi identical with the stem) of the main verb, previously an *Aktionsart* form (Lienhard 1961): H. *boltā hū̃* 'I speak', but *bol rahā hū̃* 'I am speaking'. This latest feature of the NIA Aspect-marking system is more securely established in some languages (e.g., Hindi) than in others. Even in Punjabi, it is not used in the negative, being replaced by the {*-(n)d-*} form, which is otherwise also more widely substitutable for it than is the case in Hindi.

The question of the substitutability of "unmarked" for "marked" forms in *some* contexts (and different degrees thereof, e.g., Hindi vs. Punjabi) needs to be distinguished from its *total* substitutability in *all* contexts (which may be the situation in certain other NIA languages), or perhaps, its substitutability except for considerations of emphasis or *style.* In these cases, the "marked" form, still "marked" no doubt, is also *optional.* Exclusion of "marked" forms from certain environments (i.e. neutralization), as in the case of the Punjabi negative, is another possible scenario. Bhojpuri provides another example of this: since the Past Tense marker in this language, {*rahal-*}, is homonymous with the Continuous marker {*rahal-*}, the "marked" Continuous is excluded from the Past environment in favor of the "unmarked" general Imperfective, to avoid the sequence **rahal rahal* (cf. Shukla 1981: 111–12). Field investigation of the status of {*rah-*} Continuous forms in the various NIA languages that have them would be a good project for someone, which would contribute to our understanding both of Markedness and of the processes by which aspectual systems expand. The influence of Modern Standard Hindi complicates the situation, however, particularly in the "Hindi area" itself.

Another case in point is Sindhi. Here there is a Continuous, marked by {*rahyo*}, and a Habitual, marked by the participle in {*-ando/īndo*},[11] but unlike elsewhere these have not driven the Aspect-unspecified Old Present into exclusively "Subjunctive" status. Buttressed by the auxiliary *thō (thā, thī, thiū̃)* (which differs from the usual Present Tense auxiliary *āhē*, used with the Continuous, Habitual, and Perfective), it also continues to express, in the Present at least, both continuous and habitual (= general Imperfective) meanings. With respect to the

Unspecified stems both Habitual and Continuous are no doubt "marked", but with respect to each other, are they "equipollent"? Probably not, since {*and-/ īnd-*} (rather than the Unspecified stem as elsewhere in NIA) also serves as the basis of the Definite Future in Sindhi, and thus has a wider function than {*rahyo*}, even if it is not substitutable for it (and earlier descriptions indicate that it may once have been).

A more serious difficulty regarding the general NIA system is posed by the "Habitual Aorist" of Sindhi (Trumpp) = "Past Habitual" (Grierson), "Imperfect" (Shahani), "Past Iterative–Durative" (Egorova): that is, the Perfective followed (or preceded) by *thē* (invariant: Oblique of the auxiliary *thō*), which makes it *imperfective.* A somewhat similar construction with the auxiliary *pyo* (= Addleton and Brown, *payō*), variable with the "Simple Present", invariable (= *paē*, according to Grierson, *pē*) with the Perfective, again frequently *preceding* the main verb, gives a specifically Continuous meaning (Present/Past): *likhē payō* 'he is writing', *likhiō paē* 'he was writing' – according to Addleton and Brown. According to Egorova and Zograph it is essentially an intensifier, an *Aktionsart* form "outside the system" (although the construction as well as the meaning are different from when the same verb – *pavaṇ*ᵘ 'to fall' – is used as a *"vector"* in "Compound Verb" forms as described in section 9.7). In any case, both the *thē* and the *pē/paē* construction as it were *countermand* the basic Perfectivity of -Y-, and are thus at odds with the general NIA system of Aspect marking. It resembles, however, the kind of Aspect marking found in neighboring Iranian, where Imperfectives or Duratives are formed from Perfectives by the addition of a prefixed particle: cf. Persian *gof-t-am* 'I said', *mi-gof-t-am* 'I was saying'.

On another periphery of NIA, the Sinhalese language is not very often brought into general NIA discussions of this kind, perhaps because it is taken to be too aberrant. Non-specialist understanding of its verbal system is also complicated, as with Sindhi, by noncongruent descriptions and dialectal problems, and unlike Sindhi, by strongly-marked diglossia, as well as by the desirability of bringing Dravidian (particularly Tamil) parallels to bear on many of its features. We have already noted the conservatism (often disguised by drastic phonological developments) of its Past Participle formation.

In Literary Sinhala, the inherent imperfectivity of the stem forms (+ PC-I) in the Present is replaced in the Past, as so generally in NIA, by use of a Present Participle (+ PC-II), which also serves (or served – even in the modern Literary language the form has largely given way to others) as a Contrafactual and – as in Sindhi – as a Future. The form in question, in *-nn(e)-*, is not derived by Geiger (1938: 134) from *-anta.* (He suggests that the underlying adjectival participle in *-na* – the /n/ is doubled in inflected forms – might come from a Skt adjectival suffix *-na.*) However, it behaves as if it were so derived. Dravidian Telugu has adjectival participles in *-na*, *-unna*, but not neighboring Tamil.

In modern Colloquial Sinhala, what seem to be related forms (minus PC) in {*-navā*} and {*-nne*} (the former used in "ordinary," the latter in "emphatic" sentences) have pushed the "Old Present" out of the General Imperfective Present slot, again as often elsewhere in NIA, but they have not retained Past Imperfective or Contrafactive functions. Meanwhile the Continuous has come to be expressed either by a form in {*-min*} + Past/Present Aux (also Literary: . . . *kisivak kara-min siṭiyāya* '[When I entered the room she] was . . . doing something' [Bel'kovich 1970: 790]), or more commonly by the *reduplicated conjunctive participle* + Present/Past Aux: *minihā gáha kápa kápā innavā/hiṭiyā* 'The man is/was cutting the tree' (Garusinghe 1962:88).

This arrangement would seem to provide no means of expressing Past Habitual. Is the so-called Simple Past really Unspecified in this language, rather than Perfective? Bel'kovich (1970) thinks so, and makes a case independent of Pořízka for localizing perfectivity in the vector ('take', 'put', 'go') of the compound verb construction: *avurudu dekak gevī giyēya* 'Two years passed [having passed *went*]' (ibid.: 786). However, these vectors can also occur in the Present, in clearly non-Perfective contexts: *kūḍællā lē bī-gannavā* 'the leech sucks up blood' (Garusinghe 1962: 67). Moreover, the examples that persuade Bel'kovich of the aspectual neutrality of the "Simple Past" seem to be of the same kind as those cited by Pořízka. That is, they involve time periods delimited by *'until, as long as'*: *orlōsu kaṇuvehi rǣ hatahamāra vanaturu da mama esē mē ata æviddemi* 'And so I *walked* back and forth *until* the clock on the tower showed 7:30 p.m.' (Bel'kovich 1970: 785). Possibly such environments demand a Perfective in Indo-Aryan and an Imperfective in Slavic. If so, that is a matter of feature *usage*, not of the distinction itself. More work needs to be done both on this point and on Aspect in general in Sinhalese, ideally from a comparative perspective.

Less problematic is the specification of Perfect (or "Resultative") under Perfective in Bengali, Oriya, Literary Sinhala, Nepali, Kumauni, and Kashmiri. (As we have seen, in Assamese there are special problems.) Rather than the Past Participle, the Conjunctive Participle (also implying "completed" or "preceding" action) + Present/Past Aux is employed for this purpose in the first three languages named (and Assamese), and special forms in *-eko*, *-a*, *-mut* in the next three respectively. Too much need not be made of this difference, since the Simple Perfective and Perfect forms between them parallel the range of Tense-unspecified and Tense-specified forms using the Past Participle in languages like Hindi and Marathi.

Mention of the Conjunctive Participle brings up another point. Recent general studies of aspect (e.g., Hopper 1982, with references especially to Forsyth 1970) emphasize as the chief role of the perfective the chronological sequencing of past events, as against the provision of background and scene-setting for the imperfective. In NIA languages, however, such functions are to a much larger extent than in European languages the province of non-finite forms (particularly of the Conjunctive Participle or "Absolutive" in the first case and the Imperfective Participle in the second). A full picture of Aspect in NIA would have therefore to include such forms and their functions, although such a grand synthesis, which necessarily involves syntactic considerations, will not be attempted here.

There are additional specialized Aspect features in the finite verb in some NIA languages, for example, the "Prospective" Aspect (marked by {*-ṇār*}) in Marathi, for action "about to" take place. This is not an instantiation of "Aspect" because of some general criterion of what aspect is semantically, but because it behaves structurally like such an instantiation in the language concerned: mutual exclusiveness with other Aspect markers, cooccurrence with the full range of T/M markers. There are related constructions in some other NIA languages (H. *-nevālā* + T/M, S. *-ṇavārō* + T/M), but none has quite achieved the paradigmatic status of M. {*-ṇār*}. For one thing, the latter is added directly to the verb stem, like other aspectual markers. In the other languages the construction is with the Oblique Infinitive (H. *-n-e* + *vāl-ā*, S. *-ṇ-a* + *vār-ō*). The Marathi form is differentiated from the agent-suffix (*-ṇārā*); in Hindi and Sindhi the forms coincide with those of the agent-suffix.

The general development of aspectual oppositions in NIA (that is, without reference to the particular markers involved, or to the aberrant features of Sindhi, Sinhalese, Assamese, etc.) is summarized in Figure 9.2.

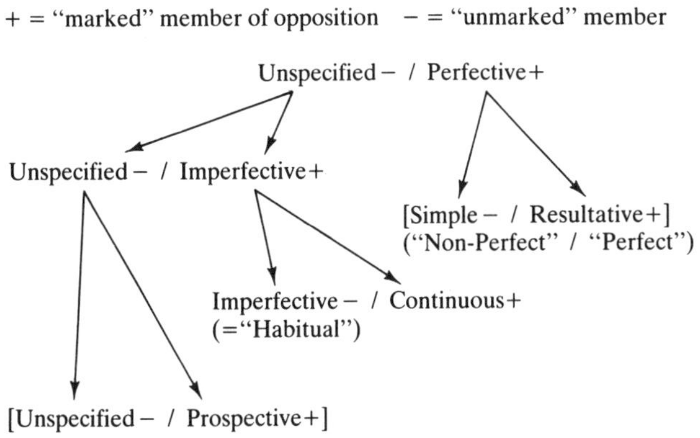

Figure 9.2 Development of aspectual oppositions in NIA

Comments on Figure 9.2

1. Oppositions in square brackets [ ] are less generally distributed.
2. The domain of Unspecified is progressively restricted as further oppositions develop.

-Y- = marker *-y-*, but with significant survival of historic *-t-*, *-n-* forms

(*-y-*) = marker occurs only after vowel-stems, or otherwise severely restricted

[ ] = marker used with Tense-marked ("Perfect") forms, if different

[ ]* = "Perfect" marker same as Conjunctive ("Absolutive") Ppl

|| = Colit Bhasa vs. Sadhu Bhasa Bengali

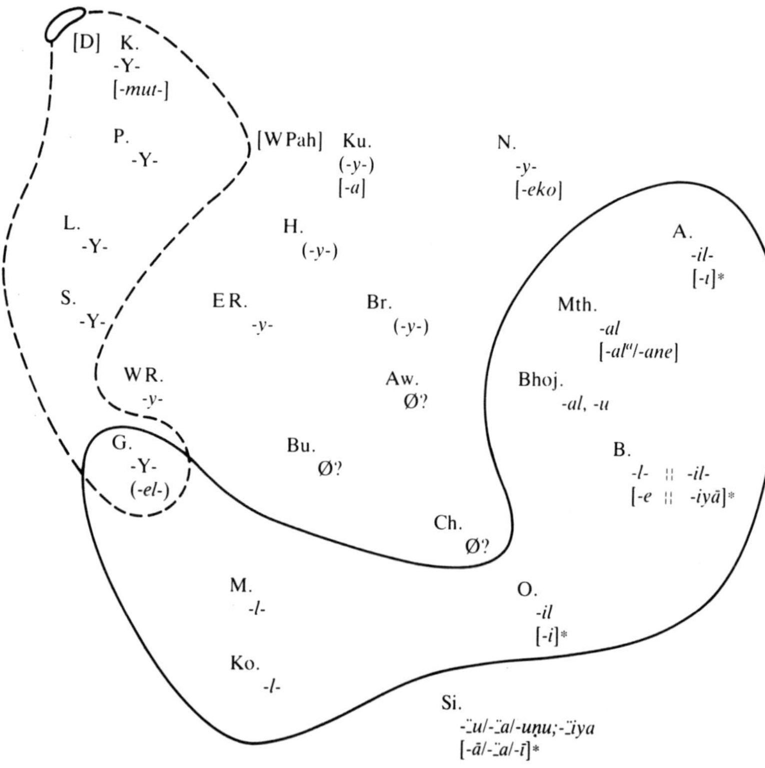

Figure 9.3 Perfective markers in NIA

Comments on Figure 9.3

1. Even with the almost complete disappearance of the {-y-} morpheme from Awadhi, Bagheli, Bundeli, and Chhattisgarhi (i.e. even after vowel stems: H. *gayā* 'went', *khāyā*

'ate' = Bu. *gaō*, *khāo* [Jaiswal 1962]) the stem is still in some sense specified, or invisibly marked, so that it may take secondary endings (in some of which the /y/-element may be subsumed) and contrasts with the true unmarked stem ("Old Present" = Contingent Future in these languages), which takes primary endings: Aw. *dekhau˜/dēkhī* '(if) I/we see', *dekheu˜/dekhan* 'I/we saw'. Helpfully, some of these Perfective stems show other (irregular) differences: 'give' = *dē-*, Pfv. stem *dih-*, 'take' = *lē-*, Pfv. stem *lih-* (Aw., Ch.).

2. The Halbi dialect of Bastar (between Marathi and Oriya, not shown) also has the {*-l-*} marker, thus making the use of this extension continuous from the Konkan to Assam, as indicated.
3. Colloquial Sinhalese has a Conjunctive Participle or "Absolutive" in *-lā*, which is also used as a finite – "Perfect" – verb (*minihā gedara gihillā* 'The man has gone home' [Garusinghe 1962: 57]), but this is derived by Geiger not from *-illa* but from a verb *lanu* 'to put'. (Cf. certain Tamil constructions.)

   Most of the Sinhalese Perfective allomorphs (that is, all except the modern *-uṇu* and irregular inherited forms) entail umlaut of a preceding vowel as shown (*-a* also entails doubling of the preceding consonant), indicating the presence of the high front vowel of the Prakrit *-i(y)a* in their formation at some stage. The / marks conjugational differences; *-iya* is found with verbs of all three conjugations.[12]

9.4 Tense/mood

Tense and Mood together constitute a category in NIA, in terms of mutual substitutability in a particular slot in the paradigm: a verbal expression may have Tense *or* Mood (or neither) but not both, while either combines more or less freely with Aspect, just discussed. (Interestingly, the Sanskrit grammarians stand accused of failing to distinguish Mood from Tense [Jha 1958: 456, Jaiswal 1962: 140], grouping both under the label *lakāra*. In Dravidian also, it is convenient to treat the two as one.)

While it is customary and convenient to refer to a complete verbal form (Aspect + T/M, with ^{CONCORD}) as a "tense", the real Tenses are Present and Past, to which we may for most NIA languages add Future. (Arguments as to whether Future is a "Tense" or a "Mood" are irrelevant in NIA. Future does have some peculiarities, however, chief among which is its ability to combine only with Aspect-Unspecified stems.)

The usual Moods (so distinguished by their ability to occur in the T/M slot) are Subjunctive, Presumptive, and Contrafactive: some languages have more; others have less. An attempt has been made to choose labels which are the most common and/or the least confusing: the Subjunctive has also been called the *Contingent*, the *Potential* or the *Conjunctive*; the Presumptive also the *Probabilitive* or the *Conjectural*; the Contrafactive the *Past Conditional* – or *Conjunctive* (Tiwari 1960); all three have been called the *"Hypothetical"*. What has more widely come to be called the Conjunctive Participle (in old-fashioned descriptions, the *"Absolutive"*) has also been called simply the *"Conjunctive"* (Jha 1958: 513).

Avoiding such confusion is not easy, however. The term *contrafactive* was used in the preceding section to describe a *function* of the Past Imperfective. In many

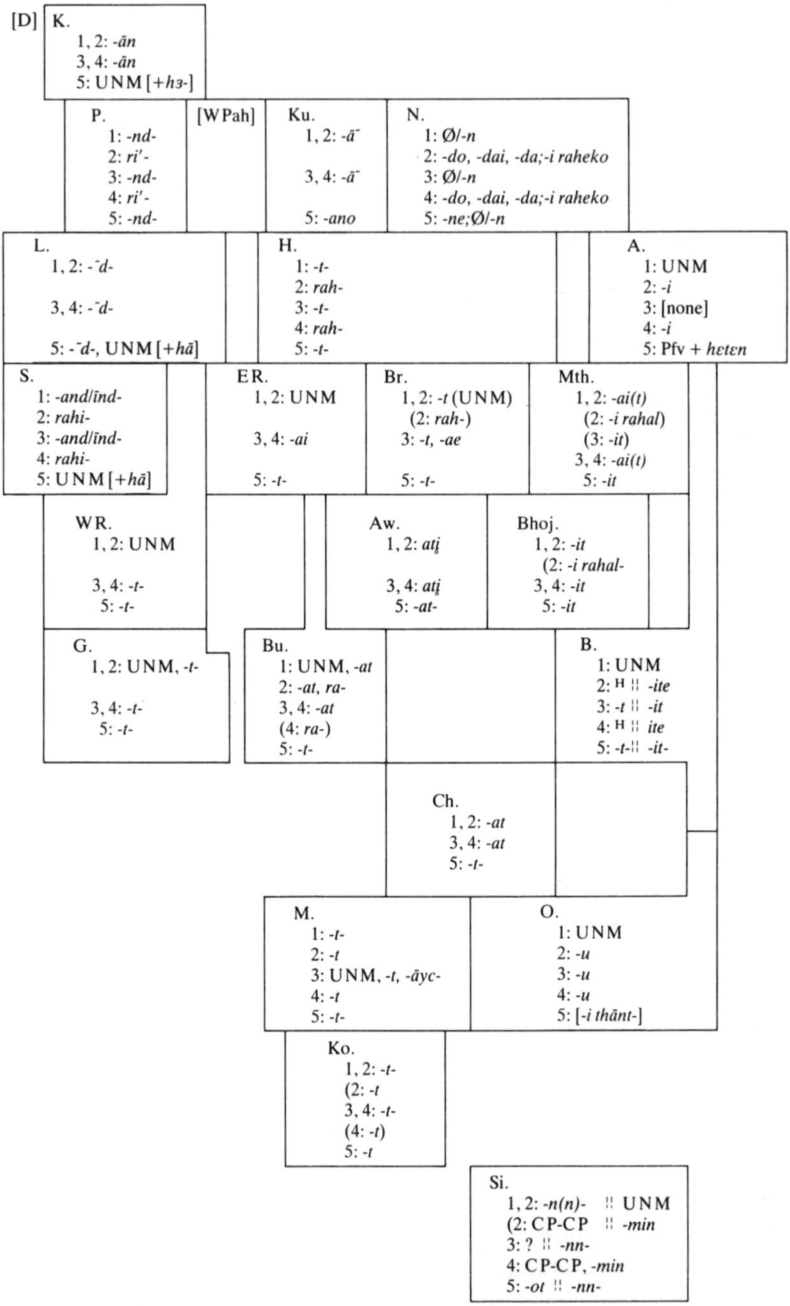

Figure 9.4 Habitual, Continuous, Contrafactual and General Imperfective marking in NIA, in Present and Past

1 = Habitual (in Present)
2 = Continuous (in Present)
1, 2 = General Imperfective (Habitual or Continuous, in Present)
3 = Habitual (in Past)
4 = Continuous (in Past)
3, 4 = General Imperfective (Habitual or Continuous, in Past)
5 = Contrafactual (usually = 3; distinguished syntactically)
( ) = optional contrast
UNM = unmarked and unspecified plain stem (+ CONCORD and/or T/M) used
N.B. T/M and CONCORD markers, essential to complete construction, not shown, but presence of some variety of the latter shown by hyphen following marker-symbol (-x-). See paradigmatic section 9.5 for full forms.

Comments on Figure 9.4

1. The above figure is designed to show the widespread but uneven substitution of forms built on the *-anta* participle for unmarked forms in various Non-Perfective functions in different NIA languages, and the substitution in turn of forms built on the verb *rah-* 'remain' for the former.
2. Whether or not they have Continuous forms, regular or facultative, using *rah-* with the Conjunctive Participle, many NIA languages have constructions with the Imperfective Participle in *-t-* + *rah-*, so-called "Continuatives", giving the emphatic–aspectual (or *Aktionsart*?) reading 'keep on, continue V-ing': H. *boltā rahtā hai* 'continues, keeps on speaking'. Although these constructions have not been discussed here, their overall relation to the "Continuous" forms in terms of distribution and history would make an interesting investigation.
3. The symbol | | again distinguishes *Colit* from *Sadhu* Bengali, and also Colloquial from Literary Sinhala. The symbol H among the *Colit* forms indicates a (H)igh Vowel stem.
4. "Continuous" (Durative) vs. "Habitual" (Iterative) functions are not always clear for some of the less-commonly described languages (to say nothing of their obligatory vs. optional status), as authors writing in English for whom it is not a native tongue sometimes seem uncertain of the English equivalents of the distinctions, which can be tricky, and other accounts are written in languages (German, Russian, French) where such a distinction is not regularly made. A more detailed cross-linguistic and historical investigation would therefore be useful.
5. The nasal element in P. {*-nd-*}, L. {*-̃d-*}, N. {*ø/-n*} is often described as "automatic" after vowel stems, but in view of its possible historical legitimacy and for comparative purposes it seems better to describe it as suppressed after consonant stems.
6. Lack of a Habitual/Continuous distinction is indicated by 1,2 or 3,4 on the same line. Such languages may be said to possess a General Imperfective. (The Oriya Past Habitual and Past Continuous are distinguished by different T/M markers. The Marathi Present Habitual and Present Continuous are distinguished – in the written language – by use vs. non-use of CONCORD and T/M markers; in the spoken language the two merge; the Present Habitual and Contrafactive are distinguished by use (in the 2nd and 3rd persons) of PC-11a vs. AC CONCORD markers.)

languages it is not a *form* separate from the latter, however, so the term can be salvaged for use here. Where it does have a separate form, we shall have to resort to *"Contrafactive I"* (Simple) and *"Contrafactive II"* (T/M marker). The T/M form has evidently evolved to facilitate the expression of aspectual distinctions ("if you had been working" vs. "if you had finished that job") along with contrafactivity. *Subjunctive* is often also used for what we shall try to remember to call *Contingent Future* here – "Old Present" forms with an array of vaguely future references: optative, "imperative", permissive, as well as narrowly subjunctive (in subordinate clauses dependent on verbs of wanting, ordering, etc.). It is necessary to keep the latter separate from the T/M-marked aspectual forms in question here (used in dependent clauses and also with adverbs of doubt, but not in the other contexts mentioned). *"Hypothetical"* might be a good term for these, were it not already in use in several contrary senses.

Some descriptions call Presumptive Perfectives, on the analogy of "Tense"-based descriptions of Western languages, *"Future Perfect"*: H. *vah bāhar gayā hogā* 'he will have (= must have) gone out'. English forms such as *will have gone* indeed also may have a conjectural sense, even in non-Indian English. This is strengthened and standardized in English as used in India, obviously on the NIA model, and begins to sound after a while quite normal, since a native English speaker has no grounds, other than vague considerations of frequency and style, to reject it. Adding to the confusion is the fact that the Future of the verb 'to be', when used as an independent verb, may have *either* a Future or a Presumptive sense – 'he [will be/probably now is] in that room', and it is this form which functions as the Presumptive marker. It should be noted that the Presumptive and the Future markers are different (although the former "contains" the latter).

The T/M functions normally reside in an auxiliary, or what was once an auxiliary, although in some languages the Future is marked by an inherited suffixal element: in either case, we may refer simply to the T/M *marker.* The auxiliary may contain what in another context (e.g., in a main verb, including the case where the auxiliary verb itself functions as a main verb) would be an Aspect marker (or as just noted above, even a T/M marker): e.g., the Hindi Contrafactual marker *hotā* as a main verb "contains" what in the context of a main verb would be the Habitual marker *-t-* (*hotā hai*, *hotā thā*, *nahī̃ hotā* '[generally] is, [generally] was, [generally] is not'): this is irrelevant to its T/M function (*gayā hotā*, *jātā hotā*, *jā rahā hotā* '[if X] had gone, were to go, were going') – or at least, is not to be considered separately from the function of the T/M marker as a whole. (Similarly, the Continuous Aspect marker {*rah-*} in some languages, such as Sindhi, Nepali, and Maithili, has overt ostensible Perfective markers, {*i*}, {*eko*}, {*al*}. These also are to be regarded as "deactivated" in this position, irrelevant to the function of the grammaticalized whole, as is the erstwhile Conjunctive Participial *-i* that precedes this element in a number of languages.) Recognition of the different status of certain elements occurring in both main verbs and auxiliaries may in fact be a prerequisite to discerning the system.

T/M markers also contain, in most but not all cases, CONCORD elements, which do retain their function of indicating relationships within the sentence. The Present T/M marker, which is usually either the same as the Present of the verb 'to be' (often the only verb in the language having such a Present) or a reduced form of it, typically takes PC-I – often, however, in a slightly different version from that found with other verbs. These, along with those for the Past marker, may be inspected in Figure 9.5.

Pres = Present 1 2 3 4 5 6 = 1sg. 2sg. 3sg. 1pl. 2pl. 3pl. or equiv.

/ = gender contrast: M/F/ (N)

K.	Pres	Past
1	*chus/chas*	*ōsus/ɜsɨs*
2	*chukh/chakh*	*ōsukh/ɜsɨkh*
3	*chu/cha*	*ōs/ɜs*
4	*chi/cha*	*ɜs'/āsɨ*
5	*chivɨ/chavɨ*	*ɜsivɨ/āsɨvɨ*
6	*chi/cha*	*ɜs'/āsɨ*

	P. Pres	P. Past	Ku. Pres	Ku. Past	N. Pres	N. Past
1	*h-ā˜*	*sā˜*	*chū˜*	*chiyū˜*	*chu*	*-the˜*
2	*hɛ˜*	*sɛ˜*	*chai/(chē)*	*chiyē/chī*	*chas/(ches)*	*-this*
3	*hɛ*	*sī*	*ch/(che)*	*chiyo/chi*	*cha/(che)*	*-thyo/-thī*
4	*h-ā˜*	*sā˜*	*chū˜*	*chiyā˜*	*chau˜*	*-thyau˜*
5	*ho*	*sɔ*	*chā*	*chiyā*	*chau/(chyau)*	*-thyau*
6	*han*	*san*	*chan*	*chiya/chin*	*chan/(chin)*	*-the/-thin*

	L. Pres	L. Past	H. Pres	H. Past	A. Pres	A. Past
1	*hā˜*	*ham*	*hū˜*	*thā/thī*	*-so˜*	*-silo˜*
2	*he˜*	*have˜*	*hɛ*	*thā/thī*	*-sɒ*	*-sili*
3	*he*	*hā/hāī*	*hɛ*	*thā/thī*	*-se*	*-sil*
4	*hise*	*hāse*	*hɛ˜*	*the/thī˜*	*-so˜*	*-silo˜*
5	*ho, hive*	*hāve*	*ho*	*the/thī˜*	*-ssā*	*silā*
6	*hin*	*han*	*hɛ˜*	*the/thī˜*	*-se*	*-sil*

	S. Pres	S. Past	ER. Pres	ER. Past	Br. Pres	Br. Past	Mth. Pres	Mth. Past
1	*āhīā˜*	*hōs/huīas*	*chū˜*	*cho/chī*	*hao˜*	*hō/hī*	*chī*	*chalahu˜*
2	*āhī˜*	*huiī˜/huī˜a*	*chai*	*cho/chī*	*hae*	*hō/hī*	*chae˜*	*chalāha*
3	*āhē*	*hō/huī*	*chai*	*cho/chī*	*hae*	*hō/hī*	*achi*	*chal*
4	*āhīū˜*	*huāsī˜/huīū˜sī˜*	*chā˜*	*chā/chī*	*hae˜*	*hē/hī˜*	*chī*	*chalahu˜*
5	*āhīō*	*huā/huīū˜*	*cho*	*chā/chī*	*hao*	*hē/hī˜*	*chaha*	*chalāha*
6	*āhin*	*huā/huīū˜*	*chai*	*chā/chī*	*hae˜*	*hē/hī˜*	*achi*	*chal*

	WR. Pres	WR. Past	Aw. Pres	Aw. Past	Bhoj. Pres	Bhoj. Past
1	*hū˜*	*ho/hī*	*hau˜*	*rahau˜*	*bānī*	*rahalī˜*
2	*he*	*ho/hī*	*hai*	*rahai*	*bāṛe*	*rahale*
3	*he*	*ho/hī*	*hai*	*rahai*	*bāṭe*	*rahal*
4	*hā˜*	*hā/hī*	*han*	*rahan*	*bānī*	*rahalī˜*
5	*ho*	*hā/hī*	*hau*	*rahau*	*bāṛa*	*rahal*
6	*he*	*hā/hī*	*hai˜*	*rahai˜*	*bāṛe*	*rahale*

	G. Pres	G. Past	Bu. Pres	Bu. Past	B. Pres	B. Past
1	*chu˜*	*hato/hatī/hatu˜*	*ho˜*	*(ha)tō/(ha)tī*	*-chi*	*-chilum*
2	*che*	*hato/hatī/hatu˜*	*hai*	*(ha)tō/(ha)tī*	*-chiʃ*	*-chili*
3	*che*	*hato/hatī/hatu˜*	*hai*	*(ha)tō/(ha)tī*	*-che*	*-chilo*
4	*chīe*	*hatā/hatī/hatā˜*	*hai˜*	*(ha)tē/(ha)tī˜*	*-chi*	*-chilum*
5	*cho*	*hatā/hatī/hatā˜*	*hō*	*(ha)tē/(ha)tī˜*	*-cho*	*-chile*
6	*che*	*hatā/hatī/hatā˜*	*hai˜*	*(ha)tē/(ha)tī˜*	*-chen*	*-chilen*

Figure 9.5 Present and Past markers in NIA, with concord markers

Ch.	Pres	Past
1	*hau˜*	*raheu˜*
2	*has*	*rahes*
3	*hai*	*rahis*
4	*han*	*rahen*
5	*hau*	*raheu*
6	*hai˜*	*rahin*

M.	Pres	Past
1	*āhe˜*	*hoto˜/hote˜*
2	*āhes*	*hotās/hotīs*
3	*āhe*	*hotā/hotī/hote˜*
4	*āho˜*	*hoto˜*
5	*āhā˜t*	*hotā˜(t)*
6	*āhet*	*hote/hotyā/hotī*

O.	Pres	Past
	-chi	*-thili*
	-chu	*-thilu*
	-chi	*-thilā*
	-chu˜	*-thilu˜*
	-chɔ	*-thilɔ*
	-chɔnti	*-thile*

Ko.	Pres	Past
1	*āsā*	*āʃilo˜/āʃilī˜/āʃile˜*
2	*āsai*	*āʃilosi/āʃilī/āʃilei˜*
3	*āsā*	*āʃilo/āʃilī˜/āʃile˜*
4	*āsāu*	*āʃileu˜*
5	*āsāt*	*āʃilyāth*
6	*āsāt*	*āʃile/āʃilyo/āʃilī*

Si.	Pres	Past
1	*siṭimi*	*siṭiyemi*
2	*siṭihi*	*siṭiyehi*
3	*siṭiyi/tibeyi*	*siṭiyēya/tibuṇēya*
4	*siṭimu*	*siṭiyemu*
5	*siṭihu*	*siṭiyāhu*
6	*siṭiti/tibeti*	*siṭiyōya/tibuṇōya*

Figure 9.5 (*cont.*).

Comments on Figure 9.5

1. In several of the above cases (Punjabi, Bengali, Oriya, Marathi, Gujarati) it is the "written" forms of the auxiliary that have been given, as more conservative and facilitating comparison. In Punjabi the spoken equivalents are *ā˜*, *e˜*, *e* (or *ɛ*); *ā˜*, *o*, *ne*. In Bengali and Oriya the (suffixed) auxiliary is written CH as shown, but commonly pronounced without the aspirate as /c/. In spoken Marathi and Oriya (also modern written Marathi), the nasalized vowels are denasalized. In Gujarati, *che* and *cho* are commonly pronounced [*chɛ*] and [*chɔ*], but according to Cardona 1965 the latter forms are considered less elegant even in speech. (There is no way of writing these forms in Gujarati.)
2. The Sinhalese forms are of course Literary Sinhala: the Colloquial forms (Pres *innavā*, Past *hiṭiyā*) are as usual invariant. The form to the right of the slash is used with inanimates; the *siṭi-* forms are used with animates only. There is also a *feminine* animate form in the 3sg. Past: *siṭāya.*
3. For Nepali the suffixed (shortened) forms have been given. The full form of the Past (used in certain constructions) has an extra /*i*/: *thie˜*, *thiis*, *thiyo/thiī*; *thiyau˜*, *thiyau*, *thie/thiin*.
4. For Hindi and Punjabi, the forms are given as *hɛ*, *hɛ˜*; *sɛ˜*, *sɔ* instead of the customary *hai*, *hai˜*; *sai˜*, *sau* (which will be used elsewhere in this book), to distinguish their monophthongized vowels from the diphthongs preserved in Braj, Awadhi, etc.
5. For the unwritten or unstandardized languages, it is not practicable to give all the alternative forms on the chart. Thus Chhattisgarhi has *three* Past auxiliaries: *hoyeu˜*, *bhayeu˜*, and *raheu˜* (identically conjugated), and several variants of the Present auxiliary: *havau˜*, *havo*, *ho*, *au˜*, *avau˜*, etc. (cf. Telang 1966: 147–8).
6. For Maithili and Bhojpuri, however, the paradigm given may be particularly misleading. Variants aside, the full paradigm is much more complicated than shown, because of

incorporation of direct and indirect object (along with subject) reference in the Maithili forms, and the elaborated honorific system in the Bhojpuri forms (see Figure 9.1, Comment 4).

7. Note the neutralization of number in the 1st person (= 1,4) not only in the Eastern languages (except Oriya) as far west as Bhojpuri, but also in Punjabi, and in the 3rd person (= 3,6) in Gujarati and Rajasthani. The distinctions remaining in the 2nd and 3rd persons (2,5 and 3,6) in the east have become distinctions of honorificity rather than of number.
8. The Konkani forms are again Goa Christian forms according to Katre 1966. The Saraswat dialects do not distinguish Person in the Past except the 1sg (M. *-o*˜, F. *-i*˜). They do distinguish Number: 2,3 Msg. *āʃilo*, Mpl. *āʃile*; 2,3 Fsg. *āʃili*, 2,3 Fpl. *āʃilyo*, 1 Fpl. *āʃilī*˜ (Aiyagal 1968: 67).
9. Some accounts of Sindhi add short vowels (generally unwritten) to some of the forms shown: *hōs*^{e}, *huīas*^{a}, etc. They also hear some of the full vowels differently: *huo* for *huā*, *hue*˜ for *huī*˜ (e.g., Egorova 1966). Dialectal differences may account for some of these variants; others seem to be transcriptional.
10. Sindhi has a second Present marker (not shown, see Figure 9.6 and Comments), *thō*. Its inflection is purely adjectival (AC): Msg. *thō*, Mpl. *thā*, Fsg. *thī*, Fpl. *thiū*˜.
11. The Kumauni forms given (also in Figure 9.6) are Grierson's "Standard Dialect" (*LSI 9*) rather than Apte and Pattanayak's.

There are sometimes tricky overlaps in the forms employed as T/M markers in different NIA languages. For instance, *hotā* in Hindi, just referred to, is a Contrafactual marker; in Marathi the same form is a Past marker. While Hindi *thā* is a Past marker, with Masculine Singular ^{CONCORD}, Sindhi *thā* is a Present marker, with Masculine *Plural* ^{CONCORD}. Hindi *rahe* is a Continuous Aspect marker with Masculine Plural ^{CONCORD}; the closely similar Awadhi *rahai* is a Past T/M marker. The opportunities for mutual "contamination" would appear to be great, particularly among languages which are intimately associated, for example in the "Hindi area", but the matter has not been closely studied. An incomplete idea of the shape of the formal markers and their overlap may be gleaned from Figure 9.6 (incomplete because only the 3sg. – Masculine, if gender differences are involved – is given).

A detailed history of the auxiliary (and of the closely connected existential verb and copula, the anchor of the system) in every language is too complicated and too controversial a problem to treat here. Broadly speaking it is everywhere a suppletive paradigm pieced together with elements going back to different Sanskrit roots: √BHŪ 'become', Pres. *bhávati* (> H.M.P. *ho-*, N. Ku. S. *hu-*, G. *hɔ-*); √ĀS 'sit', Pres. *ā́satē* (> Kal. *ās-*, Kho. Sh. *as-*, K. *ōs-*); √AS 'be', Pres. *ásti* (> Khash. *as-*, Si. *æti*); √KṢI 'dwell, exist', Pres. *ā́kṣēti* (> K. *chu*, G. *chɛ*, B. *-che* < *āche*, A. *-se* < *āse*, O. *-ci* < *ɔchi*, Ku. N. *cha*, M. *as-* [according to Turner 1966], H. *hai*, S. *āhē* [cf. Chatterji 1926: 1035]); √STHĀ 'stand', Ppl. *sthitá* (> H. *thā*, S. *thō*, O. *thi-*; Si. *tiyanavā* < *sthāpáyati*; Si. *siṭanavā* < *tiṣṭhati*; prob. B. *thāk-*); √VR̥T 'turn, occur, exist', Pres. *vártatē* (> Bhoj. *bāṭ-*, dial. B. *bɔṭ-*); √*RAH 'remain', MIA Pres. *rahaï* (> Aw. Bhoj. Mth. Sad. *rah-*). Future markers will be dealt with separately below.

1 = Present
2 = Past
3 = Presumptive
4 = Subjunctive
5 = Contrafactive

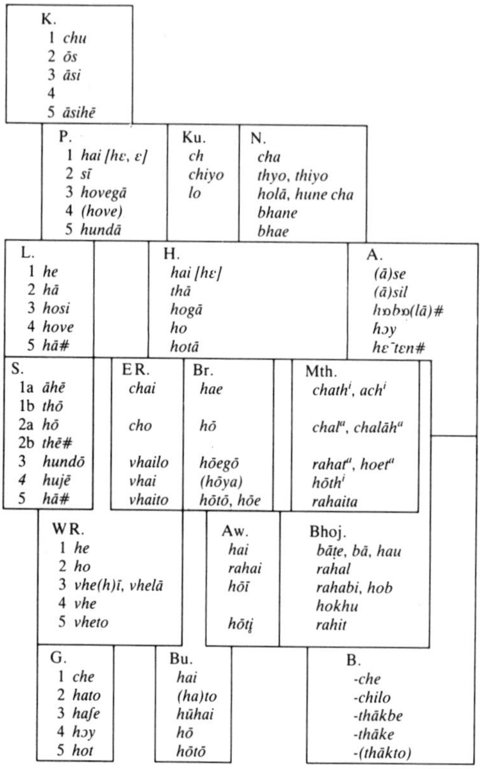

Figure 9.6 T/M markers in NIA (except Future): 3sg.M forms

Comments on Figure 9.6

1. Forms marked (#) are invariant; others may be presumed to show CONCORD in ways analogous to those illustrated in Figure 9.5. The Siraiki ("L.") Contrafactual marker *hā#* is thus different from the Past marker *hā*, which has forms *ham*, *havẽ*, *hāī*, etc. as already shown (although the two are homonymous in the 3sg. M).
2. The extra (1b and 2b) Present and Past markers in Sindhi may have as much to do with Aspect as with Tense/Mood, but they do also specify the latter: *acē* '(if) comes' [Contingent Future], *acē thō* 'he comes, is coming' [Present Imperfective]; *likhiō* 'wrote/ written' [Unspecified Perfective], *likhiō thē* 'was writing' ["Past Iterative-Durative"]; cf. *likhiō āhe* 'has written', *likhiō hō* 'had written'.
3. Maithili has a surfeit of T/M markers in addition to its other complications. They are not alternates, but specific to particular Aspect/TM combinations. (They are not placed on the same "line" with the extra Sindhi forms [1a, 1b, etc.] as they do not correspond to

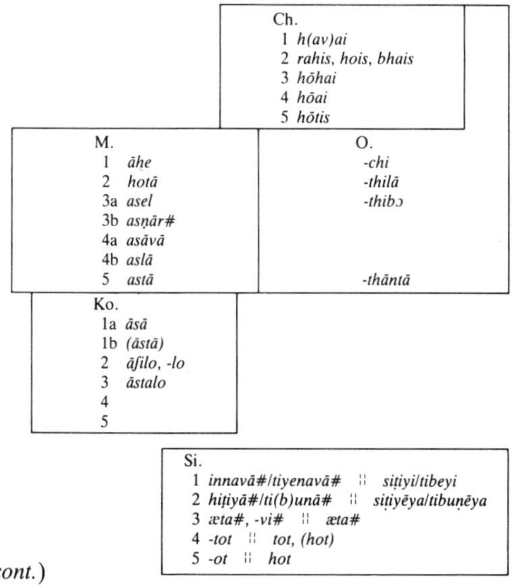

Figure 9.6 (*cont.*)

them in function.) Jha 1958 calls *hoet*[a] "Presumptive", although the translations he gives suggest it may be Subjunctive. The Maithili final ultrashort /[a]/ is specified by Jha but not by Grierson.

4. Several languages apparently lack a Subjunctive T/M marker (or use it rarely), presumably getting along with the (aspectually-unmarked) Contingent Future. Like the Contrafactual marker, it is a late development, "filling out" the system.
5. The first Bhojpuri Presumptive given is Honorific 3sg.; Tiwari 1954a: 250 says that in the 3p Ordinary and "Contemptuous" (found only in the Feminine), forms from the Future in /*-h-*/ are used instead of those in /*-b-*/ which are used with other persons. (The *hob* form is taken from Shukla's description of the Gorakhpuri dialect.)
6. Marathi is another language with a superabundance of T/M markers, apparently contrastive at least in some contexts, although some of the contrasts defy easy descriptions: *asel*, *asṇār*, and *asāvā* all involve various degrees of presumption; *asāvā* and *aslā* both involve open conditions, although the former has other, classically "subjunctive" (doubt, uncertainty, etc.) uses as well. Additional possible markers include *asto* (in combination with the Impfv it means 'keeps on'; *jāt asto* 'keeps going') and *ase* (in combination with the Impfv it means 'used to': *jāt ase* 'used to go'). These were excluded because their functions are more analogous to those of the "*Enhanced Aspect*" forms of Hindi and other languages than to T/M functions, e.g., to the H. so-called *Continuative* in V-*tā* + *rah-* and *Frequentative* in V-*(y)ā* + *kar-*. Formally it is admittedly harder to draw a line in Marathi, and at least the *ase* form is probably much more frequent than its Hindi counterpart. Konkani *āstā* seems to be equivalent to M. *asto* (and H. *rahtā hai*). Aiyagal 1968 (extra-Goan Brahmin dialect) translates *tāgelyā gharā˜tu˜pankho ċalat āstā/āsa* as 'The fan in his house runs/has been running incessantly', tagging the former in the literal equivalent 'remains', the latter 'is'.
7. For Sinhalese, ⁞⁞ separates Colloquial (left) from Literary (right). According to Gair and Karunatilaka (1974: 112, 276) the *hot* form (and according to Fairbanks, Gair and De Silva 1968: 296 the Colloquial equivalent *-ot*) is not necessarily contrafactive: *ohu nuvara yanahot mamada yami* 'if he goes to Kandy I will go too'. It is placed in line 5 because of formal parallelism. See also Garusinghe 1962: 61, but according to Fairbanks et al. a contrafactive is expressed by the Perfective + the conjunction *naŋ* 'if': *mama kaḍēṭa giyā naŋ* . . . 'if I had gone to the shop . . .' (vs. *kaḍēṭa giyot* . . . 'if I go to the shop . . .').

Traditional and historically-minded descriptions usually divide NIA finite verbal forms into "Radical Tenses", "Participial Tenses", and "Periphrastic (or Analytic) Tenses". Such a division based on historical form does not throw much light on the functioning system of grammatical distinctions in each language or in NIA generally. We might make momentary use of it, however, to point out that only the last (plus the Future) have Tense (that is, are *marked* for Tense, or rather Tense/Mood) according to the analysis advocated here. The first two (minus the Future) may be marked for Aspect (or unmarked altogether), but are *unmarked* (= unspecified) for Tense. Present, past, or future time may be *implied* in such forms, but context may change the implication.

Thus "Simple" Perfectives may usually refer to the past, because what is completed (or more exactly, can be "viewed as a whole") is usually past, but they are not *specified* as Past. Their use also in conditional clauses referring to the future is thus no anomaly, but quite in keeping with their "open" status as far as Tense is concerned. Similarly, reference to the present or future by the Imperfective forms that function as Past Habituals-cum-Contrafactives is not excluded: H. *agar vah ātā* . . . 'if he had come/came/were to come . . .'.

There is a Future subsystem in most NIA languages that calls for special remark. As noted earlier, the unspecified "Old Present", on being crowded out of its old role by newer formations, was left with a range of vaguely future residual meanings, which are retained in most NIA languages as the Contingent Future ("Simple Subjunctive"). In Kashmiri and certain other Northwestern languages it came to function as Future per se; in other languages expression of a Definite Future came to require an additional element, {*-g-*} or {*-l-*}, usually (i.e. except in Marathi) with a further element of CONCORD, PC or AC. Of these, {*-g-*} (> H. *-gā*, Braj *-gō̃*, etc.) is clearly an auxiliary element (< MIA *gaa* < OIA *gata*, Past Participle of 'go'), albeit reduced and suffixed. The *-g-* Future is confined to Hindi and Punjabi and associated dialects (Braj, Hariyanvi, Bundeli, Dogri) and some forms of Eastern Rajasthani (Mewati, Malvi, Harauti). The form is no doubt being strengthened by the prestige of Standard Hindi. (Whether Kangri and Mandeali Futures in *-ghā* are also related to these is unclear.)

The {*-l-*} Future is more widely spread (Marathi–Konkani, Rajasthani, Nepali, most of Central and West Pahari) and more problematic. It works the same as the {*-g-*} Future, being added (sometimes with morphophonemic adjustments, as in Marathi: *jāī̃* + *-l-* = *jāī-n*) to an already conjugated form, but attempts to link it to that via the Marathi Past Participle *gelo* are thwarted by the fact that the /*l*/ is not part of the Past Participle in the other areas mentioned.

There are two other sets of Future markers in NIA. Those in {*-b-*}, which prevail in the Eastern languages and reach as far west as Awadhi, descend from the OIA Future Passive "Participle of Obligation", or Gerundive, in *-tavya*. The other set represents a survival of the OIA sigmatic Future itself (in *-sya*, *-iṣya*). An actual /s/ (or /ʃ/) has survived only in Gujarati, Eastern Rajasthani (Dhundhari), Literary Marwari (Magier 1983: 128), Gojri (Sharma 1982: 167), and some "Lahnda" dialects (including Siraiki); elsewhere (spoken Marwari, Bhili, Bundeli, Braj, Awadhi, Bhojpuri, Maithili) it is represented by /h/ (+ PC-I endings). (In the form of Marwari observed by Magier the /h/ had further weakened to a high-falling tone.) In most of these languages it co-exists with other Future markers ({*-l-*} in Rajasthan, {*-b-*} elsewhere), sometimes in complementary distribution in the same paradigm. For example, in Bhojpuri as described by Shukla *-ab-* is found with the 1st person, *-ih-* with the 2nd and 3rd persons. A similar distribution occurs in Maithili.

Although the {*-b-*}, {*-s-*} and {*-h-*} Future markers are not strictly speaking originally independent Auxiliary elements like the {*-g-*} and {*-l-*} markers, it is convenient to treat them all as simply T/M markers synchronically, and as part of a cross-linguistic Future subsystem in which this subset of T/M markers combines with a verb stem Unspecified for Aspect and thus already having future *implications*. The first set, it is true, unites directly with the stem, the second, with the stem + PC-I, but the presence or absence of CONCORD elements (and the variety employed and their position) may be treated as a secondary taxonomic matter.

There is still another type of Future in NIA, built on the Imperfective ("Present") Participle + personal endings: this type is found in Sindhi (*haland-us* 'I shall go'), Literary Sinhala (*ennēya* 'he will come'), and possibly Halbi (*dakhūnde* 'we shall see'). It is not part of the aforementioned subsystem, since it is built on an aspectually marked form. The subusage of the Hindi–Urdu Present Habitual as an immediate future (*abhī ātā hū̃* 'I'm coming right now') might be mentioned in this context.

The several Future formations in NIA lend themselves well to "mapping": see Figure 9.7.

A very different OIA method of marking Tense (= Past) by means of the augment-prefix {*á-*} apparently survives in Khowar and Kalasha: Kal. *pim/apis* 'I drink/I drank'; *kārim/akāris* 'I do/I did' (Morgenstierne 1965).[13]

Finally, it should be noted that several NIA languages (Gujarati, Marathi, Oriya, Bhojpuri, etc.) possess sets of *Negative* Auxiliaries – in which a negative particle has become fused with the auxiliary verb (sometimes with an obsolete version of it or at any rate one different from the positive) to the point where the resulting "conjugated negative" form is not entirely predictable: M. *hotā* 'Past (3sg. M)'/*navhtā* 'Past Neg (3sg. M)'; O. *(khāu)cɔ* 'you are (eating)'/*(khāu)nɔ* 'you are not (eating)'; G. *che* 'Pres (2, 3sg., 3pl.)'/*nathī* 'Pres Neg (all persons)'. (The CONCORD endings are usually but not always the same as the corresponding

; = parallel paradigms, sometimes contrastive
/ = complementary (suppletive) paradigm
[ ] = Future formation not involving any Future T/M marker
Unsp = (aspectually) Unspecified plain stem

··· = area of {*-s-*, *-h-*} Future

—— = area of {*-b-*} Future

- - - - = area of {*-l-*} Future

═══ = area of {*-g-*} Future

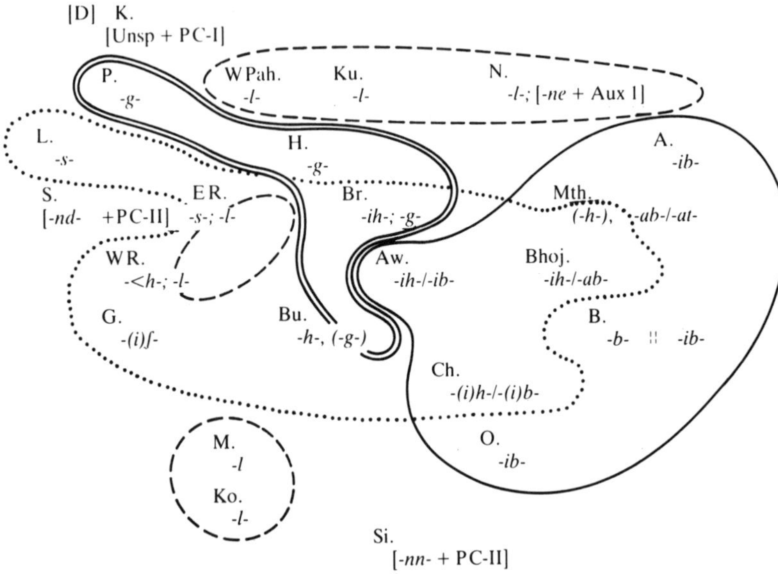

Figure 9.7 Future markers in NIA

Comments on Figure 9.7

1. As noted earlier, Sindhi, (Literary) Sinhalese, and Kashmiri do not employ Future markers. The first two have Futures based on an Imperfective ("Present") Participle. Kashmiri, together with much of Dardic, uses the Unspecified stem + personal endings ("Old Present").
2. Note also Nepali: the *-l-* Future is less "definite" than the Infinitival Future in *-ne cha* (Matthews 1984: 173, 199; Korolev 1968: 1296).
3. The suppletive paradigms of Eastern Hindi and Bihari are of special interest as a battleground between the old inflectional {*-h-*} (<∗*-sya*/*-iṣya*) and the participial {*-b-*} (<∗*-tavya*) Futures. In Awadhi, according to Saksena 1971: 264, {*-h-*} is found with all persons except 1pl. in the Western dialects, is losing ground to the {*-b-*} Future in the 2nd person in the Central dialects, and has kept only the 3rd person in the Eastern dialects. In

Bhojpuri as described by Tiwari 1954a, 1960, and in Magahi (Aryani 1965), the {*-b-*} Future has taken over the 1st person and is invading the 2nd, while the {*-h-*} Future firmly retains the 3rd. In Sadani (Jordan-Horstmann 1969) the {*-b-*} Future has taken over completely. In Chhattisgarhi (Telang 1966), the {*-b-*} Future has managed to take over only the 1st plural and 2nd singular. In Maithili, {*-h-*} is restricted to the Jolahi dialect (North Darbhanga Muslims), and to the 3rd person (Jha 1958: 496). Elsewhere the {*-b-*} Future is now still confined to the 1st and 2nd persons: in the 3rd, a newer form in *-t-* has taken over.

4. In the west of the Hindi area, the competition is rather from {*-g-*}. It has prevailed in Mewati and Malvi (NE and SE Rajasthani), but {*-h-*} is still common in Bundeli.

positive forms: note the Gujarati forms just cited.) The Bhojpuri forms *naikhī̃*, *naikhe* etc. seem to preserve the controversial root √KṢI (see above) in a purer form than is usually found (although Bhojpuri also has positive forms in *hokhī̃*, *hokhe* [Tiwari 1954a: 277, 282–3]).

9.5 Finite verb paradigms of the principal NIA languages

The main NIA verbal inflectional components have now been discussed (although not much has been said about the Imperative[14]). The point may be clear that Aspect and Tense/Mood are to a large extent independent variables, the different combinations of which (not all are possible), together with the appropriate CONCORD elements, produce the various finite verb types – traditionally called "tenses" – of NIA. The total picture will no doubt be clearer, however, with some illustration of how they fit together. Space considerations forbid giving complete paradigms for each language, but it is hoped that some indication may be obtained from the truncated paradigms given below (for the principal languages only). These will consist of the 1st and 3rd persons singular (with gender variations, if any) of each "tense" of an intransitive verb, usually *come*. Both 1st and 3rd are given (rather than, for example, 3rd alone) because different principles of conjugation (particularly at the level of CONCORD) are sometimes illustrated thereby. The other persons are not lacking in special points of interest: some idea of them can be gleaned from Figures 9.1 and 9.5 above. The reason for choice of an *Intransitive* verb will become clear in Chapter 10.

Since the system is particularly well articulated in Modern Standard Hindi–Urdu, and readers are most likely to be familiar with that language (or those languages), we depart from our usual order and present that pattern first, followed by Punjabi and the other principal NIA languages in counterclockwise geographical sequence, finishing with Nepali. In the formulas, as in the figures given earlier, Unsp = Unspecified (i.e. ZERO marker) Aspect or Tense/Mood, Pfv = Perfective, Pf = Perfect, Impfv = Imperfective, Hab = Habitual (Iterative), Cont = Continuous (Durative, "Progressive"), P = Past, Pr = Present, F =

Future, Pmv = Presumptive, Sjv = Subjunctive, Cfv = Contrafactive, PC-I = primary person-concord, PC-II = secondary person-concord (and mixed PC/AC concord), AC = adjectival concord, AC* = adjectival concord with tertiary person-concord, (X) = no concord.

Hindi–Urdu: V = *ā-* 'come' (Inf. *ānā*)

1. V + Asp:Unsp (ZERO) + PC-I + TM:Unsp (ZERO) = *Contingent Future*
   1sg. *āū̃* '(that) I may come'
   3sg. *āe* '(that) he/she/it may come'
2. V + Asp;Unsp (ZERO) + PC-I + TM:F (*-g-*) + AC = *Definite Future*
   1sg. *āū̃gā/āū̃gī* 'I shall come (M/F)'
   3sg. *āegā/āegī* 'He/she will come'
3. V + Asp:Hab (*-t-*) + AC* + TM:Unsp (ZERO) = *Unsp Habitual-Contrafactual*
   1,3sg. *ātā/ātī* 'I (M/F) he/she would come; had I he/she come'
4. V + Asp:Hab (*-t-*) + AC(*) + TM:Pr (*hai*) + PC-I *Present Habitual*
   1sg. *ātā hũ/ātī hū̃* 'I (M/F) come'
   3sg. *ātā hai/ātī hai* 'He/she comes'
5. V + Asp:Hab (*-t-*) + AC + TM:P (*thā*) + AC* = *Past Habitual*
   1,3sg. *ātā thā/ātī thī* 'I (M/F) he/she used to come'
6. V + Asp:Hab (*-t-*) + AC + TM:Pmv (*hogā*) + PC, AC = *Presumptive Habitual*
   1sg. *ātā hoū̃gā/ātī hoū̃gī* 'I (M/F) probably come'
   3sg. *ātā hogā/ātī hogī* 'He/she probably comes'
7. V + Asp:Hab (*-t-*) + AC + TM:Sjv (*ho*) + PC-(I) = *Subjunctive Habitual*
   1sg. *ātā hoū̃/ātī hoū̃* '(perhaps) I (M/F) come'
   3sg. ātā ho/ātī ho '(perhaps) he/she comes'
8. V + Asp:Hab (*-t-*) + AC + TM:Cfv (*hotā*) + AC = *Contrafactual Habitual*
   1,3sg. *ātā hotā/ātī hotī* 'had I (M/F), he/she come (regularly)'
9. V + Asp:Cont (*rah*) + AC + TM:Pr (*hai*) + PC-I = *Present Continuous*
   1sg. *ā rahā hū̃/ā rahī hū̃* 'I (M/F) am coming'
   3sg. *ā rahā hai/ā rahī hai* 'He/she is coming'
10. V + Asp:Cont (*rah*) + AC + TM:P (*thā*) + AC* = *Past Continuous*
    1,3sg. *ā rahā thā/ā rahī thī* 'I (M/F) am, he/she is coming'

11. V + Asp:Cont (*rah*) + AC + TM:Pmv (*hogā*) + PC, AC = *Presumptive Continuous*
    1sg. *ā rahā hoū̃gā/ā rahī hoū̃gī* 'I (M/F) must be coming'
    3sg. *ā rahā hogā/ā rahī hogī* 'He/she must be coming'
12. V + Asp:Cont (*rah*) + AC + TM:Sjv (*ho*) + PC-(I) = *Subjunctive Continuous*
    1sg. *ā rahā hoū̃/ā rahī hoū̃* '(perhaps) I (M/F) am coming'
    3sg. *ā rahā ho/ā rahī ho* '(perhaps) he/she is coming'
13. V + Asp:Cont (*rah*) + AC + TM:Cfv (*hotā*) + AC = *Contrafactive Continuous*
    1,3sg. *ā rahā hotā/ā rahī hotī* '(if) I he/she had been coming'
14. V + Asp:Pfv ([*y*]) + AC* + TM:Unsp (ZERO) = *Unspecified Perfective*
    1,3sg. *āyā/āī* 'I (M/F) he/she came'
15. V + Asp:Pfv ([*y*]) + AC + TM:Pr (*hai*) + PC-I = *Present Perfective*
    1sg. *āyā hū̃/āī hū̃* 'I (M/F) have come'
    3sg. *āyā hai/āī hai* 'He/she has come'
16. V + Asp:Pfv ([*y*]) + AC + TM:P (*thā*) + AC* = *Past Perfective*
    1,3sg. *āyā thā/āī thī* 'I (M/F), he/she had come'
17. V + Asp:Pfv ([*y*]) + AC + TM:Pmv (*hogā*) + PC, AC = *Presumptive Perfective*
    1sg. *āyā hoū̃gā/āī hoū̃gī* 'I (M/F) must have come'
    3sg. *āyā hogā/āī hogī* 'He/she must have come'
18. V + Asp:Pfv ([*y*]) + AC + TM:Sjv (*ho*) + PC-(I) = *Subjunctive Perfective*
    1sg. *āyā hoū̃/āī hoū̃* '(if) I (M/F) have come'
    3sg. *āyā ho/āī ho* '(if) he/she has come'
19. V + Asp:Pfv ([*y*]) + AC + TM:Cfv (*hotā*) + AC = *Contrafactive Perfective*
    1,3sg. *āyā hotā/āī hotī* '(if) I (M/F) he/she had come'

Comments: English glosses of the 3sg. can of course also refer to 'it'. The relic morpheme {*-y-*} is represented by a ZERO-allomorph after consonant stems (*dekh-* 'see' > Pfv. *dekhā*) and fuses with the Feminine ending *-ī*, although *āī* can also be written *āyī*. Glosses of the Subjunctive forms are selected "tags"; the actual equivalent depends very much on the specific context. The CONCORD element in the common modern form of the Subjunctive marker is somewhat truncated, but basically PC-I. Fuller forms (*hove*, etc.) also exist, especially dialectally and in older Hindi. The Past Perfective is often equivalent to an English Simple Past in Hindi and other NIA languages (as well as to the Past Perfect as shown).

Except in combination with the negative *nahī̃* (*ājkal koī nahī̃ ātā* 'Nowadays nobody comes') the Habitual without T/M specification has a past sense, for historical reasons suggested earlier – that is, when it does not have a contrafactual sense; the choice depends on larger syntactic factors. In its contrafactual function the form does not necessarily have any "habitual" sense.

Glosses of the Continuous forms are somewhat misleading in that in English forms like *am coming* often refer to the future – a subfunction proper rather to the Present Habitual (<Imperfective) in Hindi as well as other NIA languages. An Unspecified Continuous form occurs (uncommonly) only with negatives: *nahī̃ ā rahā* 'he/it isn't coming (on his/its way)'.

Punjabi: V = *āu-*, *āv-/ā-* 'come' (Inf. *āuṇā*)

1. V + Asp:Unsp (ZERO) + PC-I + TM:Unsp (ZERO) = *Contingent Future*
   1sg. *āvā̃* '(that) I may come'
   3sg. *ā(v)e* '(that) he/she/it may come'
2. V + Asp:Unsp (ZERO) + PC-I + TM:F (*-g-*) + AC = *Definite Future*
   1sg. *āvā̃gā/āvā̃gī* 'I (M/F) shall come'
   3sg. *āegā/āegī* 'He/she will come'
3. V + Asp:Hab (*-nd-*) + AC + TM:Unsp (ZERO) = *Unsp Habitual-Contrafactive*
   1,3sg. *āundā/āundī* 'I (M/F) he/she would come; had I he/she come'
4. V + Asp:Hab (*-nd-*) + AC + TM:Pr (*hai*) + PC-I = *Present Habitual*
   1sg. *āundā hā̃/āundī hā̃* 'I (M/F) come'
   3sg. *āundā hai/āundī hai* 'He/she comes'
5. V + Asp:Hab (*-nd-*) + AC + TM:P (*sī*) + PC-I = *Past Habitual*
   1sg. *āundā sā̃/āundī sā̃* 'I (M/F) used to come'
   3sg. *āundā sī/āundī sī* 'He/she used to come'
6. V + Asp:Hab (*-nd-*) + AC + TM:Pmv (*hovā̃gā*) + PC, AC = *Presumptive Habitual*
   1sg. *āundā hovā̃gā/āundī hovā̃gī* 'I (M/F) probably come'
   3sg. *āundā hovegā/āundī hovegī* 'He/she probably comes'
7. V + Asp:Hab (*-nd-*) + AC + TM:Sjv (*hove*) + PC = *Subjunctive Habitual*
   1sg. *āundā hovā̃/āundī hovā̃* '(perhaps) I (M/F) come'
   3sg. *āundā hove/āundī hove* '(perhaps) he/she comes'

8. V + Asp:Hab (*-nd-*) + AC + TM:Cfv (*hundā*) + AC = *Contrafactive Habitual*
   1,3sg. *āundā hundā/āundī hundī* 'had I/he/she come (regularly)'
9. V + Asp:Cont (*ri'/ra'*) + AC + TM:Pr (*hai*) + PC-I = *Present Continuous*
   1sg. *ā ri'ā hā˜/ā ra'ī hā˜* 'I (M/F) am coming'
   3sg. *ā ri'ā hai/ā ra'ī hai* 'He/she is coming'
10. V + Asp:Cont (*ri'/ra'*) + AC + TM:P (*sī*) + PC-I = *Past Continuous*
    1sg. *ā ri'ā sā˜/ā ra'ī sā˜* 'I (M/F) was coming'
    3sg. *ā ri'ā sī/ā ra'ī sī* 'He/she was coming'
11. V + Asp:Pfv (*-i-*) + AC + TM:Unsp (ZERO) = *Unspecified Perfective*
    1,3sg. *āiā/āī* 'I (M/F) he/she came'
12. V + Asp:Pfv (*-i-*) + AC + TM:Pr (*hai*) + PC-I = *Present Perfective*
    1sg. *āīā hā˜/āī hā˜* 'I (M/F) have come'
    3sg. *āiā hai/āī hai* 'He/she has come'
13. V + Asp:Pfv (*-i-*) + AC + TM:P (*sī*) + PC-I = *Past Perfective*
    1sg. *āīā sā˜/āī sā˜* 'I (M/F) had come'
    3sg. *āiā sī/āī sī* 'He/she had come'
14. V + Asp:Pfv (*-i-*) + AC + TM:Pmv (*hovegā*) + PC, AC = *Presumptive Perfective*
    1sg. *āiā hovā˜gā/āī hovā˜gī* 'I (M/F) must have come'
    3sg. *āiā hovegā/āī hovegī* 'He/she must have come'
15. V + Asp:Pfv (*-i-*) + AC + TM:Sjv (*hove*) + PC-I = *Subjunctive Perfective*
    1sg. *āiā hovā˜/āī hovā˜* '(if) I (M/F) have come'
    3sg. *āiā hove/āī hove* '(if) he/she has come'
16. V + Asp:Pfv(*-i-*) + AC + TM:Cfv (*hundā*) + AC = *Contrafactive Perfective*
    1,3sg. *āiā hundā/āī hundī* '(if) I (M/F), he/she had come'

Comments: The Perfective marker {*-i-*} (= {*-y-*}) is much better preserved in Punjabi, i.e. after consonant stems as well as after vowel stems: *vekh-* 'see' > Pfv. *vekhiā* (although again assimilated to CONCORD endings in front vowels: Fsg. *āī*, *vekhī*). The /n/ of the Habitual (<Imperfective) marker {*-nd-*}, however, is lost after consonant stems: *vekhdā*. In spoken Punjabi, a version of the Habitual marker with {*-n-*} alone is more common in the Present: *āunā vā˜* 'I come', *vekhnā vā˜* 'I see'. It is not used with all Persons, with other T/Ms, or in the negative.

In contrast with Hindi, the Punjabi Past marker varies with Person (and the 1pl. *hā˜*, *sā˜* is distinct from the 3pl. *han*, *san*, although identical with the 1sg.) In spoken P. the 1sg. Pres (=*ā˜*) takes a /*v*-/ after a preceding /-*ā*/: *vekhnā vā˜* 'I see'.

The complex subjunctives are said to be "rare" in Punjabi (Smirnov 1976: 325), which is hardly the case in Hindi, although I know of no comparative study of the subject. The Continuous occurs (though commonly enough) only with the Present and Past, and only in the positive, and is thus somewhat less well established (and not recognized as a full-fledged Aspect by some authorities) than in Hindi where the other T/Ms are possible, if uncommon. In the negative the Habitual is used instead, which thus reverts to a general Imperfective with two possible meanings: *na'ī˜ sī āundā* = (1) 'didn't use to come' (2) 'wasn't coming'. The marker *ri'ā*, *ra'ī*, *ra'e*, *ra'īā˜*, with high tone, is *spelled* RIHA, RAHI, RAHE, RAHIA˜. It is actually *pronounced* [*rĕā*, *rĕe*, *rĕī*, *rĕīā˜*] (Shackle 1972: 47).

The Future suffix is not simply added to the Contingent Future (in -*īe*, not shown) in the case of the 1pl., but to the singular form in -*ā˜* instead. According to Gill and Gleason (1969: 40) there is also a tone difference in some stems. (They also cite a 1sg. Future in -*ū˜gā*, but this would appear to be an influence from Hindi.) The 1sg. Future form is often transcribed -*āngā*, -*engā* (and the Presumptive auxiliary *hovāngā*).

In addition to more morphophonemically conditioned variation, Punjabi has more lexically conditioned variation (irregularities) than Hindi. Notable are a series of Perfective Participles preserving a -*t*-: *kītā* 'done', *pītā* 'drunk', *suttā* 'slept', *dittā* 'given', *sītā* 'sewn', *t'otā* 'washed'; cf. also *diṭṭhā* (<*dekh*-) 'seen', *pīṭhā* (<*pīh*-) 'torn', *khā˜dā* (<*khā*-) 'eaten'. The verb *ho*- 'be, happen' has a regular Perfective (*hoiā*, vs. Hindi *huā*) but an irregular Imperfective participle (*hundā*), something unknown in Hindi.

Kashmiri: V = *y(i)*-/*ā*- 'come' (Inf. *yun*)

1. V + Asp:Unsp (ZERO) + PC-I + TM:Unsp (ZERO) = *Future*
   1sg. *yimɨ* 'I'll come; (if) I come'
   3sg. *yiyi* 'He/she/it will come; (if) he/she/it comes'
2. TM:Pr (*chu*) + AC∗/PC-II + V + Asp: Impfv (-*ān*) + (X) = *Present Imperfective*
   1sg. *chus*/*ches yivān* 'I (M/F) come, am coming'
   3sg. *chu*/*che yivān* 'He/she comes/is coming'
3. TM:P (*ōs*) + AC∗/PC-II + V + Asp:Impfv (-*ān*-) + (X) = *Past Imperfective*
   1sg. *ōsus*/*ɜsɨs yivān* 'I (M/F) used to come, was coming'
   3sg. *ōs*/*ɜ̄s yivān* 'He/she used to come, was coming'

4. TM:Pmv (*āsi*) + PC-I + V + Asp:Impfv (*-ān-*) + (X) = *Presumptive Imperfective*
   1sg. *āsɨ yivān* 'I probably, may come, will be coming'
   3sg. *āsi yivān* 'He/she/it probably comes, may come, will be coming'
5. TM:Cfv (*āsihē*) + PC-I + V + Asp:Impfv (*-ān-*) + (X) = *Contrafactive Imperfective.*
   1sg. *āsɨhɜ̄ yivān* 'Had I been coming'
   3sg. *āsihē yivān* 'Had he/she/it been coming'
6. TM:Unsp (ZERO) + V + Asp:Pfv A ([*-y-*]) + AC, PC = *Unspecified Perfective A*
   1sg. *ās/āyes* 'I (M/F) came (recently)'
   3sg. *ā/āyi* 'He/she came (recently)'
7. TM:Pr (*chu*) + AC, PC-II + Asp:Pf (*-mut*) + AC = *Present Perfect*
   1sg. *chus āmut/ches āmɨċ* 'I (M/F) have come'
   3sg. *chu āmut/che āmɨċ* 'He/she has come'
8. TM:P (*ōs*) + AC, PC-II + V + Asp:Pf (*-mut*) + AC = *Past Perfect*
   1sg. *ōsus āmut/ɜ̄sɨs āmɨċ* 'I (M/F) had come'
   3sg. *ōs āmut/ɜ̄s āmɨċ* 'He/she had come'
9. TM:Pmv (*āsi*) + PC-I + V + Asp:Pf (*-mut*) + AC = *Presumptive Perfect*
   1sg. *āsɨ āmut/āsɨ āmɨċ* 'I (M/F) may, shall, must have come'
   3sg. *āsi āmut/āsi āmɨċ* 'He/she may, will, must have come'
10. TM:Cfv (*āsihē*) + PC-I + V + Asp:Pf (*-mut*) + AC = *Contrafactive Perfect*
    1sg. *āsɨhɜ̄ āmut/āmɨċ* 'Had I (M/F) come'
    3sg. *āsihē amut/āmɨċ* 'Had he/she come'
11. V + Asp:Unsp (ZERO) + PC-(I) + TM:Cfv (*hē*) + PC-I = *Contrafactive Unspecified*
    1sg. *yimɨhɜ̄* '(if) I had come'
    3sg. *yiyihē* '(if) he/she/it had come'

Comments: Kashmiri has a number of peculiar features, even while in comparison with its Dardic neighbors conforming in important ways to some of the linguistic patterns of the Indo-Gangetic plain. The most striking peculiarity is the placement of the T/M auxiliary to the left of the main verb – a matter for syntax, but unavoidably before our eyes here. It does not distinguish Habitual and Continuous, or Definite from Contingent Future (a matter which affects the T/M auxiliary we are still calling "Presumptive" in this paradigm). On the other hand it distinguishes Perfect from Perfective, and according to Grierson (1973), three varieties of Perfective (in his terminology, "Pasts"), "Recent", "Indefinite", and "Remote", only the first of which is included above. The verb *yun* is irregular: Grierson gives *āyov* as 3sg. M of Pfv B.[15] Kachru's (1973) version of the markers and the endings (also of the T/M marker: *cha* for *che(h)*) differs somewhat from Grierson's (and Bailey's) – partly but perhaps not entirely a question of transcription of the elusive Kashmiri vowels.

The paradigm has also been simplified by non-inclusion of the pronominal clitics referring to direct and indirect objects which can complicate the inflection of both auxiliaries and of such forms as the Unspecified Perfective. For example, *ās*, in addition to meaning 'I (M) came', can also mean 'It (M) came to him', and *āyes* 'I (F) came/she came to him', *ōsus* 'I (M) was/it (M) was to him', etc.

An /m/ is said to be "inserted" in the 1sg./pl. Future of vowel stems (Grierson 1973: 60) [cf. *yi-m-ɨ* above, 1pl. *yimau*], but, like the "inserted" /y/'s of Hindi, it is likely a historical relic: cf. the Sinhalese PC-I endings.

Sindhi: V = *ac-/ā, ī-* 'come' (Inf. *acaṇ^u*)

1. V + Asp:Unsp (ZERO) + PC-I + TM:Unsp (ZERO) = *Contingent Future*
   1sg. *acā̃* '(if, that) I come'
   3sg. *acē* '(if, that) he/she come'
2. V + Asp:Unsp (ZERO) + PC-I + TM:Pr2 (*thō*) + AC = *Present Unspecified*
   1sg. *acā̃ thō/acā̃ thī* 'I (M/F) come, am coming'
   3sg. *acē thō/acē thī* 'He/she comes/is coming'
3. V + Asp:Unsp (ZERO) + PC-I + TM:Cfv (*hā*) + (X) = *Contrafactive Unspecified*
   1sg. *acā̃ hā* 'Had I come'
   3sg. *acē hā* 'Had he/she/it come'
4. V + Asp:Impfv (*-and/īnd-*) + PC-II = *Definite Future*
   1sg. *īndus/īndīas* 'I (M/F) shall come'
   3sg. *īndō/īndī* 'He/she will come'
5. V + Asp:Impfv (*-and/īnd-*) + AC + TM:Pr1 (*āhē*) + PC-I = *Present Habitual*
   1sg. *īndō āhīā̃/īndī āhīā̃* 'I (M/F) come'
   3sg. *īndō āhē/īndī āhē* 'He/she comes'
6. V + Asp:Impfv (*-and/īnd-*) + AC + TM:P (*hō*) + PC-II = *Past Habitual*
   1sg. *īndō hōs/īndī huīas^i* 'I (M/F) used to come'
   3sg. *īndō hō/īndī huī* 'He/she used to come'

7. V + Asp:Cont (*-ī/ē+rahī*) + AC + TM:Pr1 (*āhē*) + PC-I = *Present Continuous*
   1sg. *acī rahīō āhīā̃/acī rahī āhīā̃* 'I (M/F) am coming'
   3sg. *acī rahīō āhē/acī rahī āhē* 'He/she is coming'
8. V + Asp:Cont (*-ī/ē+rahī*) + AC + TM:P (*hō*) + PC-II = *Past Continuous*
   1sg. *acī rahīō hōs/acī rahī huīas*[i] 'I (M/F) was coming'
   3sg. *acī rahīō hō/acī rahī huī* 'He/she was coming'
9. V + Asp:Impfv (*-and/īnd-*) + AC + TM:Pmv (*hūndō*) + PC-II = *Presumptive Imperfective*
   1sg. *īndō hūndus/īndī hūndīas* 'I (M/F) probably come, am coming'
   3sg. *īndō hūndō/īndī hūndī* 'He/she probably comes, is coming'
10. V + Asp:Impfv (*-and/īnd*) + AC + TM:Sjv (*hujē*) + PC-I = *Subjunctive Imperfective*
    1sg. *īndō hujā̃/īndī hujā̃* '(perhaps) I (M/F) come'
    3sg. *īndō hujē/īndī hujē* '(perhaps) he/she comes'
11. V + Asp:Pfv (Y) + PC-II + TM:Unsp (ZERO) = *Unspecified Perfective*
    1sg. *āīus/āīasi* 'I (M/F) came'
    3sg. *āīō/āī* 'He/she came'
12. V + Asp:Pfv (Y) + AC + TM:Pr1 (*āhē*) + PC-I = *Present Perfective*
    1sg. *āīō āhīā̃/āī āhīā̃* 'I (M/F) have come'
    3sg. *āīō āhē/āī āhē* 'He/she has come'
13. V + Asp:Pfv (Y) + AC + TM:P (*hō*) + PC-II = *Past Perfective*
    1sg. *āīō hōs/āī huīas* 'I (M/F) had come'
    3sg. *āīō hō/āī huī* 'He/she had come'
14. V + Asp:Pfv (Y) + AC + TM:Pmv (*hūndō*) + PC-II = *Presumptive Perfective*
    1sg. *āīō hūndus/āī hūndīas* 'I (M/F) must have come'
    3sg. *āīō hūndō/āī hūndī* 'He/she must have come'
15. V + Asp:Pfv (Y) + AC + TM:Sjv (*hujē*) + PC-I = *Subjunctive Perfective*
    1sg. *āīō hujā̃/āī hujā̃* 'I (M/F) may have come'
    3sg. *āīō hujē/āī hujē* 'He/she may have come'
16. V + Asp:Pfv (Y) + PC-II + TM:? (*thē*) + (X) = "*Past Iterative*"
    1sg. *āīus thē/āīasi thē* 'I (M/F) used to go; was going'
    3sg. *āīō thē/āī thē* 'He/she used to go; was going'

Comments: The status of "Tense" no. 16 in the system is not clear, especially in view of its equivalents in *paē* instead of *thē* (*pa-* in various forms is found as an "intensifier" with several Tense/Aspect forms: *acā˜ thō payō*, *payō acā˜ thō* 'I am coming') (see above, section 9.3). The status of *thē* as a T/M marker is in doubt: note that while in nos. 12–15 (where also the Perfective clearly retains its Perfective function) the T/M markers are added to a Pfv form with *AC* endings, in no. 16 the marker (or particle) is added to a form with *PC* endings. Like the *pa-* intensifiers, and unlike the normal T/M markers, it can *precede or follow* the main verb. For that matter, is the related *thō* in no.2 a T/M marker? Is it really a marker of Present *Tense*, or does it specify (or "explicate") an aspectual function?

In its basic differentiation of the Imperfective, Sindhi is less advanced than Hindi, or even than Punjabi, although as just noted it has experimented in other directions. While more recent descriptions assign a specifically Habitual function to the forms in nos. 5 and 6 (as against a more generally Imperfective one in earlier descriptions [see note 11]), no. 9 seems to retain the old wider meaning. The Imperfective participle also serves as the basis for the Future. A Habitual–Future link is characteristic of Dardic languages like Kalasha (as well as of certain Dravidian languages, i.e. Telugu). Note also that the Unspecified Contrafactual ("Past Conditional") is built on the Contingent Future ("Present Conditional") like that of Kashmiri rather than on the Imperfective Participle as elsewhere in NIA.

NIA languages differ in the number of "irregular" (historically conditioned) forms they retain. Probably Hindi has the fewest, and Sindhi the most: Grierson 1919 (*LSI*), following Trumpp, lists approximately 126 irregular Perfective ("Past") Participles (as against 5 in Hindi); in addition there are a respectable number of irregular Imperfective ("Present") Participles, including that of the verb *come* utilized here.

Gujarati: V = *āv-*, 'come' (Inf. *āvvu˜*)

1. V + Asp:Unsp (ZERO) + PC-I + TM:Unsp (ZERO) = *Contingent Future*
   1sg. *āvu˜* '(if) I come'
   3sg. *āve* '(if) he/she/it comes'
2. V + Asp:Unsp (ZERO) + TM:F: (*-(i)ʃ-*) + PC-(I) = *Definite Future*
   1sg. *āviʃ* 'I shall come'
   3sg. *āvʃe* 'He/she/it will come'
3. V + Asp:Unsp (ZERO) + PC-I + TM:Pr (*che*) = *Present Unsp (Imperfective)*
   1sg. *āvu˜ chu˜* 'I come, am coming'
   3sg. *āve che* 'He/she/it comes, is coming'

4. V + Asp:Impfv (-*(a)t)* + (X) + TM:Unsp (ZERO) = *Unspecified Contrafactual*
   1,3sg. (pl.) *āvat* 'Had I/he/she (etc.) come'
5. V + Asp:Impfv (-*t*-) + AC + TM:Unsp (ZERO) = *Unspecified Imperfective*
   1,3sg. *āvto/āvtī/āvtu˜* 'I/he/she/it used to come'
6. V + Asp:Impfv (-*t*-) + AC + TM:P (*hato*) + AC = *Past Imperfective*
   1,3sg. *āvto hato/āvtī hatī/āvtu˜ hatu˜* 'I/he/she/it used to come, was coming'
7. V + Asp:Impfv (-*t*-) + AC + TM:Pmv (*haʃe*) + PC-(I) = *Presumptive Imperfective*
   1sg. *āvto hɔiʃ/āvtī hɔiʃ* 'I (M/F) probably come, am coming'
   3sg. *āvto hato/āvtī hatī/āvtu˜ hatu˜* 'He/she/it probably comes, is coming'
8. V + Asp:Impfv (-*t*-) + AC + TM:Sjv (*hɔy*) + PC-I = *Subjunctive Imperfective*
   1sg. *āvto hɔu˜/āvtī hɔu˜* '(if) I (M/F) come, am coming'
   3sg. *āvto hɔy/āvtī hɔy/āvtu˜* '(if) he/she/it comes, is coming'
9. V + Asp:Impfv (-*t*-) + AC + TM:Cfv (*hɔt*) + (X) = *Contrafactive Imperfective*
   1,3sg. *āvto hɔt/āvtī hɔt/āvtu˜ hot* '(if) I/he/she/it had come (regularly), had been coming'
10. V + Asp:Pfv (-*y*-) + AC + TM:Unsp (ZERO) = *Unspecified Perfective*
    1,3sg. *āvyo/āvī/āvyu˜* 'I/he/she/it came'
11. V + Asp:Pfv (-*y*-) + AC + TM:Pr (*che*) + PC-I = *Present Perfective*
    1sg. *āvyo chu˜/āvī chu˜* 'I (M/F) have come'
    3sg. *āvyo che/āvī che/āvyu˜ che* 'He/she/it has come'
12. V + Asp:Pfv (-*y*-) + AC + TM:P (*hato*) + AC = *Past Perfective*
    1,3sg. *āvyo hato/āvī hatī/āvyu˜ hatu˜* 'I/he/she/it had come'
13. V + Asp:Pfv (-*y*-) + AC + TM:Pmv (*haʃe*) + PC-(I) = *Presumptive Perfective*
    1sg. *āvyo hɔiʃ/āvī hɔiʃ* 'I (M/F) must have come'
    3sg. *āvyo haʃe/āvī haʃe/āvyu˜ haʃe* 'He/she/it must have come'
14. V + Asp:Pfv (-*y*-) + AC + TM:Sjv (*hɔy*) + PC-I = *Subjunctive Perfective*
    1sg. *āvyo hɔu˜/āvī hɔu˜* '(if) I (M/F) have come'
    3sg. *āvyo hɔy/āvī hɔy/āvyu˜ hɔy* '(if) he/she/it has come'

15. V + Asp:Pfv (*-y-*) + AC + TM:Cfv (*hɔt*) + (X) = *Contrafactive Perfective*
    1,3sg. *āvyo hɔt/āvī hɔt/āvyu˜ hɔt* '(if) I, he/she/it had come, came, would come'

Comments: Gujarati retains an aspectually unmarked form (no. 3) in the function of Present Imperfective, although a marked form (*āvto nathī* 'doesn't come, isn't coming') replaces it in the negative. Like Kashmiri, the language is more conservative even than Sindhi in retaining an undifferentiated Imperfective. It has, however, evolved an optionally specified Habitual in the Present (*āvto hɔy che* 'he generally comes', cf. Cardona 1965: 107–8); no. 5 already serves that function in the Past. Note that the Unspecified Imperfective (= "Past Habitual") is differentiated from the Unspecified Contrafactual ("Past Conditional") by the presence of AC CONCORD markers.

The PC-I markers used with the Future (and the Presumptive Auxiliary) have undergone some vicissitudes: the 1sg. has lost its *-u˜*, which has become instead the marker of the 1pl.

There is a second form of the Perfective using a marker {*-el-*} rather than {*-y-*}, basically the attributive adjectival form of the Perfective (see below, section 9.8), but used also predicatively by some speakers interchangeably with the {*-y-*} form (Cardona 1965: 135, Savel'eva 1965: 39, Zograph 1976: 278): *āvelo*, *āvelo che*, *āvelo hato*, etc. Six additional formulas could thus be added, but they would involve non-contrastive, merely alternative forms. These forms are interesting in that they link Gujarati with Marathi to the south (see Figure 9.3) rather than with the Central and Northwestern languages as is more often the case. More in line with the last connection, it also has a respectable number of "irregular" Perfectives: *khādhu˜* 'ate', *pidhu˜* 'drank', *dīṭhu˜* 'saw', *līdhu˜* 'taken', *sutu˜* 'slept', etc.

Marathi: V = *ye-/ā-* 'come' (Inf. *yeṇe˜*)

1. V + Asp:Unsp (ZERO) + PC-I + TM:Unsp (ZERO) = *Old Unspecified* ("*Past Habitual*" 1)
   1sg. *yeī˜* 'I used to come'
   3sg. *yeī* 'He/she/it used to come'
2. V + Asp:Unsp (ZERO) + PC-(I) + TM:F (*-l*) = *Future*
   1sg. *yeīn* 'I shall come'
   3sg. *yeīl* 'He/she/it will come
3. V + Asp:Impfv (*-t-*) + PC-IIa + TM:Unsp (ZERO) = *Present Habitual*
   1sg. *yeto˜/yete˜* 'I (M/F) come'
   3sg. *yeto/yete/yete˜* 'He/she/it comes'

4. V + Asp:Impfv (*-t-*) + PC-IIb + TM:Unsp (ZERO) = *Unspecified Contrafactual*
   1sg. *yetõ/yetẽ* 'Had I (M/F) come'
   3sg. *yetā-yetī/yetẽ* 'Had he/she/it come'
5. V + Asp:Impfv (*-t*) + (X) + TM:Pr (*āhe*) + PC-(I) = *Present Continuous*
   1sg. *yet āhẽ* 'I am coming'
   3sg. *yet āhe* 'He/she/it is coming'
6. V + Asp:Impfv (*-t*) + (X) + TM:P (*hotā*) + PC-II = *Past Continuous*
   1sg. *yet hotõ/yet hotẽ* 'I (M/F) was coming, (used to come)'
   3sg. *yet hotā/yet hotī/yet hotẽ* 'He/she/it was coming, (used to come)'
7. V + Asp:Impfv (*-t*) + (X) + TM:Pmv1 (*asel*) + (X) = *Presumptive Imperfective 1*
   1sg. *yet asen* 'I probably come, am coming'
   3sg. *yet asel* 'He/she/it probably comes, is coming'
8. V + Asp:Impfv (*-t*) + (X) + TM:Pmv2 (*asṇār*) + (X) = *Presumptive Imperfective*
   1,3sg. *yet asṇār* 'I/he/she/it (etc.) will probably come, be coming'
9. V + Asp:Impfv (*-t*) + (X) + TM:Sjv1 (*asāvā*) + AC* = *Subjunctive Imperfective 1*
   1,3sg. *yet asāvā/yet asāvī/yet asāvẽ* 'maybe I (he/she/it) come(s), am (is) coming'
10. V + Asp:Impfv (*-t*) + (X) + TM:Sjv2 (*aslā*) + PC-IIb = *Subjunctive Imperfective 2*
    1sg. *yet aslõ/yet aslẽ* '(if) I (M/F) come (regularly)'
    3sg. *yet aslā/yet aslī/yet aslẽ* '(if) he/she/it comes, is coming'
11. V + Asp:Impfv (*-t*) + (X) + TM:Cfv (*astā*) + PC-IIb = *Contrafactive Imperfective*
    1sg. *yet astõ/yet astẽ* '(if) I would come, would have come (regularly), had been coming'
    3sg. *yet astā/yet astī/yet astẽ* '(if) he/she/it would come, would have come (regularly), had been coming'
12. V + Asp:Impfv (*-t*) + (X) + TM:HabP (*ase*) + PC-I = "*Past Habitual*" *2*
    1sg. *yet asẽ* 'I used to come'
    3sg. *yet ase* 'He/she/it used to come'
13. V + Asp:Pfv (*-l-*) + PC-IIb + TM:Unsp (ZERO) = *Unspecified Perfective*

1sg. *ālo˜/āle˜* 'I came (M/F)'
3sg. *ālā/ālī/āle˜* 'He/she/it came'

14. V + Asp:Pfv (*-l-*) + PC-IIb + TM:Pr (*āhe*) + PC(I) = *Present Perfective*
    1sg. *ālo˜ āhe˜/āle˜ āhe˜* 'I (M/F) have come'
    3sg. *ālā āhe/ālī āhe/āle˜ āhe* 'He/she/it has come'
15. V + Asp:Pfv (*-l-*) + PC-IIb + TM:P (*hotā*) + PC-IIb = *Past Perfective*
    1sg. *ālo˜hoto˜/āle˜hote˜* 'I (M/F) had come'
    3sg. *ālā hotā/ālī hotī/āle˜hote˜* 'He/she/it had come'
16. V + Asp:Pfv (*-l-*) + PC-IIb + TM:Pmv1 (*asel*) + (X) = *Presumptive Perfective 1*
    1sg. *ālo˜asen/āle˜asen* 'I (M/F) probably came'
    3sg. *ālā asel/ālī asel/āle˜asel* 'He/she/it probably came'
17. V + Asp:Pfv (*-l-*) + PC-IIb + TM:Pmv2 (*asṇār*) + (X) = *Presumptive Perfective 2*
    1sg. *ālo˜asṇār/āle˜asṇār* 'I (M/F) must have come'
    3sg. *ālā asṇar/ālī asṇār/āle˜asṇār* 'He/she/it must have come'
18. V + Asp:Pfv (*-l-*) + PC-IIb + TM:Sjv1 (*asāvā*) + AC* = *Subjunctive Perfective 1*
    1sg. *ālo˜asāvā/āle˜asāvī* 'I (M/F) might have come'
    3sg. *ālā asāvā/ālī asāvī/āle˜asāve˜* 'He/she/it might have come'
19. V + Asp:Pfv (*-l-*) + PC-IIb + TM:Sjv1 (*aslā*) + PC-IIb = *Subjunctive Perfective 2*
    1sg. *ālo˜aslo˜/āle˜asle˜* '(if) I (M/F) have come'
    3sg. *ālā aslā/ālī aslī/āle˜asle˜* '(if) he/she/it has come'
20. V + Asp:Pfv (*-l-*) + PC-IIb+ TM:Cfv (*astā*) + PC-IIb = *Contrafactive Perfective*
    1sg. *ālo˜asto˜/āle˜aste˜* '(if) I (M/F) had come'
    3sg. *ālā astā/ālī astī/āle˜aste˜* '(if) he/she/it had come'
21. V + Asp:Pro (*-ṇār*) + (X) + TM:Unsp (ZERO): = *Unspecified Prospective*
    1,3sg. *yeṇār* 'I am, he/she/it is (definitely) going to come'
22. V + Asp:Pro (*-ṇār*) + (X) + TM:Pr (*āhe*) + PC(I) = *Present Prospective*
    1sg. *yeṇār āhe˜* 'I'm going to come'
    3sg. *yeṇār āhe* 'He/she/it is going to come'
23. V + Asp:Pro (*ṇār*) + (X) + TM:P (*hotā*) + PC-IIB = *Past Prospective*

1sg. *yeṇār hoto˜/yeṇār hote˜* 'I (M/F) was going to come'
3sg. *yeṇār hotā/yeṇār hotī/yeṇār hote˜* 'He/she/it was going to come'

24. V + Asp:Pro (*-ṇār*) + (X) + TM:Pmv1 (*asel*) + (X) = *Presumptive Prospective*
    3sg. *yeṇār asel* 'He/she/it must be going to come'
25. V + Asp:Des (*-āv-*) + AC∗ + TM:Unsp (ZERO) = *Unspecified Desiderative*
    1,3sg. *yāve˜* 'I/he/she/it should come'
    1,3sg, *yāvā/yāvī/yāve˜* 'I/he/she/it might come'
26. V + Asp:Impfv2 (*-āyc-*) + PC-IIb + TM:Unsp (ZERO) = "*Past Habitual*" *3*
    1sg. *yāyċo˜/yāyce˜* 'I (M/F) used to come'
    3sg. *yāyċā/yāycī/yāyce˜* 'He/she/it used to come'

Comments: The older spellings of Literary Marathi are given for comparative purposes (with *anusvāra* distinguishing the 1st person from the 3rd – in some cases). To arrive at the reformed spellings (and modern literary pronunciation), remove the *anusvāra*. Arriving at the colloquial pronunciation is slightly more complicated: in the 3sg. Neuter, replace *-e˜* with [*-ə:*]; various contractions of Aux and participial stem also take place: e.g., no. 15, *ālo˜hoto˜* becomes *ālohvto* (see Kavadi and Southworth 1965: 201–3).

Marathi differentiates the Imperfective as Habitual and Continuous – with the help of CONCORD and T/M components – only in the Present (nos. 3 and 5). Despite this, it has a large number of "tenses", achieved through contrastive elaboration of all three inflectional components (Aspect, Tense/Mood, and CONCORD). For instance, different CONCORD markers in the 3rd person differentiate nos. 3 and 4. (Since this is insufficient in the 1st person, no. 4 is generally replaced by nos. 11 and 20.) Even more "tenses" could be added. The Imperative/Optative has endings distinct from either those of the form that represents the "Old Present" (the "Past Habitual 1") or of the newer "Subjunctives": *yeu˜* 'shall I come?'

Elaboration of the Aspect component provides additional forms of the auxiliary for elaboration of the T/M component. A grasp of the system is complicated by the fact that it is "in motion": newer forms are in the process of crowding out older forms with similar functions: note the three "Past Habituals" (nos. 1, 12, 26) along with the not completely abdicated Past Habitual function of no. 6. At the same time, real specializations exist: Marathi differentiates the "doubtful" function of the "Subjunctive" (nos. 9, 18) from the "conditional" function (nos. 10, 19), and both from the "optative" function as just stated. The Future is also frequently used in open conditions in Marathi. The Unspecified Perfective can also be used (as in Hindi), no doubt the source of the T/M form in nos. 10 and 19.

It is sometimes difficult to find appropriate terminology: *Prospective* is fairly standard for nos. 21–24, but unsuitable for the T/M function in nos. 8 and 17. For want of anything better, Berntsen and Nimbkar's *Desiderative* is used for no. 25 although the sense is one of "mild obligation" rather than desire. (They also call it *Subjunctive*, when used in a different construction with the subject of Intransitives.) Often the newer forms (e.g., the "Impfv2" of no. 26) are verbal nominals or adjectivals pressed into service – but such after all is the history of many older forms also throughout NIA.

How many of these forms actually function in a given register or regional or class dialect is an important question that unfortunately cannot be answered here. While the term "*Marathi*" does not cover a collection of distinct languages the way the term "*Hindi*" sometimes does, a form that is obsolete in one region or at one social level is often found to be vigorously alive in another.

The Prospective forms are much more frequent than the roughly corresponding *-nevālā* forms of Hindi, and often replace the Future.

Sinhalese (Colloquial): V = *e-*, *āv-*, *æv-* 'come' (Inf. *enavā*)
(Colloquial Sinhalese lacks verbal CONCORD, but certain forms occur only with the 1st Person, or only with the 2nd and 3rd. Hence the designations *1p* and *3p* will be used only to mark the latter cases. However, there is an important distinction in the language between Non-Emphatic ("Simple") and Emphatic verb forms. These will be indicated by NE and E.)

1. V + Asp:Unsp (ZERO) + TM:Sjv (*-vi*) = *Unspecified Subjunctive*
   3p *ēvi* 'He/she/it might come'
2. V + Asp:Unsp (ZERO) + TM:F (*-nnam*) = *Unspecified Future*
   1p *ennam* 'I'll come/may I come?'
3. V + Asp:Impfv (*-n-*) + TM:Unsp (ZERO) = *Unspecified Imperfective*
   NE *enavā* 'I (he/she) come(s)/am (is) coming/will come'
   E *enne* 'I (he/she) come(s)/am (is) coming/will come'
4. V + Asp:Impfv (*-n-*) + TM:Pmv (*æti*) = *Presumptive Imperfective*
   NE *enavā æti* 'I (he/she) probably come/am (is) coming/will come'
5. V + Asp:Impfv2 (*-t-*) + TM:Cond (*-ot*) = *Conditional Imperfective*
   etot 'if I he/she come(s)'
6. V + Asp:Pfv ("-Y-") + TM:Unsp (ZERO) = *Unspecified Perfective*
   NE *āvā* 'I/he/she came'
   E *āve* 'I/he/she came'

7. V + Asp:Pfv ("-Y-") + TM:Cond (*-ot*) = *Conditional Perfective*
   āvot 'if I/he/she came/happen to come'
8. V + Asp:Pfv2 (*-nna[ṭa]*) + TM:Pmv (*æti*) = *Presumptive Perfective*
   enna(ṭa) æti 'I/he/she must have come/been coming'
9. V + Asp:Pf ("L" + *-lā*) + TM:Unsp (ZERO) = *Unspecified Perfect*
   ævillā 'I have come; he/she has come'
10. V + Asp:Pf ("L" + *-lā*) + TM:Pr (*tiyenavā/tiyenne*) = *Present Perfect*
    NE *ævillā tiyenavā* 'I have come; he/she has come'
    E *ævillā tiyenne* 'I have come; he/she has come'
11. V + Asp:Pf ("L" + *-lā*) + TM:P (*ti[b]unā*) = *Past Perfect*
    ævillā ti[b]unā 'I/he/she had come'
12. V + Asp:Cont ("L" × 2) + TM:Pr (*innavā*) = *Present Continuous*
    ∗*katā kara kara innavā* 'I am talking; he/she is talking'
13. V + Asp:Cont ("L" × 2) + TM:P (*unnā, hiṭiyā*) = *Past Continuous*
    ∗*katā kara kara unnā* 'I/he/she was talking'
14. V + Asp:Hab ("L" × 2 + *-t*) + TM:P (*hiṭiyā*) = *Past Habitual*
    ævi ævit hiṭiyā 'I/he/she used to come'

Comments: The above and following account is based mainly on Fairbanks, Gair and DeSilva 1968 (with a modification of the transcription in the direction of a transliteration of the Sinhala spelling), with additional input from Garusinghe 1962, Geiger 1938, Bel'kovich 1970, and Gair 1970. It may not be complete, but I have hesitated to extrapolate beyond these sources: e.g., no Emphatic forms are given for nos. 11–14, although they probably exist; the use of the inanimate auxiliary *tiyenavā* (rather than *innavā*) is puzzling in nos. 10 and 11: the contrast is consistent in Literary Sinhala (Bel'kovich 1970:790). A different verb is used in nos. 12 and 13, since according to Fairbanks et al. (1968: II. 159), the verb *come* lacks such a form (although cf. Garusinghe p. 88, the source of no. 14).

The symbol "Y" is an arbitrary one for the complex formation of the Sinhalese Perfective, reflecting the input of MIA ∗*-i-*. The symbol "L" is Gair's for the complex formation of the Conjunctive Participle Base (*Past* Participle in Fairbanks et al., *Perfect* Participle in Gair 1970).

What we are calling the Sinhalese *Imperfective* retains a very wide meaning – it can be future as well as iterative or durative. The Specific Future (confined to the 1st person) in *-nnam* (pronounced [*nnaŋ*]), which has Dravidian echoes, is given by Geiger (p. 163) as *-ññā* (sg.) and *-ññamu* (pl.).

The distinction between the *etot* and *āvot* Conditionals is Garusinghe's. Neither seems to be contrafactual. Conditionality is also expressed by simple Imperfective or Perfective + the particle *nam* 'if': *enavā nam* 'if he (etc.) comes'.

No. 8 is Perfective according to Bel'kovich, who is mainly describing Literary Sinhala: it is really the Dative of the Infinitive (Bel'kovich calls it the General Participial Noun II ["*prichastnoe imia obshchego deistviia* II"] and the Mood in question the *Potential*). The Colloquial form omits the Dative -*ṭa*.

Oriya: V = *ās-* 'come' (Inf. *āsibā*)

1. V + Asp:Unsp (ZERO) + PC-I + TM:Unsp (ZERO) = *General Unspecified* (>*Present Habitual*)
   1sg. *āse˜* 'I come'
   3sg. *āse* 'He/she/it comes'
2. V + Asp:Unsp (ZERO) + TM:F (-*ib*-) + PC-IIb = *Future*
   1sg. *āsibi* 'I shall come'
   3sg. *āsibɔ* 'He/she/it will come'
3. V + Asp:Cond (-*ɔnt*-) + PC-IIa + TM:Unsp (ZERO) = *Unspecified Conditional*
   1sg. *āsɔnti* 'I would come'
   3sg. *āsɔntā* 'He/she/it would come'
4. V + Asp:Cont (-*u*-) + TM:Pr (-*chi*) + PC-IIc = *Present Continuous*
   1,3sg. *āsuchi* 'I am coming; he/she/it is coming'
5. V + Asp:Cont (-*u*-) + TM:P (*thilā*) + PC-IIa = *Past Continuous*
   1sg. *āsuthili* 'I was coming'
   3sg. *āsuthilā* 'He/she/it was coming'
6. V + Asp:Cont (-*u*-) + TM:Pmv (*thibɔ*) + PC-IIb = *Presumptive Continuous*
   1sg. *āsuthibi* 'I will be coming'
   3sg. *āsuthibɔ* 'He/she/it will be coming'
7. V + Asp:Cont (-*u*-) + TM:Cfv (*thāntā*) + PC-IIa = *Contrafactive Conditional*
   1sg. *āsuthānti* '(if) I had been coming'
   3sg. *āsuthāntā* '(if) he/she/it had been coming'
8. V + Asp:Pfv (-*il*-) + PC-IIa = *Unspecified Perfective*
   1sg. *āsili* 'I came'
   3sg. *āsilā* 'He/she/it came'
9. V + Asp:Pf (-*i*-) + TM:Pr (*chi*) + PC-IIc = *Present Perfect*
   1,3sg. *āsichi* 'I have come; he/she/it has come'
10. V + Asp:Pf (-*i*-) + TM:P (*thilā*) + PC-IIa = *Past Perfect*
    1sg. *āsithili* 'I had come'
    3sg. *āsithilā* 'He/she/it had come'

11. V + Asp:Pf (*-i-*) + TM:Pmv (*thibɔ*) + PC-IIb = *Presumptive Perfect*
    1sg. *āsithibi* 'I will have come'
    3sg. *āsithibɔ* 'He/she/it has come'
12. V + Asp:Pf (*-i-*) + TM:Cfv (*thāntā*) + PC-IIb = *Contrafactive Perfect*
    1sg. *āsithānti* 'I would have come, (if) I had come'
    3sg. *āsithāntā* 'He/she/it would have come, (if) . . . had come'

Comments: The Oriya system is quite straightforward. The main points to notice are the use of the Old Present or Unspecified form as a Present Habitual, the clearly differentiated Continuous forms, the lack of a Subjunctive, and the lack of a Past Habitual. No. 3 above, the form without T/M auxiliary derived from the MIA Present Participle, is not used in Oriya in the function of both a Contrafactual and a Past Habitual as is the case in a number of other NIA languages (including neighboring Bengali), Tripathi (p. 193) is at pains to warn us.

As with Marathi, nasalization in the 1sg. (no. 1) has been indicated following traditional spelling (Mahapatra 1955), although modern descriptions of the colloquial ignore it. The spelling has also been followed in using /*ch*/ rather than /*c*/ (although not the older /*ɔch-*/ for the Present forms. Mahapatra (1955) lists three additional "tenses" that are combinations of the Continuous with the Perfect: *kɔriāsuɔchi* 'He has been doing', *kɔriāsuthilā* 'He had been doing', and *kɔriāsuthibɔ* 'He will have been doing'. If these are really in use and not merely attempts to render English forms, they would seem to be unique in NIA.

Bengali (Colloquial): V = *āʃ-*, *e-* 'come' (Vbl. N. *āʃā*)

1. V + Asp:Unsp (ZERO) + PC-I + TM:Unsp (ZERO) = *General Unspecified* (>*Present Habitual*)
   1p *āʃi* 'I (we) come'
   3p *āʃe* 'He/she/it comes (they come)'
2. V + Asp:Unsp (ZERO) + TM:F (*-b-*) + PC-IIb = *Future*
   1p *āʃbo* 'I (we) shall come'
   3p *āʃbe* 'He/she/it (they) will come'
3. V + Asp:Impfv (*-y-*) + PC-IIa + TM:Unsp (ZERO) = *Past Habitual/Contrafactual*
   1p *āʃtum* 'I (we) used to come/(if) I (we) had come'
   3p *āʃto* 'He/she/it (they) used to come/(if) he, etc. had come'
4. V + Asp:Cont (^{H}) + TM:Pr (*-che*) + PC-I = *Present Continuous*
   1p *āʃchi* 'I am (we are) coming'
   3p *āʃche* 'He/she/it is (they are) coming'

5. V + Asp:Cont (^{H}) + TM:P (*-chilo*) + PC-IIa = *Past Continuous*
   1p *āʃchilum* 'I was (we were) coming'
   3p *āʃchilo* 'He/she/it was (they were) coming'

6. V + Asp:Cont2 (-te*) + TM:Pmv (*thākbe*) + PC-IIb = *Presumptive Continuous*
   1p *āʃte thākbo* 'I (we) shall be coming'
   3p *āʃte thākbe* 'He/she/it (they) will be coming'

7. V + Asp:Pfv (*-l-*) + PC-IIa + TM:Unsp (ZERO) = *Unspecified Perfective*
   1p *āʃlum (elum)* 'I (we) came'
   3p *āʃlo (elo)* 'He/she/it (they) came'

8. V + Asp:Pf (*-e-*) + TM:Pr (*che*) + PC-I = *Present Perfect*
   1p *eʃechi* 'I (we) have come'
   3p *eʃeche* 'He/she/it has (they have) come'

9. V + Asp:Pf (*-e-*) + TM:P (*chilo*) + PC-IIa = *Past Perfect*
   1p *eʃechilum* 'I (we) had come'
   3p *eʃechilo* 'He/she/it (they) had come'

10. V + Asp:Pf (*-e-*) + TM:Pmv (*thākbe*) + PC-IIb = *Presumptive Perfect*
   1p *eʃe thākbo* 'I (we) shall, must have come'
   3p *eʃe thākbe* 'He/she/it (they) will/must have come'

11. V + Asp:Pf (*-e-*) + TM:Sjv (*thāke*) + PC-I = *Subjunctive Perfect*
   1p *eʃe thāki* '(if) I (we) have come'
   3p *eʃe thāke* '(if) he/she/it has (they have) come'

Comments: In brackets following the stem allomorphs, what is given in all the above paradigms is the "dictionary form" of the verb, not necessarily the Infinitive. In Bengali and Assamese this is a verbal noun. As a reminder of the fact that there are no number distinctions in the Bengali verb, plural pronoun references are given in brackets.

In Bengali we meet the unique phenomenon of High and Low verb stems, a kind of historical vowel harmony, where the conditioning factors are no longer always present. In the Colloquial Continuous the High stem itself (^{H}) is all that remains of the Aspect marker. (Verbs with /ā/ + consonant, such as *āʃ-* shown here, do not illustrate the phenomenon as well as some others, e.g., *ʃon-e* 'he, she listens'/*ʃun-che* 'is listening'.) Synchronically, an alternative analysis is possible, taking *-ch-* as the Continuous marker and the distinctive PC-I endings themselves as the Present marker (Bender and Riccardi 1978: 21), but such a segmentation, while perhaps fitting the current state of the language, would violate the historical facts and thus disturb the comparative side of this presentation.

The *Sadhu Bhasa* Continuous marker, {*-ite*}, shows a more obvious relation to the MIA Present Participle, the usual source of NIA first-stage Imperfectives. A truncated form of it is kept in the Colloquial form in no. 6, which has more a Future than a Presumptive sense. The Presumptive label fits no. 10 better, however. The *Sadhu Bhasa* has several additional forms (complex Imperfective and Perfective Contrafactives, Imperfective Subjunctive) that are apparently absent from the Colloquial. As in most NIA languages where the Old Present retains its primary function, it also serves as a contingent future ("Simple Subjunctive"): *āʃe* also = 'he may come, (if) he comes'.

Partly as a result of loss of gender, CONCORD is marked only once in the verb forms of the Eastern group (vs. twice in the Central and Western languages) – albeit using three partially contrasting sets of PC markers.

Assamese: V = *āh-*, *ɒh-* 'come' (Vbl. N. *ɒhā*)

1. V + Asp:Unsp (ZERO) + PC-I + TM:Unsp (ZERO) = *General Unspecified* (>*Present Habitual*)
   1p *āho˜* 'I (we) come'
   3p *āhe* 'He/she/it comes (they come)'
2. V + Asp:Unsp (ZERO) + TM:F (*-ib-*) + PC-IIb = *Future (Unspecified)*
   1p *āhim* 'I (we) shall come'
   3p *āhibɒ* 'He/she/it (they) will come'
3. V + Asp:Cont/Pf (*-i-*[1,2]) + TM:Pr (*-se*) + PC-I = *Present Continuous/Perfect ("Present Definite")*
   1p *āhiso˜* 'I am (we are) coming; I (we) have come'
   3p *āhise* 'He/she/it is (they are) coming; he . . . has (they have) come'
4. V + Asp:Cont (*-i*[1]) + TM:Pr2 (*āse*) + PC-I = *Disambiguated Present Continuous*
   1p *āhi āso˜* 'I am (we are) coming'
   3p *āhi āse* 'He/she/it is (they are) coming'
5. V + Asp:Cont (*-i-*[1]) + TM:P2 (*āsil*) + PC-IIa = *(Disambiguated) Past Continuous*
   1p *āhi āsilo˜* 'I was (we were) coming'
   3p *āhi āsil* 'He/she/it was (they were) coming'
6. V + Asp:Pfv (*-il-*) + PC-IIa + TM:Unsp (ZERO) = *Unspecified Perfective*
   1p *āhilo˜* 'I (we) came; (. . . have come)'
   3p *āhil* 'He/she/it (they) came; (. . . has [have] come)'

7. V + Asp:Pfv (*-il*) + PC-IIa + TM:Cfv (*he˜ten*) + (X) = *Contrafactive Perfective*
   1p *āhilo˜ he˜ten* 'Had I (we) come; I (we) would come'
   3p *āhil he˜ten* 'Had he/she/it (they) come; he . . . (they) would come'

8. V + Asp:Hab (-i+thāki-*) + TM:P (*sil*) + PC-IIa = *Past Habitual*
   1p *āhithākisilo˜* 'I (we) used to come'
   3p *āhithākisil* 'He/she/it (they) used to come'

Comments: The ambiguity of Perfect and Continuous ({*i*}[1,2]) in Assamese was noted earlier. Although the Present seems to have more often the Continuous sense, and the Past the Perfect sense, according to Kakati (1962: 369) only context differentiates them. In any case it is the Continuous which has special disambiguated forms (nos. 4 and 5), by employing the full forms of the auxiliary.

The unusual form of the 1p Future (*-im*) represents a fusion of the Future marker {*-ib-*} with the 1st person marker {*-o˜*}: cf. the analogous development in Marathi ({*-l*} + {*-o˜*} = *-n*).

Brown (1848) lists a Present Subjunctive (no. 1 + *he˜ten*), but according to Kakati (p. 360), such a form (he gives *hā˜te* rather than *he˜ten*) is Middle Assamese and has not survived. Both Babakaev (1961) and Kakati (and the *LSI*), however, list an additional form with the Past (or "Perfect") Participle in *-ā* (invariant) + *he˜ten*, *hɔle*, or *hɔli* usable (without 'if') in the protasis of a contrafactual conditional sentence: *hā he˜ten*, 'if X had come' (=*zɔdi . . . āhil/āhilo˜/āhili/āhilā he˜ten*).

Babakaev (1961) also lists Presumptive forms, involving the addition of *hɔbɔlā*, *hɔbɒ* or *hɔbɒ pāy* to finite forms: *āhise hɔbɔlā* 'He must have come'. According to the scheme employed here, these would involve a "*second*" T/M marker (*-se* + *hɔbɔlā*) rather than the paradigmatic substitution of a Presumptive marker as in the rest of NIA.

Assamese has been said to lack a Past Habitual (Kakati 1962: 359), but the form in no. 8 seems to have evolved to supply this need.

Nepali: V = *āu-*, *ā-* 'come' (Inf. *āunu*)

1. V + Asp:Unsp (ZERO) + PC-I + TM:Unsp (ZERO) = *Contingent Future ("Desiderative", "Injunctive")*
   1sg. *āu˜* 'I would like to come; may I come?'
   3sg. *āos* 'Let him/her/it come'
2. V + Asp:Unsp (ZERO) + PC-(I) + TM:F (*-lā*) + AC* = *Presumptive Future*

1sg. *āu˜lā/āu˜lī* 'I (M/F) may, probably shall, come'
3sg. *āulā/āulī* 'He/she/it may, probably will, come'

3. V + Asp:Prox (*-ne*) + TM:Pr (*cha*) + PC-IIa = *Proximate Future*
   1sg. *āunechu* 'I shall come'
   3sg. *āunecha/āuneche* 'He/she will come'
4. V + Asp:Prox (*-ne*) + TM:P1 (*thiyo*) + PC-IIb = *Proximate Contrafactual*
   1sg. *āune thie˜* 'I would have come'
   3sg. *āune thiyo/thiī* 'He/she would have come'
5. V + Asp:Impfv-1 (*-(n)-*) + TM:Pr (*-cha*) + PC-IIa = *Present Habitual*
   1sg. *āu˜chu* 'I come; (I shall come)'
   3sg. *āu˜cha/āu˜che* 'He/she comes; (he/it will come)'
6. V + Asp:Impfv-1 (*-(n)-*) + TM:P2 (*-thyo*) + PC-IIb = *Past Habitual (and Contrafactual)*
   1sg. *āu˜the˜* 'I used to come/would come'
   3sg. *āu˜thyo/āu˜thī* 'He/she used to come/would come'
7. V + Asp:Impfv-2a (*-˜dai*) + (X) + TM:Pr (*cha*) + PC-IIa = *Present Continuous 1-A*
   1sg. *āu˜dai chu* 'I am coming'
   3sg. *āu˜dai cha/che* 'He/she is coming'
8. V + Asp:Impfv-2b (*-˜d-*) + AC + TM:Pr (*cha*) + PC-IIa = *Present Continuous 1-B*
   1sg. *āu˜do/āu˜dī chu* 'I (M/F) am coming'
   3sg. *āu˜do cha/āu˜dī* 'He/she is coming'
9. V + Asp:Cont (*-i+rahek-*) + AC + TM:Pr (*cha*) + PC-IIa = *Present Continuous 2-A*
   1sg. *āiraheko/āirahekī chu* 'I (M/F) am coming'
   3sg. *āiraheko cha/āirahekī che* 'He/she is coming'
10. V + Asp:Cont (*-i+rahe*) + (AC) + TM:Pr (*cha*) + PC-IIa = *Present Continuous 2-B*
    1sg. *āirahe/āirahi chu* 'I (M/F) am coming'
    3sg. *āirahe cha/āirahi che* 'He/she is coming'
11. V + Asp:Impfv-1a (*-˜dai*) + (X) + TM:P1 (*thiyo*) + PC-IIb = *Past Continuous 1-A*
    1sg. *āu˜dai thie˜* 'I was coming'
    3sg. *āu˜dai thiyo-thiī* 'He/she was coming'
12. V + Asp:Impfv-1a (*-˜dai*) + (X) + TM:Pmv (*holā*) + (*) = *Presumptive Continuous 1-A*

1sg. *āu˜dai hu˜lā/hu˜lī* 'I (M/F) probably am/was/shall be coming'
3sg. *āu˜dai holā/holī* 'He/she probably is/was/will be coming'

(13–16: Past and Presumptive Continuous 1-B and 2-A can be made by substituting *thie˜/thiyo/thiī* and *hu˜lā/hu˜lī/holā/holī* for *chu/cha/che* in nos. 8 and 9 above. There seem to be no corresponding forms for no. 10, that is, for Continuous 2-B [Verma and Sharma 1979: 200, 205].)

17. V + Asp:Pfv (*-y-*) + PC-IIb + TM:Unsp (ZERO) = *Unspecified Perfective*
1sg. *āe˜* 'I came'
3sg. *āyo/āī* 'He/she came'
18. V + Asp:Pfv (*-y-*) + PC-IIb + TM:Sjv (*bhane*) + (X) = *Subjunctive Perfective*
1sg. *āe˜bhane* 'if I come'
3sg. *āyo/āī* 'if he/she comes'
19. V + Asp:Pfv (*-y-*) + PCIIb + TM:Pmv (*holā*) + (*) = *Presumptive Perfective*
1sg. *āe˜hu˜/lā* 'I probably came'
3sg. *āyo/āī* 'He/she probably came'
20. V + Asp:Pf (*-ek-*) + AC + TM:Pr (*cha*) + PC-IIa = *Present Perfect*
1sg. *āeko/āekī chu* 'I (M/F) have come'
3sg. *āeko cha/āeki che* 'He/she has come'
21. V + Asp:Pf (*-ek-*) + AC + TM:P1 (*thiyo*) + PC-IIb = *Past Perfect*
1sg. *āeko/āekī thie˜* 'I (M/F) had come'
3sg. *āeko thiyo/āekī thiī* 'He/she had come'
22. V + Asp:Pf (*-ek-*) + AC + TM:Pmv (*holā*) + AC* = *Presumptive Perfect*
1sg. *āeko hu˜lā/āekī hu˜lī* 'I (M/F) must have come'
3sg. *āeko holā/āekī holī* 'He/she must have come'

Comments: In luxuriance of forms, Nepali rivals Marathi. Quite a number of them (e.g., nos. 7–10 and their corresponding T/M forms) are merely alternates, however. Still others could be listed; cf. Korol´ev (1968). Although the full array of gender variants has been given, gender tends to be lost in Spoken Nepali (Matthews 1984: 44–5). With Nepali, however, we return to an area, albeit marginally, accustomed to making number distinctions in verbs (as well as honorific distinctions – an elaborate system not given here). The plural forms are distinct from those given above.

The term *Proximate* for the Aspect form in nos. 3 and 4 is borrowed from Verma and Sharma (1979b). Matthews (1984) calls the forms in question the *Infinitival Future* and *Infinitival Conditional*. Korol´ev calls no. 3 the *Indefinite Future* (*"budushchee neopredelennoe deistvie"*), which is something of a misnomer since this is the most definite of the Nepali Futures (Matthews 1984: 226). The use of the Present Habitual to refer to future action (particularly shortly impending future action) is widespread in NIA but is taken special note of in the gloss of no. 5 because it is apparently more common in Nepali.

The verb *āunu* is perhaps not the best for illustrating certain morphological features. The /n/ element in nos. 5 and 6 is reduced to /˜/ after stems having such a phonological shape (and lost entirely after consonant stems): this /˜/ should not be confused with the /˜/ in no. 2 (and in the Presumptive Auxiliary), where it is part of the 1st person marker *-u˜*.

This concludes our tour of NIA paradigms. Their general structure should now be clear. It is hoped that this together with the information in the preceding sections will help in approaching languages and dialects not covered in section 9.5.

9.6 **Verb stem I: valence and voice**

The *inflectional component* of the NIA verbal system treated in the preceding sections (9.2–9.5), while complex and not without interest, particularly in the capacity for expansion and refinement of its three categories, is really not so different from that of many languages around the world. A more distinctive feature of NIA appears when we turn our attention to the remaining element, the *verb stem* itself (V). Although the mechanisms involved are arguably "derivational" rather than "inflectional", those dealt with in this section are at any rate "morphological". The topic of this section might therefore be called *morphologically related stems*.

Theoretically, Voice and Valence are quite different matters and should be kept distinct (Magier 1983: 223). *Valence* is concerned with the number of necessary arguments ("participants") implied by a verb stem, and thus with transitivity (two arguments, three in the case of "double transitives" such as *give* and *feed*) intransitivity (one argument), and causativity (more than one argument, often three, sometimes four). With a handful of exceptions in each language, a NIA primary stem is inherently marked as transitive or intransitive. This *basic* valence can be *altered* (increased or decreased) *morphologically*, resulting in secondary stems. In the ideal world of classical transformational grammar, *Voice* involves a shift of focus from Agent to Patient (or, in some languages, possibly to certain other arguments also), *without* altering the total number of arguments (or the "meaning" of the sentence whatsoever). (Passivization in this sense has probably received far more attention than its importance in most NIA systems warrants. But as will be seen, it has other senses, or functions, in NIA.)

In practice, however, the distinction between the two is blurred. Historical passives come to have an intransitive sense (i.e. with no second argument implied). Derived intransitives often can be translated only by English passives (which suggests the latter may have a double function), producing a secondary confusion at the level of description. NIA passives have characteristic functions that do alter the "meaning" of the sentence. Finally, the influence of English on journalistic and scholarly writing has affected the function and behavior of passives in ways that may obscure these more typical functions.

The initial raw material for the NIA system comes, as usual, from Sanskrit – from the passive in {*-yá*}, following the weak grade of the root, and the causative in {*-áya*}, with an alternate *-paya* after roots ending in /*-ā*/, following a strengthened grade of the root (basically *guṇa*, but *vr̥ddhi*, that is, /*ā*/, in the case of /*a*/). Reanalyzed as *-āpaya*, the alternate became the productive form of the causative, extended to other roots early in the history of Sanskrit itself.

In Early MIA, the passive developed (apparently in the west) as *iyya*, thence (in Prakrit and Apabhramsa) as *ijja*. This was the transparent source, in accordance with regular NIA phonological developments (VCCV > V:C, but > S. VC), of the so-called inflectional passives found in the Western languages: Marwari, Siraiki *-īj-*, Sindhi *-(i)j-*, Shina *-iʒ-* (information is lacking for other "Dardic" languages, except Kashmiri, where the suffix is absent). The weak root-vowel pattern of OIA continues to prevail (except in secondary passives from causatives): Sir. *mār-/marīj-* 'beat/be beaten', *ḍē/ḍivīj* 'give/be given' (Shackle 1976). In Sindhi, it should be noted that passives have a different imperfective Participle and therefore Future formation, in *-ibō* instead of the *-ando* of primary intransitives (themselves sometimes of earlier passive origin).

The *īj*-suffixes were formerly more widespread in the west (e.g., in Old Marathi), and were not totally unknown in the center (e.g., in Old Braj [McGregor 1968: 157]) and east, but there another version of the suffix, in *ī(y)a* or *i(y)a*, seems to have prevailed (Chatterji 1926: 910–18), one which was phonologically more vulnerable. Although its NIA reflex, *-ī-*, is found in Early Bengali, Maithili, Oriya, Hindi, etc., it has been preserved (except for isolated forms, such as H. *cāhiye* 'is wanted', B. *cāi*) only in Nepali (*gar-/gari-* 'do/be done' and almost all verbs). (The *-ī* suffixes of Dogri and of Shahpuri "Lahnda" may be from this, or they may be reduced forms of *-īj*.) In Sinhalese, this MIA suffix was the original source of the Third or *-e-* Conjugation, intransitive or "involitive" in meaning (and thus a matter of *Valence*), extended as a productive formation to nearly all verbs (Geiger 1938: 139): *palanavā/pælenavā* 'split (tr/intr)'.

In some NIA languages, notably Gujarati (and marginally in Bhojpuri, Maithili, Magahi, and Awadhi), there is a different passive suffix, *-ā*: *āp-/apā-* 'give/be given'. Chatterji (1926), following a suggestion of Grierson's, supports its derivation from the OIA *denominative* suffix *-āya*. See also Saksena (1971: 293–4). Bloch (1965: 238) objects that the OIA form had "no special force" and clear antecedents go back only to MIA.

With the decay of passive suffixes, or even with their preservation, NIA languages turned to periphrastic methods of expressing a passive. In Marathi, Gujarati, and Kashmiri, it was to a case form (Ablative or Locative) of the Infinitive + the verb *come*: M. *karṇyāt ye-* 'be done'; in Sinhalese to the Infinitive + *labanu* 'receive'. In the majority of NIA languages, however, it was, in its later phase, to the Perfective Participle (in *-(y)ā*, or *-al* in the Bihari group), or in the easternmost languages to an invariant verbal noun in *-ā* resembling it, + the verb *jā-* 'go', which serves as the conjugational base.

Chatterji supports an earlier suggestion of Beames that this choice was influenced by the resemblance of *jā-*, particularly in the earlier version of the construction using the Conjunctive Participle in *-i* (=*-i + jā-*, still preserved in Dogri) instead of the Perfective, to the Apabhramsa *-ijja*. Although the latter was more Western than Eastern, it was Western Apabhramsa that served as the basis of the literary medium prevalent across northern India during this formative period. In view of this, the passive with *jā-* may be regarded as a complex verbal stem rather than a syntactic construction, albeit derived quasi-analytically rather than morphologically. Similar kinds of reinterpretation of weakening morphological material in terms of phonologically similar independent words, thereby snatching it, as it were, from the brink of destruction, reoccur a number of times in the development of both NIA and Dravidian, and may be called a characteristic feature of pan-Indic linguistic dynamics. It is the reverse side of the process that has turned originally independent words into morphemes.

Periphrastic or suffixal, the NIA passives are notable in their applicability to intransitives as well as transitives. The result is impersonal (or "involitive") verbs, expressing the helplessness or non-volitionality of the erstwhile agent, if any.

Turning now to the causative line of development, the MIA reflex of the original *strengthened grade* + *-aya* was (*long vowel stem*) + *-ē*. That is, except in Konkani, where *-aya* itself (like the *-th* of the OIA 2pl.) mysteriously survives – a reminder that Literary MIA shows only a limited part of the historical picture. Otherwise, the original causative morpheme eventually merged with personal endings (*-ayati* > *-ēti* > *ēdi* > *ēi*) and did not survive except indirectly in the Marathi and Sindhi transitive endings, as noted earlier. The strengthened grade of the root entailed by the lost morpheme, however, survived as a mark of transitivity in most languages – albeit not a 100 per cent reliable one, since primary *intransitives* with long vowels as well as primary *transitives* with short vowels also existed. In any case, the pattern Weak Grade: Intransitive::Strong Grade:Transitive was extended by analogy in both directions, above all in Hindi, where a whole series of *derived intransitives* has been produced by "re-weakening" a root which had not been strengthened in the first place: H. *mãjh-* 'be scoured', from *mā̃jh-* 'scour' < OIA *mārjati*. (Because of the obligatory English translation, these are sometimes miscalled Passives, or Passive-Neuters, but they are reduced-Valence verbs rather than passives.)

Meanwhile, the pseudo-allomorph *-āpaya*, launched on its independent career, became (with normal *-p-* > *-v-*) *-āvē-* in MIA, which even after the fusion of the *-ē* with the personal endings was substantial enough to resist total phonetic erosion. The basic causative marker through much of NIA today is in fact this same *-āv-* (in Bhojpuri, Awadhi, Gujarati, West Rajasthani), generally pronounced [*āw*], or equivalent *-āu-* (in Nepali, Punjabi, Braj). In Kashmiri it is *-(an)āw*; in Maithili the /*v*/ is hardened to *-āb-*; in Marathi the vowel is shortened in accordance with the peculiar stress effects in that language (see Chapter 7) to *-av-*. In Kumauni only *-ū* remains (Apte and Pattanayak 1967: 44). Here care must be taken: the /*u*/ element is dropped in a number of conjugational forms (for example in Punjabi with the Perfective morpheme *-i-*: *ban-* 'take shape' > *banāu-* 'make', but Pfv. Msg. *banāiā*), leading some descriptions to treat it as a "euphonic element" coming in at certain points, and to take the suffix as *-ā-*. In view of its historical legitimacy, it is preferable to take the suffix as *-āu*/*āv-* if the /*u*/ or /*v*/ is regularly present at any point in the conjugation. It is only lost entirely, giving way completely to *-ā-*, in Standard Hindi–Urdu, Bengali, Oriya, Sindhi (where it is followed by the transitive conjugation-sign *-i-*), "Lahnda", Eastern Rajasthani, Bundeli, and Sinhalese. In Assamese, it is still present in an alternative form of the suffix, *-uwā*. (In Bengali it may also be said to lurk in the "alternative" causative marker {*-o*, *-u*} [Seely 1985: 168–70], and even in Hindi, in the isolated causative *bhigo-* 'wet, drench' < *bhīg* 'get wet': **-āu* > **-au* > *-o*.)

There are also, however, competing causative suffixes of more obscure origin. Chief among these are *-ār* or *-ar*, the regular suffix in Shina, also found in Kashmiri, Sindhi (frequently: *uṭh-*/*uṭhār-* 'rise/raise', *ɗhu-*/*ɗhuār-* 'be washed/wash'), Awadhi, Chhattisgarhi, the perhaps related *-āḍ* (Gujarati, Malvi), and *-l*, *-āl* (Hindi, Nepali, Siraiki). The different suffixes, or the same suffix, may combine, giving *double causatives*: G. *-āvḍāv*, *-āḍāv*, Mth. *-abāeb*, S. *-ārā(i)*, Bhoj. WR. *-(a)vāv*. This procedure has preserved a /*v*/ even in those languages which have lost it, by resegmentation, as the initial of a *Second Causative* marker: **-āv + āv* > **-avāv* > **-(a)vā(v)* > *-vā*. Bengali, Oriya, and Marathi have no Second Causatives in this sense.

The purpose of a Second Causative can best be understood by looking at the purpose of a First Causative, which is twofold: (1) to turn primary intransitives into transitives (by an alternative and simpler procedure than the vowel-strengthening inherited from OIA): H. *uṭh-/uṭhā-* 'rise/raise, lift', *cal-/calā* 'go/drive, operate (make go)' alongside *mar-/mār-* 'die/kill, beat', *khul-/khōl-* 'open' (intr/tr); G. *cal-/calāv-* alongside *ughaḍ-/ughāḍ-* 'open' (intr/tr); (2) to turn primary transitives, *or* transitives derived by the "old" method, into indirect causatives, that is, entailing getting something done by another person: *kar-/karā-* 'do/have done by someone', *kāṭ-/kaṭā-* 'cut/have cut by someone'.[16] A (morphological) Second Causative enables the formation of (functional) indirect causatives from secondary transitives made with the First Causative (H. *uṭhā-/uṭhvā-* 'lift/have lifted by someone'. Otherwise, i.e. in a language without a Second Causative such as Bengali, indirect causatives can be formed only from primary transitives: *kɔr-/kɔrā-* 'do/get done by someone'. Secondary transitives derived by the "old" (vowel-strengthening) method (a residual rather than a productive category in Bengali, and involving only the alternation /ɔ/ā/) can add the causative *-ā*, but the result, according to Seely (1985: 166–7), is not an indirect causative but only a kind of doublet: *pɔṛ-/pāṛ-*, *pāṛā-* 'fall/throw down, fell, lay (an egg), pluck (fruit)'; *cɔl-/cāl-*, *cālā* 'move/cause to move, drive, operate' (also: 'shake down or pick fruit from a tree, cause to fall'). Indirect causation is expressed in such cases periphrastically.

In the languages that have it, the Second Causative also forms doublets without basic semantic contrast (though one or the other may be preferred in a given situation) when used with a primary transitive: H. *kar-/karā*, *karvā-* 'do/get done by someone'. (The case of semi-transitives [see note 16] must be distinguished: *paṛh-/paṛhā-/paṛhvā-* = 'read, study/teach/have taught by someone'.) However, in some languages, notably Sinhalese, it has replaced a weakened First Causative. (There is some disagreement over whether the formally Second Causative of Assamese in *-owā* is a contrasting – i.e. indirect – or merely an alternative form: *dekh-/dekhā-/dekhowā-* [Babakaev 1961] 'see/show/have someone show' or *dekhā-*, *dekhowā-* = 'show'?) To compound the confusion, in some languages, e.g., Braj, Siraiki, the Second Causative morpheme is used with vowel stems to form their First Causative: Br. *khā-/khabāu-*, Sir. *khā-/khavā* 'eat/feed'.

The unpredictable and therefore derivational character of the causative formations is underlined by the fact that (First) Causatives (derived transitives) will be found to be formed from the same root by the "old" (strengthened-vowel) method in some languages and by the "new" (suffixal) method in others (and sometimes by both methods in the same language): M. *car-/cār-* 'graze (intr/tr)', H. *car-/carā-*; S. *caṛh-/cāṛh-* 'climb/cause to go up, offer', H. *caṛh-/caṛhā-*; N.

khul-/khol- ‘open (intr/tr)’, also N. *khul-/khulā-*. However, interesting parallels run across many languages, e.g., the stem *khā-* ‘eat’ has the allomorph *khu-* (or *kho-*) before the causative marker in Oriya, Assamese, Nepali, Punjabi (alternate), Kumauni, Maithili, etc.

The more basic of the above facts are summarized on Figure 9.8 below. Only

P = morphological Passive marker
(P) = “analytic” Passive formation
I = First Causative marker (including original Second Causatives that have replaced First Causatives)
II = Second Causative marker

[Sh. P: *-iʒ-;* I: *-ar-*]

K.
(P: Inf.^{ABL}+*yi-*)
I: *-(in)āw-*

P.
(P: Pfv.+*jā-*)
I: *-āu-*
II: *-vāu-*

Ku.
P: *-ī-*
I: *-ā-*, *-ū-*

N.
P: *-i-*
I: *-āu-*

L.
P: *-īj-*
I: *-ā-*
II: *-vā-*

H.
(P: Pfv.+*jā-*)
I: *-ā-*
II: *-vā-*

A.
(P: *-ā* + *zā-*)
I: *-ā-*, *-uwā-*
?II: *-owā-*

S.
P: *-(i)j*
I: *-ā-*, *(-ār-)*
(II: *-ārā-*)

ER.
(P: Pfv+*jā-*)
I: *-ā-*
II: *-vā-*

Br.
(P: Pfv+*jā-*)
I: *-āu-*
II: *-bāu-*

Mth.
(P: Pfv+*jā-*)
I: *-āb-*
II: *-abāeb-*

WR.
P: *-īj-*
I: *-āv-*
II: *-vāv-*

Aw.
P: *-ā-*
(P: Pfv.+*jā-*)
(P: ^{OBL}+*āv-*)
I: *-āv-*
II: *-avāv-*

Bhoj.
P: *-ā-*
(P: Pfv.+*jā-*)
I: *-āv-*
II: *-(a)vāv-*

G.
P: *-ā-*
I: *-āv-*, *-āḍ-*
II: *-ā(v)ḍāv-*

Bu.
(P: Pfv.+*-jā-*)
I: *-ā-*
II: *-vā-*

B.
(P: *-ā* + *jā-*)
I: *-ā-*, *(-o-)*

Ch.
I: *-ā-*, *(-o-)*
II: *-(a)vā-*

M.
(P: Inf^{LOC}+*ye-*)
I: *-av-*

O.
(P: *-ā* + *jā-*
I: *-ā-*

Ko.
I: *-ay(a)-*

Si.
< P: *-e-*
I: *-va-*

Figure 9.8 Regular Passive and Causative markers in NIA

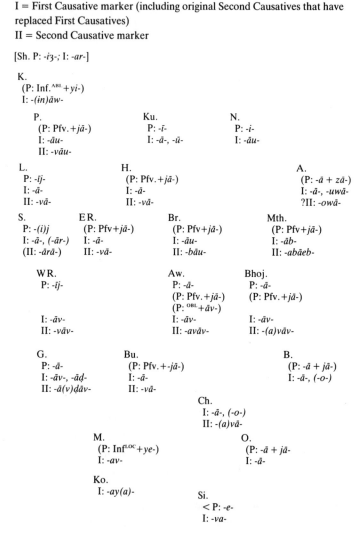

Comments on Figure 9.8

1. The "irregular" Sindhi and Gujarati causatives in *-ār-*, *-āḍ-* have been included because they are very common.
2. According to Egorova (1966: 78), the Sindhi Second Causative in *-ārā-* is used only to "emphasize" indirect causation. Otherwise the First Causative is used for indirect causation also.
3. There is a distinctive Second Causative marker only in some languages. In others (Awadhi, Bhojpuri, Maithili, Gujarati), the marker is a mechanical combination of two First Causative markers (from which the distinctive markers also originated through phonetic reduction). The Gujarati combinations are quite varied and irregular (see Cardona 1965).
4. Where passive formation is not shown, clear information has not been available.

the "regular" formatives are shown (the vowel-alternating method, though extended analogically in some languages, being considered for the purposes of Figure 9.8 "irregular" for NIA as a whole).

9.7 **Non-finite forms**

In anticipation of the next chapter, as well as of the final section of this chapter, it is necessary to give a brief survey of the more important non-finite forms of the verb, as they provide part of the raw material for those discussions. Some of them, namely the Imperfective and Perfective Participles (and more briefly the Conjunctive or Absolutive Participle) have already made their appearance in the preceding discussion of finite forms, into which they have entered as component parts, albeit generally not labelled as such, and disguised by our concern at that point with distinguishing the Aspect and the CONCORD markers. (We will now assume that these have been distinguished, and treat the full forms as they occur as words.) Their role in the finite verb may be called, historically rather than functionally speaking, secondary; here we meet them in their primary identity. To be sure, not all non-finite forms play a role in the finite verb. Moreover, those that do are sometimes now distinguished morphologically in their non-finite roles, which are "secondary" functionally even if not historically. In this section we shall not be concerned with their functions – except insofar as they suggest some basic labels[17] – but only with their formal identities.

NIA non-finite forms are basically of three kinds: (1) those with *nominal* functions (=N); (2) those with *adjectival* functions (=A); and (3) those with *adverbial* (or *adjunctual*) functions (=D). That is, the first may serve as subject or object and take case-endings and postpositions, the second may modify nouns (particularly attributively), and the third may serve as essentially adverbial adjuncts to the main sentence predication. NIA languages differ considerably in the number of forms over which these functions are spread. In some languages, there is partial overlap of forms with functions N and A, or A and D, or even N and D. These basic functions are sufficiently distinct, however, that it is easiest to consider them as separate forms in spite of this.

For example, in Hindi the "*-nā* form" is both *noun*, taking an oblique (*-ne*) + case-particles, and *adjective*, with gender variation (*-nī*) – but in quite different contexts and with quite different meanings. It is best to consider that there are two forms here, an *Infinitive*, as it is usually called, and a *Future Passive Participle* (some would add "*of Obligation*") = an adjective, albeit occurring only in predicative position: *aisī ciṭṭhī likhnā muśkil hai* 'To write such a letter is difficult' vs. *aisī ciṭṭhī likhnī hai* 'Such a letter is to be written (=You/someone has to write such a letter)'. The position is much the same with Gujarati *-vu˜*, Punjabi *-ṇā*, Sindhi *-aṇ*^{u}/*-iṇ*^{u}, and Kashmiri *-un*. In Figure 9.9 below, variable adjectival (A) forms will be given in the Masculine Singular Direct form (in Gujarati this is *-vo* not *-vu˜* which would be the Neuter form), with * to indicate their variability for gender (and number and sometimes case). Oblique nominal (N) forms will be listed separately (as N^{o}).

It is trickier where there is neither gender nor (primary) case to guide us. Both the Oriya (*-ibā*) and the Sinhalese (*-nnə*) "Infinitives" may be used as either nouns or adjectives, as may the Bengali form in *-ā*, *-oā*, *-no* (the differences are morphophonemic). In the latter case, however, the semantic difference between the nominal usage (*tā kɔrā ucit nɔe* '*To do* that is not proper') and the adjectival usage (in a *perfective* and passive sense: *tār lekhā ækkhānā boi* 'a book *written* by him' [cf. Page 1934]) is great enough to justify positing both a Verbal Noun and a Perfective (or "Past") Adjectival Participle – even though the two have a common origin (Chatterji 1926: 945, 1016). Further synchronic justification might be sought in the fact that before case-endings *-bā* (originally a separate form, now almost regardable as an "oblique base" – although Bengali nouns do not have oblique forms) is commonly substituted: *jābār dɔrkār* 'necessity of going' (*jāoār dɔrkar* is possible but less frequent), a feature obviously absent from the "participle".

The case is the opposite with the Bengali Infinitive and Imperfective ("Present") Participle, both in *-(i)te*. According to Chatterji, the former is the Locative (=B. *-te*) of an old verbal noun in *-i* (it has nothing to do with the Sanskrit Infinitive in *-tum*), the latter a Locative (in *-e*) of the MIA Present Participle in *-anta* > B. *-ita*. In function, however, there is an area of overlap where it is difficult to sort out the two. Unlike the Oriya and Assamese Infinitives in *-ibā*, *-ibɒ* (or the Infinitives of Hindi, Punjabi, etc.), the Bengali Infinitive is only used as a complement of the predicate, never as a subject – perhaps because there is the Verbal Noun in *-ā* available for that function (although such Verbal Nouns also exist in the first two languages). It is probably also the oblique case status of the

Bengali Infinitive that militates against such usage. (The Imperfective Participle is similarly restricted: it is used only adverbially, never attributively.)

The Marathi Verbal Noun in *-ṇe˜*, Obl. *-ṇyā-* (technically not an infinitive, in M. a separate form in *-ū˜*, despite its similarity to the Hindi form) has no such identity problems: its functions are purely nominal. However, it shares the nominal functions, not only with the Infinitive just mentioned (of very restricted usage as the complement of certain modals) but in the oblique case area with what Katenina calls "*Supines*", the forms *-āylā* 'in order to V' and *-āyċā∗*, a "Desiderative" adjectival (<Gen.) form with some nominal complement functions.

Most NIA languages have both Adjectival (A) and Adverbial (D) Imperfective (traditionally "Present") and Perfective (traditionally "Past") Participles, as well as the (adjectival) Future Participles "of obligation" already alluded to. (According to our scheme the latter would be *Unspecified.*) In the Eastern group, except perhaps Oriya, Adjectival Imperfective Participles based on the MIA Present Participle (B. *-ɔntɔ*, A. *-ɒntɒ*, O. *-ɔntā*) tend to be archaic and literary (Oriya, however, uses the *-ibā* form as an Imperfective Adjectival), but these languages also have a *Conditional* (adverbial) Participle (B. *-le*, O. *-ile*, A. *-ile/-ilɒt*). It can signify 'when' as well as 'if.' (The two Assamese forms are used with Future and Past main verbs respectively.)

In several Central–Western languages, Adjectival Participles, particularly when used attributively, are distinguished from their Finite Verb counterparts by special morphological or analytic extensions: M. Pfv. *-lelā∗*, G. Pfv. *-elo∗*, S. Pfv. -(Y)*al*^{u}∗ (thus extending Perfective *-l-* forms one step further northwest [see Figure 9.3]), S. Impfv. *-andaṛu∗/ -īndaṛu∗*, P. *-ndā∗ hoyā∗*, H. *-tā huā∗*. Imperfective Adverbial Participles (most commonly equivalent to 'while . . . -ing') are typically distinguished by use of "oblique" or of completely different forms: H. *-te (hue)*, S. *-andē/-īndē*, G. *-tā˜*, M. *-tā˜nā*, A. *-o˜te*, Si. *-min/-ddi*.

In the function of a Perfective Adverbial Participle (='*having* . . . *-ed*'), we have what is usually called the *Conjunctive* Participle (also variously the *Past* or *Past Active* Participle, or the *Absolutive* Participle), no doubt the most important NIA non-finite form (see Chapter 10 as well as section 9.8). Its usual form is *-ī* (O., A. *-i*). B. has *-e*, G. *-ī(ne)*, S. *-ī/-ē*, M. *-ūn*, K. *-ith*, Si. *-(l)lā* (Literary *-ā/-a/-ī*), but in H. and P., which use the extensions *kar*, *-ke*, one form (the "short" form) of the Conjunctive Participle, having lost the *-i*, coincides with the verb stem. In Nepali the *Absolutive* in *-i* is distinct from the Conjunctive Participle in *-era*, *-ī*, *-īkana*.

In most NIA languages, except apparently the Eastern group, there is also a regular secondary nominal formation (usually from the Oblique Infinitive) of an Agentive Adjective > Noun: H. *-vālā∗*, P. *-vāḷā∗*, S. *-vārō∗*, G. *-nār(o∗)*, M. *-ṇārā*. This also functions as a "Prospective Participle" ('about to V'), except in Gujarati and Marathi, where such forms are distinct (G. *-vāno∗*, M. *-ṇār*).

N = nominal forms:
- N1 = infinitives
- N2 = verbal nouns
- N3 = other
- N° = oblique of nominal form

A = adjectival forms:
- A1 = Unspecified ("future")
- A2 = Imperfective
- A3 = Perfective
- A4 = Desiderative and other
- * = gender (and other) variation

D = adverbial forms:
- D2 = Imperfective
- D3 = Perfective (Conjunctive Participle)
- D4 = Absolutive (if different from D3)
- D5 = Conditional
- D2a,b,c, etc. = subvarieties

Kashmiri

N1: *-un*
N1°: *-anis* (Dat.)
A1: *-un**
A3: *-mut**
D2: *-ān*
D3: *-ith*

Punjabi

N1: *-ṇā*
N1°: *-(a)ṇ-*
N1b: *-ṇo*
N2: *-iyā*
N2°: *-iye-*
A1: *-ṇā**
A2: *-ndā* hoyā**
A3: *-Yā* hoyā**
A4: *-idā**
D2a: *-ndiā̃*
D2b: *-nde*
D3a: *-ke*
D3b: ZERO

Nepali

N1: *-nu*
N1°: *-nā-*
N1b: *-na*
A1: *-ne*
(A2: *-ne*)
A3: *-eko**
D2a: *-da, dā, dai*
D2b: *-do**
D3a: *-era*
D3b: *-ī*
D3c: *-īkana*
D4: *-ī*

Hindi

N1: *-nā*
N1°: *-ne-*
(N2: *-yā*)
A1: *-nā**
A2: *-tā* (huā*)*
A3: *-(y)ā* (huā*)*
D2: *-te (hue)*
D3: *-kar, -ke*
D3b: ZERO

Assamese

N1: *-ib*
(N1°: *-ibɒ-*)
N2: *-ā*
[A2: *-ɒntɒ*]
A3: *-ā*
D2: *-õte*
D3: *-i*
D5a: *-ile*
D5b: *-ilɒt*

Figure 9.9 Principal non-finite forms in principal NIA

Comments on Figure 9.9

1. An objection to regarding the Punjabi "Short Infinitive" in *-(a)ṇ* as the *oblique* of the infinitive in *-ṇā* is that no other obliques are formed in this way. However, it has all the functions of oblique infinitives in other NIA languages.

Sindhi

N1: *-aṇu/iṇu*
N1°: *-aṇa-/iṇa-*
A1a: *-aṇu*/iṇū**
A1b: *-aṇo**
A2: *-andaṛu*/īndaṛu**
A3: *-Yalu**
D2: *-andē/īndē*
D3a: *-ī/ē*
D3b: *-ī/ē karē*
D3c: *-iō* (dial. *-iā*)

Gujarati

N1: *-vu˜*
N1°: *-vā-*
N3: *-yā*
A1: *-vo**
A2: *-to**
A3: *-elo**
A4: *-vāno**
D2: *-tā˜*
D3a: *-ī(ne)*
D3b: *-yā˜*

Bengali

N1: *-te*
N2: *-ā, oā, no*
N2°: *-bā-*
A3: *-ā, oā, no*
D2: *-te*
D3: *-e, ie*
D5: *-le*

Marathi

N1: *-ū(˜)*
N2: *-ṇe˜*
N2°: *-ṇyā-*
N3: *-āylā*
A2: *-t aslelā**
A3: *-lelā**
A4a: *-āvā**
A4b: *-āyčā**
D2a: *-tā˜nā*
D2b: *-t astā˜*
D3a: *-ūn*
D3b: *-lā* astā**

Oriya

N1: *-ibā*
(N1°: *-ibā-*)
N2a: *-ā*
N2b: *-lā*
A1: *-ibā*
A2a: *-ɔntā*
A2b: *-ibā*
A3: *-lā*
D2a: *-ɔnte*
D2b: *-u(˜)*
D3: *-i*
D5: *-ile*

Sinhalese

N1: *-nnə*
N2a: *-īma*
N2b: *-illa*
N3: *-nā/nī*
A1: *-nnə*
A2: *-na*
A3a: *-u/ā/uṇu/iya*
A3b: *-(ā)pu, icca*
D2a: *-min*
D2b: *-ddi*
D3: *-(l)lā* [L.S.*-ā/a/ī*]

2. *Unextended* Pfv and Impfv participles are found in attributive adjectival function in Gujarati and Marathi only in fixed expressions, mainly dealing with time: G. *āvte aṭhvāḍie* 'next week', *gae aṭhvādie* 'last week'; M. V-*te samayī˜/veḷī˜* 'at the time when . . .'

9.8 Verb stem II: Aktionsart and the compound verb

Besides that discussed in section 9.6 above (which might be represented as V ⟶ V+, V−) the V (*verb stem*) component may be expanded in another way: V ⟶ Vv. It will be found that any descriptive grammar of a NIA language has a section (usually inadequate) devoted to the phenomenon most commonly known as the *compound verb*.[18] This is one of the true innovations of NIA, unknown to Sanskrit. It does, however, have clear analogues in Dravidian, and perhaps further afield as well.

The compound verb, as might be guessed from its usual but possibly confusing label ("compounds" of *nouns* or *adjectives* with the verbs *do* and *become* also have an important place in NIA: these are now usually called *conjunct* verbs to distinguish them, although that term might have been really more appropriate for the phenomenon now under discussion), consist of a close union of *two verbs* (Vv). The "first" or main verb (V) is in the form of the Conjunctive Participle: a more precise formula would therefore be V ⟶ $V^{conj\,ppl}v$. The "second" verb (v) is drawn from a small set of special auxiliaries, which have been called *intensifiers*, *operators*, *explicators*, or more recently *vectors*: typically *go*, *come*, *give*, *take*, *fall*, *rise*, *throw*, *put*, *sit*. Partially emptied of their lexical content, these modify the meaning of the main verb in various ways not unrelated to that content, which might best be described as *manner-specification* (including directionality, completeness, suddenness, violence, deliberateness, stubbornness, benefaction, affectivity, etc.).

In Hindi and Punjabi a Short Form of the Conjunctive Participle is used which is identical with the stem – thus in effect directly compounding two stems.[19] In other languages, the Conjunctive Participle in this function does not have its usual implication of "prior action" and might better be termed an Absolutive. In Nepali, where the Absolutive is distinct from the Conjunctive (or Perfective Adverbial) Participle, it is only the former that is used in these forms. Whatever the form of the "first" verb, the two behave as a unit (separable only by certain emphatic particles) – although conventionally *written* separately – with the "vector" normally taking the Aspect, Tense/Mood, and CONCORD markers pertaining to the whole: H. *ā jāo*, *ā jāegā*, *ā jātā thā*, *ā gayā* 'Come!, he/it'll come, he/it used to come, he/it came'.

(It is necessary to say "normally", and to put "first" and "second" in quotes above, because under certain circumstances, usually entailing emphasis on the speed of the action, the ordering can be reversed, in which case the *main* verb – now in second position [=vV], takes the desinence: *ciṭṭhī likh mārī* '[He] dashed off a letter' [normal] *ciṭṭhī mār likhī* [reversed, further emphasizing the speed]. The example is Hook's [see Hook 1974: 55–65 and 1978b: 135–6]. At least this is possible in Hindi. Other languages, especially those where the Conjunctive Participle suffix does not have a ZERO allomorph, need more investigation.)

The Hindi example *ā jāo* is an appropriate one for illustrating two additional points: the untranslatability of the vectors in many instances (into English, at any rate), and their loss of lexical meaning: the vector used here, *jā-*, from the H. verb *go*, obviously does not mean 'go' in this context, since the meaning of the whole expression is 'come'!

Compound verbs occur with all Tense/Mood and Aspectual combinations (except perhaps the {*rah-*} Continuous, with which they are extremely rare), but are most common with the Unspecified Perfective and the Imperative, and less frequent with the Future. In Hindi, although they may occur with the negative under conditions of special emphasis, and are even preferred in certain formally negative expressions (e.g. *until*-clauses), under negation they are normally replaced by simple verbs, so that Hook makes such deletability part of the definition of the *vector* (distinguishing it, for example, from the second of two clausal verbs conjoined under the Conjunctive Participle construction [see Chapter 10]). The compound verb is rare with modals and in certain non-finite forms, especially the Conjunctive Participle. (Different NIA languages have slightly different rules, however.) Hook also points out that it may not occur in catenation with "phasal" verbs (*begin*, *stop* + V).

Although compound-verb formation is obviously a matter of derivation rather than inflection, it is highly structured, as Hook (1974 and 1978b) has demonstrated, in spite of also including some phenomena which must be described as idiomatic. Advice given in some manuals that they "must be learned as vocabulary items" ignores the massive generalizations that can be made. To be sure, the latter often involve levels of cognition unfamiliar to speakers of Western European languages and difficult to formulate in terms of them.

As noted earlier (section 9.3), certain similarities between functions of NIA vector verbs and those of the verbal prefixes in Slavic languages have led Pořízka followed by Hook to postulate an "aspect"-marking role for the vectors, and a perfective-marking role in particular. Some objections to this have already been listed: (1) there is already an aspect-marking *morphological* system in place in NIA, which is consequently ignored (or confused with tense, which is thereby also misconstrued); (2) the aspect-marking role of the Slavic prefixes themselves can be questioned (Aronson 1985); (3) use of *vectors* in NIA is not uniform for all verbs, but governed by lexical semantics. More objections may now be added.

Although the NIA vectors – like the Slavic prefixes – have been held to be markers of Perfective Aspect, both are compatible with non-perfective forms on the suffixal level: H. *ā jātā thā* 'used to come', *pardā girā jātā hai* 'the curtain falls (down)' [stage direction], e.g., with Imperfective {*-t-*}. (The last example is quoted by Pořízka 1981 in an article trying to make the opposite argument. When such arguments are being made, the Imperfective Participle is not called that, but "*present participle*" or "*participle I*".) If it has already been decreed that such forms are "tense"-indicating rather than aspectual, then of course they do not constitute counter-examples, but the argument becomes circular. The pivotal case purporting to show that the {*t*} form is aspectually either perfective or imperfective in H., namely the non-finite construction V-*te hī*, taken to be equivalent to 'as soon as [X] V-ed', can be interpreted more literally as 'while [X] was yet V-ing', retaining its imperfectivity.

The argument for perfectivity hinges on the alleged common behavior of the Slavic prefixes and the NIA vectors (or, more properly, the Hindi vectors: Hook's position is that, for example, the Marathi vectors, which do not meet these tests, have not developed into such a system) *collectively*: there is very little correspondence in detail, in terms of individual prefixes and vectors. Thus such characteristic Slavic prefixes as *po-* 'do something for a little while' and *za-* 'begin to do something' have no counterparts in NIA, nor do the most basic NIA transitive vectors, *give* (do something for someone else) and *take* (do something for oneself), have functional counterparts among the Slavic prefixes. Those few for which some vague equivalence may be found have, as noted earlier, equally plausible "equivalents" among the (non-aspect-marking) German prefixes and English adverbial particles (*smash up*). A much closer analogy is to be found in the resultative verbs of Chinese and allied languages – starting with the fact that it is *verbs* that are involved – and, of course, even more with the compound verbs of Dravidian languages, which have much the same set of lexical verbs in much the same range of functions. (It must be reported that "aspectual" claims have also been made for the latter: see Schiffman 1979, Fedson 1981. The merits of these cannot be discussed here.)

The clinching argument against locating Aspect in the compound verb rather than in the suffixal morphology of NIA, however, is the chief problem of NIA syntax, namely *split ergativity* (see next chapter). It hinges on perfectivity in the latter sense, never in the former sense. (To avoid the use of the term *perfective* here, rather elaborate circumlocutions are necessary: e.g., Hook and Koul's [1984] "verb forms based on the OIA past passive participle".)

All things considered, the functions of the NIA vector verb are best described under *Aktionsart* rather than Aspect. Conceivably, in the case of the vectors of most general meaning (*go* with intransitives, perhaps also *give* and *take* with transitives) we might speak of incipient grammaticalization in the direction of something sometimes called "aspect". Even with these, however, there is something further involved in each case besides whatever general meaning is deemed to be there, in the case of *give/take* especially, something (the benefactive/affective distinction) of seemingly greater importance. Whatever quasi-aspectual implication may also be there is different in kind from Aspect as it is usually understood (and usefully understood) cross-linguistically. It is a question of "completeness" vs. "completion", of a *specification of the latent semantics of individual verbs*. E.g., the action of a transitive verb is potentially either for the benefit of the agent or for the "benefit" of someone or something else – directed back toward or away from the agent, in other words, but this remains *latent* in NIA until specified by vectors *take* and *give*, even when, as in the case of verbs like *eat*, *strike* (or the main verbs *take* and *give* themselves), such information appears redundant: see Katenina 1957, Hacker 1958, Bahl 1967, and Masica 1976.

A totally different name would be less confusing, ideally one more descriptive of the elusive common function of such elements in a number of languages (i.e. the Slavic, German, Greek, and Hungarian – and Sanskrit – prefixes, NIA and Dravidian vector verbs, Chinese and Southeast Asian resultatives). Let me therefore tentatively propose one: *specification*; the elements themselves would be *verbal specifiers*. There is perhaps some analogy, in the deeper semantics of language, to specification (or *definiteness marking*) in the noun, although the verbal system is richer.

To be sure, the set of vectors might be looked upon as a reservoir of potential grammatical markers. The Continuous marker (in many NIA languages) {*rah-*} may have had such an origin (Lienhard 1961). If so, it is important to note that in the process of its grammaticalization it has lost certain properties, namely the ability which vectors normally have to take any finite desinence. As a Continuous marker, {*rah-*} occurs only in a form (appropriate to each language) formally homonymous with (but having lost the value of) the Perfective: H. -(Ø) *-ā*∗, S. *-yo*∗, Bhoj. *-al*, N. *-eko*∗. (The form apparently originated from an expression literally meaning 'He has/had/will have *remained* [>*continued*] doing so-and-so'.)

One of the interesting facts about the NIA vector sets looked at cross-linguistically is their *semantic* rather than etymological equivalence. Naturally some vectors are etymologically equivalent also: *go* ("transition") = *jā-*, *ja-*, *zā-*, *ya-* in most languages (but Sindhi *vañ-*), and *give* ("benefactive") = *de-*, *di-*, *ḍi-*, *dā-*. But *take* ("affective" or "reflexive") = H.G. *le-*, M. *ghe-*, S. *vaṭh-*, B. *nā-*, O. *ne-*, Si. *gan-*, and *throw/drop* ("do violently/carelessly/suddenly") = H. *ḍāl-*, G. *nākh-*, Raj. *nāk̄h-*, M. *ṭāk-*, B. *phæl-*, O. *pakā-*, A. *pedā*, N. *hāl-*, Si. *dama-*. Naturally there is some variation in inventory and function over the NIA area, but the basic core correspondences carry on into Dravidian.

Moreover, what Hook (1974: 120–44) calls "unusual vector verbs" (bringing his total to twenty-two) in Hindi often involve playful or slangy substitution of another lexical verb with semantic implications similar to those listed (e.g., *mār-* 'strike', for *ḍāl-*, 'with more extreme connotations'; *khaṛā** *ho-* 'stand up' for *paṛ-* 'fall' or *baiṭh-* 'sit', denoting suddenness and/or a regrettable act; *dhar-* 'put, throw', for *ḍāl-*, *rakh-*). Cf. Gujarati *āp-* as well as *de-* ("benefactive"). The vector set, while limited, is thus permeable, to new shades of meaning and new distinctions also. An absolute boundary for the vector set is somewhat difficult to draw (at least in Hindi) because of what Hook calls the *sub-synonymy* phenomenon: reinforcement of a given main verb by another verb close to it in meaning: *kho choṛā* 'losing-left behind', *ā pahũcā* 'coming-arrived'.

The close parallels to the compound verb in Dravidian have raised questions concerning its possible origin. Results have been inconclusive. Although Hook notes the phenomenon can be traced back in Indo-Aryan as far as Pali, its flowering seems to have been in recent NIA. Historical study is handicapped by the fact that the phenomenon seems to be colloquial in origin (cf. English *he up and did it*), finding its way only slowly and incompletely into written records. Descriptive studies of other NIA languages complementary to Hacker's (1958) and Hook's basic studies for Hindi need to be undertaken, but as Hook has shown, they cannot rely exclusively on literature, but must also make use of eavesdropping and multiple-informant judgment techniques, since the cutting edge of this phenomenon is clearly in everyday speech and some of its manifestations are still to be found only there.

10

Syntax

10.1 **Introduction**

If historical phonology was the queen of the older linguistic sciences, it is clearly syntax that has occupied the throne since the Chomskyan revolution. What had been an often perfunctory appendage (in traditional, and also structuralist, grammars), has become the starting-point as well as the driving force of grammars in the new mold. To be sure, by no means all traditional grammars neglected syntax. The treatment in Kellogg's old (second edition, 1892) grammar of Hindi, for example, is very extensive (152 pages), perhaps more so than that of any modern *general* work (although now we have whole books devoted to specific syntactic problems). Such interest in syntax was at the discretion of the author, however, and could not be generally expected. Phonology and morphology could not be avoided in treatment of a language, but syntax could be and often was. The new breed of linguist typically begins to grapple with syntax at the outset. Even work consciously outside the transformational–generative framework (TG), such as that in typology, tagmemics, and so-called functionalist grammar, has focused unprecedented attention on syntax. Much of the work on NIA languages over the past three decades has accordingly been in this field.

The relegation of this chapter to end-position, and its sketchy nature, imply no lack of recognition of this fact, but are due rather to the difficulty of making efficient use of it in the context of a language-family handbook. Our concern here is with cataloguing the main features of NIA in an accessible form. A great deal of the work on NIA languages just mentioned is what might be called theory-driven: it tests one phase or another of standard or anti-standard TG theory (and others), which have usually been framed on the basis of English, against the data of a NIA language.[1]

This is not to say that such work has not also, in the course of its theoretical preoccupations, managed to unearth many new facts about NIA, as well as to shed new light on previously-known ones. To attempt to review all this work, however, with due attention to all the intricate arguments and issues involved, would be tantamount to writing a history of linguistics over the past thirty years, which is not the purpose of this book. Even to try to distill from it all the hard "information" it contains (especially that specific to NIA languages as distinct from "any" language), embedded as it is in many different theoretical models, submodels, and stages of models, and to present it in a coherent form satisfactory to all would be very difficult. One would have to make a choice (already in itself not satisfactory to all) among various theoretical options still undergoing rapid evolution, and try to maintain this consistently, which would mean also extending it to untried areas. Even within particular models, a number of important issues pertaining to NIA are still unresolved. Moreover, many issues have not been explored to an equal degree in all the languages with which we are concerned. Often they have been explored mainly with reference to Hindi–Urdu, and the danger of extrapolating from that to other NIA languages will soon be apparent if it is not already.

It is convenient, in traditional terms, to divide the subject into the syntax of simple and of complex sentences. The new syntax – in some of its forms more than others – sees a great many things as complex (that is, as the result of combining two "underlying" sentences) that used to be treated as part of the grammar of the simple sentence or of the phrase: attributive adjectives, modal verbs, even causative morphology. This "derivational" approach is perhaps more rigorous than traditional parsing and taxonomy, especially in forcing consideration of all the grammatical relations involved. There is not, however, complete agreement as to what these underlying sentences (or derivational stages) are. In some formulations, underlying sentences are posited that cannot exist in the language concerned. At a further extreme of abstraction, we have moved from language to the realm of logic. That approach having been eschewed here as impractical, the *ad hoc* solutions which are adopted instead may be unsatisfactory to some, but it is hoped they are at least intelligible.

The domain of traditional syntax, properly conceived, was already very large: with the new syntax, which explores covert as well as "surface" relations, it has expanded exponentially. It must be understood, therefore, that what can be discussed below, especially in view of our multilingual concerns here, has to be very selective.

10.2 **The simple sentence: preliminaries**

10.2.1 *Word order*

The central fact of NIA syntax is the final position of the verb. In terms of basic types, the sentence consists (deferring the question of the roles of the NPs, and prior to any transformational reorderings or deletions) of:

a. NP + Vb (intransitive):
   1 (H.) *vah/ro rahī hai* 'She is weeping'
   2 (B.) *āmi/jābo* 'I shall go'
   3 (M.) *to/ālo* 'He came'
   4 (O.) *āme/kheluthilu* 'We were playing'

b. NP + NP + Vb (transitive):
   5 (Ko.) *tānne˜/mūsu/mārlo* 'He killed a fly' (Katre 1968: 169)
   6 (Si.) *mama/bat/kanavā* 'I eat rice'
   7 (B.) *rām/āmār boi/niāſbe* 'Ram will bring my book'

c. NP + NP + NP + Vb (double transitive):
   8 (G.) *modī/baīne/sāḍīo/batāve che* 'The dealer is showing some saris to the woman' (Lambert 1971: 30)
   9 (A.) *χikhɔkhe/sātɔribilākɔk/pāth/pɔrhāy* 'The teacher teaches the lesson to the students' (Babakaev 1961: 105)
   10 (O.) *mu˜/tumɔku/bɔhi/debi* 'I shall give you the book'

Indirect causatives, which also have the basic form of (c), are usually considered non-basic sentences.

The caveat "prior to deletions" must be particularly noted, because in Type (b) sentences, for example, either NP may be deleted in context (a type of pronominalization, unknown in English), yielding a sentence superficially similar to type (a), but not intransitive:

7a. *——/āmār boi/niāſbe* '(He) will bring my book'
7b. *rām/——/niāſbe* 'Ram will bring (it)'

This order also characterizes the neighboring Dravidian, Munda, Tibeto-Burman, Iranian, and Turkic languages (Masica 1976). It was also (despite many permitted stylistic permutations) the basic order of OIA (Speijer 1980 [1886]: 9–10), and very possibly of Proto-Indo-European itself (for a contrary view see Friedrich 1975). Depending on the answer to this last question, and apart from certain more specific instances in individual languages (e.g., Sinhalese), the extent of areal influence on the basic order of clause elements in NIA is unclear, and may have played mainly a reinforcing role. The differences between NIA and other IE languages would then presumably be due to contrary areal influences on the latter. Postpositions are another matter: Indian areal influence seems quite clear.

Adjuncts are placed normally somewhere before the verb (except for certain negative and interrogative elements in some languages, again really a matter of non-basic sentences, and to be treated separately below):

11 (B.) *āmi ṭrene gelām* 'I went *by train*'
12 (O.) *mu˜ bɔjārɔku gɔli* 'I went *to the bazaar*'
13 (Ko.) *pora˜ ghārā dhāvli˜* 'The children ran home' (Aiyagal 1968: 22)
14 (G.) *hu˜ thoḍi varmā˜ 'āvu˜ chu˜* 'I'm coming *soon*'
15 (B.) *tini āmāke bhitore ḍaklen* 'He called me *inside*'
16 (B.) *āmi tār kāch theke ciṭhi enechi* 'I have brought a letter *from him*' (Page 1934: 133)

Regarding the ordering of adjunctal elements (Time, Manner, Place, etc.) vis-à-vis one another, attempts have been made to state a normative order, but the nuances of emphasis – in which order plays a major role – are so delicate that it may be difficult to establish a truly "neutral" order, where no constituent has any implied prominence. Other things being equal, the position closest to the verb entails greatest prominence.

"Normally" implies a contrary possibility, and what is nowadays usually referred to as "rightward displacement", that is, movement to the right of the verb of either an adjunctual element or of one or another of the basic NP elements, is a not uncommon transformation (and thus again a matter of non-basic sentences) in most NIA languages.

Adjunct displacement:
17 (M.) *saraḷ zāytsə tyā devicyā devḷāparyanta* 'Go straight *as far as that temple of the goddess*' (Berntsen and Nimbkar 1975: 75)
18 (B.) *æmerikā ābiʃkār hɔe ʃāṛe cārʃo bɔchor age* 'America was discovered *four and one half centuries ago*' (Dimock et al. 1964: 61)

Basic NP displacement:
19 (A.) *χuniso˜mɔi 'I'm* listening' (Babakaev 1961: 105)
20 (Ko.) *koṇāk zāyi tuzo duḍu!* 'Who wants *your wealth*!' (Aiyagal 1968: 15)
21 (B.) . . . *(tāder ʃustho nā kore) tini ʃustho korechilen ʃiriyā-nibāʃi næmānke* '(Not curing them) he cured [instead] *Naaman the Syrian!*' (Luke 4:27, paraphrase)
22 (H.) *kisne bulāyā thā is nigorī īd ko?* 'Who asked for *this wretched Eed?*' (Premchand, *Idgah*)

The purpose of rightward displacement is either greater emphasis than can be attained in a position to the left of the verb (as in all the above examples), or in some cases, *de*-emphasis in the sense of "afterthought" or redundancy:

23 (H.) *nadī-kināre vāle jangal kā saudā karnā hai pāpā ko* 'He wants to negotiate for some riverbank woods (Papa does)' (Gulshan Nanda, *Ajnabi*, p. 126)

24 (H.) *aur kyā kahā usne?* 'What else did (he) say?' (ibid.: 126)

The difference between emphasis and de-emphasis seems to involve juncture and intonation, and deserves further study, but the emotional content of the two sentence types is so different that minimal pairs are unlikely. In any case, either kind of displacement is infrequent (2 per cent) in proportion to normally ordered sentences, and mainly confined to affective conversation (rare in literary prose). It would be useful to undertake actual counts in various registers. It is also likely that different NIA languages vary in the displacements they tolerate.

One clear exception to the above generalizations is Colloquial Sinhalese. There the frequently used so-called Emphatic forms of the verb regularly ("though not invariably") entail the rightward displacement of an emphasized constituent:

25 (Si.) *mē bas-eka kalutaraṭa yanavā* 'This bus is going to Kalutara'

25a (Si.) *mē bas-eka yanne kalutaraṭa* 'It is to K. that this bus is going'

25b (Si.) *mē bas-eka yanne dæŋ* 'This bus is going *now*'

25c (Si.) *kalutaraṭa yanne mēka* '*This one* is going to Kalutara' (Fairbanks et al. 1968: I.7, modified)

Because of this phenomenon, quasi-rule-governed rather than merely a stylistic option, there are proportionally many more sentences in Sinhalese where the verb is not final.

The case of Kashmiri is altogether different. As students of NIA have long noted, the *normal* order of constituents in this language differs strikingly from that of the rest of the family. Most notably, in main clauses the verb is not final. The result has been loosely compared to English (for example, by Grierson), but as Hook has shown in a series of papers exploring the question (1976a, 1984b, 1985, the last with Manaster-Ramer), the analogy is more with German. That is, the order is not NP Vb NP (NP), but rather V-2, as in German or Dutch: the finite verb comes second, whatever the first constituent, NP or Adjunct:

26 (K.) *rāman khyav batɨ* 'Ram ate food' (Hook 1976 < Kachru)

27 (K.) *rāth pyauv seṭhāh rūd* 'yesterday fell much rain' (Hook 1976 < Grierson)

Moreover, if the verb consists of an auxiliary or modal + a non-finite element, the latter is (usually) pushed to the end, again as in German:

28 (K.) *rāmɨ chu cāy cavān* 'Ram is/tea/drinking'
29 (K.) *rāmɨ heki batɨ khyath* 'Ram can/food/eat' (Hook 1976: 134
30 (K.) *prath vɜrī chus ɜmis guris trei phiri nāl laganāvān* 'Every year I-am/to this horse three times shoes/attaching' (Bailey 1937: 26)

Such separation of verbal elements never occurs elsewhere in NIA. When the phrase is kept together in Kashmiri, the normal NIA order of V + Aux, V + Modal is reversed:

31 (K.) *rāmɨ chu cavān cāy* (cf. ex. 28).
32 (K.) *rāmɨ heki khyath batɨ* (cf. ex. 29) (Hook 1976: 135)

When an Adjunct begins the sentence, the Verb-Second Rule has the effect of forcing the Subject to follow the verb:

33 (K.) *gāmas ɜkis manz ōs rōzān akh grūstā* 'In a certain village *was living* a farmer' (Bailey 1937: 25)

Stylistically marked[2] verb-initial sentences are also characteristic of the language. Finally, in some (but not all) types of subordinate clauses – which are not under consideration at the moment – the verb comes last, as in German. Hook finds it more economical to explain all this by applying Movement Rules to an underlying verb-final ("SOV") order, which fits the areal and historical relationships of Kashmiri. (Even closely-related dialects such as Poguli, Kishtawari, and Rambani are verb-final.) The complexity of Kashmiri word order is such, however, that Hook is forced to bring in discourse considerations in addition to the Movement Rules (which are unavoidable) to account for its many quirks and apparent exceptions, especially those involving subordinate clauses. (For details, see the papers cited.)

10.2.2 *The nominal sentence*

Not all NIA basic sentences have verbs, however. It is customary in traditional grammar to distinguish between verbal and nominal sentences (or more accurately, *predications*). In NIA languages which have overt copulas (Hindi, Punjabi, Kashmiri, Sindhi, Gujarati, Rajasthani, Marathi, Nepali), the latter do not differ greatly from verbal predications, except of course that the semantic relationship is different: the predicate identifies, defines, or locates. The copula is in final position like any verb (or in Kashmiri, in second position), and in particular like the T/M auxiliary with which it is usually identical. (Preceding nominal, adjectival, or locative complements can be displaced to the right of it for emphasis.) The participial component of many NIA verbal constructions has led some observers to remark on the "nominal" nature of the verbal predication itself: cf. H. *vah acchā hai* 'he is good'/*vah jātā hai* 'he goes', although such an analysis is perhaps not very helpful.

In eastern NIA, however, and in Sinhalese, verbless constructions (NP + NP, NP + Adj) are normative in such situations:

34 (B.) *eṭā/hinduder ekṭi tirthɔsthān* 'This is a sacred place of the Hindus'
35 (B.) *cā/toiri* 'Tea is ready'
36 (A.) *mɔi/ezɔni kerānī* 'I am a clerk' (Baruah 1980: 24)
37 (O.) *āji/mo jɔnmɔdinɔ* 'Today is my birthday'
38 (O.) *e khɔbɔrɔ/michɔ* 'This news is false' (Pattanayak and Das 1972)
39 (Si.) *eyā/hoňda minihek* 'He is a good man' (Garusinghe 1962: 94)
40 (Si.) *ē minihā/hoňda-y* 'That man is good'

No. 40 may or may not qualify, depending on how we treat the final {*-y*} (required only on adjectives ending in vowels: *magē yāluvā/pohosat* 'My friend is rich' = Literary *pohosat-i*). It is called an "assertion marker" by Fairbanks et al., a "particle" by Garusinghe, but a "verb of incomplete predication" by Bel'kovich.

Such constructions often entail an overt distinction between copular and existential/locative *be*-verbs in a language, with the former but not the latter "deleted" in the Present. (In languages like Hindi, there is no such distinction, and no deletion.) Such is the case in Sinhalese (ZERO 'copula' vs. *tiyenavā/innavā* 'exist [Inan/Anim]') but the matter is more complex in the Eastern group. In some cases, a verbless Locative predicate is also used:

41 (B.) *āmār bāṛī/ʃekhāne* 'My house is there' (Dimock et al. 1964: 37)
42 (A.) *mor sāti/duwārɒr osɒrɒt* 'My umbrella is near the door' (Baruah 1980: 36)
43 (O.) *morɔ bɔsā/ehi nikɔtɔre* 'My residence is right next door' (Karpushkin 1964: 89)

In other cases, the existential verb (Bengali *āche*, Oriya *ɔchi*) is put in, apparently dependent on discourse considerations, some of them having to do with *duration*. (It is always used when the construction is equivalent to *have*.) Even with adjectives, Oriya has such constructions as *se mo kāmɔre khusi ɔchɔnti* 'He is happy with my work', referring to a "definite segment of time" (Karpushkin 1964: 91) – rather than an identifying characteristic? This recalls certain Dravidian distinctions, where NP + NP sentences also constitute a regular type. Verbless predications are also characteristic of Sanskrit, however, often accompanied in the case of adjectives by a peculiar reversal of subject and predicate: *śītalā rātriḥ* 'Cold [is the] night'; *taruṇo'śvaḥ* 'Young [is the] horse' (Speijer 1980 [1886]: 1, 3).

Marginal to the Eastern area, Magahi and its Sadani offshoot have NP + NP but apparently not NP + Adj or NP + Loc: Mag. *ī macchiyā* 'This is a fly', Sad. *i to mor sahodar bhāi* 'This is my true brother!' (Jordan-Horstmann 1969: 115). The construction is present in Early but not in Modern Maithili (Jha 1958: 583), and seems not to characterize Bhojpuri. Nepali distinguishes, although not consistently, between definitional and locational–existential predicates by means of different verbs, *ho* vs. *cha* (Matthews 1984: 23), but the former is not deleted. Far to the south, Konkani has both constructions in what appear to be similar contexts:

44 (Ko.) *to pisso, tā˜ budvantu* 'He is dull, you are clever' (Katre 1966: 164)

45 (Ko.) *tiyo bāu uśār <u>assā</u>* 'Your brother is clever' (ibid: 164)

46 (Ko.) *to hagūr manuṣyu* 'He is an unassuming person' (Aiyagal 1968: 32)

47 (Ko.) *bāyl zoru <u>āsa</u>* '[His] wife is a shrew' (ibid: 32)

General suppression of the copula of the above kind should be distinguished from its (optional) deletion in pragmatically specific contexts, e.g., Marathi and Gujarati often delete the copula in predications involving deixis (including "introductions"):

48 (M.) *hī/bæŋk* 'This is the bank [pointing]' (V. Dharwadker, personal comm.)

49 (M.) *mī/bāpaṭ* 'I'm Bapat' (Berntsen and Nimbkar 1982)

50 (G.) *ā/māhrā moṭā bhāi* 'This is my elder brother' (Cardona 1965: 104)

Copula deletion of either kind in independent basic sentences should of course also be distinguished from *ellipsis* in linked sentences as well as from the stylistically marked deletion that characterizes proverbial utterance, abuse, and poetic registers in NIA.

Copula deletion is normally confined to the Present Tense, and the copula reappears in other Tense/Mood contexts:

51 (B.) *tini prophesar* 'He's a professor'
52 (B.) *tini prophesar chilen* 'He was a professor'
53 (B.) *khābār toiri* 'The food is ready'
54 (B.) *khābār jodi toiri hɔe* . . . 'If the food is ready . . .' (Bender and Riccardi 1978: 78)

Possibly Assamese behaves a bit differently:

55 (A.) *χɔti zɔymɔti/mɒhārāz gɒdādhɒr ʃiŋhɒr ghɔiniyek* 'Sati Joymati was ["is"] a wife of King Gadadharsingha' (Baruah 1980: 954)

This may be related to another peculiarity of Assamese, namely the regular use of the Present in past habitual and historical contexts (Babakaev 1961: 87–88).

The tenuous Bengali definitional/existential distinction (B. *hɔ-/āch-*) becomes still more problematic in the Past, with e.g., *chil-* often functioning as the Past equivalent of both (suppressed) copular *hɔ-* and existential *āch-*, while *hol-* takes on connotations of 'become' or 'happen': *tini prophesar holen* would mean 'He *became* a professor'.

Not much more can be said about the properties of the simple sentence in NIA, i.e. concerning the function of the enumerated NPs and the roles of case, agreement, and position, until we confront the problem of *Subject* in these languages.

10.3 The problem of Subject in NIA

The notion of Subject has been used, crucially but somewhat uncritically, in both traditional grammar and, explicitly or implicitly, in more recent theories and typological work. As linguists working with South Asian languages have not been slow to point out, this notion is problematic in these languages. It is problematic because the various properties which are associated with it at various levels of grammar, which for the most part conveniently coincide in familiar European languages *and especially in English*, do not coincide, that is, do not unanimously point to the one and the same Noun Phrase in NIA (or in Dravidian or Tibeto-Burman) languages. Such properties include, at the semantic level: ideally Actor/Agent, and also the top end of the animacy–personhood hierarchy among sentence NPs; at the surface-syntactic (sometimes called the "grammatical") level: verb agreement, Nominative case, and first position among Noun Phrases in the sentence;[3] at the "behavioral" or covert syntactic level: *control* of reflexivity, coreferential deletion and a number of other processes (and *selection* by others); at the pragmatic level: topicality.

By no means all NIA sentences are problematic in this regard. (It is not even clear whether the problematic sentences are a minority or a majority. It might be useful to determine the average proportion by textual counts. The proportion in different NIA languages will differ, for reasons that will soon be apparent.) In such sentences as the following the Subject criteria do coincide:

56 (H.) *gopāl ciṭṭhī likh rahā thā* 'Gopal was writing a letter'
57 (B.) *āmi choṭo meeke ekṭi kukur dilām* 'I gave the little girl a dog'
58 (M.) *sanjay tikiṭə zamavto* 'Sanjay collects stamps' (Berntsen and Nimbkar 1982: 197)

In these sentences, the NP in first position, in the Nominative (or "Direct") case, semantically the Agent, and highest in animacy-personhood (or in no. 57, egocentricity), also controls verbal agreement, with which any other NP in these examples happens to be discordant. Everything points unambiguously to its Subjecthood. (The covert-syntactic criteria do not show, of course, until we perform various operations on the sentences, and topicality cannot be determined apart from a discourse context.) Not so the following:

59 (H.) *gopāl ne ciṭṭhī likhī thī* 'Gopal had written a letter'
60 (B.) *amāke choṭo meeke ekṭi kukur dite hɔbe* 'I will have to give the little girl a dog'
61 (M.) *sanjaylā tsāŋglī tikiṭə āvaḍtāt* 'Sanjay likes nice stamps'

In these sentences, which in English have the same Subjects as nos. 56–8, the NP in question, while remaining in first position, is not in the Nominative case and does not control verb agreement. Semantically it is an Experiencer rather than an Agent in nos. 60–1, although it remains an Agent in no. 59, and retains its animacy primacy in all three. In nos. 59 and 61, other NPs (*ciṭṭhī* 'letter', *tikiṭə* 'stamps') control verb agreement. They are in the Nominative case, but low on the animacy hierarchy. In no. 60, *kukur* 'dog' is in the Nominative case but does not control verb agreement: the verb *hɔbe* does not agree with any NP in the sentence and is in the 3rd person because that is the "neutral" form. So, where is the Subject? One solution, which sidesteps the issue, has been to call the first NP the "logical" (more recently, the "underlying") Subject and the second NP (in nos. 59 and 61) the "grammatical" (or "surface") Subject – the latter primarily on grounds of verb agreement. But as was just noted, in no. 60 there is no agreement. It has been held (although this is a minority position) that such sentences lack a Subject altogether. Although sentences like those above have much in common, they involve several different constructions which are among the most interesting in NIA and deserve special examination. These are principally the *Ergative and Quasi-Ergative* and the *Dative-Subject* constructions, to which may be added the *New Passive* and *Topicalized Locative* constructions.

10.3.1 *Ergative and quasi-ergative constructions*

No. 59 above is an example of a construction, in older accounts often called the "passive construction of transitive verbs in the perfective", inherited by all NIA languages from a Sanskrit so-called passive construction employing the past passive participle instead of a finite verb, with the passive agent (the erstwhile subject) in the Instrumental and the participle, as the adjective it is, agreeing with the promoted passive subject (the erstwhile object):

62 (Skt) *mandirē tēna darśanaṁ labdham* 'He had a vision in the temple' (lit. "in the temple by-him [a] vision obtained [was]")

Or rather, it was inherited from an Early MIA construction which was abundantly reflected in Late Sanskrit, and eventually drove finite active "past" forms out of existence in later MIA. In NIA it has ceased to be a "passive" construction, since there is no longer any corresponding "active", but its ancestry accounts for the verb agreement (with the Patient in Hindi and the languages west of it, up to but not including Khowar), the special marking of the Agent (a vestige of the old Instrumental or a new form replacing it), and restriction to the Perfective (sometimes inaccurately called the "past tense": cf. no. 62), the forms of which derive from the OIA/MIA past passive participle. (One feature of the Sanskrit construction which was apparently *not* passed on to NIA, however, was its use with *intransitives*, as in, e.g., *dēvadattēna suptam* 'Devadatta slept' = "By D. [it] was slept" [Cardona 1976b: 4]. Although the later NIA ergative construction is found with certain intransitives also in some languages, the usage is not general and these seem to form a special class, and perhaps a later development. See, however, Hock 1985: 251.)

Is the Patient, as the controller of verb agreement, the Subject in this construction? That would mean that sentences with very similar if not identical semantic relations, such as nos. 56 and 59, have different Subjects. There is every indication, mainly in the form of covert syntactic behavior, that this is not the case. It is the Agent, which remains the first NP, that still controls or is uniquely accessible to such operations making crucial reference to Subject[4] as Reflexivization (no. 63), Coreferential Subject Deletion (no. 64: Y. Kachru's term is *Conjunction Reduction* – perhaps the clearest term of all in an IA context would be *Conjunc-*

tive Participle Formation), and Raising (of Subject to Object in an embedded sentence: no. 65), despite its Oblique case marking:

> 63 (H.) *gopāl ne apnī ciṭṭhī likhī thī* 'Gopal had written his (own) letter'
>
> 64 (H.) *andar jākar gopāl ne ciṭṭhī likhī* '(Gopal) going inside Gopal wrote a letter'
>
> 65 (H.) *mohan ne gopāl ko ciṭṭhī likhte hue dekhā* 'Mohan saw Gopal write the letter'

Interestingly enough, at least the first two of these apply also to the (Classical) Sanskrit parent construction (Hock 1982: 131). Together with the fact that the Agent is normally not moved from its erstwhile first-NP/Subject position in Sanskrit (discounting for the moment stylistic permutations of word order), this raises questions both concerning the "passive" status of the Sanskrit construction itself and of its motivation. With respect to the latter, it is worth noting that the mountain borders of Indo-Aryan on the north are home to languages (Tibetan dialects and Burushaski) of strongly "ergative"[5] type. Chatterji (1926) sees a Dravidian parallel in the use of a "nominal" sentence (i.e. the participle as predicator) in the first place, but there is no trace of ergativity in Dravidian.

The candidacy of the Patient (normally still the second NP) for the Subject role in the ergative constructions is further weakened by the fact that it has later come to be marked, in the case of personal and/or definite Patients, with an Object case marker, which moreover blocks (except in Gujarati, Rajasthani, and some rural Marathi[6] dialects) the only claim the Patient has on Subjecthood, that of agreement with the verb (that is, concord is neutralized):[7]

> 66 (P.) *ustād ne kuṛī nū̃ pucchiā* 'The teacher asked the girl'
>
> 67 (S.) *māṇhun kutani khē kuṭhō* 'The men killed the dogs' (Addleton and Brown 1981: 225)

but:

> 68 (Raj. [Marw.]) *mhẽ sītā ne dekhī hī* 'We had seen Sita' (Magier 1983: 321)

The Patient is thus basically still the Object, and the sequence NP + NP + Vb in a NIA ergative construction may be interpreted as a subtype of SOV ("AgOV"), alongside the parallel non-ergative (nominative–accusative) constructions (such as no. 56 above).

The classic NIA split ergative (quasi-ergative case-marking and agreement patterns in the Perfective only, vs. nominative–accusative patterns in non-Perfective tenses) could be regarded as a historical accident without any function – but it should be noted that very similar splits are characteristic of ergativity in a number of languages (e.g., Georgian) unrelated to and distant from Indo-Aryan (as well as in some of the aforementioned non-Aryan northern border languages), implying that it is perhaps not accidental. Conformity to a natural and universal tendency (which has been explained with reference to the greater transitivity and more complete affectedness of the Patient in Perfective predications: Givón 1984: 156, 161; Hopper and Thompson 1980) may thus merely have been facilitated for NIA by the "accident" of the Sanskrit participial construction – or the latter itself may have been similarly motivated.

Be this as it may, a number of NIA languages have tinkered with their inherited ergative, perhaps in an attempt to make greater sense out of it. The case marking of the Patient as Object (in certain cases) has already been noted. (In NIA for the most part this does not result in what has been called an "antipassive", since the Agent retains its ergative case marking in such sentences, if such marking exists in the language in question: i.e. Object marking is not in complementary distribution with Agent marking, as it is in Eskimo and Georgian. Hook points out that Kashmiri and nearby dialects do exhibit such a distribution, however.) The Subjecthood of the ergative Agent has been further strengthened in some languages (Assamese, Nepali, Shina, Gawarbati) by making the verb agree with it rather than the Object/Patient. In some cases, this appears to have been brought about through an intermediate stage where the verb agreed with both Object (as an adjective) and Subject/Agent (through suffixed pronominal clitics):

69 (K.) *me chelim palav gari* 'I washed the clothes at home' [*cheli* 'washed' (Mpl.) agrees with the Object *palav* 'clothes', while *-m* represents the 1sg. Agent (Erg) *me*] (Hook and Koul 1984b: 128)

70 (S.) *khēs guzrēl mahinē ciṭī likhī hōmi* 'I wrote him a note last month' [*likhī* 'written' (Fsg. Perfective) and *hō* (3rd person Past marker) agree with the Object *ciṭī* 'note', while *-mi* represents the (deleted) 1sg. Agent (Erg) *mū̃*] (Addleton and Brown 1981: 341)

Such a "stage" is preserved in some of the northwestern languages: Kashmiri, Sindhi, Siraiki and other "Lahnda" dialects. Something similar occurs in Marathi in the 2nd person only:

71 (M.) *tu tyālā kiti payse diles* 'How much money did you give him?' [*dile* 'given > gave' (Mpl. Perfective) agrees with *payse* 'money', while *-s* agrees with *tu* 'you'] (Kavadi and Southworth 1965: 200)

The total loss of the ergative construction, that is, its replacement by a nominative–accusative construction, which has occurred (for example) in Standard Bengali, Oriya,[8] and Sinhalese, could plausibly have come about from double-agreement constructions like the above with the waning of gender–number concord in these languages along with merger of nominative–ergative case marking, but the picture is not a clear one (Chatterji 1926: 970–2). There is no evidence for double agreement at any point in the history of Eastern Magadhan; the double agreement of modern Maithili and Magahi is of a different sort (pronominal clitic + pronominal clitic rather than gender-number + clitic) and of recent origin (Jha 1958: 469–74):[9]

> 72 (Mth.) *ham^a torā beṭa-ke dekhal-i-ah^u* 'I saw your son' [*-i-* = 1sg. Nom, agreeing with *ham^a* 'I'; *-ah^u* = 2sg. non-Nom, agreeing with *torā* 'your'] (Jha 1958: 473)

Although OIA had enclitic pronouns and they may have survived in the west reinforced by Iranian influences (Chatterji 1926: 971), the actual history of the Northwestern forms is not clear. (Like the Maithili one, the *Kashmiri* system of pronominal clitics goes much beyond representation of the Subject/Agent, but unlike the Maithili case, they are mainly in addition to, not in place of, adjectival agreements of the verbal forms. For details, see Hook and Koul 1984b.)

Where distinctive marking of the ergative Agent is retained, it has taken several forms:

1. a direct phonological descendant of the Sanskrit Instrumental (*-ēna*, *-ina*, *-unā*, *-ayā*, *-yā*; *-aiḥ*, *-bhiḥ*, etc.) in the form of the common Oblique case into which it has merged (different in Masculine and Feminine, and in singular and plural) is the marker – in Sindhi and "Lahnda" (including Siraiki), most forms of Rajasthani (lost except as an alternate with 3rd person pronouns in the form of Marwari studied by Magier 1983), Bhadarwahi, and several Dardic dialects; in Kashmiri where the old cases are less completely merged, some declensions preserve a recognizably Instrumental form (*-an*, *-en*) in the singular; in Kalasha and Khowar, where they are even better preserved, the ergative construction does not exist (the old Preterite also having been preserved), and the case retains a purely instrumental function, primarily with inanimate nouns (Morgenstierne 1947, 1965);

2. one (most common) direct phonological descendant (*-ēna* > *-e͂* > *-e*) is generalized for all genders and both numbers as an agglutinized marker – in Gujarati, Assamese (with some East Bengali dialects and Bishnupriya [K. P. Sinha 1981: 81]), and most West Pahari dialects (Kangri, Jaunsari, Baghati, Sirmauri, Kiunthali, Kului, Mandeali, Churahi, but Standard Chameali and

Bhadarwahi show gender variants); this suffix partly coincides with the Locative (the Eastern languages attempt to keep them separate by means of new Locatives in *-t-*), but new suffixes (G. *-thī*, A. *-ere*) compete for the properly "instrumental" function, leaving it almost as a distinctively "Agentive" case;

3. "reinforced" versions of an instrumental marker characterize Hindi, Punjabi, and Marathi, distinct as Agentives from new Instrumentals in the first two (*-ne* vs. H. *se*, P. *-nāḷ*), retaining an instrumental function (and distinct singular/plural forms) in Marathi (*-ne*, *-nə̄/-nī*);

4. "new" instrumental markers have usurped the agentive function in Nepali and Kumauni (*-le*), also partly in Shina (*-s/se* – possibly borrowed from the neighboring Balti dialect of Tibetan), with still newer markers coming in (N. *-bāṭa*) to pick up the ordinary instrumental function.

Many NIA languages have neutralized the Nominative/Agentive distinction in 1st and 2nd person pronouns, often in favor of the Agentive in the former: P. *maĩ*, Marw. *mhẽ* 'I (Nom/Ag)' (vs. G. *hũ/mɛ̃* 'I (Nom)/I (Ag)'). Hindi pleonastically reinforces *maĩ*, originally Agentive, as *maĩ-ne*.

It remains to discuss changes in the *domain* of the ergative or ergative-derived constructions. While Hindi, Punjabi, "Lahnda", Sindhi, Gujarati, Marathi, West Pahari, Rajasthani, and Kashmiri have preserved the original split-ergative pattern (although in Marathi it has "lost" some transitives – 'learn', 'forget', 'drink' – to a nominative–accusative construction), Assamese, Bishnupriya Manipuri, and Shina have extended what they preserve of it, namely distinctive case marking of the transitive Agent, to all tenses of transitive verbs (and of some intransitives), thus evolving a more consistent marking of the category of transitive Agent as such.

73 (A.) *χikhɒke̲ sātɔribilākɒk pāth pɔrhāy* 'The teacher teaches the lesson to the students' (Babakaev 1961: 105)
74 (A.) *rintiy̲e̲ sɒndɒnɒr hātī kinise* 'Rinti has bought a sandalwood elephant'
75 (A.) *bubule̲ pɔrhi āse* 'Bubul is reading'
76 (A.) *bubule̲ bhāt khāise neki?* 'Has Bubul eaten (rice)?' (Baruah 1980: 212, 230)
77 (Bshn.) *rāme̲ kām ehān karla* 'Ram has done this work'
78 (Bshn.) *pramīlā-y̲ leirik ceirī* 'Pramila reads books'
79 (Bshn.) *bāghe̲ mānu kheitā ā* 'Tigers eat human beings' (K. P. Sinha 1981: 109–10)

Intransitive verbs, with the exceptions mentioned, take Nominative Subjects as usual:

80 (A.) *bubul sowā nāi* 'Bubul has not slept'
81 (A.) *bipul kɒlɔi gɔise?* 'Where has Bipul gone? (Baruah)
82 (Bshn.) *pāhiyāga pharder* 'The bird is flying' (Sinha)

In Assamese and Bishnupriya the distinction is absent with pronoun subjects, for all of which (A. *mɒi*, *tɒi*, *āmi*, *tumi*, *χi*, *tāi*) there is a single form, derived from an old Instrumental (Kakati 1962: 311–16). (In Shina, however: *ma/mas*, *tu/tus*, *anu/anus*, etc.)

Nepali, while not going quite this far, has extended the Instrumental (*-le*) marking of transitive Agents beyond the Perfective (and Perfect), where it is obligatory, optionally to the Presumptive (*-lā*) Future and Present General/Habitual (*-ncha*: when used with Future meaning?), and sometimes even elsewhere "for emphasis" (Clark 1977: 93, 100, 224, 286):

83 (N.) *rāmle timīlāī ke bhanyo?* 'What did Ram say to you?'
84 (N.) *āja maile besarī bhāt khāeko chu* 'I have eaten too much rice today'
85 (N.) *nānīle tyo ghaḍī phāllā, hai* 'Baby will knock the clock down'
86 (N.) *rāmele ali dinpachi ghaḍī pāũcha* 'Rame will get a watch in a few days' time'

This distribution roughly coincides with that of several Tibeto-Burman languages of Nepal, including the previously culturally dominant Newari. Nepali verb agreement, as previously noted, is with the Agent.

10.3.2 *The Dative Subject construction*

The Dative Subject construction gets its name from the fact that one of the NPs which is a prime candidate for the syntactic role of Subject is marked by the Dative case in many NIA (and non-NIA) languages. (Not in all: in Bengali and to a lesser extent in Assamese and Oriya it is marked in many of its manifestations by the Genitive case.) It should not, however, be confused with the similarly marked Indirect Object (although this is implied or even stated in some traditional descriptions, which refer to it as the "Indirect Construction"): unlike the latter, it normally occurs in first – that is, "Subject" – position. The two are also distinguished by behavioral, that is, covert syntactic, characteristics.

On the semantic level, unlike the Ergative Subjects dealt with in the preceding section which are Agents marked as such, the Dative Subject is not an Agent but an *Experiencer*. What is "experienced" includes

a) physical sensations and conditions:

87 (H.) *bacce<u>ko</u> ṭhaṇḍ lag rahī hai* 'The child is feeling cold'
88 (P.) *tu`<u>ānu˜</u> buxār lagdā ai* 'Do you have fever?' (U. S. Bahri 1973: 119)
89 (K.) *ʃīla<u>s</u> lɜj bɔchi* 'Sheela is feeling hungry' (Kachru 1973: 386)
90 (S.) *mū˜ <u>khē</u> mathē me˜ sūrᵘ āhē* 'I have a headache' (Addleton and Brown 1981: 91)
91 (G.) *mah<u>ne</u> dā˜tmā˜ dukhe che* 'I have a toothache' (Cardona 1965: 110)
92 (M.) *tyā<u>lā</u> khoklā yetoy* 'He has a cough' (Berntsen and Nimbkar 1982: 431)
93 (Si.) *mahattayā<u>ṭa</u> mahansiyi* 'The gentleman is tired' (Fairbanks et al. 1968: II. 103)
94 (O.) *mɔ<u>te</u> nidɔ heuci* 'I'm sleepy' (Pattanayak and Das 1972: 214)
95 (B.) *amā<u>r</u> triʃnā peyechile* 'I was thirsty' (Matthew 25: 35)
96 (A.) *mo<u>r</u> bhok lāgisil* 'I was hungry' (Matthew 25: 35)
97 (N.) *rām<u>lāī</u> aulo lāgyo* 'Ram has contracted malaria' (Wallace 1985b: 131)

b) psychological or mental states, including liking, perceiving:

98 (H.) *mujh<u>e</u> apne deʃ kī yād ātī hai* 'I'm homesick'
99 (P.) *sā<u>nū˜</u> umēd e ki . . .* 'We hope that . . .' (Shackle 1972: 65)
100 (K.) *tɜmi<u>s</u> lagi dakɨ* 'She will be shocked' (Kachru 1973: 386)
101 (S.) *mū˜ <u>khē</u> χabar na āhē* 'I don't know' (Addleton and Brown 1981: 308)
102 (G.) *ma<u>ne</u> te bābatmā˜ ras nathī* 'I have no interest in the matter' (Dhruva 1920: 143)
103 (M.) *tu<u>lā</u> tī pāṇḍhrī imārat diste kā?* 'Can you see that white building?' (Berntsen and Nimbkar 1982: 434)
104 (Si.) *mā<u>ṭa</u> ē katāva matakay* 'I remember that story' (Fairbanks et al. 1968: I. 379)
105 (O.) *tebe mɔ<u>te</u> sikārɔ bhɔlɔ lāge ni˜* 'But I don't like hunting' (Pattanayak and Das 1972: 207)
106 (B.) *tā<u>r</u> obhimān hoyeche* 'He was piqued' (Klaiman 1980: 277)
107 (A.) *rātulrinti<u>r</u> bɒr ānɒnd lāgise* 'Ratul and Rini have felt very happy' (Baruah 1980: 212)
108 (N.) *syām<u>lāī</u> ris uṭcha* 'Shyam is angry' (Wallace 1985b: 123)

c) wanting or needing:

109 (H.) *āpko kyā cāhiye* 'What do you want/need?'
110 (P.) *tu`anū˜ kī cā'īdā ai* 'What do you want/need?'
111 (K.) *tse kyah gatshīy* 'What do you want/need?'
112 (S.) *tavhā˜ khe chā khapē* 'What do you want/need?'
113 (G.) *tamne ʃu˜ joīe che* 'What do you want/need?'
114 (M.) *tumhālā kāy pāhije* 'What do you want/need?'
115 (Si.) *obaṭa mokada ōnæ* 'What do you want/need?'
116 (O.) *āpɔṇɔŋkɔrɔ kɔɔnɔ dɔrɔkār* 'What do you need?
117 (B.) *āpnār ki cāī* 'What do you want/need?'
118 (A.) *āponāk ki lāge* 'What do you want/need?'
119 (N.) *tapāīlāī ko cāhincha* 'What do you want/need?'

d) obligation or compulsion:

120 (H.) *mujhe jānā hai* 'I have to go'
121 (P.) *mainū˜ kī karnā cā'īdā ai* 'What should I do?' (Bahri 1973: 54)
122 (S.) *tavhā˜ khē hī kitāb*[a] *paṛhaṇa pavandā* 'You will have to read these books' (Addleton and Brown 1981: 195)
123 (M.) *malā mumbailā jāvə lāglə* 'I had to go to Bombay' (Kavadi and Southworth 1965: 205)
124 (Si.) *māṭa payin yanna vanā* 'I had to go on foot' (Fairbanks et al. 1968: I. 263)
125 (O.) *mɔte jibaku hebɔ* 'I shall have to go' (Pattanayak and Das 1972: 231)
126 (B.) *āmāke kɔrte hɔe* 'I must do (it)' (Zbavitel 1970: 16)
127 (N.) *malī kām garnuparcha* 'I have to work' (Clark 1977: 127)

e) having kinship relations (several languages, marked * *below*, show Genitives here):

128 (P.)* *o'dī keval ik bai'ṇ e* 'He has only one sister' (Shackle 1972: 64)
129 (S.) *huna khē ɓa puṭ*[a] *āhin* 'He has two sons' (Addleton and Brown 1981: 92)
130 (G.)* *tamāre keṭlā˜ chokrā˜ che* 'How many children do you have? (Dhruva 1920: 131)
131 (M.) *āmhālā cār mulə āhet* 'We have four children' (Kavadi and Southworth 1965: 100)

132 (Si.) *minihāṭa lámay kī denek innavā da* 'How many children does the man have?' (Garusinghe 1962: 54)

133 (B.)∗ *ei bhɔdrɔloker konoʃɔntān neī* 'That gentleman has no sons' (Bender and Riccardi 1978: 17)

134 (N.)∗*usko pā̃cjanā chorāchorī chan* 'He has five children' (Matthews 1984: 55)

f) external circumstances or events affecting but not controlled by the Dative (or Genitive*) NP:

135 (K.) *mohnas yeli mōkɨ lagi su yiyi* 'When Mohan gets an opportunity he will come' (Kachru 1973: 387)

136 (G.)∗*mare hamṇā̃ vakhat nathī* 'I have no time just now' (Dhruva 1920: 134)

137 (M.) *tilā mulgī zhālī* 'She had a daughter' (Berntsen and Nimbkar 1982: 431)

138 (Si.) *mahattayāṭa æksidanṭ ēkak vanā* 'The gentleman had an accident' (Fairbanks et al. 1968: II. 104)

139 (O.)∗*amɔrɔ kahari kichi heini* 'Nothing happened to any of us' (Pattanayak and Das 1972: 173)

140 (N.) *malāī ḍhilo cha* 'I will be late' (Verma and Sharma 1979b: 30)

Under the latter head we might put the common verbs of *receiving/finding* in at least the Central and Western NIA languages:

141 (H.) *mujhe mor kā ek pankh milā* 'I found a peacock feather'

142 (K.) *asi mēli tankhā pɨtsimi doh* 'We will receive our salary on the fifth day' (Kachru 1973: 367)

143 (M.) *tumhālā pustak milālə kā?* 'Did you receive the book?' (Berntsen and Nimbkar 1982: 428)

144 (G.) *kɔne inām maḷyu*? 'Who got the prize?' (Lambert 1971: 130)

145 (P.) *o'nū̃ ṭaiksi na'ī̃ la'bbī* 'He didn't get a taxi' (Shackle 1972: 79)

146 (S.) *mū̃khē ajjᵘ hikaṛō χatᵘ milīō* 'I got a letter today' (Addleton and Brown 1981: 265)

In the Eastern languages, verbs in direct construction tend to be used here, e.g., Bengali *pāoā*. In any case, the predications in the group 135–46 above undercut the generalization, which is sometimes made, that the predications in Dative

Subject constructions are always *stative* predications (although it may be true that most of them are, or express an "event" which is only a *change of state* rather than an "action").

What, then, do these constructions have in common? My own earlier attempt (Masica 1976: 160) to characterize it as "subjective" experience (i.e. perceived only or primarily by the Experiencer) does not capture it: cf. the last group above. A more accurate diagnosis has been developed most fully in the context of NIA by Klaiman 1979 and 1980 (building on the work of N. McCawley 1976 on Old and Middle English; see also Sridhar 1976, on the Dravidian language Kannada). Klaiman notes that many such expressions in Bengali have Direct-construction counterparts (while others do not), e.g.,

147 (B.) *tār nāk ḍāke* 'He snores' (Klaiman 1980: 284)
148 (B.) *ʃe nāk ḍāke* 'He snores' (ibid.: 84)
149 (B.) *āmār doʃ hoyeche* 'I am guilty' (ibid.: 279)
150 (B.) *āmi doʃ korechi* 'I have done wrong' (ibid.: 279)

She observes, on the basis of trial insertion of adverbials such as "deliberately", "pretendingly", that the general semantic parameter distinguishing all such pairs seems to be *volitionality*. Moreover, among non-paired predications, those showing no Direct counterpart are such that (to a Bengali at least) the matter may be viewed only as nonvolitional (no. 151 below), while with those showing no "Dative" (i.e. Genitive) counterpart it may often be viewed only as volitional (no. 152 below):

151 (B.) *tār* [Gen] *ghum bhāŋglo* 'He awakened' (Klaiman 1980: 288)
152 (B.) *ʃe* [Nom] *upoʃ bhāŋglo* 'He broke his fast' (ibid.: 288)

It should be noted, however, that the contrast is not *volitional/nonvolitional*, but rather *neutral* (unmarked)/*nonvolitional* (marked). (See especially Wallace 1985b.) It is not that Direct constructions are necessarily volitional, but rather that they are unmarked as to volitionality and thus *may* be (where the contrast is present, may even *tend* to be) volitional, whereas the Dative construction is definitely nonvolitional.

Such an analysis appears to be valid, not only for NIA generally, but for Dravidian (and for other *Indo-European* languages where the construction appears) as well, and perhaps universally. ("*Involitive*" verbs have long been recognized in grammars of Sinhalese, since they are distinguished morphologically in the verb itself, and the formation is a productive one. Studies of them have generally focused on this rather than on the case of the Subject they govern, however.) Languages obviously differ, synchronically and diachronically (cf. the history of English and N. McCawley 1976) in their interest in such a specifying of nonvolitionality. South Asian languages, both NIA and Dravidian, show what may be a maximum interest in such specification, and it is one of their most characteristic features. This is not to say that they are "consistent" in this regard, in accordance with some external canon of logic or semantic theory.

These constructions are sometimes compared with English constructions of the "It is pleasing to me"-type, but the comparison is not particularly apt, because there is no question of *to me* being a candidate for Subject (in Modern English): that role has been usurped by the dummy *it*. The underlying semantics (as well as the Old English surface construction) are another matter.

Naturally there is variation in the way certain situations are viewed even within NIA. Thus *understand* is neutral (Direct) in Hindi (*mai˜ samjhā* 'I [m.] understood') and Bengali (*āmi bojhlum*), but potentially marked as nonvolitional, that is, taking a "Dative Subject", in Marathi (*mī samazlo* or *maḻā samazlə̄/kaḻalə̄*) and Sinhalese (*maṭa tērenavā*). More surprisingly, "compulsion" (*must*), which is marked as nonvolitional in most NIA languages, is unmarked (= Direct) in Sinhalese:

153 (Si.) *mama* [Nom] *yānna ōna* 'I must go' (Fairbanks et al. 1968: I. 41)
cf. 154 (Si.) *maṭa* [Dat] *yānna ōna* 'I want to go' (ibid.: 34)

(There is a similar case contrast in Tamil in these constructions.)

In the same semantic sub-area (compulsion/obligation) there is variation in the particular non-Nominative case used to mark the Experiencer in a few languages. In Bengali, where the Genitive is the usual case of the Experiencer (the result of a deleted body-part reference, Klaiman suggests), a Dative may be used here.

155 (B.) *cākɔrer* [Gen]/*cākɔrke* [Dat] *roj kāj kɔrte hɔe* 'The servant has to work every day' (Bender and Riccardi 1978: 49)

In Gujarati, in the 1st and 2nd persons a special form (*māre/amāre/tamāre* = "Agentive/Locative of the Genitive"?) varies freely with the Dative (*mane/amne/tamne*), while in the 3rd person the Dative varies freely with the regular Agentive:

156 (G.) *māre*[10] [Ag?]/*mane* [Dat] *ghɛr javu˜ joie* 'I ought to go home' (Cardona 1965: 95)
157 (G.) *e māṇase* [Ag]/*māṇasne* [Dat] *ghɛr javu˜ joie* 'That man ought to go home' (ibid.)

The normal Agentives of the 1st and 2nd person pronouns in Gujarati are *me˜*, *tɛ˜*

and in the plural (merging with the Nominative) *ame*, *tame* (see note 10). In contrast with Sinhalese, the distinction between *want* and *must* is expressed not through case marking but by simple vs. extended verbal adjective:

158 (G.) *māre/mane ghɛr javu˜ che* 'I want to go home'
159 (G.) *māre/mane ghɛr javānu˜ che* 'I have to go home' (Cardona 1965: 95)

Noting that the use of *māre*, etc. also in statements of kinship relation militates against identification of the */-e/* with the Agentive, Cardona (1965: 96) remarks that these constructions "are among the most confusing in Gujarati, not only to the linguistic analyst, but also to speakers of the language; there is great variation both regionally and within regions among individual speakers with regard to the preferred usage." (See also Lambert 1971: 60–1, 108–9.)

In Punjabi also there is a slight anomaly in that with what Shackle (1972: 84) calls a "weaker" form of the obligation construction (using *hoṇā* rather than *paiṇā* as the modal auxiliary), the Experiencer is in the Agentive rather than in the Dative case (a usage which is often transferred to the Urdu of Pakistan and the Hindi of Delhi in the characteristic *mai˜ne jānā hai* for the standard *mujhe* [Dat] *jānā hai* 'I have to go'). Perhaps the external compulsion is felt weakly enough to allow some scope for the initiative (i.e. agentivity) of the Experiencer. Possibly also the historical precedent of the Sanskrit gerundives in *-(i)tavya*, *-ya*, *-anīya*, which are not phonologically antecedent but also expressed obligation or necessity, and governed an "agent" in the Instrumental, may have played a role:

160 (Skt) *atra bhavitavyam anayā* [Instr] 'Here she must stay' [= "Here (it is) to-be-stayed by-this-one (F)"] (Gonda 1981: 94)

In Oriya also there is variation (between Genitive and Nominative) in some kinds of obligational constructions:

161 (O.) *moorɔ* [Gen]/*mu˜* [Nom] *jibarɔ ɔchi* 'I am supposed to go' (Pattanayak and Das 1972: 205)
but: 162 (O.) *mɔte* [Dat – no variation] *jibaku hebɔ* 'I shall have to go' (ibid. 231)

Kashmiri also shows Nominatives here:

163 (K.) *bɨ gotshus gatshun* 'I should go' (Hook: pers. com.)

Assamese shows a peculiar construction, Nominative but "impersonal" (the modal auxiliary does not agree with the Nominative Experiencer, but is in a neutral, i.e. 3sg. form):

164 (A.) *mɔi* [Nom] *kɔribɔ lāge* 'I am obliged to do' (Babakaev 1961: 93)

165 (A.) [*jɔdi āponār lɒgɒt*] *mɔi* [Nom] *mɔribɔ-o lāge* [*tɒthāpi āponāk āχɔi nā-mātim*] 'Even [if with you] I must die [I will not deny you]' (Matthew 26: 35)

cf. 166 (B.) [*jodi āpnār ʃɔŋge*] *āmāke* [Dat] *morte-o hɔe* [*ʃeobhi acchā, tobu āpnāke oʃʃikār korbo nā*] = no. 165 (ibid.)

167 (A.) *mɔi kɔribɔ lāgo͂* 'I *begin* to do' (Babakaev 1961: 93)

This Assamese peculiarity is not due to non-availability of a Dative (= A. *mok*), which otherwise is perhaps more widely used in Assamese than it is in Bengali.

Finally (for our purposes here: other NIA languages and dialects need further study) in Nepali and Marathi also there is variation in case marking with obligational constructions. In Nepali, the Experiencer is Nom/Ag/Dat when the verb is intransitive, Ag/Dat when it is transitive in the *must* construction; Nom-intransitive/Ag-transitive in the *should* construction. (For further details, see Wallace 1985b: 168–9, 175.) In Marathi, it is Dat or Dat/Inst in *must* constructions, Instr in the *should* construction, and Dat/Inst in the "weak" obligational (*is to*, *wants to*) construction (Berntsen and Nimbkar 1975b: 122–6).

In fact obligational constructions differ from other "Dative-Subject" (Experiencer) constructions in significant ways, of which case assignment is only a reflection. (They warrant a separate chapter in Wallace 1985.) Most importantly, they involve not a simple predication, but an embedded sentence, the Subject of which, deleted in favor of the coreferential Experiencer, is generally an Agent, whether marked Nominative or Agentive (Ergative) in the original. The nonvolitionality of the Experiencer role is as it were superimposed on the agentivity of the underlying Subject, hence the conflict. In Nepali, verb agreement is neutralized in these constructions; in Hindi, Marathi, etc. it agrees with the underlying Object (if the latter is unmarked):

168 (N.) *mai-le* [Ag] *dherai kitāpharu* [pl.] *paṛnu parcha* [3sg.] 'I have to read many books' (Wallace 1985: 174, modified)

169 (H.) *mujhe* [Dat] *bahut kitābe͂* [Fpl.] *paṛhnī* [F] *paṛtī* [F] *hai͂* [pl.] 'I have to read many books'

170 (M.) *malā* [Dat] *āmbe* [pl.] *toḍāylā pāhije āhet* [3pl.] 'I have to pick the mangoes' (Berntsen and Nimbkar 1975b: 124)

171 (M.) *tyānī* [Inst] *gāḍyā* [Fpl.] *durusta kelyā* [Fpl.] *pāhijet* [pl.] 'He must repair the cars' (ibid.: 125)

To return to the original question: do these obliquely-marked Experiencers qualify as Subjects? Or to put the question another way, what *is* the Subject of such a construction? According to some, such constructions are Subject-less. According to traditional grammar, another NP, which governs verb agreement in the sentence, is the Subject.

As we have seen, on the pragmatic level the marked Experiencer is usually also the Topic (i.e. occupies Subject "position"), unlike the superficially similar (in some languages) Indirect Object. The latter entails the existence of another, more "agentive" animate or human NP in the sentence, one with greater claims to Subjecthood, whereas the Experiencer is itself the most conscious (albeit non-agentive) – and often the only – human NP in the sentence. On the other hand, on the level of surface grammar, not only is it (generally) non-Nominative in case, but it never[11] controls verb agreement (unlike Quasi-Ergative Subjects, which in languages like Nepali and Assamese have come to do so). The verb either agrees with some other NP in the sentence, or is in neutral (3sg.) form.

The most telling evidence is in the form of behavioral characteristics (covert syntax). Like Nominative Subjects and marked Agents (Ergative Subjects) the marked Experiencer controls the reference of the reflexive possessive (in languages where this exists) and other reflexives:

172 (H.) *laṛke ko apne dost yād āe* '*The boy* remembered *his* friends' (Kachru et al. 1976: 91)

173 (N.) *malāī āphno kāraṇa-mā duhkh lāgcha* '*I* am unhappy for *my own* reasons' (Wallace 1985: 136)

This is not true of Indirect Objects:

174 (H.) *usne laṛkī ko apnā koṭ diyā* 'He gave the girl his coat' [i.e. not *her* coat]

Except, Hook points out, in Kashmiri:

174a (K.) *mye dyits laḍkas paniny kyitāb (vāpas)* 'I gave the boy back *his* book' (Hook: pers. comm.)

The marked Experiencer behaves like the (Nominative) Subject of a matrix sentence also with respect to control of the coreferential Subject-deletion entailed by the Conjunctive Participle construction (see below, section 10.9):

175 (H.) *kitāb paṛhkar laṛkā* [Nom] *so jāegā* '*The boy* will go to sleep after *he* reads the book' (Kachru et al. 1976: 88)

176 (H.) *skūl kā maidān dekhkar laṛke ko* [Dat] *dost yād āe* '*The boy* remembered his friends when *he* saw the schoolyard' (ibid.: 91)
177 (N.) *dinbhari daurā kāṭera malāī* [Dat] *tirkhā lāgcha* 'After cutting wood all day, *I'm* getting thirsty' (Wallace 1985b: 137)

There appear to be significant differences among NIA languages in this area, however. The Dative–Experiencer (unlike the Nominative or Ergative Subject) cannot be the *victim* of such deletion in Hindi, Punjabi, or Kashmiri (Kachru et al. 1976: 91, 99), but it can be in Nepali (Wallace 1985b: 140). However, only certain matrix Experiencers can *control* deletion in Nepali, namely those involved in what Wallace (see below) calls "intransitive" Dative Subject Constructions. In the languages studied by Kachru et al. (1976), there is apparently no such restriction (cf. no. 176 above). The matter obviously needs more cross-linguistic study.

Remaining behavioral tests for Subject yield equivocal results. A marked Experiencer may both control the deletion of coreferential Subjects of embedded infinitival clauses (the so-called EQUI-Control) and itself be deleted (EQUI-Deletion) when belonging to such a clause in Hindi, Punjabi, and Kashmiri, but only the former in Nepali. When belonging to an embedded participial clause, it may be Raised to the status of Object of a matrix clause in Nepali, but not in the other three languages. (Again, see Kachru et al. 1976 and Wallace 1985b for this data.)

Ignoring these language differences for the moment, it may be noted that Nominative and Ergative Subjects check out positive for all the above processes, Indirect Objects (except in Kashmiri) for none of them.[12] Marked Experiencers ("Dative Subjects") are thus somewhat less Subject-like than the former, but vastly more so than the latter, and should on no account be identified with the latter.

This analysis leaves one prominent loose end. If the marked Experiencer is recognized as a kind of Subject, what then is the status of the Other NP often found in Dative Subject constructions, for example, the NP naming the "sensation"/"experience"? Leaving obligational constructions (with their underlying Objects, Goals, etc.) out of consideration for the moment, in the linguistic literature on South Asian languages alone, the Other NP in non-embedded Dative Subject constructions has been called everything from *Subject* itself (as we have seen, in traditional grammar, on the basis of grammatical agreement), to *Object* (despite the lack of a transitive verb in these predications: cf. Mistry 1976, also Sridhar 1979, concerning the Dravidian language Kannada, where – as in Tamil and Malayalam – overt optional accusative markers appear on the NP in question under causativization or when paraphrased by a Nominative construction; to my knowledge this does not happen in Indo-Aryan, but I stand to be corrected), to *Actor* (Fedson 1985, writing on Tamil).

Wallace (1985b), however, has drawn attention to the fact that there are *two kinds* of Other NPs in Dative Subject constructions, because there are two kinds of (non-embedded) Dative Subject predications (in Nepali, but the insight may be extended to the other languages). The first, which he calls "intransitive", involves either a simple verb (*cilāũcha* 'itches') or a "sensation" NP + carrier verb (*bhok lāgcha* 'is hungry', *ris uṭcha* 'is angry', *jaro cha* 'has fever'). The second, which involves a variable "patient" in addition to the simple verb, or in addition to the carrier verb + "sensation" NP, he calls "transitive" ([*kitāp/bhāt man parcha* 'likes [the book/rice]', [*bihā-ko/hamro*] *smaraṇa bhayo* 'remembered [the wedding/us]'). It makes some sense to view the *variable NP* in the latter type – which must be carefully distinguished from an *embedded transitive* predication in an obligational construction – as in some sense a Patient (although it is not affected by any "action") or indeed an Object. Such "Objects" – and not the Sensation NP, where both are present – control verb agreement in Nepali (and indeed in Hindi also) when unmarked by a postposition:

178 (N.) *rām-lāī ti mānche<u>haru</u>* [pl.] *man pardaina<u>n</u>* [pl.] 'Ram doesn't like those men' (Wallace 1985b: 113)
179 (H.) *rām ko ve log yād ā<u>e</u>* 'Ram remembered those people' (Hook, pers. comm.)

Recall that *embedded* Objects do not control agreement in Nepali, also that Objects of ergative constructions do control agreement in most NIA languages (though not in Nepali).

Sensation NPs themselves are not Objects in NIA (whatever may be the case in Dravidian). It is perhaps best to view them as the nominal part of compound predicates, akin to so-called conjunct verbs (see section 10.4 below). Some are purely "intransitive"; as we have just seen, some may take complements, "quasi-Objects", in the form of additional NPs, and thus be "quasi-transitive".

10.3.3 *The Passive Agent*

Although the Passive Agent is often deleted in NIA, as in other languages, when it is present the construction differs from the type familiar in English in that the Agent retains certain properties of the underlying Subject, including its head *position* (i.e. it does not undergo demotion-by-*movement*, as in English):

180 (G.) *sarkārthī garibone paisā apāyā* 'Money was given to the poor *by the government*' (Cardona 1965: 116)
181 (M.) *sarkārkaḍūn pratinidhī nemle zātāt* 'The representatives are appointed *by the government*' (Berntsen and Nimbkar 1975b: 128)
182 (B.) *ʃɔttojit rāyer dārā poricālnā kɔrā hɔe* 'It is directed *by Satyajit Ray*' (Seely 1985: 129)

It also retains the properties of Reflexive Control and Control of Coreferential Subject Deletion in Conjunctive Participle formation. The former may be retained even by a deleted Agent (Wallace 1985b: 220), which makes Subjecthood candidacy for even a Deleted Agent not totally unreasonable. In the positive, sentences such as nos. 180–2 with overt Agents have an official or journalistic ring. In everyday speech, however, sentences with overt Agents are used, in the negative or in questions, with the implication of *incapacity* in a number of NIA languages:

183 (P.) *mere to˜ rāt p`ar sutta na'ī˜ giā* 'I was not able to sleep the whole night' (U. S. Bahri 1973: 213)
184 (H.) *rājan se makke kī roṭiyā˜ khaī jāe˜gī?* 'Will Rajan be able to eat corn bread?' (Kachru 1980: 107)
185 (Marw.) *mhārā sū˜ savere cyār bajiyā nī˜ jāgiyo jāvelā* 'I can't get up at 4 a.m.' (Magier 1983: 216)

Such an implication (and restriction to negative and interrogative contexts) is not obligatory in the Nepali passive, according to Wallace, and may be absent:

186 (N.) *rām-bāṭa rukh kāṭiyo* 'Ram was able to cut down the tree/ The tree was cut down by Ram' (Wallace 1985b: 212)
187 (N.) *jaŋgal-bāṭa baḍhi rokincha* 'Floods are stopped by the jungle' (ibid. 211)

Cf. also Gujarati:

188 (G.) *ɛnā-thī ā kāgaḷ va˜cāī gayo* 'This letter was read by him = He accidentally read this letter' (Cardona 1965: 124)
189 (G.) *mārā-thī vadhāre khavāī gayu˜* 'Too much was eaten by me = I ate too much without meaning to' (ibid. 124)

As nos. 182 and 184 indicate, another peculiarity of this NIA passive is its ability to occur with intransitive verbs. This feature, like the others such as position retention, also characterized the Classical Sanskrit passive construction (Hock 1982).

In both Sanskrit and NIA, this "incompletely demoted" Passive Agent is marked by an Instrumental. In NIA, this involves use of a postposition different from that which marks the Agentive (itself often descended from the Sanskrit Instrumental) in Ergative or Quasi-Ergative constructions: H. *se, ke dvārā* (vs. *ne*), N. *bāṭa* (vs. *le*), M.-*[cyā]kaḍūn* (vs. *-ne*/*-nī*), G. *-thī, vaḍe* (vs. *-e*).

A further complication is the influence of English on, especially, journalistic and expository prose, superimposing another model and function of passive in certain registers. It is not possible to say, at the present stage of investigation of the subject, exactly what this influence has been across the NIA spectrum, but it may include the possibility of Agent displacement for other than the normal NIA stylistic reasons (see section 10.8.3 below):

190 (B.) *corṭāke pūliʃer dārā dhɔrā gælo* 'The thief was caught by the police' (Bender and Riccardi 1978: 41)

A number of different constructions are expressive of "passive" in the Eastern group. For the fullest discussion on Bengali, see Seely 1985: 128–35.

10.3.4 *Other candidates for Subjecthood*

These may be passed over more briefly, although each has its interest as well as its complications. The *Temporary Possession* construction parallels the Dative construction closely, except that the Possessor has Locative marking of some kind (followed by object possessed and an existential verb) rather than Dative marking:

191 (P.) *muṇḍe koḷ kalam e* 'The boy has a pen' (Shackle 1972: 65)
192 (S.) *mū̃ vaṭʲ ɓa rupīā āhē* 'I have two rupees' (Addleton and Brown 1981: 92)
193 (G.) *tamārī pāse koi sārũ kāpaḍ che?* 'Do you have any good [cotton] cloth?' (Dhruva 1920: 149)
194 (M.) *tujhyāzavaḷ sāykal āhe kā?* 'Do you have a bicycle?' (Berntsen and Nimbkar 1982: 82)
195 (Si.) *māma lāňga sigaræṭ tiyenavā* 'I have cigarettes [on me]' (Fairbanks et al. 1968: I. 103)
196 (O.) *mo pākhɔre se bɔhi āu nāhĩ* 'I don't have that book [with me]' (Pattanayak and Das 1972: 134)
197 (B.) *tomār hāte ki pɔeʃā āche?* 'Have you got [any] money?' (Hudson 1965: 48)

198 (A.) *tār hātɒt pɔisā nāi* 'He does not have any money [with him]' (Baruah 1980: 95)

199 (N.) *ma-sanga pā̃c rupiyā̃ mātrai cha* 'I only have 5 rupees [with me]' (Matthews 1984: 55)

200 (H.) *mere pās sirf das rupaye kā noṭ hai* 'I have only a 10-rupee note'

[201 (K.) *tɔhi chavɨ ṭūkɨr?* 'Do you have a basket?' (Kachru 1973: 235)]

The Locative expression usually denotes 'near', but Bengali and Assamese prefer a more body-oriented 'in the hand'. (The Kashmiri expression is in brackets, as it makes use of a simple Dative for temporary possession also. This is also the *unmarked* expression in Sinhalese.)

Distinguished from these only slightly (although various behavioral tests need to be explored) are existential expressions with *Topicalized Locatives*, often but not necessarily involving inanimates or at least non-humans:

202 (H.) *kamre me᷈ do khiṛkiyā̃ thī̃* 'The room had two windows' [= 'There were two windows *in the room*']

203 (H.) *hāthiyo᷈ me᷈ baṛī tākat hotī hai* 'Elephants have great strength' (Hook 1979: 81)

204 (H.) *rāju me᷈ baṛā dhairya hai* 'Raju has great patience' (Y. Kachru 1980: 122)

205 (M.) *rastyāvar puṣkaḷ gharə̄ āhet* 'There are many houses *on the road*' (Berntsen and Nimbkar 1982: 97)

206 (N.) *tyo gāũmā ciyāpasal rahenacha* 'It seems that there is no teashop *in that village*' [= it seems that that village has no teashop] (Matthews 1984: 55)

207 (G.) *koī koī gāmmā̃ prāthamik ʃāḷā hɔy che* '*In some villages* there are primary schools' [= Some villages have primary schools] (Lambert 1971: 64)

208 (O.) *āmerikāre jhiɔmānɔŋkɔ pāĩ ɔlɔgā sālun ɔchi* 'There are separate saloons for girls *in America*' [= "America has . . ."] (Pattanayak and Das 1972: 224)

When the relation is one of "integral" part to whole (animate or inanimate), the NP in Subject position has Genitive marking:

209 (H.) *kamre kī tīn hī dīvāre᷈ hai᷈* '*The room* has only three walls'

210 (P.) *muṇḍe dā ba'ut vaḍḍā sir sī* '*The boy* had a very big head' (Shackle 1972: 65)

Hindi, Gujarati, and probably other languages have also (as an alternate but often preferred construction) peculiar *invariant* Genitives here, used also in expressing kinship relations:

211 (H.) *uske sirf ek bahan hai* 'He has only one sister' [rather than *uskī*, feminine]
212 (H.) *harek ke nāk hotī hai* 'Everybody has a nose' [rather than *kī*, agreeing with *nāk*, f.] (Hook 1979: 80)
213 (G.) *māre bɛ hāth che* 'I have two hands' (Lambert 1971: 43)
214 (G.) *māre traṇ kākā che* 'I have three paternal uncles' (ibid.) [rather than normal Mpl., which is *mārā*]

The normal variable Genitive is usually used for expression of non-temporary (sometimes defined as "non-portable") possession – landed property, etc.:

215 (G.) *amāro moṭo bangalo che* 'We have a large bungalow' (ibid.)
216 (P.) *o´de puttar de tin k`ar ne* 'His son has three houses' (Shackle 1972: 65)

On the other hand, in Marathi, Sindhi, and other languages the Dative is used in many of these situations:

217 (M.) *gāīlā ʃiŋgə āhet* 'A cow has horns' (Berntsen and Nimbkar 1975b: 135)
218 (S.) *mū˜ khē ba ghar^{a} āhin* 'I own two houses' (Addleton and Brown 1981: 92)
219 (S.) *hina ghar^{a} khē panj^{a} darivāzā āhin* 'This house has five doors' (ibid. 93)

Subject-candidates (so defined by their control of Coreferential Subject Deletion in conjunctive participle clauses) with Genitive or Locative marking outside of these contexts need further exploration:

220 (H.) *(jangal me˜ pahu˜ckar) uskā ḍakuo˜ se pālā paṛā* '(Arriving in the jungle), he encountered bandits' (Dwarikesh 1971)
221 (H.) *(zahar kā pyālā pīkar) us-par koi asar nahī˜ huā* 'She drank the cup of poison and there was no effect *on her*' (ibid.)

All of the above involve NPs in Subject "position", and in some cases at least with certain behavioral properties pertaining to Subjects, but not controlling verb agreement. In the remaining cases, namely the *Passive Patient* and the *Ergative Patient*, there is something like the opposite situation. That is, these entities have come to control verb agreement – their main claim on Subjecthood – in some languages (Hindi, Punjabi, Sindhi, Kashmiri, Gujarati, and Marathi, primarily), and under certain conditions (when the Patient is unmarked) – but their normal position is still Object position, not Subject position. Moreover, (except in Kashmiri) they may still take overt Object-marking (see section 10.4 below) under certain conditions, in which case (except in Gujarati and Rajasthani) even the agreement is neutralized:

Passive Patient:

222 (H.) *maĩ* [Nom] *fauran pahcān lī jāū̃gī* 'I[(F] will be recognized right off' (Hook 1979: 120)

223 (H.) *mujhe* [Dat–Acc] *fauran pahcān liyā jāegā* 'I'll be recognized right off' (ibid.: 120)

Ergative Patient:

224 (H.) *mere beṭõ ne yah film* [Nom (Fsg.)] *dekhī* (Fsg.) 'My sons saw this film' (Hook 1979: 19)

225 (H.) *mere beṭõ ne is film ko* [Dat–Acc] *dekhā* (msg.) 'My sons saw this film' (ibid.: 19)

In several respects, then, the "promotion to Subject" of the Object in NIA passive constructions may be called *incomplete*. In the case of the Ergative constructions, the claim of the Agent on Subject status is especially strong, but the close parallelism of the two constructions may be noted. In Bengali the Passive Patient (there is of course no Ergative) always retains its Object-marking if it had it (Seely 1985: 130, Bender and Riccardi 1978: 40–1):

226 (B.) *bɔchor khānek pɔre khukuke nāki kɔlkātāe dækhā geche ābār* 'Several years later Khuku was again seen in Calcutta' (Seely 1985: 130)

On the other hand, in such languages as Hindi, Punjabi, and Kashmiri (investigated by Kachru et al. 1976), the Passive Patient (the Ergative Patient does not enter the picture) has apparently acquired (marginally) the additional Subject property of Reflexive Control:

227 (H.) *laṛke ko apnī jagah par biṭhā diyā gayā* 'The boy was seated at his place' (Kachru et al. 1976: 93).

The authors admit the sentence is ambiguous: the *apnī* could refer to a deleted Agent. Since either Agent or Patient can control Reflexives in Passive constructions, such ambiguity is not uncommon (Pandharipande 1981: 62). Disambiguation is through extra-linguistic context. Cf. Nepali:

228 (N.) *rām-dvārā sitā-lāī āphnā kathā-le ruvāiyo* 'Sita was made to cry by Ram through (hearing) her own story' (Wallace 1985b: 220)
229 (N.) *ma-bāṭa syām-lāī āphno ṭhaũ-mā paṭhāiyo* 'Syam was sent by me to his/my room' (ibid. 220)

10.3.5 *Summary*

NP constituents that have some Subject properties in NIA thus range from unmarked Agents of transitive verbs in non-Perfective tenses, which may be said to have the maximum (including topic-position, verb agreement control, Nominative case, agentivity and volitionality, and control of or accessibility to all relevant covert-syntactic rules), to Ergative Patients, which have the minimum (verb agreement control under some conditions; in Kashmiri, even some non-Ergative Patients can control verb agreement). Thus Subjecthood in NIA would appear to be a cluster of properties, distributed on a cline.

If this is unacceptable – although such fuzzy boundaries would seem to be a fact of linguistic life (e.g., agentivity is a cline [cf. Hook 1976b], volitionality is a cline [cf. Pandharipande 1982], ergativity is a cline [cf. Masica 1982], transitivity is a cline [cf. Hock 1985]) – there are several alternatives. One is to declare Subject an irrelevant concept for NIA languages – which, in view of the crucial reference made to it by several syntactic processes, hardly seems acceptable. Another is to take one property as definitional, ignoring the others. This has been the method of traditional grammar, taking Subject to be "that NP with which the verb agrees" (such as, e.g., Ergative and Passive Patients), even though this conflicts with other criteria (making Subject indeed a concept of very limited utility) and leaves many sentences "subjectless" (the traditional term is *impersonal*).[13]

It is possible, however, to take another property to be definitional (or diagnostic), one around which a maximum of other useful properties cluster. All so-called Subject-properties are not of equal weight. (Verb agreement may actually be one of the least important, easily acquired and easily lost.) Such a property may well be first or "topic" *position* (in unmarked sentences, before any displacement transformations have been applied). While many hint at this, Mistry (1976) (on Gujarati) makes it explicit. It may be noted that in terms of the usual generative models of syntax, this coincides neatly enough in NIA with "that NP [whatever its case-marking] immediately dominated by the S-node in a sentence," i.e. (using simple Hindi examples for convenience):

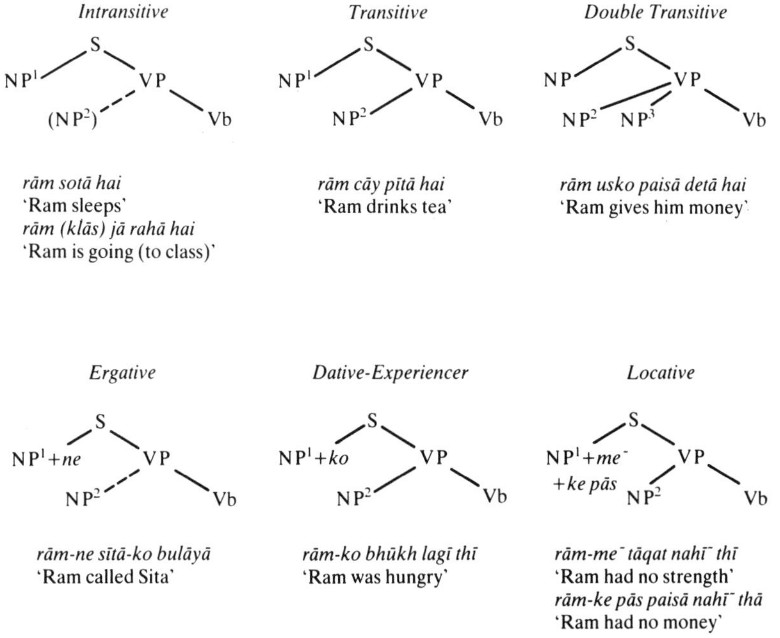

Figure 10.1 Simple verbal sentence types in NIA in terms of "subject"

(The fact that these languages are SOV rather than SVO, which seems to have bothered some investigators, does not seem to affect this argument in the least.) As Mistry points out, this does not mean identity of Topic and Subject: after the Subject is displaced through a topicalization transformation, and something else becomes the Topic, the Subject does not cease to be the Subject (as proven by various behavioral characteristics). This formulation also does not preclude recognition of the fact that, as Kachru et al. (1976: 102) conclude, "some subjects are more subject-like than others," i.e. that Dative Experiencers and Passive Agents may lack certain alleged Subject properties. It does exclude Ergative and Passive Patients from Subjecthood, despite the presence of certain alleged Subject properties.

It does not, of course, solve every problem. For example, are first-place Locative NPs used with existential predications primary, or are they the result of a topicalization permutation? May Passive Patients, when the Agent is unspecified, be said to occupy first position (and therefore qualify)?

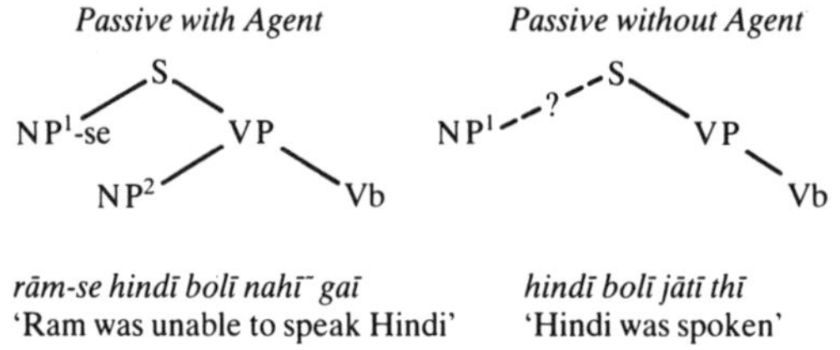

Figure 10.2 Passive sentences with and without agent

The Subject problem has generated several important symposia with resulting publications. See Li (ed.) 1976 (which includes the important paper by Edward L. Keenan, "Towards a universal definition of 'Subject'"), Verma (ed.) 1976a, and Zide et al. (eds.) 1985. The most extensive work by a single author on the subject is Wallace 1985b on Nepali, which also has sections on the handling of the problem (or inadequacies in doing so) in Relational Grammar and Government and Binding Theory for the theoretical-minded. (For the latter, see also Davison 1985, in Zide et al.) Otherwise, for NIA passives, see Pandharipande 1981, 1982; for Sanskrit passives, see Hock 1982; for the Dative Subject construction, see Klaiman 1980, 1981 as well as Sridhar 1976, 1979 (on Kannada); for a succinct history of the Ergative construction, see Pray 1976 (in the Verma volume); for an account of its distribution and permutations in the area, see Masica 1982.

10.4 **Object in NIA**

The Object problem is the obverse of the Subject problem – at least in part. That is, in a number of cases we must decide whether a given NP is essentially a Subject or an Object, since it appears to have attributes of both. As some of these arguments have already been reviewed in the Subject section, this aspect of our treatment of Objects may accordingly be more brief.

Normal Object *position* in non-interrogative clauses (non-finite as well as finite) is immediately before the verb:

230 (H.) *suresh jeb me˜ cābhī rakhtā hai* 'Suresh keeps *a key* in his pocket' (Y. Kachru 1980: 16)

231 (G.) *paṭāvāḷo sṭeʃan parthi sāmān lāvyo hato* 'The messenger brought *the luggage* from the station' (Lambert 1971: 97)

232 (B.) *āmrā bier rāttre gān gāibɔ* 'We shall sing *songs* on the night of the wedding' (Dimock et al. 1964: 114 [modified])

233 (Si.) *mama dæŋ sumāneak vitara rejisṭar liyumak balāporottuveŋ innavā* 'I have been expecting *a registered letter* for about a week now' (Fairbanks et al. 1968: I. 100)

The Object is not distinguished from the Subject by *case marking* in many NIA sentences, including those above. Both may be in the Nominative. Unlike Sanskrit – or Dravidian – (but rather like Tibeto-Burman) there is generally no distinctive Accusative Case in NIA.[14] Historically, the Indo-Aryan Accusative merged with the Nominative. (This may be one factor in the persistence of an Agent Case in a number of NIA languages: if the Object is not marked, at least the Subject may be, by way of distinction. Note, however, that only a minority of Subjects are so marked, and only in certain languages. Moreover, the Agentive is a *unique* marker only in Hindi, Punjabi, and to some extent in Kashmiri. Nepali *-le*, Marathi *-nī/ne*, Assamese and Gujarati *-e* also have retained certain instrumental functions, and in the last case Locative functions as well. In Sindhi, the General Oblique without a postposition is used for the Agentive: it is not always distinct from the Nominative, and may have other functions.)

This is not to say that Objects are always bereft of case marking. They may take it, in the form of the Dative marker (in the absence of an Accusative: the marker is sometimes called a *Dative–Accusative* as a result). Its functions, however, are often more pragmatic than syntactic. That is, in the case of non-human nouns, it generally indicates a "definite" object, that is, one that is already known (see Masica 1981, 1986 for extended discussion); in the case of human nouns, it stresses their Patienthood, a marked status (human nouns normally being Agents). In languages with other means of marking definiteness (or indefiniteness, in the case of Sinhalese) (see section 10.5 below), the first of these functions is minimalized. Except in Sinhalese, it nevertheless exists (e.g., in Bengali).

234 (H.) *usne kamre ko har taraf se dekhā* 'He looked around *the room*' (Usha Priyamvada, "Kagaz ke phul")

235 (P.) *o´ nīlī kitāb nū˜ mez te rākkho* 'Put *that blue book* on the table' (Shackle 1972: 70)

236 (B.) *boi-ṭā-ke ṭebiler opor dāo* 'Put the book on the table' (Page 1934: 126)

237 (G.) *kutrā-ne pāchaḷ rākho* 'Keep the dogs back' (Dhruva 1920: 159)

No. 237 is slightly different in that it involves an *animate* (though non-human Object). It is difficult to find good examples of definitized *inanimate* Objects in Gujarati and Marathi; although the construction is said to exist in those languages (Savel'eva 1965: 26, Katenina 1963: 58), it would appear to be much less common than in Hindi or Punjabi. (Significantly, it is not used with *pronouns* referring to such Objects in those languages, unlike Hindi.) This usage should be distinguished from that with Objects that have complements, where it is frequent though perhaps not required in all cases:

238 (G.) *dhobie mārā̃ kapḍā̃-ne {istari} barābar karī nathī* 'The washerman has not ironed [= done the iron to?] my clothes well' (Dhruva 1920: 153)

239 (G.) *ʃekspiyare potāna kavitva-ne {mahān} banāvyũ* 'Shakespeare made his poetry great' (Savel'eva 165: 26)

Often Objects with complements are +human, and would take the Dat–Acc marker on those grounds also. The Human Patient-marking function, unlike the identification functions, *is* general in all the languages except Sinhalese:

240 (M.) *to āplyā mitrā-lā soḍūn gelā* 'He forsook his friend' (Katenina 1963: 58)

241 (G.) *chokarī mā-ne jue che* 'The girl sees [her] mother' (Lambert 1971: 36)

242 (N.) *keṭā-lāī kina piṭchau?* 'Why do you beat the boy?' (Mathews 1984: 70)

243 (Si.) *gunapāla hamibavenna ōna da?* 'Do you want to see Gunapala [unmarked]?' (Fairbanks et al. 1968: II. 206)

The Dat–Acc marker can be omitted with +human Objects, but this has the effect of making them "non-referential", i.e. generic:

244 (H.) *rānī ne laṛkā janmāyā* 'The queen gave birth to *a boy*'

The Object + Complement construction is close to that of the double transitive requiring an Indirect Object. The latter, usually +human in any case, obligatorily takes the Dative in all NIA languages (except Kashmiri in certain cases, where it may be Nominative, and unlike Sanskrit, where it may be Accusative) and has priority over Direct Objects (which it also normally precedes positionally) in such marking:

245 (H.) *yogesh ne ajay ko apnī tasvīre˜ dikhāī˜* 'Yogesh showed his pictures to Ajay' (Kachru 1980: 100)

246 (G.) *lok dukāndār-ne paysa āpe che* 'People give money to the shopkeeper' (Lambert 1971: 30)

247 (O.) *mu˜ apɔnɔ-ŋku goṭie bhɔlɔ bɔhi debi* 'I shall give you a good book' (Pattanayak and Das 1972: 137)

but: 248 (K.) *temy hyēchinōv-us* [1sg. M] *bi* [Nom – 'I'] *jāgrephyī* 'He taught me geography' (Hook: pers. comm.)

Indirect Objects of verbs semantically requiring them (e.g., 'tell', 'invite') are never advanced to Direct Object status in NIA but retain Dative (or sometimes other oblique case) marking, even in Sinhalese:

249 (Si.) *api sēna-ṭa-t enna kiyamu* 'Let's invite Sena, too' (Fairbanks et al. 1968: II. 155)

250 (G.) *ahī˜ pāṇī laī āv, ɛm māḷī-ne kaho* 'Tell the gardener to bring some water' (Lambert 1971: 37)

Keeping all these distinctions in mind, it could be revealing to do a frequency count of marking of inanimate Direct Objects (and perhaps also animate non-human Objects) – *only* – for definiteness in different NIA languages. It might strengthen – or refute – the suggestion (see Masica 1981) that this comparatively new phenomenon owes something to Turkic and Persian influence, strongest in Hindi and Punjabi. It is absent, for example, in the transmontane languages Kashmiri and Shina (Hook, pers. comm.).

The Object marker is an excellent example of the multifunctionality of most case markers in NIA, that is, their failure to coincide on a one-to-one basis with any syntactic roles (the only exception, as noted previously, being the Agentive *-ne* in Hindi). The Dative marker can mark the Indirect Object (its "proper" role), the Direct Object under several distinct sets of conditions, and the Subject (when it is an Experiencer), as well as certain adverbial adjuncts (e.g., of time) in some languages, and other functions.

The only unequivocal indicator of the Object role in NIA syntax is thus again *position*. By this measure, as well as in consideration of the fact that Object markers (assigned according to the above criteria) are often retained by ergative and passive Patients, the latter are more Object-like than Subject-like, in spite of the control of verb agreement they exercise when Object markers are not present. Presence or absence of Object markers has more to do with pragmatic and other factors than with syntactic roles: that is, in active sentences, their presence or absence does not *change* the syntactic role of an NP. The "promotion to Subject" of the Patient in passive constructions may thus be regarded as incomplete at best when this pattern is retained. On the other hand, as Hook (1985a: 277) notes, in at least some styles of Modern Hindi prose *ko*-marked human Patients *may* lose their *ko*'s in the passive (in about half the cases) and thus have a stronger claim on promotion to Subjecthood. (Other languages need investigation: see, however, Magier 1985 and Mistry 1976 for counterevidence pertaining to Marwari and Gujarati.)

There is one additional problem with Objects in NIA that must be noted. This arises from the ubiquitousness of so-called *conjunct verbs* – compounds made up of a noun or adjective + a verbalizer such as *do*: H. *madad karnā* 'to help'; *band karnā* 'to close', *ʃurū karnā* 'to begin', *pratīkṣā karnā* 'to await'. When the non-verbal element is a noun, it may be treated syntactically as the verb's Object (never taking Dat–Acc marking, but governing verbal agreement in Perfective and Infinitival constructions in the Central and Western languages). The semantic Patient of the Conjunct Verbal expression is often expressed syntactically as a Genitive adjunct of such a noun:

251 (H.) *maĩne rām kī madad* (F) *kī* (F) 'I helped Ram'

252 (G.) *āṭhme divase teo chokrā-nī sunat karvā āvyā* 'On the eighth day they came to circumcise the boy'

253 (G.) *teṇe potānā lok-nī mulākāt laine teo-no uddhār karyo che* 'He has visited and redeemed his people' (St Luke 1: 68)

254 (M.) . . . *tyāne tyā̃cī suṭkā* (Fsg.) *kelī* (Fsg.) *ahe* 'He has released them' (ibid., Living NT version)

On the other hand the Patient may be treated as a syntactic Object:

255 (H.) *unhõne hamārā nimantraṇ svīkār kiyā hai* 'They have accepted our *invitation*'

256 (H.) *maĩne kām ʃurū kiyā hai* 'I have begun *work*'

Y. Kachru, whose 1982 article on Hindi and Persian conjunct verbs is one of the few devoted to the subject (see also Hook 1979: 106–7, Pořízka 1963: 436–7), would call only the latter "true conjunct verbs"; the former she says are just "verb phrases". Impressionistically speaking, both types appear to be more numerous in the languages of the north, possibly again due to Persian influence. In Bengali, where the Genitive seems already over-used, the Genitival construction nevertheless occurs commonly enough (although the question is complicated by the merger of the Dative and Genitive cases in the plural):

257 (B.) *āpnā-ke* [Dat] *ʃāhājjɔ korechilam* 'I helped you'

258 (B.) *tini ei rɔhɔʃʃer* [Gen] *udghāṭon korte pāren nā* 'He is unable to solve this mystery' (Seely 1985: 263–6)

Here, it would seem, is another area where detailed cross-linguistic comparison (with frequency counts) would be fruitful. {Adjectival} elements must be carefully distinguished, as they behave differently (forcing treatment of Patients as Objects):

259 (H.) *rāj ne angrezī gāne* (Mpl.) *{pasand} kiye* (Mpl.) 'Raj liked English songs' (Y. Kachru 1982: 119)
260 (H.) *darvāzā {band} kar dījiye* 'Please close the door'
261 (B.) *tini nijo prɔjāder* [Gen] *tɔttābɔdhān* [noun] *korte eʃechen, tāder* [Gen/Dat] *{mukto} kɔrechen* 'He has visited and redeemed his people' (St Luke 1: 68) [cf. no. 253]

The main point to be noted about all three subtypes of these formations, which probably exist in most languages (cf. English *take place*, *catch hold [of N]*, *make use [of N]*), is that they are especially numerous in NIA, and are often the sole equivalents of simple verbs in other languages. Another point of some importance, however, is that where a *noun* is involved, it is bereft of any attribute of definiteness, that is, it is neither specified nor unspecified nor generic: it cannot take (without change of function) either a specifying Dat–Acc marker or a Determiner (nor, in those languages which have them, a Definitizing or Indefinitizing Suffix). Even when treated syntactically (in some respects) as an Object, it represents the bare idea of the noun, verbalized by the lexically empty verb which accompanies it. The latter is thus equivalent to a denominal verb-forming suffix (examples of which also exist in NIA – more copiously, it may be noted, in those languages, such as Marathi and Sinhalese, in which the "conjunct verb" construction appears to be less used). Here we have another example of the unclear boundary between syntax and morphology (in this case derivational) in NIA.

10.5 The Noun Phrase

Although modern theoretical treatments of the NIA Noun Phrase (i.e. mainly the Hindi NP – Verma 1971, Kachru 1980, Subbarao 1984, but cf. also Mistry 1969 on Gujarati and Shukla 1981 on Bhojpuri) differ somewhat in their analyses, the basic facts need not detain us long. If we may leave embedded clauses involving predications other than *be* for later consideration, the structure of the "simple" Noun Phrase in NIA (with certain exceptions to be noted presently) may be called straightforwardly *left-branching* (Modifier + N).

Regular cooccurrence possibilities – which in many of the languages need more study than they have received – force us to postulate several distinct functional slots within the Modifier. Immediately to the left of the Head Noun come attributive Adjectives,[15] if any: B. *dhārmik mohilā* 'religious woman', N. *purāno mandir* 'old temple', Si. *sudu eladenā* '(the) white cow'. To the left of these, much as in Germanic, comes the Determiner'[16] which specifies definiteness (identification) or indefiniteness (introduction) in various ways: H. *us choṭe gā̃v (me)̃* '(in) that small village', B. *ʃei purāno ʃāp* 'that ancient serpent', G. *ek moṭo tāro* 'a great star', A. *eṭā bɒgā gho̜rā* 'a white horse', P. *koī purāṇī kitāb* 'some old book'.

Is the Determiner an optional element or is it obligatory (with ZERO as one of its terms)? Perhaps neither: nouns used in a *generic* sense do not require it, nor do those entering into conjunct-verb relations (see section 10.4), but NIA is not like Russian: specification of definiteness-status relative to discourse is not entirely optional, and it could be argued that in certain syntactic contexts, ZERO is one of its terms (cf. Y. Kachru 1980: 22). That is, in most NIA languages an unstressed form of the word 'one' (K. *akh*, S. *hik[aṛo]*, P. *ik*, H.G.M. *ek*, etc.) is close to becoming an Indefinite Article[17] (and is so treated in some descriptions). Accordingly, nouns not so marked (or specified as "indefinite" by another, more specific Determiner, such as H. *koī* 'some/any') may be regarded – *at least in the context of Subject and of Object of a Postposition* – as "definite" (identified) and so specified by the ZERO-Determiner. (They may of course be more overtly specified by the Demonstratives *this/that.*) Another and perhaps better way of looking at the matter, however, would be to posit a privative opposition with "*indefinite*" as the marked member. Indefiniteness is marked (that is, made explicit) primarily where (1) the distinction matters, and (2) it differs from the status implied by the syntactic role of the noun: e.g., Subjects are usually previously known, *identified* = "definite"; for them (and for Objects of Postpositions) *unidentified* status is a marked status (see Masica 1986).

The question is further complicated by the part played in the overall Definiteness marking (as distinct from merely Determiner) system by the differential use of the Acc–Dat case marker on Direct Objects (simultaneously marking syntactic, and in the case of personal nouns, semantic roles [section 10.4 above]), and by the so-called (definite) specifier *suffixes* (*-ṭā*, *-ṭī*, etc.) of the eastern group (Chapter 8, section 5): B. *boiṭā* 'the book'. These suffixes are simultaneously part of (but not coterminous with) a *numeral classifier* system, suffixed to numerals (including '*one*' in its Indefinite Article function in Bengali–Assamese–Bishnupriya = *ekṭi/etā/etā*, but not in Oriya = *ekɔ*), in which case they do *not* indicate definiteness. (In Nepali, such elements function as numeratives only – *duijanā mānche* 'two men', *euṭā kitāb* 'one/a book' – and never as definite noun-suffixes.) The relationship of the Definite Suffixes to the pan-Indian system of definiteness–

status marking needs more study: they appear to be used (redundantly but by no means consistently) mainly with nouns whose definiteness is already implied by their position, or even overtly, marked by a demonstrative: B. *ʃiʃu-ṭi-r̲ pitā* 'the baby's father', *ʃiʃu-ṭi-k̲e̲ jāber pātre ʃoyāno dekhte pælo* 'they found *the* babe lying in a manger' (St Luke 2: 16), *ei lækhā-ṯi-te* 'in this letter' (Bender and Riccardi 1978: 109); O. *e ṭɔŋkā-tāe* 'this money (Subj.) [is] . . .', (*rājā*) *bɔṛɔ rāṇī-ṭi-k̲u̲* (*dekhi parɔnti nāhī*) '(The king could not look at) the elder queen' (Karpushkin 1964: 86). It should be noted, however, that most nouns with definite status in a discourse seem not to be marked with the Definite Suffixes. Their relationship, if any, to the Determiner system is therefore unclear (although see the extensive discussion in Dasgupta 1983). Of more direct concern to NP phrase structure is the aberrant postnominal position (but not *areally*: cf. neighboring Tibeto-Burman languages) of the Demonstrative in Bishnupriya: *pāni e̲t̲ā̲* 'this water' (K. P. Sinha 1981: 88).

In Sinhalese, as already noted, it is the Indefinite Article which has been morphologized (as the suffix *-ek*/*-ak*). There are possibly incipient similar developments in Shina (*muʃā-k* 'a man': Bailey 1924: 82–3), Assamese (cf. no. 55), and Oriya. In the latter, the suffix {*-e*}, added to time units, measure words, and inanimates in general signifies "singularity" according to Tripathi (1962: 126) (*rɔtnɔhāre̲* 'one [= a?] jewelled necklace'), but is apparently still in free variation with the preposed Determiner *ekɔ: māse̲* = *ekɔ māsɔ* 'one month' (Pattanayak and Das 1972: 25). A phonologically identical suffix {*-e*} is used with "rational" nouns as a *plural* marker: *puɔ-pue̲* 'son/sons', *pilā*/*pilāe̲* or *pile̲* 'child/children' (a Dravidian loanword) (Tripathi 1962: 128, Karpushkin 1964: 27). Whatever their status, the Shina and Assamese suffixes have not driven out preposed indefinite Determiners.

A somewhat unusual device, both in the context of NIA and generally, entering into the definiteness-marking system is the *definite adjectival suffix* ({*-(k)k-*}) described for Northern Bhojpuri by Shukla (1981: 85–6, 93–4: *ham n̲ī̲k̲e̲ pēḍe par caḍhab* 'I will climb on *a good* tree'/*ham n̲i̲k̲k̲ā̲ pēḍe par caḍhab* 'I will climb on *the good* tree'.

In Bengali the Determiner (or at least its Indefinite instantiations) can be moved to a position *between* the adjective and head noun: *khub bɔṛo æ̲k̲ṭ̲ā̲ pukur* 'a very big tank' (Page 1934: 191), *ʃundor ʃundor k̲ɔ̲æ̲k̲k̲h̲ā̲n̲i̲ pākhā* 'a number of very beautiful fans' (ibid. 191), *birāṭ e̲k̲ṭ̲i̲ nɔkkhɔttro* 'a huge star' (Rev. 8: 10). This is a marked order, not the normal one.[18] The Central and Western NIA languages seem not to permit this, but the other Eastern languages might well be looked into further, although I have so far found no examples.

Between the Determiner (in our narrow sense) and the Adjective can come numerals and other quantity-indicating elements ('all', 'some'): H. *ye do laṛke* 'these two boys', G. *ā badhā kāgaḷo* 'all these ["these all"] letters' (Lambert 1971: 57). This forces us to posit for most NIA languages another optional NP slot, that of *Quantifier*: Det + (Quant) + (Adj) + N. The constituent (Quant) may be further differentiated internally. In Sinhalese, however, cardinal (not ordinal) numerals beyond 'one' (*eka*) along with words for 'some', 'many', 'how much', 'how many' (cf. H. *kitne paise* '*how much* money?' = Si. *salli koccara?*) come *after* the noun, followed in turn where relevant by the indefinite suffix mentioned earlier, which thus turns out to be a kind of clitic (and even further from the meaning 'one'): *lamay tundenā* 'the three boys'/*lamay tunden-ek* 'three boys (indefinite)'; *pol huṅgak* '*many* coconuts'. The Sinhalese NP thus has a structure Det¹ + (Adj) + N + (Quant) + Det², where Det¹ (= Definite, i.e. Demonstratives and ZERO) and Det² (= Indefinite, i.e. *-ek*/*-ak*) are mutually exclusive.

Dasgupta points out that the Bengali Quantifier may also follow the noun, and when it does, this conveys *definiteness*: *duṭo khām* 'two envelopes'/*khām duṭo* 'the two envelopes' (Dasgupta 1983: 18). Something else seems to be going on in Kashmiri: *zɨ jāyi* 'two places' (B. Kachru 1973: 560), *zɨ neciv´* 'two sons' (Bailey 1937: 39 [Prodigal Son], *neciv´ zɨ* 'two sons' (ibid. 36 [Hatim's Tales]), *tihɨnzɨ vēlinji zɨ* 'their two hearts' (ibid. 37), *hūn´ zɨ* 'two dogs' (ibid. 37); the contexts are, except for the fourth, indefinite rather than definite.

Preceding the Determiner on the left are modifying *Genitive Phrases*: H. *ʃarmilā kī ve do lāl kitābẽ* 'Those two red books *of Sharmila's*' (Y. Kachru 1980: 41), B. *āmār ei kɔthā* [lit.] "my this-thing" = 'these words *of mine*' (St Luke 1: 20), G. *mārā ā be mitra* 'these two friends of mine' (Cardona 1965: 88). Note that with Quantifiers such as 'all' and 'both' the NIA rule is more general than its English counterpart, resulting in different orders in NIA and English: H. *uske do bhāī* = 'her two brothers' but *uske donõ bhāī* 'both her brothers'; G. *mārī sarva sampatti* '*all* my wealth' (1 Cor. 13: 3). Determiners and Quantifiers modifying a subordinated noun must of course be distinguished from Determiners and Quantifiers modifying the Head: *[ʃɔb jānoār]eri māmā* 'the uncle of [*all* the animals]' (Page 1934: 182).

In at least some NIA languages a Locative phrase may also be used as an attribute. In Hindi it takes a Genitive marker: *mez par kī kitābẽ* 'the books on the table' (Subbarao 1984: 15). The same construction is found in Gujarati: *pyālā-mā-nũ pāṇī* 'the water in the cup' (Mistry 1969: 53). In Marathi, there is a special (variable) suffix {*-lā∗*} (Literary {*-il*}) for this purpose: *tyā kapāṭ-āt-il bhāṇḍī* 'the pots in that cupboard', *tyā deʃāt-il lok* 'the people in that country' (Berntsen and Nimbkar 1975: 139). Like other phrasal attributes that follow the Head in English, these are placed at the far left of the NP in NIA. Locative attributes may usually also be expressed by a relative clause. (This may not be the case in every language, however: Marathi, Oriya, and Sinhalese need special scrutiny here.) Another such construction is "by the name of": M. *suman nāvā-c̲ī̲ mulgī* 'a girl by the name of Suman' (ibid. 137); N. *pokharā nāu˜gareko arko euṭā sāno tar atyanta sundar ʃahar* 'another small but extremely beautiful city called Pokhara' (Matthews 1984: 146).

Pending finer tuning, then, the basic NIA Noun Phrase may be represented as:

$$\begin{array}{l}\{\text{Gen P}\}\\ \qquad\qquad + \text{Det} + (\text{Quant}) + (\text{Adj P}) + \text{N}.\\ \{\text{Loc P}\}\end{array}$$

10.6 The Adjective Phrase

As might be expected in a generally left-branching phrasal syntax, qualifiers of adjectives precede them: H. *bahut baṛā*, B. *khub bɔṛo*, S. *tamām vaddo*, M. *phār moṭhā*, Si. *bohoma loku* 'very large'.

Comparative constructions constitute a special variety of (phrasal) qualifier. There being no inflection of the adjective for comparative degree in NIA, comparison is expressed by prefacing the adjective with the thing (i.e. noun or pronoun) with which comparison is made (in the case of the superlative with the word 'all') in the Ablative case (or equivalent expression) – an idiom also found in neighboring non-IA languages: i.e. 'bigger than X' = H.X *-se baṛā*, G.X *-thī moṭo*, P.X *-to˜ vaḍḍā*, K.X *-khɔtɨ boḍ*, M.X *-pekʃā moṭhā*, O.X *-ṭhāru bɔṛɔ*, B.X *-er ceye bɔṛo*, A.X *-ɒt koi dāŋɒr*. Sinhalese uses the Dative + *vaḍā* 'more' (X-*ṭa vaḍā loku*); the superlative has a special suffix *-ma*.

10.7 The Verb Phrase

According to traditional generative grammar, the VP includes at least the Direct and Indirect Object and probably also the Goal/Source of Motion. In a sense the verb is indeed incomplete without these essential arguments, and as we have seen (end of section 10.4 above), there is one common situation in NIA, that of the conjunct verb, where the verb itself and a quasi-object component form what is in effect a lexical unit. These components all occur to the *left* of the main verb stem (except in aberrant Kashmiri). What concerns us here, under the label Verb Phrase (for the sake of notational consistency we should perhaps call it Vb), occurs to the *right* of the main verb stem (= V) – again, except in Kashmiri.

How do we decide what is the "main" verb stem? For NIA generally a simple rule-of-thumb holds good: it is the *leftmost* verb stem in the Verb Phrase (always excepting Kashmiri, for which analogical equivalence of components to those of the common NIA pattern will have to suffice here, although analysis in its own terms should yield the same result). The first fact to be noted about the NIA Verb Phrase is that the (Tense/Mood) auxiliary is its *rightmost* element, "closing" the phrase. (Here exceptions are to be found not only in Kashmiri but also in Punjabi and Sindhi *negative* sentences [see section 10.8.2 below]. These may be regarded as *modified*, i.e. non-basic, sentences, however.) It makes some sense, as will be seen, to define an element Aux containing both the Tense/Mood "auxiliary" proper and the *Aspect* marker immediately preceding it (sometimes as a quasi-analytic element). In its simplest form, the Verb Phrase would be, in syntactic terms, thus V + Aux.

Between the main (initial) V and the Aux, however, there may occur a limited set of "secondary" stems (Pattanayak 1972: cf. the common notation V^1 V^2 in e.g., Southworth 1961 on M.) with special functions. In some of the now older literature, particularly of the London school (Burton-Page 1957, Raeṣide 1958 on M.), they are labeled *Operators*. In terms of function, they are described by Kachru (1980) as "modals" and "secondary aspect" markers; for Cardona (1965) they are all "modals". The problem is to distinguish these from sequences of verbs which are the result of embedding (*learn* to V, *forget* to V, *enjoy* V-ing, etc.) on the one hand,[19] and from "Vv" or Main Verb + Specifier (Explicator) "vector" on the other. This is not always a simple matter, since, in the first case, some may perceive embeddings where others do not, and in the second, the Specifier class can with some justification be seen as merely a special subclass of V^2. We may in general, however, first adopt Cardona's criterion (1965: 119) that *The sentence containing the sequence is not derivable from two sentences, each containing a form of one of the verb roots*, adding that the reference is to real sentences of the language and not to artificial constructs by linguists that do not occur as sentences. It may also be noted that, unlike English ("I *can't*", "You *must*", etc.) such "modals" (many of them, at least: more work needs to be done in this area in the different NIA languages) do not occur outside these combinations in sentences by themselves – either absolutely (H. *saknā* 'to be able'), or (perhaps arguably, depending on one's imagination) "in the same meaning" (H. *rahnā* 'stay', > as V^2, 'keep on', B. *pāoā* 'get', H. *pānā* 'find' > as V^2, 'manage to'). With regard to the Explicator subclass, we may again follow Cardona (1965: 122, 124) in setting these apart on the basis of *more restricted distribution*, i.e. potential cooccurrence with only certain subsets of main V^1 rather than with all (or most) of them.[20]

Another and perhaps even more delicate problem arises from V^2 having "secondary aspectual" functions: how do we decide when such elements have passed into the primary tense–aspect paradigm of a language? In the (re)construction of the NIA paradigms such sequences were prime sources of material.

At bottom the matter is bedevilled by the fact that it is a question of *degrees* of grammaticalization, with (judging from disagreeing descriptions) a certain arbitrariness necessarily involved in the making of cuts along this cline. (V^2s having more narrowly "modal" meanings are less problematic, for semantic reasons – at least from a modern Indo-European perspective: in other language groups these too may suffer obvious incorporation into paradigms, even morphologization.)

Arbitrariness may also be detected at the other end of the descriptive spectrum, in the matter of identifying embedded sentences. Equivalents of *want to* and *have to* are particularly problematic here, since *want to* from some standpoints at least appears to be no different from *learn to*, *forget to*, etc., and *have to* usually involves in any case a *transformation*, the erstwhile Subject being transformed into a Dative Subject. Arbitrarily or not, I shall include them in the basic inventory below, primarily on the basis of the fact that (unlike *learn to*, etc.) they too seem to be subject to deletion restrictions [∗] similar to those governing clearly modal verbs like *be able to* in most NIA:

262 (U.) *kyā āp usko dekh sakte hai˜? jī hā˜, dekh saktā hū˜* 'Can you see that? Yes, I can (see it).' [∗*jī hā˜, saktā hū˜*]
262a (U.) *kyā āpko jānā hai? jī hā˜, jānā hai* 'Do you have to go? Yes, I have to (go).' [∗*jī hā˜, hai*]
262b (U.) *kyā āp us film ko dekhnā cāhte hai˜? jī hā˜, dekhnā cāhtā hū˜* 'Do you want to see that film? Yes, I want to (see it).' [∗*jī hā˜, cāhtā hū˜*][21]

One of the more elaborate and careful subclassifications has been attempted (for Marathi) by Berntsen and Nimbkar (1975). They distinguish *Verb Operators* (*begin to*, *keep on*) from *Sentence Operators* (*say that*, *know that*), and both of these from *Unary Transformations* (*want to*, *have to*) and *Binary Transformations* (coordinated, subordinated, and nominalized clauses). Their criteria result in the inclusion of *try to* in the first set, a departure from the most common NIA pattern – but this may simply be a fact of Marathi.

Various V^2 are attached to various forms of the main verb (V^1) – usually referred to as the Infinitive, Inflected Infinitive, Imperfective ("Present") Participle, Perfective ("Past") Participle, Verbal Noun, and Absolutive Participle (equivalent to the "Bare Stem" in some languages, notably Hindi and Punjabi, which will be indicated by -Ø below). It will be most convenient here to follow, e.g., Southworth 1961 and treat these formants (*-Aff* in his and Raeside's notation, "complementizers" in Hook's terminology) as part of the description of the V^2 itself (since the "meaning" of the V^2 is most often not independent of the

-*Aff* in any case). The basic inventory below will be classified in semantic terms, although that may not be the best (and certainly is not the only) approach.

In the patterns charted in the tables below, the "*Operator/Modal*" (V^2) given in stem form may be understood to carry for the Vb as a whole the full range of *Aspect* and *Tense/Mood* (and ^{CONCORD}) markers, unless otherwise specified. Gender-number variation in the Main Verb formant will be indicated by the symbol ^{C}, however. The symbol ^{E} (for Experiencer) before V indicates the construction is used with a so-called Dative Subject; the symbol ^{A}, that it is used with an Agentive Subject in *other than* Perfective constructions.

Table 10.1 *Be able to V*

(K. *hek-* + V-*ith*)		
P. V-Ø + *sak-*	N. V-*na* + *sak-*	A. V-*ibɒ* + *pār-*
S. V-*ī/ē* + *sagh-*	H. V-Ø + *sak-*	B. V-*te* + *pār-*
G. V-*ī* + *ʃak-*		O. V-*i* + *pār-*
M. V-*ū* + *ʃak-*		
	Si. ^{E}V-*nna* + *puluvani*	

The center/west vs. east pattern is obvious, although the M. and N. constructions involve (like those of the Eastern group + Sinhalese) an Infinitive rather than an Absolutive Participle. A K. construction ^{E}*tag-* + V-*un* is not included here: the verb *tagun*, which can occur by itself, may best be glossed as 'be possible for'. (K. *hek-* or *hyak-* is cognate with the *sak-* forms.) Compare the N. construction with that given in Table 10.3 below.

263 (K.) *ʒkis dohas manz chā vāpas hekān yith?* 'Can one come back the same day?' (B. Kachru 1973: 492)

263a (P.) *tusī̃ panjābī bōl sakdē ō?* 'Can you speak Punjabi?' (U. S. Bahri 1973: 111)

264 (S.) *hitā̃ tavhī̃ hunanjō ghara ɗisī saghō thā* 'You can see their house from here' (Addleton and Brown 1981: 207)

265 (G.) *tame āvi ʃakʃo?* 'Will you be able to come?' (Cardona 1965: 123)

266 (M.) *mī kevhāhi yeū ʃakto* 'I can come at any time' (Berntsen and Nimbkar 1975: 116)

267 (Si.) *maṭa pattarē kiyavanna puluvani* 'I can read the paper' (Fairbanks et al. 1968: I. 167)

268 (N.) *pauṛi ta khelna saktina, tara ghoṛā caṛhna sakchu* 'I cannot swim but I can ride a horse' (Matthews 1984: 141)

269 (H.) *kāmnā yah namūnā utār sakegī* 'Kamna will be able to copy this design' (Y. Kachru 1980: 49, modified)

270 (A.) *χi bhālkoi rāndhibɒ pāre* 'He can cook well' (N. Sarma 1963: 37)

271 (B.) *koi, āmi to dekhte pācchinā* 'Well, *I* can't see it!' (Page 1934: 109)

272 (O.) *mo stri kɔnɔ sālunre bāḷɔ kāti pāribe* 'Will my wife be able to have her hair cut in a saloon?' (Pattanayak and Das 1972: 224)

Table 10.2 *Manage to V*

(K. ?)		
P. ?	N. V-*na* + *pāu-*	A. V-*ib* + *pā-*
S. ?	H. V-Ø + *pā*	B. V-*te* + *pā-*
G. ?		
(M. ᴱV-*tā* + *ye-*)		O. ?
	Si. ?	

A second modal also often glossed as 'can, is able', but with a narrower meaning, such as 'manage to' or 'succeed in', and based on the verb *get, find*, is found in some NIA languages. Y. Kachru (1980: 50) explains the distinction as ability which "is a result of some effort on the part of the agent" (*pā-*) vs. neutrality with respect to this feature (*sak-*). Often the context is negative, i.e. *inability* despite effort. (The modals *sak-*, *pār-*, etc. sometimes have connotations of "permission" or "possibility" as well as "capability". They can be used epistemically – 'It could rain today' – which *pā-* cannot be.)

Some NIA languages have other verbs in this area also, but it is not clear without further investigation whether they are equivalent, although the M. construction ᴱV-*tā* + *ye-* seems to be close: cf. nos. 276–7 below. K. S. *pār-* 'finish, perform' are cognate with B. *pār-* (Table 10.1); P. *lai-* according to Bahri means 'is able to swim/read/walk, etc.' (cf. similar use of H. *le-*) – not quite the same thing. P. does have a verb *pāu-* 'find, get' cognate with H.B.A. *pā-*.

273 (H.) *vah baṛī koʃiʃõ ke bād kalkatte se nikal pāyā* 'He managed to leave Calcutta after much effort' (Y. Kachru 1980: 50)

274 (A.) *mɔi eito kɔribɒ pālõ* 'I succeeded in doing it'

275 (B.) *āmrā ḍānponthī bɔktāṛ kɔthā ʃunte pācchi nā* 'We can't hear the Rightist speaker's words' (Seely 1985: 236)

276 (M.) *malā tyālā bheṭṭā nāhī ālə* 'I didn't succeed in meeting him' (Hook: pers. comm.)

277 (M.) *tyālā sarv khātā yeīl kā?* 'Will he be able to eat everything?' (Southworth 1961: 204)

Table 10.3 *Finish V-ing/have already V-ed*

(K. *mokal-* + V-*ith*)?		
P. V-Ø + *cuk-*	N. V-*i* + *sak-*	A. V-*i* + *ɒ̃tā-*
S. V-*ī/ē* + *cuk-*	H. V-Ø + *cuk-*	B. ?
G. V-*ī* + *cuk-*		O. V-*i* + *sār-*
M. (V-*un* + *ho-*)?		
	Si. ?	

This modal set (it is not clear if the Eastern items are precisely equivalent) denotes completion often prior to something else (conveying the idea of 'already'). Dative Subject predications appear to be excluded. For N. (for which again compare Table 10.1), Matthews (1984) specifies completion "once and for all", but it seems to overlap a bit with the H. V + *jā-* Specifier–Compound construction (cf. no. 284). For G. *cuk-*, Cardona (1965) specifies "completion and inability to continue": the second G. construction with *rah-* seems not to have this connotation, and to be equivalent to some cases of H.P.S. *cuk-*. Oriya has a peculiar suffix *-ṇi*, added to finite forms (i.e. at the *end* of the Vb), which has this function (cf. no. 288) among others (Tripathi 1962: 194–7).

278 (K.) *yeli zyun tsɜtith mɔklyau* 'When he had finished cutting wood' (Bailey 1937: 25)

279 (P.) *oˊ tā̃maĩ vekh cukiā ā̃* 'I have already seen that [film]' (U. S. Bahri 1978: 114)

280 (S.) *ṭapālī acī cukō āhē?* 'Has the postman already come?' (Addleton and Brown 1981: 303)

281 (G.) *hũ bhani cukyo hũ* 'I've studied as much as I can' (Cardona 1965: 124)

282 (G.) *tame khāi rahyā?* 'Have you finished eating?' (ibid. 123)

283 (N.) *sinemā ʃurū bhaisakyo* 'The film has already started' (Matthews 1984: 238)

284 (N.) *hāmro buṛho nokar mari sakyo* 'Our old servant has just died' (ibid.)

285 (H.) *vah sab kuch batā cukā hai* 'He's already told all' (Hook 1979: 25)
286 (A.) *mɔi kāmto kɔri ɒ̃tālõ* 'I finished [doing] the work' (Babakaev 1961: 98)
287 (O.) *tumemāne āsilābelɔku mũ khāisarithibi* 'By the time you come I shall have finished eating' (Pattanayak and Das 1972: 95)
[288 (O.) *hɔri puri gɔlāni* 'Hari has already gone to Puri' (Mahapatra 1955: 77)]

Table 10.4 *Want to V*

(K. *yatsh-* + V-*un*)		
P. V-ṇā/ + cā-	N. V-*na* + *cāha-*	A. V-*ibɒ* + *khuz-*
S. V-*aṇ*^{u} + *cāh-*	H. V-*nā* + *cāh-*	B. V-*te* + *cā-*
G. $^{A/E}$V-*vũc* + *ho-*		O. ?
M. ^{E}V-*āytsā*^{c} + *as-*		
	Si. ^{E}V-*nna* + *ōna*	

The root used in Assamese means 'seek' in other languages. Note the indirect construction and use of 'be' in G.M.[22] An analogous construction in H. also often translates 'want to' instead of the usually glossed 'have to' (see below) – perhaps especially often in the Hindi of peninsular India (Dakhini).

289 (K.) *bɨ chus tamis vuchun yatshān seṭhā* 'I want very much to see him' (Hook 1987: 6 [respelled])
290 (P.) *maĩ tā̃ kise pā̀ṛ te jāṇā ca'õdi ā̃* 'I would like to go to some hill station' (U. S. Bahri 1973: 65)
291 (S.) *hū likhan*^{u} *cāhe thō* 'He wants to write' (Addleton and Brown 1981: 370)
292 (G.) *māre/mane ghɛr javũ che* 'I want to go home' (Cardona 1965: 95)
293 (M.) *tyālā kām karāytsə̄ hotə̄* 'He wanted to work' (Berntsen and Nimbkar 1975: 123)
294 (Si.) *maṭa palaturu ganna ona* 'I want to buy some fruit' (Fairbanks et al. 1968: II. 34)
295 (N.) *ma pradhānmantrīlāī bhetna cāhanchu* 'I want to meet the Prime Minister' (Matthews 1984: 131)
296 (H.) *tum kise lanā cāhte ho?* 'Who do you want to bring?' (Hook 1979: 24)

297 (A.) *χi ghɒrɒlɔi zābɒ khuzise* 'He wants to go home' (N. Sarma 1963: 8)

298 (B.) *ʃe bāŋlādeʃer khābār khete cāe* 'He wants to eat Bengali food' (Bender and Riccardi 1978: 47)

299 (O.) ? [expression of *want to* is avoided in Oriya]

Table 10.5 *Have to V* ("weak") + *have to V* ("strong")

(K. *ās-* + ^{E}V-*un*^{C})		
(K. *pyo-* + ^{E}V-*un*^{C})		
P. ^{A}V-*nā*^{C} + *ho-*	N. $^{E/A}$V-*nu* + *par-*	A. ^{E}V-*ibɒ* + *lɔgiyā*
^{E}V-*nā*^{C} + *pai-*		V-*ibɒ* + *lāg*[3p]
S. ^{E}V-*aṇō*^{C} + *hu-*	H. ^{E}V-*nā*^{C} + *ho-*	B. ^{E}V-*te* + *hɔ-*
^{E}V-*aṇō*^{C} + *pav-*	H. ^{E}V-*nā*^{C} + *paṛ-*	
G. $^{E/A}$V-*vānu*$^{\sim C}$ + *ho-*		O. ^{E}V-*ibāku* + *he-*
$^{E/A}$V-*vu*$^{\sim C}$ + *paḍ-*		^{E}V-*ibāku* + *pɔṛ-*
M. ^{E}V-*lā* + *pahije*∗		
^{E}V-*āvā*^{C} + *lāg-*		
	Si. ^{E}V-*nna* + *tiyanavā*	
	^{E}V-*nna* + *venavā*	
	V-*nna* + *ōna*	

The distinction between the lower and upper items is generally between "external" compulsion, "outside the control of the Agent", most often indicated by the verb 'to fall' (H. *paṛnā*), and a category neutral with respect to this feature – that is, possibly *within* the control of the Agent, at least in the sense of the Agent's involvement in making a *prior arrangement*, and indicated most often by 'to *be/become*' (H. *honā*, Si. *tiyenavā*). It sometimes can be glossed 'is supposed to'. Significantly, the latter takes an Agentive Subject in P., and optionally in G. and N., while the former usually (except in Si. and A., and again optionally in G.) takes an Experiencer (= "Non-Volitional") Subject (in the Dative).

The distinction appears to be flattened in N. and B. (although "emphatic" compulsion may be expressed in B. by use of an emphatic particle (*jete-ī hɔbe*). The difference between the two A. constructions seems to be "idiomatic" rather than of the type in question here. The second A. construction is distinguished from one meaning *begin* only by the neutralization of person-agreement.

300 (K.) *tot vātɨnɨ khɜ̄trə pei me akh zampāna biye nāv kirāyi karɨñ* 'To go there I must hire a palanquin and a boat' (Grierson 1973: 111)

301 (P.) *kurī ne jāṇā e* 'The girl has to go' (Shackle 1972: 84)

302 (P.) *o'nā̃ nū̃ muṛnā piā* 'They had to come back' (ibid. 84)

303 (S.) *mū˜khē kētrā-ī kam karaṇa āhin* 'I have to do a number of things' (Addleton and Brown 1981: 193)

304 (S.) *tō khē subhāṇī subūha jō savēr uthaṇō pavandō* 'You'll have to get up early tomorrow morning' (ibid. 194)

305 (G.) *māre mārā bhāine thoḍā paysā āpvānā che* 'I have to give some money to my brother' (Cardona 1965: 109)

306 (G.) *māre ghare rahɛvu˜ paḍyu˜* 'I was forced to stay home' (ibid. 122)

307 (M.) *malā mumbailā zāylā pāhije* 'I have to go to Bombay' (Berntsen and Nimbkar 1975: 124)

308 (M.) *tyānī gelə pāhije* 'He must go' (ibid. 125)

309 (M.) *malā kām karāvə lāgel* 'I will have to work' (ibid. 126)

310 (Si.) *oheṭa pahaṭa kolam̆ba inna tiyenavā* 'You are to be in Colombo at 5' (Fairbanks et al. 1968: I. 167)

311 (Si.) *maṭa payin yanna unā* 'I had to go on foot' (ibid. 263)

312 (Si.) *mama yanna ōna* 'I must go' (ibid. 41)

313 (N.) *ʃaharbāṭa hiṇṛerai āunuparyo* 'I had to walk back from town' (Matthews 1984: 128)

314 (H.) *mujhko agle sāl banāras zarūr jānā hai* 'I must definitely go to Banaras next year' (Y. Kachru 1980: 50)

315 (H.) *tumhe˜ gāy lanī paṛegī* 'You'll have to bring the cow' (Hook 1979: 24)

316 (A.) *mor khābɒ lɔgiyā* 'I must eat' (Babakaev 1961: 80)

317 (A.) *χi kɔribɒ lāgil* 'He had to do it' (ibid. 93)

318 (B.) *āmāke ʃekhāne jete hɔe* 'I must go there' (Page 1934: 163)

319 (O.) *bɔhu lokɔthile āpɔṇɔŋku bāhāre bɔsibāku hebɔ* 'If there are many people you will have to sit outside' (Pattanayak and Das 1972: 224)

Table 10.6 *Ought to V*

K. V-*un* + *gatsh-*		
P. ^{E}V-*ṇā*^{C} + *cā́idā*^{C}-	N. V-*na* + *hu-* (Pres)	A. ?
S. ^{E}V-*aṇ*^{uc} + *ghur-*	H. ^{E}V-nā^{C} + *cāhiye*∗	B. ^{E}V-*te* + *āche/nei*
G. $^{A/E}$V-*vu*$^{˜C}$ + *joie*∗		O. ?
M. $^{A/E}$V-*āylā* + *pāhije*∗		
^{A}V-*tā* + *kāmā naye*		
	Si. ?	

Another modal construction, encoding "moral" obligation, is found in some NIA languages. It sometimes involves an old passive stem of *want/need*, construed indirectly (in the Dative or Agentive), or a *be* verb (N. and B.). In both cases, it is usually defective, except in P. taking only number agreement (in H., S., and M., none in G.) and only Present/Past T/M-marking, with the first usually unmarked.

320 (P.) *mainū˜ ka'l jāṇā ca'idā sī* 'I ought to have gone yesterday' (Shackle 1972: 83)

321 (S.) *asā˜ khē ētrī dēr hutē rahaṇ^{u} na ghurbo ho* 'We ought not to have stayed there so long' (Addleton and Brown 1981: 191)

322 (G.) *mārelmane ghɛr javu˜ joie* 'I ought to go home' (Cardona 1965: 95)

323 (M.) *tyānnī dillilā zāylā pāhije hotə̄* 'He should have gone to Delhi' (Berntsen and Nimbkar 1975: 124)

324 (M.) *tyānī tithe zātā kāmā naye* 'He ought not to go there' (ibid. 126)

325 (N.) *keṭaketīharūle raksī khāna hundaina* 'Children should not drink *raksī*' (Matthews 1984: 129)

326 (H.) *unko socnā cāhiye* 'They should think [about it]' (Hook 1979: 25)

327 (B.) *bhitɔre tomār ʃigāreṭ khete nei* 'You should not smoke inside' (Seely 1985: 237)

Table 10.7 *Begin to V* (a) and *allow to V* (b)

K. (a) *lag-* + V-*un*^{c}		
(a) *hye-* + V-*un*^{c}		
(b) *di-* + V-*ɨnɨ*)		
P. (a) V-*aṇ* + *lagg-*	N. V-*na* + *lāg-*	A. V-*ibɒ-* + *lāg-*
	V-*na* + *thāl-*	
(b) V-*aṇ* + *de-*	V-*na* + *di-*	V-*ibɒ-* + *di-*
S. (a) V-*aṇ*^{a} + *laʄ-*	H. V-*ne* + *lag-*	B. V-*te* + *lāg-*
(b) V-*aṇ*^{a} + *ɗī-*	V-*ne* + *de-*	V-*te* + *de-*
G. (a) V-*vā* + *lag-*		O. V-*u* + *thi-*
(a) V-*vā* + *maṇḍ-*		
(a) V-*tu˜*+*thā-*		
(b) V-*vā* + *dɛ-*		?
M. (a) V-*ū* + *lāg-*		
(a) V-*āylā* + *lāg-*		
(b) V-*ū* + *de-*		
	Si. (a) V-*nna* + *paṭaŋ gannavā*	
	(a) V-*nna* + *gannavā*	
	(b) V-Ø + *-dden*	

These two common modals are grouped together here because they share a common construction (with the Oblique Infinitive, where it exists) in most NIA languages, and employ verbs which in other contexts mean 'attach' and 'give' (as modals, *begin* and *allow* respectively). K., G., N., and Si. have additional modals with different shades of inceptive meaning. The first M. construction is "more formal" according to Berntsen and Nimbkar..

328 (K.) *ɜm´ hyut panɨni safruk pai tɨ patɨ vanun* 'He began to recount his trip' (Bailey 1937: 26)
329 (K.) *pānas-sɨt´ dih me pakɨnɨ* 'Allow me to go with you' (Grierson 1973: 74)
330 (P.) *o´ jān lagge* 'They began to go' (Shackle 1972: 88)
331 (P.) *o´nā˜ne sānu˜ jāṇ ditte* 'They allowed us to go' (ibid. 88)
332 (S.) *hunanjī chōkirī rōaṇ*^{a} *lagī* 'Their daughter started to cry' (Addleton and Brown 1981: 352)
333 (S.) *mā+ tavhā˜khē pāhīnjō kitāb paṛhaṇ*^{a} *ɗīndus* 'I will let you read my book' (ibid.)
334 (G.) *e kām karvā lāgyo* 'He began to work' (Cardona 1965: 121)
335 (G.) *ɛṇe bhāʃaṇ karvā māndyu˜* 'He began to give a speech' (ibid. 285)
336 (G.) *brahmaṇo pahelā˜ iṇḍā˜ khātā na hatā, paṇ have te khātā thayā che* 'Previously Brahmins did not eat eggs, but now they have started to eat them' (ibid. 108)
337 (G.) *chokrāne āmārī sāthe āvvā dɔ* 'Let the boy come with us' (ibid. 121)
338 (M.) *to vātsū lāgto* 'He begins to read' (Southworth 1961: 204)
339 (M.) *tī raḍāylā lāglī* 'She began to cry' (ibid. 204)
340 (M.) *tyālā yeū det* 'Let him come' (Berntsen and Nimbkar 1975: 127)
341 (Si.) *mahattayā væḍa karanna paṭaṇ gannavā* 'The master is starting to work' (Fairbanks et al. 1968: I. 140)
342 (Si.) *vahinna gannāṭa digaṭama vahinavā* 'When it starts raining it keeps right on' (ibid. 148)
343 (Si.) *api gaha kapa-dden* 'Allow us to cut the tree' (Garusinghe 1962: 72)
344 (N.) *pānī parna lāgyo* 'It came on to rain' (Matthews 1984: 142)
345 (N.) *usle angrejī sikna thālyo* 'He began to learn English' (ibid. 72)
346 (N.) *khālī hinduharūlāī matrai jānā dinchan kyāre* 'I think they only let Hindus go inside' (ibid. 136)

347 (H.) *pānī barasne lagā* 'It began to rain' (Hook 1979: 25)

348 (H.) *sīmā ne mujhe tasvīr dekhne dī* 'Sima allowed me to look at the picture' (Y. Kachru 1980: 51)

349 (A.) *tɔi kɔribɒ lāgili* 'You began to do it' (Babakaev 1961: 93)

350 (A.) *tāk zābɒ[lɔi] diyā* 'Let him go' (ibid. 98)

351 (B.) *tārā āmāder pechone pechone dourote lāglo* 'They began to run after us' (Page 1934: 135)

352 (B.) *tomāder ʃɔŋge ki āmāke jete debe?* 'Will you let me go with you?' (Seely 1985: 234)

353 (O.) *ghɔṇṭā ṭhɔnṭhɔn bājuṭhāe* 'The bell began to ring' (Karpushkin 1964: 70)

Table 10.8 *Keep on V-ing + go on V-ing: make a habit of V-ing*

K.	V-*ān* + *rōz*^{c}-				
	V-*ān* + *gatsh*^{c}-				
P.	V-*ndā*^{c} + *rai´ndā*^{c}-	N.	V-*do* + *rah*-	A.	V-*i* + *thɒk*-
	V-*ndā*^{c} + *hundā*^{c}-		V-*i* + *rah*-		V-*ā* + *kɒr*-
	V-*yā* + *kar*-		V-*ne* + *gar*-		
S.	V-*andō/īndō*^{c} + *rah*-	H.	V-*tā*^{c} + *rah*-	B.	V-*te* + *thāk*-
	V-*andō/īndō*^{c} + *vañ*-		V-*tā*^{c} + *jā*-		V-*e* + *thāk*-
	V-*andō/īndō*^{c} + *ac*-		V-*(y)ā* + *kar*-		*V-e* + *cɔl*-
G.	V-*tu*$^{\sim c}$ + *rah*-			O.	V-*i* + *thi*- (Pres.)
	V-*tu*$^{\sim c}$ + *ja*-				V-*i* + *rɔh*-
	V-*tu*$^{\sim c}$ + *āv*-				
	V-*yā* + *kar*-				
M.	V-*at/īt* + *rah*-				
	V-*at/īt* + *zā*-				
		Si.	?		

This group of Secondary Aspectuals enables NIA languages to combine such meanings as continuance (expressed by the modal) and completion (expressed by the Asp slot), as well as to "emphasize" continuation or regularity. (As we have seen, these languages have other devices for emphasizing completion and "perfectivity", including the Explicator auxiliaries.) Generally speaking, it may be said that the use of *stay* (*rah*-, *thāk*-) in this position expresses continuation *at* the point of reference,[23] the use of *go* (*jā*-, *vañ*-, *cɔl*-), expresses continuation *from* the point of reference, and the use of *come* (*ac*-, *āv*-, *ā*-), continuation *up to* the point of reference, while the use of *do* (*kar*-, *gar*-) expresses regularity or custom. Whether through idiosyncrasy of description or gloss, or real differences among the languages, there is some confusion here, however (particularly between the first and the last of these categories), and the area needs more careful cross-linguistic study. Note that *stay*, *go*, and *come* are used with the Imperfective Participle, typically, and *do* with an invariant Verbal Noun.

354 (K.) *bɨ rōzɨ kɜ karān* 'I'll keep working' (Hook: pers. comm.)
355 (K.) *bāj gatsh tārān* 'Keep taking tribute' (Bailey 1937: 39)
356 (P.) *os veḷe maĩ o'dar jāndā rai'ndā sā̃* 'At that time I used to make a habit of going there' (Shackle 1972: 119)
357 (P.) *ajkal maĩ pāṇī pīndā hundā vā̃* 'Nowadays I always drink water' (ibid. 19)
358 (P.) *onā̃ de koḷ jāyā karo!* 'Keep on going to them!' (ibid. 120)
359 (S.) *ɠāīndā rahō!* 'Keep on singing!' (Addleton and Brown 1981: 328)
360 (S.) *hunajō hālu χarāb thīndō vīō* 'His condition went on getting worse' (ibid. 329)
361 (S.) *hī qaom taraqī kandī acē thī* 'This nation keeps on making progress' (ibid. 330)
362 (G.) *tame kām kartā raho* 'You go on working' (Cardona 1965: 120)
363 (G.) *loko uʃkerātā jatā hatā* 'People went on getting more and more excited' (ibid. 120)
364 (G.) *kām thatũ ave che* 'The work is coming along' (ibid. 120)
365 (G.) *loko kaṇṭalyā hatā, chatā̃ ɛṇe bhāʃaṇ karyā karyũ* 'The people were bored, but still he went on lecturing' (ibid. 121)
366 (M.) *divasbhar pāūs paḍat rāhilā* 'It went on raining all day long' (Berntsen and Nimbkar 1975: 115)
367 (M.) *to kām karīt zāto* 'He goes on working' (Southworth 1961: 204)
368 (N.) *nepālī ta rāmrai bolnuhundo rahecha* 'Why, you speak Nepali quite well' (Matthews 1984: 227)
369 (N.) *umaleko pāni piune garnuhos* 'Keep on drinking boiled water' (ibid. 170)
370 (N.) *bas naāesamma ma yahī̃ basirahanchu* 'I'll keep sitting here until the bus comes' (ibid. 236)
371 (H.) *vah kal din bhar paṛhta rahā* 'He kept on reading all day yesterday' (Y. Kachru 1980: 48)
372 (H.) *vah kahtā gayā aur maĩ likhtā gayā* 'He went on dictating, and I went on writing' (Phillott 1918: 102)

373 (H.) *ham tīn baje khānā khāyā karte haĩ* 'We make a habit of eating at 3' (Hook 1979: 214)

374 (A.) *mɔi pɔrhi thākõ* 'I read [all the time/go on reading]' (Babakaev 1961: 99)

375 (A.) *zowā kɒr* 'Go regularly' (ibid. 98)

376 (B.) *ʃe tāder bāṛir dike hẽṭe jete thāklo* 'She continued walking toward their house' (Seely 1985: 156)

377 (B.) *e deʃer lokerā bhāt khee thāke* 'The people of this country eat rice' (Page 1934: 148)

378 (B.) *jɔtɔkhon nā ghūm pāe tɔtɔkhon āmi kāj kore colbo* 'I shall keep on working until I get sleepy' (Bender and Riccardi 1978: 61)

379 (O.) *e kɔthā mɔnɔre pānci se pāthɔsāḷārɔ piṇḍāre sɔrbɔdā bɔsithāe* 'Burning with this desire, he would always sit near the school' (Karpushkin 1964: 70)

380 (O.) *cārimitɔ ghɔrɔku nɔ jāi bɔnɔre luci rɔhile* 'The four friends didn't go home but remained hiding in the forest' (Karpushkin 1964: 72)

There are no doubt other candidates for inclusion in the V^2 category, more specific to particular languages. The foregoing may be sufficient, however, to make the point that this is a major, albeit optional, constituent of the pan-NIA Verb Phrase, the most general formula for which may thus now be given (using m – for Modal – for this category in preference to, e.g., O for "Operator" which is too easily confused with O for "Object") as:

V (+ v) + (m) + AUX [= Asp + T/M]

10.8 **Modifications of the simple sentence**

These are chiefly the following:

10.8.1 *Question formation*

Question formation is quite straightforward in NIA. No inversions or alterations of phrase structure are involved (except in Kashmiri). In so-called WH-questions, those asking for information, the question word comes normally in the focal position right before the verb (ignoring negation markers), unless it is an adjectival question word modifying a noun (which then itself occupies this position):

381 (P.) "Director" *saʼb huṇ kithe ne*? '*Where* is the Director now?' (U. S. Bahri 1973: 55)

382 (S.) *hū <u>kēr^{u}</u> āhē?* '*Who* is that?' (Addleton and Brown 1981: 37)

383 (M.) *nāgpūrce pāhuṇe <u>kitī</u> tārakhelā yeṇār āhet* '*On what* date are the guests from Nagpur coming?' (Berntsen and Nimbkar 1982: 303)

384 (H.) *āp ne <u>kyo͂</u> nahī͂ batāyā?* '*Why* didn't you tell [me]?'

385 (B.) *jeleke <u>kɔto</u> dām dilen?* '*How much* did you pay the fisherman?' (Dimock et al. 1964: 171)

386 (O.) *āpɔnɔ <u>kou</u> ghɔre rɔhucɔnti?* '*In which* house are you staying?' (Pattanayak and Das 1972: 49)

Sometimes, however, a Direct Object or Goal retains its claim on this position, the question word then coming immediately to its left:

387 (G.) *āp <u>kyāre</u> ghēr javānā cho?* '*When* are you coming *home*?' (Lambert 1971: 120)

388 (B.) *orā <u>kæno</u> e boiguli nielo?* '*Why* did they bring *these books*?' (Page 1934: 13)

Sinhalese is exceptional: the question word follows what it governs, which most often puts it last, *preceded by* the special Emphatic verb form:

389 (Si.) *mahatmayā yanne <u>kohēda</u>?* '*Where* are you going?' (Garusinghe 1962: 29)

390 (Si.) *mahatmayā kanne <u>mokak</u> <u>da</u>?* '*What* are you eating?' (ibid. 29)

Interrogatives of quantity, like the numerals they replace, immediately follow the *noun* they refer to:

391 (Si) {*lamay*} *<u>kīdenek</u> innavā da?* '*How many* {children} are there?' (Fairbanks et al. 1968 I. 75)

392 (Si.) *ohē lañga* {*salli*} *<u>koccara</u> tiyenavā da?* '*How much* {money} do you have on you?' (ibid. 137)

In Bengali there is a tendency to prefer final position for the word *why* – *kæno*:

393 (B.) *āpni oʃɔb nie māthā ghāmācchen <u>kæno</u>?* '*Why* are you bothering your head about all that?' (Page 1934: 63)

394 (B.) *oder ekhāne thākte bɔloni <u>kæno</u>?* '*Why* didn't you tell them to stay there?' (ibid. 53)

Kashmiri, exceptional as always, puts question words in second position, even if this means moving them out of their own clauses (no. 396):

395 (K.) *yeti pyaṭhɨ kūṭ dūr chu nehrū pārk?* '*How far* is Nehru Park from here?' (B. Kachru 1973: 148)

396 (K.) *tsɨ kus chuhan yatshān bɨ gotshusan anun?* '*Who* do you want me to bring?' (Hook: pers. comm.)

Yes/no questions may be marked simply by intonation: Gujarati and to a lesser extent Oriya seem to prefer this option. Most NIA languages may also employ a question-marker particle, placed either sentence-initially (Standard Hindi, Sindhi, Punjabi) or finally (Bengali, Marathi, Sinhalese). The first is reminiscent of the Persian construction, the second of the Dravidian one. The question marker is often but not always identical with an unstressed form of the word *what* (unlike either Dravidian or Persian). Not, however, in Sinhalese ('what' = *mokak*, question particle = *da*) where it moreover cooccurs with question-words: in the rest of NIA they are mutually exclusive. In Kashmiri, the question marker is *-ā -ɨ* (vs. 'what' = *kyāh*), added to the finite verb (in position 2) – except for position oddly reminiscent of the Dravidian marker (*-ā*).

397 (H.) *kyā āp in logoˇ ko jānte haiˇ* 'Do you know these people?'

398 (S.) *chā hū ustādā āhin?* 'Are those [people] teachers?' (Addleton and Brown, 1981: 38)

399 (P.) *kī "beer" pīṇī ca'oge?* 'Would you like to drink beer?' (U. S. Bahri 1973: 66)

400 (B.) *mānuʃ āʃe ki?* 'Does the man come?' [also *mānuʃ ki āʃe*, i.e. in *preverbal* position] (Bender and Riccardi 1978: 10–11)

401 (M.) *tumhī udyā sakāḷī ɔfismadhe asāl kā* 'Will you be in the office tomorrow morning?' (Berntsen and Nimbkar 1982: 273)

402 (N.) *tapāīˇ sāˇjhmā kunai kasrat garnuhuncha ki* 'Do you take any sort of exercise in the evening?' (Dasgupta and Karmacharya 1964: 166)

403 (Si.) *mahattayā kalutaraṭa yanavā da?* 'Is the gentleman going to Kalutara?' [also *mahattayā {yanne} kalutaraṭa da* and *mahattayā kalutara da {yanne}*, with Emphatic forms = 'Is it to K. that the gentleman is going?'] (Fairbanks et al. 1968: I. 43)

Cf. 404 (Si.) *mahattayā {yanne} kohāṭa da* [or *mahattayā kohāta da {yanne}*] '*Where* is the gentleman going?' (ibid. 43)]

405 (K.) *yih bandūkh chu-ā bormot?* 'Is this gun loaded?' (Grierson 1973: 121)

406 (G.) *tamˇ temne oḷkho cho?* 'Do you know him?' (Dhruva 1920: 155) [no marker]

Except in Sinhalese, text-frequency counts might well show that *yes/no* questions are marked most often in NIA in general by intonation alone. For Nepali Matthews (1984) describes an additional type rather reminiscent of Chinese, where a question is asked by posing the alternatives "is it or isn't it?"

407 (N.) *tarkārī mīṭho cha ki chaina?* 'Are the vegetables any good?' (Matthews 1984: 31)

408 (N.) *tyo mānche chetrī ho ki hoina?* 'Is that man a Chetri?' (ibid. 31)

Most NIA languages also make use of (invariant) tag questions ('Isn't it?') of the type of Japanese *ne* – in fact, in Gujarati the particle is also *ne?* (in Hindi it is *na?*):

409 (G.) *tɛnī pāse jāo ne?* 'Go and see him, won't you?' (Lambert 1971: 204)

410 (G.) *ka˜ ī to laī javu˜ joīe ne?* 'I must take something with me, mustn't I?' (ibid. 204)

10.8.2 *Negation*

The tag-question particles just mentioned (G. *ne?*, H. *na?*, M.K. *nā?*, Si. *nædda?*) are an appropriate preface to the next topic, negation, which unlike question formation in NIA, is neither straightforward nor simple. From the single OIA negative particle *na* has grown up, through fusion with other elements and other processes, a luxuriance of forms and constructions that we can only note the high points of here.

Sanskrit did have an additional "prohibitive" or "precative" particle, *mā*, used in negative commands and some other contexts. It survives (H.P. *mat*, S. *ma*, K. *mā*, *maṭi*, G. *mā*) mainly in the center and west; in the Eastern and Southern languages other devices have evolved. It usually precedes the verb, except in Gujarati, where according to Cardona it always follows (Savel´eva 1965 has a counterexample, however):

411 (P.) *mat jā!* 'Don't go!' (Rabinovich and Serebryakov 1961: 997)

412 (G.) *jāo mā* 'Don't go!' (Cardona 1965: 139)

413 (G.) *darvājo band mā karo!* 'Don't close the door' (Savel´eva 1965: 57)

414 (K.) *yim pōʃ ma* [= *mɨ*?] *tsaṭu-kh* 'You must not pick-them [= don't pick] these flowers' (Grierson 1973: S. 749)

There are other means of expressing negative commands/requests both in languages retaining reflexes of OIA *mā* (nos. 415–19) and in those which have lost it (nos. 420–4):

415 (H.) *na jāiye* 'Please do not go!' (Y. Kachru 1980: 110)

416 (P.) *nā likhio* 'Please don't write!' (Rabinovich and Serebryakov 1961: 997)

417 (G.) *āvāj na karto* 'Don't make noise' (Cardona 1965: 139)

418 (G.) *e khātā nahī̃* 'Don't eat that' (ibid. 139)

419 (S.) *hōḍā ''ha ̃na vaño* 'Don't go there' (Addleton and Brown 1981: 106)

420 (O.) *kichi cintā kɔrɔ nāhĩ* 'Don't worry' (Karpushkin 1964: 82)

421 (O.) *tu epɔri āu hɔṭɔhɔṭā kɔrɔ nā* 'Don't joke any more like that' (ibid. 82)

422 (M.) *mājhī vāṭ pāhū nakos* 'Don't wait for me' (Berntsen and Nimbkar 1982: 135)

423 (Ko.) *nidevnu poḍnākā* 'Don't go to sleep' (Aiyagal 1968: 127)

424 (Si.) *mē bas eken yanna epā* 'Don't go by this bus' (Fairbanks et al. 1968: II. 186)

Turning now to the larger matter of negated statements (and questions), we find that in a number of NIA languages the task of negation is divided between (at least) two markers (besides *mā*): H. *na/nahī̃*, P. *nā/na'ī̃*, G. *na/nahi (nahī̃)/nathī*, M. *na-/nāhī^c/-nā*, O. *nɔ-/nā/-ni/nāhĩ*, B. *nā/-nā/-ni*, N. *na-/-na^c*. Among the major languages, Sindhi and Kashmiri get along with the one inherited particle *na* (K. *-nɨ*). Assamese essentially also has only one negator, *"nɒ-"*, but in a phenomenon unique in NIA, its vowel assimilates to that of the verbal root (if it begins with a consonant): *nɒkɒre* 'doesn't do', but *nimile* 'doesn't agree', *nobole* 'doesn't speak', *nubuze* 'doesn't understand', *nepāy* [also represented as *næpāy*] 'doesn't get' (Kakati 1962: 345, 140; Babakaev 1961: 91; Baruah 1980: 121 gives *nākhāy* 'doesn't eat'). With vowel-initial roots, other assimilations take place: *nɒ + ā- = nā-* (e.g., *nāhe* 'doesn't come'), *nɒ + i- = noi, nɒ + u- = nou*.

Unlike Sanskrit, where *na* could go anywhere in the sentence, including often at its very beginning far from the verb (*na mayā suciramapi vicārayatā tēṣām vākyārtho'dhigataḥ* 'Though I have been reflecting on it quite a while I *do not understand* what it is they speak of' [Speijer 1980 (1886): 315]), NIA negators of predications are attached to the verb, commonly in a fixed position or positions. Various patterns of choice among the possibilities (i.e. preposed, prefixed, postposed, suffixed, or inserted between the main verb and auxiliary) may be seen in individual languages; there is not even a regional consensus: B. *-nā/-nī*, O. *-ni* are postposed; closely related A. *nɒ-*, Bishnupriya *nā-* are preposed; O. *nɔ-*, preposed to the Past and Future of the verb *be* (*nɔthili* 'I was not', *nɔthibi* 'I won't be'), thus finds itself in the middle of verb phrases involving the auxiliary: *jāi pārinɔthili* 'I could not go' (Pattanayak and Das 1972: 124). Cf. also N. *garenachu* 'I have not done'. S. *na-* is preposed, K. *-nɨ* postposed. Again attraction to the auxiliary may place both of them *inside* the VP:

425 (S.) *asā̃ na samjhīō* 'We didn't understand' (Addleton and Brown 1981: 223)
426 (S.) *hū kaʼhin khē disī na rahīō āhē* 'He isn't seeing anyone' (ibid. 206)
427 (S.) *āū̃ paʼhinjā kapṛā na dhōīndō āhīā̃* 'I don't wash my own clothes' (ibid. 149)
428 (K.) *tim gatshan nɨ dili* 'They won't go to Delhi' (Kachru 1973: 182)
429 (K.) *ɜs´ chinɨ sokūlas manz mēlān* 'We do not meet inside the school' (ibid. 368)
430 (K.) *am´ hyɜc nɨ akh gɨr lɜbith*[24] 'He could not find even one mare' (Bailey 1937: 25)

H. and P. *nahī̃* (*naʼī̃*) are generally preposed (postposed for emphasis[25]), while G. *nahi/nathī*, M. *nāhī*, and Si. *næ̆* are postposed. (The G. and less often the M. forms may also be preposed: this is "emphatic" in G. according to Tisdall 1892, and in M. involves a denial of a previous assertion, according to Hook. The suffixation of the clitic *-(a)j* in G., equivalent to M. *-(a)ts*, to the main verb may be more common as an emphatic device in these languages, however.)

431 (H.) *maĩ nahī̃ gayā* 'I didn't go'
432 (H.) *maĩ gayā nahī̃* 'I didn't *go*'
433 (G.) *hũ gayo nahi* 'I didn't go'
434 (G.) *hũ nahi gayo* 'I *didn't* go'
435 (M.) *mī gelo nāhī* 'I didn't go'
436 (M.) *mī nāhī gelo* 'I *didn't* go'
437 (Si.) *mama giyē næ̆* 'I didn't go'
438 (G.) *e kām karto nathī* 'He isn't working' (Cardona 1965: 138)
439 (G.) *ame tyā̃ nathī rahɛtā* 'We do not live here' (ibid. 138)
440 (G.) *mane hamdardī kyā̃y maḷti j nathī* 'I don't get sympathy anywhere' (Anul Savaani, tr. *Anton Chekhov, laghunavalo ane navalikaao*, Moscow 1979: 125)

441 (M.) *tū kāy mhaṇtes te malā kaḷt-ats nāhī* 'I don't know what you're talking about' (Mark 14: 68)

Regarding the functional differentiation of these markers, B. *-ni* is used only (with the Unspecified Present) to form the negative of the Present and Past Perfective, which thus lose their contrast in the negative. O. *-ni* is of much wider application.

442 (B.) *āmi jāi ni* 'I haven't/hadn't gone, didn't go'
443 (B.) *āmi ækhon jete pāri nā* 'I can't go now' (Page 1934: 146)
444 (B.) *āmi jābo nā* 'I shall not go'
445 (O.) *mu˜ jāeni* 'I don't go' (Pattanayak and Das 1972: 131)
446 (O.) *tume jibɔni* 'You will not go' (ibid. 131)
447 (O.) *āpɔnɔ gɔleni* 'You (hon.) didn't go' (ibid. 131)

H. *na* and *nahī˜* are both usable with many finite forms, although the latter is more common. Only *na* occurs with the Contingent Future ("Simple Subjunctive": *ʃāyad vah na jāe* 'Perhaps he/she won't go') and Polite Imperative (*na jāiye* 'Please don't go'), however, and the contrast between the two distinguishes the Contrafactive (*na jātā* '[if he] didn't go/hadn't gone') from the Present Habitual (*nahī˜ jātā* '[he] doesn't go'). M. *-nā* is used with the Past Habitual (= Old Present: *[tyālā] boltā yeīnā* 'he could not speak'); *na-* is prefixed to the several tense forms of the auxiliary in this language, producing not fully predictable amalgams: *na + hoto, hotī*, etc.. = *nahvto, nahvtī*; *na + asto* = *nasto*, *na + asel* = *nasel*, *na + hoy* = *navhe*. (G. similarly has the allegro forms *nɔhtu˜*, *nɔhto*, etc. corresponding to the negative with forms of the past auxiliary *na hatu˜*, *na hato*, which however continue to exist.) Elsewhere the M. negator is *nāhī*.

Although Turner (*CDIAL* 7035) prefers to derive at least H. *nahī˜* from OIA *na hi* 'surely not', others (e.g., Katenina 1963: 269 on M.) insist that these forms (which probably include B. and O. *-ni*, corresponding to E.B. and Sadhu Bhasa *nāi*, Si. *nǣ*, shortened from *næhǣ*, and possibly N. *-na*) are contractions of *na-* with some form of the *Present* auxiliary. On the side of this view is the fact that in M. this form is partially inflected (for 2sg. and 3pl.: *tū ālā nāhīs* 'You didn't [haven't] come', *mulə̄ aikat nāhīt* 'The children don't listen' [Berntsen and Nimbkar 1982: 345, 210]), occurs in the auxiliary position, and fills a place in the paradigm that would otherwise be vacant. (The N. form has a complete inflection: *-na˜*, *-nas*, *-na*, *-nau˜*, *-nau*, *-nan*.) Against it is the lack of justification for the vowel *-ī* (or H.P. *-ī˜*), and the fact that in H.P. *nahī˜*, *na'ī˜* come (normally) not in the auxiliary position but before the verb. On the other hand again, it does entail (or permit) the dropping of the Present Auxiliary in complex verb forms in these languages (H. *jātā hai* 'goes'/*nahī̃ jātā* 'doesn't go'). The cooccurrence of the present of *be* as a predicator, while common enough, might be seen as redundant (H. *laṛkā lambā nahī̃ hai* 'The boy is not tall' [Y. Kachru 1980: 109]). *Be* with a Dative Subject is perhaps more often dropped (H. *mujhe bhūkh nahī̃* 'I'm not hungry', *koī āpattī nahī̃* '[You] have no objection' [Upendra Nath Ashk, *girtī divārẽ*, 4th edition, Allahabad 1967: 45–6], *mujhe mālūm nahī̃* 'I don't know' = also *mujhe nahī̃ mālūm* [colloquial]). Quite possibly the *nahī̃*/*nāhī* forms owe something to both *na* + *hi* and *na* + Present Auxiliary, with verb-like features predominating in some languages (Marathi) and particle-like features in others (Hindi).

In any case, so-called "negative verbs" are often cited as one of the features in which NIA has come to parallel Dravidian. Unlike the negative verbs of the latter, however, those of NIA betray their origin in a fusion of the negative particle (*na*) with a following stem, even if the stem in question is not always precisely identifiable: that is, they generally begin with *n-*. In addition to the fairly transparent M. auxiliaries cited above, and the more elusive *nahī̃*/*nāhī*, some others that might be mentioned are the B. negative Present copula (corresponding to positive ZERO) *noi*, *nɔo*, *noʃ*, *nɔe*, *nɔn*, the B. negative existential verb *nei* (= E.B., Sadhu Bhasa – also A. – *nāi* [Seely 1985: 308], again cf. *nahī̃*), the G. negative Present auxiliary *nathī* (from OIA *nāsti*, but synchronically equivalent to *na* + *che*), and further afield, A. *nowār-* 'not to be able' and the M. prohibitive *nako-* mentioned earlier.

448 (B.) *āmi klānto noi* 'I'm not tired' (Bender and Riccardi 1978: 11)
449 (B.) *tini nei* 'He's not here' (ibid. 59)
450 (A.) *tār hātɒt pɔisā nāi* 'He has no money' (Baruah 1980: 118)
451 (G.) *e ɔphismā̃ nathī* 'He is not in the office' (Cardona 1965: 138)
452 (A.) *mɔi kobo nowārõ* 'I cannot say' (Sarma 1963: 4)

A further complication is that in several languages the negative particle is used with an aspect stem different from the positive:

453 (G.) *e kām kare che*/*karto nathī* 'He is working/not working' (Cardona 1965: 138)
454 (Si.) *minihā gedara yanavā*/*yanne næ̆* 'The man is going/is not going home' (Garusinghe 1962: 24)
455 (N.) *garcha*/*gardaina* 'He does/doesn't' (Matthews 1984: 68)
456 (N.) *garyo*/*garena* 'He did/didn't' (ibid. 94)

457 (B.) *āmrā to bolechi/bolini* ‘We have/have not said [it]’ (Page 1934: 146)

Finally, inversion (of V and Aux), otherwise unknown in NIA, is entailed by negation in some languages, mainly Punjabi (in the Past) and Sindhi (in the Present):

458 (P.) *jāndā sī/na´ī̃ sī jāndā* ‘[He] used to/didn’t use to go’ (Shackle 1972: 35)
459 (P.) *giā sī/náī̃ sī giā* ‘[He] had/hadn’t gone’ (ibid. 77)
460 (S.) *vañā̃ tho/na tho vañā̃* ‘[I] am/am not going’ (Addleton and Brown 1981: 113)

In one respect in this complicated picture, however, there seems to be a NIA consensus: with *non-finite forms* the negator is always a preposed *na* (in the east, *nā*), even when all other negators are postposed: N. *nagarera* ‘not having done’, *nagardo* ‘not doing’, B. *nā āʃte* ‘not to come’, *nā āʃbār [kāron]* ‘[cause] of not-coming’, *nā āʃle* ‘if [X] doesn’t come’, etc. Similarly, the *neither . . . nor* construction is *na . . . na* (or *nā . . . nā*).

10.8.3 *Displacement*

Although required inversions of the type found in West European languages are rare or non-existent in NIA (the auxiliary inversion under negation in P. and S. noted above, plus the V-2 > SOV order change in K. subordinate clauses [see below] is all that comes to mind), violations of normal order in the form of *meaningful* displacements of constituents (of the Simple Sentence, which is still the focus of this discussion) are an important syntactic feature. These may be tentatively classified as follows, although the categories both intersect and interact.

1. *Topicalization:* various clausal constituents, but most commonly the Object, may be topicalized by displacement leftward to the Topic (initial) position. This is really a kind of deemphasis, usually involving concomitant (emphasis) of another constituent.

461 (H.) *dhan {sab log} cāhte haĩ* ‘Wealth, {everybody} wants’ (S. K. Verma 1981: 64)

In Bengali apparently such fronting does not entail deemphasis:

462 (B.) *ʃāṛiṭā āmār bhāi kālke purāno bāṛite diye āʃben* ‘It is *the sari*

that my brother is going to take to the old house tomorrow' (Seely 1985: 101)

For discussion of a more specific Hindi mechanism for thematization (*jo hai*), "characteristic of speech and not of writing", see Gambhir 1983.

2. *Question–answer focus:* information supplied in answer to a question normally occupies the position of the question word in the corresponding question, i.e. the *focal position* just before the verb.[26] This also involves Displacement (usually leftward, and therefore often Topicalization) of the constituent that would normally occupy that position, if it is not itself the "answer".

463 (H.) *roṭī mai͂ne khāī hai* '*I* ate the bread' (S. K. Verma 1981: 60) [answer to *roṭī kisne khāī?* 'Who ate the bread?']

3. *Rightward displacement:* a constituent may be displaced to the right of the VP for a kind of emphasis (in some cases at least – Hindi and Bengali appear to differ here – the "emphasis" is really on the preceding VP [see note 26]).

464 (H.) *mai͂ samajh gayā uskī cāl* '*I understand* what his moves are' (Y. Kachru 1980: 130)
465 (H.) *mai͂ne khāī hai roṭī* '*I ate* the bread' (S. K. Verma 1981: 60)
466 (B.) *bāṛi pācchi nā to kothāo* 'I'm not finding a house *anywhere*' (Seely 1985: 324, from Jibanananda Das)

4. *Scrambling:* other reorderings, particularly those involving displacement of the VP to initial position, are as Y. Kachru notes, "stylistically marked" (and often emotionally marked):

467 (H.) *kar cuke tum hamārī madad!* 'I [do not] trust you to help us' [Lit. "You have already helped us"] (Y. Kachru 1980: 130) [order VSO, normal SOV]
468 (H.) *khāī hai roṭī mai͂ne* 'I have eaten *bread*' (S. K. Verma 1981: 60) [order VOS, normal SOV]
469 (H.) *khānā pakānā bhī nahī͂ sikhāyā. kisī kambaχt ne tumhe͂!* 'No miserable person has even taught you to cook!' (Ashk, *girtī divāre͂* 311) [order [DO/V/S/IO, normal S/IO/DO/V]

There are limits to scrambling. Usually constituents of a *phrase* are not separated, although occasionally "outer" constituents of the NP – Genitive and Participial Phrases – may be displaced rightward for stylistic reasons (or appended as "afterthought"). Poetic diction permits much greater freedom in this respect:

470 (H.) *sunkar bār-bār bāt vahī unki* 'Having heard many times these same words of theirs' (Maithilisaran Gupta, as quoted in R. Shukla 1961: 76)

471 (U.) *jhulse haĩ mũh ʃikār kiye par bhī ʃer kā* 'They must scorch the face of a lion after he hath been struck dead in the chase' (Zauq, as quoted in Sadiq 1964: 170)

Much more work needs to be done on the constraints of displacement cross-linguistically in NIA, and even in Hindi–Urdu (between which there may be significant differences also). For example, it is often claimed that *non-finite clauses* tolerate almost no displacement, but in poetry, it would seem (cf. no. 470), almost anything goes. Not all NIA languages may permit it to the degree Hindi–Urdu does. Even when all the marked word-order variants are given their due, however, the vast majority of sentences in all the languages will no doubt be found to conform to the normal order – which of course is what gives the variants their marked character.

One area that especially needs investigation is whether, as Dezsö (1968) observed for Hungarian, increasingly radical violations of word order norms correlate with increasingly marked intonation patterns. A feature of NIA syntax that must also be kept in mind, however, is the set of *emphatic particles* (clitics) (H. *hī*, B. *i*, G. *j*, M. *ts*, etc.) which make it possible to express "emphasis" without the help of either word order variation or intonation (although also not incompatible with either).

10.8.4 *Deletion*

Various clausal constituents may be deleted, although the precise rules for such ellipsis have not been well worked out for NIA languages as a whole or for any one of them. It is perhaps not surprising that linguists have described what is there before turning their attention to what is not there. We are not talking here of the compulsory EQUI-deletion so beloved by recent transformationalists, which "deletes" identical constituents which are present only theoretically somewhere in the derivational "tree", but of optional (though frequent) deletion in a discourse context – not necessarily under identity conditions – of constituents which *could* be present. Coordinate structures are involved [see below, 10.9], but are only a small part of the problem. This is an important area of NIA syntax, and its rules seem to be moreover not quite the same in the different languages. (For example, Subject pronouns appear to be not quite as readily deletable in Bengali as in Hindi, despite the clearer person marking in the former.)

In the case of certain anaphoric pronouns, particularly those with 3rd person referents, it is not always clear (see no. 472) whether actual *deletion* is involved, or the use of ZERO itself as a kind of anaphoric pronoun (represented by [ø] in the following examples:

472 (U.) *mistrī āj sandūq banāegā aur kal* [ø] *le āegā* 'The carpenter will make the box today and will bring *it* tomorrow' (Bailey 1956: 141, also quoted by Davison 1986b: 13)

473 (P.) *p`āī o´ tā˜ mai˜ vekh cukiā ā˜ / terī k`arvālī vī* [ø] *vekh cukī ai?* 'Oh, I have already seen it/that one' [referring to movie]/'Has your wife seen *it* also?' (U. S. Bahri 1973: 114)

Deletion (X) would seem to be the best explanation for the following, however:

474 (M.) *mulə kāy kartāyat? /* (X) *patte kheḷtāyat* 'What are the children doing? / *They* are playing cards' (Berntsen and Nimbkar 1982: 316)

475 (O.) *tumɔku khoji khoji* (X) *thɔkile* '*He* was tired looking for you' (Pattanayak and Das 1972: 104)

476 (U.) *jab kabhī* (X) *āū˜gā* (X) *āp ke ghar ṭhahrū˜gā* 'Whenever I come, I shall stay with you' (Bailey 1956: 141) [*mai˜* deleted]

477 (G.) (X) *āvīe chīe, tame jāo* 'We are coming, you go ahead' (Lambert 1971: 239) [*ame* deleted]

Verbs as well as nominal constituents are subject to deletion:

478 (H.) *rameʃ ne sanemā dekhā aur ʃīlā ne bhī* (X) (X) 'Ramesh saw the movie and so did Sheela' (Koul 1981: 186 [*sanemā* and *dekhā* deleted]

Care must be taken not to confuse deletion with the non-expression of certain referents as part of the idiom of the language, for example non-use of possessives with parts of one's body, or sometimes with kinship terms. In the case of so-called impersonal constructions, the question might be raised, is the (Dative or Genitive) referent deleted, or is it (optionally) added?

479 (H.) *peṭ me˜ dard hai* 'I have a pain in "my" stomach'

480 (N.) *āghu˜ ta pūrvatir jāne bicār cha* 'But later I intend to go to the east' [Lit. 'There is an idea . . .'] (Matthews 1984: 168, 281)

10.9 Coordinate structures and the "conjunctive participle"

Coordinating conjunctions – little words occurring between sentences, phrases, or words of equal status with the function of connecting them – are common in most NIA languages. But not in all: in Sinhalese there is no 'and' or 'or', their functions generally being performed by *coordinating suffixes* (or particles): . . . *-y* . . . *-y*, . . . *-t* . . . *-t*, . . . *da* . . . *da*, . . . *hari* . . . *hari*. This is the Dravidian idiom (Tamil . . . *-um* . . . *-um*, . . . *-ō* . . . *-ō*).

481 (Si.) *nōna-y daruvo-y gama navatinavā* '(My) wife and children are staying home' (Fairbanks et al. 1968: I. 91)

482 (Si.) *mahattayāṭa liyanna-t puluvani, kiyavanna-t puluvani* 'The gentleman can write as well as read' (ibid. II. 25)

483 (Si.) *tē da kōpi da?* 'Tea or coffee?' (ibid. I. 229)

484 (Si.) *elōlu hari mas hari gēnna* 'Bring either vegetables or meat' (ibid. I. 347)

The *-t* suffix (which means 'also', like Tamil *-um*) may be used alone to string together sentences which (in the sense of Koul 1981: 184–5) are not "coordinate in deep structure":

485 (Si.) *babālā iskōle; nōnā-t sāppu giyā* 'The children are at school; and my wife went shopping' (ibid. I. 228)

The postposition *hā* 'with' (< *saha*) may be used to connect words but not sentences:

486 (Si.) *midulehi hā istōppuvehi bohō minissu ræsvī siṭiyōya* 'Many people collected *in the compound and on the veranda*' (Bel'kovich 1970: 795)

Coordinators of the more familiar type need not detain us long, except to note that there are apparently stronger constraints on their use, both structural and semantic, than on their English equivalents (see Y. Kachru 1980: 144–9, and Koul 1981: 183–204 for further discussion). There is also an interesting regional patterning of the most common conjunctions, e.g., the equivalents for 'and' fall into three groups:

1. H. *aur* [ɔr], Bhad. *aur*, most WPah. *hor*, ER. *ar*, N. *au*, Bhoj. *ao*, Mth. *ao*, *o*, *aor*, *ār*, B. *ār*, *o*, A. *āru*, O. *āu*, *o*
2. M. *āṇi*, Ko. *āni*, G. *(a)ne*, Marw. *nai*, S. *aē̃*
3. P. *(a)te*, L. (Sir.) *(a)te*, K. *tɨ*, Goj. *dɛ*, Chameali *atē*

Objects or persons which form a natural pair generally form a *dvandva* compound rather than being linked with 'and': H. *bhāī-bahan* 'brothers and sisters', *hāth-mũh* 'hands and face'.

Remaining for consideration is a construction which, while by no means unique to Indic languages (see Masica 1976: 108–40), is nevertheless highly characteristic of them, namely the so-called *Conjunctive Participle* construction. Its key element, a non-finite and indeclinable verbal form (having antecedents in Sanskrit, although its role has been greatly expanded in NIA to approach that of similar forms in Dravidian), has been given many names (ibid. 109–11), of which "conjunctive participle" is now perhaps the most common. However, that is a misnomer if it implies that this is another device for *conjoining* sentences – as it is sometimes taken to do because of its frequent equivalence in *usage* to (for example) English sentences conjoined with '*and*'. The NIA clause having the participle is generally clearly subordinate, formally and semantically, to the other clause, the one with the finite verb. For formal arguments in favor of such an assertion, see Davidson 1981, 1986b.

The precise semantic relation of the CP clause to the main clause ranges from temporal priority through cause to manner and a host of others (for the latter see especially Dwarikesh 1971):

487 (H.) *banie ke beṭe ne ciṭṭhī likhkar ḍāk me˜ ḍālī* 'The shopkeeper's son wrote a letter and mailed it at the post office' (Davison 1986b: 1)

488 (H.) *mujhe in cīzo˜ ko dekhkar bahut gussā āyā* 'When I saw those things [= as a result], I became very angry' (ibid. 1)

489 (H.) *dauṛke jāo varnā nārāz hū˜gā* 'Go quickly [lit. 'run and go'] or I will be annoyed' (Davison 1986b: 2)

Although it is interesting that the three 'meanings' illustrated turn up in most descriptions of CP constructions, even for non-IA languages (Tamil, Japanese), Davison argues that they as well as the more specialized meanings are best attributed to inference from the specific material contained + the pragmatic context (+ a general 'perfective' aspectual meaning inherent in the CP form itself), rather than to derivation from a number of different underlying structures.

The "meaning" of the CP construction may thus be very general, "adverbial" if subordinate clauses must be so classified, but in a very non-specific sense compared with other adverbial clauses. It is indeed very close to coordination, except that (1) the Subject of the two clauses must be the same (in the NIA sense of Subject discussed in section 10.3 above) – with certain very specialized exceptions (apparently wider in some NIA languages); and (2) they must be compatible in (underlying) Tense and Aspect, that is, with a "perfective" reading of the CP (i.e. one can't use it to say "I was going to the store, and decided to drop in on you.")

490 (H.) **banie ke beṭe ne ciṭṭhī likhkar, uskī bahan ne ḍāk me˜ ḍālī* 'The shopkeeper's son wrote a letter and his sister mailed it at the post office'

⟶ 491 (H.) *banie ke beṭe ne ciṭṭhī likhī aur uskī bahan ne ḍāk me˜ ḍālī*

Moreover, as Lindholm (1975) has argued for Tamil, not just any two clauses may be so linked: they must have what he calls "natural relevance" – an elusive concept when one tries to define it, but independently cited by other investigators (e.g., Berntsen and Nimbkar 1975: 149, 1982: 244: "closely related actions").

The most common reading, temporal priority, lends itself to various translations, "After X did Y", "When X had done Y", as well as "X did Y and . . ." and the most literal version, "Having done Y, X . . ." Examples from the other main NIA languages follow:

492 (K.) *aki dɔhɨ zɨ tsōr mīl gari nīrith, samkhyis zɜn' jorā* 'One day when he had gone out a couple of miles, he encountered a pair of men' (Bailey 1937: 25) [NB the CP here refers to a Dative Subject, coded by *-s*]

493 (S.) *mā˜ kapṛā dhōī ārām kandus* 'After washing the clothes, I'll rest' (Addleton and Brown 1981: 201)

494 (P.) *ca' pī ke jāṇā* 'Have some tea and then go' (Bahri 1973: 81)

495 (N.) *ma havāījahāj mā carhī belāyat gae˜* 'I boarded the plane and went to Britain' (Matthews 1984: 116)

496 (G.) *strīo vahɛlī ūṭhīne mandire gaī* 'The women got up early and went to the temple' (Lambert 1971: 99)

497 (M.) *pustak hātāt gheūn to vātsāylā lāglā* 'He took a book in his hand and began to read' (Berntsen and Nimbkar 1975: 150)

498 (O.) *se dekhi pɔsɔndɔ kɔribɔ* 'He will see it and make a choice' (Pattanayak and Das 1972: 183)

499 (B.) *āmi tār kāche gie ʃɔb bolbo* 'I'll go to him and tell him everything' (Page 1934: 157)

500 (A.) *āmi khowālowā kɔri relɒt uṭhilo˜* 'After taking food and so forth we entered the train' (Baruah 1980: 839)

501 (Si.) *minihā gedara gihillā bat kanavā* 'The man goes home and eats rice' (Garusinghe 1962: 57)

Some Sinhalese examples appear to violate the same-Subject constraint in non-trivial ways:

502 (Si.) *mahattayā gihillā maṭa mokut karanna bæri unā* 'The

master having gone, I couldn't do a thing' (Fairbanks et al. 1968: II. 90)

503 (Si.) *gedara vædaṭa unnu gǣni gihillā dæn gedara sērama væḍa karanne eyā* 'The woman who did the housework having gone, she now does all the housework herself' (ibid. 90)

10.10 **Complex sentences**

10.10.1 *Preliminaries*

As in other languages, complex sentences in NIA may be defined as sentences which include other sentences, either more or less complete or "reduced", in the role of one or another clausal component (Subject, Object, Complement, Adverbial Adjunct), or in the role of a phrasal component (mainly as adjectival modifiers of nouns). These included (embedded) sentences may involve either finite or non-finite predications. The latter are often, but not necessarily, "reduced" sentences – missing one internal clause component, typically because of identity with a component in the main sentence. The overlap here, however, (i.e. non-reduced non-finite clauses), and the frequent non-equivalence of these two formal categories functionally not only to similar categories in European languages but also cross-linguistically in NIA, make the usual division into non-finite forms and their functions vs. subordinate clauses difficult when dealing with many languages simultaneously as we are attempting to do here. We shall approach the subject instead from a general functional standpoint.

Subordinate clauses are marked as such in NIA by elements ("complementizers" as they are called by some: because of great variation in the use of the word *complement* itself [cf. Berntsen and Nimbkar 1982: 255] let us call them here simply *subordinators*) which may come either at the beginning or at the end of the clause in question – and occasionally even inside it. Clause-initial subordinators prevail in Northwestern NIA, with clause-final ones becoming more and more predominant as we move south toward the border with Dravidian, until in Sinhalese they in turn prevail completely, on the Dravidian model. (A strong preference for clause-final subordinators may also be seen on the border with Tibeto-Burman in Nepali, and in some forms of Shina, but the same is not true of Assamese.)

NIA clauses with final subordinators are normally found to the left of the main sentence, in accordance with general typological principles (Kuno 1974); in a replay on a larger scale of the Displacement operations on components of the simple sentence discussed in section 10.8.3 above, they may, however, occasionally be moved to its right – a stylistically highly marked position. The corollary of this would be that clauses with initial subordinators are found to the right of the main sentence – moved there from their presumed starting point, the internal position of the sentence component they replace, to avoid center-embedding (which often remains a possible option, decreasing in stylistic comfort as the length of the clause increases). However, in NIA the normal position of many clauses of this type also is to the *left*. It would seem that the general left-branching tendency of an SOV language has prevailed over the specifics of subordinator placement. (There is one major class of exceptions to this generalization, to be discussed shortly.) One might also suspect strong pressures to develop clause-final subordinators. It is possible that the *correlative constructions* so characteristic of NIA (although by no means of recent origin: cf. Speijer 1980 [1886]: 347–79) furnish a means by which this pressure may be partly deflected. In some cases (Marathi) they themselves have been the source of a clause-final subordinator.

Reduced non-finite clauses (participial, infinitival) are generally embedded in the position of the main sentence constituent they replace. Such clauses are often permitted in NIA where English would require a finite subordinate clause.

The complexities of complex sentences have been investigated very unevenly – and described very differently – across NIA. The subject itself is vast, and there are a number of theoretical preliminaries that cannot be sorted out here. Therefore this discussion must confine itself to a few major features.

10.10.2 *Nominal clauses*

Sentential Objects, after verbs of saying, telling, hearing, thinking, knowing, etc., corresponding to English *that*-clauses constitute the main NIA exceptions to the leftward placement of subordinate clauses. They also constitute a major watershed within NIA, in that in Hindi–Urdu, Punjabi, Kashmiri, and Sindhi they involve clause-initial subordinators and go to the right; in Bengali, Assamese, Oriya, Gujarati, Nepali, and Marathi either clause-initial or clause-final subordinators are possible (mainly the former in Bengali, mainly the latter in Oriya, Marathi, and Nepali), with concomitant placement rightward or leftward respectively, while in Sinhalese there are only the latter. According to Patnaik and Pandit (1986) in Oriya the postposed clause with initial marker (*je* . . .) is less preferred and is due to English influence. In Nepali the use of a postposed clause with initial marker *ki* . . . is borrowed from Hindi (Matthews 1984: 118). In Marathi the postposed clause with initial marker *kī* . . . is said to be stilted in some contexts (Klaiman 1976a: 11) and also probably due to Hindi influence according to Bloch (1920). In Gujarati also, the preposed clause with final marker is preferred (Tisdall 1961: 99).

In Sinhalese, Dakhani Urdu, Oriya, Bengali, Assamese, and also Nepali, the use of a postposed marker based on the CP of the verb *say* (Si. *kiyalā*, D. *bolke*, O. *boli*, B. *bole*, A. *buli*, N. *bhanera*) has often been remarked upon as a Dravidian calque (Telugu *ani*, Tamil *eṉṟu*, etc.), although it is also found in some Tibeto-Burman languages. Marathi *mhanūn* (with same the literal meaning of 'having said') is sometimes also cited in this connection, although as a subordinator it is mostly used in the more specialized meanings of 'because' or 'so that' (meanings also found in Bengali, Dakhani, etc.); reported speech is mainly indicated by other markers (*asə̄*, *-tsə̄*). Assamese, while using *buli* as a clause-final subordinator, uses *bole* as a clause-*initial* subordinator.

There is no sequence of tenses in NIA: the embedded sentence retains its original tense. In some languages, there is no clear distinction between indirect and direct quotation, the subordinator sometimes obtruding itself with the latter and being dropped with the former. In the examples that follow, the embedded clause is in brackets, while its subordinator (= "complementizer") is underlined.

504 (H.) *mālik ne naukar se kahā [ki tum ghar jāo]* 'The master asked the servant [to go home]' (Subbarao 1984: 46)

505 (P.) *mainū̃ kise ne ākhiā sī [ki pajāme kamīzã mailīā̃ ne]* 'Did anyone tell me [that pyjamas and shirts were dirty]?' (Gill and Gleason 1969: 132)

506 (K.) *panɨń dilan vonnas [zi yimɨvɨī āsi gur nīmɨts]* 'His own heart said to him [that it was by them that this mare must have been taken]' (Bailey 1937: 26)

507 (S.) *tavhī̃ sabhu cio thā [ta mā̃ paṛhiṇa aẽ khāiṇa khā̃ sivā ko kamu na jāṇā̃]* 'You all say [that I don't know how to do anything except read and eat]' (Egorova 1966: 99]

508 (G.) *te jāṇto hato [ke te āvvānī hatī]* 'He knew [that she was coming]' (Lambert 1971: 205)

509 (G.) *teṇe ɛm bolyo [ke tɛno nāno bhāī pās thayo]* 'He said that his younger brother passed' (ibid. 205)

510 (G.) *[tɛno bhāī pās thayo ɛm] te bolyo* '[ditto]' (ibid. 205)

511 (M.) *[mavʃīcī prakruti bari aslyātsə̄] tyānnī kaḷavlə̄* 'He informed me [that my aunt was in good health]' (ibid. 171)

512 (M.) *[tū ātā gharī zā, asə̄] mulīlā sāŋgā* 'Tell the girl [to go home now]' (Lambert 1943: 256)

513 (M.) *malā vaṭlə̄ [kī tumhī yeṇār nāyh]* 'I thought [you wouldn't come]' (ibid. 256)

514 (M.) *malā vaṭlə̄ [payse phār paḍtīl]* 'I thought [it would cost too much'] (Kavadi and Southworth 1965: 184)

515 (O.) *[kɔṭɔkɔ jibɔ boli] hɔri kɔhilā* ‘Hari said [he would go to Cuttack]’ (Patnaik and Pandit 1986: 236)

516 (O.) *hɔri kɔhilā [je kɔṭɔkɔ jibɔ]* ‘[ditto]’ (ibid. 236)

517 (B.) *ʃe bolechilo [je kāj hocche]* ‘He said [that the work was going on]’ (Page 1934: 169)

518 (B.) *ʃe bolechilo [kāl āʃbe]* ‘He said [he would come tomorrow]’ (ibid. 169)

519 (B.) *[ʃe kichu korbena bole] protigge korechi* ‘He has vowed [he won’t do anything]’ (ibid. 170)

520 (B.) *[ʃe je mārā gæche e kɔthā] tumi kār kāche ʃunechile* ‘From whom did you hear [that he was dead]?’ (ibid. 170)

521 (A.) *lɔrātowe kɒle [ze χi χidinā pɒrhāχālilɔi nezābɒ]* ‘The boy said [that he was not going to school that day]’ (Babakaev 1961: 111)

522 (A.) *teo ezɒn bhāl khelwār buli] mɔi χunisɔ̃* ‘I have heard that he is a good sportsman’ (N. Sarma 1963: 12)

523 (A.) *māke mīnuk χuddhisil [bole ɒχɒmkhɒn tāir kene lāgisil]* ‘Mother asked Minu [how she liked Assam]’

524 (N.) *usle [ma bholi āũchu bhanera] bhanyo* ‘He said he would come tomorrow’ (Matthews 1984: 117) [= He said, ‘I will come tomorrow’]

525 (N.) *tyasle bhanyo [ki ma bholi āũdai chu]* ‘[ditto]’ (ibid. 118)

526 (Si.) *nōnā [maṭa salli dunnā kiyalā] kivvā.* ‘The lady said [she gave me the money]’ (Fairbanks et al. 1968: I. 344)

527 (Si.) *[eyā væḍa karapu bava] mahattayā kivvā* ‘The master said [that he worked]’ (ibid. II. 54)

528 (Si.) *[ovun enṭa pera maṭa lamayā muda ganṭa puluvan veyi dæyi] mama magenma prasna kalemi* ‘I asked myself – [Would I be able to free the child before their arrival?]’ (Bel′kovich 1970: 821)

In the function of *Subject*, it is generally clauses (often reduced) with nominalized verb forms (Verbal Nouns in Bengali–Assamese, nominalized Present Participles in Sinhalese, Infinitives in most other NIA languages) that do duty. The Subject of the embedded clause, when expressed, is demoted to the Genitive in the languages of the north, but this appears not to be true for all of NIA (note Sinhalese below).

529 (H.) *[āpkā yahā̃ rahnā] zarūrī hai* ‘[Your staying here] is necessary’ (Y. Kachru 1980: 41) = “It is necessary for you to stay here”

530 (P.) *[tu`āḍā jānā] ba'ut zarūrī ai* '[Your going] is a must' (U. S. Bahari 1973: 85)
531 (S.) *[dū'ā ghuraṇu] sumhaṇu khā˜ vadhik suṭhī āhē* '[To pray] is better than to sleep' (Addleton and Brown 1981: 189)
532 (G.) *[gujarātī akʃaro lakhvānu˜] agharu˜ che* '[To write Gujarati characters] is difficult' (Lambert 1971: 113)
533 (M.) *[ati khāṇe] tsāŋgle nāhī* '[To eat too much] is not good' (DasGupta and Pandit 1975: 130)
534 (Si.) *[ē minihā pōt liyana eka] hoňda næ* '[That he ("that man")] writes books isn't good' (Fairbanks et al. 1968: II. 55)
535 (O.) *iŋgrejī nɔ jāṇile [cākiri ghɔṭibā] bɔṛɔ muskil thilā* 'Without knowing English, [counting on a job] was very difficult' (Karpushkin 1964: 102)
536 (B.) *[tomār āmāder ʃɔŋge ʃɔhɔre jāoā] ucit* 'You should go to the city with us' (Bender and Riccardi 1978: 41)
537 (A.) *[khāl bā ku˜wār pɒrā nɔlire pānī ɒnā, zuit pānī dhɒlā, bāli sɔhiowā ādi] ɒnek kām* 'To bring water by pipe from tank or well, to pour water on fire, to sprinkle sand, etc.] are our duty' (Baruah 1980: 810)
538 (N.) *[saberai ḍulnu] svāsthyako lāgi asal cha* 'To walk in the morning is good for health' (DasGupta and Karmacharya 143)

In Hindi, at least, it is possible to have an embedded sentence as Subject which has not undergone the nominalization transformation:

539 (H.) *[vo kahā˜ gayā] mujhe mālūm nahī˜* '[Where he went] I don't know' (M. Verma 1971: 106)

In the end it may be preferable to use the more general term *complement* (following Y. Kachru 1980) for these embedded sentences. While their syntactic function may sometimes be equated with that of a simple sentence element, it is at other times more complicated. Not only verbs, but adjectival (and other) predications take such "complements" also. As in English, they may be appositive (hence a "complement") to a "dummy" element occupying the normal syntactic position: *It is true [that the basis of a language is some dialect or other]* = H. *yah satya hai [ki bhāʃā kā ādhār koī-na-koī bolī hī hotī hai]* (H. Bahri 1980: 5). Unlike English, such a "dummy" is often present in NIA with postposed so-called Object clauses as well (cf. no. 489 above), so that Subbarao (1984) prefers to analyze them all as if it were present in the derivation (and subsequently deleted):

mālā ko (yah) patā calā [ki vah gā sakegī] 'Mala just learnt (this) [that she could sing]' (Subbarao 1984: 23–4).

Clauses with nominalized verbs are also found in Object functions, typically with a different set of main-clause verbs from the Finite Object Clauses, and unlike the latter, generally in Object *position* as well. They may undergo drastic reduction, but not necessarily:

540 (H.) *maĩ [apnā usse milnā) ṭhīk nahī̃ samajhtā* 'I do not consider [my meeting him) proper' (Y. Kachru 1980: 142)
541 (B.) *āpnī ki tāke [tɔblā bājāno] ʃekhāben?* 'Will you teach him [to play the tabla]? (Seely 1985: 246)
542 (O.) *āme [oṛiā kɔhibā, pɔṛhibā o lekhibā] sikhibu* 'We will learn [to speak, read, and write Oriya]' (Pattanayak and Das 1972: 73)
543 (N.) *ma [ghumna] parāũchu* 'I like [to walk]' (Verma and Sharma 1979: 95)
544 (M.) *tyānī [bhāratāt parat zāytsə] ṭharavlə* 'He decided [to return to India' (Berntsen and Nimbkar 1975: 170)
545 (G.) *tyārthī mɛ̃ [tɛne tyā̃ javānũ] choḍī dīdhũ* 'Since then I have given up [going to his house]' (Lambert 1971: 113)
546 (S.) *aña tāī̃ hū [sindhī likhaṇu] na thō fāṇē* 'So far he doesn't know how [to write Sindhi]' (Addleton and Brown 1981: 323)

As in most languages other than English, the verb *want* takes an infinitival complement when the Subjects of the main and embedded clauses are the same, but demands a clausal complement when they are different:

547 (H.) *pitāji [ānā] cāhte haĩ* 'Father wants [to come]'
548 (H.) *pitāji cāhte haĩ [ki āp āẽ]* 'Father wants [you to come]' (= "that you come" ')

Kashmiri may have the English construction here:

549 (K.) *su chu [rāmas yun] yatshān* 'He wants Ram to come' (Hook: pers. comm.)

In some languages a casal form of the nominalized verb, generally a Dative, is common in the Object function with main verbs of both types. It is especially favored by Assamese.

550 (M.) *āmhālā [marāṭhīt patra lihāylā] ʃikvā* 'Teach us [to write a letter in Marathi]' (Berntsen and Nimbkar 1980: 251)

551 (M.) *mī lālālā [gāḍī durusta karūn ghyāylā] sāŋgen* 'I will tell Lala [to have the car fixed]' (Berntsen and Nimbkar 1975: 172)

552 (O.) *ḍāktɔr bi mɔte [bisramɔ nɔbāku] kɔhicɔnti* 'The doctor also told me [to take rest]' (Pattanayak and Das 1972: 201)

553 (A). *dewiye [rātir bhitɒrɒte etā khɒtkhɒti bāndhi dibɒlɔi] koisi* 'The Goddess asked him [to construct a staircase overnight]' (Baruah 1980: 652)

554 (A.) *mɔi [ɒχɒmiyā kɒbɒlɔi] χikiso˜* 'I am learning [to speak Assamese]' (Sarma 1963: 43)

555 (A.) *teo˜ āmāk [teo˜r ghɒr sābɒlɔi] mātise* 'He invited us [to see his house]' (Baruah 1980: 666)

These shade off into *Purpose Clauses.* For these, some NIA languages (I) use verbal nominals in the Dative of the above type; others (II), Oblique Infinitives (in the case of obliqueless Sinhalese, an ordinary Infinitive); others (III), various specialized markers of Dative type (i.e. "for"):

I. 556 (M.) *lok [ṭivhī baghāylā] yetāt* 'People come [to watch television]' (Berntsen and Nimbkar 1975: 168)

557 (A.) *[kitāp pɔrhibɒlɔi] zāo* 'I am going (in order) to read a book' (Babakaev 1961: 79)

558 (O.) *se [sɔudā kiṇibāku] gɔlā* 'He went [to buy groceries]' (Karpushkin 1946: 48)

559 (Si.) *minihā [bat kæmaṭa] gedara giyā* 'The man went home [to eat (for the purpose of eating)] rice' (Garusinghe 1962: 87)

II. 560 (H.) *mai˜ zarūr [film dekhne] jāū˜gā* 'I will definitely go [to see the film]' (Y. Kachru 1980: 143)

561 (N.) *hāmi [bhāt khāna] jānchau˜* 'We are going (in order) to have dinner' (Matthews 1984: 130)

562 (G.) *teo mane [ʃahɛr jovā] laī gayā* 'They took me [to see the city]' (Lambert 1971: 81)

563 (Si.) *minihā [jivatvenna] væḍa karanavā* 'Man works [to live]' (Garusinghe 1962: 87)

III. 564 (B.) *[tomāke e kɔthā bolbār jonne] eʃechī* 'I came [to tell you this]' (Page 1934: 156)

565 (G.) *hu˜ [ɛne maḷvā māṭe] āvyo* 'I've come to see him' (Cardona 1965: 136)

566 (M.) *[mantrānnā bheṭnyāsāṭhī] te numbaīlā gele āhet* 'He (hon.)

has gone to Bombay to meet the minister' (Berntsen and Nimbkar 1975: 168)

567 (K.) *byākh zon voth [paninyin guryen-hund gīth gyevani]* 'Another man rose to sing his own horses' song' (Bailey 1937: 26 [Ablative of Infinitive]

Other casal forms of verbal nominals, with their attached clausal arguments, play syntactic roles analogous to the corresponding case forms of nouns. Among them (I) adjuncts of cause, instrument, and time, and (II) genitival modifiers of nouns, are particularly important.

I. 568 (N.) *[dherai nai ṭhūlo bhaekole] maile kinina˜* '[Because it was too big] I did not buy it' (Matthews 1984: 297)

569 (P.) *[mere jāṇ nāl] tu`āḍā kām na'ī˜hoṇā* 'You won't get the work done [by my going]' (U. S. Bahri 1973: 87)

570 (H.) *[āne ke kuch din bād] mujhe zukām ho gayā* '[A few days after arriving], I came down with a cold' (Pořízka 1963: 327)

II. 571 (H.) *[chātro˜ kī heḍ se milne kī] icchā thī* 'The students wanted [to meet with the headmaster]' (Hook 1979: 95) (= "There was a desire of meeting . . .")

572 (B.) *[ʃekhāne jāoār] dɔrkār nei* 'There is no need [to go there]' (Page 1934: 155)

573 (M.) *tyānī [te durusta karāytsā] prayatna kelā* 'He tried [to repair it]' (Berntsen and Nimbkar 1975: 170)

574 (S.) *hāṇe [sumhaṇa jo] vaqt āhe* 'Now it's time [to sleep]' (Addleton and Brown 1981: 188)

10.10.3 *Adjectival clauses*

Apart from the genitival modifiers noted above, NIA languages generally have available two more salient means of embedding sentences as modifiers of nouns: the relative clause and the adjectival participle (or participial clause). That is, except for Sinhalese, which like neighboring Tamil[27] has only the latter. (Certain Southern forms of Konkani as well as the Indo-Aryan linguistic island of Saurashtri in the middle of Tamilnadu are also said to have lost the relative construction.)

The participial constructions are straightforward enough: they typically come in at least Perfective ("Past") and Imperfective ("Present") varieties, which may either be identical with the participial forms that are components of the finite verb paradigms, or have special {markers} of their adjectival status (suffixal in Sindhi,

Gujarati, Marathi, and Sinhalese, analytic in Hindi and Punjabi). They typically show concord with the noun they modify in gender, number, and Level I case like a variable adjective if adjectives in the language show these categories.

Verbal adjectives in the Eastern group are not quite like this. In (Standard) Bengali there is only one category (with two forms, *-ā* and *-no*, selected by phonological criteria), and it is identical with the verbal noun rather than connected with components of the finite verb. Assamese and Oriya (and dialectal Bengali, according to Tripathi 1962: 181) have more bits and pieces from the pan-NIA system, but not always closely connected with their own finite paradigms.

575 (N.) *[maile khāeko] bhāt kā˜co thiyo* 'The rice [that I ate] was not well cooked' (Verma and Sharma 1979: 22)

576 (N.) *[pātan jāne] bāṭo kuncāhi˜ho, dāi* 'Which is the road [that goes to Patan] (brother)?' (Matthews 1984: 161)

577 (S.) *cānd jī rauʃanīa mē˜, [sandase badan tē avaḍhīyala] kapṛā thē ɗisē saghise* 'By the light of the moon I could see the clothes [that had been put upon her body]' (Egorova 1966: 58)

578 (S.) *naraīndara jī ʃādī [īndare] janvarīa mē˜ tae thī cukī huī* 'Naraindar's marriage has been set for the [coming] January' (ibid. 57)

579 (G.) *[cār divas pahɛlā˜mokalelo] kāgaḷ mane hajīpaṇ maḷyo nathī* 'I haven't yet received the letter [which was sent four days ago]' (Lambert 1971: 131)

580 (G.) *[ā kām māṭē joīto] sāmān hu˜ lavyo chu˜* 'I have brought the things [needed for this work]' (ibid. 136)

581 (G.) *[aphīsmā˜ janāṛā] lokone savāre vahɛlā nīkaḷī javu˜paḍe che* 'The people [who go to (work in) offices] have to start early in the morning' (ibid. 138)

582 (M.) *[tyānnī˜ lihilelyā] laghukathā . . .* 'Short stories [written by them] . . .' (Katenina 1963: 196)

583 (M.) *[kapḍe dhuṇārī] bāī . . .* 'The woman [who washes clothes] . . .' (Berntsen and Nimbkar 1975: 139)

584 (Si.) *[mama ē minihāṭa dunna] salli dækkā da* 'Did you see the money [I gave to that man]?' (Fairbanks et al. 1968: II. 52)

585 (Si.) *banḍā kaḍapu] pol adinna* 'Fetch the coconuts [that Banda has picked]' (ibid. 344)

586 (Si.) *[gedara yana/giya] minihā bat kanavā* 'The man [who is going/who has gone home] eats rice' (Garusinghe 1962: 59–60)

587 (H.) *devtāo˜ko [cakhe hue] phal caṛhāe nahī˜ jāte* 'You don't

offer to the gods fruits [that have already been tasted]' (Hook 1979: 201)

588 (H.) *[caltī (huī)] gāṛī se kūd paṛnā bevukūfī hai* 'To jump from a [moving] train is stupidity' (McGregor 1972: 156)

589 (H.) *[sāmne se ānevālī] moṭar merī moṭar se ṭakrā gaī* 'The car [that was coming from the opposite direction] collided with my car' (Hook 1979: 16)

590 (P.) *[suttā hoyā] muṇḍā o´ kamre vic sī* 'The boy [who was asleep] was in that room' (Shackle 1972: 106)

591 (P.) *[rondī hoī] kuṛī mān koḷ gaī* 'The [weeping] girl went to her mother' (ibid. 106)

592 (P.) *[kam karanvāḷīā˜] kuṛīā˜ ne ṣanū˜ vekhiā* 'The girls [who were working] saw us' (ibid. 95)

593 (A.) *[kitāp pɒrhā] mānuhzɒn kɒn āsil* 'Who was the man [who read the book]?' (Babakaev 1961: 80)

594 (A.) *[kitāp pɔrhi thɒkā] mānuhzɒn mor bɔndhu* 'The man [who is reading the book] is my friend' (ibid. 79)

595 (O.) *[dɔyā kɔrilā] pɔṭṭɔ-sthitti . . .* 'the settlement of the charter [granted as a favor or grace]' (Tripathi 1962: 181 – inscriptional)

596 (O.) *[pācilā] kɔḍɔḷī* '[ripened] bananas' (Karpushkin 1964: 51)

597 (O.) *[cori kɔrithibā] pilā* 'the boy [who has committed a theft]' (Patnaik and Pandit 1986: 237)

598 (O.) *tɔ pɔre se [upɔrɔ mɔhɔlāku uṭhibā] siṛitɔḷe bɔsi rɔhilā* 'Then she sat under the stairway [leading to the upper storey]' (Karpushkin 1964: 46)

599 (B.) *[tār nijer jonne toiri kɔrāno] ghɔre āmi thākbo kæno?* 'Why should I stay in a house [that he has had built for himself]?' (Page 1934: 157)

600 (B.) *āmi [tār lekhā] ækkhāṇā boi poṛechi* 'I've read a book [written by him]' (ibid. 157)

Relative clauses present a much more complicated picture. For one thing they involve the characteristic Indo-Aryan (Old as well as New) *relative–correlative* construction, where the modifying clause, marked by a member of the "J"-set of relative pronouns, adverbs, and other words, is "represented" by a *correlative* in its role-slot (i.e. basically that of Modifier in the NP) in the main clause. The correlative is usually identical with the remote demonstrative in the language (except in Sindhi and Dakhani, where the correlative *so* preserves the form of an *earlier* IA demonstrative). In most languages the modifying clause (we may call it the J-clause, although represented in Kashmiri and Assamese by cognate Y- and Z-) may occur either to the *left* of the main clause, immediately *after* the Head Noun ("center-embedded"), or to the *right* of the main clause, after its final verb. In the first case, which is the most characteristic and common, the Head Noun of the main clause is generally deleted (leaving the correlative to mark its place) while its coreferent in the modifying clause is allowed to remain:

601 (P.) *[je'ṛā bandā ā ri'ā e] mai˜ o'(bande)nū˜ na'ī˜ pachāṇdā* 'I don't recognize *the man who* is coming' (Shackle 1972: 103) = "Which *man* is coming, I *him* (that man) don't recognize"

There are certain constraints on the three options, however. The classic distinction between restrictive and non-restrictive clauses plays a role in these: a non-restrictive clause comes after the Head, or to the right of the main clause – and requires no correlative.

602 (H.) *ūpar se usne apne dono˜ aiyāro˜ ko [jinkā nām nājim-alī aur ahmadkhā˜ hai] is bāt kī takīd kar dī hai ki barābar ve log mahal kī nigahbānī kare˜ kyo˜ki* . . . 'And moreover he has instructed his two *sorcerers*, [whose names are Nazim Ali and Ahmad Khan], to keep a constant watch on the palace, because (etc.) . . .' (Devakinandan Khatri, *candrakāntā*; n.d. [1892]: 2)

603 (H.) *mujhko to yah khabar nājim ne pahu˜cāi thī [jo āj kal mahal ke pahre par mukarrar hai]* 'But Nazim, [who these days has been appointed to the palace watch], gave me this information' (ibid. 26)

604 (O.) *rāmɔ bābu [jie oḍiā re ɔnɔrgɔlɔ bɔktrutā dei pārɔnti], prɔkrutɔre oḍiā nuhɔnti* 'Rama Babu who can deliver speeches in fluent Oriya is not really an Oriya' (Patnaik and Pandit 1986: 237)

Subbarao (1984: 13) has noted that, in Hindi, relative clauses tributary to *indefinite* Head Nouns also must go to the right. (To be sure, the two categories – indefinite Head and non-restrictive clause – often overlap, but not entirely.)

605 (H.) *vahā˜ use ainiyās nām jhole kā māra ek manuṣya milā, [jo āṭh varṣ se khāṭ par paṛā thā]* 'There he found *a* man named Aeneas, stricken with paralysis, [who had been bedridden for eight years]' (Acts 9: 33)

On the other hand, Marathi and Gujarati seem to avoid using their J-relative in this position, although examples can be found:

606 (G.) *sankrā˜t, jɛnu˜ bīju˜ nām utarāṇ che . . .* 'Sankrant, the other name of which is Utaran . . .' (Lambert 1971: 222)

More typically, what looks like parataxis seems to be preferred, e.g., in the same passage from Acts cited above (no. 605):

607 (G.) *tyā˜ tene eniyās nāme ek māṇas malyo, [te pakṣghātī hato, ane āṭh varasthī khātle paḍelo hato]*

608 (M.) *tethe aineyās nāmatsā ek māṇūs tyālā bheṭlā, pakṣghāt dzhālyāmuḷe to āṭh varṣ antharuṇālā khiḷalā hotā*

And further:

609 (G.) *tenī pāse ek adhurī masjid che, te bā˜dhṇī tathā ʃobhāmā˜ hindustānmā˜ bīji koi paṇ imāratthī utartī nathī* 'Near it is an unfinished mosque [which for its proportions and beauty is second to no other building in Hindustan]' (Taylor 1908: 236)

It may be open to question whether non-restrictive clauses, which are usually marked by distinctive junctures, are really part of the NP. On the other hand, in both these languages there is a distinct tendency to *delete* the J-element (Lambert 1971: 133, Berntsen and Nimbkar 1975: 146), leaving the correlative to mark the connection (see below). Whether this is what is going on with the above sentences needs to be determined by a careful study of intonation and juncture. (If it is, it would mean that the sentences may be analyzed differently, with the first clause as a relative clause with a deleted J-element, essentially no different from a restrictive clause, and the second clause as the main clause – another problem.)

In any case, it is the restrictive clause that constitutes the heart of the matter. Here investigators of various languages (e.g., Shackle 1972: 103 on Punjabi, Patnaik and Pandit 1986: 237 on Oriya) agree that the preposed variety is the normal NIA construction. It is possible that in some languages it is the only construction. (Subbarao 1984 avers that in Hindi there is a "preference" for rightward placement when the Head Noun is an Object. For a contrary example, cf. no. 618 below.)

610 (B.) *[je lokṭi māṭhe kāj korche] ʃe cāʃā* 'The man [who is working in the field] is a farmer' (Bender and Riccardi 1978: 61)

611 (A.) *[zi ɔinɒr upɒkār kɔribɒ nowāre] tæo˜ nizɒrɒ mɒŋgɒl nubuze* 'He [who doesn't know how to help others] doesn't understand his own happiness' (Babakaev 1961: 108)

612 (O.) *[jou pilā cori kɔrichi] sei pilā . . .* 'the boy who has committed a theft . . .' (Patnaik and Pandit 1986: 237)

613 (M.) *[kal jyānī gāṇə mhaṭlə] tyācə nāv kāy?* ‘What is the name of the man [who sang a song yesterday]?’ (Berntsen and Nimbkar 1975: 147)

614 (G.) *[je māṇas mārī sāthe āvyo] te paṭelno bhāī che* ‘The man [who came with me] is the Patel’s brother (Lambert 1971: 128)

615 (S.) *[jō kitābu tuh̃injē hatha mē˜ āhē] sō mū˜ khē ɗēkhārīō* ‘Show me the book [which is in your hand]’ (Addleton and Brown 1981: 261)

616 (P.) *[je'ṛī kursī te tusī˜ baiṭhe hoe o] o'ī kursī ṭuṭṭī hoī ai* ‘The chair [on which you are seated] is broken’ (U. S. Bahri 1973: 165)

617 (H.) *[jo log zyādā cāy pite hai˜] ve kam so pāte hai˜* ‘People [who drink a lot of tea] sleep less’ (Subbarao 1984: 102)

618 (H.) *[vahā˜ jo log baiṭhe hai˜] unko mai˜ nahī˜ jāntā* ‘I do not know the people [who are sitting there]’ (Y. Kachru 1980: 28)

Such constructions constitute a typological anomaly, in that they have a preposed marker, yet are preposed themselves. (Preposed subordinators usually imply rightward movement of the clause.) As noted earlier, Gujarati and Marathi frequently delete the preposed J-element, leaving in effect the correlative (T-) element as a postposed subordinator and thus “correcting” the anomaly:

619 (G.) *[hu˜ (je kām) karto hato] te kām bahu agharu˜ hatu˜* ‘The work that I was doing was very difficult’ (Lambert 1971: 128)

620 (M.) *[āz sakāḷī (zo) tumcyābarobar ālā hotā] to koṇ āhe?* ‘Who was that [who came with you this morning]?’ (Berntsen and Nimbkar 1975: 146)

Such constructions are foreign to Hindi and its Indo-Gangetic neighbors, but are highly characteristic of the southern form of Hindi–Urdu, Dakhani:

621 (D.) *[āp kharīde] so ghar mere kū pasand hai* ‘I like the house [you bought]’ (Y. Kachru 1986: 171)

622 (D.) *[baṛe kamre me˜ thā] so mez par vo kitābā˜ rakh diyā* ‘He put the books on the table [which was in the big room]’ (ibid. 172)

Here there is no question but that the correlative has already been reanalyzed as a clause-final subordinator, and the modifier clauses should be bracketed, intonationally and otherwise, as *[āp kharide so], [baṛe kamre me˜ thā so]*.

Note that the coreferential nouns in the two clauses may occasionally both be left in (as in no. 612 above), or both may be deleted (as in nos. 611, 613) resulting in pronominalized relatives.

The alternative orders, i.e. with rightward placement (O. *sei pilā [jie cori kɔrichi] . . .*, cf. no. 612, and H. *ve log [jo zyādā cāy pite haĩ] kam so pāte haĩ* or *ve log kam so pāte haĩ [jo zyādā cāy pite haĩ]*, cf. no. 617), are becoming increasingly common, although in most languages they probably still are far behind the "normal" order. (Careful frequency counts in different registers and genres need to be undertaken.) In the case of Oriya, Patnaik and Pandit (1986) do not hesitate to attribute the postposed restrictive construction (as well as the nonrestrictive one exemplified by no. 604) to the influence of English.

Other possibilities deserve some consideration, however, at least for NIA as a whole. One is the influence of Persian, the prevailing official language for half a millennium before English was a factor, in which the relative clause is rightward-placed (and also normally contains a kind of correlative, although not precisely analogous to the NIA usage):

623 (Pers.) *yek mard vāred ʃod [ke man ū-rā na-miʃenāχtam]* 'A man came in [that I didn't know]' (Lazard 1957: 222)

Persian has no distinct relative pronoun, using the general subordinator *ke* (= H. *ki*). Here it is noteworthy that some users of Hindi append a *ki* to the H. relative pronoun when it introduces a postposed clause = *jo ki.* Elena Bashir reports (pers. comm.) that this is very common in the Urdu of Pakistan, e.g., in radio news.

I have been able to find Kashmiri relatives only of the postposed variety:

624 (K.) *su nāvivōl (yus ḍalgēṭɨ rōzān chu] niyi asi niʃāth bāg* 'That boatman [who lives at Dal Gate] will take us to Nishat Garden' (B. Kachru 1973: 517)

625 (K.) *sɔndar tɨ javān kūr [yɔs yōr ɜ̄s āmɨts] gɜyi az dili* 'The beautiful and young girl [who came here] went to Delhi today' (Koul 1976: 195)

If this is not somehow due to the peculiar syntax of Kashmiri itself, it is more likely attributable to Persian than to English influence. Finally, a few postposed J-clauses occur in the late sixteenth century Braj prose texts studied by McGregor (1968: 148), where no English influence is possible.

There is a second factor that may have a role, however. It was noted earlier that preposing a clause with a preposed subordinator is something of a typological anomaly. One way of resolving this is to develop a postposed subordinator. Another is to move the clause to the right.

Relativization is a fascinating area of NIA syntax which merits more extensive investigation. It is a question not only of identifying the constraints and tendencies that govern the three placement strategies in all the NIA languages mutually compared, but of these vis-à-vis the participial option. It appears that the latter is strikingly more favored by Marathi, and also by Nepali (and according to Hook, also by Shina), than by Hindi, for instance, but this needs detailed demonstration. In Nepali, relative pronouns seem to exist (Korol'ev 1968: 1261), but it is difficult to find examples of their use: all the likely contexts turn out to have participles.[28] Both Dravidian and Tibeto-Burman prefer participles.

10.10.4 *Adverbial clauses*

There are many kinds of adverbial clauses, which it is not possible to give a full account of here. One variety, the most general, is exemplified by the so-called Conjunctive Participle construction already discussed in section 10.9 above. Another, very specialized type, the Conditional, will be discussed in the next section. Here we may merely sample one representative adverbial adjunct type, the temporal.

Sentences to be embedded as temporal adjuncts have available to them the same two strategies (besides the verbal noun + postposition) that were employed by those embedded as noun modifiers, the J-clausal and the participial. The former are again normally preposed, and entail a correlative within the main clause:

626 (H.) *[jab mai˜ kalkatte me˜ thā] tab har garmīme˜ ḍarjīling jātā thā* 'I used to go to Darjeeling every summer [when I was in Calcutta]' (Kachru 1980: 139)

627 (G.) *[jyāre kām pūrū thaſe] tyāre hu˜ ghɛr jaīſ* 'I shall go home [when the work is finished]' (Lambert 1971: 120)

628 (M.) *[jevhā tumhī kolhārpūrla zāl] tevhā tyāncyākaḍe zāūn bheṭā* '[When you go to Kolhapur] go and meet him' (Berntsen and Nimbkar 1975: 147)

629 (B.) *[tārā jɔkhon cole jābe] tɔkhon āmrā āſbo* 'We'll come [when they go away]' (Page 1934: 167)

630 (S.) *[jēstāī˜ asānjā mizmān hitē āhin] tēstāī asī˜na vēndāsī˜* '[As long as our guests are here] we won't go' (Addleton and Brown 1981: 355)

Just as in adjective clauses, the J-element may be deleted in Gujarati and Marathi, leaving the correlative as postposed quasi-marker. As in adjective clauses, the J-element may come second rather than at the beginning of the clause, especially in Bengali.

The participial option primarily means the Imperfective Participle, used in an

Oblique case form where it exists, or with special endings (A. *-o˜te*, M.*-ānā*), or reduplicated, to indicate action concurrent with that of the main verb ("while", "during").

631 (H.) *[kamre se nikalte hue] usne dekhā ki dhobī barāmde baiṭhā huā hai* '[As he came out of the room], he saw that the washerman was sitting on the verandah' (Nilsson 1975: 22–5)

632 (P.) *o´ [caldī gaḍḍī te ca´ṛde ca´ṛde) ḍig piā* 'He fell [while (trying to) board the moving train]' (U. S. Bahri 1973: 154)

633 (K.) ... *yā hekiv [pakān pakān] gɜtshith tim tre mīl* 'Or, you can cover those three miles [on foot ("walking-walking")]' (B. Kachru 1973: 441)

634 (S.) *chōkirō [rōandē] āīō* 'The boy came crying' (Addleton and Brown 1981: 318)

635 (G.) *hu˜ [ahī āvtā˜] rasto cūkī gayo* 'I lost my way [as I was coming here]' (Lambert 1971: 144)

636 (M.) *to [kām kartānā] gāṇə mhaṇat āhe* 'He is singing [while he is working]' (Berntsen and Nimbkar 1975: 155)

637 (O.) *mu˜ [jāu jāu] goṭie bāghɔ dekhili* 'I saw a tiger [while going]' (Pattanayak and Das 1972: 169)

638 (B.) *[douṛote douṛote] tārā citkār kollo* 'They shouted [as they ran]' (Page 1934: 162)

639 (A.) *χi [puthi pɒrho˜te] hā˜hile* 'He laughed [as he read the book]' (Babakaev 1961: 80)

640 (N.) *tyo [landanmā cha˜dā], harek haptā sinemā herna jānthyo* '[When he was in London] he used to go to the pictures every week' (Matthews 1974: 224)

The Sinhalese equivalent is made by duplicating the stem of the "Past" (= Conjunctive) participle:

641 (Si.) *[kæma kakā kakā] karanna epā* 'Don't talk [while eating]!' (Fairbanks et al. 1968: II. 159)

The Perfective equivalent of these, indicating sequenced rather than simultaneous action, is the Conjunctive Participle. There are "adverbial" uses of Perfective participles themselves, but they are not *temporal* uses:

642 (H.) *ek ādmī [pā˜v par pā˜v rakhe (hue)] farʃ par baiṭhā (huā) thā* 'A man was sitting on the floor [with his legs crossed]' (McGregor 1972: 160)

Imperfective participles, however, are used in other temporal constructions in various languages:

643 (H.) *[hamāre ghar pahuc̃te hī] pānī barasnā band ho gayā* '[*As soon as* we got home] it stopped raining' (Hook 1979: 137)
644 (B.) *[āmi boʃte nā boʃte-i] ʃe uṭhe dā̃ṛālo* '[I had *scarcely* sat down when] he stood up' (Page 1934: 162)
645 (M.) *[divas uzāḍtā-ts] to bāher nighālā* '[*As soon as* day dawned] he set out' (Berntsen and Nimbkar 1975: 159)

A third type of temporal clause, characteristic especially of Marathi and Sinhalese, and to some extent also of Oriya, is formed by attaching postpositions or "adverbial nouns" referring to time to the *adjectival participle.* It is very similar to constructions in Dravidian:

646 (M.) *[tikḍe gelyānantar] to kāy karṇār?* '[After going there] what is he going to do?' (Berntsen and Nimbkar 1975: 151)
647 (M.) *[ithe yāycyāagodar] āmhī dahā divas mumbaīlā rāhilo* '[Before coming here] we stayed in Bombay for ten days' (ibid. 160)
648 (Si.) *[sandŭda enakoṭa] rupiyal pahē muddareak gēnna* '[When you come on Monday], bring a 5-rupee stamp' (Fairbanks et al. 1968: I. 104)
649 (Si.) *[væḍa paṭangattāma] gunapāla giyā* 'Gunapala went away [when (after) the work started]' (ibid. I. 326)
650 (O.) *kintu semanɔŋku kuhɔ je [āsilabeḷe o gɔlābeḷe] phāṭɔkɔ bɔnd kɔri deuthibe* 'But tell them that they should close the gate [while coming and going]' (Pattanayak and Das 1972: 161)

Except for its formation with a Perfective participle, the Oriya form using a noun meaning 'time' has parallels (although perhaps not in frequency of usage) in other NIA languages:

651 (H.) *[barf girte samay] andar raho* 'Stay inside [when it snows]' (Hook 1979: 137)
652 (S.) *[mōṭandē vaqt] mū̃ khā̃ rastō visarī viō* '[On the way back (when returning)] I forgot the way' (Addleton and Brown 1981: 319)

10.10.5 *Conditional constructions*

Although they often involve special tense forms, on the syntactic level conditional clauses might appear to be merely a special case of adverbial clause involving a correlative (*if . . ., then . . .*), but they merit attention because: (1) the initial *if* is often dropped, leaving in effect a postposed subordinator (the correlative), even in languages such as Hindi where this does not happen with other correlative constructions; (2) Sinhalese and Nepali have only postposed subordinators; (3) the three Eastern languages also have conditional *participles*. The finite clausal type may be illustrated by the following:

653 (H.) *[agar kitābo˜ vālī dukāne˜ subah khul jātī ho˜] to ham āj hī le sake˜ge* '[If the bookstores open in the morning] we could get it today' (Hook 1979: 48)
654 (B.) *[ʃe jodi āʃto] tɔbe āmi cole jetum* '[If he had come] I should have gone away' (Page 1934: 168)
655 (A.) *[χi zɔdi āhe] tente mɔi zām* '[If he comes], I shall go' (Babakaev 1961: 109)
656 (G.) *[(jo) tame sā˜je āvʃo] to hu˜ tamne paisā āpīʃ* '[If you come this evening] I'll give you the money' (Lambert 1971: 174)
657 (M.) *[(zar) tū gelās] tar mīhī zāīn* '[If you go] I will go too' (Berntsen and Nimbkar 1975: 161)

In Sinhalese and Nepali there is no correlative with the clause-final marker:

658 (Si.) *[minihā væḍa karanavā nam] mama salli denavā* '[If the man works], I give him money' (Garusinghe 1962: 61)
659 (N.) *[roṭī bhaena bhane] ma bhāt nai khānchu* '[If there is no bread] I'll just have boiled rice' (Matthews 1984: 107)

The participial construction of the Eastern group does not require the correlative:

660 (B.) *[ʃe kichu jānle], tomāke niʃcɔy bolto* '[If he knew something] he would certainly have told you' (Bender and Riccardi 1978: 48)
661 (A.) *[mɔi āhile] tumi zābā* '[If I come,] you will leave' (Babakaev 1961: 81)
662 (O.) *[ketebeḷe ṭikie subidhā kɔri āpɔṇɔ āsipārile] bhɔlɔ huɔntā* '[If some time at your convenience you could come] it would be good' (Pattanayak and Das 1972: 191)

The conditional participles often have a temporal meaning. In Assamese this sometimes has a special form, *-ilɒt*:

663 (A.) *[mɔi āhilɒt] tumi gɔlā* 'You left [after I came/upon my arrival]' (Babakaev 1961: 81)

Sinhalese and Nepali may also be said to have conditional participles, not cognate with those of the Eastern group, although the Sinhalese forms are cognate with general NIA Contrafactives (though not themselves necessarily contrafactive):

664 (Si.) *[minihā væḍa karatot(in)] mama salli denavā* 'If the man works, I will give him money' (Garusinghe 1962: 61)
665 (N.) *[bhok lāge] phul pakāera khānuhos* '[If you feel hungry], cook yourself an egg (and eat it)' (Matthews 1984: 182)

The form used in the Nepali construction is not exclusively conditional in its function.

10.10.6 *Causative constructions*

Being a prominent feature of NIA languages, causative constructions have received a fair share of attention, but remain a tough nut to crack. Some modern syntacticians see them as complex, the result of combining two underlying sentences. The trouble with this is that one of those sentences (**cause to*) is purely an abstraction. Despite the undeniable relationships between causative and non-causative sentences, and the morphological relationship of their verb forms, it is probably best to see the construction as a special subtype of simple sentence, the verb of which (like *give*) happens to entail an additional argument. When such clear relationships are apparent, the linguist naturally feels a strong compulsion to reduce them to rules if possible. For extended discussions in the transformational-generative mode see Mistry (1969: 130–70) (on Gujarati) and A. Saksena (1982) (on Hindi). For causative *morphology* see Chapter 9, section 6.

Appendix I

INVENTORY OF NIA LANGUAGES AND DIALECTS

Although the problem of the distinction between *language* and *dialect* cannot be resolved absolutely (see discussion in Chapter 2), a basic classification which is far from arbitrary (the distinction is clear enough in many cases) will be imposed on the alphabetized list below by means of typographical conventions, partly following those of Turner's *CDIAL*. That is:

1. a *dialect* (= essentially, a regional subvariety of a larger entity) will be written with an initial lower-case letter;
2. a *language* (= cluster of dialects) will be written with an initial capital letter: thus *Shina* is a language, *gilgiti* is one of its dialects. However,
3. When a language possesses an established modern *literary standard* (= "language" in Sense B [see Chapter 2]), it will be written entirely in capitals: e.g., *PUNJABI* rather than *Punjabi*.
4. Languages cultivated for pre-modern but not modern literary purposes are given in capitals enclosed by square brackets: *[AWADHI]*.
5. Languages attempting to develop a modern literary standard are given in capitals enclosed by round brackets: *(KHOWAR)*.
6. In certain cases, both qualifications may apply: *([MAITHILI])*.

The same conventions are followed on Map 1, although space allows the inclusion of only a few dialect names. (These conventions are not followed in the text of Chapters 1–10.)

There are certain anomalies which these typographic distinctions cannot handle. One is Konkani, where several dialects (from a Marathi point of view, *sub*dialects) – according to Pereira (1973) as many as seven – have been cultivated as literary media. It would distort the overall picture to put all these in capital-letter entries. Another is the Hindi–Urdu situation, where not even different dialects, but different *styles* based on the same dialect, are widely (and also officially) regarded as different *languages*. We can only acknowledge this cultural (and political) fact.

Although the intention is to be as comprehensive as possible, we cannot pretend to be exhaustive: for some investigators, every village has its own "dialect". We shall attempt to include, however, names the reader may encounter in the literature as well as all those given by respectable numbers of respondents in the census.

Alternative names will be enclosed in *single quotes*, and the reader directed to the main entry: *'Laria': see Chhattisgarhi*. An attempt will be made to use the most recently current name as the main entry. Names which are philological inventions and/or represent philological constructs will be enclosed in *double quotes*: *"Central Eastern Rajasthani"*. The so-called Nuristani (or "Kafiri") languages which are not strictly part of Indo-Aryan but are referred to in the literature are listed preceded by an asterisk: **Ashkun*.

The list is alphabetized according to the order of the Roman (not the Nagari or other

Indian) alphabet. Moreover, if the speech variety has an established name in English the entry will be alphabetized under that, with the native name transcribed after a diagonal line: e.g., *BENGALI/bāŋlā, bɔŋgo bhāʃā.* With regard to *chh/ch* vs. *ch/c*, *sh* vs. *ṣ/ś* (or *ʃ* if this distinction is unwarranted), the former are used in the "English" names, the latter in the transcriptions; *w/v* are used for the most part according to the usual back vowel/front vowel allophonic rendering. To simplify the printer's task, outside this list, that is, in the remainder of the text, the "English" name, beginning with a capital, will be used to refer to the language or dialect, without diacritics (which will be reserved for *cited Indo-Aryan forms*): e.g., Shina, not *ṣiṇā.*

Statistics are particularly problematic in Indo-Aryan. To quote Lockwood (1972: 199): "Where there are no clear boundaries, there can be no exact statistics." Paradoxically, for India at least we do have at the same time the enormous resource represented by the census. Its figures must be used with extreme caution, however, particularly with respect to what Khubchandani (1983) calls the "Fluid Zone" (= the Hindi area, plus Punjab and Kashmir), where there have been radical statistical swings from one census to another. Here "mother tongue" responses indicate not so much the respondent's actual speech as his (often shifting) cultural identification.

Moreover, this is sometimes made for him. Apparently alarmed by the great increase in "regional language" identity assertion in the Hindi area in the 1961 census, the authorities decreed that in the 1971 and subsequent censuses, all such language claims should be counted as *Hindi* (Khubchandani 1983: 104). Even without this assistance, many regional language speakers in every census put down their language as *Hindi*, representing what Khubchandani calls an "assimilative" trend competing and often oscillating with the "assertive" trend. To be sure Hindi *is* replacing the regional language as the effective home language among certain urban elite groups, but these are likely to be smaller than the figures indicate. There is no reliable way of knowing how far this process has really gone – and thus, of ascertaining the real number of *native speakers* of Standard Hindi (the figures are likely to be fairly reflective of would-be *users* for formal purposes) vs. the regional languages. To give some indication of the numbers behind some of these languages, however, an attempt will be made to provide estimates based on the population increases of the areas concerned according to the provisional figures of the 1981 census. In what Khubchandani calls the "Stable Zone" – the rest of the country – language statistics themselves are more reliable, but are not as yet available for 1981, so again supplemental estimates must be made. To give an idea of the trends toward assimilation or assertion and also of the problems connected with the Indian census data, both 1961 and 1971 statistics are given below, and where particularly relevant, *LSI* statistics as well. For Pakistan there is much less to go on.

Abbreviations

n. = name	alt. = alternative	AP = Andhra Pradesh
lg. = language	N = north(ern)	UP = Uttar Pradesh
dial. = dialect	S = south(ern)	MP = Madhya Pradesh
Dt = District	E = east(ern)	HP = Himachal Pradesh
	W = west(ern)	NWFP = Northwest Frontier Province
acc. = according to	*LSI* = *Linguistic survey of India*	
est. = estimate	m. = million	

'Afgon' – see *Par'ya.*
'Ahirani'/ahirāṇī – usual name in Maharashtra for *Khandeshi.*
'Ahiri'/ahīrī – another name for *Malvi*, as spoken by non-Rajputs.

ahīrī – a *Bhili* dialect of Kutch (or *GUJARATI* dialect with *Bhili* substratum).

ahīrvāṭi – a dialect of *Mewati*, spoken in W Gurgaon Dt, Haryana, SW of Delhi.

ajmeri – a subdial. of *"Central Eastern Rajasthani"* in E Ajmer Dt, Rajasthan.

anāwlā – subdialect of *GUJARATI*, spoken by cultivator-Brahmans in S part of Surat Dt; alt. *bhaṭhelā, anavla, anaola.*

Angika/angikā – new name first appearing in 1961 census (5,598) in E Bihar, roughly corresponding to *LSI*'s *chhikāchhikī bolī* "dialect" of *([MAITHILI)]*; acc. P. Pandey 1979 an independent language; other alt. *'angā'*, *'bhagalpurī'* (94, 401 in 1971).

'Antarbedi' – alt. n. for both *[BRAJ]* and *Kannauji* < 'language of the sacrificial holy ground between the Ganges and the Jumna'.

antruzi – name (Pereira 1973) of *(KONKANI)* dialect of Hindus in most parts of Goa (= Katre's *'g.'*?); considerable prose literature in twentieth century < Antrus = Ponda (taluka), in the Novas Conquistas.

**Ashkun/aṣkū̄* – lg. of about 2,000 persons in nine villages in Afghan Dt of Ashkun, Nuristan, S of *Kati* area.

ASSAMESE/ɒχɒmiyā – lg. (ca. 12,000,000) of Brahmaputra valley, especially middle and upper portions, in State of Assam; literary tradition from fourteenth century, divided into Early (fourteenth–sixteenth centuries), Middle (seventeenth–eighteenth centuries), and Modern (nineteenth–twentieth centuries); literary standard based on Eastern dialect of Sibsagar, old seat of Ahom kings; easternmost cultivated NIA language; has absorbed many indigenous Tibeto-Burman (esp. Bodo) and Austro-asiatic elements. Script identical to Bengali except for characters for /r/ and /w/; characters often have different values, however (e.g., B. CH = A. S).

astori – dialect (or dialectal subdivision) of *Shina* (Azad Kashmir, Pakistan; in latter sense also in mts. of Indian Kashmir, N and NE of Srinagar).

[AWADHI]/avadhī – lg. (or acc. Grierson principal "dialect" of his lg. construct "Eastern Hindi") of east-central Uttar Pradesh, from just W of Banaras to somewhat W of Lucknow, roughly corresponding to old kingdom of Oudh (Awadh); literary cultivation sixteenth–eighteenth centuries, including the *Rāmacaritamānasa* of Tulsidas ("the Hindi Ramayana") and Sufi romances; present no. of speakers impossible to determine, since most give their lg. as *'Hindi'*. ([AWADHI] area one of most densely populated UP tracts: one-third of 1981 UP total would give roughly 37m.; Bahri 1980 est. 18m.); alt. n. *'Baiswari'* and *'Kosali'*.

awāṇkārī – subdial. of *Hindko* (a form of *"Northern Lahnda"*), S Attock Dt, NW of Salt range, Pakistan.

'Bachadi' – see *Malvi.*

'bāghalī' – local name and possibly subdial. of *Handuri* (HP).

Baghati/baghāṭī – W Pahari lg. of parts of HP just N of Chandigarh, centering on former hill state of Baghat.

Bagheli – lg. of NE MP Dts of (= "Baghelkhand") Rewa, Satna, Shahdol, Sidhi, as far as Jabalpur and Mandla; closely related to *[AWADHI]*; no meaningful figures (557,034 returns in 1961, only 231,231 in 1971; most speakers return as *'Hindi'*; alt. *Riwai* (Kellogg's *Grammar*), *Baghelkhandi.*

bāgṛī – dial. of *([MARWARI])* (acc. Grierson) spoken in E Churu and

Ganganagar Dts, Rajasthan (= the NE of former Bikaner State) and adjoining sections of Haryana; 309,903 returns in 1961, 1,055,607 in 1971(!); not to be confused with *vāgḍī*.

'Bahawalpuri' – see *(SIRAIKI)* (< the former Bahawalpur State on the east bank of the Middle Indus).

baigānī – dial. of *Chhattisgarhi* spoken by Baiga tribe in SE MP; 11,113 in 1971.

Baluj – lg. of IA-speaking semi-nomads of Soviet Central Asia, first noted by Wilkins in 1879; not closely related to *Par'ya*; Indians call *'Paniraj'*, Afghans *'Jatt'*.

banāpharī – mixed dial. of *Bundeli* and *Bagheli* spoken in Hamirpur Dt., UP; lg. of *Alhakhand* folk epic; < Banaphar Rajputs.

banārasī – subdial. of *Western Bhojpuri*, spoken in city of Banaras.

'Bangaru'/bāngarū – see *Haryanvi*.

'Banjari'/banjārī – see *Lamani*; (also *'Banjuri'*).

bāorī – *Bhili* dial. of nomadic tribe of Punjab and parts of Rajasthan; 9,697 in 1971 (vs. 2,045 in 1961).

'Baraik', *'Barik'* – n. of *Bhojpuri* in W Bengal.

'barāṛī' – see *śarācholī*.

barel – important *Bhili* dial. of MP/Gujarat border area; 230,034 in 1971.

barhdexi – *(KONKANI)* dial. of Christians of N Goa (taluka of Bardez, capital Mapusa); literary cultivation from later nineteenth-century; pron. [*barhdeʃi*].

'bashahri' – alt. n. for *kochi* dial. of *Mahasui* (< Bashahr, former large princely state in Simla hills).

**'Bashgali'* – non-native n. for **Kati*.

Bashkarik – Central Dardic lg. spoken in upper valleys of Panjkor and Swat in N Pakistan (Dir and Kalam, NWFP); acc. Fussman, quoting Biddulph, speakers numbered 12–15,000 in 1880; no current figures; also called *Diri*, *Gawri*, *Garwi*.

BENGALI/bāŋlā; (formal) *bɔŋgo bhāʃā* – ca. 148,000,000 speakers, incl. ca. 94m. in Bangladesh and 54m. in India (in W Bengal, Tripura, and Assam, where Bengali-speaking immigrants and their descendants are said to outnumber native Assamese); dialects: *central* or *standard* (Calcutta, Nadia, Murshidabad, E Burdwan, N. Midnapore); *western* (Manbhum, Singhbum, W Burdwan, W Birbhum) + *malpaharia* subdial. in Santal Parganas (Bihar); *southwestern* or *midnapore* (SW Midnapore); *northern* (Dinajpur, E Malda, partly in Bangladesh) + subdial. *siripuria* of Purnea (Bihar), *bogra*, and *koch* of Malda (S. K. Chatterji calls this group *north central*); *rajbangshi* (Rangpur in Bangladesh, Jalpaiguri and Cooch Behar in northern W Bengal., and Goalpara Dt of Assam) + subdial. *bahē* of Darjeeling Terai (Chatterji calls this group *western kamarupa*); *eastern* (Dacca, Jessore, Mymensingh, etc. in Bangladesh) + *haijong* subdial. of Mymensingh tribals (Chatterji calls these *western vanga*); and *southeastern* (Bangladesh: Noakhali, Chittagong) + subdial. *chittagong* and *chakma* (acc. Chatterji, *eastern vanga*); literary cultivation from twelfth century or earlier; divided into Old (1000–1300), Middle (1300–1750), and Modern (1750–present); older literary standard (*ʃādhu bhāʃā*) a composite of several dialectal elements; newer literary standard (*colit bhāʃā*) based on Calcutta Colloquial.

bhadauri – dial. of *Bundeli* spoken mainly in Gwalior Dt, MP, and S of Agra, but not as far as Bhadaura town itself.

Bhadrawahi, or *bhadarwāhī* – W Pahari lg. or dialect group; spoken in Bhadarwah area of SE Kashmir; 40,200 in 1971.

'bhagalpuri' – local n. for *Angika.*

bhalesi – N dial. of *Bhadarwahi*, with two subdial.

Bharmauri – W Pahari lg. of SE Chamba Dt, HP; 70,217 in 1971; alt. n. *Gaddi* or *Gadi.*

bhateāḷī – dial. of *(DOGRI)* spoken in W of Chamba Dt, HP; 31,922 in 1961 (*LSI* est. 10,000), 5,907 in 1971.

bhatri – aberrant dial. of *ORIYA* spoken in NE Bastar Dt, MP; 103,766 in 1971.

bhaṭṭiānī – Grierson's n. for a SW dial. of *PUNJABI* "merging into Rajasthani", spoken in S Ferozepore and N Ganganagar Dts < area known as *Bhattiānā*, 'country of the B*haṭṭis*'.

Bhili – group of dialects, including *bhīlī/bhīloḍī* proper plus about thirty others with special names, spoken mainly in the hilly areas between Gujarat, Rajasthan, MP, and Maharashtra, in the Aravallis of Rajasthan, and in a few cases (*bāorī*) further afield in Punjab and UP; see also *bhilālī, ahīrī, bāorī, barel, chāṛaṇi, chodhrī, dhankī, dehāwalī, ḍhoḍiā, ḍublī, dungri, gāmṭi, girāsiā, konkaṇī-3/koknā, koṭalī, magrā kī bolī, māwchī, nāharī/baglānī, naikaḍi, panchālī, pahāḍī, pāradhī, ranāwat, kāthoḍī, rānī bhīl, rāṭhvī, pawri, tadvi, tetaria, vāgḍī*, and *walvī*; 1,250,312 returned *bhīlī/bhiloḍī* in 1971, at least 1.5m. under other names = total, ca. 2,750,000, perhaps 3+m.

bhiḍlaī – dial. of *Bhadrawahi.*

bhilālī – a *Bhili* dial. of Gujarat-MP border; 246,724 in 1971.

bhitrauti – subdial. (?) of *([MARWARI])* spoken in "the valley to the immediate W of the Aravalli Range and which trends NE-ward from Abu Road through Tartoli towards Sirohi" (Hook and Chauhan 1986), S Rajasthan; notable for use of inflected adverb in place of compound verbs (ibid.); est. 500,000 (ibid.).

Bhojpuri – lg. of E UP and W Dts of Bihar (Shahabad, Saran, part of Champaran); dialects: *western* (incl. Banaras and Azamgarh), *southern* (Ballia and Shahabad), and *northern* (W subdial. *sarwaria* in Basti Dt, *gorakhpuri*, and *madhesi* in Champaran); carried by emigrants to Fiji, Guyana, and Calcutta; 1971 figures (14,340,564) probably underrepresent, with many speakers returning as *'Hindi'* (but not to same extent as *[AWADHI]* and *[BRAJ]* speakers).

'Bhopali' – see *Malvi.*

bhoyari – dial. (?) of *Malvi* in Maharashtra; 5,388 in 1961.

'Bhuani' – see *Nimadi.*

bhuliā – dial. of *Chhattisgarhi* spoken in Bolangir and Sambalpur Dts, Orissa, also adjoining section of MP.

"Bihari" – a language construct of Grierson's, comprising *([MAITHILI])*, *Magahi*, and *Bhojpuri* (all spoken at least in part in Bihar); rejected by partisans of some of these languages; returned as mother tongue, however, by 14,940 in 1961, 23,222 in 1971 – but by emigrants in Assam and MP, none from Bihar itself; census data from Bihar show increasing assertion of local lg. identities, some previously unheard of.

bīkānerī – dial. (or subdial.) of *([MARWARI])*.

bilāspurī-1 – dial. (or local n.) of *PUNJABI* spoken in Bilaspur Dt, HP; Bailey and Grierson both report little difference from *PUNJABI* of Jalandhar and Hoshiarpur (*doābī*), but separate identity strongly entrenched; one of principal "Pahari dialects" returned in CIIL survey of HP; 66,868 in 1971, with many speakers returning as *"Pahari"*.

bilāspurī-2 – dial. (or alt. n.?) of *Chhattisgarhi*; 11,959 in 1971; < Bilaspur Dt, MP, but returns esp. from emigrants in Bihar and W Bengal.

binjhwārī – dial. of *Chhattisgarhi* spoken by tribe related to Baigas in Raigarh Dt, MP and Orissa border.

birir – dial. of *Kalasha* (Turner).

Bishnupriya, or *Bishnupriya Manipuri* – lg. spoken in parts of Manipur, and in Cachar Dt (Assam), Tripura, and Bangladesh (Sylhet) by early nineteenth-century emigrants from Manipur; related to but not a "dial. of" Bengali or Assamese; though once regarded (*LSI*) as Bengali–Meithei creole, retains pre-Bengali features; Sinha 1981 est. 150,000; 43,813 returns in India in 1971; alt. n. (*LSI*) *Mayang* (derogatory, not used by speakers < Meithei 'foreigner'); two (now non-territorial) dial. *mādai gāng* and *rājār gāng* = 'queen's village dial.' and 'king's village dial.'

'bishshau/biśśau' – local n. of *giripārī*.

[BRAJABULI] – an artificial literary lg., concocted of a mixture of *([MAITHILI])* and *BENGALI*, which flourished in Bengal as a medium of Vaishnava poetry in sixteenth to nineteenth centuries, with a branch in Orissa; a similar independent tradition in Assam; not to be confused with *[BRAJ BHASHA]*, with which it has no connection, except symbolically.

[BRAJ BHASHA]/braj bhākhā, or simply *[BRAJ]* – lg. of W-central UP, also adjoining parts of Rajasthan (Bharatpur, Sawai Madhopur) and Haryana (E Gurgaon); principal and most characteristic "dialect" of *"Western Hindi"*; literary cultivation in sixteenth to nineteenth centuries; main *'Hindi'* vehicle for poetry into early twentieth century; no meaningful statistics: Bahri 1980 estimates ca. 12,500,000 speak it today.

brokskat – dial. of *Shina* spoken in central Ladakh, E of Kargil; unintelligible to other *Shina* speakers; sometimes called (incorrectly) *brokpa*.

Bundeli – lg. (acc. Grierson, "dialect" of *"Western Hindi"*) of W-central MP, from Gwalior and Jhansi as far S as Chhindwara, Seoni, and Hoshangabad; 376,036 in 1971 (most speakers return as *'Hindi'*); vehicle of *Ālhakhaṇḍ* epic cycle in *banāpharī* dial.; alt. n. *Bundelkhandi*.

"Central Eastern Rajasthani" – lg. (or "dial.") construct of Grierson ("the typical Rajasthani dialect") comprising four "locally recognized [sub]dialects: *Jaipuri*, *Harauti*, *Kishangarhi*, and *Ajmeri*, of which *Jaipuri* is taken as the Standard"; sometimes called *Eastern Rajasthani*.

chachhi – acc. Shackle, dial. of *"Hindko proper"* (division of "Northern Lahnda") in N Attock and S-most Hazara Dts, Pakistan; alt. n. *'hindko'*.

chakma/cākmā – subdial. of *SE Bengali* (or distinct lg.?) spoken in Chittagong hill tracts; uses script related to Cambodian; 68,711 in 1971 (mainly Tripura, Mizoram), but main body of speakers is in Bangladesh (no figures available).

Chameali/cameāḷī – W Pahari lg. of W half of Chamba Dt, HP; had own script based on improved Takri; 52,973 returns (as *'Chambeali'*) in 1971; some doubtless returned as *'Pahari Unspecified'* or as *'Hindi'*.

charani/caraṇī – *Bhili* dial. (MP and Panch Mahals, Gujarat).

charotari/carotari – dial. of *GUJARATI*, spoken by peasants in the Charotar (a tract of fertile land in Kaira Dt).

chaurasi/caurāsī – a dial. of *Dhundhari* in NW Tonk Dt, Rajasthan, around Lawa; only 436 returns in 1961, mostly from Maharashtra.

Chhattisgarhi/chattīsgaṛhī – distinctive *"Eastern Hindi"* dial. (or lg.), spoken in SE MP (Raipur, Bilaspur, Raigarh, E Balaghat, N Bastar); 6,693,445 returns in 1971 (high rate of "assertion" compared with *AWADHI* or *BRAJ*); < 'country of the 36 forts'; alt. n. *Laria*.

chhikacchiki/chikā-chiki (bolī) – alt. n. for *Angika*; previously regarded as dial. of *([MAITHILI])*; SE Monghyr, Bhagalpur, N fringes of Santal Parganas (Bihar).

chibhali/cibhālī – "N Lahnda" dial. spoken in hills running from border of Jammu NW to Murree and Muzaffarabad (W Kashmir).

chilasi/cilāṣī-1 – dial. of *Shina* spoken in Chilas, along first great bend of the Indus, above Nanga Parbat, NW Kashmir; (also n. of a dial. of *Pashai*).

'chinawari'/cināvaṛī, also *cinhāvaṛī* – local n. for *jhangi* dial. of *(SIRAIKI)*.

chodhari/codharī – *Bhili* dial. of Scheduled Tribe in Surat Dt, Gujarat; 138,978 in 1971.

choṭā bangāḷī – Bailey's term for a dial. of *Mandeali* spoken in extreme N of Mandi and beyond.

Churahi/curāhī – lg. (or dial.) of Chamba group, spoken in NW of Chamba Dt (Chaurah tehsil, capital Tissa); 34,669 in 1971, 43,762 in 1961.

[dakhini], also *dakani* – dial. of *HINDI–URDU*, centered in Hyderabad, Bijapur, Gulbarga, and other towns of the Deccan Plateau having large Muslim populations; brought from N India in the wake of the Muslim conquest of the S; literary cultivation in fifteenth to seventeenth centuries.

daldi – a *(KONKANI)* dial. of Muslim fishermen, coastal Karnataka.

(*)Dameli/damɛ̃ḍī (Turner), *dāmia-bāṣa* (Fussman) – lg. of single village in Gid valley of S Chitral, Pakistan; classification doubtful: has both *"Dardic"* and *Nuristani* traits.

dāmī – subdial. of *bilaspuri* spoken in W Arki tehsil, Mahasu Dt and SE Bilaspur Dt (HP).

'Dangarik'/ḍangarik(wār) – the Khowar n. for *Phalura* < 'lg. of the cow-people'; reported now to be used by speakers themselves.

dāngbhāng – dial. or subdial. of *[BRAJ]* spoken in Sawai Madhopur Dt, Rajasthan.

ḍāngī-1 – set of dial. of *[BRAJ]* spoken mainly by Gujars in the Dang or hill country of Sawai Madhopur Dt (Rajasthan), near Chambal river.

'ḍangī-2' – n. of *Khandeshi* in Dangs Dt, Gujarat; 80,533 returns under this n. in 1971.

dehāwālī – a *Bhili* dial. of Dhulia and Jalgaon Dts, Maharashtra ("Khandesh"); over 100,000 acc. *LSI*; not returned in 1961 or 1971.

'derāwāl' – local n. for the *ṭhalī* dial. of *(SIRAIKI)* in Dera Ismail Khan Dt, and for the *multānī* dial. in Dera Ghazi Khan Dt; (both also called *'hindkī'*).

desia – an *ORIYA* dial., acc. K. Mahapatra the link lg. and "second natural lg." of the non-Aryan tribals of the highly polyglot Koraput Dt, Orissa, from the fifteenth century.

'deswālī' – a n. for *Haryani*, esp. in Hissar Dt.

'dhamdi' – a n. (or form) of *Chhattisgarhi* in Maharashtra.

'dhanderi/dhandi' – see *Malvi.*

dhanki – a *Bhili* dial. of Gujarat and Maharashtra; see also *tadavi.*

dhannī – dial. of NW *"Lahnda"*, in W Jhelum Dt, Pakistan.

ḍhaṭkī – dial. transitional between *SINDHI* and *MARWARI*, spoken in Thar-Parkar Dt of Sind, and SW Jaisalmer Dt, Rajasthan; < *ḍhaṭ*, 'desert'; alt. n. *ṭharelī.*

ḍheḍ gujarī – see *Khandeshi.*

dhoḍiā – a *Bhili* dial. of Dadra-Nagarhaveli and extreme S Gujarat; 75,657 in 1971.

Dhundhari/ḍhū˜ḍhāṛī – important "Rajasthani" lg. or dial., centered on Jaipur; Grierson's statement that it "has a large literature" (*LSI v.9.2*: 32) must be taken with caution pending linguistic analyses of these texts (some of which may be in *[PINGAL]* or *([MARWARI])*; lg. assertion plunged from a high of 1,591,826 in 1961 to 155,040 in 1971; most speakers return as *'Hindi'* – or very possibly as *"RAJASTHANI"*, which registered significant gains.

dhūnḍī, also *dhūnḍī-kairālī* – "Lahnda" dial. of the Murree hills, Pakistan; called *'pahāṛī'* in Rawalpindi section of hills.

[DINGAL]/ḍīṁgaḷa – a form of *[OLD MARWARI]*, acc. some authorities based on the caste dialect of the Charans (bards), cultivated for heroic poetry from the fifteenth century; one of earliest NIA literary lgs.

'Diri' – see *Bashkarik.*

'DIVEHI' – see *MALDIVIAN.*

doābī – dial. of *PUNJABI* spoken in the Jalandhar Doab between the Beas and the Sutlej.

ḍoḍā sirājī – see *'Siraji'*-4.

(DOGRI)/ḍogrī – lg. of Jammu currently agitating for recognition; formerly treated as "dial." of *PUNJABI*, now considered (Nigam 1971) more closely related to *W Pahari*; had own Takri-derived script; now uses Nagari; 1,298,855 in 1971.

drāsī – dial. of *Shina*, or acc. Bailey, subdial. of *astori*; with *guresi*, more archaic than other *Shina* dial.: case preserved in adjectives; retroflex /ḷ/.

ḍublī – *Bhili* dial. of S Gujarat and Thana Dt, Maharashtra.

Dumaki/ḍumākī – "Dardic" lg. spoken by a caste of blacksmiths in Hunza (in Burushaski-speaking territory); some think it may be a remnant of the ancestor of *Romany*; < *ḍoma* – 'n. of caste of blacksmiths and musicians' (also > *Rom* 'Gypsy' in *Romany*).

ḍūgar-wāṛā – dial. of *BRAJ* (or, of *Dhundhari*), spoken SW of *dangī.*

"Eastern Hindi" – a Grierson lg. construct, comprising *[AWADHI]*, *Bagheli*, and *Chhattisgarhi.*

'Gaddi', also *'Gadi'* – see *Bharmauri.*

gahora – dial. of *Bagheli* in E Banda Dt, UP, S of *tirhari.*

gāmaḍiā – village dial. of *GUJARATI*, Ahmadabad Dt.

**Gambiri* – Morgenstierne's n. for **Tregami.*

'gāmit' – see *gāmṭi*; also *mawchi.*

gāmṭī – *Bhili* dial. of S Gujarat (Surat and Navsari); 1971 census puts together *gāmṭi* and *gāvit* (136,209), but separates *mawchi*, said to be almost the same or identical; *gāvit* is n. in Maharashtra < *gāv* 'village' (Gujarati *gām*).

gangoi – dial. of *Kumauni* (pargana of Gangola, central Kumaun beyond Almora); alt. *gangola*.

gaoli – *Bundeli* dial. of a caste in Chhindwara Dt, S MP.

Garhwali/gaṛhwālī – "Central Pahari" lg. of Garhwal and Tehri Garhwal Dts, UP Himalayas; 1,277,151 in 1971 (assertion up from 809,746 in 1961).

'Garwi'/gārwī – see *Bashkarik*; (n. used by Biddulph, Grierson).

'gāvit' – see *gāmṭī*.

Gawar-Bati – "Dardic: lg. spoken near Afghan–Pakistani frontier where Bashgal and Chitral rivers merge to form the Kunar"; alt.n. *Narisati*.

ghebi – subdial. of *"Hindko proper"* in central Attock Dt (Pindi Gheb Tehsil), N. Pakistan.

ghisāḍī – *GUJARATI* dial. of wandering blacksmiths in Maharashtra; alt. n. *tarimuki*; 1,776 in 1961.

gilgiti – dial. of *Shina*, Azad Kashmir, Pakistan (Gilgit valley).

girāsiā – a *Bhili* dial. of Sirohi Dt and nearby areas, Rajasthan; 27,156 in 1971; alt. n. *'garāsiā'*, *'nyār'*.

girīpārī – dial. of *Sirmauri* N of Giri river; < 'across the Giri'; local n. *'biśśau'* in S of former Jubbal State; Bailey calls later subdial. *south jubbal*.

goḍwāṛī – subdial. of *([MARWARI])* (acc. *LSI*) in 'Godwar' region on W flank of Aravallis, NE of Sirohi; notable for use of an inflected particle in place of *([MARWARI])* compound verbs (Hook 1982: 33–4); *LSI* est. (1908) 147,000; see also *bhitrauti*.

Gojri – lg. of Gujjars in Jammu and Kashmir, exp. in mountains (Punch Dt) SW of Vale of Kashmir; also in Azad Kashmir (Pakistan) and beyond; related to *Mewati* form of "Rajasthani"; 330,485 in India in 1971, ca. 200,000 in Pakistan (Sharma 1982); possibly ca. 7,000 additional speakers (*'Gujjari'*, *'Gujari'*) in HP, mountains of UP, etc.; numerically third lg. of Jammu-Kashmir (after *KASHMIRI* and *(DOGRI)*); alt. *'Gujuri'*.

gonḍwānī – dial. of *Bagheli* in Mandla Dt, MP, spoken by Gonds and others; Dt was center of a medieval Gond kingdom; alt. n. *'manḍlāhā'*.

gorakhpuri – subdial. of *'northern' Bhojpuri*, E of Gorakhpur, UP.

'Gorkhali', *'Gurkhali'* – old n. for *Nepali*.

govari – a MARATHI dial. of cowherds in Chanda and Bhandara Dts, E of Nagpur; 7,893 in 1971; acc. Tulpule 1971 a "tribal dial. [=unwritten lg.] so much influenced by Marathi it has become a dial. of Marathi."

gowro – dial. of Chhattisgarhi spoken by members of Baiga tribe (of MP) settled as workers in Assam; 4,802 in 1961.

GUJARATI/gujarātī – lg. of Gujarat in W India; 25,656,274 in 1971; est. 32,600,000 in 1981; many speakers found outside state, including nearly 1m. in Bombay; colonies abroad (Africa, USA); literary cultivation from fourteenth or possibly thirteenth century; Old (to 1450), Middle (1450–1800), Modern (early nineteenth century to present); *[OLD GUJARATI]* was used as literary lg. also in S Rajasthan; distinctive script replaced Nagari (retained longer by Nagar Brahmans) only in nineteenth century; four basic dial. divisions (Cardona 1965): *standard* (central

Gujarat from Ahmadabad to Baroda), *kathiawāḍī* (the Kathiawar peninsula), *'northern'* or *paṭṭanī*, and *'southern'* or *surati* – plus dial. of special caste or religious groups (e.g., *parsi gujarati*).

'Gujari' – acc. Grierson a "mechanical mixture of local Panjabi and true *Gujuri* [=*Gojri*] spoken in sub-montane Punjab"; the speech of Gujars of the plains of Punjab.

guresi – a dial. of *Shina* (or subdial. of *astori* dial.) in Kishanganga valley N of Vale of Kashmir.

haijong – a *BENGALI*-based creole spoken by originally Tibeto-Burman speaking tribals in NE Bangladesh and Cachar Dt, Assam; 23,978 in 1971 in India alone.

hakkipikki – a form of *MARATHI* reported from Karnataka.

Halbi, also *Halabi* – lg. of semi-Aryanized Gonds of Bastar Dt, MP; once regarded as dial. of *MARATHI* but this is now questioned (R. A. Singh 1971), as it has too little structurally and lexically in common with the latter, and features also of *ORIYA* and *Chhattisgarhi*; 346,377 in 1971.

Handuri/haṇḍūrī – lg. or acc. some a dial. of *Mahasui*, around and E of Nalagarh on border of Punjab and HP (N of Chandigarh, W of Simla); transitional between *PUNJABI* and *"West Pahari"* of *Mahasui* type.

hāṛauti – form of *"Rajasthani"*, acc. Grierson subdial. of *"Central Eastern Rajasthani"*, in Bundi and Kota Dts; 334,377 in 1971; < *hāṛā* (old ruling house of Bundi and Kota); locally *hāḍautī*; acc. Allen *LSI*'s *hāṛauṭī* (with retroflex) is wrong.

Haryanvi/haryānvī – main lg. of Haryana State (formerly E and S Punjab) and of rural parts of Union Territory of Delhi; a "dialect" of Grierson's *"Western Hindi"* construct; most speakers return lg. as *'Hindi'*, but projected population of Haryana (1981) was 12,850,902, exclusive of Delhi and Chandigarh; until recently most common n. was *'Bangaru'*; other alt. n. *'Deswali'* or *'Desari'* (around Hissar), *'Jatu'* (especially in Delhi Terr.), *Hariani*.

'hazara hindki' – see *kagani*.

high rudhārī – dial. of *Khashali* (Turner).

"Himachali"/himācalī – recently coined term for the W Pahari lgs. of HP, or of a proposed synthesis of them.

HINDI – this term has several, confusingly overlapping meanings: (1) *MODERN STANDARD HINDI*, the standard modern literary language, based on *Khari Boli*, now the official lg. of six Indian states (UP, MP, Haryana, HP, Bihar, and Rajasthan) and the proclaimed national lg. of India (see Chapter 2, section 3); (2) the literary traditions and speech of the *"Eastern Hindi"* and *"Western Hindi"* (q.v.) areas, e.g., the "Hindi Ramayana" = the *Rāmacaritamānasa* written in *[OLD AWADHI]*; (3) more loosely still, the regional speech and literary traditions of the whole area (see Chapter 2, section 1.1) lying between Bengal and the Punjab (i.e. the six north and central Indian states listed above) which from a linguistic point of view differ significantly; < earlier *Hindu-i*, *Hindvi* 'language of the Indians (from the standpoint of the Persian or Turki-speaking Muslim conquerors)'; (4) in the latter sense, occasionally also further afield, e.g., beyond the Indus, = NIA speech as distinguished from the Pashto of later invaders (see *hindki/hindko*); (5) also in that sense, = *URDU*, especially before 1800; although 153,729,062 persons gave *"Hindi"* as their lg. in 1971, it is difficult to tell for how many of these *HINDI* in sense 1 was their mother tongue, or whether it was *'Hindi'* in sense 2 or 3, or given as the literary medium they normally employed (and thus knew it at least as a second lg.: this was the case, for example, among many Hindus in the Punjab), or merely indicated allegiance to the Hindi cultural tradition, or to the official status of *HINDI* in their state; since the *population* of these areas was considerably greater, ca. 290,000,000 in 1981, evidently not all of it made any of these identifications; *HINDI* is now the language of education and formal communication throughout the area, and is thus known to all persons with some education; on the other hand, the area has the lowest literacy rates in India (UP 27 per cent, Bihar 26 per cent, Rajasthan 24 per cent in 1981); paradoxically, the Hindi state with the highest rate was HP (42 per cent), where the actual spoken lgs. are not among those sometimes described [e.g., by Bahri 1980] as "dialects" of *HINDI*; although *MODERN STANDARD HINDI* is a latecomer to the NIA literary scene, really getting under way only in the twentieth century, more books and periodicals are published in it today than in any other NIA lg.

'hindki' – see *Hindko*, *'hindko'*; slightly pejorative acc. Shackle 1980.

Hindko – most common n. for NW *"Lahnda"* including *awāṇkārī*, *ghēbi*, *chachhī* (Attock Dt and S Hazara) and lg. of Kohat and Peshawar cities; < 'lg. of Indians' (vs. Pathans).

'hindko' – (1) local n. or dial. of *(SIRAIKI)* in Dera Ismail Khan Dt, W of Indus in central Pakistan; (2) alt. n. for lg. of N Hazara; see *Kagani*; (< [see *Hindko*]).

'Hindostani' – Grierson's n. (also *Vernacular Hindostani*) for the popular lg. spoken N of Delhi and W to Ambala; see *Kauravi*.

'Hindustani' – term referring to common colloquial base of *HINDI* and *URDU* and to its function as lingua franca over much of India, much in vogue during Independence movement as expression of national unity; after Partition in 1947 and subsequent linguistic polarization it fell into disfavor; census of 1951 registered an enormous decline (86–98 per cent) in no. of persons declaring it their mother tongue (the majority of *HINDI* speakers and many *URDU* speakers had done so in previous censuses); trend continued in subsequent censuses: only 11,053 returned it in 1971, mostly from S India; [see Khubchandani 1983: 90–1].

'jadeji' – see *Kachchhi*.

'jadobāṭī' – dial. or alt. n. of *[BRAJ]* as spoken by members of Yadava (*jādō*) caste in plains between Gwalior, Karauli, and Shivpuri (N "lobe" of MP).

'Jaipuri' – see *Dhundhari*.

jānglī – subdial. of *(SIRAIKI)* spoken by nomads of Jangal Bar tract in Lyallpur Dt, Pakistan.

jashpuri – dial. of *ORIYA* in NE Raigarh Dt, MP; 7,211 in 1971.

'Jatki'/jaṭkī – alt. n. for *(SIRAIKI)* in localities where Jatts are numerous (esp. Jhang, Lyallpur, and Muzaffargarh Dts).

'Jatu'/jāṭū – alt. n. for *Haryani*, or of variety spoken by Jats.

Jaunsari – W Pahari lg. of N Dehra Dun Dt, UP; probably 54,122 in 1971 (the total 554,122 given in Nigam's *Handbook*, followed by 53,957 for UP – almost all speakers reside in Dehra Dun Dt – must be a typographical error) down from 56,556 in 1961; Sirmauri variant of Takri script had been in use.

jhangi – dial. of *(SIRAIKI)* spoken in most of Jhang Dt.

jharia – an *ORIYA* dial. of Koraput Dt (acc. K. Mahapatra).

jijelut – a dial. of *Shina* in Punial region NW of Gilgit.

'jubbali' – see *saracholi*; < former Jubbal State.

jūṛar – dial. of *Bagheli* in Banda Dt, UP between Ken and Bagain rivers.

Kachchhi/kacchī – lg. of Kutch (desert wilderness in far NW Gujarat); sometimes considered a dial. of *SINDHI*; cultural allegiance is to *GUJARATI*, which serves as written lg.; 470,991 in 1971.

kacchṛī – subdial. of *(SIRAIKI)* in alluvial plain SW of Jhang town (Pakistan); alt. *kāchṛī* (Turner).

Kagani/kāγānī – acc. Bailey 1915, dial. of "Lahnda", spoken in Kagan valley, Hazara Dt, Pakistan, from Abbottabad as far as Chilas; also called *'Hindko'* (like all "NW Lahnda"); apparently = Turner's *'hazara hindki'* (*LSI* est. 308,867); returns also from Indian Kashmir in 1961 census.

'kahlūrī' – see *bilāspuri-1*.

'kairālī' – see *ḍhunḍī-kairālī*.

Kalasha/kalaṣa – archaic "Dardic" lg. of SW Chitral, Pakistan; about 3,000 speakers acc. Fussman 1972.

**Kalaṣa-alā* – *Nuristani lg. of Waigal valley, Afghanistan; not to be confused with the "Dardic" *Kalasha* of Chitral; alt. n. *Waigali*, *Wai-ala*, *Veron*; 4–5,000 speakers acc. Fussman 1972.

kālīmāl – dial. of *BRAJ* closely resembling *dāngbhāng*, Sawai Madhopur Dt, Rajasthan.

kamari – dial. of *MARATHI* spoken by a caste in MP; 10,106 in 1971.

**kamdeshi* – dial. of **Kati* in lower Bashgal valley, Afghanistan (near Pakistan border); acc. Strand, significantly different from other **Kati* dialects.

kandia – acc. Fussman, a variety of *Maiyã*, spoken in "the valley of a tributary on the right bank of the Indus, between Duber and Tangir."

kanḍiālī – acc. *LSI*, a dial. of *DOGRI* "mixed with Panjabi" spoken in hills NE of Gurdaspur, (Indian) Punjab; but 1961 census returns were from Maharashtra.

Kangri – acc. *LSI*, a "mixture of Dogri and Panjabi"; acc. Turner a "subdialect of Dogri dialect of Punjabi"; now considered (Nigam 1971), to form, with *DOGRI*, a "subgroup of Western Pahari"; in any case, the largest respondent speech group in the CIIL survey of HP, where it was found to hold first rank also among HP "dialects" in A.I.R. programme listenership; census declarations have however been rather low (7,808 in 1961, 55,386 in 1971, as against *LSI* est. 636,000).

Kannauji – conventionally, a "regional lg." of the "Western Hindi" group; acc. Grierson, "really a form of Braj Bhasha, given separate consideration only in deference to public opinion"; spoken in E-central Doab and area to the N of it: Kanpur, Farrukhabad, Etawah, Hardoi, Shahjahanpur, Pilibhit; lingering identity is that of medieval imperial capital destroyed by the Muslim conquest nearly 800 years ago; speakers almost all return *'Hindi'*; est. 4,400,000 (Bahri 1980: 97).

kanyawālī – a dial. of *Maiyã*, spoken in village of Bankari, isolated in the Tangir valley amid *Shina* speakers (Fussman 1972).

karwari – acc. Pereira 1973, the *KONKANI* dial. of Hindus of N Kanara (of Chitrapur Saraswats, Katre's *'s-'*?); cultivated for literature, esp. for drama in Bombay.

([KASHMIRI])/kǝ̄ʃur – numerically dominant (54 per cent) lg. of Kashmir, although speakers not found much outside Vale of Kashmir; cultivated for poetry from fourteenth century (*Old Kashmiri* period, ca. 1300–1500; *Middle*, 1500–1800; *'Modern'* from 1800) but a modern prose tradition did not develop; although *KASHMIRI* is an "official lg." of India (i.e. listed in Schedule VIII of the Constitution) paradoxically it is not in official use in Kashmir itself; despite attempts to encourage the lg. and solve its problems (particularly relating to script), *KASHMIRI* speakers continue to prefer *URDU*, which continues in official use in the state; Sharda script, in use from the tenth century, has fallen into disuse as a result of the Islamic cultural orientation of four-fifths of the speech community and consequent preference for the Perso-Arabic script; neither script is well-suited to express the sounds of the lg.; traditional dial. divisions (B. Kachru 1973: 6): *marāz* (S/SE), *kamrāz* (N/NW), *yamrāz* (Srinagar and environs), plus (acc. some) *Kashtawari* outside the Vale; 1,421,760 returns in 1971; est. 3,500,000 in 1981.

Kashtawari, also *Kishtwari/kaṣṭawārī* – "Dardic" lg. of the Kashmir group; sometimes regarded as a "dial." of *KASHMIRI*; written in Takri script; Kishtwar is a town (and valley) in Udhampur Dt, SE of the Vale on Upper Chenab; 12,166 in 1971.

'Kaṭārqalā(i)' – see *Woṭapūrī*.

kaṭheriyā – dial. or alt. n. of *BRAJ* in Budaun Dt, UP.

kāthiyāwāḍī – dial. of *GUJARATI* spoken in Kathiawar peninsula (Saurashtra); returned in census (*"kaithyawadi"*) mainly by émigrés; *LSI* est. 2,596,000.

kāthoḍī – tribal dial. of mountains of Konkan and Sahyadris (Kolaba, Thana, Dadar-Nagarhaveli); alt. n. *kātkarī*; 6,562 under both names in 1961; described (Tulpule 1971) as "originally a *Khandeshi* dial. but now a form of *MARATHI*"; acc. *LSI* it was a *Bhili* dial.

**Kati* – an important *Nuristani lg. of Afghanistan, spoken in two discontinuous areas of the Hindu Kush, with some settlements across the border in Chitral; W area centered on upper tributaries of Alingar; E on Bashgal valley; hence alt. n. *Bashgali*; bifurcation of area appears recent, not reflected in dial. divisions *katǝviri*, *kamviri*, *mumviri* (Strand 1973).

'kātkarī' – see *kāṭhoḍī*.

'Kauravi' – n. advocated by H. Bahri and others for the regional variety of W Hindi called *Vernacular Hindostani* by Grierson and often loosely *Khari Boli* (q.v.); < the ancient kingdom of the *Kurus*.

kerali – Pereira's term for the Hindu *KONKANI* dial. centered at Cochin; acc. J. Rajathi (Survey of Konkani in Kerala, Census Monograph No. 4, 1971) there are at least eight dial. of *KONKANI* in Kerala, spoken by various caste-communities (Kudumbis, Saraswat and Gowd Saraswat Brahmins) in different localities from Trivandrum in the S to Kasaragod in the N, i.e. not confined to Cochin; see also *kudubi*.

kewaṭī – a subdial. of *nagpuri MARATHI* with *Bagheli* admixture; 3,468 in 1961.

khairāṛī – a dial. of *MARWARI* spoken by Minas in small area of E Rajasthan NE of *Mewari* area, SW of Tonk; registers continuous decline: 228,264 acc. *LSI*; 111,050 in 1961; 20,848 in 1971.

khalṭāhī – dial. of *Chhattisgarhi* spoken in E tehsils of Balaghat Dt, MP; alt. n. *khaloṭī* (< local n. of Balaghat Dt).

Khandeshi – vernacular lg. of Dhulia and Jalgaon Dts in Maharashtra (the former *Khandesh*) and partly of Gujarat Dt of the Dangs, i.e. of the main valley of the Tapti river; variously considered a "dial." of *MARATHI*, of *GUJARATI*, or a separate lg. allied to *Bhili*; better known locally as *Ahirani* (in Maharashtra), *Dangi* (in Gujarat), or *Dhed Gujari*, but still best known to scholars as *Khandeshi*; returns under all names show a decline: *LSI* 1,253,066; 428,104 in 1961; 147,219 in 1971 – perhaps in favor of the state lg., *MARATHI*.

Khaṛī Bolī, sometimes *Kharī Bolī* – term in use since 1800 (first by Lallu Lal, acc. Bahri 1980: 40) for the vernacular base of Modern Standard Hindi and Urdu, identified with the variety of W Hindi spoken N and NE of Delhi from Ambala in the NW to Muradabad in the SE (called *'Vernacular Hindostani'* by Grierson, *'Sirhindi'* by Dhirendra Varma); Bahri (who advocates the n. *'Kauravi'* for the latter) and other investigators have pointed out that these are not the same; the regional vernacular has features, such as a retroflex /ḷ, ṇ/, not shared by the standard dial. or the speech of Delhi on which it was based; < *khaṛī* 'standing, erect' (vs. *paṛī* 'fallen, prone' applied to *BRAJ*) + *kharī* 'straightforward, plain' + *kaṛā* 'hard, strong' (vs. the "softness" of *BRAJ*); 6m. returned as mother tongue in 1961, nearly all from Rajasthan, apparently in modern sense as synonymous with *MODERN STANDARD HINDI*; not repeated in 1971.

kharawa, *kharwa* – *GUJARATI* dial. of Muslim seamen of Kathiawar.

'Khas-kura' – a n. for *NEPALI*.

khasparjiya – a dial. of *Kumauni*, spoken in Almora Dt.

khaṭolā – a dial. (or local n.) of *Bundeli* found in region of E Bundelkhand called Panna and adjacent areas (Bijawar, Damoh), MP; *LSI* gave 891,000; no separate returns in 1961 or 1971.

'khatri' – see *Saurashtri*.

Khetrānī – NIA or dial. of Marri hills in Baluchistan (not to be confused with Murree hills in N Punjab); Grierson called it a dial. of *"Lahnda"*; acc. Morgenstierne 1932 it may be a remnant of IA spoken in Baluchistan before arrival of the Baluchis and Pathans; *LSI* gave 14,581.

(KHOWAR) – main lg. of Chitral (NWFP), spilling into W parts of Gilgit; expanding S at expense of *Kalasha*, the original lg. of Lower Chitral; recently (Buddruss 1976) trying to develop a literary standard; modified Perso-Arabic; 90,000 in 1951 acc. Fussman, citing Morgenstierne; n. from Kho tribe; Morgenstierne (1973/1936) thought (because of the "many peculiarities" of *KHOWAR* when compared with neighboring lgs.) that they may have been invaders from N of Hindu Kush, who drove a wedge between "the originally homogenous Dardic population of Kafiristan, Chitral, and Gilgit"; alt. n. *'Chitrali'*.

kirārī – dial. of *Bundeli* spoken by Kirar caste in Chhindwara Dt, MP; 4,750 acc. *LSI*; only 632 in 1961.

kīrnī – dial. of *Mahasui* (*Kiunthali*) of extreme E of Mahasu Dt (HP), along border with Dehra Dun Dt, in former princely states of Tar(h)och and parts of N Jubbal; 3,938 acc. *LSI*; no returns in 1961.

'kishanganjia' – see *siripuria*; 56,921 returns under this n. in 1971 (from Bihar).

kishangarhi – subdial. of *"E Rajasthani"* in former Kishangarh State NE of Ajmer; 8,608 in 1961; decline in 1971.

Kiunthali/kiū̃ṭhalī-Mahasui – principal W Pahari lg. of the Simla hills, now Mahasu Dt, HP; also "group" including *handuri*, *simla siraji*, *barari*, *sarachali*, *kirni*, and *kochi*, sometimes classed as "dial. of Kiunthali"; n. (*LSI*) after Keonthal, the chief among the former Simla hill states; modern preferred n. seems (cf. CIIL Survey) to be *Mahasui*, after Mahasu valley, the local n. of the Satlej and n. of the new Dt; but oddly unrepresented in the census: only 133 under *Kiunthali* in 1961, none under either n. in 1971 Provisional Figures; perhaps returned under *'Pahari Unspecified'*, or *'Hindi'*, or local names; *LSI* gave 43,577 for *Kiunthali* "proper", 188,763 for "group".

kochi/kōcī – lg. or dial. (of Kiunthali "group") in E Mahasu Dt, HP, corresponding to W half of former princely state of Bashahr; acc. Bailey 1915, a generic n. of dialects he lists as *rohṛū*, *rāmpurī*, *surkhuḷī*, *kuārī*, and *bāghī* – none of which turns up in the census except *rāmpurī*, derived from n. of old capital of Bashahr State; *LSI* gave 51,882 for *kochi*; Bailey est. 45,000; alt. n. *'bashahri'*.

koddialli/koḍiāḷī – Pereira's n. for the Hindu *KONKANI* dial. of S. Kanara; < Kodial (another n. for Mangalore).

(*'kohistānī'* < Pers. *koh* 'mountain' + *-istān* + *-ī*, lit. 'of the mountain country'; descriptive term like *'pahāṛī'*, *sirājī*.)

'Kohistani'-1 – alt. n. for *Maiyã*.

"Kohistani"-2 – collective n. (Grierson's) for *Maiyã*, *Garwi* (*Bashkarik*), and *Torwali*; or (Strand's) for these + *Wotapuri* and *Tirahi*; also called the *"Central group"*.

kohistani-3 – one of three main dial. of *Shina* acc. Bailey 1924; spoken in Chilas and down the Indus N of and including "Indus Kohistan".

kohistani-4 – a subdial. of *kohistani-3* (vs. *chilasi*), i.e. the *Shina* of Jalkot, Palas, and Indus Kohistan (locally *kohistyõ*, acc. Schmidt and Zarin 1981).

koknā, also *kokni*, *kukna* – a *Bhili* dial. of N Konkan, Surat, and Dadar-Nagarhaveli; 152,987 in 1971; same (?) as *LSI*'s *konkaṇī-3*.

koḷī – subdial. of *konkan* dial. of *MARATHI*, spoken by Koli caste in Thana, Kolaba, and Bombay; *LSI* gives 189,186; no significant returns from later censuses (e.g., 232 in 1961); essentially = general *konkan* dial.

(KONKANI)-1 – S-most contiguous NIA lg., main lg. of Goa (and of Savantvadi area immediately to N), and important lg. of the polyglot N and S Kanara Dts of coastal Karnataka to the S; also spoken by large emigrant colonies in Bombay and Kerala; literary cultivation of so-called [*STANDARD KONKANI*] in sixteenth–seventeenth centuries seems to have been mainly of foreign inspiration (grammars, dictionaries, catechisms, translations); of an alleged earlier literature, supposedly destroyed by the Inquisition, no trace has been found; considerable literary cultivation of several modern dialects, however (see *bardhexi*, *manglluri*,

antruzi, karwari, saxtti); efforts underway to develop unified modern literary lg.; now commonly written (and printed) in Devanagari, Kannada, Roman, and (occasionally) Malayalam script; 1,522,684 in 1971.

konkani–2 – also *konkan standard*; form of *MARATHI* spoken in coastal Maharashtra (= the Konkan), i.e. in Thana, Kolaba, Janjira, and N. Ratnagiri Dts; many local names acc. to caste; not to be confused with *KONKANI–1*.

konkani–3 – see *kokna*.

koshti – n. refers to a community of silk weavers in Vidarbha (Berar) and the Chhindwara Dt of MP; acc. Grierson "there is no such thing as a special Koshti dial."; they speak "a varying mixture of *Bundeli*, *Chhattisgarhi*, and *MARATHI*"; Nigam 1972 distinguishes *koshti–1*, a *MARATHI* subdial. of former Berar, and *koshti–2*, a *Bundeli* dial. (mixed with *MARATHI*) of Chhindwara; total of both in 1961 was 27,313, mostly from Maharashtra; down to 9,445 in 1971.

koṭalī – a *Bhili* dial. of Khandesh; 455 in 1961.

'koṭguru, koṭguruī, koṭgaṛhī' – see *Sodochi*.

koṭkhaī – Bailey's term for a subdial. of *simla siraji*; n. < former British tract of Kotkhai in middle of Simla hill states (now a tehsil of Mahasu Dt, HP); a variety of *'eastern Kiunthali'*.

kuḍālī – *KONKANI* dial., main lg. of Savantvadi and S Ratnagiri as far as Rajapur (coastal Maharashtra); alt. n. *'mālvanī'*; (Tulpule 1971 calls it a *MARATHI* dial., but he considers *KONKANI* itself, and *Khandeshi*, to be *MARATHI* dialects); *LSI* est. 90,000.

kudubi, also *kudumbi* – *KONKANI* dial. of non-Brahmin settlers in Kerala; 7,840 in 1961; 7,554 in 1971.

Kului, also *Kuluhi*, *Kulvi* – W Pahari lg. of the Kulu valley on the Upper Beas, in N of Kulu Dt (other dialects spoken in S of Dt); formerly written in local variety of Takri script; *Kulvi* seems preferred modern term (census, CIIL); 63,715 in 1971.

Kumauni – *"Central Pahari"* lg. of subhimalayan tract known as Kumaun (= Almora Dt and N of Naini Tal Dt, UP); also extends into W Nepal; normal literary lg. is *HINDI*, but there is a *Standard Kumauni* not equivalent to any local dial. but the speech of the educated classes all over Kumaun, and used in writing to some extent; acc. Grierson it derives from the speech of the old capital at Champavat in the *kumaiyā* dial. area, subsequently influenced by the *khasparjiya* dial. of Almora; 1,234,939 in 1971.

kunḍri–1 – a subdial. of the *jūṛar* dial. of *Bagheli*, NW border of Banda Dt, UP.

kunḍri–2 – a dial. of *Bundeli*, E Hamirpur Dt, UP; *LSI* est. 11,000.

'Kuṭhārī' – see *Baghati*.

'Labhani' – see *Lamani/Lambadi*.

"Lahnda" – a term (< "Western") used (although not invented) by Grierson (*LSI*) for a grouping of dial. (now entirely in Pakistan, apart from émigrés) W of *PUNJABI* (narrowly defined, q.v.) and N of *SINDHI*, which he recognized as a distinct "language", noting that its existence "has long been recognized under various names such as Jatki, Multani, Hindki or Hindko, and Western Punjabi," each of which names is misleading or too limited; some modern scholars prefer the feminine form

Lahndi; neither n. has any currency among speakers; Grierson recognized three main dialectal divisions: *"Southern"*, *"Northwestern"*, and *"Northeastern"*, each with numerous subdivisions and alternate, sometimes overlapping, names; modern investigators commonly recognize an important linguistic boundary associated with the escarpment of the Salt range separating forms of *"Southern Lahnda"* from the dialects to the N, but on the basis of better information the validity of the other two divisions is challenged; acc. Shackle 1979 the "emerging consensus" in Pakistan is crystallization around four identities: *SIRAIKI* in the S centered in Multan, *Hindko* in the NW centered in Peshawar, *Pothohari* in the N centered in Rawalpindi, and *PUNJABI* in the center and E, centered (in Pakistan) in Lahore; est. 10–16,000,000 (*LSI* 1891 est. 7,092,781). See also *multani*, *thali*, *derawal*, *hindki*, *Hindko*, *chinawari*, *niswani*, *kacchri*, *jangli*, *peshawari*, *tinauli*, *sawain*, *dhanni*, *Pothohari*, *dhundi-kairali*, *chibhali*, *punchi*, *awankari*, *ghebi*, *Kagani*, *thalochri*, *jatki*, *khetani*, and *SIRAIKI*.

Lamani/Lambadi – lg. of "Rajasthani" provenance belonging to a people now especially employed in construction, noted for the colorful dress of their women; sometimes erroneously called "Gypsies", with whom they have no connection; found all over India but esp. in the Deccan (Maharashtra, Andhra, Karnataka); alt. n. *Banjari*; 1,203,338 under *Lamani/Lambadi* in 1971; 471,853 under *Banjari*.

lārī – *SINDHI* dial. of Lower Sind, from Hyderabad to the sea, including hinterland of Karachi.

'Laria' – alt. n. of *Chhattisgarhi*, q.v.; 46,108 returns under this n. in 1971.

lāsī – *SINDHI* dial. spoken NW of Karachi in former princely state of Las Bela (along with other lgs.).

lodhāntī – dial. of *Bundeli* in NW of Hamirpur Dt, UP, and adjacent parts of Jalaun Dt spoken mainly by Lodha caste; alt. n. *'rāṭhorā'*; not to be confused with *lodhi*.

lodhi – dial. of *Bundeli* mixed with *MARATHI* spoken by immigrant peasants (originally *lodhanti*-speakers?) in Balaghat Dt, S MP; 44,074 in 1971.

ludhiānī – a subdial. of *powadhi* dial. of *PUNJABI*, taken as the basis of a written standard by European missionaries (instead of *mājhī*).

madhesi – dial. of *Bhojpuri* spoken E of Gandak river in Champaran Dt, Bihar; 11,029 returns in 1971 probably underrepresent.

Magahi – spoken lg. of central Bihar (from Son river E to Monghyr town and S to Hazaribagh, including Patna, Gaya); 6,638,495 in 1971 (NB population of Bihar was 69,823,154 in 1981; many return as *'HINDI'*); written for informal purposes in Kaithi script; normal literary lg. is *HINDI*.

magra ki boli – *Bhili* dial. of Merwara, Rajasthan.

'Mahasui' – see *Kiunthali*.

mahlogi – W Pahari dial. tentatively classified under *Handuri*; 5,093 in 1971.

([MAITHILI]) – lg. of N Bihar (Tirhut), excepting Champaran Dt, and of parts of Nepal; formerly considered to extend S of Ganga E of Monghyr (see *Angika*); literary cultivation from fifteenth century; formerly had own script akin to Bengali; now Nagari mainly used; although there is some *MODERN MAITHILI* prose, hampered by lack of official

recognition, particularly in educational system in the capacity of a medium, as distinct from a subject, of study; also by identification with an elite; by low level of literacy in N Bihar; and by inability to compete with *HINDI* (see Brass 1974: 51–116 for a detailed analysis); est. 1961 (Brass 1974: 64) 16,500,000, of whom only one-third declared it their mother tongue in the census (6,121,922 in 1971); recognized as a "language" by the Sahitya Akademi in 1965; some official recognition in Nepal.

Maiyã – the "Dardic" lg. of a few villages on the right (W) bank of the Indus, opposite Palas, in Indus Kohistan (Pakistan); poorly known; alt. n. *'Kohistani'-1*; see also *kanyawali.*

mājhī – dial. of *PUNJABI* centering on Amritsar; basis of *STANDARD PUNJABI.*

MALDIVIAN – official lg. of Republic of the Maldives in the Arabian Sea SE of India; related to *SINHALESE*; may have been brought by colonists from Sri Lanka a thousand years ago, or (de Silva 1979: 18–19) from the Indian mainland at the same time as the colonization of Sri Lanka (fifth century BC); in any case now quite distinct; written right to left in a special script (*Tana*); indigenous literary tradition; 100,000 speakers; also spoken on Minicoy Island, hence 5,034 return in 1971 Indian census; alt. (indigenous) n. *'DIVEHI'* < "lg. of the islands [*div*]".

mālpahāṛiā – a dial. of *BENGALI* spoken in Santal Parganas, Bihar; 99,313 in 1971.

'mālvanī – see *kuḍālī.*

Malvi – form of *"Rajasthani"* spoken in W MP (Indore, Ujjain, Bhopal); < Malwa, traditional n. of region; *HINDI* allegiance predominant; only 644,032 returns in 1971; alt. n. *Ahiri*, *Ujjaini*, *Bhopali.*

mālwaī – dial. of *PUNJABI* spoken SW of Ludhiana (Ferozepore, Faridkot, Bhatinda).

Mandeali/maṇḍeāḷī – a major W Pahari lg. of Mandi Dt, HP; used in administration at all levels more than any other W Pahari lg.; said to be taken as basis of proposed *"Himachali"* lg.; 241,443 in 1971.

'manḍlāhā' – see *gonḍwānī*; < Garha Mandala, n. of old Gond kingdom.

manglluri/mangaḷuri – *(KONKANI)* dial. of Christians of S Kanara and Mangalore (Katre's '*x.*'); considerable literary cultivation (journalism, poetry, fiction) esp. in twentieth century; center of literary activity shifted to Bombay in 1940s.

marāri – *Bagheli* dial. of caste of tribal gardeners (Marars), concentrated in Balaghat Dt, MP; 78,832 in 1971 (up from 37,742 in 1961).

MARATHI/marāṭhī – major NIA lg. with literature from thirteenth century (inscriptions from eleventh); conventionally divided into *Old* (to 1350), *Middle* (1350–1800), and *Modern* or *New* (1800–present); one of earliest NIA lgs. to develop strong prose tradition in modern functions; standard based on dial. of Pune (Poona) or *deśī*; other dial. include *konkan standard*, *varhādī* (of Vidarbha), and *nagpuri*; spoken mainly in consolidated Maharashtra with outliers in MP and southern states where Maratha dynasties had ruled; earlier distinctive Modi script replaced by Balbodh (= Nagari with special character for /*ḷ*/ and a different way of writing /*r-*/ conjuncts) after 1800; recently spelling reformed to bring closer to pronunciation of colloquial standard, mainly by dropping unpronounced nasals; Maharashtra 1981 literacy rate highest among NIA-speaking areas (47.37 per cent) excepting Goa (55.86 per cent); 41,723,893 in 1971; 1981 total probably over 50m.

marheṭī – dial. of *MARATHI* spoken as main lg. in polyglot Balaghat Dt, MP.

marmati – subdial. of *khashali* (W Pahari) acc. Turner.

([MARWARI])/mārvāṛī – premier *"Rajasthani"* lg., spoken in various dial. throughout Rajasthan W of Aravallis; some also include *Mewari* as a dial.; large traditional literature; divided into *Old* and *Middle* periods; one variety of *[OLD MARWARI]* known as *[DINGAL]*; in its modern incarnation as a literary lg. most often called *('RAJASTHANI')* ; 4,714,094 in 1971, to which should be added many of the *'RAJASTHANI'* returns (2,093,557) as well as those under various dialectal names, e.g., *bagri*, *mewari*, *thali*, *godwari*, *sirohi*, and *bikaneri.*

mawchi – an important *Bhili* dial. of the Gujarat–Maharashtra border area; 44,236 in 1971.

'Mayang' – see *Bishnupriya.*

merwāṛī – subdial. of *mewari*, spoken in Merwara (around Beawar in Ajmer Dt, Rajasthan); not another n. for *mewari*, as sometimes used.

mewāṛī – spoken lg. of old princely state of Mewar (except for Bhil-majority areas S of Udaipur city), modern Udaipur, Bhilwara, and Chitorgarh Dts, Rajasthan; acc. *LSI* a "dial." of *([MARWARI])*; never cultivated for literary purposes; 817,974 in 1971.

Mewati/mewāṭī – principal lg./dial. of Grierson's "Northeastern Rajasthani" construct: Alwar and NW Bharatpur Dts, Rajasthan + SE Gurgaon Dt, Haryana; < Meos, a local tribe; 94,687 in 1971.

mirgānī – a dial. of *Halbi* in Raigarh and Raipur Dts, E MP; 2,250 in 1961.

moopan – dial. or alt. n. of a dial. of *(KONKANI)* in Kerala; 473 in 1971.

'Multani', *multani* – main dial. and alt. n. of *(SIRAIKI)*; < Multan city, Dt, and Division, Pakistan; *LSI* gave 2,176,983; 15,692 returns from India in 1971, presumably refugees after Partition.

nagarchal/nāgarcāl – subdial. of *Dhundhari* (Jaipuri) of N Tonk Dt, Rajasthan; 7,090 in 1971 (down from 28,637 in 1961, and *LSI*'s 71,575).

nagpuri – eastern dial. of *MARATHI*; < Nagpur city.

'Nagpuria' – see *Sadani.*

nāharī–1 – dial. of *MARATHI* (or possibly of *Halbi*) in MP.

nāharī–2, or *nāharī-bāglanī* – dial. of *Bhili* in N Nasik Dt, Maharashtra.

naikaḍi – a *Bhili* dial. of NE Gujarat; 5,351 in 1971.

**Nangalami* – a *Nuristani lg. (acc. Strand 1973; acc. Fussman 1972 a "Dardic" lg. "of Gawarbati type") spoken along Pech river in Afghanistan, in two small islands in Pashto-speaking territory; also *'Ningalami'*, *'Grangali'*.

natakani – a form of *MARATHI* spoken in AP (6,360 in 1971, 5074 in 1961).

nawait – a dial. of *(KONKANI)* spoken by Muslim petty traders, mostly in coastal Karnataka, a few in Kerala; 749 in 1961.

'neelishikari' – alt. n. for *paradhi* in AP; 223 in 1961.

NEPALI – state lg. of kingdom of Nepal since Gurkha conquest in eighteenth century; attested much earlier in W Nepal (royal edicts and inscriptions from fourteenth century); known to 84 per cent and mother tongue of 66 per cent in "hill areas" acc. Clark 1977 (1963) based on 1952–4 census data; percentages no doubt higher now; has also been spreading significantly along Himalayas E of Nepal; literary record divided into Early (1300–1670), Middle (1670–1900), and Modern (post-1900); acc. Srivastava 1962 Grierson's assertion that *NEPALI* is derived from *mewari* brought by Udaipur Rajputs to Garhwal, Kumaun, and W Nepal in early sixteenth century is "not correct", since – whatever its relation to Garhwali and Kumauni – it has been shown (partly by evidence that has come to light since Grierson's time, when Nepal was closed to outsiders and not well known) that it was the lg. of W Nepal long before that; est. 8,000,000, including 1,286,824 in India (mainly Darjeeling Dt in W Bengal, and Sikkim) in 1971; speakers in India have begun agitating for recognition; second lg. of many Tibeto-Burman-speaking hill peoples in Nepal and Sikkim; Devanagari script; alt. n. *'Gorkhali'*, *'Khas Kura'*, *'Parbatiya'*.

Nimadi/nimāḍī – peculiar dial. or lg. of "Rajasthani" group spoken in two enclaves (E and W Nimar Dts) in MP S of Indore, surrounded by *Bhili* and *Khandeshi* except on the E; 794,246 in 1971.

niswānī – subdial. or local n. of "Southern Lahnda" (*SIRAIKI*), N Jhang Dt, Pakistan; *LSI* gives 9,432.

'nyar' – see *girāsiā*.

ORIYA/oḍiā – lg. of 82.3 per cent of population of Orissa (rest mainly Munda and Dravidian tribal lgs.); literary cultivation from fifteenth century, inscriptions from the tenth ("connected lines" only from the mid-thirteenth); *Modern* period late in arriving (1950–60) because of domination of *BENGALI* in nineteenth century; unique and difficult script; 19,726,745 in 1971; at least 21,600,000 in 1981.

Padari/pāḍarī – W Pahari lg. of Padar area in S Kashmir, between Pangi and Kishtwar; 7,927 in 1971 (6,359 in 1961); Turner considers it a subdial. of *Bhadarwahi*; alt. n. *'Pondri'*.

pahāḍī – acc. *LSI*, a *Bhili* dial. of E Gujarat; not recorded in 1961–71; < Gujarati 'of the hills'.

"Pahari"–1 – Grierson's n. for a group of NIA lgs. and dialects in the Himalayas, divided into *Eastern* (= *NEPALI*), *Central* (= *Kumauni* and *Garhwali*), and *Western* (stretching from *Jaunsari* in NW UP to *Bhadarwahi* in Kashmir).

'Pahari'–2, or 'Pahari Unspecified' – term used by speakers themselves (= "lg. of the hills/mountains") for their own and related dialects, to express differentiation from plainsmen's speech; 1,269,651 such returns in 1971, mostly from the "*Western* Pahari" area.

'pahāṛī'–3 – local n. for *Bilaspuri/Kahluri* in hilly part of Hoshiarpur Dt, Punjab.

'pahāṛī'–4 – local n. for *dhundi-kairālī* subdial. of *"NE Lahnda"* in Rawalpindi Dt.

paidi – dial. or n. of *ORIYA* in AP; 3,967 in 1961; [= *'pamidi'*? = *'paki'*?].

'palesi' – subdial. of *Shina*; < Palas; see *kohistani–4*.

panchpargania – E dial. of *Magahi* spoken in E Ranchi Dt, Bihar; 160,085 in 1971 (up from 57,974 in 1961); "mixed with Mundari and *BENGALI*".

Pangwāḷī – W Pahari lg. of "Chamba group"; in some ways agrees more with "Bhadrawahi group"; 9,800 in 1971 (8,195 in 1961).

pāradhī – dial. of *Bhili* in Maharashtra, MP, and AP; 10,691 in 1971 (10,153 in 1961); alt. n. (AP) *'pittala bhasha'*, *'neelinshkari'*.

'pardesi' – n. for *[AWADHI]* in Maharashtra; 22,093 in 1971 (32,423 in 1961).

parsi gujarati – subdial. of S *GUJARATI* spoken by Parsis; only 15,463 so report in 1971.

parvari – form of *MARATHI* in MP; 59,586 in 1961; none in 1971?

Par'ya – recently discovered (1954) NIA lg. of Soviet Central Asia (in the Gissar valley W of the Tadzhik capital of Dushanbe); alt. n. *'Afgon'*.

Pashai – a group of mutually unintelligible dialectal fragments in the poorer and smaller valleys N of the Kabul river in Afghanistan, surrounded by Pashto; remnants of a NIA-speaking population, once part of the Indian civilization (Fussman 1972: 25–6) that dominated the region from Buddhist times until at least the ninth century; around 100,000 speakers acc. Fussman (i.e. before the war in Afghanistan).

pāṭīdārī – a *GUJARATI* peasant dial. of Kaira Dt *outside* the Charotar tract; see *charotari*; close to the *"standard"* dial.

'Paṭṇūlī' – see *Saurashtri*.

paṭṭani – n. for the "N" dial. of *GUJARATI*; < Patan, the capital of pre-Muslim Gujarat.

pāwarī/pāwrī – a *Bhili* dial. of Maharashtra; 176,018 in 1971 (38,593 in 1961).

pa˜wārī/panwārī – dial. (or local n.) of *Bundeli* in Datia Dt, N MP; < *Pa˜war* (Paramara) Rajputs; 25,400 in 1971; see also *powari*, *powa˜ri*.

peshawari, *peshawari hindko/pifaurī* – dial. of "NW Lahnda" spoken in and around Peshawar city; beginnings of literary cultivation as most prestigious variety of NWFP *Hindko* (Shackle 1980: 509).

Phalura/phalūṛa – "Dardic" lg. of several villages in SE Chitral; an archaic offshoot of *Shina*; 800–1000 acc. Morgenstierne 1941; still spoken 1988 (Elena Bashir: pers. comm.); alt. n. *'Dangarikwar'* (most common local n.), *'Palola'*, *'Palula'*; see also *Sawi*.

[PINGAḶ] – n. for literary *BRAJ* as written in (esp.) E Rajasthan, incorporating occasional Rajasthani forms; early medieval period.

Poguli – "Dardic" lg. of "Kashmir group" spoken in mountain valleys of Doda Dt, Kashmir, W of Kishtwar but E of the highway leading from Jammu to Srinagar; 9,508 in 1961; Hook estimates 10–20,000.

Poṭhohārī, also *Poṭhwārī* – N. "dial. of Lahnda" spoken around and S of Rawalpindi; some attempts to cultivate.

powādhī, also *puādī* – E dial. of *PUNJABI* (of Ludhiana, Patiala, part of Ambala Dt).

powārī – mixed dial. of *Bundeli* in Chhindwara Dt and adjacent Maharashtra; 64,078 in 1961.

po˜wārī – dial. of *Bagheli* spoken in Balaghat and Bhandara Dts, MP; < Paramara Rajputs of Malwa; see also *pa˜wari*.

**Prasun* – *Nuristani lg. of Prasun valley, central Hindu Kush, Afghanistan (between the two sections of **Kati*); est. 2,000–3,000 (Fussman 1972); alt. n. *Wasi-weri*, *Wa˜si-weri*, *Veron*.

puncchi/punchī – dial. of "NE Lahnda", spoken in Punch region of Kashmir, below (SW of) Pir Panjal range; much influenced by *KASHMIRI*; 13, 385 in India in 1971 (+speakers in Pakistan).

PUNJABI/panjābī – lg. of state of Punjab in India and of adjacent parts of

Pakistan (Lahore, Gujranwala); colonies of "Central" *PUNJABI* speakers also further W in "Lahnda" area of Pakistani Punjab; little literary activity before 1600; modern prose standard developed only in twentieth century; standard, associated in India with Sikh community, based on *mājhī* dial. of Amritsar; other dialects: *powādhī*, *bhaṭṭiānī*, *malwaī*, *doābī*, *raṭhī*; 13,900,202 in India in 1971; Aksenov estimated a total (India + Pakistan) of 25–30,000,000 in 1961; Gurmukhi script used in India; Perso-Arabic in Pakistan; some Punjabi linguists in both India and Pakistan would still include *"Lahnda"* under *PUNJABI*; on their side is the fact that "all varieties of language in the Panjab are collectively closer to one another than they are to even the most closely related adjacent NIA languages" (Shackle 1979: 199–200); defining such a *"Greater Panjabi"* entity is another matter, however (ibid.: 199–200): *SIRAIKI*, for instance, lacks one criterion commonly advanced, namely tone, but has distinctive implosive consonants.

'purbi' – (lit. "eastern") a n. for the *western* dial. of *Bhojpuri*, more loosely used for both *[AWADHI]* and *Bhojpuri* when spoken by settlers in the "Western Hindi" area; 8,073 returns under this n. in 1971.

"Rajasthani"-1 – a Grierson construct, grouping the dialects lying between *"Western Hindi"* and *GUJARATI* into one lg.; comprising *"Western"* (*([MARWARI])* with *Mewari*, *Bagri*, etc.), *"Central Eastern"* (*Jaipuri* or *Dhundhari*, *Harauti*, etc.), *"Northeastern"* (*Mewati*, *Ahirwati*), and *"Southeastern"* [outside the geographic boundaries of Rajasthan/Rajputana] (*Malvi*, *Nimadi*); Kellogg had previously treated all these as "dialects of *HINDI*"; Tessitori subsequently (1914–16) used the term *Old Western Rajasthani* to refer to a lg. which acc. J. D. Smith (1975: 434) is really *[OLD GUJARATI]*, although it was widely employed as a literary medium in Rajasthan; the non-contiguous *Gojri* and *Lamani* have also been found to be affiliated to the group; excluding these and *Malvi* + *Nimadi*, the population of Rajasthan was 34,102,912 in 1981.

('RAJASTHANI')-2 – increasingly used as n. of new literary lg., based primarily on *([MARWARI])*; decline of certain local dial. names in Rajasthan, partly in favor of '*RAJASTHANI*' (over 2m. in 1971) may be an indication that linguistic consolidation is proceeding: Devanagari script used.

rajbangshi – dial. of *BENGALI* spoken in N Bangladesh (Raṅgpur), N. Bengal (Jalpaiguri, Cooch Behar), and Goalpara Dt of Assam.

Rāmbanī – "Dardic" lg. of "Kashmir group" in Jammu; current local n. *'Zundhārī'* (Hook: pers. comm.).

rampuri – subdial. of *kochi*; 517 in 1961.

rangari-1 – a *MARATHI* dial. of dyers in Berar, acc. *LSI*.

rāngaṛī – variety of *Malvi* spoken by Rajputs in SW MP; alt. n. *rājwāṛī*.

rāṭhaurī – acc. *LSI*, local n. of *bhaṭṭiānī* dial. of *PUNJABI* in Ferozepore; but 1961 census returns (584 only) mostly from Maharashtra.

rāṭhī-1 – a dial. of *PUNJABI*, strongly mixed with *Haryani*, spoken in Ghaggar valley; alt. n. *pacchāḍī*, *naili*, *jāṇḍ*.

rāṭhī-2 – a dial. of *Garhwali*; 63,057 acc. *LSI*; alt. n. *rāṭhwālī*.

rāṭhī-3 – a subdial. of *sirohi* spoken on Mt Abu; 8,669 in 1971; alt. n. *ābu lok kī bolī*.

'raṭhora' – see *lodhanti*.

rāṭhvī – a *Bhili* dial. of E Gujarat.
'REKHTA' – an old n. for standard literary *URDU*.
relli – a dial. of *ORIYA* in AP; 11,151 in 1971 (5,295 in 1961).
'Rewapari', *'Riwāī'* – alt. names for *Bagheli* (e.g., in Kellogg).
roḍiyā – a *SINHALESE* dial., or argot, of a particular community.
rohrui – a subdial. of *kochi* (HP).
Romany, also *Romani* – lg. of the Gypsies; three main dial. divisions: *asiatic* (Syro-Palestinian), *armenian*, and *eụropean* (with many subdial.); numbers difficult to ascertain: Voegelin and Voegelin 1977 estimate 450,000–900,000; no true Gypsies in Indian subcontinent, but probable linguistic connection with *Dumaki* in Hunza.
rudhārī – with subdial. *"high"*, *"middle"*, and *"low"*; acc. Turner, a subdial. of *Khashali.*
Sadan/Sadani, also *Sadri* – vernacular and lingua franca of E Chota Nagpur plateau (Palamau and Ranchi Dts, SW Bihar); arguments over whether it is a "dial. of *Bhojpuri*" or a "dial. of *Magahi*" might better give way to considering it as a separate lg.; now recognized as a subject at the University of Ranchi; alt. n. *'Nagpuria'*; total under both n. in 1971 (with *Sadan/Sadri* predominating) was 1,142,310, up from 626,124 in 1961.
sāēṭh kī bolī – subdial. of *sirohi* in SW of Sirohi Dt; transitional to or mixed with *GUJARATI*; *LSI* gives 6,000.
sainji – W Pahari dial. spoken in valley of Sainj r. in S Kulu Dt, HP (Bailey 1915).
saracholi/śorācolī – dial. of *Kiunthali/Mahasui*, spoken in Jubbal tehsil of E Mahasu Dt; alt. n. *barāṛī* (sometimes considered a separate dial., pertaining to E portion of above territory); *LSI* gives 2,428 for *saracholi* and 7,894 for *barāṛī*; barely returned in later censuses.
sarākī – Jain subdial. of *"western"* dial. of *BENGALI*, spoken in Ranchi, Bihar.
sā̃sī, *sansi* – acc. Bailey, dial. of a "criminal tribe" in N Himalayas; returns (467 only) in 1961 from Rajasthan and MP, not HP; acc. *LSI* pertains to "UP and Punjab"; alt. n. *sā̃siyā.*
Saurashtri – lg. of a weaver community in S India, centering on Madurai (Tamilnadu); originally connected with *GUJARATI*, but colony dates back 1000 years; written in Tamil script; 181,289 in 1971 (under alt. n. *'Saurashtra'*); other alt. n. *'Paṭnūlī'*, *'Khatri'*.
Savi, *Sāwī* – "Dardic" lg. (or dial. of *Phalura*, with which it is mutually intelligible) spoken in villages (Sau, Narsat, etc.) on Kunar river in Afghanistan, S of *Gawarbati* area.
sawain – subdial. of "NW Lahnda" (acc. Grierson) in Fatehjang Tehsil, Attock Dt, Pakistan; alt. n. *'sohain'*.
[saxtti]/saṣṭī – *(KONKANI)* dial. of Christians of S Goa (Salcete), cultivated in eighteenth and nineteenth centuries (songs, hymns); superseded in literature by *barhdexi* dial. in twentieth century.
seuṭī – acc. Turner, a subdial. of *Khashali.*
shahpuri – transitional dial. (< Shahpur town on Jhelum river, Sargodha Dt, Pakistan) unfortunately taken by Grierson as base of reference for *"standard Lahnda"*, but acc. Shackle 1979: 201 now better classed as a dial. of *PUNJABI.*
shekhāwāṭī – dial. of *([MARWARI])* in N Rajasthan, S of *bāgṛī* dial., mainly

in Jhunjhunu Dt of Jaipur; 22,160 in 1961; does not appear in 1971; acc. Bahl 1972, several important *('RAJASTHANI')* writers are from this area.

Shina/ṣiṇā – main "Dardic" lg. after *KASHMIRI*; spoken in Gilgit, Upper Indus valley (Indus Kohistan, Chilas, enclaves in Baltistan, i.e. Skardu, and in Ladakh), and mountainous area N and E of Vale of Kashmir (Astor, Gurais, Dras); acc. Bailey, three main dialectal divisions: *gilgiti*, *kohistani* (incl. *chilasi*, *palesi*), and *astori* (incl. *guresi*, *drasi*), plus *broks-kat*; Voegelin and Voegelin 1977 est. 100,000 speakers, mostly in Pakistan; 1971 census found 9,902 in India; may once have occupied more of Baltistan and Ladakh than it does at present.

sikarwāṛī – dial. of *[BRAJ]* spoken between Gwalior town and Chambal river, MP.

SINDHI – distinctive lg. of Lower Indus valley (Pakistan, Sind Province); pre-modern literary cultivation mainly by Sufi poets; *Modern* literary development mainly in twentieth century, now vigorous, including journalism; most firmly established regional lg.-identity in Pakistan; influx of Hindu refugees from Sind has led to its recognition (in Schedule VIII) as an official lg. of India also; dialects: *vicholi*, *lāṛī*, *lāsī*, *'siraiki'* (doubtful: see below); sometimes *Kacchi* also considered a *SINDHI* dial.; *vicholi* is basis of the standard; specially modified Perso-Arabic script (see Chapter 6); Hindus had also used for informal purposes the Landa script; proposals to adopt Devanagari for *SINDHI* in India inhibited by desire not to break unity of lg.; 5–6,000,000 in Pakistan; 1,204,678 in India in 1971.

SINHALESE/siŋhala – IA lg. of Sri Lanka (Ceylon), established from sixth century BC; literary cultivation from tenth century, inscriptions earlier; 10,585,000 speakers; unique cursive script of S Indian type.

(SIRAIKI)–1 – new literary lg. based on "S Lahnda" dialects, especially *multani* and *bahawalpuri*; < *SINDHI siro* 'north'.

['siraiki']–2 – n. of "Lahnda" (= *SIRAIKI*) as spoken particularly by immigrants in Sind acc. *LSI*; formerly in some literary use; alt. n. *siraiki hindki* (*LSI*), *sindhi siraiki* (Shackle 1976).

'siraiki'–3 – acc. Trumpp, n. of *SINDHI* dial. spoken in N Sind (the Siro); acc. to Grierson the lg. there does not differ from standard *vicholi* except in "clearer articulation", and in any case, local officials always used the term in sense 2 (hence > modern sense 1), never in Trumpp's sense.

siraji–1 – a dial. of *Kului* (or lg. of "Kulu Group"); alt. n. *inner siraji*, *kulu siraji*.

siraji–2 – a dial. of "Sutlej Group" closely allied to *Shodochi*, also spoken in Kulu Dt, but S of Jalor range, in valleys tributary to Satlej, i.e. S of *inner siraji*; alt. n. *outer siraji*; NB 1971 figure of 56,135, though probably from Kulu (92 per cent of CIIL Survey *"Shiraji"* respondents were from Kulu), could be either *siraji–1* or *siraji–2*.

siraji–3 – dial. of *Kiunthali/Mahasui* spoken in Kotkhai and adjacent areas, E. of Simla, S of *Shodochi*; alt. n. *simla siraji*.

Siraji–4 – a dial., or lg. of "Kashmir group", spoken in and around town of Doda on Chenab river, Kashmir, S of Kishtwar; 19,978 in 1971; alt. n. *Doda Siraji*.

'Sirhindi' – Dhirendra Varma's term for *Khari Boli*.

Sirmauri – W Pahari lg. of Sirmaur Dt, HP (and of Chaupal tehsil of Mahasu

Dt); dialects: *girīpārī* (with subdial. *bissau*) and *dhārṭhī* (S of Giri rivers); special variety of Takri script used for informal writing; 111,385 in 1961; only 14,542 in 1971 (returned under *"Pahari Unspecified"?*).

sirohi – *([MARWARI])* dial. spoken in Sirohi Dt + Jalor, Rajasthan; 179,000 acc. *LSI*.

Sodochi – W Pahari lg. of S bank of Satlej river in Mahasu Dt, HP; akin to *'outer siraji'* of N bank; 18,893 acc. *LSI*; alt. n. *'Koṭgurū'* (Bailey), *'Sadochi'*.

sondwārī – dial. of *Malvi* in Rajasthan; 31,488 in 1971.

'sohain' – see *sawain*.

'Suketi' – the same lg. as *Mandeali*; 4,906 under this n. in 1961.

surajpuri – a dial. (?) of *([MAITHILI])*; 28,092 in 1961; 159,677 in 1971.

surati – the southern dial. of *GUJARATI*.

surgujia – a dial. of *Chhattisgarhi* in Surguja Dt, NE MP.

tadavi/tadvi – a *Bhili* dial. of Maharashtra; 4,097 in 1961; 10,229 in 1971.

'tamaria' – see *panchpargania*.

thaḷī-1 – *([MARWARI])* dial. spoken in E Jaisalmer and NW Jodhpur Dts.

thaḷī-2 – a NW dial. of *(SIRAIKI)* ("S Lahnda") spoken W of Jhelum in Mianwali Dt, and beyond the Indus in Dera Ismail Khan Dt; alt. n. *'jaṭkī'*, *'hindko'*, (W of Indus) *'derāwāl'*.

thareli – dial. intermediate between *SINDHI* and *([MARWARI])* spoken in Thar-Parkar desert region of E Sind + SW Jaisalmer (Rajasthan); alt. n. *ḍhaṭkī*, *tharechi*.

tinauli – subdial. of "NW Lahnda" spoken by Tinawal tribe in Hazara, Pakistan.

Tirahi – "Dardic" lg. spoken (or once spoken – only a few old people remembered the lg. acc. Fussman 1972) in an enclave of three villages in Pashto territory S of Jalalabad, Afghanistan; S-most "Dardic" lg.

tirhari-1 – dial. of *Kannauji* spoken on N bank of Jamuna in Kanpur Dt, UP, opposite Hamirpur.

tirhari-2 – dial. of *Bagheli* spoken on S bank of Jamuna in Banda, Fatehpur, and Hamirpur Dts, UP.

'TIRAHUTIYA' – see *([MAITHILI])*.

torāwāṭī – subdial. of "Central E Rajasthani" spoken N of Jaipur; *LSI* gives 342,554; not returned in later censuses.

Torwali – "Dardic" lg. of a few villages in the upper Swat valley; numbers have greatly declined since first discovered (Fussman 1971: 27).

'to˜wargarhi' – see *bhadauri*; < Tomara Rajputs.

**Tregami* – *Nuristani lg. of three villages (*tre gām*) situated in a small valley W of the Kunar; alt. n. (Morgenstierne) *'Gambiri'* (< n. of one of the villages).

'Ujjaini' – see *Malvi*.

URDU – national lg. of Pakistan and one of the official lgs. of India; a Persianized development of *Khari Boli*; spoken in Delhi, Lucknow, Hyderabad, and other Indian cities with large Muslim populations; originally not native to Pakistan, though cultivated in Lahore; now Karachi is an expanding *URDU*-speaking enclave; est. 32,000,000, incl. 28,600,428 in India in 1971; modified Perso-Arabic script (see Chapter 6).

vaḍodarī – n. of dial. of uneducated in Baroda, but basically the same as general "standard" *GUJARATI*.

vāgḍī (also *wagdi*) – the main dial. of *Bhili* spoken in S Rajasthan (Dungarpur, Banswara, S Udaipur); 756,786 in 1961; missing in 1971.

varhāḍī – the *MARATHI* of Vidarbha (Berar): Amraoti, Buldana, Akola Dts.

vārlī–1 – a *Bhili* dial. of the Dangs in S Gujarat.

vārlī–2 (also *warli*) – a *MARATHI* dial. of a tribe in Thana Dt allegedly of Bhil origin; 1971 figure of 113,291 (up from 45,605 in 1961, mostly from Dadra-Nagarhaveli and Gujarat) may not distinguish *varli–1* and *varli–2*.

vedda – a dial. of *SINHALESE*, spoken by small aboriginal group in Sri Lanka, who have lost their own lg.

vicholi – dial. of *SINDHI* on which the standard lg. is based, spoken in central Sind ("Vicholo"), focusing on Hyderabad.

'Wai-ala', *'Waigali'* – see **Kalaṣa-alā*.

'Wasi-weri' – see **Prasun*.

wazirabadi – a NW variety of Central *PUNJABI* (N of Lahore), the basis of Bailey's descriptions (1904).

"Western Hindi" – a Grierson construct comprising *Braj Bhasha*, *Kannauji*, *Bundeli*, *Bangaru* (= *Haryanvi*), and *"Vernacular Hindostani"*.

"Western Pahari" – lg. group, though sometimes treated as a "language" with "dialects", including as chief members (E to W) *Jaunsari*, *Sirmauri*, *Kiunthali/Mahasui*, *Baghati*, *Sodochi*, *Kului*, *Mandeali*, *Kangri*, *Dogri*, *Chameali*, *Bhadrawahi*, and *Khashali*; the group stretches from NW UP to S Kashmir, mainly occupying HP.

Wotapuri – "Dardic" lg. of Wotapur and Katarqala on lower Pech river in Afghanistan.

'Zundhari' – see *Rāmbanī*.

Appendix II

SCHEMES OF NIA SUBCLASSIFICATION

What is usually meant by linguistic classification is *genetic* classification, implying a systematic divergent development (primarily though not exclusively *phonological*) from a common ancestor, and portrayable in a branching-tree diagram (*Stammbaum*). Other kinds of classification (e.g., typological) should be kept rigorously separate from this one, although in practice – and especially in the NIA field – they have often been mixed into it, greatly confusing the picture.

A *Stammbaum* represents historical linguistic reality with minimal distortion in a situation where the diverging branches lose contact with one another and remain thus, because of geographical or longstanding political separation. If they remain in contact, or come into contact again (through further migrations, or assimilation of intervening peoples), the effects of mutual borrowing may greatly obscure the relationships, or make it difficult to construct a *Stammbaum* at all.

This is preeminently the case with Indo-Aryan, which has developed primarily in an area with few internal natural barriers, where unstable political units have often not coincided with linguistic units, and where significant internal migrations have taken place. The resulting dialectal continuum thus creates problems for NIA subclassification as well as for the identification and delimitation of languages and dialects (Chapter 2).

The so-called *wave theory* may describe many of the linguistic facts better than a *Stammbaum*. Individual linguistic features spread, pond-ripple fashion, first from one center, then from another, weakening as the distance increases, and thereby affecting sometimes only certain dialectal subdivisions of a "language", sometimes only certain subsystems thereof, sometimes only particular items. In terms of such centers of diffusion, there has been, along with more localized movements, a large-scale shift of the center of gravity of Indo-Aryan culture and power from the western end of the Indo-Gangetic plain to the eastern, and then back again, at least to the vicinity of Delhi. Closely connected with this has been the influence of prestige languages far beyond their natural dialectal constituencies: first of northwestern Vedic, then midland Sanskrit, eastern Magadhi, midland Sauraseni Prakrit and Apabhramsa, alien Persian, and finally midland Hindi.

The effects of all this overlie whatever "original" pattern of relationships there was, and are often difficult to sort out from it. Wave theory, by the very nature of the effects it is concerned with, does not offer an alternative basis for *classification* of languages. It does permit the drawing of *isoglosses*, which at least can make the pattern of overlays clearer.

Leaving aside earlier speculations that led nowhere, the first attempt to sort out the Indo-Aryan puzzle that had lasting effects was that of Hoernle in 1880. He classified the NIA languages he knew about into four groups: "*Northern*" (Nepali, Kumauni, Garhwali). "*Western*" ("Western Hindi" under which he included Marwari and "Eastern Rajputani",

Punjabi including "Multani", Sindhi, and Gujarati), "*Southern*" (Marathi with Konkani), and "*Eastern*" (Bengali, Oriya, and "Eastern Hindi" by which he meant primarily Bhojpuri, with Maithili and "Magadh", and marginally "Baiswari", that is, Awadhi, which he felt was mixed with "Western Hindi"). There were to be sure certain errors and omissions here, along with use of a nomenclature often differing from the one that has since prevailed (mainly because of Grierson's *LSI*): e.g., his term *Gaudian* for continental NIA, or his use of *Eastern Hindi* primarily in the sense of "*Bihari*".

Hoernle believed that "at a former period each of these four groups constituted a single language." Moreover, affinities between the "*Southern*" and the "*Eastern*" groups, on the one hand, and between the "*Northern*" and the "*Western*", on the other, pointed to "a still more remote period" when these four reduced themselves to *two*, a northwestern speech, which he proposed to call "*Sauraseni*", and a southeastern, which he proposed to call "*Magadhi*" – not to be confused with Literary Sauraseni and Literary Magadhi Prakrit. (Maharashtri he considered, on the basis of a number of arguments, to be merely another form of Sauraseni and to have nothing to do with Maharashtra or Marathi, attributing such an identification to a mistake by Prakrit grammarians in the east, never by those in the west who had first-hand knowledge of the situation. The basically descriptive term *mahā-rāṣṭra* 'great country' could allegedly have been applied to any powerful kingdom.) Hoernle's scheme is thus explicitly historical and genealogical, and attempts to keep separate the questions surrounding the literary languages. it yields a fairly neat *Stammbaum* with only one anomalous element: see Figure II.1.

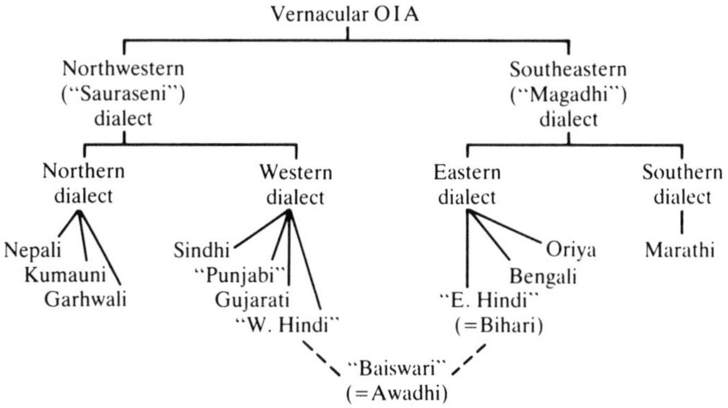

Figure II.1 NIA subclassification according to Hoernle

Hoernle moreover viewed the situation as dynamic. Speakers of the Southeastern dialect had, he thought, once occupied the northwest, but had been pushed back by a later invasion of "Sauraseni" speakers – leaving, however, tokens of their former presence in some of the later languages of the west and north.

It was this two-invasion hypothesis of Hoernle's that led Grierson, armed with a better knowledge of the number and extent of NIA languages, to develop his well-known *Inner–Outer* model. It also postulated two basic branches but differed in important respects from Hoernle's model. Certain languages belonging to Hoernle's "Western" group (Western Hindi, Punjabi, Gujarati, Rajasthani – recognized as distinct from Hindi, along with Bhili and Khandeshi) plus the "northern" group were taken to constitute an *Inner sub-branch*, the speakers of which were also the bearers of the Vedic religion, Sanskrit, the caste system, and Hindu civilization in general (always associated with the *Madhyadeśa*, the area between Ambaḷa and Allahabad). The remaining "Western" languages (i.e. Sindhi plus Western Punjabi or "Lahnda", which was recognized as distinct partly for the sake of this scheme) he combined with the "Southern" and "Eastern" languages (including Assamese and the cluster of dialects he called "Bihari") to constitute an *Outer sub-branch* surrounding the "*Inner*" languages in a semi-circle interrupted only at Gujarat, where "*Inner*" speakers had "broken through to the sea."

Considering the connection between Marathi and the Eastern languages to have been established by Hoernle, Grierson concentrated his efforts on trying to prove that the "Northwestern" languages (Sindhi and "Lahnda"), as he called them, also belonged to that group and not with what he called the "Central" languages headed by Western Hindi. (Hoernle had held an explicitly opposite view, although he had noted, as an indication of the supposed former occupancy of the northwest by "Magadhan", certain alleged "Magadhan" features in the Iranian language Pashto, as well as in "Kafiri".)

Although it is often associated with his Inner–Outer theory, Grierson was careful to dissociate himself from the two-invasion hypothesis as such (*LSI 1.1*: 116, and footnote 2), maintaining only that there were earlier and later "immigrants", either of which could have constituted the core of the Inner or of the Outer branches, by any of several possible scenarios. It is plain from his comments elsewhere, however, that he inclined to the view that the Outer represented the earlier and the Inner the later arrivals.

He was compelled to recognize a third or *Mediate sub-branch* also, consisting of Awadhi with the related Bagheli and Chhattisgarhi, which inconveniently manifested characteristics of both the Inner and the Outer sub-branches. He labeled this dialect cluster "*Eastern Hindi*" and it was this usage, rather than Hoernle's, that prevailed, at least in English. (In Hindi, the term *Purbi*, 'Eastern', usually denotes Bhojpuri, as it did for Hoernle.) Bhojpuri was assigned to the new "*Bihari*" cluster or "language": one effect of this, according to partisans of Maithili, has been to skew "*Bihari*" more toward *Hindi* than it should have been.

The Inner and the Outer sub-branches consisted of further branches, or "*groups*". As a *Stammbaum*, Grierson's first model therefore looked something like Figure II.2.

Grierson did not concern himself much (and Hoernle not at all) with the extra-Indian members of the family, Sinhalese and Romany. The implication was that the former went with the Outer branch ("its nearest relative in India is Marathi, but the relationship is distant" – *LSI 1.1:* 145), while Romany was regarded as of "Dardic" affinity. (The "Dardic" question will be summarized later. Grierson did not consider the so-called Dardic languages to be Indo-Aryan at all, although he held that their most prominent representative, Kashmiri, had been subjected to strong Indo-Aryan influence.)

Grierson immediately began to hedge on his basic classification. Punjabi, "Rajasthani", and Gujarati were Inner languages, but superimposed on an Outer *substratum*, most tangible in Gujarati. "Lahnda" showed weaker traces of expanding Inner influences, but Outer characteristics retained the upper hand. Sindhi and "Lahnda" were superimposed in turn on a "Dardic" substratum – itself having a substratum of the non-Aryan Burushaski. Grierson indeed found traces of "Dardic" in many places, e.g., in the Romany, Pahari, and Bhili dialects and as far afield as Konkani. The "Inner" character of Pahari was allegedly the result of the rather recent superimposition of Rajasthani on a complex substratum that included Munda, Tibeto–Burman, "Dardic", and foreign elements.

S. K. Chatterji, in an appendix to the introduction to his monumental *Origin and development of the Bengali language* (1926), took strong exception to the whole Inner–

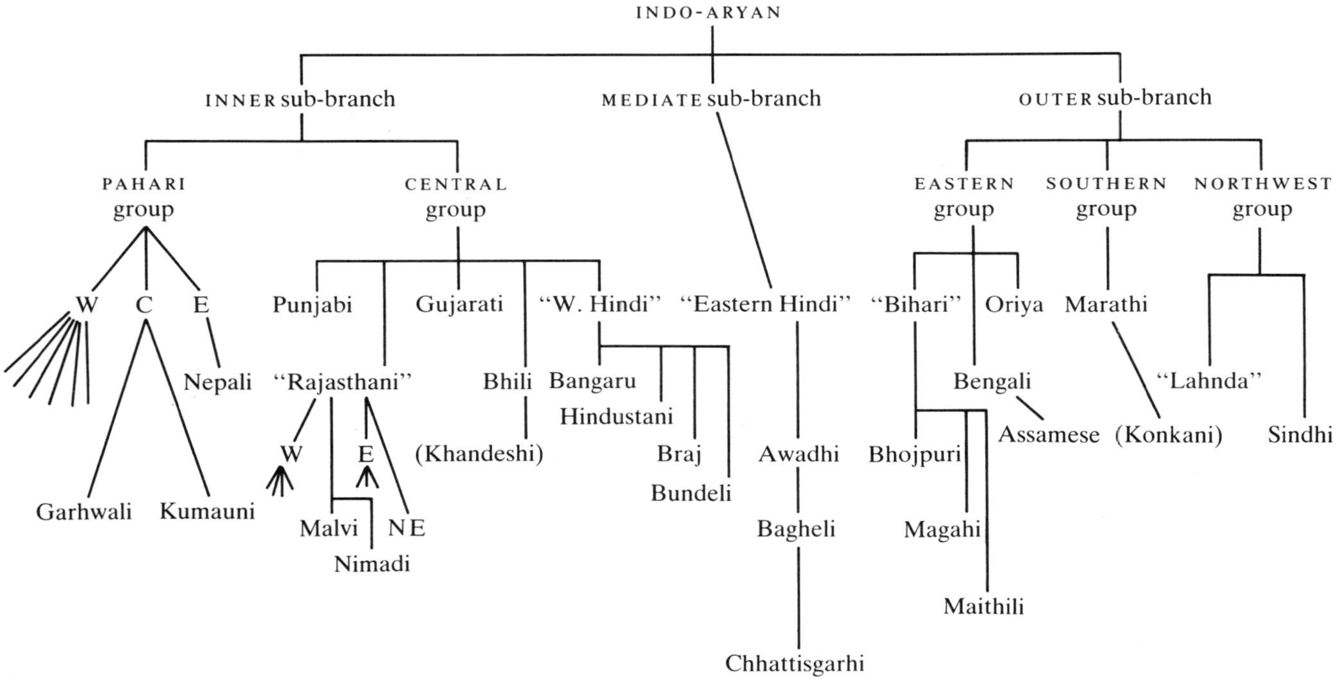

Figure II.2 NIA subclassification according to Grierson (LSI): tree-diagram

Outer premise. Grierson's criteria for this basic division were a mixed bag of phonetic, morphological, and what would have to be called typological characteristics, e.g.,

1. Inner preservation of /*s*/ (<OIA /*ś*, *ṣ*, *s*/) vs. Outer substitution of other sounds;
2. Inner loss vs. Outer retention of final short vowels (actually a matter of relatively recent linguistic history);
3. Inner Past suffix {*-i-*} vs. Outer {*-l-*};
4. the "analytic" character of the Inner languages vs. the alleged "synthetic" character of the Outer languages.

Chatterji attempted to refute these on (briefly) the following grounds:

1. some alleged "Outer" features are often demonstrably late and independent developments (e.g., the Pasts in {*-l-*}): it will be recalled that the Inner–Outer division was supposed to go back to the beginning of the Indo-Aryan period;
2. they are not found in all the so-called "Outer" languages (e.g., the {*-l-*} Past is not found in "Lahnda");
3. they are also found in so-called "Inner" languages (the {*-l-*} suffix *is* found in Gujarati; the deformation of /*s*/ to [*h*] is found in Punjabi, non-standard, and Bhili – and in the future suffix, even in Braj (OIA *kariṣyati* > MIA *karissati* > Braj *karihaī*; paradoxically, "Outer" Lahnda preserves an [*s*] in such forms: *karēsī*);
4. they are stages through which all NIA languages have passed (e.g., the retention of final short vowels, where in any case no real Inner–Outer pattern is discernible);
5. they are superficial coincidences resulting from *different local non-Aryan* influences (e.g. the dental articulation of /*c*, *j*/ as [*ts*, *dz*] in Marathi, Southern Oriya, Eastern Bengali, and certain Pahari languages, under the respective influence of Dravidian [Telugu] and Tibeto-Burman languages);
6. they result from universal phonological tendencies ([*s*] > [*h*], found also in Greek, Welsh, Iranian, dialectal Spanish, etc.; in certain classes of words, e.g., numerals, the change of medial *-s-* to *-h-*, often subsequently lost, is universal in Prakrit and NIA: OIA *aṣṭāsaptati* 'seventy-eight' > MIA *aṭṭha-hattari* > Hindi–Punjabi–Lahnda *aṭhattar*);
7. they represent a heterogeneous collection of features (e.g., the "deformation of [*s*]": the change of [*s*] to [*ʃ*] before front vowels in Marathi is not the same thing as the merger of the three OIA sibilants into [*ʃ*] in Magadhi Prakrit; neither of these developments is the same as the shift of medial [*-s-*] to [*-h-*] in Sindhi, Lahnda, and Punjabi);
8. the Outer languages are "agglutinative" in structure, not "synthetic"; truly synthetic elements, inherited from OIA, are mere fragments preserved randomly in both "Inner" and "Outer" languages; "Inner" languages are arguably as agglutinative as "Outer" languages; finally, such typological arguments are of no relevance for genetic subclassification.

In short, Chatterji saw no unity among the "Outer" languages, and more importantly, even less unity going back in time: the earliest reliable record, that of the Asokan inscriptions, shows "profound differences" between the Northwestern and the Eastern Prakrits. Instead, he saw more abiding differences along a simple east/west axis, with the Eastern and Northwestern groups at two extremes and the Midland (= Central) group in between.

The Eastern and Midland groups share certain important innovations vis-à-vis the northwest, such as the change VCC > V:C, the northwest being in all respects more conservative. In some other matters, such as the preservation of the so-called "passive" construction of transitive verbs in the perfective, the Midland languages align themselves with the northwest (and Marathi). Chatterji finally quoted his mentor Meillet to the effect that there was almost nothing in IA that could not be explained from Vedic, and nothing indicating that there had ever been an Aryan dialect in India in ancient times "which differed from that which is represented by the Vedic except in details of secondary importance."

Further considerations (e.g., the retention of /v/ in Gujarati, Punjabi, Sindhi, and Marathi, as against its shift to /b/ in Hindi and the Eastern languages) led Chatterji to set up somewhat different subgroupings also. Rajasthani and Gujarati were put in a *Southwestern* group and the Pahari languages in a separate *Northern* group, while Punjabi was put in the *Northwestern* group. This left a *Midland* group consisting only of Western Hindi. Eastern Hindi was added to the Eastern group. Marathi with Konkani he viewed as standing alone. Sinhalese he regarded as having more affinity with Gujarati than with Marathi. Romany was brought out of Dardic and into the Northwestern group. Dardic itself was still viewed as outside IA.

The original Grierson model and the Chatterji model are compared below (Figures II.3 and II.4) using instead of a tree diagram a stylized map diagram which shows the contact relations of the main languages (taking these in Grierson's terms for convenience).

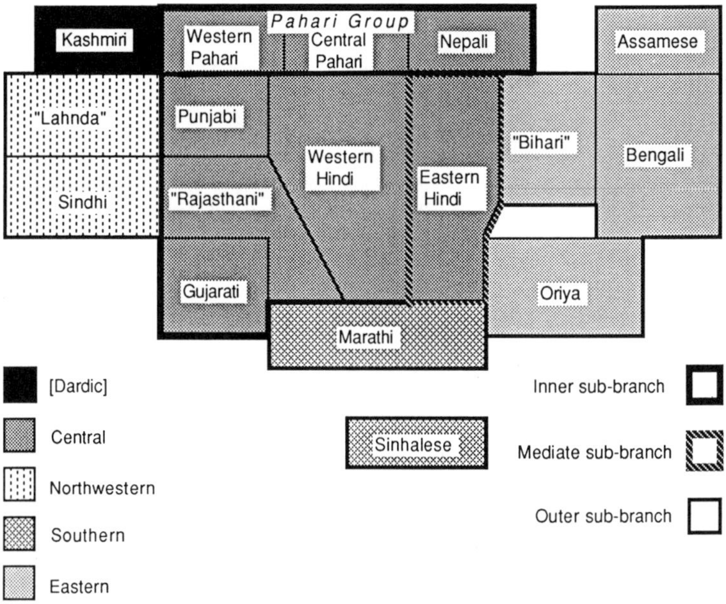

Figure II.3 NIA subclassification according to Grierson (LSI): map-diagram

Chatterji tried to trace his groupings back to early MIA or even OIA dialectal differences, attested or hypothetical. The east/west difference he saw as going back at least to the Vedic period, partly as the natural result of the greater effect of non-Aryan languages on the advancing Aryan spearhead while the Aryan of the west continued to be influenced by the neighboring and related Iranian. He too felt the need to postulate various inter-group influences within IA, especially Midland influence on Punjabi, Rajasthani, Gujarati, and

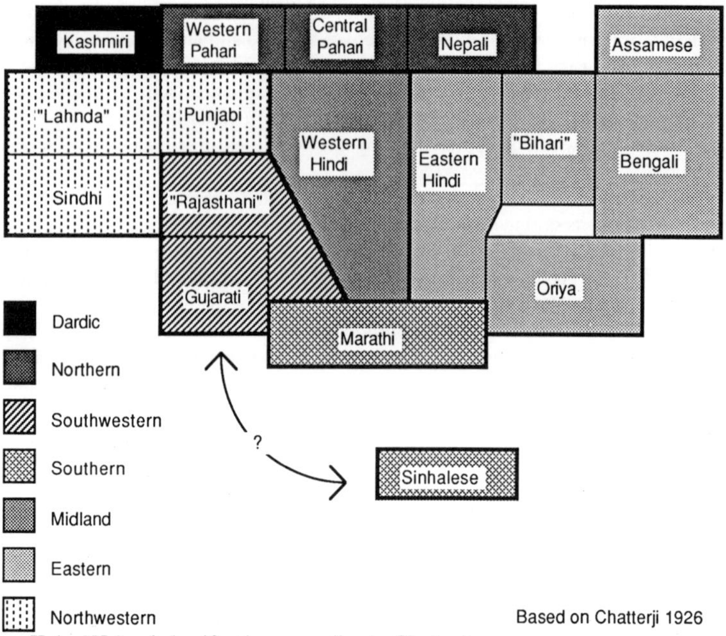

Figure II.4 NIA subclassification according to Chatterji

Eastern Hindi. He agreed with Grierson in seeing Rajasthani influence on Pahari and "Dardic" influence on (or under) the whole Northwestern group + Pahari.

Grierson was not persuaded by Chatterji's arguments. Against one of the most telling of them, namely that many of the points of agreement among so-called "Outer" languages were of modern and therefore independent origin, he mounted a surprising defense, which is worth quoting at length:

> If, for the sake of argument, we admit that every single case of agreement between the North-Western and the Southern and Eastern languages was in each case an instance of independent development, it would also have to be admitted by my critic that for so many coincidences of independent development there must have been a common cause. This I find in what may be called the hereditary tendencies of languages or of language groups. Assuming that several languages can be traced to a common stock, even though that stock contains no signs of what will be the ultimate forms developed in after years, still these languages will in the main develop on the same lines and have similar resultant forms, while other related languages, not descended from that common stock, but from some other stock related to it but not containing the same seeds of tendency, will develop on different lines . . . (Grierson: 1931 51–2)

On the subject of subgroupings Grierson was more flexible, the original subgroupings being largely a working plan (based on preliminary impressions) *for* the Linguistic Survey, not conclusions *based* on it. In a revised version of his scheme published in 1931–3, he confined the Inner or Midland branch (now equivalent terms) to Western Hindi alone. The "*Intermediate*" branch, as it was now called, was expanded to include Punjabi, Rajasthani,

Gujarati, and Pahari. Removal of these from the Central group had the merit of removing the major sources of embarrassment for "Outer" features in the "Inner" branch. It is obviously easier to defend the character of one "language" against all others. It does not, however, make it easier to defend a common origin for the others. (In the case of Hindi, Chatterji had noted, and it is worth emphasizing here, that it owed some of its character to the purely gratuitous circumstance that it had been more influenced by Persian than any other NIA language.)

Bhili and Khandeshi were now regarded as "dialects" of Gujarati and Rajasthani, respectively. (Mixed or transitional forms of speech present obvious problems for this type of classification. One way of "solving" – actually of hiding – them is to decree that such a language is a "dialect" of an already safely classified language. Khandeshi has suffered the fate of being regarded as a dialect of Marathi, of Gujarati, of Bhili, of Rajasthani, and as an independent language.) Figure II.5 shows the revised Grierson scheme.

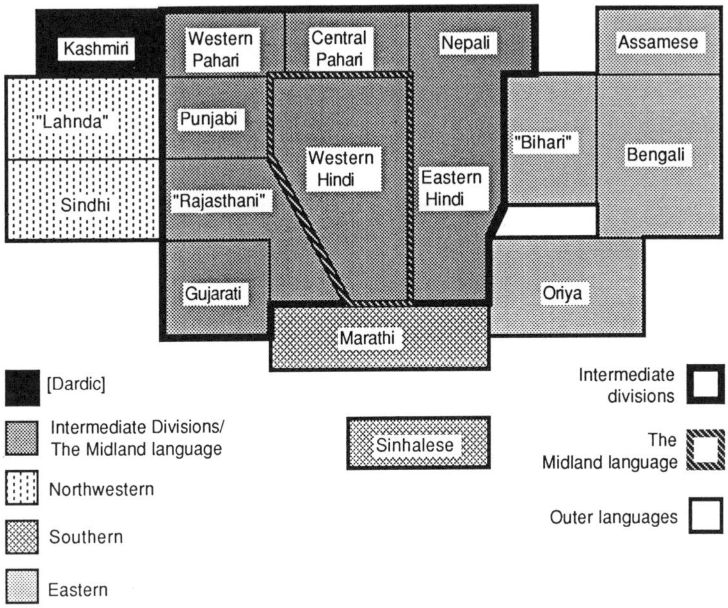

Figure II.5 Revised NIA subclassification according to Grierson 1931

Meanwhile and subsequently, other scholars have perceived somewhat different relationships. Although Turner apparently nowhere sets forth a complete classification as such, he seems to have worked out a fairly definite model in his head, the outlines of which can be pieced together (see Figure II.6) from repeated references to one or another part of it in his various articles (mostly fairly early: 1975 [1921, 1926, 1927]). It is partly based on the work of Bloch, with whom, however, he did not hesitate to differ when he felt the evidence demanded it. First of all, he brought Kashmiri and the rest of "Dardic" (although recognizing the special nature of "Kafiri") into Northwestern Indo-Aryan proper, along with Punjabi and *West* Pahari. Central and Eastern Pahari (that is, Nepali, on which he had particular expertise), however, he saw as part of an enlarged Central group, including Eastern Hindi, Rajasthani, ancestral Romany (also the object of his special investigation), and possibly "Bihari", but probably not Gujarati, on the subject of which he seems to have had difficulty making up his mind, in spite of (or perhaps because of) a detailed study devoted to it (1921). In spite of its alleged common ancestry with Rajasthani (according to Tessitori 1916 – a matter on which J. D. Smith has recently cast some doubt), there were reasons to put it with Marathi. There were likewise reasons to put Sinhalese in this Southwestern group, although in the (later) introduction to his *Comparative dictionary* (1966: xi) he expresses the conviction that it is connected "rather with the eastern languages, especially Oriya."

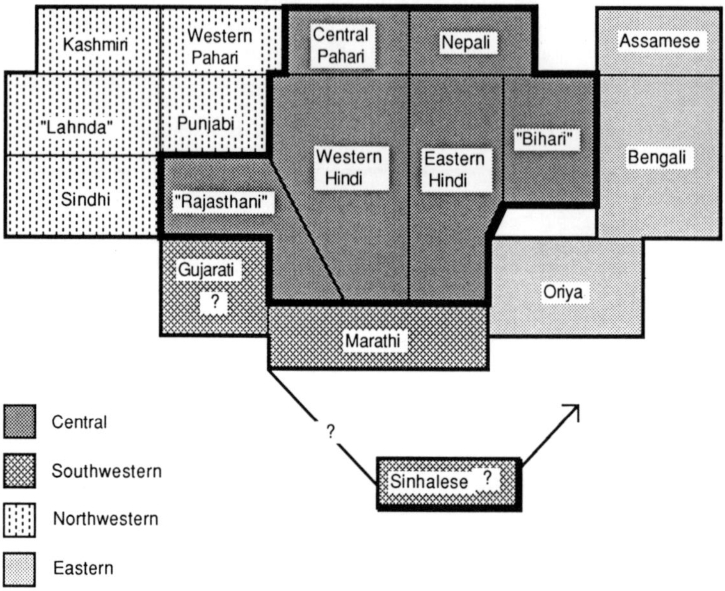

Figure II.6 NIA subclassification based on Turner

Katre 1968 (Figure II.7) expanded the Central group further to again include Gujarati, Punjabi, and West Pahari, although excluding "Bihari". He saw "Dardic" as a special *branch* of IA, including "Kafiri" as a subgroup, and Sinhalese as going with Marathi.

Cardona 1974 (Figure II.8) reattached Bihari to the central group, but again took out Gujarati to put it with Marathi and Sinhalese in a category called "Western and Southwestern groups", and Punjabi to put it in an enlarged Northwestern group including this time all of Pahari as well as "Dardic" (although recognizing the disputed position of the latter).

As a final example (more could be given), relational statements in Nigam 1972 when put together yield a classification (most easily expressed as a *Stammbaum*, Figure II.9) that among other things sees a southern group (Marathi and Sinhalese) as an offshoot of a *Proto-Central* group.

There have also been tinkerings with smaller points in the taxonomy. It is proposed, for example, that Dogri, with the closely related Kangri, belongs with West Pahari rather than Punjabi of which it had previously been considered a "dialect", and that Sadani is an offshoot of Magahi rather than of Bhojpuri (Nigam 1972).

It may seem that just about every conceivable way of carving up the NIA pile has been advocated by one scholar or another. Marathi, whose connection with the Eastern group was for Hoernle and Grierson so obvious as to hardly need comment, for others tends to be a language of "Western" or at least "Southwestern" affinity, or even (Nigam) of "Central"

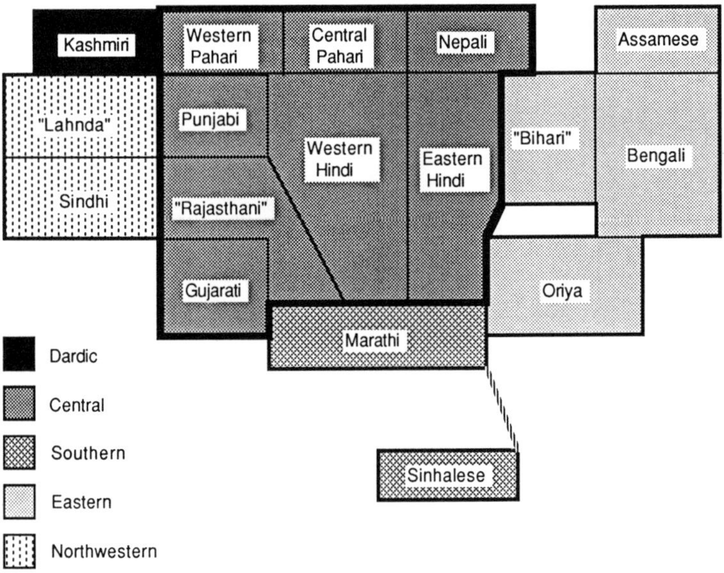

Figure II.7 NIA subclassification according to Katre

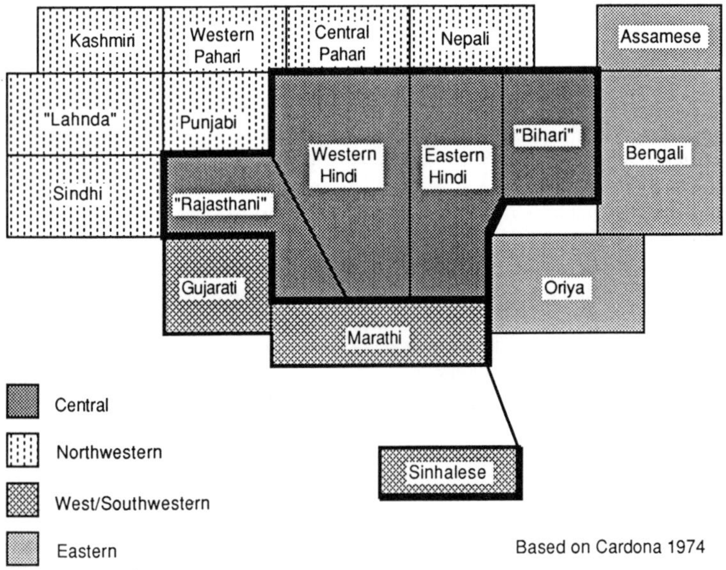

Figure II.8 NIA subclassification according to Cardona

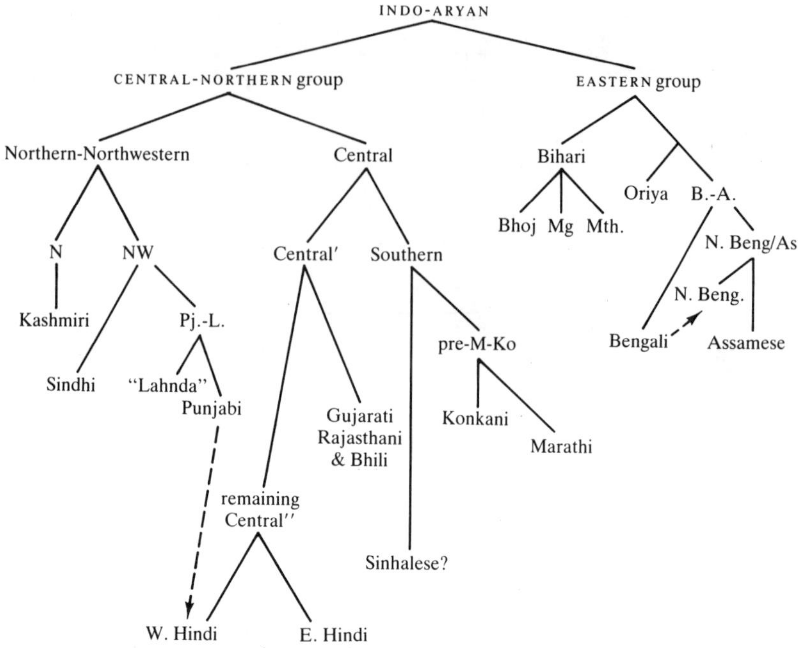

Figure II.9 NIA subclassification according to Nigam

affinity. Eastern Hindi, which was for Hoernle, Grierson, and also Chatterji not only a different language from Western Hindi but also a member of a different branch of Indo-Aryan, is put together with Western Hindi in more recent taxonomies (Turner, Katre, Nigam, Cardona, Zograph) – which at least has the merit of greater congruence with popular feelings: "Hindi" is "Hindi".

There have been, to be sure, a few constants: the "core" if not the boundaries of the peripheral Eastern and Northwestern groups have remained stable in all the classifications, that is, Bengali–Assamese–Oriya and Sindhi–"Lahnda". The problem has been with literally everything in between. It should be recalled that Grierson's controversial Inner-Outer hypothesis (which has by no means been abandoned by all scholars) rested on trying to link precisely these two extremes.

The *criteria* for these varied classifications are given in very few cases (exceptions being Turner, Bloch, and to some extent Cardona). In fairness to the scholars concerned it must be acknowledged that spelling them out would involve an amount of philological detail inappropriate to the contexts in which such overall classifications are usually presented. The fact is that criteria do exist for all the above taxonomies, and some others besides – and they conflict. One scholar is struck by the differences between Gujarati and Marathi, e.g., that Gujarati uses the Perfective suffix {*-i-*} (like Hindi and Punjabi) while Marathi uses {*-l-*} (like Oriya and Bengali), and that Gujarati forms its Future with {*-ʃ-*} (like Lahnda with {*-s-*}, while Marathi forms it with {*-l-*} (like Nepali). A second scholar may note that both languages preserve three genders, the "passive" construction of transitive verbs in the Perfective, the distinction *v*/*b*, and have /*-ḷ-*/ as the reflex of MIA /*-l-*/ and /*ch*/, progressing to /*s*/ as the reflex of OIA /*kṣ*/. A taxonomic decision thus appears to have to rest on giving priority to some criteria over others.

A non-arbitrary way of doing this might appear to lie in giving priority to phonology. The achievements of historical and comparative linguistics after all mainly rest on it elsewhere – why not in Indo-Aryan? As Turner never tired of stressing, regularities underlie even apparent exceptions to the regularity of sound change – certain classes of frequently used words, grammatical endings, etc. (P. D. Gune Memorial Lectures, 1960).

Unfortunately phonology is precisely the area where exceptions of another sort are most in evidence, namely those due to borrowing of words from other dialects. Turner himself (writing on Gujarati historical phonology) is rather pessimistic on the subject:

> The result [of the extensive mixture of dialects in India from the earliest times] has been that the sound-changes, which chiefly distinguish the modern Indo-Aryan languages from the primitive as represented more or less in the Veda, were shared in common over the greater part of the area; and even the differences, such as the varying evolution of /r̥/ or of /*kṣ*/, have been so confused by mutual borrowings of vocabulary, early as well as late, that it is in many cases well nigh impossible to unravel their history.
>
> (1921: 329)

And again:

> The early sound-changes which differentiate definite dialect areas are comparatively few, such as the varying developments of the vowel /r̥/, of /*kṣ*/, and of /r/ + dental. But the extension of words exhibiting these changes from one area to another has been so widespread that, assuming as we must that a similar degree of borrowing affected words not happening to contain these particular sounds, it is almost impossible to say which words in any particular language have been handed down in unbroken succession from generation to generation within that language. (1960: 47)

A good example of the difficulty is provided by the reflexes of Sanskrit /r̥/ and /*kṣ*/ in Marathi and Gujarati. Although it may be held that the "characteristic" developments of these in these two languages are respectively /*a*/ and /*ch* > *s*/, there are a great many words in both (but especially in Gujarati) that show the more or less pan-Indian /*i, u*/ and /*kkh* > *kh*/ instead. That is,

OIA	Marathi	Gujarati
tr̥na 'blade of grass'	*tan*	*taraṇ(u˜)*
kr̥tti 'skin, hide'	*kātḍī*	*kātṛī*
mr̥ttikā 'earth, clay'	*mātī*	*māṭī*
ghr̥ta 'ghee'	*ghī*	*ghī*
dr̥śyatē 'appears'	*disṇe˜*	*dīsvu˜*
pr̥cchati 'asks'	*pusṇe˜*	*prichvu˜*
akṣa 'axle'	*ās*	*ā˜k*
kakṣa 'grass'	*kās*	*kāchar*
ikṣu 'sugarcane'	*ūs*	*ūs*
kṣaṇa 'festival'	*·saṇ*	*khaṇ*
kṣetra 'field'	*ʃet*	*khetar*
kṣāra 'alkali'	*khār*	*khār*
kṣatra 'rule, authority'	*khate˜*	*khātu˜*
kṣōḍa 'post'	*khoḍ*	*khoṛ*
upalakṣayati 'beholds'	*oḷakhne˜* 'know'	*oḷakhvu˜*

Whatever data does not fit a particular rule must be attributed to borrowing or substratum or otherwise explained. The exceptions are typically so numerous that it is often hard to tell which cases constitute a rule and which are the exceptions. Deciding this calls for an exercise of scholarly judgment based on many considerations. It is not surprising that one scholar's rule is sometimes another scholar's exception. In the cases just given, if we decide (on the weight of other evidence) that Gujarati is basically a Southwestern language allied to Marathi, the examples showing /*r̥* > *ī*, *ri*/ and /*kṣ* > *kh*/ are exceptions due to Midland influence; if we decide it is basically a Central language, then the examples showing /*r̥*> *a*, *ā*/ and /*kṣ* > *ch*, *s*/ are the exceptions, due either to borrowing from Marathi or to a common local "substratum". Often the borrowed element (usually of Midland origin) is so massive in the standard languages that determining the underlying phonological character of a language may depend to some extent on unearthing obscure and sometimes obsolete dialectal forms.

The above example has been simplified by leaving out the MIA stage. Bringing in MIA data complicates the picture further, although it is also helpful. The "Southwestern" development of /*r̥*> *a*/ (so called because it is characteristic of the Asokan inscription at Girnar on the Kathiawar peninsula, Gujarat – the southwesternmost inscription in "Aryan" territory, the rest being in Dravidian Karnataka, skipping Maharashtra) is common also, among MIA literary languages, not only in Maharashtri but also in Pali (often thought to be of Midland origin), though not, it is true, in Sauraseni (the later Midland Prakrit), Magadhi, or the Asokan inscriptions of the northwest and east. (It is also found in Ardhamagadhi, thought to be of Eastern Midland origin, but whose texts are affected more and more by Maharashtri after the shift of the center of Jainism to Gujarat and the Deccan [Bloch 1920: 9–10].) Unfortunately, all the treatments (/*r̥*> *a*, *r̥*> *i*, *r̥*> *u*/) are found in all the MIA literary dialects to some measure, reflecting not only dialectal mixture well under way but also, as a holdover from an earlier period, exemplified by Prakritisms in Sanskrit, when the treatment was phonologically rather than geographically conditioned (/*r̥*> *i*/ before /*i*/ or in the neighborhood of a palatal consonant, /*r̥*> *u*/ before /*u*/ or in the neighborhood of a labial consonant, /*r̥*> *a*/ elsewhere).

Similarly, the "Southwestern" (also "Dardic") development of /*kṣ* > *(c)ch*/ (vs. /*kṣ* > *(k)kh*/ normally elsewhere) turns up often enough in the other MIA dialects (and thence in NIA dialects) also. Pischel (1981 [1900]: sec. 317–19) suggested some of this could be explained by differing origins of /*kṣ*/ (<IE $*k^w + s$ vs. < IE $*k' + s$) as reflected in Iranian cognates (see also Burrow 1955: 90–7) and exceptions to Sanskrit sandhi rules, but admitted the existence of many doublets in the same dialects, difficult to account for by that or any other rule (e.g., Skt *akṣi-* 'eye', Pali *akkhi*, *acchi*).

Although we are thrown back on dialectal differentiation and subsequent mixture as the best explanation for much MIA data, the precise geographical distribution of the dialects concerned, as well as their relation to later NIA, is far from clear. It is suspected that several of them shifted their location during the long MIA period itself (1,500 years): for example, that early Magadhi was located further west up the Ganges valley. Turner thought that the dialect of the Girnar inscription (third century BC) was closer to Marathi than to Gujarati, the ancestral speakers of the latter having then presumably pushed the Proto-Marathi speakers further south. (Later he may have changed his mind.) Regarding the later MIA literary dialects with specific "regional" names, Bloch pointed out that such names coexisted with names having other kinds of reference, and were first associated with groups of actors or singers (Bloch 1920: 11–12).

One thing is clear from a comparison of NIA phonological developments with MIA: NIA languages often continue dialectal lines not represented in the MIA documents (just as recorded MIA itself shows evidence of the existence of dialects not represented in either

Vedic or Classical Sanskrit – the most famous case being the resurfacing in Pali of the Indo-Iranian **idha* 'here', already reduced to *iha* in Vedic). To confine ourselves to the cases already discussed, for Skt *vr̥kṣa*, Pali has *vaccha*, the Girnar inscription *vracha*, Prakrit *vakkha*/*vaccha*/*vuccha*, but the Kochi dialect of West Pahari has *bīkh* (which cannot go back to *vakkha* with an /*a*/), while Nepali has *buk* (which cannot go back to *vuccha* with a /*cch*/).

In addition to the problems involved in establishing them, the phonological rules and dialectological isoglosses (in Kurath's terms, *heterophones*) derivable from them moreover still "conflict". This may be illustrated by superimposing several such isophones (ignoring for the moment the problems involved in establishing them for each language) on a simplified geographical grid of the type we have been using (Figure II.10).

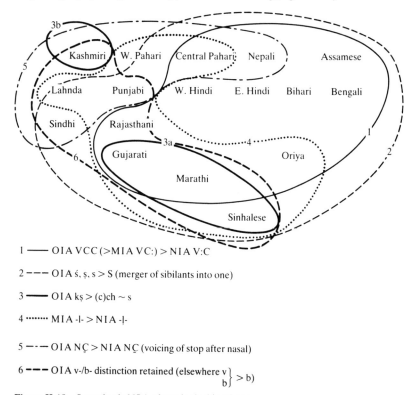

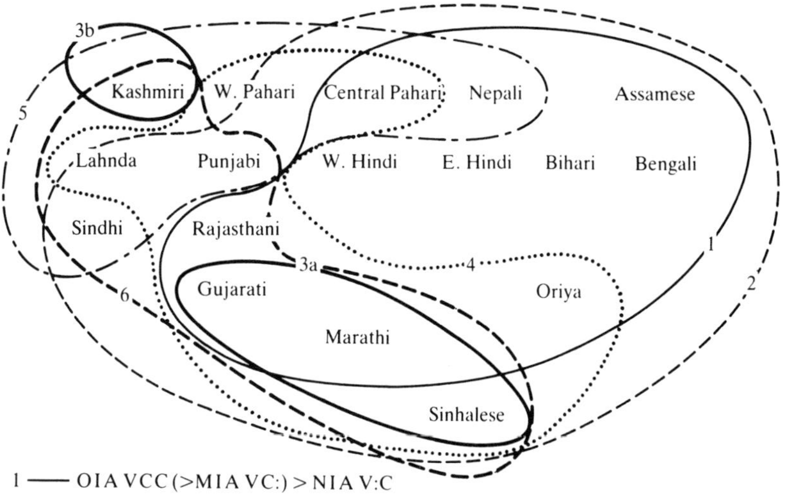

1 —— OIA VCC (>MIA VC:) > NIA V:C

2 – – – OIA ś, ṣ, s > S (merger of sibilants into one)

3 ▬▬ OIA kṣ > (c)ch ~ s

4 ········ MIA -l- > NIA -ḷ-

5 —·— OIA NC̥ > NIA NC̰ (voicing of stop after nasal)

6 ▬ ▬ ▬ OIA v-/b- distinction retained (elsewhere v, b > b)

Figure II.10 Some basic NIA phonological isoglosses

Comments on Figure II.10

1. Languages not participating in the "Central/Eastern" development VCC > V:C do not all reflect the same development. Some apparently did not pass through the "Prakrit" stage of reducing internal clusters to geminates and shortening long vowels before them. Sindhi preserves the original (OIA) vowel *length* in such cases, although reducing -CC- to -C- (except when -CC- = -C + /*r*-/). Sinhalese has reduced -CC- to -C-, but has neither lengthened the preceding vowel nor kept the original length: all such vowels are short. E.g., Skt *yātrā* 'journey'. Pkt *jattā*, but Sindhi *jāṭra*, Sinhalese *yata*.

2. The notation *ś*, *ṣ*, *s* > S refers to the reduction of the three OIA sibilants to one, irrespective of the phonetic value of the latter (*ʃ* in Magadhi) and of subsequent developments (Marathi *s* > *s*, *ʃ*) – as contrasted with the *preservation* of at least a two-way distinction in the "Dardic" and part of the West Pahari area.
3. Note that beside the "Southwestern" *kṣ* > *ch* area, there is a second and quite separate *kṣ* > *ch* area in the far northwest among the "Dardic" languages, imperfectly represented on this simplified diagram by only Kashmiri; it sometimes affects western West Pahari and northern "Lahnda" dialects also, and is thought to be the source of a few individual items that have spread further: Skt *ṛkṣa* 'bear' > P. *ricch*, H. *rīch* (vs. Garhwali–Kumauni *rīkh*, according to the usual rule).
4. In Sinhalese, /ḷ/ is written but no longer pronounced differently from /l/. In the Pahari area, /ḷ/ is reported by the *LSI* and by Bahri 1980 (who gives minimal pairs) for Kumauni but not by Apte and Pattanayak 1967; Bahri but not the *LSI* reports it for Garhwali; the *LSI* does not record it for the easternmost West Pahari languages/dialects (Jaunsari, Baghati, Sirmauri). However, the closely related *n*/*ṇ* distinction is reported for all these languages from Kumauni westward. Note that Sindhi does not have /ḷ/; it does often show /r/ in these positions however: S. *tharu* 'desert' < OIA *sthala*.
5. The voicing of voiceless stops after nasals in the northwest (and as far east as Nepali in the Himalayas) is post-Prakritic but also affected the Romany dialects.
6. The /*v* > *b*/ isophone is stated backwards for convenience, in terms of preservation rather than innovating merger. In Marwari the distinction /*v*/*b*/ is preserved as /*b*/*ɓ*/ (implosive); it appears to be lost in Eastern Rajasthani, and in most "Dardic" languages other than Kashmiri. Dogri in this respect goes with West Pahari (which experienced the merger) and not with Punjabi (which retains the distinction).

In view of these conflicting data it is small wonder that many have turned to morphological and other criteria. Unfortunately morphological criteria conflict just as much as phonological criteria. We can set up a rigid taxonomy only at the price of ignoring some criteria.

Perhaps a wiser course would be to recognize a number of *overlapping genetic zones*, each defined by specific criteria. Such may in fact be what Turner has had in mind in his use of regional labels rather than any absolute taxonomy. Some zones would indeed be more strongly defined than others, but the mixed dialectal ancestry of most NIA languages (even apart from external, non-Aryan influences) would at least be clear.

We might therefore be well-advised to give up as vain the quest for a final and "correct" NIA historical taxonomy, which no amount of tinkering can achieve, and concentrate instead on working out the history of various features, letting such feature-specific historical groupings emerge as they may, with their overall non-coincidence as testimonial to the complexity of the situation.

Meanwhile, all should be aware of the fact that despite the authoritative position which the *LSI* continues to hold, its classifications, and the data on which they are based, are hardly the last word on the subject. With regard to phonology in particular, the material left much to be desired, as Grierson was the first to admit. The science of phonetics was in its infancy when the Survey started, and in any case the collectors of the material in the field were not trained phoneticians. Although gramophone records were collected toward the end of the Survey as an enterprising afterthought, the analysis rested not on them but on written materials using the imperfect transcriptions available through various local alphabets or their standard government transliterations. Finally, there was no awareness of phonemic principles, nor was there enough material collected to permit their later application.

Although what was achieved within these limitations is remarkable, one of the deficiencies of subsequent attempts at overall taxonomies has been the tendency to accept the conclusions of the *LSI* without rechecking them, particularly regarding aspects of the subject with which the writer is not well-acquainted personally. A few recent specialized studies have brought this out. For example, Grierson put "Bihari" in the Eastern group with Bengali, and almost no one ventured to question this (except Cardona) until Jeffers (1976) established conclusively that there are no *phonological grounds* for such an assignment. More startlingly, Učida plausibly suggests that "Kauravi" (="Vernacular Hindostani"), on which Modern Standard Hindi and Urdu are mainly based, is (along with Hariyanvi) not a "Hindi" dialect at all, but a "Punjabi" dialect. At least, that is one way of looking at the data: i.e. where Braj and Awadhi have a true "Hindi" form, such as *mākhan* 'butter' (with V:C), Standard Hindi and Urdu often prefer a "Punjabi" form, *makkhan* (with VCC), as do Kauravi and Hariyanvi.

Even less should Grierson's tentative classification be taken as the last word on the "Dardic" question. These languages of the difficult mountain country between Kashmir and Afghanistan were very imperfectly known in Grierson's time, and much has been learned about them since. There is no question that they contain much of interest for linguistic science both in the way of archaic survivals and peculiar local developments. The question is, are they Indo-Aryan or something else?

Grierson's view (now definitely obsolete, and incorrect also in its details, but unfortunately often still given in works of reference) was that the group as a whole was something else, namely an independent branch of Indo-Iranian (if anything, slightly inclined toward Iranian: *LSI 1.1*: 100). He saw it as consisting of three subgroups: "Kafiri", "Central" (=Khowar), and "Dard proper". Khowar was allegedly aberrant and represented a later intrusion from the Pamirs across the Hindu Kush. Inconsistently, he also saw his "Outer" IA languages as having some affinity with "Dardic" – going so far as to say "if they are not

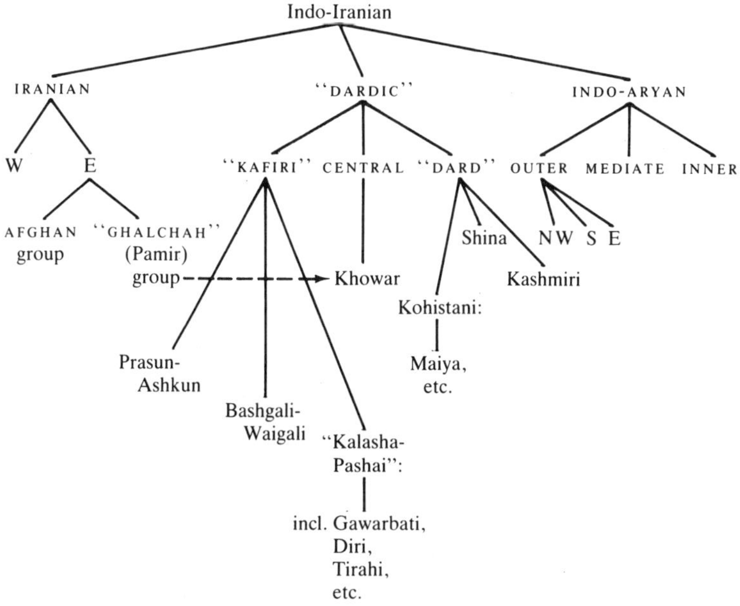

Figure II.11 "Dardic", according to Grierson

one and the same thing". At another point he tried to connect "Dardic" with the Paiśācī Prakrit. Except for these latter speculations, Grierson's classification may be represented by Figure II.11 for comparative purposes.

In reaction to this, Morgenstierne (1926) at first maintained that the group as a whole was a branch of Indo-Aryan, chiefly on the basis of vocabulary, in which it almost always agrees with Indo-Aryan rather than Iranian when the two differ. Its apparent agreements with Iranian were archaisms preserved from a period when Indo-Aryan and Iranian differed very little, or later borrowings, or independent developments. The latter would include the loss of the voiced aspirates in Iranian and "Dardic" – where, however, it is not everywhere complete (e.g., in Pashai). Later, after a lifetime of study, Morgenstierne considerably modified this view: the "Kafiri" subgroup alone (differently constituted from Grierson's, that is, not including Kalasha or Pashai) was indeed an independent branch of Indo-Iranian. The remainder (for which the term *Dardic* is now reserved) were purely Indo-Aryan languages of the Northwestern type, without any common defining feature, although preserving archaic features in varying degrees due to their isolation from MIA developments.

This view is now the one generally accepted by most close students of this special field (Fussman, Strand, Buddruss). Among the archaisms preserved in the Dardic area are OIA clusters such as *st*, *str*, *śr*, *br*, *rt* (e.g. in Khowar) and lexical items such as *aśva* (Shina *aſp*) which have been replaced elsewhere in NIA. The crux of the "Kafiri" (Nuristani) matter is the preservation of a distinction between IE $*g'/*g^w$ before front vowels (as Nur. *dz/j*, vs. IA *j*), and of a more archaic form of IE $*k'$ (as *ts*, vs. IA *ś*). Figure II.12 below is based on Strand 1973. More recent affirmations of this consensus are Buddruss 1977 and Nelson 1986.

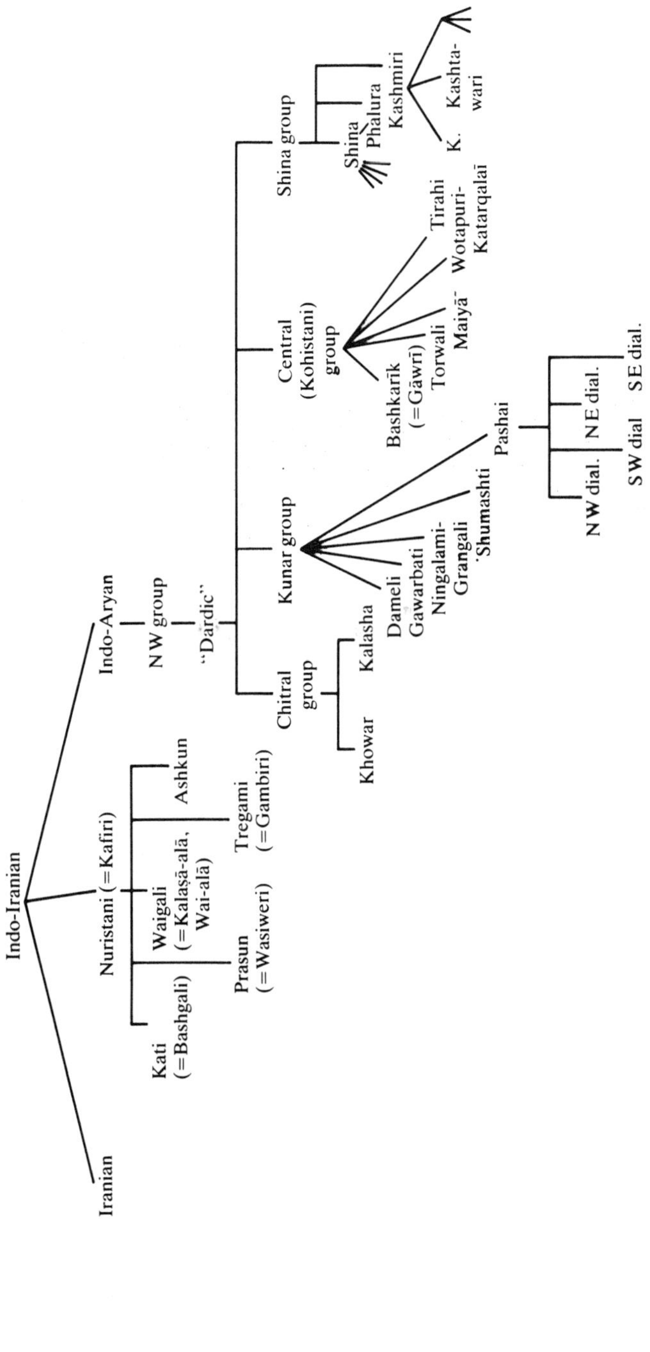

Figure II.12 Nuristani and "Dardic", according to Strand

NOTES

1. Introduction

1. On Indian English, see Vermeer 1969a and B. Kachru 1983.
2. Their impact is particularly felt in the realm of the printed word. India has emerged as a major world center for publishing in English.
3. This figure, which includes those knowing English only as a second language (the figure for native speakers of English is an infinitesimal 0.054 per cent) is taken from Schwarzberg (1978: 102, 235–6), which in turn is based on various census data. The range is from 0.1 per cent in Nepal to 8.0 per cent in Sri Lanka, with the highest local unit figure being 16.4 per cent in the Union Territory of Delhi, where highly educated professionals are concentrated. Bombay, Calcutta, and Madras do not constitute comparable political units, but the percentages there are no doubt also high. Among states in the Indian Union, the percentage is highest (4.3 per cent) in West Bengal. These figures are somewhat dated, and several factors are involved in the current sociolinguistic dynamics. On the one hand, the "decline" of English competence, especially in the Hindi-using north, is often lamented. On the other hand, the huge middle class is sparing no effort to see that its children acquire English (which is seen as the key to social and economic advancement), preferably through private English-medium education. Institutions of varying quality have sprouted like mushrooms across the land (although primarily in cities) to cater to the latter demand. The net effect of all this may be a diluted but wider diffusion of English, albeit still not affecting the masses of peasants and workers, or even certain rural elites.
4. That is, areas corresponding geographically to southern Vietnam, the center of the early Indianized kingdom known to the Chinese as *Funan*, later part of Greater Cambodia (until the seventeenth century), and to central Vietnam about Hue and Quang-nam, the center of the kingdom of Champa (Coedès 1966, 1968). The Vietnamese themselves, who stem originally from the Red River delta region in northern Vietnam, were never in the orbit of Indic civilization. The definitive Vietnamese move into the previously Indianized south did not come until the seventeenth century. On the other hand, Sanskrit loanwords in Philippine languages (e.g., Tagalog *guru* 'teacher') show that ripples of Indic influence went beyond Indonesia to reach even those islands. Scripts of Indic origin were once in use throughout Southeast Asia (except by the Vietnamese), including to a limited extent the southern Philippines. They still are in use in Laos, Cambodia, Thailand, and Burma.
5. See Mukherjee 1968: 91–6.
6. Republished by George Allen & Unwin, 1970.
7. E.g., on Assamese by B. Kakati (1962) and on Maithili by Subhadra Jha (1958). After Uday Narayan Tiwari's *hindī bhāṣā kā udgam aur vikās* = 'The origin and development of the Hindi language' (1961), there are numerous derivative titles in Hindi dealing with the regional languages of the Hindi area.
8. For an idea of the gradual unfolding of the understanding of Panini abroad, see Staal (ed.) 1972 and Cardona 1976.
9. This is to be sure an oversimplification. For details, see Irawati Karve 1965. The point is that "southern", that is, Dravidian, modes of marriage and kinship, which permit or even favor marriages with cross-cousins, are found also in the southern Indo-Aryan-speaking zone, i.e. Maharashtra. Village exogamy is the rule on the northern plains, and weakens as one moves away from that area.
10. For discussion of Trinidad Bhojpuri in terms of "*language death*", see Mohan 1978 and Mohan and Zador 1986.

11. For perhaps the best recent account of the Gypsies available in English, see Jean-Paul Clébert 1967 (French original 1961). Better from a philological point of view is Bloch 1953.
12. Despite the preference of the government of Sri Lanka for "Sinhala", and the policy of the Central Institute of Indian Languages, Mysore, for use of the "native name" of each language, the present author prefers to use the established English name where such exists and is not offensive, rather than "Bangla", "Sinhala", etc. We do not speak of Français, Deutsch, or Italiano. It might indeed almost be taken as a mark of status for a language to have an established name in English. The "native name" policy is difficult to apply consistently, particularly where alien sounds are involved, and it is in fact not applied consistently. Thus the "native name" of Assamese is [*ɔχɔmi*], not [*asāmī*] – although the latter will do in *Hindi*. Similarly the advocates of the policy do not ordinarily refer to Kashmiri as [*kə̄shur*] or for that matter to Tamil as [*tamiR̲*] (using the peculiar retroflex consonant of that language). Moreover, the usual spelling of the native name, without diacritical marks, may result in its mispronunciation: the Sinhalese name for their language is [*ˈsiŋhaɭa*] not *[*ˈsin-hala*] or *[*sin-ˈha:la*].

    On the other hand, if a common term is in fact a derogatory nickname, as is the case with certain previously current tribal names, or is otherwise offensive to the speakers of the language(s), as in the case of "Kafiri" (see Chapter 2), a change is in order.

    Each case should be judged individually. Elsewhere in the South Asian context, Kannada seems to have established itself, albeit shorn of its Dravidian retroflexion, in place of the older (and misleading, because of the implied reference to Kanara District) Kanarese; perhaps Sinhala, mispronunciation and all, will eventually do the same. We no longer call, e.g., Telugu "Gentoo", as English-speakers did in the eighteenth century, although some persist in spelling it "*Telegu".
13. For Sinhalese diglossia see Gair 1960, 1986a.
14. The interested reader might start with Burrow 1955.

2. The modern Indo-Aryan languages and dialects

1. Shackle (1979: 195) notes that Grierson was not the first to use the term: Tisdall had used it before him in his *Simplified grammar and reading book of the Panjabi language* (1889), Appendix C, "Notes on the Lahinda Dialect", albeit not quite in the same sense. The latter writes that the term applies, according to "the Granthis [Sikh scholars] of Amritsar", primarily to the dialects *north of the Ravi* – which would exclude "Multani" but include under "Lahinda" Wazirabadi and other dialects of Central Punjab that Shackle and others consider definitely "Punjabi".
2. See Shackle 1977a for an account of the Siraiki language movement.
3. The extent of academic confusion in this area may be gauged by the ethnolinguistic map. *Peoples of South Asia*, published by the National Geographic Society in Washington in December 1984. It shows the dialects *west* of Kashmiri (i.e. in Azad Kashmir) as "West Pahari".
4. It is not clear where Professor Bahri gets these figures. They would seem to be impressionistic. The Braj Bhasha/Bundeli figure of only "50–75 per cent" mutual intelligibility is particularly odd since according to Grierson and Bahri himself (1980: p. 92) these two are almost the same.
5. I use the word *terminology* here to get around the special case of U. *wālid*/*wālidā* for 'father/mother' (vs. H. *pitā*/*mātā*). Basic kinship terms may be part of core vocabulary according to some formulations, but these particular terms belong to the realm of special cultural terminology – and are borrowed items.
6. This writer for one suspects that Persian and even Turkish would also turn out to be

components of that mixture (in areas other than merely vocabulary) if it were properly investigated.

7. It is worth recording that Narula (1955: 66–7, 77) disputes this, claiming that the role of Khari Boli is in fact due to the official status accorded to Urdu later by the British, and that, in effect, the "language of the capital" (Delhi) had *not* become the standard for the Hindi area before the promulgation of Modern Standard Hindi – as shown by the fact that, for example, "Sur Das and Tulsi did not have any commonly evolved colloquial language for this whole area to serve as their medium . . . *Sur Sagar* and *Ram Charit Manas* could not, therefore, perform a function in the evolution of a common language for the whole of northern India, as was done by Luther's Bible."
8. A truncation of the earlier *zabān-e-urdū-e-muallā* 'language of the Exalted Camp' – *urdū* meaning 'camp' and referring to the imperial bazaar.
9. This honor is generally given to the poet Mashafi ([sic] Tiwari 1961: 207, Rai 1984: 33; according to my colleague C. M. Naim and also Muhammad Sadiq, the name should be ***Mus-hafi***). Dates for the couplet in question range from 1776 to 1800. Worth noting is the fact that even Mus-hafi "calls his chronicle of Urdu poets by the name Tazkira-i-*Hindi*" (Rai 1984: 178).

3. The historical context and development of Indo-Aryan

1. Often called Satem; opposed to Centum. The initial *s-* vs. *k-* of these words for 'hundred' in Avestan and Latin respectively made them convenient tags for the languages which changed the *IE palatals (or palato-velars) into sibilants vs. those which retained them. This overall division is no longer considered quite as fundamental as was once the case.
2. The reconstructed *IE series **k^*, **g^*, **gh^* is variously named in the literature: Burrow (1955), following Brugmann (1886), is content with *palatal*; another school, which includes Meillet (1922) and Bloch (1965), prefers *prepalatal*, probably to distinguish it from the Sanskrit palatal series *c*, *ch*, *j*, *jh*; Hudson-Williams (1935) even has *front palatal*. From a phonetic point of view the latter term seems ill-chosen, in that **k^* would seem to have been further back than *c*, not further forward. Entwhistle and Morison (1949) refer to it as *postpalatal*. (Perhaps either *pre-* or *post-* could mean "further back" – depending on which way we are going.) Since the sounds in question are now thought to have been in complementary distribution with (plain) *velars*, the term *palatovelars* (opposed to the other reconstructed series, the *labiovelars*), might be most appropriate. Chatterji (1960: 27) calls them simply *velars* "(or so-called 'palatals')".
3. The palatalization and ultimate assibilation of [*k*] before front vowels represents a general tendency, amply attested in non-IE languages, which manifested itself eventually in many Centum languages also, most obviously in the Romance group (Latin *cocina* /*kokīna*/ > Italian *cucina* /*kučina*/, Amer. Spanish *cocina* /*kosina*/), but also elsewhere (cf. the evolution of the same word as a loan in Germanic: German *Küche* /*kyχə*/, Swedish *kök* /*cœk*/, Old Eng. *cycene* /*kykene*/ > Mod. Eng. *kitchen*). The *timing* of this change is accordingly an important consideration. (See Bynon 1977: 28, 219–22.) Generally original labiovelars have been slower to share this fate (see Allen 1958): if the labial element was lost, at least the velar was safeguarded, except in Romanian (Latin *quis* /*kwis* 'who' > Fr. *qui*, It. *chi* /*ki*/, but Romanian *cine* /*čine*/; Lat. *quinque* / *kwinkwe*/, Vulg. Lat. *cinque* /*kinkwe* 'five' > It. *cinque* /*činkwe*/, Amer. Sp. *cinco* /*sinko*/, but Romanian *cinci* /*činč*/). Another exception is Greek (see Allen 1958). In Indo-Aryan later palatalization of velars is rare.
4. It shares them also with Armenian, but that language has in other respects been so much influenced by its Caucasian neighbors that it presents on the whole a very different appearance.

5. See Burrow 1955 for the best short discussion of all these points.
6. According to Collinder (1965: 29), Indo-Iranian loanwords common to Finno-Ugrian "were probably supplied by the Scythians who lived north of the Black Sea." Historically this is not impossible since the Scythian presence is attested from the ninth century BC – long before the movement of the Finns northwestward into Finland (which occurred about the beginning of the Christian era). However, according to Burrow (1955: 25) it is not possible phonologically: the loanwords show none of the sound changes (e.g. *ś* > *s*, *s* > *h*) that are characteristic of Iranian. (Note: Gamkrelidze and Ivanoff [1984: 921], however, claim that the words are Iranian.)
7. This displacement is associated with the appearance of the Grey Ware culture and the spread into Iran of the allegedly Proto-Indo-European Kurgan culture, according to Gimbutas, who has adopted a higher chronology on the basis of C-14 reckonings. Previously she had dated her Middle Kurgan, corresponding to these developments, around 3000–2200 BC.
8. The theories of the Maharashtrian polymath (and nationalist hero) B. G. Tilak (1893, 1903) that the *Vedas* themselves (along with the *Avesta*) contain forgotten references, not only to an earlier home, but to the Ice Age itself ("the oldest traditional record preserved by human memory") – albeit mythologized to an extent where their meaning was not intelligible – do not constitute an exception to this, since they do not represent a living cultural memory, but a previously unheard of interpretation, very much at variance with Indian tradition, as Tilak himself was fully aware. Whatever we may think of them, Tilak's arguments were thoroughly modern, and bristle with astronomical, geological, and philological data. He asked himself (1903: 7–8) "why the real meaning [of the passages in question] should have remained so long hidden," and attributed his present ability to discern that meaning solely to recent scientific progress.
9. See Masica 1979 for further details.
10. In most of this I follow Mayrhofer 1956–72. The reader is cautioned that Mayrhofer's revised edition is now beginning to appear.
11. There is some dispute about the etymology of *mayūra* (Tamil *mayil*, Tulu *mairu̥*), since the name could conceivably come from the peacock's characteristic loud cat-like cry.
12. Apart from speculations linking it with everything from Japanese and Korean on the one hand to the languages of Senegal in West Africa on the other, there have been two serious proposals regarding the extra-Indian relationship of Dravidian which merit attention here. McAlpin (1974, 1975, 1979) has tried to connect it with the extinct Elamite language of southwestern Iran. Persistent hypotheses of a relationship with Uralic (Caldwell 1961 [1856], Schrader 1925, Burrow 1944, Tyler 1968) have been greatly advanced by the full length study of Marlow (1974), which systematically examined 786 etyma and attempted to set up phonological correspondences. The Munda link with Mon-Khmer to constitute Austroasiatic, however, is more generally regarded as established.
13. The term "Kolarian" was invented by Sir George Campbell in 1866. It was favored by S. K. Chatterji (1926: 2, fn. 1) and others who objected that the term "Munda" properly refers to only one tribal group (the Mundari speakers). Grierson counterobjected that: (1) the term "Kolarian", insofar as it is derived from a term "Kol" used by Hindus to denote certain North Munda peoples as well as the Dravidian-speaking Oraons, is also overspecific and at the same time overgeneral; (2) despite a possible connection with Munda words for 'man', it also has insulting connotations, denoting 'pig' in Sanskrit; (3) the stem "Kolar-" rests on a mistaken identification with the Kolar goldfields in South India, or with a Kannada word *kaḷḷar* 'thieves' – mistaken and insulting at the same time; (4) in any case, after the fashion in botany, the term proposed by the original

"discoverer" – in this case Max Müller in 1854 – should by scientific courtesy be allowed to stand. As usual, Grierson's view prevailed, even in Hindi, where (as in other Indian languages) a third alternative exists, namely *niṣād(a)*. This goes back at least to the *Valmiki Ramayana*, where (*Ayodhyakanda* 50: 33ff) is described Rama's encounter with Guha, who helps him cross the Ganges. The latter is styled *niṣād-ādhipatiḥ* 'the Nishada chief', *nisādajātyo balvān sthapitiḥ* 'mighty lord of the Nishada race', and *tatra rājā* 'king of that place'. The *Manak Hindi Kos, v. 3*: 301 defined *niṣād* as: "(1) an ancient non-Aryan forest people . . .; (2) an ancient country near Sringaberapura [on the north bank of the Ganges near Allahabad]; the Nishadas are taken to be the original inhabitants of this same country and their language is reckoned among the Munda languages; (3) a lowcaste person; (4) an individual born of a Shudra mother and a Brahman father." All this together suggests that: (1) in Valmiki's time Munda-speaking peoples were found *north* of the Ganges in what is now UP; (2) they were probably absorbed into the lower strata of Hindu society in the same area, with the usual genealogical rationalizations. The term "Nishada" is sometimes used by Indians writing in English, in an ethnographic or cultural historical sense; it does not seem to have found favor with linguists, however.

According to Kakati (1962: 26–41) the specifically Khasi element in Assamese, while present (a couple of dozen lexical items are cited) is less prominent than another Austroasiatic element with closer affinity to Munda. The latter presumably entered the language "in its formative period" further to the west of its present center, that is, in what is now northern Bengal, when "Kol" tribes also inhabited that region. There is a further "Austric" element not further identifiable except by analogies in Mon-Khmer languages and Malay (possibly borrowed from Mon-Khmer, i.e. from the indigenous Semang of the Malay peninsula). Most of these words are not found in Bengali, he notes, and "Assamese seems to have been foisted on an Austric-speaking people."

15. The inaccessibility of these areas is vividly described by Morgenstierne (1932 et al.). They are often to be reached only by narrow paths along deep gorges rendered impassable by winter ice, which moreover cross and recross the stream below by rickety pole bridges frequently swept away by spring floods.
16. Important figures after 1000 AD include the poets Bilhana and Jayadeva (*Gīta Govinda*), the "novelist" Somadeva (*Kathāsaritsāgara*), the historian Kalhana (*Rājataraṅgiṇī*), and the grammarian Hemacandra. Warder (1975: 193) states that "about 90% of extant Sanskrit literature belongs to the periods since 1200 and was written in the regions remaining under Indian [i.e. Hindu] rule." This is partly no doubt a historical accident: much of the previous literature was destroyed by the Turks. Nevertheless a whole genre, the mixed prose and verse *campū*, belongs mainly to this period.
17. Traugott (1972: 113) calls attention to an example of this from the history of English: "most direct Scandinavian influence ceased with the death of King Canute in 1042; nevertheless [Scandinavian loans] are largely not attested until the twelfth century."

4. The nature of the New Indo-Aryan lexicon

1. For an important study of one example of early (*c.* 1600) Braj prose, see R. S. McGregor 1968.
2. The form *pomma* also exists, in Maharashtri and Ardhamagadhi, but as a later special development from *pauma: au* > *o* + *-m-* > *-mm-*. See Pischel 1981 (1900): sections 166, 195.
3. With the exception of Maldivian.
4. A similar lexical split may be developing in Sindhi, as emigrant Hindu Sindhis in India replace abstract and technical words of Perso-Arabic origin with Tss. Recent develop-

ments (for example, in the matter of script) indicate a concern to preserve the unity of the language, however.

5. The standard work on the subject is still Soares 1936, *Portuguese vocables in Asiatic languages*, an augmented translation of a Portuguese original by Msgr. Sebastião Rodolfo Dalgado (an Indian, native to Goa), Lisbon 1913. There have been supplemental studies of the Portuguese element in Sinhalese by Hettiaratchi (1965, 1968).
6. The only exception known to the writer is the attempt of Osmania University, Hyderabad (Deccan), to teach them through Urdu from its inception in 1918 (an experiment terminated in 1948). However the terminology problem was solved there, it had no connection with Neo-Sanskrit terminology-building. More relevant may have been the popular encyclopaedias published in Marathi, and some of the educational activities of the Arya Samaj in Hindi.

5. NIA descriptive phonology

1. The Arabic letters in question are ث , ح , ذ , ص, ض, ط, ظ, and ع. These are usually transliterated *th* (=θ), *h*, *dh* (=$\eth$), *ṣ*, *ḍ*, *ṭ*, *ẓ*, ᶜ, but in the South Asian context the use of subscript dots for the (originally) pharyngealized consonants conflicts with their use for *retroflex* consonants (it is a curious fact that the two series almost never occur in the same language), while "th" and "dh" represent aspirates rather than dental fricatives. In Urdu (as in Persian) these letters are pronounced as follows: TH = [*s*], Ḥ = [*h*], DH = [*z*], Ṣ = [*s*], Ḍ = [*z*], Ṭ = [*t*], Ẓ = [*z*], ᶜ = (usually ignored).
2. Although in some systems the symbol for the [*ts*] sound is *c*, the confusion entailed by using this symbol cross-linguistically in the Indo-Aryan field, where *c* customarily represents *č*, will be apparent. Nevertheless in works devoted to single languages, it will sometimes be found so used, e.g., in Berntsen and Nimbkar's *Marathi reference grammar*, the reason no doubt being that *most* orthographic *c*'s become [*ts*] in Marathi. Lambert 1943 uses *ts*, however. Bloch 1920 and Turner 1966–71 use *ċ*, which may be best, in that it conveys the notion of a unit phoneme rather than of a cluster.
3. These examples are cited as the authors, who subscribe to a qualitative rather than a quantitative analysis of the Hindi vowels, give them. In the transcription used in most of this book, they would be *māŋnā*, *mānnā*, *māngnā*; *paŋkhī*, *kankhī*, *pangkhī*.
4. Bloch (1965: 73) is mistaken on this point.
5. I am puzzled by the assertion sometimes made that it is also reflected in the general use of the letter Ś to write /s/ in the Kaithi script used until recently in Bihar, because the very examples that are supposed to illustrate this (e.g., *LSI 5.2*: 123–5, 129, 133, 135) do not in fact do so.
6. The Rajasthani opposition is supported by Allen 1957a, b, Lalas 1962, and Bahl 1980. It is disputed for Marwari by Magier 1983: 30–3, who maintains that even if there are two *h*'s phonetically (which he doubts) the "voiceless" one would be an allophone of /s/ (as in Sanskrit: see Chapter 7), not a separate phoneme. This might be true of the northwestern dialect described by Allen 1957b, where *c has developed only as far as [*ts*], but in the Southern Mewari case a "new" *s* has arisen from *c, *ch*, and the situation may be different. On the question of phonetic difference, I recall Peter Ladefoged attempting to test for it in India some twenty years ago (using, I believe, palatography) on a Marwari speaker who claimed to make (and hear) two distinct *h*-sounds, but I am not sure what conclusion was reached. The Gujarati cases (Pandit 1954: 44; Vyas 1974: 135, 142, 147), along with the related Bhili cases, need more study.
7. According to Allen (1983) they are also similar to those of Classical Arabic.
8. A handful of final clusters do occur, generally involving radicals ending in *r* + C: *ūrk* 'strength'. They have themselves been simplified from -*r*CC forms dictated by the grammar. For further discussion, see Chapter 7.

9. This may appear to contradict what was just said regarding final clusters in Sanskrit, but the clusters in question were not final in Sanskrit, only becoming so in NIA *tatsamas* with loss of a final vowel or syllable, e.g., Skt *kaṣṭa(m)* > H. *kaṣṭ*.
10. For example, that described by Magier (1983), which maintains a distinction between /*b*/, /*v*/, and /*ɓ*/. In a variety described by Allen, **v* is represented by [*b*], while **b* is represented by [ɓ].

6. Writing systems

1. Raykar's script combines certain characteristics of the Kannada and Nagari scripts (e.g., cursive shapes, but suspended from a straight top line) with several unique features (e.g., vowel *matras* placed only above or to the right of the consonant, never below or to the left). Raykar was a commercial artist living in Sirsi, a town in North Kanara District (Karnataka State), one of the Konkani strongholds outside of Goa.
2. E.g., with you = Nepali *tapāī̃-sa˜ga* तपाईंसँग, Marathi *tumcyā-barobar* तुम्च्याबरोबर; but Hindi *āp ke sāth* आप के साथ (One syllable postpositions are commonly written attached to *pronouns* in Hindi also: 'from/by that one' = *us-se* उससे. *āp* 'You [hon.]' does not behave like a pronoun.)
3. In alphabets which include retroflex Ḷ, this follows H in Marathi, Gujarati, and Sinhalese, but in Oriya it precedes ordinary L. The Gurmukhi order is different at the beginning: (U, Ū), O, A, (Ā, AI, AU), I, (Ī, E), S, H then K, KH, G . . . as usual. Items in parentheses are not considered separate letters, but are alphabetized (e.g., in dictionaries) in that order under O, A, I.
4. There is some inconsistency about writing Oriya Ṛ (Karpushkin 1964: 15): e.g., the name of the language itself = OṚIĀ/OḌIĀ.
5. A murmured segment is recognized here following Cardona 1965. (He transcribes it *mahro*.)
6. To be sure, the Brahmi-descended Shāradā and Lāṇḍā scripts were used to write Kashmiri and Sindhi (also Multani) respectively, which have their share of exotic sounds. From Grierson's *LSI* account, it would appear that in the various mercantile scripts of Laṇḍā type used in Sind, the distinctive Sindhi implosives were written with the symbol originally standing for the voiced plosive, while the ordinary voiced and aspirate voiced plosives (*g*/*gh*, etc.) were both written with another set of symbols and not clearly distinguished from one another, As will be seen this situation is similar to that involving the employment of Nagari for writing Rajasthani.

7. Historical phonology

1. More stress is laid on the existence of other OIA dialects by Chatterji and by Burrow than by other scholars. Turner goes so far as to declare (*CDIAL* ix) that "the phonetic systems of nearly all the New Indo-Aryan languages are descended directly from that of the Ṛgveda with one exception [the Kafiri retention of the Indo-European palatals as dental affricates]." On the other hand the need for so many postulated alternative forms in the *CDIAL* itself would seem to suggest that, for some matters of detail at least, the recorded tradition is not enough.
2. Dating even the received texts of the epics is fraught with problems, since the *Mahābhārata* especially was in the process of composition over a long period. Van Buitenen and others give 400 BC to 400 AD as the probable limits of this. The *Rāmāyaṇa* is usually put within a narrower frame, *c.* 200 BC–200 AD, but the latest opinion on the subject, Goldman 1985, places it much earlier, back to the sixth or possibly the seventh century BC. The important point for us here is that Epic Sanskrit is linguistically post-

Vedic but pre-Classical – although (for most authorities at least) post-Paninian. See Burrow 1955: 51–3. According to Sen (1960–5), Epic Sanskrit represents Sanskritized MIA rather than irregular OIA.

3. Eric P. Hamp (personal communication).
4. The existence of the so-called "independent" *svarita* does not materially affect this argument.
5. It does not, of course, explain the presence of the long vowels *ī*, *ū* in the first column and of *ā* in the first and second columns of Table 7.1, which I have avoided in the illustration. These are "original" long vowels, due to the presence of a following laryngeal (**a*H, **e*H, **o*H, **i*H, **u*H) in Indo-European rather than to the processes under discussion here; they nevertheless may be made to fit the scheme also. For further details see Burrow 1955: 109–10.
6. "Prakritic" is placed in double quotes because Sir George Grierson was undoubtedly right in insisting that "Prakrit" really means only the language in its "natural" or vernacular state (as opposed to Sanskrit or "cultivated" speech), be it OIA ("Primary Prakrits"), MIA ("Secondary Prakrits"), or NIA ("Tertiary Prakrits"). Nevertheless, the terms "Prakrit" and "Prakritic" have come to be primarily associated with MIA, and particularly with the mainstream Central–Eastern–Southern developments about to be described. They are also used, however, for contemporary forms of Indo-Aryan outside that areal focus, e.g., in the northwest or in Sri Lanka. More narrowly, "Prakrit" refers to the literary languages of the Second Stage of MIA, especially the Prakrits of the Drama (Sauraseni, Magadhi, Maharashtri), as opposed to Pali. More specifically still, "Prakrit" without further qualification often means the most cultivated (and advanced in phonological development) of these, Maharashtri. It is in the last sense that "Prakrit" will be used in the citation of forms in this chapter (which are mostly those given in Turner's *CDIAL*) unless otherwise specified. For a more thoroughgoing discussion of the term "Prakrit" and its usage, see Woolner 1975 (1928): 2–4.
7. Although Misra (1967) asserts that length contrast in final vowels was lost (and *ē*, *ō* > *i*, *u*) much earlier in the Central group (i.e. in Asokan to early AD times), it is not clear to me what this is based on, other than loc. sg. *-ē* > *-i* (*gṛhē* > Saur. *ghari*). The Asokan inscriptions (although as we have seen there are really none representing the Central group) retain final long vowels, as does Literary Sauraseni. Cf. Chatterji and Sen, *A Middle Indo-Aryan Reader* (1957), or the Lanman edition of the *Karpuramanjari*.
8. In some cases it may be possible to postulate other motivations, such as emphasis (as noted earlier with respect to gemination in Sanskrit itself), deformation or special treatment of taboo words and words referring themselves to deformities (a category noted by Turner), or contamination with semantically related words. For the possible role of stress, see below. Such "motivations" may also apply in cases involving other recognized linguistic processes, such as metathesis (often but not always sporadic), not dealt with here.
9. At least one authority, namely Bloch, disputes the existence of a stress system (as distinct from "rhythm") in MIA, or for that matter in NIA. Most, however (e.g., Jacobi, Pischel, Geiger, Grierson, Chatterji, Turner), hold that there was one, although they are split into two camps as to its nature. See below.
10. By Bloch, on grounds that there was no stress, and by Jacobi followed by Grierson on grounds that the Vedic system nowhere survived, the new system of Classical Sanskrit having prevailed everywhere.
11. According to Tagare (1948: 60), "Literary Apabhramsa does not attest to diphthongization of *udvṛtta* vowels," although he suggests there is evidence for its existence in the spoken language.

12. For further discussion see Allen 1973 and 1983.
13. This seems to be the case in Bengali, Gujarati, Nepali, Sinhalese – and Marathi, whether the theory of the Vedic-derived stress stage in Proto-Marathi is accepted or not.
14. Except, as always, for isolated irregularities: cf. Chatterji (1926: 525) on *rāṇī* 'queen' in Oriya, but this is also the form in Sindhi–Lahnda–Punjabi–Kumauni–Marwari–Gujarati–Marathi–Konkani: in other words in a continuous band of languages, which Oriya joins across the Bastar tract.
15. Even this is not quite true. Chatterji notes its apparent presence in some marginal West Bengali dialects according to *LSI 5:1* 91ff.
16. Grierson writes $^{-e}$ instead of $^{-i}$, Trumpp explicitly hesitates between *-e* and *-i*, and others sometimes write *-a*, sometimes nothing, due to the shortness and indistinct quality of the vowel. This phonetic fact having been noted here, the reader is asked to remember it: Sindhi (and Maithili) examples in the remainder of this book will be transcribed using simply *-a*, *-i*, *-u*, not only for typographical reasons but because the final ultra-short vowels may be taken as positional allophones of the short vowels, which do not otherwise occur finally. Transcriptions using superscript vowels to convey their special phonetic quality in final position are phonologically overdifferentiated.
17. Turner in his later writings (1975 [1967, 1970]) was inclined to place it somewhat earlier ("completed by 9th/10th c.") than he and most others had previously (1975 [1926b]: 275).
18. The initial *v-* that occurs in deictics in several of these languages (Hindi *vah* 'that') is not OIA *v-* but a secondary development from OIA *-m-*.
19. According to Bloch (1920: 97–9; cf. also Chatterji 1926: 437–9) such aspiration in MIA or NIA may be motivated by a following *r* or *s*, or by a lost **s* + C- in pre-Sanskrit (i.e. Indo-European). That explanation does not account for voiced aspirates like *jhan-*, *bhon-*, for forms like *phāṇī* or for final aspiration in Kashmiri.
20. Some observers (Ohala 1983 is not among them) have contended that aspiration is lost in final position in Hindi also. If this is so, it is a question of neutralization (morphophonemics), since it definitely reappears when followed by a vowel in inflection (obl. pl. *hāthõ*), which is quite different from an actual historical loss as in Bengali *hāt*.
21. That is, they are aspirated when *not* followed by the unpronounced (as vowels) *mātrā-* constructs postulated by Grierson and his source, Pandit Ishwar Kaul. There seem to be no simple solutions to the complexities of Kashmiri phonology that preserve any segmental transparency. Alternatively, an elaborate system of morphophonemic or even suppletive alternations is unavoidable.
22. For further details, stated in terms of phonological interpretation of the historically-based Gurmukhi writing system, see Shackle 1972: 142–4.
23. Not all general writers on the subject (Chatterji, Bloch) have made this distinction, but cf. Kakati 1962: 63.

8. Nominal forms and categories

1. I must acknowledge my indebtedness in this and the following chapter to Zograph's *Morfologicheskii stroi novykh indoariiskikh iazykov* (1976). Although I have ventured to differ with him on a few points and in some strategies of presentation and have seen fit to bring in some additional data along with some historical information, his work has been an invaluable guide through the jungle of NIA morphology. Since that is a book and these are merely chapters, however, I cannot do justice to all his insights here, and can only recommend it for further reading.

2. Most writers (Beames, Grierson, Bloch, Turner) have avoided the question of its etymology even while discussing the suffix. Bhandarkar's (1877) attribution of it to the MIA Feminine Plural in *-āō* (*mālāō* 'garlands', an analogical formation from Feminine Plurals in *-īō*, *-ūō*, from sandhi forms of NIA *-ayas*, *-avas*), later *-āu* (which would nicely give NIA *-o* presumably then extended to other nouns – *re*-extended in the case of Feminines in *-ī*, *-ū*), suffers from the fact that the suffix is new (eighteenth century), and apparently not attested in either Old Gujarati or the subsequently uncovered Old West Rajasthani (where the Feminine Plural has no suffix: Tessitori 1914: 183). P. B. Pandit (1961: 66), after noting the recent date of the suffix and the obscurity of its origin, speculates not very convincingly that it represents an extension of masculine *Singular* *-o*. Other possibilities that have been raised are the Hindustani general *Oblique* Plural in *-ō˜* (intervening NIA dialects have *-an* or *-ā˜*, but such Oblique plurals apparently *have* taken over Direct functions often enough in NIA, particularly in the Bihari group) and the late MIA Vocative Plural in *-(a)hō* > *-ahu* > *-au*. The Bhandarkar thesis looks more attractive when one considers that Konkani (and the Marathi dialect of the Chitpavan Brahmins) has Feminine Plurals in *-o* (*bāyl*/*bāylo* 'wife/wives'). The historical difficulty can perhaps be laid to rest by remembering that Gujarati, like many languages, has mixed antecedents as well as diverse dialects: it has connections with Konkani as well as with Rajasthani. The "new" suffix may simply have spread from a dialect not represented in Old or Middle Gujarati literature.
3. After much soul-searching, I have decided to transliterate the traditional orthography in the matter of *ī*/*i* and *ū*/*u* in such languages as Gujarati, Bengali, and Marathi in this and subsequent sections where phonology is not the issue. The reader is asked to remember that the contrast has been lost between the erstwhile long and short high vowels in these languages. The orthography sometimes reflects the ancestral vowel, sometimes is allophonic, sometimes purely arbitrary. I also propose to normalize (in the direction of the standard Orientalist transcription) the various representations of vowels found in some sources, e.g., *a* for ə, ʌ; *i* for I, y; *u* for U, w; and of course *ā* for *aa*, *a*: and also *a* (in languages where [ə] has become [ɔ, ɒ]).
4. This suffix seems to have multiple origins, complicated by its partial merger with the Locative. It cannot simply come, as is sometimes asserted, from OIA Instr. Sg. *-ēna* which by the time of Early NIA would give simply *-i* (which is in fact attested in mss.). According to Pandit (1961), it most likely represents a coalescence of the Instr. and Loc. Plural (Pkt *-ehi*, *esu* via *-ei-*, *eu* > Early NIA Instr./Loc. Pl. *-e*, also attested) with the Instrumental Singular of *extended* nouns (see below) (OIA *-akēna* > *-ahim* > *-ai˜* > *-e˜* > *-e*). A third possibility, supported by Grierson and Tagare, is from the Loc. Sg. of the *pronominal* declension in *-asmin* via Ap. *ahi˜* > *-ai˜* > *-e˜* > *-e*.
5. To my knowledge, first by A. Juilland.
6. There are of course many Bhili dialects. The neuter marker is nasalized in the Bhili of Dangs as described by Kulkarni 1976. In some material I collected from a careful speaker of the Vagdi dialect (southern Rajasthan) in 1981, however, it seems not to be, in which case see below concerning at least lip-rounding.
7. The first member of this opposition is generalized to include descriptions such as "*-ū* tending toward *-o*" (Shina, Bailey) and "*-a*, noted . . . in the majority of cases [as] *-ɔ*" (Gawarbati, Morgenstierne).
8. Despite its crucial importance, the history of the extended forms as such is not discussed at all by Pischel, Woolner, Sen, or Tagare (or, I believe, by Turner) and only very sketchily by Bloch. Here it would seem is a topic inviting the attention of future researchers.
9. This according to Bloch. According to Chatterji (1926: 723), H. *ghōṛē* is from the Instrumental plural **ghōṭēbhiḥ*, via *ghōṛahi*, transferred to the Nominative.

10. This particular shift is not an unexpected one, to be sure, since with the early demise of the Dative in MIA the Genitive took over many of its functions, and indeed had shared them even in OIA (Bloch 1965: 156). One of Bloch's problems (1920: 197–9) with a Genitive derivation of the Marathi Dative in *-s* is the lack of any remnant of Genitive function in the Marathi form (also true of the Kashmiri form, although he is not concerned with it here). However, it would seem that with the old Genitive becoming the case of all work (and typically the source, insofar as one can be posited, for the General Oblique), the quintessential "genitive" functions (possession, etc.) were soon expressed in any case by circumlocutions, which became the source of most NIA Layer II Genitives.
11. Kakati (1962: 305–6) says they are confined to certain repetitive phrases, such as *ʃukhe-dukhe* 'in prosperity and in adversity', *bate-bate* 'on every road', *ghɒre-ghɒre* 'house to house'.
12. The conditioning of the allomorphs of the Bengali (Instrumental-) Locative is somewhat more complicated than indicated here. See Dasgupta 1985.
13. Marathi, for example, seems to avoid this in favor of a construction with a resumptive pronoun: *rām āni śyām tyānnī*, lit. 'Ram and Shyam, to them'.
14. Kavadi and Southworth 1965: 213. (The {ċ} in *tyāċ* is an emphatic particle, not a Genitive.) Compare, however, Hindi *is-ke liye* 'for him/her/this one', *isliye* 'on account of this/therefore'. See also Katenina 1963: 131.
15. The long *ā* is not an Oblique, but the result of the application of Sanskrit sandhi in a Tss.: see Katenina 1963: 266–7 for more discussion.
16. I am grateful to Bh. Krishnamurti for reminding me of this, and to Vijayarani Fedson for further particulars.
17. The historically-minded conversely sometimes prefer to treat it as the *only* "case", very general in function, with specifying postpositions added.

9. Verbal forms and categories

1. We neglected to mention in Chapter 8 that in the nominal paradigm also these Northwestern languages have a tiny handful of *pre*positions, of the Layer III or secondary type, that is, preceding a base with a Layer II marker. From another point of view, taking the two elements together as one (discontinuous) complex, they are *ambipositions*, "straddling" the nominal base. Chief among them are words for 'without': Siraiki, etc. *baɣær/binā* + N° + *de*.
2. For qualifications and explanations in the context of the larger problem of Kashmiri word order in general, see Hook 1976a.
3. It could be argued, however, that in some of the Eastern languages at least the categories of Definiteness (combined with Size-Shape Classification) and of Number (combined with Animacy and other considerations) are also expandable, not in the sense that there are many instantiations ("features") of the categories Definiteness (Definite, Indefinite, etc.?) and Number (Singular, Plural, etc.?) but because the actual category is something else. There is evidence that the categories in question are in complementary distribution and therefore constitute one supercategory for which we have not found an adequate name. Number and definiteness are only two of several possible features, among which "refinement" is possible. The formula for the inflected noun would therefore be:
   NOUN STEM + "Number/Definiteness/Other Specification" + Case (I, II, III)
4. The use of the *-t*-increment is optional in Marathi (in the forms cited).
5. Similarly, the basis of the Sinhalese Third or *-e* Conjugation lies in Sanskrit Passives in

-ya, MIA *-iya*: Skt *māryatē* 'he dies' > Pkt *māriyati* > Si. *mæreyi* > *mærē* (with umlaut of *ā* due to *i-* and subsequent change of *-iya* to *-e* as regular developments). The (Literary) Sinhalese Imperative singular still retains *-iya* (Geiger 1938: 139, 149). However, this has since become a productive mechanism for forming intransitives from transitives in modern Sinhalese (see section 9.6). Sinhalese verbs of the Third Conjugation do not necessarily go back to Sanskrit passives, indeed frequently do not.

6. Grierson (*LSI*), following Brown 1848, recognizes three conjugations in Assamese, on the basis of types of morphophonemic treatments of the stem. The endings are not affected, except that in the "First Conjugation" (stem ending in a vowel), the 3sg. is *-y* rather than *-e*. There is, however, a more important difference in the conjugation of intransitive vs. transitive verbs in Assamese, namely that the 3sg. Perfective ("Simple Past") in the former ends in *-il*, in the latter in *-ile*. Similar phenomena are found in some (North and West) Bengali dialects (Chatterji 1926: 983–6). Also to be noted in this connection are the Maithili Perfect formations employing *-ala* (intransitive) vs. *-ane* (transitive): *gēla chathi* 'he has gone'/*dekhane chathīnha* 'he has seen him' (Jha 1958: 526–9).
7. This is not at all to say that aspect is a primary structural–semantic feature in all languages. In the course of historical development, while some languages have maintained such primacy, others – including Old Indo-Aryan itself – have evolved "tense" systems, in which tense and aspect have been conmingled, sometimes obscuring the latter. Why later Indo-Aryan has developed in the way it has, underlining as it were the primacy of aspect, is an interesting typological question. While a Dravidian model for NIA nominal morphology seems clear, the verbal problem is more complex. The way aspect is marked in Dravidian is sometimes different from, sometimes parallel to NIA – with parallels sometimes extending to the material morphemes themselves (e.g., the Telugu Durative marker {*-t-*}). Moreover, somewhat different methods seem to be employed by different Dravidian languages. The question deserves a careful exploration that cannot be attempted here – preferably one with a historical dimension, if the problem of the direction of influence is to be addressed.
8. I am relying here on the judgment of my colleague C. M. Naim, who attributes it to the limitation inherent in *jab tak* 'as long as'.
9. The quasi-invariant (i.e. except 3pl.) Alternative Transitive Perfect in *-ē* – *dēkhē hau͂* beside *dēkheu͂ hai* 'I have seen' – is a less likely candidate, as it seems to be modern. (In all of this I am relying on Saksena 1971.) This should be distinguished from the representation of the regular reflex of the morpheme in descriptions of Mandeali, Chameali, Churahi, etc. (West Pahari) by *-ē-*, just another way of writing *-y-*. There is a development of an alternative *-ē* marker in Garhwali, however.
10. There seem to be Perfective markers in *-ū*, however, in Kului–Pangwali–Bharmauri (West Pahari) independent of the *-illa* developments.
11. Extant accounts of Sindhi are not completely consistent with one another. I have consulted mainly Trumpp 1872, Grierson 1919 (*LSI*), Shahani n.d. (pre-1947), Steinmetz et al. (Peace Corps materials prepared at the University of Minnesota in the early 1960s under the direction of Robert F. Spencer), Egorova 1966, Zograph 1976, and Addleton and Brown 1981, giving more weight to the more recent. Addleton and Brown agree with Egorova, Steinmetz et al., and Shahani in describing the {*-ando/indo*} + Aux forms as Habituals, but Trumpp (pp. 294–5) describes them as General–Imperfective (Continuous *or* Habitual) and Grierson as Continuous. Neither of the latter report the {*rahyo*}-Continuous forms.
12. Certain (mainly III Conj.) verbs in Colloquial Sinhalese also have a Perfective (not shown) in *-icca* (*pipenavā* 'open [of flowers]' > *pipicca*), which appears to be a borrowing from Tamil.

13. Bloch wondered (1965: 235) whether such forms might not be secondary formations (which would in itself be remarkable), but these doubts are not widely shared.
14. Imperatives generally have a ZERO ending in the 2sg. (except in Sindhi) and an *-ō* or *-au* ending in the 2pl, coinciding with the "Subjunctive" or "Old Present", as they do in other Persons. Some languages have special 3p Imperative endings, however: M. *-o/-ot*, B. *-(u)k*, A. *-ɔk*. (Marathi also has a 1sg. Imperative in *-u*˜, coinciding with other NIA Imperative/Subjunctives but distinct from other Marathi 1sg. endings.) Bengali, Assamese, Maithili, Gujarati, Sindhi, Punjabi, and certain other languages have *Future* as well as Present Imperatives, in the Western languages with a distinctive ending, *-jo* (P. *-yo*).
15. "Past II" and "Past III" in Grierson's terminology.
16. In this simplified presentation I am omitting reference to (1) morphophonemics (some languages such as Hindi shorten or *reshorten* the root vowel upon adding the causative suffix in accordance with general rhythmic rules; others such as Gujarati do not); (2) to the matter of semi-transitive or "affective" verbs (*see*, *hear*, *eat*, *understand*, which form (secondary in NIA) double transitives – *show*, *tell*, *feed*, *explain* – rather than indirect causatives when the First Causative suffix is added (H. *dēkh-/dikhā-*, *sun-/sunā*, *khā-/khilā*, *samajh-/sam´jhā-*): failure to distinguish this class of verbs from ordinary transitives confuses many conventional descriptions); and (3) to the qualification that (sometimes) primary intransitive + First Causative = indirect causative of the intransitive rather than a transitive (e.g., *uṭhā-* can mean 'cause to get up' as well as 'lift').
17. On labels: at one period in the history of structural linguistics, from which unfortunately some of our best modern descriptions come, traditional grammatical terminology was avoided in favor of *ad hoc* terms arising supposedly only from the exigencies of the language being described, often taken from the form in question itself: "the *-te* form". Whatever the merits of this position in, for example, language teaching, it makes cross-linguistic comparison of different forms with similar functions difficult. For that general labels are needed, and traditional terminology is probably the best source for them, although it needs refinement and standardization.
18. At least one NIA language (and not a peripheral one) seems to lack the construction, substituting an equivalent declinable particle. This is the Godwari dialect of Pali District, Rajasthan. See Hook 1982: 33–4. Subsequently the same thing has been discovered in the nearby Bhitrauti dialect (Hook and Chauhan 1986).
19. Hook 1978b objects that, even for Hindi, "compound verbs" are not true compounds, in the sense that the result is not a combination of the meanings of two verbs taken as independent lexical items. Nevertheless, he too continues to use the term for want of anything better. One might argue that the formation still involves two verb stems, even if one of them has a specialized function.

10. Syntax

[The transcription of Marathi examples used in this chapter differs slightly from that used in earlier chapters, in that the affricates [ts, ^{d}z] are represented by /*ts*, *z*/ rather than by /*c̀*, *j̀*/. The latter, which are those used by Turner's *CDIAL*, are confusing to some people, and more difficult for the printer. We apologize for the inconsistency, but it may be good for the reader to learn to cope with both.]

1. This is not to say that there have not also been some attempts by such linguists to present complete descriptions of a particular language (Y. Kachru 1966 on Hindi is an example), or at least of its syntax. Such work is necessarily also data-driven, even though it may also strive for theoretical consistency.

2. According to Hook, such verb-initial clauses have a specific stylistic function, namely to move a narrative forward.
3. Other positions do occur among the languages of the world, such as Malagasy, but this is typologically rare and must presumably first be identified on other grounds.
4. Hook 1985a would therefore say that these rules make crucial reference to *Agent* rather than to *Subject* – but this has the (to me undesirable) consequence of forcing us to call the Experiencer also an "Agent".
5. DeLancey (1985) notes that while most Tibetan dialects are "ergative or aspectually-split ergative," the system of Lhasa Tibetan is better characterized as *active/stative*. For Burushaski see Bashir 1985 and Tiffou and Morin 1982.
6. Hook (personal communication).
7. This Neutralization rule, where applicable, normally blocks 1st and 2nd person Object agreement in the verb – which could only be carried by the Tense/Mood auxiliary – since such Objects will always be definite. It is even blocked in Gujarati and Marwari, where the rule otherwise does not apply: *teṇe mane joyo* <u>*che*</u> 'He has seen me,' i.e. not **chũ*, the 1st person form. In Kashmiri, however, 1st and 2nd person agreement is possible, thanks to what Hook and Koul (1984b) call the Absolutive set of suffixes and to the fact that no such Object-marking rule has disturbed the original Nominative (="Absolutive") case of the ergative Patient in that language: (K.) *tse onuthas bɨ yōr* 'You brought me here' [*-th* = 2nd Sg. Agent, agreeing with *tse* 'you'; *as* = 1st. Sg. Patient, agreeing with *bɨ* 'I') (Hook 1984: 127).
8. A fragmentary relic of the old Instrumental construction of the Subject is found in the Oriya Nominative *plural* suffix *-māne* occurring with animate nouns (which are more likely to be Agents), contrasting with *-mānɔ* occurring with inanimates (Tripathi 1962: 128).
9. Double agreement of the type under discussion may have existed in Early Maithili for a brief period and also in Early Awadhi (Pray 1976: 198; but Saksena 1971 curiously avoids the subject). See also R. R. Smith (1974: 79–82), concerning double concord produced by border-zone combination of Agent- (Awadhi) and Patient- (Kannauji) concord patterns.
10. Cardona hears a breathy vowel, which he represents as vowel + */h/*, in many of these forms, e.g., */mahre/*, */mahne/*, */ahme/*. In retranscribing these forms for citation according to the more or less pan-Indian system employed here, we omit this where it is not represented in the Gujarati script (or other transcriptions).
11. That is, not in Indo-Aryan, as a general rule, although I am informed (Asif Agha, personal communication) that sometimes it may do so in Tibetan. Hook informs me it may also do so in the neighboring Aryan Shina of Dras and Skardu.
12. Certain types of "EQUI", however, apparently can be controlled by Indirect Objects, at least in Hindi. Subbarao (1984: 57, 61) cites such sentences as these:
    a) *hamne rekhā se tez dauṛne ko kahā* 'We asked Rekha to run fast' ("Indirect Object" *rekhā se* – albeit not Datively marked – controlling deletion of Subject of **Rekha run*);
    b) *hamne rām ko vahā̃ bhejne kā vacan diyā* 'We promised Ram to send him there' (Indirect Object *rām ko* controlling deletion of Direct Object **send Ram*).
    Wallace (1985b: 86) rejects this for Nepali, although the context is somewhat different. It may be that EQUI is too multifaceted a process to serve as a useful test.
13. Noting that "the syntactic typology of the Indo-Aryan language family has changed over the past 2500 years to such an extent that [the Paninian categories of] *karaka* and *vibhakti* alone no longer provide adequate classifications to account for regularities in the cooccurrences of the Hindi noun phrase," Hook (1985a) goes on to propose a (non-Paninian) category of Subject rather similar to the traditional (Western) one. That is, unmarked Passive Patients and Sensation NPs in Dative-Experiencer constructions

(with which the verb agrees) are recognized as Subjects (but not Ergative Patients, with which the verb also agrees, because they behave differently under nominalization). The common behavioral characteristics of the various NPs discussed in the above subsections are attributed (see note 4) to an entity called "Agent" rather than "Subject". (Hook notes that the Experiencer category, present in Sanskrit although not in such a developed form as in NIA, is essentially ignored by Panini.)

14. Exceptions are the marginal and apparently recent {*-va*} suffix in Sinhalese (noted by Garusinghe 1962, Fairbanks et al. 1968: 2. 132, Gair 1970: 27–8) and distinctive Accusative suffixes in Poguli, the Gultari dialect of Shina, and possibly other NW languages (Hook: pers, comm.)
15. It has been held since the early days of transformational-generative grammar, of course, that attributive adjectives are basically embedded sentences, derived via relative clauses. There are a number of arguments for this view, among them the fact that in all but the most self-consciously literary *texts* of a language (and perhaps even in them), predicate adjectives obviously outnumber attributive adjectives; whatever the impression we may get from grammar books, the latter are actually rather rare in "normal" texts. It may be noted further that the attributive (the so-called *ezāfat*) construction in neighboring Persian appears to be derived even historically from a relative construction. There seems to be no limit to the multiplication of such embeddings in literary Persian: *motāle'e-ye daqīq-e neveſtehā-ye movarreχān-e qadīm* 'the careful study of the works of ancient historians' (Lazard 1957: 63). In Indo-Aryan, on the other hand, Mistry (1969: 57) points out that in Gujarati at least "there is no sentence . . . that allows more than one layer of relativization in its surface structure, though there is no limit to the number of adjectives in any of the prenominal positions." (He concludes from this, not that the derivation in transformational terms is wrong, but that "adjectivization" is obligatory in certain cases.) In any case, it is necessary to posit an (optional) adjectival "slot" in the NP at some stage in the derivation, and for the purposes of this presentation we will focus on that, rather than on the complicated hypothetical process required in order to transform an adjectival predication into an attribute.
16. Needless to say, but so there may be no confusion: I am not using *Determiner* in the general sense of "all modifying elements" (=French *déterminant*, as used, for example, by Lazard) as is done in some descriptions.
17. Perhaps this is more the case in some languages (Hindi, Bengali) than in others (Sindhi): the question, like so many others, needs more extensive comparative study.
18. I am grateful to Edward C. Dimock, Jr., for clarifying this for me.
19. Hook 1979, in his pedagogical grammar, treats both kinds of sequences alike, under the heading "*complementizers*". I shall avoid the latter term here, since it seems to mean different things to different people: for e.g., Subbarao (1984) and Sinha (1970), it refers specifically to embedding devices (in Hindi, two according to Subbarao, three according to Sinha); in Hook (1979) the term refers to any device for "attaching verb to verb", whether involving embedding or not (and there are "7 or 8" of them in Hindi).
20. Hook points out that this criterion has apparently yet to be tested using actual counts and statistics.
21. For the record, I have checked these examples with, among others, my long-suffering colleague, C. M. Naim (native speaker of Urdu from Bara Banki, UP, India), and Asif Agha (native speaker of Urdu from Pakistan). Both say *cāhtā hū̃* is doubtfully acceptable (perhaps because it can occur with a Noun Object in approximately the same meaning), but *dekhnā cāhtā hū̃* definitely sounds better. The starred forms of *have to* and *can* are completely out. To be sure, this information pertains only to (Hindi)–Urdu. In Bengali, *pār-* 'be able' does occur (in context) without the Infinitive on which it is dependent: *āmi chāgɔler dāṛi kāmāte pārbo nā* 'I can't shave the goat's beard'/*kæno*

pārbe *nā* *bābu?* 'Why can't you?'. I am grateful to C. B. Seely for digging up this example for me (from a book of children's stories, *bāgher māʃi beṛāl*), after Douglas Varley had suggested it was the case. Oriya *pār-* seems to behave similarly. On the other hand, in the B. structure Inf. + *hɔbe* 'have to V', the Infinitive cannot be deleted.

22. Sinhalese *ōna* (Lit. *ōnæ*) does not literally mean *be*: according to Bel'kovich and Vykhukholev (1970) it means 'necessary, wanted'. I have been unable to ascertain its etymology: the resemblance to the ubiquitous Dakhani *honā* (<OIA *bhavati* > Si. *venavā* according to *CDIAL*) used in these constructions is perhaps only coincidental.
23. This is Cardona's observation with respect to Gujarati, but it appears to have wider validity.
24. Emended at Hook's suggestion. Bailey gives *lɜbthiī* for *lɜbith* but this may be a misprint. Cf. Table 10.1.
25. Not all speakers accept this interpretation (or these examples). Further investigation is necessary. Meanwhile, some genuine examples in context are:
(a) *mujhe to nahī̃ jān paṛtā, maĩne to kuch aisā dekhā nahī̃./pūrā viʃvās hai?/maĩ kyā kah saktī hū̃? par lagtā to nahī̃.* 'I don't think so; I didn't see any such thing./Are you sure?/What can I say? But I *feel* like I didn't' (Yashpal, *JhuuThaa Sac*, 3rd edn 1963: 93)
(b) *hori cupcāp suntā rahā, minkā tak nahī. jhũjhlāhaṭ huī, krodh āyā, khūn khaulā, ā̃kh jalī, dā̃t pise; lekin bolā nahī* 'Hori went on listening silently. He didn't utter a sound. He was irritated, he was angry, his blood boiled, his eyes burned, he ground his teeth; but he didn't speak' (Premchand, *Godaan*, 13th abridged edn, 1960: 34)
(c) *āge zarūr paṛho! guṇ apne pās ho to kyā burā hai? koī chīn to legā nahī̃* 'By all means study further! If you have the talent what harm is there? No one is going to snatch it away from you' (Ashk, *girtī divārẽ*, 4th edn. 1957: 46)
It may be a question of what we mean by "emphasis": perhaps what is truly emphasized is the verb itself, not the negation, and this is merely a special instance of the Rightward Displacement phenomenon discussed in note 26 below.
26. Kachru (1980: 130), while calling for more work on the subject, suggests that the end position in Hindi is the focal position. From S. K. Verma's (1981) observations on the placement of the tonic or sentence stress, however, it would appear that the *second-from-the-end* position is the focal (or contrastive) one. This accords with conclusions reached independently by M. H. Klaiman, and with the fact that, as Verma notes (p. 61), quoting Halliday with approval, "the verb is not readily associated with any form of prominence in the discourse"; indeed, to achieve such prominence, Rightward Displacement of another clausal constituent is required. Although this postverbal position is sometimes dubbed "emphatic", the constituent in question will generally be found to bear no real prominence. Its extraposition seems merely to bring the VP itself into focal position. At least this is the case in Hindi: it may not hold for other NIA languages. Note, however, the presence of emphatic particles, especially the contrastive *to*, in both H. and B. VPs, and also in the H. postposed negatives in note 25 above.
27. Dravidian Telugu and certain varieties of Kannada have marginal relative-correlative clauses (modeled on Sanskrit according to Krishnamurti and Gwynn 1985: 361) using interrogatives in place of the Indo-Aryan relatives for which there is no equivalent. This in turn is imitated by some varieties of Konkani (see Nadkarni 1975) and Dakhani Urdu. However, speakers of some varieties of Shina do this also (Hook: pers. comm.).
28. Matthews (1984: 187) does provide an example of such usage (postposed at that), which he says is largely a feature of written Nepali. Whatever the influence of English, some of these postposed clauses in NIA generally may also be due to the unprecedented requirements of complex modern prose.

BIBLIOGRAPHY

With the aim of facilitating access to works on individual Indo-Aryan languages, the bibliography below is divided into two sections. The first, or *general*, section includes works on general linguistic theory, Indo-Aryan or South Asian languages in general, historical and regional background, and on individual non-Indo-Aryan languages of the area referred to in the text. The second section is organized under individual Indo-Aryan language names, given alphabetically. (When a reference that seems to belong in Section I does not appear there, it is likely to be found under *Sanskrit* in Section II. Note that Section II includes subsections on both *Middle Indo-Aryan* and *Prakrit*.) References to works of fiction, Bible translations, etc. from which some examples have been drawn are given in the text, but are not included below.

Abbreviations

[B]SO[A]S = [Bulletin of the] School of Oriental [and African] Studies (University of London)

CIIL = Central Institute of Indian Linguistics (Mysore)

CLS = Chicago Linguistic Society

IJDL = International Journal of Dravidian Linguistics

IL = Indian Linguistics

[J]AOS = [Journal of the] American Oriental Society

[J]RAS = [Journal of the] Royal Asiatic Society

Lg. = Language (Journal of the Linguistic Society of America)

LSI = Linguistic survey of India

NSSAL = The notion of subject in South Asian languages (Manindra K. Verma, ed.)

NTS = Norsk Tidsskrift for Sprogvidenskap

PCPR = Proceedings of the Conference on Participant Roles: South Asia and Adjacent Areas (Zide, Magier, and Schiller, eds.)

SALA = South Asian Language Analysis (Papers from annual meeting); formerly "South Asian Literary Association"

THL-2 = Topics in Hindi Linguistics, vol. 2 (Omkar N. Koul, ed.)

Section I: *General*

Abbi, Anvita. 1987. *Reduplicative structures in South Asian languages: a phenomenon of linguistic area.* New Delhi: Jawaharlal Nehru University, Centre of Linguistics and English

Allen, W. S. 1958. Some problems of palatalization in Greek. *Lingua* 7: 11–33

Allen, W. S. 1959. Indo-Aryan. *Phonetica* 4: 33–6

Allen, W. S. 1973. *Accent and rhythm.* Cambridge University Press

Allen, W. S. 1977. The PIE aspirates: phonetic and typological factors in reconstruction. In Alphonse Juilland (ed.), *Linguistic studies offered to Joseph Greenberg*. Saratoga, CA: Anma Libri: 237–47

Allen, W. S. 1978. The PIE velar series. Neogrammarian and other solutions in the light of attested parallels. *Transactions of the Philological Society 1978*. 87–110

Allen, W. S. 1983. Some reflections on the 'penultimate' accent. *Illinois Classical Studies* 8.1: 1–10

Arden, A. H. 1937. *A progressive grammar of the Telugu language*. 4th edn. Madras: Christian Literature Society

Arden, A. H. 1942. *A progressive grammar of common Tamil.* 5th edn, revised by A. C. Clayton. Madras: Christian Literature Society

Aronson, Howard I. 1985. Form, function, and the "perfective" in Bulgarian. In Michael S. Flier and Alan Timberlake (eds.), *The scope of Slavic aspect.* Columbus, Ohio: Slavica (= *UCLA Slavic Studies*, vol. 12): 274–85

Bailey, T. G. 1938. *Studies in North Indian languages.* London: Lund, Humphries

Bashir, Elena. 1985. Toward a semantics of the Burushaski verb. In Zide et al. (eds.) *PCPR*: 1–32

Beames, John. 1872–9 (repr. 1970). *A comparative grammar of the modern Aryan languages of India.* New Delhi: Munshiram Manoharlal

Beskrovny, V. M., E. M. Bykova, and V. P. Liperovski (eds.). 1968. *Iazyki Indii, Pakistana, Nepala y Tseilona* (Papers from a conference held in Moscow in January, 1965). Moscow: Nauka

Bhandarkar, R. G. 1887 (repr. 1974). *Wilson Philological Lectures on Sanskrit and the derived languages.* Poona: Bhandarkar Oriental Institute

Bhatia, Tej. 1978. A syntactic and semantic description of negation in South Asian languages. (University of Illinois Ph.D. dissertation)

Bickerton, Derek. 1981. *Roots of language.* Ann Arbor: Karoma

Bloch, Jules. 1963. *Application de la cartographie à l'histoire de l'Indo-aryen.* Paris

Bloch, Jules (trans. A. Master). 1965. *Indo-Aryan from the Vedas to modern times.* Paris: Adrien-Maisonneuve

Boyce, Mary. 1979. *Zoroastrians, their religious beliefs and practices.* London: Routledge & Kegan Paul

Bronkhorst, Johannes. 1982. Some observations on the Padapāṭha of the Ṛgveda. *Indo-Iranian Journal* 24: 181–89.

Brass, Paul R. 1974. *Language, religion and politics in North India.* Cambridge University Press

Burrow, T. 1944. Dravidian Studies IV: the body in Dravidian and Uralian. *BSOS* 11: 328–56

Burrow, T. 1973. The Proto-Indo-Aryans. *JRAS*: 123–40

Burrow, T., and M. B. Emeneau. 1960. *A Dravidian etymological dictionary.* London: Oxford University Press

Bynon, Theodora. 1977. *Historical linguistics.* Cambridge University Press

Caldwell, Robert. 1961 (1856). *A comparative grammar of the Dravidian or South-Indian family of languages.* Repr. Madras: University of Madras

Cardona, George. 1974. The Indo-Aryan languages. *Encyclopedia Britannica.* 15th edn. 9: 439–50

Cardona, George, H. M. Hoenigswald, and Alfred Senn (eds.). 1970. *Indo-European and Indo-Europeans.* Philadelphia: University of Pennsylvania Press

Chatterji, Suniti Kumar. 1960. *Indo-Aryan and Hindi.* Calcutta: K. L. Mukhopadhyay

Chatterji, Suniti Kumar. 1968. *India and Ethiopia, from the 7th century BC.* Calcutta: Asiatic Society (Monograph 15)

Coedès, G. (trans. H. M. Wright). 1966. *The making of South East Asia.* Berkeley and Los Angeles: University of California Press

Coedès, G. (trans. Susan Brown Cowing). *The Indianized States of Southeast Asia.* Honolulu: East–West Center press

Collinder, Björn. 1965. *An introduction to the Uralic languages.* Berkeley: University of California Press

Comrie, Bernard. 1976. *Aspect.* Cambridge University Press

Crosby, Alfred W. 1972. *The Columbian exchange: biological and cultural consequences of 1492.* Westport, Conn.: Greenwood

Davison, Alice. 1980. Peculiar passives. *Lg.* 56: 42–66

DeLancey, Scott. 1985. Categories of non-volitional actor in Lhasa Tibetan. *PCPR*: 58–70

Deshpande, Madhav M., and Peter Edwin Hook (eds.). 1979. *Aryan and Non-Aryan in*

India. Ann Arbor: University of Michigan Center for South and Southeast Asian Studies

Dezsö, L. 1968. Einige typologische Besonderheiten der ungarischen Wortfolge. *Acta Linguistica* 18: 125–59

Elizarenkova, T. Y. 1974. *Issledovaniia po diakhronicheskoi fonologii indo-ariiskikh iazykov*. Moscow: Nauka

Emeneau, M. B. 1956. India as a linguistic area. *Lg*. 32: 3–16

Emeneau, M. B. 1969. Onomatopoetics in the Indian linguistic area. *Lg*. 45.2: 274–99

Emeneau, M. B. 1980. *India and linguistic areas*. In Anwar S. Dib (ed.) *Language and linguistic area: essays by Murray B. Emeneau*. Stanford, CA: Stanford University Press: 126–66

Emeneau, M. B. 1983. Demonstrative pronominal bases in the Indian linguistic area. *IJDL* 12.1: 1–7

Entwhistle, W. J., and W. A. Morison. 1949. *Russian and the Slavonic languages*. London: Faber & Faber

Fairservis, Walter A. 1975. *Roots of ancient India*. 2nd edn. University of Chicago Press

Fedson, Vijayarani Jotimuttu. 1981. The Tamil serial or compound verb. (University of Chicago Ph.D. dissertation)

Fedson, Vijayarani Jotimuttu. 1985. Agency modulation and other facets of participant roles in Tamil. *PCPR*: 104–18

Ferguson, Charles A., and John J. Gumperz (eds.). 1960. Linguistic diversity in South Asia: studies in regional, social, and functional variation. *International Journal of American Linguistics* 26:3, pt. 2

Ferreiro, Emilia. 1971. *Les relations temporelles dans le langage de l'enfant*. Paris: Droz

Forsyth, John. 1970. *A grammar of aspect: usage and meaning in the Russian verb*. Cambridge University Press

Fox, Robert Grady Allen. 1978. Individual variability in the perception of vowels. (University of Chicago, Ph.D. dissertation)

Friedrich, Paul. 1970. *Proto-Indo-European trees*. University of Chicago Press

Friedrich, Paul. 1975. *Proto-Indo-European syntax: the order of meaningful elements*. Butte: Montana College of Mineral Science and Technology (*Journal of Indo-European Studies*, Monograph 1)

Gamkrelidze, T. V., and V. V. Ivanov. 1984. *Indoevropeiskii iazyk i indoevropeitsy: rekonstruktsiia i istoriko-tipologicheskii analiz praiazyka*. Tbilisi: Izd. Tbil. Univ.

Gimbutas, M. 1970. Proto-Indo-European culture: the Kurgan culture during the 5th, 4th and 3rd millennia BC. In Cardona et al., 253–65

Givón, T. 1984. *Syntax: a functional-typological introduction*, vol. 1. Amsterdam/Philadelphia: John Benjamins

Gnoli, Gherardo. 1980. *Zoroaster's time and homeland: a study on the origins of Mazdeism and related problems*. Naples: Istituto Universitario Orientale

Goyal, S. R. 1979. Brahmi: an invention of the Early Mauryan period. In Gupta and Ramachandran: 1–53

Grierson, George A. 1903–28. *Linguistic survey of India*. vols. I–XI. Calcutta. Repr. Delhi 1968: Motilal Banarsidass

Grierson, George A. 1917. The Indo-Aryan vernaculars. *BSOS* 1: 247: 81

Grierson, George A. 1922. Spontaneous nasalization in the Indo-Aryan languages. *JRAS*: 381–8

Grierson, George A. 1931–3. On the modern Indo-Aryan vernaculars. *Indian Antiquary*

Gupta, S. P. and K. S. Ramchandran (eds.). 1979. *The origin of the Brahmi script*, Delhi: D. K. Publications

Halliday, M. A. K. 1967. Notes on transitivity and theme in English, Parts 1–2. *Journal of Linguistics* 3: 37–81, 177–244

Halliday, M. A. K. 1968. Notes on transitivity and theme in English, Part 3. *Journal of Linguistics* 4: 179–215

Hock, Hans Henrich. 1985. Transitivity as a gradient feature? Evidence from Indo-Aryan, especially Sanskrit and Hindi. *PCPR*: 247–63

Hoernle, R. 1880. *A comparative grammar of the Gaudian languages*. London

Hook, Peter E. 1977b. The distribution of the compound verb in the languages of North India and the question of its origin. *IJDL* 6.2: 336–49

Hook, Peter E. 1982. India as a semantic area. In Mistry (ed.): 30–41

Hook, Peter E. 1984a. Kashmiri and types of split accusativity in South Asian languages. *SALA* 6

Hook, Peter E. 1985a. Coexistent analyses and participant roles in Indo-Aryan. *PCPR*: 264–83

Hook, Peter E. 1987a. Differential S-marking in Marathi, Hindi–Urdu, and Kashmiri. *CLS* 23

Hook, Peter E. 1987b. Linguistic areas: getting at the grain of history. In George Cardona and Norman Zide (eds.), Henry H. Hoenigswald commemorative volume. Tübingen: Gunter Narr Verlag: 155–68

Hopper, Paul J. 1982. *Tense-Aspect: between semantics and pragmatics*. Amsterdam/ Philadelphia: John Benjamins

Hopper, Paul J. and Sandra A. Thompson. 1980. Transitivity in grammar and discourse. *Lg.* 56.2: 251–99

Hudson-Williams, T. 1935. *A short introduction to the study of comparative grammar (Indo-European)*. Cardiff: University of Wales Press

Indian Institute of Advanced Study, Simla. 1969. *Language and society in India. Transactions of the Indian Institute for Advanced Study*, vol. 8

Jain, Banarsi Das. 1927. Stress accent in Indo-Aryan. *BSOS* 4: 315–23

Johnson, David E. 1976. *Toward a theory of relationally-based grammar*. Bloomington: Indiana University Linguistics Club

Johnson, David E. 1977. On relational constraints in grammar. In Cole and Sadock (eds.), *Syntax and Semantics* 8: 151–78

Junghare, Indira Y. 1972. The perfect aspect in Marathi, Bhojpuri, and Maithili. *IL* 33.2: 128–34

Junghare, Indira. 1983. Markers of definiteness in Indo-Aryan. *IL* 44: 43–53

Kachru, Braj B. 1983. *The Indianization of English: the English language in India*. Delhi/ New York: Oxford University Press

Kachru, Yamuna, Braj B. Kachru, and Tej K. Bhatia. 1976. The notion 'Subject', a note on Hindi–Urdu, Kashmiri, and Panjabi. *NSSAL*: 79–108

Kachru, Yamuna and Rajeshwari Pandharipande. 1979. On ergativity in selected South Asian languages. *SALA* 1: 193–209

Karve, Irawati. 1965. *Kinship organization in India*. 2nd edn. Bombay/New York: Asia Publishing House

Katre, S. M. 1965. *Some problems of historical linguistics in Indo-Aryan*. Poona: Deccan College

Katre, S. M. 1968. *Problems of reconstruction in Indo-Aryan*. Simla: Indian Institute of Advanced Study

Keenan, Edward L. and Bernard Comrie. 1977. Noun phrase accessibility and universal grammar. *Linguistic Inquiry* 8: 63–99

Keenan, E. L. 1976. Towards a universal definition of subject. In Li (ed.): 303–33

Khubchandani, L. M. 1983. *Plural languages, plural cultures: communication, identity, and sociopolitical change in contemporary India*. Honolulu: University of Hawaii Press

Klaiman, M. H. 1976a. A functional view of some syntactic movement typologies. (Master's essay, Department of Linguistics, University of Chicago)

Klaiman, M. H. 1976b. Correlative clauses and I E syntactic reconstruction. In *Papers from the Parasession on Diachronic Syntax* (S. Steever, C. Walker, and S. Mufwene, eds.): 159–68 (CLS)

Klaiman, M. H. 1981. Arguments against the "ingestive verb" hypothesis. *THL-2*: 135–45

Klaiman, M. H. 1985. Subjecthood as a marker of affected entity status in several languages. *PCPR*: 179–88

Klimov, G. A. 1974. On the character of languages of active typology. *Linguistics* 131: 11–25

Krishnamurti, Bh. (ed.). 1986. *South Asian languages: structure, convergence and diglossia*. Delhi: Motilal Banarsidass

Krishnamurti, Bh., and J. P. L. Gwynn. 1985. *A grammar of modern Telugu*. Delhi: Oxford University Press

Kuno, Susumu. 1974. The position of relative clauses and conjunctions. *Linguistic Inquiry* 5.1: 117–35

Kurylowicz, Jerzy. 1964. *The inflectional categories of Indo-European*. Heidelberg: Carl Winter

Lazard, Gilbert. 1957. *Grammaire du persan contemporain*. Paris: Librairie C. Klincksieck

Li, Charles N. (ed.). 1976. *Subject and topic*. New York: Academic Press

Lindholm, James M. 1975. The conceptual basis of the Tamil adverbial participle. (University of Chicago Ph.D. dissertation)

Lindholm, James M. 1976. Nested case relations and the subject in Tamil. *NSSAL*: 152–82

Lockwood, William Burley. 1972. *A panorama of the Indo-European languages*. London: Hutchinson

Mahapatra, B. P. 1983. Scope of Indo-Aryan tribal language research. *IJDL* 12.1: 60–75.

Marlow, Elli Johanna Pudas. 1974. More on the Uralo-Dravidian relationship. (University of Texas Ph.D. dissertation)

Masica, Colin P. 1976. *Defining a linguistic area: South Asia*. Chicago: University of Chicago Press

Masica, Colin P. 1979. Aryan and non-Aryan elements in North Indian agriculture. In Deshpande and Hook (eds.): 55–151

Masica, Colin P. 1981 (1982). Identified object marking in Hindi and other languages. *THL-2*: 16–50

Masica, Colin P. 1982. Ergativity in South Asia. In Mistry (ed.): 1–11

Masica, Colin P. 1986. Definiteness-marking in South Asian languages. In Krishnamurti (ed.): 123–46

Mayrhofer, M. 1966. *Die Indo-Arier im alten Vorderasien*. Wiesbaden: Otto Harrassowitz

Mayrhofer, M. 1973. *Die Arier im vorderen Orient: ein Mythos?* Wien: Oesterr. Akad. der Wissenschaft

McAlpin, David W. 1974. Elamite and Dravidian: the morphological evidence. *IJDL* 3.2: 342–58

McAlpin, David W. 1975. Elamite and Dravidian: further evidence of relationship. *Current Anthropology* 16: 105–15

McAlpin, David W. 1976. Dative subjects in Malayalam. In Verma (ed.), *NSSAL*: 183–94

McAlpin, David W. 1979. Linguistic prehistory: the Dravidian situation. In Deshpande and Hook (eds.): 175–88

McCawley, Noriko A. 1976. From O E/M E 'impersonal' to 'personal' constructions: what is a 'subject-less' S? In *Papers from the Parasession on Diachronic Syntax* (S. Steever, C. Walker, and S. Mufwene, eds.): 192–204 (CLS)

Meenakshi, K. 1986. The quotative in Indo-Aryan. In Krishnamurti (ed.) 1986: 209–18

Meillet, A. 1922. *Les dialectes indo-européens*. Paris: Librairie de la Société de Linguistique de Paris

Mistry, P. J. (ed.) 1982. *South Asian review: studies in South Asian languages & linguistics*. Jacksonville, FL: South Asian Literary Association (= *SALA Journal* 6.3)

Mukherjee, S. N. 1968. *Sir William Jones: a study in eighteenth-century British attitudes to India*. Cambridge University Press

Nigam, R. C., 1972. *Language handbook on mother tongue in Census* (Census of India, 1971). New Delhi: Government of India (Census Centenary Monograph No. 10)

Nowotny, Fausta. 1967. Schriftsysteme in Indien. *Studium Generale* (Berlin) 20: 527–47.

Pandharipande, Rajeshwari. 1981. Syntax and semantics of the passive construction in selected South Asian languages. (University of Illinois [Urbana] Ph.D. dissertation)

Pattanayak, D. P. 1966. *A controlled historical reconstruction of Oriya, Assamese, Bengali, and Hindi*. The Hague: Mouton

Pattanayak, D. P. (ed.) 1978. *Papers in Indian sociolinguistics*. Mysore: *CIIL*

Pike, Kenneth L. 1988. *Tone languages*. Ann Arbor: University of Michigan Press

Pořízka, Vincenc. 1954. Notes on R. N. Vale's theory of verbal composition in Hindi, Bengali, Gujarati and Marathi. *Archív Orientální* 22: 114–28

Pray, Bruce R. 1976. From passive to ergative in Indo-Aryan. *NSSAL*: 195–211

Rao, S. R. 1982. *The decipherment of the Indus script*. Bombay: Asia

Renfrew, Colin. 1988. *Archaeology and language: the puzzle of Indo-European origins*. Cambridge University Press

Schiffman, Harold. 1979. *A reference grammar of spoken Kannada*. Seattle: Department of Asian Languages, University of Washington.

Schrader, F. Otto. 1925. Dravidisch und Uralisch. *Zeitschrift für Indologie und Iranistik* 3: 81–112

Schwarzberg, Joseph E. (ed.) 1978. *A historical atlas of South Asia*. University of Chicago Press

Sebeok, Thomas A. (ed.) 1969. *Current trends in linguistics, vol. 5: South Asia*. The Hague: Mouton

Shapiro, Michael C., and Harold F. Schiffman. 1981. *Language and society in South Asia*. Delhi: Motilal Banarsidass

Singh, Udaya Narayana, K. V. Subbarao, S. K. Bandyopadhyay. 1986. Classification of polar verbs in selected SA languages. In Krishnamurti (ed.): 244–69

Soares, Anthony Xavier (ed.). 1936. *Portuguese vocables in Asiatic languages*. Baroda: Oriental Institute. (From the Portuguese original by Sebastião Rodolfo Dalgado, with additions and comments)

Sridhar, S. N. 1976. The notion of 'subject' in Kannada. *NSSAL*: 212–39

Sridhar, S. N. 1979. Dative subjects and the notion of subject. *Lingua* 49: 99–125

Starosta, Stanley. 1985. The locus of case in South Asian languages. *PCPR*: 211–46

Thapar, Romila. 1966. *A history of India–1*. Harmondsworth (England): Penguin Books

Thieme, P. 1960. The 'Aryan' gods of the Mitanni treaties. *JAOS* 60: 301–17

Tiffou, Etienne, and Yves Charles Morin. 1982. A note on split ergativity in Burushaski. *BSOAS* 45.1: 88–95

Tilak, B. G. 1893. *Orion, or researches into the antiquity of the Vedas*. Bombay: Mrs Radhabhai Atmaram Sagoon

Tilak, B. G. 1903. *The Arctic home in the Vedas*. Poona: Kesari

Traugott, Elizabeth Closs. 1972. *The history of English syntax: a transformational approach to the history of English sentence structure*. New York: Holt, Rinehart & Winston
Turner, R. L. 1960. Some problems of sound change in Indo-Aryan. Poona: University of Poona (Gune Lectures)
Turner, R. L. 1966–71. *A comparative dictionary of the Indo-Aryan languages (CDIAL)*. vols. 1–2. London: Oxford University Press; vol. 3 (*Addenda and Corrigenda*) London: SOAS
Turner, R. L. 1975. *Collected papers, 1912–1973*. London: Oxford University Press
Turner, R. L. 1979. Preservation of original Indo-Aryan vocabulary in the modern languages. *BSOAS* 42: 545–60
Tyler, Stephen A. 1968. Dravidian and Uralian: the lexical evidence. *Lg.* 44: 798–812
Vale, Ramchandra Narayan. 1948. Verbal composition in Indo-Aryan. Poona: Deccan College
Varma, Siddheshwar. 1929. *Critical studies in the phonetic observations of Indian grammarians*. London: RAS (James G. Furlong Fund, vol. 7)
Varma, Siddheshwar. 1939. Indian dialects in phonetic transcriptions. *IL* 7: 281–9
Varma, Siddheshwar. 1965. Aspiration in North-west Sub-Himalayan Indo-Aryan dialects. *IL* 26: 175–88
Verma, Manindra K. (ed.). 1976a. *The notion of subject in South Asian languages* (*NSSAL*). Madison: University of Wisconsin, South Asian Studies
Vermeer, Hans J. 1969a. *Das Indo-Englische: Situation und linguistische Bedeutung*. Heidelberg: J. Groos
Vermeer, Hans J. 1969b. *Untersuchungen zum Bau Zentral-Süd-Asiatischer Sprachen*. Heidelberg: J. Groos
Warder, A. K. 1972. *Indian Kavya literature*. Delhi: Motilal Banarsidass
Weinreich, Uriel. 1957. Functional aspects of Indian bilingualism. *Word* 13.2: 203–33
Wyatt, W. F., Jr. 1970. The Indo-Europeanization of Greece. In Cardona et al.: 89–111
Zide, Arlene R. K., David Magier, and Eric Schiller (eds.). 1985. *Proceedings of the conference on participant roles: South Asia and adjacent areas* (*PCPR*). Bloomington: Indiana University Linguistics Club
Zograph, G. A. 1976. *Morfologicheskii stroi novykh indoariiskikh iazykov*. Moscow: Nauka
Zograph, G. A. 1983. *Languages of South Asia*. London: Routledge & Kegan Paul

Section II: *By individual Indo-Aryan language or dialect*

Angika

Pandey, Paramanand. 1979. *pratham angikā-vyākaraṇ* [in Hindi]. Patna: Paramashram
[A journal, *Angapriyā*, is published in this language by the Akhila Bharatiya Angika Sahitya Kala Manca, Bhagalpur (Bihar).]

Apabhramsa

Sen, Subhadra Kumar. 1973. *Proto-New Indo-Aryan*. Calcutta: Eastern Publishers
Srivastava, Virendra. 1965. *apabhraṁśa bhāṣā kā adhyayan* [in Hindi]. Delhi: Bharati Sahitya Mandir
Tagare, G. Y. 1948. *Historical grammar of Apabhramsa*. Poona: Deccan College

Assamese

Babakaev, V. D. 1961. *Assamskii iazyk*. Moscow: Vostochnoi Literatury
Babakaev, V. D. 1980. *Ocherk morfologicheskoi struktury assamskogo iazyka*. Moscow: Nauka

Barua, Hem Chandra. 1965. *The Assamese–English dictionary: Hem-Kosha*. Sibsagar: Hem Chandra Library
Baruah, P. N. Dutta. 1975. Negative formation in Asamiya and Oriya. *IL* 36.2: 144–51
Baruah, P. N. Dutta. 1980. *An intensive course in Assamese*. Mysore: CIIL
Brown, N. 1848. *Grammatical notes on the Assamese language*. Sibsagar: American Baptist Mission Press
Goswami, Golok Chandra. 1966. *An introduction to Assamese phonology*. Poona: Deccan College
Goswami, S. N. 1971. The case suffixes in Assamese. *IL* 32.2: 139–47
Goswami, Upendranath. 1976. A historical note on the negative particles in Asamiya. *IL* 37.2: 143–5
Hazarika, Biswanath. 1968. Negative formation in Assamese. *IL* 29: 34–9
Kakati, Banikanta. 1962. *Assamese, its formation and development*. Gauhati: Lawyer's Book Stall
Sarma, Nirmaleswar. 1963. *A guide to Assamese*. Gauhati: Lawyer's Book Stall
Sarma, Paresh Chandra Deva. 1962. *Assamese tutor*. Gauhati: Lawyer's Book Stall

Assamese, dialects

Goswami, Upendra. 1957–8. OIA sibilants in Kamrupi. *Bulletin of Deccan College* 18: 309–12
Goswami, Upendranath. 1970. *A study on Kamrupi: a dialect of Assamese*. Gauhati: Department of Historical and Antiquarian Studies, Assam

Awadhi

Saksena, Baburam. 1971 (1937). *Evolution of Awadhi*. 2nd edn. Delhi: Motilal Banarsidass

Bajjika

Arun, Awadeshwar. 1972. *bajjikā, hindī aur bhojapurī: tulnātmak adhyayan* [in Hindi]. Muzaffarpur: Kumud Prakashan
Tivari, Srisiya. 1964. *bajjikā bhāṣā aur sāhitya* [in Hindi]. Patna: Bihar Rashtrabhasha Parishad

Bangaru (see Hariyanvi)

Bengali

Anderson, J. D. 1917. The phonetics of the Bengali language. *BSOS* 1: 79–84
Basu, Dwijendranath. 1955. On the negative auxiliary in Bengali. *IL* 15: 9–13
Bender, Ernest, and Theodore Riccardi, Jr. 1978. *An advanced course in Bengali*. Philadelphia: University of Pennsylvania (South Asia Regional Studies)
Bykova, E. M. 1960. *Podlezhashchee i skazuemoe v sovremennom bengal'skom iazyke*. Moscow: Vostochnoi Literatury
Bykova, E. M. (ed.) 1964. *Voprosy grammatiki bengal'skogo iazyka*. Moscow: Nauka
Bykova, E. M. 1966. *Bengal'skii iazyk: voprosy grammatiki*. Moscow: Nauka
Chatterjee, Ranjit. 1980. Aspect and Aktionsart in Slavic and Indo-Aryan. (University of Chicago Ph.D. dissertation)
Chatterjee, Suhas. 1986. Diglossia in Bengali. In Krishnamurti (ed.) 1986: 294–301
Chatterji, Suniti Kumar. 1926. *The origin and development of the Bengali language*. 3 vols. Calcutta. Repr. London: Allen & Unwin
Chatterji, Suniti Kumar. 1957. *Bengali self-taught*. London: Marlborough
Dabbs, Jack A. 1971. *A short Bengali–English English–Bengali dictionary*. College Station (Texas): Department of Modern Languages, Texas A&M University

Dasgupta, Probal. 1977. The internal grammar of compound verbs in Bangla. *IL* 38.2: 57–67
Dasgupta, Probal. 1979. The Bangla -wa/-no forms as participle and gerund. *IL* 40.3: 185–97
Dasgupta, Probal. 1982. Phonology and the Bangla verb. *IL* 43.1–2: 17–28
Dasgupta, Probal. 1983. On the Bangla classifier *Ta*, its penumbra, and definiteness. *IL* 44: 11–26
Dasgupta, Probal. 1984. Bangla emphasizers and anchors. *IL* 45: 102–17
Dasgupta, Probal. 1985. On Bangla nouns. *IL* 46.1–2: 37–65
Dev, A. T. 1962. *Students' favorite dictionary (Bengali to English)*, 18th edn. Calcutta: S. C. Mazumder, Dev Sahitya Kutir Pvt Ltd.
Dev, A. T. 1971. *Students' favorite dictionary, English to Bengali*, 25th edn. Calcutta: S. C. Mazumder, Dev Sahitya Kutir Pvt Ltd.
Dimock, Edward C. Jr. 1957. Notes on stem-vowel alternation in the Bengali verb. *IL* 17: 173–7
Dimock, Edward C. Jr. 1958. Symbolic forms in Bengali. *Bulletin of Deccan College* 18: 22–9
Dimock, Edward C. Jr., Somdev Bhattacharji, and Suhas Chatterjee. 1964. *Introduction to Bengali, Part 1*. Honolulu: East–West Center
Ferguson, Charles A., and Munier Chowdhury. 1960. The phonemes of Bengali. *Lg*. 36.1: 22–59
Forbes, Duncan. 1861. *Grammar of the Bengali language*. London: Sampson Low, Marston & Co
Gupta, Gautam Sen. 1941. Nasal aspirates in Bangla. *IL* 41.3–4: 125–8
Hai, Md. Abdul. 1958. Aspiration in Standard Bengali. *IL* (Turner vol.): 142–8
Hai, Md. Abdul. 1960. *A phonetic and phonological study of nasals and nasalization in Bengali*. Dacca University
Hudson, D. F. 1965. *Teach yourself Bengali*. London: English Universities Press
Klaiman, M. H. 1976c. Subjecthood, reflexivization, emphatic pronominalization and clause matedness in Bengali. *NSSAL*: 137–51
Klaiman, M. H. 1977. Bengali syntax: possible Dravidian influence. *IJDL* 6.2: 303–17
Klaiman, M. H. 1980. Bengali dative subjects. *Lingua* 51: 275–95
Klaiman, M. H. 1986. Semantic parameters and the South Asian linguistic area. In Krishnamurti (ed.) 1986: 179–94
Litton, Jack. 1966. *Russko-bengal'skii slovar'*. Moscow: "Soviet Encyclopedia"
MacLeod, A. G. 1967. *Colloquial Bengali grammar*. Calcutta: Mission Press
Page, W. Sutton. 1934. *An introduction to colloquial Bengali*. Cambridge: Heffer
Pal, A. K. 1966b. Problems of the Bengali verb and syntax. *Journal of the Asiatic Society of Calcutta* 8.4: 219–38
Pal, A. K. 1970. Aspect in Bengali verbal compounds. *Journal of the Asiatic Society of Calcutta* 12: 110–14
Ray, Punya Sloka, and Lila Ray. 1966. *Bengali language handbook*. Washington, DC: Center for Applied Linguistics
Seely, Clinton B. 1985. Intermediate Bengali. Chicago: by the author
Singh, U. N. 1980. Comments on rule ordering in Bengali morphology. *IL* 41.2: 91–101
Svetovidova, I. A. 1968. Vremia, vid i sposob deistviia v sovremennom bengali (=Tense, aspect, and Aktionsart in contemporary Bengali). In Beskrovny et al. (eds.): 214–223
Zbávitel, Dušan. 1970. *Non-finite verbal forms in Bengali*. Prague: Czechoslovak Academy of Sciences

Bengali, Middle

Sen, Sukumar. 1956–7. Syncopated aspiration in Middle Bengali. *IL* 17b: 19–20

Bengali, Old

Mukherji, Tarapada. 1963. *The Old Bengali language and text.* University of Calcutta

Bengali, dialects

Chaudhuri, Sambha Chandra. 1939. Notes on the Rangpur dialect. *IL* 7: 297–315
Chaudhuri, Sambha Chandra. 1940–4. North Bengal dialects: Rajshahi. *IL* 8: 418–31
Goswami, Krishnapada. 1939. Linguistic notes on Maimansing dialect. *IL* 7: 247–55
Goswami, Krishnapada. 1940–4. Linguistic notes on Chittagong Bengali. *IL* 8: 493–536
Karan, Sudhir Kumar. 1962. South Western Bengali and the language of the *Srīkrṣṇakirtan. Bulletin of the Philological Society of Calcutta* 3.1: 28–34
Pal, A. K. 1966a. Phonemes of a Dacca dialect and the importance of tone. *Journal of the Asiatic Society of Bengal* 7: 1–2
Ray, Punya Sloka, Roushan Jahan, and Muzaffer Ahmad. 1966. *Introduction to the Dacca dialect of Bengali.* (mimeo). University of Chicago, Committee on Southern Asian Studies [available in University of Chicago Library]
Sen, Nilmadhav. 1972. Some dialects of Bangla Desh: an outline. *IL* 33.2: 143–52
Učida, Norihoko. 1970. *Der Bengali-Dialekt von Chittagong.* Wiesbaden: Otto Harrassowitz

Bhadarwahi-Bhalesi

Varma, Siddheshwar. 1931. The neuter gender in Bhadarwahi. *IL* 1: 55–92
Varma, Siddheshwar. 1948. *The Bhalesi dialect.* Calcutta: Royal Asiatic Society.

Bhili

Jain, Nemicand. 1971. *bhīlī kā bhāṣāśāstrīya adhyayan* [in Hindi]. Indore University
Jain, Nemicand. 1962. *bhīlī-hindī-koś* [in Hindi]. Indore: Hira-Bhaiya
Kulkarni, S. B. 1976. *Bhili of Dangs.* Poona: Deccan College
Srivastava, G. P. 1968. Bahelia phonology. *IL* 29.1: 67–79

Bhitrauti

Hook, Peter E., and M. S. Man Singh Chauhan. 1986. The perfective adverb in Bhitrauti. To appear in *Word*

Bhojpuri

Mohan, Peggy. 1978. Trinidad Bhojpuri: a morphological study. University of Michigan Ph.D. dissertation
Mohan, Peggy, and Paul Zador. 1986. Discontinuity in a life cycle: the death of Trinidad Bhojpuri. *Lg.* 62: 291–320
Shukla, Shaligram. 1981. *Bhojpuri grammar.* Washington, DC: Georgetown University
Singh, Kripa Shankar. 1972. A sketch of the hierarchical structure of Bhojpuri. *IL* 33.1: 42–58
Singh, Kripa Shankar. 1973. Bhojpuri morphophonology. *IL* 34: 163–66
Tiwari, U. N. 1954a. *bhojpurī bhāṣā aur sāhitya* [in Hindi]. Patna: Bihar Rashtrabhasha Parishad
Tiwari, U. N. 1954b. Bhojpuri verbal roots. *IL* 14: 64–76
Tiwari, U. N. 1960. *The origin and development of Bhojpuri.* Calcutta: The Asiatic Society

"Bihari" (see also Angika, Bajjika, Bhojpuri, Magahi, Maithili, Sadani)

Grierson, George A. 1883–6. *Seven grammars of the dialects and subdialects of the Bihari language*. Calcutta

Jeffers, Robert J. 1976. The position of Bihari dialects in Indo-Aryan. *Indo-Iranian Journal*. 18: 215–25

Bishnupriya

Sinha, Kali Prasad. 1974. Bishnupriya Manipuri: a descriptive sketch. *IL* 35: 185–99

Sinha, Kali Prasad. 1981. *The Bishnupriya Manipuri language*. Calcutta: Firma KLM

Sinha, Kali Prasad. 1986. *An etymological dictionary of Bishnupriya Manipuri*. Calcutta: Punthi Pustak

Braj

McGregor, R. S. 1968. *The language of Indrajit of Orcha*. Cambridge University Press

Varma, Dhirendra. 1935. *La langue braj*. Paris

Bundeli

Jaiswal, M. P. 1962. *A linguistic study of Bundeli*. Leiden: E. J. Brill

Chhattisgarhi

Telang, Bhalacandra. 1966. *chattīsgarhī, halbī, bhatrī boliyo˜ kā bhāṣāvaigyānik adhyayan* [in Hindi]. Bombay: Hindi Granth Ratnakar

Dakkhini

Arora, Harbir. 1986. Some aspects of Dakkhini Hindi–Urdu syntax with special reference to convergence. (University of Delhi Ph.D. thesis)

Kachru, Yamuna. 1986. The syntax of Dakkhini: a study in language variation and change. In Krishnamurti (ed.) 1986: 165–73

Matthews, David. 1976. Dakani language and literature 1500–1700 AD. (University of London Ph.D. thesis)

Pray, Bruce R. 1980. Evidence of grammatical convergence in Dakhini Urdu and Telugu. *Proceedings of the Sixth Annual Meeting of the Berkeley Linguistic Society*: 90–4

Schmidt, Ruth Laila. 1981. *Dakhini Urdu*. New Delhi: Bahri Publications

Shamatov, A. N. 1974. *Klassicheskii dakkhini (iuzhnyi khindustani)*. 17 vols. Moscow: Nauka

"Dardic" (see also Kalasha, Kashmiri, Khowar, Pashai, Shina, and Nuristani)

Buddruss, Georg. 1960. *Die Sprache von Wotapur und Katarqala*. Bonn: Selbstverlag des Orientalischen Seminars der Universität Bonn

Edelman, D. I. 1983. *The Dardic and Nuristani languages*. Moscow: Nauka

Fussman, Gerard. 1972. *Atlas linguistique des parlers dardes et kafirs*. 2 vols. Paris: École Française d'Extrême Orient

Grierson, George A. 1969 (1906). *The Piśāca languages of North-Western India*. (London: RAS) repr. Delhi: Mushiram

Grierson, George A. 1929. *Torwali: an account of a Dardic language of the Swat Kohistan*. London: RAS

Grierson, George A. 1931. Conjunct consonants in Dardic. *BSOS* 6.2: 349–68

Koul, Omkar N., and Ruth Laila Schmidt. 1984. Dardistan revisited: an examination of the relationship between Kashmiri and Shina. In Koul and Hook (eds.): 1–26

Morgenstierne, Georg. 1932. *Report on a linguistic mission to North-Western India*. Oslo: Instituttet for Sammenlignende Kulturforskning
Morgenstierne, Georg. 1935. The personal pronouns 1st and 2nd plural in the Dardic and Kafiri languages. *IL* 5: 63–7
Morgenstierne, Georg. 1940. Notes on Bashkarik. *Acta Orientalia* 18: 206–57
Morgenstierne, Georg. 1941. *Notes on Phalura: an unknown Dardic language of Chitral*. Oslo: Jacob Dybwad (*Skrifter utgitt av Det Norske Videnskaps-Akademi i Oslo II*. Hist.-Filos. Klasse. 1940. No. 5)
Morgenstierne, Georg. 1945. Notes on Shumashti. *NTS* 14: 5–28
Morgenstierne, Georg. 1947. Metathesis of liquids in Dardic. *Det Norske Videnskapsakademi i Oslo. Skrifter 2*: 145–54 (repr. 1973 in *Irano-Dardica*: 231–40)
Morgenstierne, Georg. 1950. Notes on Gawar-Bati. *Skrifter utgitt av Det Norske Videnskapsakademi i Oslo II*. Hist. Filos. Klasse: No. 1
Schmidt, Ruth Laila. 1981. Report on a survey of Dardic languages of Kashmir. *IL* 42: 17–21
Schmidt, Ruth Laila, and Omkar N. Koul. 1983. *Kohistani to Kashmiri: an annotated bibliography of Dardic languages*. Patiala: Indian Institute of Language Studies
Turner, R. L. 1927. Notes on Dardic. *BSOS* 4.3: 533–41 (repr. 1975 in *Collected Papers*: 301–9)

Dhundhari (Jaipuri)

Nandhala, Jhunthalal. 1974. *ḍhuṁḍhāṛī lok bhāsā kos* [in Dhundhari]. Jaipur: Rajasthan Bhasa Prachar Sabha

Dogri

Gupta, Bansilal. 1965. *ḍogrī bhāṣā aur vyākaraṇ* [in Hindi]. Jammu: Jammu Tavi Lalitkala va Sahitya Akademi
Gupta, Vina. 1984. *ḍogrī vākya-vinyās [Dogri syntax]*. New Delhi: Simant
Khajuria, Tej Ram. 1939a. An occurrence of the Perfective in Dogri. *IL* 7: 387–97
Khajuria, Tej Ram. 1939b. The conjunctive participle in Northern Dogri. *IL* 7: 290–6
Nath Sharma. 1969. *The Dogri language and literature*. Jammu
Shankar, Gauri. 1931. A short account of the Dogri dialect. *IL* 1: 93–176
Shankar, Gauri. 1969. Dogri prose in its making. *IL* 30: 77–80

Garhwali

Bhatt, R. P. 1941. *Comparative Rameshwari Garhwali grammar*. Lahore
Chandrasekhar, A. 1970. The phonemes of Garhwali. *IL* 31.3: 80–5

Gujarati

Cardona, George. 1965. *A Gujarati reference grammar*. Philadelphia: University of Pennsylvania Press
Dave, Radhekant. 1967. A formant analysis of the clear, nasalized, and murmured vowels in Gujarati. *IL* 28.2: 1–30
Dave, T. N. 1932. Notes on Gujarati phonology. *BSOS* 6.3: 673–8
Desai, Urmi G. 1972. Active–passive constructions in Gujarati. *Journal of the University of Bombay*
Deshpande, Pandurang Ganesh. 1984. *Gujarati–English dictionary*. Ahmedabad: University Book Production Board, Gujarat State
Dhruva, N. M. n.d. (1920) *Gujarati self-taught*. London: Marlborough (Revised edition by T. N. Dave)

Doderet W. 1925. A Gujarati–English vocabulary. *BSOS* 3: 783–98
Doderet, W. 1926. Government of 'prepositions' in Gujarati. *BSOS* 4: 65–7
Durbin, Mridula. 1979. Ergativity and antipassive in Gujarati. *SALA* 1: 169–92
Firth, J. R. 1957. Phonetic observations in Gujarati. *BSOAS* 20: 231–41
Fischer-Jørgensen, Eli. 1967. Phonetic analysis of breathy vowels in Gujarati. *IL* 28.2: 71–139
Gala, S. R., and P. S. Sodha. 1975. *viśāl śabdakoś: gujarātī-gujarātī-angreji*. Ahmedabad: Gala Publishers
Gala, L. R., B. L. Shah, and L. B. Gokani. 1980–1. *Gala's standard dictionary: English–English–Gujarati*. Ahmedabad: Gala Publishers
Joshi, D. M. 1975. Gujarati verb forms reconsidered. *IL* 36.3: 285–9
Lambert, H. M. 1971. *Gujarati language course*. Cambridge University Press
Master, Alfred. 1925. Stress accent in modern Gujarati. *JRAS Bombay Branch* 1: 76–94
Mehta, B. N., and B. B. Mehta. 1925. *The modern Gujarati–English dictionary*. Baroda
Mistry, P. J. 1969. Gujarati verbal constructions. (UCLA Ph.D. dissertation)
Mistry, P. J. 1976. Subject in Gujarati: an examination of verb-agreement phenomenon. *NSSAL*: 240–69
Modi, Bharati. 1986. Rethinking of 'murmur in Gujarati'. *IL* 47: 39–55
Pandit, P. B. 1954. Indo-Aryan sibilants in Gujarati. *IL* 14: 36–44
Pandit, P. B. 1955–6a. E and O in Gujarati. *IL* 16: 14–54
Pandit, P. B. 1955–6b. Nasalisation, aspiration, and murmur in Gujarati. *IL* 17: 165–72
Pandit, P. B. 1958. Duration, syllable, and juncture in Gujarati. *IL* (Turner vol.): 212–18
Pandit, P. B. 1961. Historical phonology of Gujarati vowels. *Lg.* 37: 54–66
Patel, M. S., and J. J. Mody. 1960. The vowel system of Gujarati. Baroda
Savel'eva, L. V. 1965. *Iazyk gudzharati*. Moscow: Nauka
Taylor, George P. 1908 (repr. 1985). *The student's Gujarati grammar*. New Delhi: Asian Educational Services
Tessitori, L. P. 1913. Origins of the dative and genitive in Gujarati. *JRAS*
Tisdall, W. St. Clair. 1961b (1892). *A simplified grammar of the Gujarati language*. (repr.) New York: F. Ungar
Turner, R. L. 1914. The suffixes -NE and -NO in Gujarati. *JRAS*: 1033–8
Turner, R. L. 1921. Gujarati phonology. *JRAS* 3: 329–65, 4: 505–44 (repr. 1975 in *Collected Papers*: 88–145)

Gujarati, Old

Bender, Ernest. 1992. *The Salibhadra-Dhanna-Carita: a work in Old Gujarātī, critically edited and translated, with a grammatical analysis and glossary*. (American Oriental Series, vol. 13). American Oriental Society: New Haven, Conn.
Brown, W. Norman. 1938. An Old Gujarati text of the Kalaka story. *JAOS* 58: 5–29
Brown, W. Norman. 1958. Some postpositions behaving as prepositions in the Old Gujarati *Vasantavilāsa*. *IL* (Turner vol.): 228–31
Desai, Urmi. 1991. Gujarātī Sāhityano navamo dāyako: bhāṣāvijñān ane koś, Parab 32. 4: 30–64 [Special issue of the *Journal of the Gujarātī Sāhitya Pariṣad* on linguistics and lexicography in the '80s]
Miltner, Vladimir. 1964. Old Gujarati, Middle Gujarati, and Middle Rajasthani sentence structure. *Bharatiya Vidya* 24: 9–31

Gujarati, dialects

Vyas, Y. D. 1974. *bolīvijñāna ane gujarātnī bolīo* (Dialectology and dialects of Gujarat) [in Gujarati]. Ahmedabad: University Production Board, Gujarat State

Gujuri (Gojri)

Sharma, Jagdish Chander. 1982. *Gojri grammar*. Mysore: CIIL

Halbi (see also *Chhattisgarhi)*

Kanshikar, Citra. 1972. A descriptive analysis of Halbi: an Indo-Aryan language. (Poona University Ph.D. dissertation)
Shukla, Hira Lal. 1985. *Sociocultural approach to tribal languages: an historico-comparative dictionary of Halbi, the lingua franca of Aryan, Dravidian, and Munda tribes.* Delhi: B. R. Publications
Singh, Ram Adhar. 1972. Survey of Halabi in Madhya Pradesh. Delhi: Census of India 1971, vol. 1, pt. 11E, Monograph No. 5.

Harauti

Allen, W. S. 1957a. Aspiration in the Harauti nominal. Oxford: *Studies in linguistics*

Hariyanvi

Khandelval, Shiv Kumar. 1980. *bāngarū bolī kā bhāṣāśāstrīya adhyayan.* Delhi: Vani Prakashan
Sharma, Nanak Chand. 1968. *hariyāṇvī bhāṣā kā udgam tathā vikās.* Hoshiarpur: Vishveshvaranand Vedic Research Institute
Singh, Jag Deva. 1970. *A descriptive grammar of Bangru.* Kurukshetra University (Haryana)

Hindi (Standard, including works dealing with "Hindi–Urdu" or "Hindi and Urdu")

Abbi, Anvita. 1977. Reduplicated adverbs in Hindi. *IL* 38.3: 125–35
Abbi, Anvita. 1980. *Semantic grammar of Hindi: a study in reduplication.* New Delhi: Bahri Publications
Abbi, Anvita. 1984. The conjunctive participle in Hindi–Urdu. *IJDL* 13.2: 252–63
Aggarwal, Narindar K. 1978. *A bibliography of studies on Hindi language and linguistics.* Gurgaon (Haryana): Indian Documentation Service
Ambike, S. 1960. The connotation of the conditional in spoken Hindi. *IL* 21: 14–16
Bahl, Kali Chavan. 1967. A reference grammar of Hindi. Chicago: South Asia Center, University of Chicago
Bahri, Hardev. 1960. *Persian influence on Hindi.* Allahabad: Bharati Press Publications
Barannikov, P. A. 1960. On the periodization of the history of the Hindi language. *Hindi Review* 5.9: 172–84
Barannikov, P. A. 1961. Style synonyms in modern Hindi. *IL* 22: 64–81
Barannikov, P. A. 1972. *Problemy khindi kak national'nogo iazyka.* Leningrad: Nauka
Barkhudarov, A. S. 1960. Sanskritskie elementy v sovremennom literarturnom khindi. In Beskrovny (ed.): 5–117
Barkhudarov, A. S. 1963. *Slovoobrazovanie v khindi.* Moscow: Vostochnoi Literatury
Beskrovny, V. M. (ed.). 1960. *Khindi i urdu: voprosy leksikologii i slovoobrazovania.* Moscow: Vostochnoi Literatury
Beskrovny, V. M. 1965. *O roli sanskrita v razvitii novoindiiskikh iazykov.* In G. P. Serdinchenko (ed.), *Sovremennye literaturnye iazyki Stran Azii.* Moscow: Nauka: 62–81
Beskrovny, V. M. (ed.), with A. S. Barkhudarov, G. A. Zograph, and V. P. Liperovskii. 1972. *Khindi-russkii slovar'.* 2 vols. Moscow: "Soviet Encyclopedia"
Bhatia, K. C. 1964. Consonant sequences in Standard Hindi. *IL* 25: 206–12
Burton-Page, J. 1957. The syntax of participial forms in Hindi. *BSOAS* 19.1: 94–104
Chaturvedi, Mahendra, and B. N. Tiwari. 1980. *A practical Hindi–English dictionary.* New Delhi: National Publishing House

Davison, Alice. 1969. Reflexivization and movement rules in relation to a class of Hindi psychological predicates. CLS 5: 37–52

Davison, Alice. 1978. Negative scope and rules of conversation. In J. Romball (ed.), *Syntax and semantics*, vol. 8. New York: Academic Press

Davison, Alice. 1981. Syntactic and semantic indeterminacy resolved: a mostly pragmatic analysis of the Hindi conjunctive participle. In *Radical pragmatics*. New York: Academic Press: 101–28

Davison, Alice. 1982. On the form and meaning of Hindi passive sentences. *Lingua* 58: 149–79

Davison, Alice. 1984. Syntactic constraints on WH- in situ: WH- questions in Hindi–Urdu. CLS 20

Davison, Alice. 1985. Experiencers and patients as subjects in Hindi–Urdu. *PCPR*: 160–78

Davison, Alice. 1986a. Binding relations in correlative clauses. CLS 22

Davison, Alice. 1986b. Hindi *-kar*: the problem of multiple syntactic interpretation. In Krishnamurti (ed.) 1986: 1–14

Dey, Pradip. 1975. A note on coordinate conjunction in Hindi. *IL* 36.2: 132–43

Dixit, R. P. 1963. The segmental phonemes of contemporary Hindi. (University of Texas M.A. thesis)

Dwarikesh, D. P. S. 1971. Historical syntax of the conjunctive participle phrase in New Indo-Aryan dialects of Madhyadeśa (Midland) of northern India. (University of Chicago Ph.D. dissertation)

Elizarenkova, T. Y. 1961. Distinctive features of the consonantal phonemes of Hindi. *Voprosi iazykoznania* 10.5: 22–33

Gaeffke, Peter, 1967. *Untersuchungen zur Syntax des Hindi*. The Hague: Mouton

Gambhir, Vijay. 1983. Theme-focussing in Hindi. *IL* 44: 27–38

Ghatage, A. M. 1964. *Phonemic and morphemic frequencies in Hindi*. Poona

Gumperz, John J., and C. M. Naim. 1960. Formal and informal standards in the Hindi regional language area. *IJAL* 26.3: 92–118

Gupta, Balvir Prakash. 1965. The problem of gender as a concord category in Hindi. *IL* 26: 49–65

Gupta, Sagar Mal. 1980. Indirect request in Hindi: a pragmatic approach. *IL* 41.2: 85–90

Guru, Kamta Prasad. 2022 V (c. 1965). *saṁksipta hindī vyākaraṇ* [in Hindi]. Varanasi: Nagari Pracarini Sabha

Hacker, Paul. 1958. *Zur Funktion einiger Hilfsverben im modernen Hindi*. Mainz: Akademie der Wissenschaften und der Literatur

Hacker, Paul. 1961. On the problem of a method for treating the compound and conjunct verbs in Hindi. *BSOAS* 24.3: 484–576

Hoenigswald, Henry M. 1948. Declension and nasalization in Hindustani. *JAOS* 68: 139–44

Hook, Peter E. 1974. *The compound verb in Hindi*. University of Michigan: Center for South and Southeast Asian Studies

Hook, Peter E. 1976b. Some syntactic reflexes of subcategories of agent in Hindi. *NSSAL*: 65–78

Hook, Peter E. 1978a. Perfecting a test for the Perfective: aspectual parallels in Russian, Lithuanian, Modern Greek, Hindi and Pashto. *University of Michigan Papers in Linguistics* 2: 89–104

Hook, Peter E. 1978b. The compound verb in Hindi: what it is and what it does. In K. S. Singh (ed.), *Readings in Hindi–Urdu Linguistics*. Delhi: National Publishing House: 129–54

Hook, Peter Edwin. 1979. *Hindi structures: intermediate level*. University of Michigan Center for South and Southeast Asian Studies

Jain, Dhanesh. 1973. Pronominal usage in Hindi: a sociolinguistic study. (University of Pennsylvania Ph.D. dissertation)

Jain, Dhanesh. 1975. The semantic basis of some Hindi imperatives. *IL* 36.2: 173–84

Jain, Jagdish. 1981. The Hindi passive. *Papers in linguistics*. 14: 217–32

Kachru, Yamuna. 1966. *An introduction to Hindi syntax*. Urbana: University of Illinois, Department of Linguistics

Kachru, Yamuna. 1973. Some aspects of pronominalization and relative clause construction in Hindi–Urdu. *Studies in the Linguistic Sciences* 3.2: 87–103

Kachru, Yamuna. 1978. On relative clause formation in Hindi–Urdu. *Linguistics* 207: 5–26

Kachru, Yamuna. 1979. Pragmatics and verb serialization in Hindi–Urdu. *Studies in the Linguistic Sciences*. 9.2: 157–69

Kachru, Yamuna. 1980. *Aspects of Hindi grammar*. New Delhi: Manohar

Kachru, Yamuna. 1981. Transitivity and volitionality in Hindi–Urdu. *Studies in the Linguistic Sciences* (Illinois) 11.2: 181–93

Kachru, Yamuna. 1982a. Conjunct verbs in Hindi–Urdu and Persian. In Mistry (ed.): 117–26

Kachru, Yamuna. 1982b. Pragmatics and compound verbs in Indian languages. *THL-2*: 69–84

Kachru, Yamuna, and Tej K. Bhatia. 1977. On reflexivization in Hindi–Urdu and its theoretical implications. *IL* 38.1: 21–38

Katenina, T. E. 1957. Kratkii ocherk grammatik: khindi. Appendix to A. Beskrovny (ed.), *Russko-khindi slovar´*. Moscow: Izdatel´stvo Inostrannykh i National´nykh Slovarei

Kelkar, Ashok R. 1968. *Studies in Hindi–Urdu I*. Poona: Deccan College, Postgraduate and Research Institute

Kellogg, Rev. S. H. 1938. A grammar of the Hindi language. 3rd edn. (2nd edn 1892). London: Kegan Paul, Trench, Trubner

Klaiman, M. H. 1979. On the status of the subjecthood hierarchy in Hindi. *IJDL* 8.1: 17–31

Koul, Omkar N. 1974. Coordinate conjunction in Hindi. *IL* 35.1: 14–30

Koul, Omkar N. (ed.). 1981b (1982). *Topics in Hindi linguistics*, vol. 2. New Delhi: Bahri Publications

Koul, Omkar N. 1981. Coordinating conjunctions in Hindi. *THL-2*: 183–204

Kumar, Suresh. 1980. A sociolinguistic view of Hindi in administration. *IL* 41.1: 21–30

Lakshmibai, B. 1973. *A case grammar of Hindi*. Agra: Central Institute of Hindi

Lienhard, Siegfried. 1961. *Tempusgebrauch und Aktionsartenbildung in der modernen Hindi*. Stockholm: Almqvist & Wiksell

Mathews, W. K. 1964. Phonetics and phonology in Hindi. *Le Maître Phonétique* 102: 18–22

McGregor, R. S. 1972. *Outline of Hindi grammar*. Oxford: Clarendon Press

Mehrotra, R. C. 1959. Hindi syllabic structure. *IL* 20: 213–37

Mehrotra, R. C. 1964. Hindi phonemes. *IL* 25: 324–46

Mehrotra, R. C. 1965. Stress in Hindi. *IL* 26: 96–105

Misra, Bal Govind. 1967. Historical phonology of Modern Standard Hindi. (Cornell University Ph.D. dissertation)

Narang, G. C., and D. Becker. 1971. Aspiration and nasalization in the general phonology of Hindi. *Lg.* 47: 646–67

Narula, Shamsher Singh. 1955. *Scientific history of the Hindi language*. New Delhi: Hindi Academy

Ohala, Manjari. 1983. *Aspects of Hindi phonology*. Delhi: Motilal Banarsidass
Ohala, Manjari. 1986. A search for the phonetic correlates of Hindi stress. In Krishnamurti (ed.) 1986: 81–92
Pandharipande, Rajeshwari, and Yamuna Kachru. 1977. Relational grammar, ergativity, and Hindi–Urdu. *Lingua* 41: 217–38
Pandharipande, Rajeshwari, 1979. Postpositions in passive sentences in Hindi. *Studies in the Linguistic Sciences* 9: 172–88
Pandharipande, Rajeshwari, 1981. Exceptions and rule government: the case of passive rule in Hindi. *THL-2*: 93–121
Pandharipande, Rajeshwari, 1982. Volitionality: more evidence for constraints on passive in Hindi. In Mistry (ed.) 89–103
Pinnow, Heinz-Juergen. 1953. Über die Vokale in Hindi. *Zeitschrift für Phon.* 7: 43–53
Pořízka, Vincenc. 1963. *Hindština: Hindi language course, Part 1*. Prague: Statni pedagogicke nakladatelstvi
Pořízka, Vincenc. 1967–69. On the perfective verbal aspect in Hindi. *Archív Orientální* 35: 64–88, 208–31; 36: 233–51; 37: 19–47, 345–64
Pořízka, Vincenc. 1977. Aspectual functions of simple verbs and verbal expression in Hindi. In *Readings in Hindi–Urdu linguistics*: 158–64
Pořízka, Vincenc. 1982. On the aspectual contrast in Hindi. *THL-2*: 122–34
Prasad, Kalika, Rajavallabha Sahay, and Mukundilal Shrivastava. 2020 V (c. 1963) *bṛhat hindī koś* [in Hindi]. Varanasi: Jnanamandal
Pray, Bruce. 1970. *Topics in Hindi–Urdu grammar*. Berkeley: University of California Center for South and Southeast Asia Studies
Pray, Bruce R. 1982. Verbs from participles in Indo-Aryan. In Mistry (ed.): 138–47
Rabinovich, I. S. and E. P. Chelyshev (eds.). 1962. *Voprosy grammatiki iazyka khindi*. Moscow: Vostochnoi Literatury
Rai, Amrit. 1984. *A house divided: the origin and development of Hindi/Hindavi*. Delhi: Oxford University Press
Ray, Punya Sloka. 1966. Hindi–Urdu stress. *IL* 27: 95–101
Saksena, Anuradha. 1978. A reanalysis of the passive in Hindi. *Lingua* 46: 339–53
Saksena, Anuradha. 1980. The affected agent. *Lg*. 51.3: 753–60
Saksena, Anuradha. 1982. *Topics in the analysis of causatives with an account of Hindi paradigms*. Berkeley and Los Angeles: University of California Press (*Univ. of Calif. Publications in Linguistics*: 98)
Saksena, Baburam. 1958. A peculiar use of the conditional in Spoken Hindi. *IL* (Turner vol.): 323–4
Satyanarayana, Pulavarthi. 1981. The syntax of *hona* in Hindi. *THL-2*: 146–70
Schwarzschild, L. A. 1959. Some aspects of the history of modern Hindi *nahī*. *JRAS* 1: 44–50
Shapiro, Michael C. 1974. Aspects of Hindi abstract verbal syntax. (University of Chicago Ph.D. dissertation)
Sharma, A. and H. J. Vermeer. 1963. *Einführung in die Hindi Grammatik*. Heidelberg: Julius Croos Verlag
Sharma, Aryendra. 1958. *A basic grammar of modern Hindi*. Delhi: Government of India, Ministry of Education
Shukla, Rambahori. 1961. *kāvya-pradīp* [in Hindi]. Jalandhar and Allahabad: Hindi Bhavan
Singh, A. B. 1969. On echo-words in Hindi. *IL* 30: 185–95
Singh, Suraj Bhan. 1979. A feature analysis of equational sentences in Hindi. *IL* 40.1: 1–17

Sinha, A. C. 1970. Predicate complement constructions in English and Hindi. (University of York Ph.D. dissertation)
Sinha, A. C. 1976. A phrase structure rule for Hindi noun phrase and universal grammar. *IL* 37.1: 45–9
Sinha, A. K. 1973. Factivity and the relation between main and subordinate clauses in Hindi. In *You Take the High Node and I'll Take the Low Node* (CLS): 155–63
Sinha, A. K. 1976. The notion of subject and agent in Hindi. *NSSAL*: 109–36
Spies, O. 1955. Türkische Sprachgut im Hindustani. *Festschrift W. Kirfel* (Bonn): 321–43
Srivastava, G. P. 1974. A child's acquisition of Hindi consonants. *IL* 35.2: 112–18
Srivastava, R. N. 1970. The problem of the Hindi semivowels. *IL* 31: 129–37
Subbarao, K. V. 1981. Syntactic criteria for some semantic class of predicates in Hindi. *THL-2*: 171–82
Subbarao, K. V. 1984. *Complementation in Hindi syntax*. Delhi: Academic Publications
Tedesco, P. 1945. Hindi *bhejna* 'to send'. *JAOS* 65: 154–63
Tiwari, U. N. 1961. *hindī bhāṣā kā udgam aur vikās* [in Hindi]. Prayag [Allahabad]: Bharati Bhandar
Učida, Norihoko. 1971 (1972). Geminierte Konsonanten im Hochhindi. *Indo-Iranian Journal*. 13: 255–73
Učida, Norihoko. 1977. *Hindi phonology*. Calcutta: Simant
Učida, Norihoko. 1978. *Studien zur Hindi–Vokalphonologie*. Wiesbaden: F. Steiner
Van Olphen, H. H. 1970. The structure of the Hindi verb phrase. (University of Texas Ph.D. dissertation)
Van Olphen, Herman. 1975. Aspect, tense, and mood in the Hindi verb. *Indo-Iranian Journal*. 16: 284–301
Van Olphen, Herman. 1976. The Hindi verb in indirect constructions. *IJDL* 5.2: 224–37
Varmma, Ramcandra. 196?–66. *mānak hindī koś* [in Hindi]. 5 vols. Prayag (Allahabad): Hindi Sahitya Sammelan
Verma, Manindra K. 1971. *The structure of the noun phrase in English and Hindi*. Delhi: Motilal Banarsidass
Verma, Shivendra K. 1981. Reflections on thematization in Hindi. *THL-2*: 51–68
Verma, Shivendra K. 1981 (1982). Reflections on thematization in Hindi. *THL-2*: 51–68

Hindi, dialects

Bahri, Hardev. 1980. *gramīn hindī boliyā̃* [in Hindi]. Allahabad: Kitab Mahal
Chernyshev, V. A. 1969. *Dialekty i literaturnyi khindi*. Moscow: Nauka
Chernyshev, V. A. 1978. *Dinamika iazykovoi situatsii v Severnoi Indii*. Moscow: Nauka
Geetha, K. R. *Classified state bibliography of linguistic research on Indian languages*. vol. 1: Hindi speaking states. Mysore: CIIL (*Occasional Monograph Series*, 28)
Gumperz, John J. 1955a. The phonology of a North Indian village dialect. *IL* 16: 282–95
Gumperz, John J. 1955b. Phonological differences in three Hindi dialects. *Lg*. 34: 212–24
Gumperz, John J. 1958. Dialect differences and social stratification in a North Indian village. *American Anthropologist* 60.4: 668–82
Harris, Richard W. 1966. Regional variation in urban Hindi. *IL* 27.1: 58–69
Kellogg, S. H. 1938. *A grammar of the Hindi language*. London: Kegan Paul, Trench, Trubner
McGregor, R. S. 1969. Some material bearing on the early history of Sanskritised prose style in Hindi dialects. *IL* 30: 65–9
Pathak, R. S. 1977. The intonation of Bagheli. *IL* 38.4: 197–209
Sharma, Gendalal. 1983. *hindī bhaṣa-parivār*. Aligarh: Somanchal Prakashan
Smith, Richard Rhodes. 1974. Awadhi/Kannauji transition phenomena and their correlates: a study in dialect geography. (Cornell University Ph.D. dissertation)

Kachchhi (see Sindhi, dialects)

Kalasha

Bashir, Elena. 1983. Some areal characteristics of Kalasha. (12th Wisconsin South Asia Conference paper)

Bashir, Elena. 1988. Topics in Kalasha syntax: an areal and typological perspective. (University of Michigan Ph.D. dissertation)

Morgenstierne, Georg. 1975. Notes on Kalasha. *NTS* 20: 183–238

Morgenstierne, Georg. 1973a. *The Kalasha language*. 2nd rev. edn. Oslo: Instittutet for Sammenlignende Kulturforskning. (*Indo-Iranian Frontier Languages*, vol. 4)

Kashmiri

Andrabi, Syed M. Inayatullah. 1983. Reference and coreference in Kashmiri: a syntactic–semantic study. (University of Poona Ph.D. thesis)

Bailey, T. G. 1935. The four-fold consonant system in Kashmiri. In *Proceedings of the 2nd Congress of Phonetic Sciences*. London: 182–4

Bailey, T. G. 1937. *The pronunciation of Kashmiri*. London: RAS (James G. Forlong Fund, vol. 16)

Grierson, George A. 1915. Linguistic classification of Kashmiri. *Indian Antiquary*: 270

Grierson, George A. 1916. On the Sarada alphabet. *JRAS*

Grierson, George A. 1973 (1911). *Standard manual of the Kashmiri language*. 2 vols. Jammu: Light and Life

Handoo, Jawaharlal. 1973. *Kashmiri phonetic reader*. Mysore: CIIL

Hook, Peter E. 1976a. Is Kashmiri an SVO language? *IL* 37: 133–42

Hook, Peter E. 1984b. Some further observations on Kashmiri word order. In Koul and Hook (eds.): 145–53

Hook, Peter E. 1984c. The anti-absolutive in Kashmiri and Sumerian. CLS 20: 181–91

Hook, Peter E. 1985b. The super-anti-absolutive in Kashmiri. *Proceedings of 1st Pacific Linguistics Conference* (Scott DeLancey and Russell Tomlin, eds.; Eugene: University of Oregon): 142–51

Hook, Peter E. 1986a. Non-referential valents in the expression of impersonal action in Kashmiri and Russian. CLS 22

Hook, Peter E., and Vijay Kumar Kaul. 1987. Case alternation, transitionality, and the adoption of direct objects in Kashmiri. CLS 23 (To appear in *IL*)

Hook, Peter E., and Omkar N. Koul. 1984a. On the grammar of derived transitives and causatives in Kashmiri. In Koul and Hook (eds.): 90–122

Hook, Peter E., and Omkar N. Koul. 1984b. Pronominal suffixes and split ergativity in Kashmiri. In Koul and Hook (eds.): 123–35

Hook, Peter E., and Omkar N. Koul. 1985a. Modal verbs of obligation in Kashmiri. *IJDL* 14.2

Hook, Peter E., and Omkar N. Koul. 1985b. Subject versus agent: a study of the Kashmiri phasal verb HYE 'begin to'. *SALA* 7 (Elena Bashir, M. M. Deshpande and P. E. Hook, eds., Bloomington: Indiana University Linguistics Club)

Hook, Peter E., and Alexis Manaster-Ramer. 1985. The verb-second constraint in Germanic and Kashmiri: towards a typology of V-2 languages. In Jan Faarhund (ed.), *Germanic linguistics: papers from a symposium at the University of Chicago*. Bloomington: Indiana University Linguistics Club: 46–58

Kachru, Braj. 1973. *A course in spoken Kashmiri*. Urbana: University of Illinois, Department of Linguistics

Kelkar, Ashok R., and P. N. Trisal. 1964. Kashmiri word phonology. *Anthropological Linguistics* 6.1

Koul, Omkar N. 1976. Noun phrases in Kashmiri. *IL* 37.3: 187–95

Koul, Omkar N., and Peter Edwin Hook (eds.). 1984. *Aspects of Kashmiri linguistics*. New Delhi: Bahri Publications

Morgenstierne, Georg. 1941. The phonology of Kashmiri. *Acta Orientalia* 19.1: 79–99. Repr. 1973 in *Irano-Dardica*. Wiesbaden: Dr Ludwig Reichert Verlag

Toporov, V. N. 1967. Fonologicheskaia interpretatsiia konsonantizma kashmiri v sviazi s tipologiei dardskikh iazykov. In *Semiotika i vostochnye iazyki*. Moscow

Zakhar′in, B. A., and D. I. Edel′man. 1971. *Iazyk kashmiri*. Moscow: Nauka

Zakhar′in, B. A. 1968. Kashmiri: fonetika i fonologiia, tekst i sistema. In *Naroday Azii i Afriki* 3

Zakhar′in, B. A. 1974. *Problemy fonologii iazyka kashmiri*. Moscow: Nauka

Khandeshi

Chitnis, Vijaya. 1964. The Khandeshi dialect as spoken by farmers in the village of Mohadi in the Dhulia Taluka. (University of Poona Ph.D. dissertation)

Khashali (see also *West Pahari dialects*)

Varma: Siddheshwar. 1938. The dialects of the Khasali Group. *Royal Asiatic Society of Bengal* 4: 1–65

Khowar

Biddulph, John. 1880. *Tribes of the Hindoo Koosh*. Calcutta: Government Printing Office. Repr. 1977 Karachi: Indus Publications

Buddruss, Georg. 1976. Khowar: a new literary language of Chitral (Pakistan). In *Proceedings of the 30th International Congress of Human Sciences in Asia and Africa* [= Orientalists], Mexico City

Buddruss, Georg. 1982. Khowar-Texte in arabischer Schrift. (Akademie der Wissenschaft und der Literatur), Wiesbaden: Franz Steiner

Endresen, Rolf Theil, and Knut Kristiansen. 1981. Khowar studies. *Acta Iranica* 21: 210–43

Morgenstierne, Georg. 1936. Iranian elements in Khowar. *BSOS* 8: 657–71. (Repr. 1973 in *Irano-Dardica*: 241–55)

Morgenstierne, Georg. 1947. Some features of Khowar morphology. *NTS* 14: 5–28

Morgenstierne, Georg. 1955. A Khowar tale. *IL* 16: 163–9

Morgenstierne, Georg. 1957. Sanskritic words in Khowar. In *S. K. Belvalkar Felicitation Volume*: 84–8; revised version in *Irano-Dardica* 1973: 256–72

O'Brien, D. J. T. 1895. *Grammar and vocabulary of the Khowar dialect (Chitrali)*. Lahore

Konkani

Aiyagal, Baindoor Deorai. 1968. *Konkani self-taught*. Bombay: Konkan Cultural Association

Desay, Shripad Raghunath. 1980. *konkaṇī śabdakoś: paylo bhāg* [in Konkani and Marathi]. Pedane (Goa): Shrisitaram Prakashan

Ghatage, A. M. 1963. *Konkani of South Kanara*. Bombay: State Board for Literature and Culture. (Survey of Marathi dialects: I)

Katre, S. M. 1965. Consonantal gemination in Konkani. *IL* 26: 237–9

Katre, S. M. 1966. *The formation of Konkani*. Poona: Deccan College

Kelekar, Ravindra. 1963. *A bibliography of Konkani literature*. Goa: Gomant Bharat Publications

Miranda, Rocky V. 1977. The assimilation of Dravidian loans to Konkani phonology. *Indo-Iranian Journal*. 19: 247–65
Miranda, Rocky V. 1978. Caste, religion and dialect differentiation in the Konkani area. *International Journal of the Sociology of Language* 16 (Aspects of sociolinguistics in South Asia, B. B. Kachru and S. N. Sridhar, eds.): 77–91
Miranda, Rocky V. 1982. The status of Konkani during the Portuguese era. In Mistry ed.: 204–13
Nadkarni, M. V. 1970. Noun phrase embedded structures in Kannada and Konkani (UCLA Ph.D. dissertation)
Nadkarni, M. V. 1975. Bilingualism and syntactic change in Konkani. *Lg*. 51.3: 672–83
Pereira, Jose. 1971. *Konkani: a language (a history of the Konkani Marathi controversy)*. Dharwar: Karnatak University.
Pereira, Jose. 1973. *Literary Konkani: a brief history*. Dharwar: Konkani Sahitya Prakashan

Kumauni

Apte, Mahadeo L., and D. P. Pattanayak. 1967. *An outline of Kumauni grammar*. Durham: Duke University, Program in Comparative Studies of Southern Asia, Monograph No. 6
Ruvali, Kesavadatta. 1982. *kumaunī bhāṣā aur sāhitya* [in Hindi]. Aligarh: Granthayan
Sah, P. P. 1974. The pragmatics of Kumauni *bal*. *IL* 35.4: 245–59

"Lahnda" (see also Siraiki)

Bahl, K. C. 1957a. A note on tones in Western Panjabi. *IL* 17b: 30–4
Bahl, Paramanand. 1941. Injective consonants in Western Panjabi. *Journal of the Panjabi Oriental Research Institute* 1:1: 32–47
Bahri, Hardev. 1962. *Lahndi phonology*. Allahabad: Bharati Press
Bahri, Hardev. 1963. *Lahndi phonetics*. Allahabad: Bharati Press
Shackle, C. 1977b. 'South-Western' elements in the language of the Adi Granth. *BSOAS* 40: 36–50
Shackle, C. 1979. Problems of classification in Pakistan Punjab. In *Transactions of the Philological Society 1979*: 191–210
Shackle, C. 1980. Hindko in Kohat and Peshawar. *BSOAS* 43: 482–510
Smirnov, Y. A. 1975. *The Lahndi language*. Moscow: Nauka
Wilson, J. 1899. *Grammar and dictionary of Western Panjabi as spoken in Shahpur District*. Lahore

Lamani

Trail, Ronald L. 1970. *A grammar of Lamani*. Norman (Oklahoma): Summer Institute of Linguistics

Magadhi (Prakrit)

Jha, Munishwar. 1967. *Magadhi and its formation*. Calcutta: Sanskrit College

Magahi (Bihari regional language)

Aryani, Sampatti. 1965. *magahī: vyākaraṇ, koś* [in Hindi]. Patna: Hindi Sahitya Sammelan
Sinha, Anil C. 1973. Gender in Bangla? *IL* 34.3: 220–8
Verma, Sheela, and Manindra Verma. 1983. The auxiliary with special reference to Magahi. *IL* 44: 97–101
Verma, Sheela. 1985. *The structure of the Magahi verb*. New Delhi: Manohar

Maithili

Grierson, George A. 1909. *Introduction to the Maithili dialect of the Bihari language*. Calcutta
Jha, Ramanath. 1964. *mithilā-bhāṣā-prakāś* [in Maithili]. Daribhanga: Granthalay-Prakashan
Jha, Subhadra. 1940–4. Maithili phonetics. *IL* 8: 435–59
Jha, Subhadra. 1958. *The formation of the Maithili language*. London: Luzac
Singh, U. N. 1983. Subjecthood hierarchy in Maithili. *IL* 44: 75–81
Yadav, R. 1979. Maithili phonetics and phonology. (University of Kansas Ph.D. dissertation)
Yadava, Yogendra P. 1982. Maithili sentences: a transformational analysis. *IL* 1982: 7–28

Maldivian

De Silva, M. W. S. 1969. The phonological efficiency of the Maldivian writing system. *Anthropological Linguistics*. 11.7: 199–209
"Iru". 1980. *Bidheyseen nah fahi Dhivehi/Easy Dhivehi for foreigners*. Male: Novelty Press
[See De Silva 1979 under *Sinhalese* for further references to extant work on Maldivian up to 1979. In the *Addenda* to the *CDIAL* (1985) Turner also makes use of unpublished Maldivian vocabularies by C. H. B. Reynolds.]

Marathi

Berntsen, Maxine, and Jai Nimbkar. 1975a. *A basic Marathi–English dictionary*. Philadelphia: University of Pennsylvania, South Asia Regional Studies
Berntsen, Maxine, and Jai Nimbkar. 1975b. *A Marathi reference grammar*. Philadelphia: University of Pennsylvania, South Asia Regional Studies
Berntsen, Maxine, and Jai Nimbkar. 1982. *Marathi structural patterns, Book One*. New Delhi: American Institute of Indian Studies
Bloch, Jules. 1920. *La formation de la langue Marathe*. Paris: Librairie Ancienne Honoré Champion
Chauhan, D. V. 1969. Origin of the consecutive conjunction *ki* in Marathi: an historical search. *IL* 30: 85–9
Chernova, L. A. 1968. Struktura sklonenie v maratkhi. In Beskrovny et al. (eds.): 232–43
Chitnis, Vijaya. 1979. *An intensive course in Marathi*. Mysore: CIIL
Darby, Alfred. 1933. *A primer of the Marathi language for the use of adults*. Bombay
Das Gupta, Bidhu Bhusan, and Smt. Tara Pandit. 1975. *Marathi self-taught*. 2nd edn. Calcutta: Das Gupta Prakashan
Dhongde, R. V. 1976. Modality in Marathi. *IL* 37.2: 91–101
Dhongde, R. V. 1979. From verbal stems to VP in Marathi: some observations. *IL* 40.2: 102–9
Gajendragadkar, S. N. 1969. Postpositions in Marathi: a controlled study. *IL* 30: 93–103
James, A. Lloyd, and S. G. Kanhere. 1928. The pronunciation of Marathi. *BSOS* 4: 791–801
Junghare, Indira Y. 1973. Restrictive relative clauses in Marathi. *IL* 34.4: 251–62
Katenina, T. E. 1963. *Ocherk grammatiki iazyka maratkhi*. Moscow: Izd. Lit. na Inostrannykh Iazykakh
Kavadi, Naresh B., and Franklin C. Southworth. 1965. *Spoken Marathi, Book I: First-year intensive course*. Philadelphia: University of Pennsylvania Press
Kelkar, Ashok R. 1958. Marathi phonology and morphophonemics. (Cornell University Ph.D. dissertation)

Kelkar, Ashok R. 1973. Relative clauses in Marathi: a plea for a less constricted view. *IL* 34.4: 274–300

Lambert, H. M. 1943. *Marathi language course*. Calcutta: Oxford/Humphrey Milford

Navalkar, G. R. 1925. *The student's Marathi grammar*. Poona: Scottish Mission Press

Raeside, I. M. P. 1958. The Marathi 'compound verb'. *IL* (Turner vol.): 237–48

Ranade, N. B. 1977 (1916). *The twentieth century English–Marathi dictionary*. 2 vols. Pune: Shubhada–Saraswat (Sharad Gogate)

Sardesai, V. N. 1930. Some problems in the nasalization of Marathi. *JRAS* 537–65

Southworth, Franklin C. 1961. The Marathi verbal sequences and their co-occurrences. *Lg.* 37.2: 201–8

Southworth, Franklin C. 1971. Detecting prior creolization: an analysis of the historical origins of Marathi. In Dell Hymes (ed.) *Pidginization and creolization of languages*. Cambridge University Press: 255–76

Southworth, Franklin C. 1974. Linguistic stratigraphy of North India. *IJDL* 3.2: 201–23

Southworth, Franklin C. 1976. The verb in Marathi–Konkani. *IJDL* 5.2: 298–326

Turner, R. L. 1916. The Indo-Germanic accent in Marathi. *JRAS* 1: 203–51; (repr. 1975) *Collected Papers*: 39–75

Wali, Kashi. 1982. Marathi correlatives: a conspectus. In Mistry (ed.): 78–88

Marathi, Old

Doderet, W. 1928. The grammar of the Jñāneśvarī. *BSOS* 4: 543–73

Master, Alfred. 1964. *A grammar of Old Marathi*. Oxford: Clarendon Press

Tulpule, S. G. 1960. *An Old Marathi reader*. Poona: Venus Prakashan

Marathi, dialects

Ghatage, A. M. 1969. *Warli of Thana*. Bombay: State Board for Literature and Culture. (*Survey of Marathi dialects*: VII)

Ghatage, A. M. 1970. Marathi of Kasargod. *IL* 31.4: 138–44

Kulkarni, S. B. 1969. An experiment in estimating transfer of information among some Marathi dialects. *IL* 30: 73–6

Pandharipande, Rajeshwari. 1986. Language and language variation: Nagpuri Marathi. In Krishnamurti (ed.) 1986: 219–31

*Marwari (*see also *Rajasthani)*

Magier, David S. 1983. Topics in the grammar of Marwari. (University of California Ph.D. dissertation)

Magier, David. 1985. Case and transitivity in Marwari. *PCPR*: 149–59

*Middle Indo-Aryan (*see also *Prakrit, Apabhramsa)*

Berger, Hermann. 1955. *Zwei probleme der Mittelindischen Lautlehre*. Munich: in K. bei J. Kitzinger

Burrow, T. 1937. *The language of the Kharoṣṭhi documents from Chinese Turkestan*. Cambridge University Press

Chatterji, S. K., and Sukumar Sen. 1957. *A Middle Indo-Aryan reader*. Calcutta University

Norman, K. R. 1960. Some vowel values in Middle Indo-Aryan. *IL* 14: 36–44

Prakash, Ravi. 1975. *Verb morphology in Middle Indo-Aryan*. New Delhi: Munshiram Manoharlal

Schwarzschild, L. A. 1955. Notes on the history of the infinitive in Middle Indo-Aryan. *IL* 16: 29–34

Schwarzschild, L. A. 1957. Notes on some MIA words in -LL-. *JAOS* 77: 203–7

Sen, Sukumar. 1953. *Historical syntax of Middle Indo-Aryan*. Calcutta
Sen, Sukumar. 1960. *A comparative grammar of Middle Indo-Aryan*. Poona: Linguistic Society of India
Vertogradova, V. V. 1967. *Strukturnaia tipologiia sredneindiiskikh fonologicheskikh sistem*. Moscow: Nauka

Nagpuria (see *Sadani*)

Nepali

Bendix, Edward H. 1974. Indo-Aryan and Tibeto-Burman contact as seen through Nepali and Newari verb tenses. In F. C. Southworth and Apte (eds.), *Contact and convergence in South Asian languages* [*IJDL* 3.1]: 42–59
Clark, T. W. 1957. The Rani Pokhri inscription, Kathmandu. *BSOAS* 20: 167–87
Clark, T. W. 1977. *Introduction to Nepali*. London: SOAS
Das Gupta, Bidhubhusan, and Madhav Lal Karmacharya. 1964. *Nepali self-taught*. Calcutta: Das Gupta Prakashan
Hari, Anna Maria. 1971. *Conversational Nepali*. Kathmandu: Summer Institute of Linguistics
Korolev, N. I. 1965. *Iazyk nepali*. Moscow: Nauka
Korolev, N. I. 1968. Kratkii ocherk grammatiki iazyka nepali. In I. S. Rabinovich et al. (eds.), *Nepal'sko-russkii slovar'*: 1211–328
Matthews, David. 1984. *A course in Nepali*. London: SOAS
Morland-Hughes, W. R. 1947. *A grammar of the Nepali language*. London: Luzac
Rabinovich, I. S., N. I. Korolev, and L. A. Aganina. 1968. *Nepal'sko-russkii slovar'*. Moscow: "Soviet Encyclopedia"
Riccardi, T. J. 1971. *The Nepali version of the Vetālapañcaviṁśati*. New Haven: AOS (Series 54)
Sharma, Tara Nath. 1980. The auxiliary in Nepali. (University of Wisconsin Ph.D. dissertation)
Srivastava, Dayanand. 1962. *Nepali language: its history and development*. Calcutta University Press
Turner, R. L. 1921. The infinitive in Nepali. *Philologica* 1.1: 101–16
Turner, R. L. 1931. *A comparative and etymological dictionary of the Nepali language*. London: Routledge & Kegan Paul; repr. (1980) New Delhi: Allied Publishers
Verma, Manindra K. 1976. The notion of subject and the data from Nepali. *NSSAL*: 270–86
Verma, Manindra K., and T. N. Sharma. 1979a. *Intermediate Nepali structure*. Delhi: Manohar
Verma, Manindra K., and T. N. Sharma. 1979b. *Intermediate Nepali reader*. Delhi: Manohar
Wallace, William D. 1985a. Constituent roles and clause union in Nepali. *PCPR*: 119–48
Wallace, William D. 1985b. Subjects and subjecthood in Nepali: an analysis of Nepali clause structure and its challenges to Relational Grammar and Government and Binding. (University of Illinois Ph.D. dissertation)

Nuristani languages (see also "*Dardic*")

Buddruss, Georg. 1977. Nochmals zur Stellung der Nuristan-Sprache des afghanischen Hindukusch. *Münchener Studien zur Sprachwissenschaft* 36: 19–38
Griunberg, A. L. 1980. *Iazyki vostochnogo Gindukhusha: iazyk kati*. Moscow
Morgenstierne, Georg. 1926. *Report on a linguistic mission to Afghanistan*. Oslo: H. Aschehoug

Morgenstierne, Georg. 1973. Die Stellung der Kafirsprachen. In *Irano-Dardica* (Wiesbaden: Dr Ludwig Reichert Verlag): 327–44

Nelson, David Niles. 1986. The historical development of the Nuristani languages. (University of Minnesota Ph.D. dissertation)

Strand, Richard F. 1973. Notes on the Nuristani and Dardic languages. *JAOS* 93: 297–305

Old Indo-Aryan, dialects

Emeneau, M. B. 1966. Dialects of Old Indo-Aryan. In H. Birnbaum and J. Puhvel (eds.), *Ancient Indo-European dialects*. Berkeley: University of California Press: 123–38

Oriya

Baruah, P. N. Dutta. 1975. Negative formation in Asamiya and Oriya. *IL* 36: 144–51

Chatterji, S. K. 1966. *The people, language, and culture of Orissa*. Bhubhaneswar: Orissa Sahitya Akademi

Dash, G. N. 1971. Structure of verb stem in Oriya. *IL* 32: 207–12

Karpushkin, B. M. 1964. *Iazyk oriya*. Moscow: Nauka

Mahapatra, Chakradhar. 1955. *Oria self-taught*. Berhampur–Cuttack–Sambalpur: The New Students' Stores Ltd

Matson, Dan M. 1971. *Introduction to Oriya and the Oriya writing system*. East Lansing: Michigan State University Asian Studies Center

Misra, Haripriya. 1975. *Historical Oriya morphology*. Varanasi: Bharata Manisha

Patnaik, B. N. 1976. Complementation in Oriya and English. (CIEFL-Hyderabad Ph.D. dissertation)

Patnaik, B. N. 1980. Persistence of borrowed forms in syntax: a study of some borrowed forms in Oriya. National Seminar on Areal Convergence in India/South Asia (July 1980), University of Delhi (paper)

Patnaik, B. N., and Ira Pandit. 1986. Englishization of Oriya. In Krishnamurti (ed.): 232–43

Pattanayak, D. P. 1959. Nasal phonemes of Oriya. *IL* 20: 159–64

Pattanayak, D. P., and G. N. Das. 1972. *Conversational Oriya*. Mysore: Smt. Sulakshana Pattanayak

Tripathi, K. B. 1959. The enclitic definitive -TI in Oriya. *IL* 20: 109–11

Tripathi, Kunjabihari. 1962. *The evolution of Oriya language and script*. Cuttack: Utkal University

Oriya, dialects

Mohapatra, Khageswar. 1985. *Desia: a tribal Oriya dialect of Koraput Orissa*. Bhubaneswar: Tribal & Harijan Research-cum-Training Institute, Govt. of Orissa. (*Adibasi* vol. 25, nos. 1–4).

Tripathi, K. B. 1956–7. Western Oriya dialect. *IL* 17b: 76–85

Pali

Elizarenkova, T. Y., and V. N. Toporov. 1976. *The Pali language*. Moscow: Nauka

Geiger, Wilhelm. 1916. *Pali Literatur und Sprache*. Strassburg: Karl J. Truebner

Junghare, Indira Y. 1979. Topics in Pali historical phonology. *IL* 33.2: 128–34

Warder, A. K. 1974. *Introduction to Pali*. London: Pali Text Society

Par′ya

Oranskii, I. M. 1964. Dva indoariiskikh dialekta iz Srednei Azii. In N. A. Dvoriankov (ed.), *Indiiskaia i Iranskaia Filologiia*. Moscow: Nauka: 3–16

Oranskii, I. M. 1977. *Fol′klor i iazyk gissarskikh par′ya: vvedenie, teksty, slovar′*. Moscow

Pashai

Buddruss, Georg. 1959. Beiträge zur Kenntnis der Pašai-Dialekte. Wiesbaden: DMG/ Franz Steiner
Morgenstierne, Georg. 1973b. *The Pashai language: 1. Grammar*. Oslo: Universitetsforlaget (*Indo-Iranian Frontier Languages*, 2nd rev. edn, vol. 3)

Poguli

Hook, Peter E. 1987c. Poguli syntax in the light of Kashmiri: a preliminary report. In *Studies in the linguistic sciences* 17.1 (Urbana: University of Illinois Linguistics Department): 63–71

*Prakrit (*see also *Magadhi* and *Middle Indo-Aryan)*

Pischel, R. 1981 (1900). (trans. Subhadra Jha). 2nd rev. edn. *A grammar of the Prakrit languages*. Delhi: Motilal Banarsidass
Vertogradova, V. V. 1978. *Prakrity*. Moscow: Nauka
Woolner, Alfred C. 1975 (1928). *Introduction to Prakrit*. 2nd edn. (repr.) Delhi: Motilal Banarsidass

Punjabi

Aksenov, A. T. 1961. Kratkii ocherk grammatiki iazyka pandzhabi. In Rabinovich and Serebriakov: 950–1039
Arun, V. B. 1961. *A comparative phonology of Hindi and Panjabi*. Ludhiana
Bahl, K. C. 1957b. Tones in Panjabi. *IL* 17: 139–47
Bahl, Kati Charan. 1969. Panjabi. In Thomas A. Sebeok (ed.), *Current Trends in Linguistics* (Linguistics in South Asia). The Hague: Mouton: 153–200
Bahri, Ujjal Singh. 1973. *Introductory course in spoken Punjabi*. Chandigarh: Bahri Publications
Bailey, T. G. 1976 (1919). *An English–Panjabi dictionary*. (repr.) Delhi: Ess Ess Publications
Cummings, T. F., and T. G. Bailey. 1925. *Panjabi manual and grammar*. Calcutta. Repr. 1961 (Patiala: Languages Department, Punjab) as second part of *Panjabi manual and grammars*
Gill, H. S., and H. A. Gleason, Jr. 1969. *A reference grammar of Punjabi*. rev. edn. Patiala: Punjabi University
Jain, Banarsi Das. 1934. *A phonology of Punjabi as spoken about Ludhiana*. Lahore: Punjab University
Newton, E. P. 1896. *Panjabi grammar*. Sialkot: Mission Press. Repr. 1961 (Patiala: Languages Department, Punjab) as first part of *Panjabi manual and grammars*.
Rabinovich, I. S., and I. D. Serebriakov. 1961. *Pandzhabsko-russkii slovar´*. Moscow: Izd. Inostrannykh i Natsional´nykh Slovareĭ
Sandhi, B. S. 1968b. The tonal system of the Panjabi language. *Parkh* 1. (Chandigarh)
Shackle, C. Punjabi in Lahore. *Modern Asian Studies* 4: 239–67
Shackle, C. 1972. *Punjabi*. London: English Universities Press
Singh, Gurcaran, Saran Singh, and Ravindar Kaur. 1981. *Panjabi–English dictionary*, 3rd edn. Amritsar: Singh Brothers, Mai Sevan
Smirnov, Y. A. 1976. *Grammatika iazyka pandzhabi*. Moscow: Nauka
Tisdall, W. St. Clair. 1961a (1888). *A simplified grammar and reading book of the Panjabi language*. (repr.) New York: F. Ungar
Tolstaya, N. I. 1960. *Iazyk pandzhabi*. Moscow: Nauka

Punjabi, Old

Shackle, C. 1981. *A Guru Nanak glossary*. Vancouver: University of British Columbia Press
Shackle, C. 1983. *An introduction to the sacred language of the Sikhs*. London: SOAS

Punjabi, dialects

Bailey, T. S. 1904. *Panjabi grammar: a brief grammar of Panjabi as spoken in Wazirabad District*. Lahore: Punjab Govt. Press. Repr. 1977, Lahore: Saadhi Panjabi Academy
Sandhu, B. S. 1968. A descriptive grammar of Puadi. *Parkh* 2. (Chandigarh)
Wilson, J. 1962 (repr.) *Shahpuri Kangri glossary: a grammar and glossary of the dialects as spoken in Shahpur and Kangra Districts*. Patiala: Languages Department, Punjab

Rajasthani (see also *Marwari, Dhundari, Harauti, Lamani, Shekhawati, Bhitrauti)*

Allen, W. S. 1957b. Some phonological characteristics of Rajasthani. *BSOAS* 20:5–11
Allen, W. S. 1960. Notes on Rajasthani verbs. *IL* 21: 4–13
Bahl, Kali Charan. 1972. *On the present state of Modern Rajasthani grammar*. Jodhpur: Rajasthani Shodh Samsthan, Chauparni. (Rajasthani Prakirnak Prakashan Pushp, 5)
Bahl, Kali Charan. 1980. *ādhunik rājasthānī ka sa˜racnātmak vyākaraṇ*. Jodhpur: Rajasthani Shodh Samsthan
Chatterji, Suniti Kumar. 1948. *rājasthānī bhāṣā* [in Hindi]. Udaipur: Rajasthan Vidyapith
Lalas, Sitaram. 1962–78. *rājasthānī sabad kos* [in Hindi]. 9 vols. Jodhpur: Rajasthani Shodh Sansthan
Menaria, Motilal. 1960. *rājasthānī bhāṣā aur sāhitya* [in Hindi]. Allahabad: Hindi Sahitya Sammelan
Sakaria, Badriprasad, and Bhupatiram Sakaria. 1977. *rājasthānī-hindī śabda-koś* [in Hindi]. Jaipur: Panch Sheel Prakashan
Smith, John D. 1975. *An introduction to the language of the historical documents from Rajasthan*. Modern Asian Studies 9.4: 433–64
Smith, John D. 1976. *The Visaladevarasa*. Cambridge University Press
Tessitori, L. P. 1914–16. Notes on the grammar of Old Western Rajasthani. *Indian Antiquary*: 43–5

Romany

Bloch, Jules. 1953. *Les Tsiganes*. Paris: Presses Universitaires de France
Clébert, Jean-Paul (trans. Charles Duff). 1967. *The Gypsies*. Harmondsworth (England): Penguin Books
Hamp, Eric P. 1987. On the sibilants of Romani. *Indo-Iranian Journal*. 30.2: 103–6
Kochanowski, Jan. 1967? The Romany language. (ms.)
Miltner, Vladimir. 1965. The morphologic structure of a New Indo-Aryan language of Czechoslovakia. *IL* 26: 106–31
Rishi, W. R. 1974. *Multilingual Romani dictionary*. Chandigarh: Roma Publications
Sergievski, M. V., and A. P. Barannikov. 1938. *Tsygansko-russkii slovar′: s prilozheniem grammatiki tsyganskogo iazyka*. Moscow: Izd. Inostr. i Nats. Slovar′ei
Turner, R. L. 1926b. The position of Romani in Indo-Aryan. *Journal of the Gypsy Lore Society* 3.5.4: 145–89 (repr. 1975, *Collected Papers*: 251–90)
Ventzel, T.V. 1983. *The Gypsy language*. Moscow: Nauka
Ventzel, T. V., and L. N. Cherenkov. 1968. Dialekty tsyganskogo iazyka i ikh vzaimootnosheniia s indoariiskimi iazykami Indii. In Beskrovny (ed.): 417–28

Rudhari (see West Pahari)

Sadani (Nagpuria)

Jordan-Horstmann, Monika. 1969. *Sadani: a Bhojpuri dialect spoken in Chotanagpur.* Wiesbaden: Otto Harrassowitz
Nowrangi, P. S. 1956. *A simple Sadani grammar.* Ranchi: D. S. S. Book Depot
Nowrangi, P. S. 1965. *nāgpuriya sadānī boli kā byākaraṇ* [in Hindi]. Ranchi: by the author

Sanskrit

Allen, W. S. 1951. Some prosodic features of retroflexion and aspiration in Sanskrit. *BSOAS* 13.4: 939–46
Allen, W. S. 1953. *Phonetics in Ancient India.* London: Geoffrey Cumberlege/Oxford University Press
Allen, W. S. 1954. Retroflexion in Sanskrit. *BSOAS* 16: 556–65
Allen, W. S. 1962. *Sandhi: the theoretical, phonetic, and historical bases of word-junction in Sanskrit.* The Hague: Mouton
Brugmann, Karl. 1886–1900. *Grundriss der vergleichenden grammatik der indogermanischen sprachen.* Strassburg: K. J. Trübner
Burrow, T. 1955. *The Sanskrit language.* London: Faber & Faber
Cardona, George. 1976a. Panini: a survey of research. The Hague: Mouton. (Series *Trends in Linguistics*, 6)
Cardona, George. 1976b. Subject in Sanskrit. *NSSAL*: 1–38
Coulson, Michael. 1976. *Sanskrit.* London: Hodder & Stoughton
Emeneau, M. B. 1946. The nasal phonemes of Sanskrit. *Lg.* 22: 86–93
Fry, A. H. 1941. A phonemic interpretation of Visarga. *Lg.* 17: 194–200
Goldman, Robert P. 1985. *The Ramayana of Valmiki: an epic of ancient India; introduction and translation.* Princeton University Press
Gonda, Jan. (trans. Gordon B. Ford, Jr.) 1981 (1966). *A concise elementary grammar of the Sanskrit language.* University of Alabama Press
Gonda, J. 1951. *Remarks on the Sanskrit passive.* Leiden: E. J. Brill
Gray, J. E. B. 1964. Aspirate Sandhi. *BSOAS* 27: 615–19
Hock, Hans Henrich. n.d. (Pre-)Rig-Vedic convergence of Indo-Aryan with Dravidian? Another look at the evidence. (conference paper)
Hock, Hans Henrich. 1982. The Sanskrit passive: synchronic behavior and diachronic development. Mistry (ed.): 127–37
Mayrhofer, Manfred. 1953–72. *Kurzgefasstes etymologisches Wörterbuch des Altindischen/ A concise etymological Sanskrit dictionary.* Heidelberg: C. Winter
Speijer, J. S. 1886 (repr. 1980). *Sanskrit syntax.* Delhi: Motilal Banarsidass
Staal, J. F. (ed.) 1972. *A reader on the Sanskrit grammarians.* Cambridge (Mass.): MIT Press
Thumb, Albert. 1958–9. *Handbuch des Sanskrit*, 3rd rev. edn by R. Hauschild. Heidelberg: C. Winter
Tikkanen, Bertil. 1987. *The Sanskrit gerund: a syntactic, diachronic, and typological analysis.* Helsinki: Finnish Oriental Society. (*Studia Orientalia*, 62)
Whitney, William Dwight. 1945 (1885). *The roots, verb-forms, and primary derivatives of the Sanskrit language.* Leipzig: Breitkopf and Härtel; repr. New Haven: AOS, vol. 30
Whitney, William Dwight. 1950 (1889). *Sanskrit grammar.* Cambridge (Mass.): Harvard University Press

Sanskrit, Vedic

Hoffmann, Karl. 1952. Wiederholende Onomatopoetika im Altindischen. *Indogermanische Forschungen* 60: 254–64

Macdonell, A. A. 1916 (repr. 1977). *A Vedic grammar for students*. Delhi: Oxford University Press

Renou, Louis. 1952. *Grammaire de la langue védique*. Paris: IAC

Saurashtri

Dave, I. R. 1976. "Saurashtri language". Ch. 4. In *The Saurashtrians in South India*. Rajkot: Saurashtra University: 101–227

Pandit, P. B. 1972. Bilingual's grammar: Tamil–Saurashtri grammatical convergence. In *India as a sociolinguistic area* (Gune Memorial Lectures, University of Poona): 1–25

Randle, H. N. 1943–4. An Indo-Aryan language of South India: Saurashtra bhasa, Parts I and II. *BSOS* 11: 104–21; 310–25

Učida, Norihoko. 1979. Oral literature of the Saurashtrans. Calcutta: Simant

Shekhawati

Agrawal, Kailash Chandra. 1964. *śekhāvāṭī bolī kā varṇātmak adhyayan*. Lucknow University

Shina

Bailey, T. G. 1924. *Grammar of the Shina (ṣiṇā)* language. London: RAS

Bailey, T. G. 1925. The sounds of ṣiṇā. *BSOS* 3: 799–802

Lorimer, D. R. R. 1924. The forms and nature of the transitive verb in Shina. *BSOS* 3: 467–93

Schmidt, Ruth Laila, and Mohammad Zarin. 1981. The phonology and tonal system of Palas Shina. *Münchener Studien für Sprachwissenschaft* 40: 155–85

Schmidt, Ruth. 1985. Morphological criteria for distinguishing categories of transitivity in Shina. *PCPR*: 33–47

Sindhi

Addleton, Hubert F., and Pauline A. Brown. 1981. *Functional Sindhi: a basic course for English speakers*. Shikarpur (Sindh, Pakistan): Indus Christian Fellowship (Baptist)

Egorova, R. P. 1966. *Iazyk sindkhi*. Moscow: Nauka

Egorova, R. P. 1968. Mestoimennye enklitiki v novoindiiskikh iazykakh. In Beskrovny et al. (eds.): 265–76

Khubchandani, L. M. 1961. The phonology and morphophonemics of Sindhi. (University of Pennsylvania MA thesis)

Khubchandani, L. M. 1964. Noun declensions in Sindhi and Hindi. *IL* 25: 275–80

Khubchandani, L. M. 1969. Sindhi. In Sebeok (ed.): 201–34

Shahani, Anandram T. n.d. *The Sindhi-instructor*. Karachi: Educational Publishing Co.

Stack, Captain George. 1849. *Dictionary, English and Sindhi*. Bombay: American Mission Press

Trumpp, Ernest. 1970 (1872). *Grammar of the Sindhi language*. (repr.) Osnabrück: Biblio Verlag

Turner, R. L. 1924. The Sindhi recursives or voiced stops preceded by glottal closure. *BSOS* 3.2: 301–15 (repr. 1975 in *Collected Papers*: 192–205)

Varyani, Pritam L. 1974. Sources of implosives in Sindhi. *IL* 35.1: 51–54

Sindhi, dialects

Acharya, Shanti Bhai. 1964. Segmental phonemes of Kachhi. *Vidya* 8: 129–42 (= Journal of Gujarat University)
Rohra, S. K. 1971. Sindhi, Kacchi, and Emigrant Sindhi. *IL* 32.2: 123–31

Sinhalese

Bel´kovich, A. A. 1970. Kratkii ocherk grammatiki singal´skogo iazyka. Appendix to Bel´kovich and Vykhukholev: 751–824
Bel´kovich, A. A. and V. V. Vykhukholev. 1970. *Singal´sko-russkii slovar´*. Moscow: Soviet Encyclopedia
Coates, William, and M. W. S. De Silva. 1960. The segmental phonemes of Sinhalese. *University of Ceylon Review* 18: 3–4: 163–75
De Silva, M. W. S. 1960. Verbal categories in spoken Sinhalese. *University of Ceylon Review* 18.1: 96–112
De Silva, M. W. S. 1979. *Sinhalese and other island languages in South Asia*. Tübingen: Gunter Narr Verlag. (*Ars Linguistica* 3)
Fairbanks, Gordon H., James W. Gair, and M. W. S. De Silva. 1968. *Colloquial Sinhalese: Parts I & II*. Ithaca: Cornell South Asia Program
Gair, James W. 1960. Sinhalese diglossia. *Anthropological Linguistics* 10.8: 1–15
Gair, James W. 1966. Colloquial Sinhalese inflectional categories and parts of speech. *IL* 27: 31–45
Gair, James W. 1970. *Colloquial Sinhalese clause structures*. The Hague: Mouton
Gair, James W. 1976. Is Sinhala a subject language? *NSSAL*: 39–64
Gair, James W. 1982. Sinhala, an Indo-Aryan isolate. In Mistry (ed.): 51–65
Gair, James W. 1986a. Sinhala diglossia revisited or diglossia dies hard. In Krishnamurti (ed.): 322–36
Gair, James W. 1986b. Sinhala focused sentences: naturalization of a calque. In Krishnamurti (ed.): 147–64
Gair, James W., and W. S. Karunatilaka. 1974. *Literary Sinhala*. Ithaca: Cornell University, South Asia Program
Garusinghe, Dayaratne. 1962. *Sinhalese: the spoken idiom*. Munich: Max Hueber
Geiger, Wilhelm. 1938. *A grammar of the Sinhalese language*. Colombo: RAS, Ceylon Branch
Geiger, Wilhelm. 1942. *Beiträge zur singhalesischen Sprachgeschichte*. Munich: Verlag der Bayerischen Akademie der Wissenschaften, in Kommission bei C. H. Beck
Guenther, Herbert. 1949. The conditional mood in Sinhalese. *JAOS* 69: 73–83
Gunasekara, A. M. 1986 (1891). *A comprehensive grammar of the Sinhalese language*. (repr.) New Delhi: Asian Educational Services
Hendriksen, H. 1949. The three conjugations in Sinhalese. *BSOAS* 13.1: 154–65
Hettiaratchi, D. E. 1959. Echo words in Sinhalese. *University of Ceylon Review* 17.1–2: 47–50
Hettiaratchi, D. E. 1965. Influence of Portuguese on the Sinhalese language. *JRAS Ceylon Branch* 9.2: 229–238
Hettiaratchi, D. E. 1968. Portuguese influence on Sinhalese. *Samskrti* 15.2: 9–24
Karunatilake, W. S., and S. Suseedirarajah. 1973. Phonology of Sinhalese and Srilanka Tamil: a study in contrast and interference. *IL* 34.3: 180–90
Malalasekera, G. P. 1971. *ingrisi-simhala sabdakosaya*. Colombo: M. D. Gunasena
Matzel, K. 1966. *Einführung in die singhalesische Sprache*. Wiesbaden
Reynolds, C. H. B. 1964. Participial forms in early Sinhalese prose. *BSOAS* 27: 129–50
Vykhukholev, V. V. 1964. *Singal´skii iazyk*. Moscow: Nauka

Wickremasinghe, Don M. 1916. *Sinhalese self-taught*. London: E. Marlborough
Wijayaratne. D. J. 1956. *History of the Sinhalese noun*. Colombo: University of Ceylon

Sinhalese, Old

Wijeratne, P. B. F. 1945–57. Phonology of the Sinhalese inscriptions up to the end of the 10th century AD. *BSOAS* 11–14, 19

Siraiki

Shackle, C. 1976. *The Siraiki language of Central Pakistan*. London: SOAS
Shackle, C. 1977a. Siraiki: a language movement in Pakistan. *Modern Asian Studies* 11: 379–403

Urdu (see also *Hindi–[Urdu] – below only works concerned specifically with Urdu are listed)*

Ansari, Zoe. 1964. *urdu-russkii slovar´*. Moscow: "Soviet Encyclopedia"
Bailey, T. G. 1956. *Teach yourself Urdu*. London: English Universities Press
Naim, C. M., with R. S. Ahmad, S. S. Nadvi, and M. A. Haq. 1975. *Introductory Urdu*. 2 vols. Chicago: University of Chicago, Committee on Southern Asian Studies
Phillott, D. C. 1918. *Hindustani manual*. 3rd edn. Calcutta: by the author
Platts, John T. 1965 (1884). *A dictionary of Urdu, Classical Hindi, and English*. London: Oxford University Press
Sadiq, Muhammad. 1964. *A history of Urdu literature*. London: Oxford University Press
Zograph, G. A. 1960. Iranskie i arabskie elementy v urdu. In Beskrovny (ed.): 152–204

West Pahari dialects (see also *Bhadarwahī–Bhalesi, Khashali)*

Bailey, T. G. 1908. *The languages of the Northern Himalayas*. London: RAS Monograph No. 1
Bailey, T. G. 1915. *Linguistic studies from the Himalayas*. London: RAS
Hendriksen, H. 1976, 1979, 1986. Himachali Studies I (Vocabulary), II (Texts), III (Grammar). *Danske Videnskabernes Selskab, Historisk-Filosofiske Meddele ser* 48.1–3 (mainly on Kotgarhi)
Misra, Bal Govind, and Hans Raj Dua. 1980. *Language use in Himachal Pradesh*. Mysore: CIIL
Patyal, Hukam Chand. 1982–84. Etymological notes on some Mandyali words. *Indo-Iranian Journal* 24: 289–94, 25: 41–9, 27: 121–32
Sharma, Shyamlal. 1974. *Kangari: a descriptive study of the Kangra Valley dialect of Himachal Pradesh*. Hoshiarpur: V. V. B. Institute of Sanskrit and Indological Studies, Panjab University
Varma, Siddheshwar. 1936. The Rudhari dialect. *IL* 6: 128–96
Varma, Siddheshwar. 1940. Notes of a linguistic tour in Kashmir. *IL* 8: 479–83
Zoller, Claus Peter. 1988. Bericht über besondere Archaismen im Bangani, einer Western Pahari-Sprache. *Münchener Studien zur Sprachwissenschaft*, Heft 49: 173–200.

INDEX OF LANGUAGES

Items in Appendix I, which is also alphabetical by language, are indicated here – in parentheses ( ) – only if otherwise mentioned in the text. Alternative names for languages will mainly be found in Appendix I rather than as blind entries in this index. Note that Section II of the Bibliography (pp. 486–510), which is not indexed, is also alphabetical by language. Readers should be alert to the fact that there may be more than one reference on a cited page. Boldface page numbers indicate material on numbered Figures and Tables, and on Map 1. Readers seeking to assemble a profile of a language should note that minor languages especially are often taken notice of in the text, and therefore below, only because of some unusual feature, and that many general descriptive statements apply to them also. Such inclusive descriptions may be accessed through the General Index which follows.

GENERAL INDEX

Authors are listed in this index only when reference is made to their work or arguments, or when directly quoted, and not as mere sources of examples, for which credit is given in the text. See also the Bibliography.

ablative: Layer I, 233, 248–9; Layer II, **246**, 248; Layer III, 238
absolutive: = conjunctive participle, 283, 375; distinct, 323, 326
accusative, 239, 365, 478 n.14
addak (Gurmukhi symbol), 149
Addleton, H. F., and P. A. Brown, 275
Ādi Granth, language of, 54
adjectival participial clause construction, 408–10, 415
adjectival participles, imperfective, 323, **324–5**
adjectival participles, perfective, 322, 323, **324–5**
adjectival endings, in verbal paradigms, 260, 261
adjectives: inflection of, 221, 224, 225, 230, 233, 250–1; position of, 370, 373
adjuncts: clausal, using non-finite forms, 408; phrasal, position of in sentence, 333–4
adverbial participial clause, "Dravidian type", 417
adverbial participles, imperfective, 322, 323, **324–5**, 415–17
-Aff, 375–6
"affective" verbs, *see* semitransitive verbs
affectivity, expressed by explicator, 326, 329, 320
affricates: dentalization of, 94, 95, 207, 450; dental/palatal opposition in, 132; transcription, xv; voicing contrast in, 100
Afghanistan: eastern, Indo-Aryan remnants in, 8, 21; northeastern, languages of, 32, 43
Africa, contact with, 42, 49
agent: in causative construction, 245; in ergative construction, 245, 341, 344–5, 346, 365, 367; in passive construction, 245, 356–8
agentive (case), 232, 278, 365; in other than Perfective construction, 376
agglutination, 212–13, 450; in NIA case marking, 231, 233, 237; in NIA plural marking 225, 241, 253; in NIA verbal paradigms 257, 258
Agha, Asif: on Tibetan, 477 n.11; on Urdu modal usage, 478 n.21
Agra, linguistic effects of removal of capital to, 28
agreement, 215, 259; as subject property in NIA, 339, 340, 362; blocked, 342, 361; defines gender, 218; double, 343, 344, 477 n.9; in compulsion constructions, 353; in "dative subject" constructions, 354–7, 477 n.11; in number, 225–6; multiple, 261, 289; with agent in ergative sentences, 343, 346, 354; with patient in ergative and passive sentences, 341, 342, 356, 361, 477 n.7; *see also* concord marking
agriculture, non-Aryan terminology in, 61
Ahoms, 50
Aktionsart, 268, 274, 275, 329

Ālhākhaṇḍ, language of, 57
Allen, W. S.: on Indo-Aryan phonetics, 94, 146, 158; on Rajasthani phonetics and phonology, 102, 104, 120, 118, 130, 204, 207, 470 n.10
allomorphs, numerous in OIA, 166
allophones, representation of in Sanskrit, 161
Alwar Dt (Raj.), language of, 13
American (New World) products, names for in NIA, 73
American structuralism, effect on descriptions of NIA, 8
analytic elements: in NIA morphology generally, 212–13; in verb paradigm, 257, 259
Andhra empire, *see* Satavahana empire
Andronovo culture, 34
animate/inanimate distinction, 220–1, 253, 254, 307
"antipassive", 343
anunāsika, 146
anusvāra, 95, 105, 146, 149, 160, 170–1
Apte, M. L., and D. P. Pattanayak, 97, 112
Arabic pharyngeal letters, pronunciation in Urdu, 469 n.1
Arabs, in Sind, 48
Aravalli hills, language of, 12
archaeological evidence: of crop plants, 49; of Indo-Aryan spread in South Asia, 37, 45; of Indo-Iranians, 34; of pre-Aryan cultures in India, 40; of writing, 134
arddhatatsama, *see* semi-tatsama
Arden, A. H., on layered case-marking in Telugu, 238
Aronson, H., on alternative view of aspect in Slavic, 268
articles, *see* indefinite articles, specifier suffixes
Arya Samaj, linguistic role of, 20, 59, 469 (Ch. 4) n.6
Aryanization, three types of, 44–5
Asokan inscriptions: language of, 51, 55, 167, 450; location, 45, 167, 199; phonology, 458, 471 n.7; script, 133, 134, 124
aspect, 237, 259, 262–77, **277**, 281, 282, 285, 326–7, 374, 376; "enhanced", 287; secondary, 374, 384; "unspecified", 268; *see also* perfective, imperfective, habitual, continuous, prospective, perfect
aspirated consonants, 101, 102, 131, 158–9; absence of, 103, 205–6; alternative analyses of, 88; flaps, 104; nasals, 103, 120, 124, 170, 173–4, 178, 183; laterals, 103; "new", 172–3, 177, 183, 184, 189; positional constraints on, 125, 130; representation in writing, 136, 148, 151, **152**; semivowels, 104; transcription, xv, 153; *see also* aspiration
aspiration: as precursor of tone, 205; dissimilation of, *see* Grassmann's Law; loss of in voiced series, 203–5; loss of positionally, 204; preservation as /h/, 184; relation to secondary phonemes, 106; transference of, 120, 203–4; unmotivated, 203, 204; *see also* aspirated consonants
Assam, 45, 50
Assamese script, 144
Assyrian records, evidence of Indo-Iranians in, 35, 37
Attock Dt (Punjab, Pakistan), languages of, 18–19
augment-prefix, 33–4, 289
Aux, vs. "auxiliary", defined, 374, 376
auxiliary: etymology of, 284–5; negative forms of, 289, 391–3; position of, 336, 277; "vector" as, 326; written vs. spoken forms of, 289; *see also* Tense–Mood markers
Avesta, language of, 32–3
Aśvaghoṣa, 167

/b/ in OIA, 158
Babakaev, V. D., 312
backrounding, of low central vowel, 207
Bactria, 34–6
Bahawalpur (Pakistan), language of, 18
Bahl, K. C.: on Punjabi tone, 119; on onomatopoeia in Hindi, 80; on Rajasthani, 77–8, 80, 104
Bahri, H.: on Hindi dialects, 465 n.4; on "Lahnda" tone, 119–20
Bailey, T. G., 86; on Kashmiri vowels, 112, 129; on Punjabi tone, 119, on Shina, 113, 261–2; on Simla dialects, 102
Baluchistan, language of, 17
Bangladesh, language of, 1

Gimbutas, M., 467 n.7
glides (vs. semivowels), 99–100, 269
glottalization, 99
glottalized stops, 104–5
Goswami, G. C., 113, 121
Goyal, S. R., 134–5
grades, vowel (in OIA), 165, **165–6**, 166
grammarians, Sanskrit: on genitive, 239; on mood vs. tense, 279
grammars, indigenous, of MIA, 55
Grantha script, 143
Grassmann's Law, 131, 158, 172, 204, 209
Greek transcriptions of MIA, 170
Grierson, G. A., 3, 66, 68, 74, 86, 121, 316, 467 n.13; on "Dardic", 461, **461**; on Kashmiri, 112, 129–30, 245, 261, 297–8; on Maithili, 287; on NIA subclassification, 447–8, **449**, **451**, 452–3, **453**, 456, 460; on Pahari, 26, 42–3, 120, 209; on Rajasthani, 111; on Sindhi, 123, 300; terminology and constructs, 9, 12, 13, 18, 18–19, 20
Gujarat: early scripts of, 144; Harappan civilization in, 40
Gujarati script, **138–42**, 143, 144
Gujars, 47–8
Gumperz, J. J., 103; phonemic stress in Hindi, 121; phonology of NW Hindi ("Kauravi") dialects, 97, 103, 125, 198
guṇa, 164, 165, **165–6**
guṇa-vṛddhi system, destruction of, 185
Gupta, S. P., 134
Gupta script, 137, 143
Gurjaras, 47–8
Gurmukhi script, 136, **138–42**, 143–4, 147–51, 470 n.3
Guru Granth Sahib, 135; *see also* Adi Granth
Gypsies 5, 6, 465 n.11

/h/, 99; *see also* "voiced *h*", voiced/voiceless *h* contrast
habitual (aspect), 273, 276; marker "deactivated", 282
habitual/continuous distinction, 269, 281; development of, 273–4
halant, 149
half-nasals, *see* prenasalized stops
Halliday, M. A. K., 479 n.26
Handoo, J., 112
Harappan civilization, 39–41, 44, 47, 134
Hazara Dt (northern Pakistan), languages of, 18–19
"head" of construction, (definitions), 215
Hemacandra, 181, 193
hiatus, 128, 163, 184, 189, 190, 206
high vowels, loss of distinctions in, 148, 207–8
Himachal Pradesh: languages of, 13, 20, scripts used in, 143
Himalayas, languages of, 13
"hindi area", 9, 26, 29, 58–9, 266, 274, 285, 464 n.7
Hindu Kush, languages of, 43
Hittite records of Indo-Aryan, 34–5, 37
Hoernle, R., 446–7, 456
homonyms, 70, 185
honorificity: in pronouns, 251, 253; in verbs, 226, 262, 265
Hook, P. E., 477 n.4; on aspect and the compound verb, 266, 267, 327–8, 330, 476 n.19, 478 n.20; on Hindi, 368; on Kashmiri, 335–6, 343, 354, 476 n.2; on Marathi, 391; on Panini, 477–8 n.13; on Shina, 121, 477 n.11, 479 n.27
Hook, P. E., and O. N. Koul, 254, 261
Hopper, P. J., 276
Hunas, 47–8
Hyderabad (Deccan), 22
"hypothetical", *see* contrafactive; presumptive; subjunctive

imperative, 260, 261, 272, 291, 476 n.14
imperfective, 266–9, 276, **277**, 288
imperfective participle: as "complementizer", 375, 404; in future formations, 289; inflection of, 261; *see also* adjectival participles, imperfective
implosives, xv, 104, 148, 203, 209, 470 n.6
indefinite articles, 219, 248, 370, 371
"indirect construction", *see* "dative subject" construction
indirect object, 347, 354, 355, 366–7, 477 n.12
Indo-Iranians, 34–7, 61
Indonesia, Indo-Aryan influence in, 2
Indus valley, (modern) language of, 17
Indus valley civilization, *see* Harappan civilization
industries, traditional, terminology in, 61